The following list outlines the state maintenance rules that apply to PIM Sparse Mode. These rules are explained in Chapter 11, "Using PIM Sparse Mode," beginning on page 240:

PIM-SM Rule 1—A sparse mode (*, G) entry is created as a result of an Explicit Join operation.

PIM-SM Rule 2—The incoming interface of a sparse mode (*, G) entry always points up the shared tree toward the RP.

PIM-SM Rule 3—A sparse mode (S, G) entry is created under the following conditions:

— Receipt of an (S, G) Join/Prune message

— On a last-hop router when it switches to the SPT

— Unexpected arrival of (S, G) traffic when no (*, G) state exists

— At the RP when a Register message is received

PIM-SM Rule 4—An interface is added to the outgoing interface list of a sparse mode (*, G) or (S, G) entry in either of the following conditions:

— When an appropriate (*, G) or (S, G) Join is received via this interface

— When a directly connected member of the group exists on the interface

PIM-SM Rule 5—An interface is removed from the outgoing interface list of a sparse mode (*, G) or (S, G) entry in either of the following situations:

— When an appropriate (*, G) or (S, G) Prune (that is not overridden) is received via this interface (and where there is no directly connected member)

— When the interface's expiration timer counts down to zero

PIM-SM Rule 6—The expiration timer of an interface is reset to 3 minutes as a result of either of the following conditions:

— An appropriate (*, G) or (S, G) Join is received via this interface.

— An IGMP Membership Report is received from a directly connected member on this interface.

PIM-SM Rule 7—Routers will send an (S, G)RP-bit Prune up the shared tree when the RPF neighbor for the (S, G) entry is different from the RPF neighbor of the (*, G) entry.

PIM-SM Rule 8—The RPF interface (that is, the incoming interface) of a sparse mode (S, G) entry is calculated by using the IP address of the source except when the RP-bit is set, in which case, the IP address of the RP is used.

Developing IP Multicast Networks
Volume I

Beau Williamson

Cisco Press

800 East 96th Street, 3rd Floor
Indianapolis, IN 46240 USA

Developing IP Multicast Networks
Volume I

Beau Williamson

Copyright © 2000 Cisco Press

Published by:
Cisco Press
800 East 96th Street, 3rd Floor
Indianapolis, IN 46240 USA

Printed in the United States of America   9 0

Ninth Printing May 2007

Library of Congress Cataloging-in-Publication Number: 98-86505

ISBN: 1-57870-077-9

Warning and Disclaimer

This book is designed to provide information about developing IP multicast networks. Every effort has been made to make this book as complete and as accurate as possible, but no warranty or fitness is implied.

The information is provided on an "as is" basis. The author, Cisco Press, and Cisco Systems, Inc. shall have neither liability nor responsibility to any person or entity with respect to any loss or damages arising from the information contained in this book or from the use of the discs or programs that may accompany it.

The opinions expressed in this book belong to the author and are not necessarily those of Cisco Systems, Inc.

Trademark Acknowledgments

All terms mentioned in this book that are known to be trademarks or service marks have been appropriately capitalized. Cisco Press or Cisco Systems, Inc., cannot attest to the accuracy of this information. Use of a term in this book should not be regarded as affecting the validity of any trademark or service mark.

Feedback Information

At Cisco Press, our goal is to create in-depth technical books of the highest quality and value. Each book is crafted with care and precision, undergoing rigorous development that involves the unique expertise of members from the professional technical community.

Readers' feedback is a natural continuation of this process. If you have any comments regarding how we could improve the quality of this book, or otherwise alter it to better suit your needs, you can contact us through e-mail at feedback@ciscopress.com. Please make sure to include the book title and ISBN in your message.

We greatly appreciate your assistance.

Publisher	John Wait
Executive Editor	Alicia Buckley
Cisco Representative	Anthony Wolfenden
Cisco Press Program Manager	Sonia Torres Chavez
Cisco Marketing Communications Manager	Tom Geitner
Cisco Marketing Program Manager	Edie Quiroz
Production Manager	Patrick Kanouse
Acquisitions Editor	Tracy Hughes
Development Editor	Katherine Trace
Project Editor	Jen Nuckles
Copy Editor	June Waldman
Technical Reviewers	Dino Farinacci
	Kevin Almeroth
	Manoj Leelanivas
	Erick Mar
	Bob Quinn
Team Coordinator	Amy Moss
Book Designer	Gina Rexrode
Cover Designer	Louisa Adair
Composition	Argosy
Proofreader	Sheri Cain
Indexer	Tim Wright

CISCO SYSTEMS

Corporate Headquarters
Cisco Systems, Inc.
170 West Tasman Drive
San Jose, CA 95134-1706
USA
www.cisco.com
Tel: 408 526-4000
    800 553-NETS (6387)
Fax: 408 526-4100

European Headquarters
Cisco Systems International BV
Haarlerbergpark
Haarlerbergweg 13-19
1101 CH Amsterdam
The Netherlands
www-europe.cisco.com
Tel: 31 0 20 357 1000
Fax: 31 0 20 357 1100

Americas Headquarters
Cisco Systems, Inc.
170 West Tasman Drive
San Jose, CA 95134-1706
USA
www.cisco.com
Tel: 408 526-7660
Fax: 408 527-0883

Asia Pacific Headquarters
Cisco Systems, Inc.
Capital Tower
168 Robinson Road
#22-01 to #29-01
Singapore 068912
www.cisco.com
Tel: +65 6317 7777
Fax: +65 6317 7799

Cisco Systems has more than 200 offices in the following countries and regions. Addresses, phone numbers, and fax numbers are listed on the
Cisco.com Web site at www.cisco.com/go/offices.

Argentina • Australia • Austria • Belgium • Brazil • Bulgaria • Canada • Chile • China PRC • Colombia • Costa Rica • Croatia • Czech Republic
Denmark • Dubai, UAE • Finland • France • Germany • Greece • Hong Kong SAR • Hungary • India • Indonesia • Ireland • Israel • Italy
Japan • Korea • Luxembourg • Malaysia • Mexico • The Netherlands • New Zealand • Norway • Peru • Philippines • Poland • Portugal
Puerto Rico • Romania • Russia • Saudi Arabia • Scotland • Singapore • Slovakia • Slovenia • South Africa • Spain • Sweden
Switzerland • Taiwan • Thailand • Turkey • Ukraine • United Kingdom • United States • Venezuela • Vietnam • Zimbabwe

About the Author

Beau Williamson is a consulting engineer in the Office of the CTO at Cisco Systems. His area of expertise is general IP networking, and he is currently focused on IP multicast. He received a B.S. degree in mathematics (with a specialty in computer science) from the University of Texas (Dallas) in 1984 and has been working in the computer and networking technology fields for more than 20 years. He is frequently called upon by Cisco customers and internal Cisco engineers around the world to provide consulting services on the design, implementation, and debugging of IP multicast networks. Beau is also the author and developer of Cisco's internal IP multicast training class and frequent presenter on topics related to IP multicast at Cisco Networkers and Cisco Certified Internetwork Expert (CCIE) conferences both at home and abroad. He lives in the Dallas, Texas, area with his wife and son. When not working on IP multicast, he enjoys a wide range of hobbies, including amateur radio, golf, woodworking, and flying his own plane.

About the Technical Reviewers

Dino Farinacci has been designing and implementing networking protocols for 18 years. He has extensive experience with distance-vector and link-state protocol implementations, as well as with multicast routing protocols, which have been his focus for the past 5 years. Dino currently works for Cisco Systems in the multimedia group. He has been an active member of the IETF for more than 10 years, where he has been involved in the design of Open Shortest Path First (OSPF), Protocol Independent Multicast (PIM), and various IPng candidates. He was a member of the IPng directorate for a short period of time, where he helped the IETF converge on a single IPng solution. Currently, he is concentrating on multicast tag switching, inter-domain policy-based multicast routing, and reliable multicast protocols. He is one of the principal engineers in the Internet to deploy Cisco multicast routers on the MBone and in many native production ISP infrastructures.

Kevin Almeroth is an assistant professor at the University of California in Santa Barbara. His research interests include computer networks and protocols, multicast communication, large-scale multimedia systems, and performance evaluation. In addition to his research activities, Dr. Almeroth is an active participant in several Internet Engineering Task Force (IETF) working groups, has helped manage multicast for Networld+Interop as part of the Network Operations Center (NOC) team, is a senior technologist for the IP Multicast Initiative, and is the multicast working group chair for Internet2.

Erick Mar is a senior systems engineer at Cisco Systems with CCIE certification in routing and switching (CCIE #3882). As a systems engineer for the last 7 years for various networking manufacturers, he has provided design and implementation support for Fortune 500 companies. Erick has an MBA from Santa Clara University and a B.S. in business administration from San Francisco State University.

Bob Quinn is senior technologist for Stardust.com, where he writes white papers and tracks IETF developments for the IP Multicast Initiative and QoS Forum. He is the principal author of the well-regarded *Windows Sockets Network Programming* (Addison-Wesley) and chairman of the WinSock 2 Editorial Board that oversees new developments and issues in WinSock application programming interfaces (APIs). You can reach him at rcq@stardust.com.

Acknowledgments

This book would not have been possible without the support of scores of people, all of whom I can't possibly enumerate but to whom I'm deeply indebted. In particular, I wish to thank Dino Farinacci; Liming Wei; and their manager, Achutha Rao, from the IP multicast development group at Cisco. Dino and Liming's support and patience through numerous questions and discussions on the topic of IP multicast went far beyond the call of duty. I also wish to express my thanks to my development editor, Kathy Trace, who suffered through all my deadline slips and bizarre manuscript format requirements, in addition to generally being my confidant when I needed to bounce ideas off of someone. Furthermore, I wish to thank my technical reviewers, Dino Farinacci, Manoj Leelanivas, Kevin Almeroth, Erick Mar, and Bob Quinn for their excellent input on the technical content of this book.

Finally, I owe a tremendous thanks to my wife and my son who provided support and patience as well as tolerating my occasional loud outbursts directed at the word processing software on my PC when it produced unexpected results.

Contents at a Glance

Table of Contents

Introduction

Even though IP multicast has actually been around for some time, it is just beginning to come of age and promises to be one of the most exciting network technologies to emerge since the introduction of the World Wide Web. Multimedia audio and video conferencing applications that have been available for some time to UNIX workstation users have now been ported to the Microsoft Windows environments. Using these applications and many other recently developed multimedia applications, network users have begun to experiment in the world of IP multicast. What they are finding is that IP multicast provides a wealth of possibilities beyond the most obvious applications of audio/video multimedia. The financial community is a primary example of where IP multicast–enabled networks can be leveraged to provide efficient delivery of important market data, as well as serve as a vehicle for communicating among stock market traders. This directly translates into a rapidly growing demand by users to migrate their unicast-only IP networks to multicast enabled networks. This demand is placing enterprise and service provider network engineers under tremendous pressure to learn IP multicast technology. Furthermore, many of the concepts of IP multicast such as distribution trees and Reverse Path Forwarding are totally foreign to most network designers and administrators because these concepts are not found in any other network discipline. Consequently, many network professionals are facing a very steep learning curve with little time and extremely limited information with which to come up to speed on IP multicast.

I was introduced to IP multicast in 1995 while working as a systems engineer for Cisco Systems. I quickly learned that enabling IP multicast on a Cisco router was extremely simple and required learning only two configuration commands. However, after IP multicast was enabled, I found that I had little idea as to what was supposed to be happening in the network. Even worse, the multicast routing and debugging information that was displayed by the router appeared to me to be nearly undecipherable. As I struggled to learn and understand this fascinating network technology, I quickly found that there was very little in the way of easy-to-understand information on the topic other than the RFCs that described the associated protocols. (Most of these RFCs proved to be more of a cure for my chronic insomnia than anything else.) Over time and with some considerable experimentation, I was able to build a clear picture of what IP multicast is and does from this limited repository of information, mostly written in serious geek-speak. I wrote *Developing IP Multicast Networks, Volume I* to provide other network professionals with an easy-to-understand book that not only addresses the fundamentals of IP multicast but also provides the necessary information to implement and debug Cisco-based IP multicast networks.

Objectives

The purpose of this book is to turn you into a qualified IP multicast network engineer. To accomplish this goal, the book clearly explains the principles involved with IP multicast and provides specific details on implementing Cisco-based IP multicast–enabled networks. Regardless of whether you are a network engineer trying to enable IP multicast services in a large Internet service provider network or the network administrator of a small enterprise network, this book is for you.

Audience

This book is intended for any person or organization that is contemplating making the transition from a unicast-only IP network to an IP multicast–enabled network. This group includes experienced network engineers responsible for designing networks as well as network operators who are responsible for the day-to-day operation and monitoring of the network. Even applications developers who have been tasked with writing new programs that will leverage the powers of IP multicast will benefit from the concepts presented in this book.

Although the book assumes no previous experience with IP multicast, it does, however, assume that the reader already has some knowledge in the area of IP unicast routing. Having said that, the material is presented in a building-block fashion that takes the reader from the basics of IP multicast concepts through sample multicast applications, into multicast routing protocols, and beyond. This building-block approach allows the book to address the needs of both IP multicast neophytes struggling with the basic concepts as well as experienced network engineers who are evolving their networks to support IP multicast.

Organization

The book is organized into five parts and an appendix:

- **Part I—Fundamentals of IP Multicast**—Chapters 1 through 4 cover the basic concepts, terminology, and mechanisms of IP multicast and provide the foundation for later chapters. These fundamentals include how IP multicast traffic is addressed at both Layers 2 and 3 of the OSI protocol model, as well as two of the most important concepts in IP multicast: distribution trees and Reverse Path Forwarding. Chapter 3, "Internet Group Management Protocol," is devoted to the mechanisms used between host and router to signal which multicast flow a host is interested in receiving. Finally, Chapter 4, "Multimedia Multicast Applications," covers several popular multimedia multicast applications and provides an introduction to some of the protocols and methodologies used by these applications.

- **Part II—Multicast Routing Protocol Overview**—Chapters 5 through 9 serve as an overview of the most well-known inter-domain multicast routing protocols, Distance Vector Multicast Routing Protocol (DVMRP), multicast OSPF (MOSPF), PIM dense mode (PIM-DM), PIM sparse mode (PIM-SM), and Core-Based Trees (CBTs). Each chapter is devoted to the concepts, mechanisms, suitability, and scalability of one of these multicast routing protocols. The coverage of DVMRP mechanisms presented in Chapter 5, "Distance Vector Multicast Routing Protocol," is of particular importance when the topic of interfacing Cisco routers to DVMRP networks is discussed in Chapter 13, "Connecting to DVMRP Networks."

- **Part III—Implementing Cisco Multicast Networks**—Chapters 10 through 13 get into the details of implementing IP multicast networks using Cisco routers and the PIM multicast routing protocol. Chapter 10, "Using PIM Dense Mode," and Chapter 11, "Using PIM Sparse Mode," dive deep into the details of using Cisco's implementation of PIM sparse mode and dense mode and pick up where Chapters 6 and 7 left off. These two chapters cover the interpretation of the Cisco multicast routing table entries as well as the state rules and mechanisms that create and maintain them. Chapter 12 addresses the topic of rendezvous point (RP) engineering and includes information on the protocols that are used to distribute Group-to-RP information to all the routers in the network. Finally, Chapter 13, "Connecting to DVMRP Networks," covers the often misunderstood Cisco DVMRP interoperability features that permit Cisco routers to function as a border router between a DVMRP network and a Cisco PIM network.

- **Part IV—Multicast at Layer 2**—Chapters 14 and 15 delve into the Layer 2 world of multicasting over campus networks and nonbroadcast, multiaccess (NBMA) networks. Chapter 14, "Multicast over Campus Networks," discusses some of the issues and problems encountered with constraining multicast traffic in campus LAN environments. Chapter 15, "Multicast over NBMA Networks," identifies the problems that can be encountered in nonbroadcast, multiaccess networks if the unique aspects of these types of networks are ignored.

- **Part V—Advanced Multicast Topics**—Chapters 16 and 17 cover some of the more advanced scenarios that can be encountered when building large, complex IP multicast networks. Chapter 16, "Multicast Traffic Engineering," addresses limiting and controlling the flow of IP multicast traffic. Finally, Chapter 17 serves as a brief introduction to the area of inter-domain multicast routing. This final chapter covers both current and future protocols that are related to solving the complexities of building multicast distribution trees across multiple domains or autonomous systems in the Internet.

Approach

You may find that this book departs from some of the more traditional Cisco Press books that devote a fairly substantial portion of their text to configuration examples of Cisco routers. The reason is quite simple: IP multicast is easy to configure on a Cisco router! As you will soon find out, as few as two Internetwork Operating System (IOS) commands are needed to enable IP multicast. The true challenge is being able to understand what happens in both the network and in the routers after IP multicast is enabled.

Case in point: The internal Cisco training class that I have taught on several occasions also departs from the traditional lab exercise style used in the Introduction to Cisco Router Configuration (ICRC) and Advanced Cisco Router Configuration (ACRC) classes. In the ICRC/ACRC class scenario, each student is primarily focused on configuring his or her own router with respect to some networking protocol or feature. However, in my internal IP multicast class, most of the lab exercises are centered around the use of IOS **show** and **debug** commands on all routers in the lab to see what happens after IP multicast is enabled. This is typically accomplished by carefully stimulating the network with active senders and receivers to see the PIM protocol mechanisms in action.

Likewise, this book focuses on first providing the conceptual fundamentals of IP multicast. Not until we reach Part 3, "Implementing Cisco Multicast Networks," beginning with Chapter 10, do we finally begin to see our first configuration examples. Even then, the material is more focused on understanding the information that is displayed by the router and exactly what it means than on any detailed configuration examples. Only when we reach some of the more advanced chapters, such as Chapter 13, do we really begin to see significantly detailed configuration examples.

Finally, as you read this book, it may appear to you that IP multicast routing is upside-down because it is more concerned with where the traffic came from than where it is going. I often have to remind students in my IP multicast classes (who are generally already knowledgeable unicast routing engineers) of this fact by telling them to "stand on their heads." I generally use this imagery to help clarify a particular point that they are struggling to understand in this upside-down world. I've yet to have a student actually resort to physically standing on his or her head. Instead, the image seems to induce a change in mental perspective that somehow causes the "lights to come on." As you read this book, you may want to "stand on your head," particularly when trying to comprehend some of the more advanced concepts and mechanisms. This technique certainly has seemed to help my students in the past.

Fundamentals of IP Multicast

This part covers the fundamental concepts of IP multicasting that are crucial to understanding more advanced topics, such as individual multicast routing protocols.

Chapter 1 presents a brief history of IP multicast along with the rationale behind its use.

Chapter 2 introduces several key concepts that will be the foundation on which a firm understanding of IP multicast is built. One of the first topics introduced is IP multicast addressing. This section covers not only Layer 3 multicast group addresses, but also how these addresses map to addresses at Layer 2 for popular network media, such as Ethernet, FDDI, and Token Ring. In addition, Chapter 2 presents the important idea of multicast distribution trees, along with the associated multicast packet forward algorithms necessary for proper multicast traffic flow.

Chapter 3 is completely devoted to the details of the Internet Group Management Protocol (IGMP), which is the host to the router signaling mechanism used in IP multicast.

Chapter 4 focuses on some of the more popular MBone multimedia audio and video conferencing applications that use IP multicast. In addition, Chapter 4 discusses some of the other protocols that these applications use to transmit and receive real-time multimedia data, as well as announce the existence of the multimedia session to others in the network.

Introduction to IP Multicast

At one end of the IP communication spectrum is IP unicast communication, where a source IP host sends packets to a specific destination IP host. In this case, the destination address in the IP packet is the address of a single, unique host in the IP network. These IP packets are forwarded across the network from the source host to the destination host by routers. The routers at each point along the path between the source and destination use their unicast Routing Information Base (RIB) to make unicast forwarding decisions based on the IP destination address in the packet.

At the other end of the IP communication spectrum is an IP broadcast, where a source host sends packets to all IP hosts on a network segment. The destination address of an IP broadcast packet has the host portion of the destination IP address set to all ones and the network portion set to the address of the subnet (see Figure 1-1). (In some cases the host portion is set to all zeros, but this form of IP broadcast address is generally no longer used.)

Figure 1-1 *IP Broadcast Addresses*

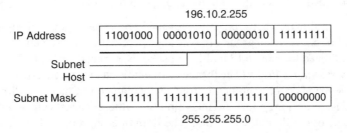

IP hosts (including routers) understand that packets, which contain an IP broadcast address as the destination address, are addressed to all IP hosts on the subnet. Unless specifically configured otherwise, routers do not forward IP broadcast packets and, therefore, IP broadcast communication is normally limited to the local subnet. Figure 1-2 clearly illustrates this point.

Figure 1-2   *IP Broadcast Being Blocked by a Router*

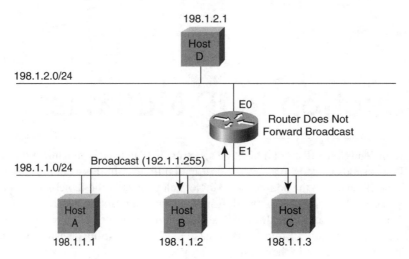

In this example, Host A sends out a broadcast to the local subnet 198.1.1.0/24. Because Hosts B and C are on the same subnet as Host A, they receive the broadcast. Host D, however, is on a different subnet (198.1.2.0/24) and does not receive the broadcast because the router does not forward broadcasts. If routers forwarded these broadcasts, route loops are likely to cause a catastrophic broadcast storm.

If your goal is to permit a host to send IP packets to other hosts not on the local subnet, then IP broadcasting is not sufficient to accomplish this goal.

IP multicasting falls between IP unicast and IP broadcast communication and enables a host to send IP packets to a group of hosts anywhere within the IP network. To do so, the destination address in an IP multicast packet is a special form of IP address called an *IP multicast group address*. (The format of IP multicast group addresses and exactly how hosts become members of a multicast group are explained in Chapter 2, "Multicast Basics.") IP multicast routers must forward incoming IP multicast packets out all interfaces that lead to members of the IP multicast group. The IP multicast group address is specified in the IP destination address field of the packet.

Exactly how the routers learn which interface to forward the packet to is part of the magic of IP multicast routing. The explanation of how this magic works is one of the goals of this book. By the time you finish reading this book, you should have a good understanding not only of how IP multicasting works in general but also of how to design efficient IP multicast networks using Cisco routers.

This chapter offers a brief history of IP multicasting, a discussion on the pros and cons of multicast, a description of various multicast applications, and an introduction to the multicast backbone.

A Brief History of IP Multicast

At Stanford University in the early 1980s, a doctoral graduate student, Steve Deering, was working on a distributed operating system project for his advisor, David Cheriton. This distributed operating system was called *Vsystem* and was composed of several computers tied together into a loosely coupled multiprocessing system via a single Ethernet segment. The computers on this Ethernet segment worked together and communicated at the operating system level via special messages sent on the common Ethernet segment. One of the operating system primitives permitted one computer to send a message to a group of the other computers on the local Ethernet segment using a MAC layer multicast.

As the project progressed, the need arose to add more computers to the multiprocessing system. Unfortunately, the only available computers were on the other side of the campus with production routers between the two networks. Consequently, the graduate students had to extend the operating system's inter-processor communications to work at Layer 3 of the OSI reference model so that the computers on the other side of the campus could function as part of the loosely coupled multiprocessor system. In addition, the MAC layer multicast messaging would also have to be extended to work at Layer 3. The task of finding a way to extend the MAC layer multicast capability across the Layer 3 routed network primarily fell to Steve Deering.

After studying the Open Shortest Path First (OSPF) Protocol and the Routing Information Protocol (RIP) IP routing protocols, Steve concluded that the link-state mechanisms of OSPF could certainly be extended to support multicasting. He also concluded that the basic mechanisms of RIP could be used as the basis for a new distance vector-based multicast routing protocol. This idea led to more research into the area of IP multicasting and ultimately resulted in Steve Deering's doctoral thesis, *"Multicast Routing in a Datagram Network,"* published in December 1991.

Dr. Deering's thesis also described a Host Membership Protocol, which became the basis for today's Internet Group Membership Protocol (IGMP) that IP multicast hosts use to signal to the router on the network that they desire to join a multicast group. In addition, Dr. Deering's thesis described a distance vector-based IP multicast routing protocol that was the basis for the Distance Vector Multicast Routing Protocol (DVMRP), also developed by Dr. Deering a few years later. These two protocols provided the first successful extensions to the IP packet network model to allow multicasting to be extended to Layer 3 of the OSI model. Since that time, advances in IP multicasting technology have continued and additional protocols such as Protocol Independent Multicasting (PIM) and multiprotocol extensions to the Border Gateway Protocol (BGP) have been developed. These protocols permit IP multicasting to scale beyond the initial limited implementations to large, enterprise-wide multicast networks and eventually on to a native, completely multicast-enabled Internet.

The Pros of IP Multicast

As the Internet and, in many cases, company intranets have grown in terms of the number of connected users, a large number of users frequently want to access the same information at roughly the same time. Using IP multicast techniques to distribute this information can often substantially reduce the overall bandwidth demands on the network. A good example of this approach is the rapidly growing area of audio and video Web content.

Here's an example: The ACME Company is using a bank of audio servers to transmit popular radio talk-show content, such as the Rush Limbaugh and Howard Stern shows, in real time to connected subscribers over the Internet. This is just one of many areas in which IP multicasting can provide significant advantages to the network providers as well as the content providers both on the Internet or within company intranets. However, it's doubtful that employees who tune in to Howard Stern through their company's Internet connection are actually performing a mission-critical task. Of course, if they happen to be in the entertainment business or do work for the FCC, this might be considered an important job-related task.

In the next few sections, the ACME Company example is used to illustrate some of the pros of IP multicasting. These include (but are not limited to) the following advantages: bandwidth, server load, and network loading.

Bandwidth

Consider, as an example, the way that the ACME Company is transmitting real-time feeds of the Rush Limbaugh talk show via an audio compression technique that requires an 8-kbps data stream to deliver. The dashed line on the graph in Figure 1-3 shows that as the number of connected *unicast* subscribers increases, the amount of network bandwidth also increases linearly. On the other hand, if you are *multicasting* the same program (represented by the solid line), a single 8-kbps multicast data stream can deliver the program to the subscribers.

Figure 1-3   *Unicast Versus Multicast Bandwidth for Audio*

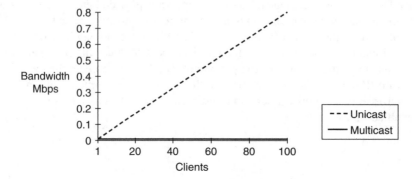

Given that ACME's revenues are based on the number of subscribers (which would somehow relate to the active number of clients at any time), it is reasonable to expect that ACME's marketing department goals are to see the number of clients in the tens of thousands. Meeting this goal is going to require engineering the network to provide bandwidths in the 100 Mbps range in order to support this single scenario.

Now, suppose that ACME has been very successful with this product and wants to extend its service offering to include highly compressed, low-rate, 120-kbps video streams to go along with the 8-kbps audio programs. Figure 1-4 shows that if the unicast model continues to be used as the delivery method, the bandwidth requirements are driven even higher.

Figure 1-4   *Unicast Versus Multicast Bandwidth for Video*

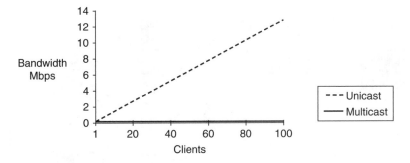

Assuming that, in the future, more and more Internet-connected subscribers have the ISDN, ADSL, or other medium-rate Internet connections necessary to watch ACME's program content and are tuned in, bandwidth demands can approach the multimegabit range.

If you further consider that some form of competition in this marketplace exists, ACME will not be the only supplier of this sort of program content. Other companies will begin offering similar services via the Internet, which will place additional demands on the Internet's infrastructure.

At this writing, several movie services were beginning to investigate the possibilities of distributing movies via data networks. Considering that a typical MPEG-2 video stream requires roughly 1.5 Mbps of bandwidth for a reasonably artifact-free video, IP multicasting is clearly an excellent choice for delivering this type of program content. Although you may have to wait some time before you can watch Arnold Schwarzenegger in the latest *Terminator III* at home via your Internet connection, you are quite likely to receive MPEG-2 multicasts of important company events over your company's IP network.

Server Load

Return to the example of the ACME Company's delivery of real-time audio to connected subscribers via the Internet. If ACME continues to use a unicast delivery mechanism, it will need to continue to increase the power and number of its real-time audio servers to meet the increasing number of connected subscribers.

Figure 1-5 shows an example of the number of flows that a real-time audio server must source to deliver Rush Limbaugh's talk show to three clients. Notice that in the unicast case (shown at the top of Figure 1-5), the server must source a separate flow for each client listening to the program.

Figure 1-5   *Server Load*

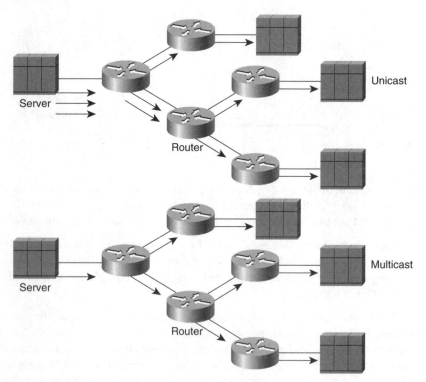

As the number of connected clients increases, the load on the server is going to increase until, at some point, the server will be unable to source the flows at the 8-kbps data rate necessary to deliver unbroken audio. At this point, ACME's customers will begin to complain about poor audio and potentially cancel subscriptions. This is a classic success/ failure situation in which the service offering is so successful that it exceeds the capability of the technology or network infrastructure to handle the demand. In this case, ACME is going to have to continue to increase the server's CPU size and its network interface bandwidth to accommodate more and more clients. Ultimately, ACME will have to provide multiple real-time audio servers to meet the demand.

On the other hand, if ACME uses IP multicast to deliver its program content (as shown at the bottom of Figure 1-5), only a single real-time data stream needs to be sourced to deliver the program to all of the connected clients. In this way, ACME will not need to purchase more and more real-time audio servers of increasing horsepower as the number of clients grows. It is obvious that IP multicasting offers a significant advantage in the area of reduced server horsepower.

Network Loading

Given that IP multicasting can significantly reduce bandwidth requirements when delivering the same content to multiple clients, the reduction in bandwidth consumption should equate to a reduction in the load placed on the routers in the network. In general, this assumption is true, but it's important to note that, in some cases, the router workload can increase at certain points in the network.

Referring once again to the multicast portion of Figure 1-5, we see that the first-hop router (the one directly connected to the server) is receiving a single data stream from the server. Note, however, that the first-hop router is replicating the single data stream into two outgoing data streams so as to deliver the data to the clients downstream. This replication process places an additional workload on the router, which needs to be considered in the overall network design. If a router does not have an efficient replication mechanism, the router load can increase significantly when the number of outgoing interfaces is high.

For example, some older implementations of multicast forwarding code require the router to duplicate the multicast packet for each additional outgoing interface. This duplication process requires a new packet buffer to be allocated from memory and the data in the original packet to be copied to the new buffer for transmission out an outgoing interface. If the number of outgoing interfaces is high, the duplication process can put a heavy burden on the router in terms of CPU and memory resources. Newer versions of forwarding code avoid this duplication process by queuing a pointer to the data in the original packet to each outgoing interface, thereby allowing each interface to share the same data buffer. This virtually eliminates the need to replicate the data for each outgoing interface and significantly reduces the CPU and memory resources necessary to forward the multicast packet.

The Cons of IP Multicast

Although there are a number of good reasons for wanting to use IP multicasting in networks, you need to keep in mind that there are limitations and downsides to this technology. These limitations need to be clearly understood, particularly if you are developing new applications that plan to use IP multicasting.

Some of the main drawbacks associated with the implementation of an IP multicast system include unreliable packet delivery, packet duplication, and network congestion.

Unreliable Packet Delivery

IP multicast, like IP unicast, is inherently unreliable. It is only through the use of TCP at Layer 4 (or some other higher layer protocol) that IP unicast data streams can be made reliable. However, because IP multicasting assumes a one-to-many communication mode, it was not designed to use the end-to-end mechanisms inherent in TCP. IP multicast packets typically use the User Datagram Protocol (UDP), which is best-effort in nature. Therefore, an application that uses IP multicasting must expect occasional packet loss and be prepared to either accept the loss or to somehow handle this at the application layer or via a reliable multicast protocol layered on top of UDP.

Dr. Deering states in his doctoral thesis that "during periods when paths are being changed immediately following a topology change, multicast packets that happen to be in flight have a lower probability of reaching their destinations than do unicast packets." Deering goes on to explain that even if erroneous unicast forwarding information exists at some routers in the network during a topology change, the network may eventually succeed in forwarding the packet to the destination. The reason this happens is that the unicast forwarding mechanism continues to attempt to forward the packet toward the destination IP address while the network topology is in transition, though the actual path may be somewhat circuitous. The forwarding mechanisms of IP multicast, on the other hand, are based on the source IP address, and to prevent loops, the packet is discarded if it does not arrive on the interface that would lead back to the source. The significance of Dr. Deering's point is a subject of some debate, particularly because the impact has not been studied. However, taken at face value, the theory is worth noting.

If the preceding material seems a bit unclear to you at this point, don't worry; Chapter 2 covers these forwarding mechanisms in greater detail. For now, it is sufficient to understand that IP multicast forwarding makes use of the source IP address, while IP unicast forwarding makes use of the destination IP address.

Packet Duplication

Duplicate packets are, just as in the UDP unicast world, a fact of life. However, a key difference between unicast and multicast routing is that routers intentionally send copies of a multicast packet out multiple interfaces. This increases the probability that multiple copies of the multicast packet may arrive at a receiver. For example, in certain redundant network topologies in which multiple paths exist to the receiver, duplicate packets can occur until the multicast routing protocol converges and eliminates the redundant path. Typically, this means that only an occasional packet is duplicated within the network, although under some transient network-error conditions, a number of duplicates may arrive at the receiver. (You'll gain a better understanding of where and when duplicate packets can occur while studying the details of different multicast routing protocols in Chapter 4, "Multimedia Multicast Applications.") Again, well-designed IP multicast applications should be prepared to detect and handle the arrival of the occasional duplicate packet.

NOTE   On one particular occasion, I recall a U.S. government agency that had designed an IP multicast application to control a critical piece of government equipment whose malfunction might result in the loss of life. Unfortunately, the application designers had failed to account for the possibility of duplicate packets caused by normal IP multicast network operation. This oversight resulted in the critical control command in the IP multicast packet being executed multiple times.

Imagine the result if such an application were used to command and control a number of tanks on the battlefield: "All tanks turn right 90 degrees," "All tanks turn right 90 degrees," "All tanks turn right 90 degrees . . ."

Network Congestion

In the TCP unicast case, the standard TCP *backoff* and *slow-start* window mechanisms automatically adjust the speed of the data transfer and therefore provide a degree of congestion avoidance within the network. Because IP multicasting cannot use TCP (due to its connectionless, one-to-many nature), there is no built-in congestion avoidance mechanism to prevent a multicast stream from exhausting link bandwidth or other critical router resources. Having said that, it is important for you to note that UDP unicast data streams suffer the same congestion avoidance problems! Furthermore, the recent growth in popularity of multimedia audio and video applications both on the Internet and within private intranets is increasing the amount of UDP unicast traffic.

As you learn more about the workings of IP multicasting, you will find that there is no provision to prevent you from joining a multicast group that is sourcing data at a rate that exceeds the total available bandwidth in your portion of the network.

Figure 1-6 shows two IP multicast servers sourcing the same video content. One server sources the program at 500 kbps, intended for use only in the local corporate headquarters network environment, while the other server sources the program at 128 kbps, intended for use by the remote sales offices.

Figure 1-6 *Exceeding Network Bandwidth with Multicast Traffic*

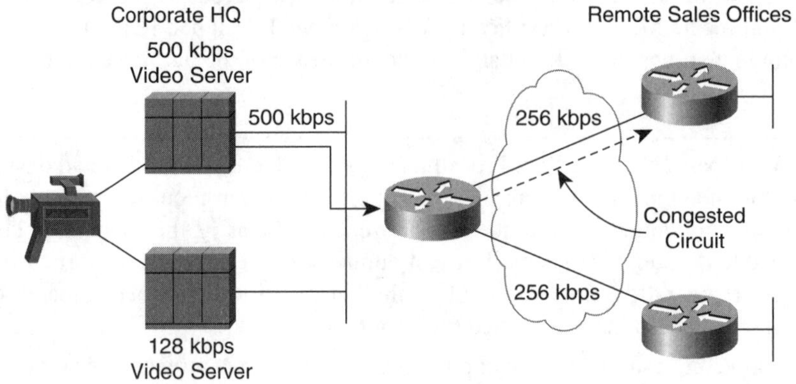

If a user at a remote sales office joins the 500-kbps multicast group by mistake, the result will be that the 256-kbps circuit to the remote sales office will be completely consumed by the 500-kbps video multicast traffic.

In Chapter 16, you will learn ways to configure the 256-kbps circuit to limit the amount of bandwidth that the multicast traffic can consume. Another alternative is to use administratively scoped boundaries to prevent users in the remote office from joining the 500 kbps group. (Administratively scoped addresses and boundaries are addressed in Chapter 2, "Multicast Basics.")

With all this in mind, it should be noted that, in all fairness, IP multicast is no worse than many of the common audio/video streaming applications in use today. These applications default to using unicast UDP and not TCP as their delivery mechanism—which means that like applications using IP multicast as a delivery mechanism, they do not use any form of congestion control!

NOTE
I'm frequently told by network designers that they do not plan to implement IP multicasting on their networks because of the lack of congestion control inherent in IP multicast's UDP-based delivery mechanisms. The real truth of the matter is that their users are probably putting up streaming-video Web servers that supply video clips of departmental training or other similar material using UDP-based, unicast applications that have no more congestion control than IP multicast. On the other hand, IP multicasting could possibly reduce the overall load in the network by sourcing a single multicast video stream instead of multiple unicast streams. (I sometimes refer to this behavior as being slightly *podiabombastic*; which is the tendency to blow off one's foot.)

The reason that some of these applications don't default to the use of TCP is that the normal retransmission mechanism in TCP provides little value because of the real-time nature of audio. By the time the retransmitted packet arrives, it's too late to be useful in the audio stream. Instead, the application designers would rather pull down the data as fast as the network permits (at the expense of possible network congestion) and not be artificially restricted by the congestion avoidance mechanism built into TCP. In most of these cases, the use of IP multicasting will reduce overall network congestion because a single transmitted data stream can reach all receivers.

NOTE   In the early days of the MBone, when the primary application was the audio conferencing tool *VAT* (which, of course, is based on UDP), the common practice in an audio conference was to clear one's throat over the microphone several times before beginning any dialog. This caused the congestion mechanisms of any active TCP streams flowing across potential congestion points in the network to kick in and back off, thereby giving the UDP-based audio conference traffic more bandwidth. I guess you might say that this was the first attempt at a crude form of resource reservation, which was set up via these initial Ahem packets. (The MBone is discussed in more detail later in this chapter.)

Multicast Applications

It's not uncommon for people to think of IP multicasting and video conferencing as almost the same thing. Although the first application to be used on an IP multicast–enabled network is often video conferencing, video is only one of many IP multicast applications that can add value to a company's business model. In fact, after some initial experiments with video conferencing over the IP multicast network, many companies find that for the bandwidth consumed, the talking head in a typical audio/video conference provides little added value to the communication process.

This section looks at some other IP multicast applications that have the potential for improving productivity, including multimedia conferencing, data replication, real-time data multicasts, and gaming and simulation applications.

Multimedia Conferencing

Some excellent IP multicast, multimedia conferencing tools were developed for the UNIX environment for use over the MBone (the next few sections discuss more about the MBone). These tools (many of which have recently been ported to the Windows 95 and NT platforms) permit a many-to-many audio-only or audio/video conference to take place via IP multicast. In addition to the audio and video tools, a UNIX-based Whiteboard tool was developed that permits users to share a common, electronic whiteboard. Besides these MBone freeware tools for multimedia conferencing over IP multicast networks, other companies are now beginning to offer commercial forms of these tools with other value-added features. (Chapter 4, "Multimedia Multicast Applications," looks at the MBone freeware tools in detail and explains how to download them.)

Many people start with audio/video conferencing because video is a particularly exciting new way to communicate over a network. After the novelty of video wears off and the realities of the bandwidths and workstation horsepower that are consumed by video conferencing (particularly if everyone in the conference is sourcing video at the same time) become apparent, it's not uncommon to see audio-only conferencing become the normal mode. Additionally, if an audio-only conference is coupled with an IP multicast-based, data-sharing application (such as the Whiteboard application previously mentioned) that allows the members of the conference to share graphics information, the result is an extremely powerful form of multimedia conferencing that does not consume much bandwidth.

Data Distribution

Data replication is another IP multicast application area that is rapidly becoming very popular. By using IP multicasting, IS departments are adopting a push model of file and database updates. Applications such as Starburst's (http://www.starburstcom.com) MFTP product, as well as work done in the area of reliable multicast by Globalcast (http://www.gcast.com), permit the reliable delivery of files and data to groups of nodes in the network. As the name MFTP implies, this product is like a multicast form of FTP. One or more files may be sent simultaneously with FTP to a group of nodes in the network by using IP multicasting.

This sort of technology permits companies to push new information such as price and product information to their remote stores every night so that the stores have up-to-date information the next business day.

Real-Time Data Multicasts

The delivery of real-time data to large groups of hosts is another area where IP multicasting is becoming popular. A good example is the delivery of stock ticker information to workstations on the trading floor. Previously, special applications were built to deliver this time-critical information to traders on the trading floor. More and more financial and investment firms are also investigating the use of IP multicasting to deliver information to their customers as another revenue-generating financial and trading service.

By assigning different financial categories (bonds, transportations, pharmaceuticals, and so forth) to different multicast groups, traders can use their workstations to receive only the real-time financial data for which they are interested.

Gaming and Simulations

IP multicasting is very well suited for use in network gaming or simulation applications. Although numerous PC games and simulations permit groups of networked gamers to battle each other in simulated dogfights or other fantasy environments such as Doom, virtually all these applications make use of unicast, point-to-point connections.

Typically, a gaming or simulation application must learn of the other participants via either manual configuration or some other special participant notification mechanism. When the notification occurs, each PC makes an IP unicast connection to all the other PCs in the game or simulation. Obviously, this is an *Order(N^2)* problem that requires on the order of N^2 interconnections between all N PCs and does not scale to large numbers of participants. The upper limit for this sort of game or simulation depends largely on the horsepower of the individual PCs or workstations being used and is usually between 5 and 10 participants.

Another method that is sometimes used in this type of networked environment is to have a central gaming or simulation server to which all participants must connect via an IP unicast connection. This places the burden of distributing the real-time game or simulation data to all of the participants on the server. Again, depending on the horsepower of the server, this solution can typically scale only to 100 or so participants.

IP multicasting can be used to extend gaming and simulations to extremely large numbers of participants. Participating PCs or workstations simply join the IP multicast group and begin sending and receiving gaming and simulation data. Dividing the simulation data into more than one stream and then communicating this information via separate IP multicast groups can further extend this concept. This division of data permits the PCs or workstations to limit the amount of simulation data that they are sending and receiving (and, hence, the number of IP multicast groups they need to join) to what they currently need to participate in a game or simulation situation.

For example, each room in a fantasy battle game could be assigned a separate IP multicast group. Only those PCs or workstations whose participants are in this room need to join this multicast group to send and receive simulation data about what is happening there. When players leave the room and go into another room, they leave the IP multicast group associated with the first room and join the IP multicast group associated with the new room.

NOTE   The U.S. military has built one of the largest IP multicast–based, war-game simulations that
I have ever seen. This simulation divides the battlefield into map grids, each of which
corresponds to a multicast group. This results in the use of thousands of IP multicast groups
to communicate between the individual participants of the simulation. As each participant,
such as a tank or an F-16 fighter, enters the map grid, the simulation application joins the
associated IP multicast group in order to receive simulation data about what is happening
in the map grid. When the participant leaves the map grid and goes to another, the
application leaves the original multicast group and joins the IP multicast group associated
with the new map grid.

As more IP networks become multicast enabled, more game and simulation application
developers are expected to make use of IP multicasting for large-scale simulations. It's not
unthinkable that sometime in the near future, thousands of gamers will be simultaneously
battling it out over the Internet in the ultimate Doom game.

MBone—The Internet's Multicast Backbone

The Internet's *Multicast Backbone (MBone)* is the small subset of Internet routers and hosts
that are interconnected and capable of forwarding IP multicast traffic.

NOTE   Note that I said "small subset," which is to say that IP multicast traffic does not flow to every
point in the Internet (yet). Newcomers to IP multicasting often mistakenly think that if they
are connected to the Internet they can receive IP multicast traffic. They believe that by just
turning on IP multicast routing on their Internet gateway router or by adding some special
application to their PC, they can receive MBone multimedia sessions via their dialup
Internet service provider. Unfortunately, this is not the case, as you will learn in the
following sections.

The next few sections describe various MBone session examples, a history of the MBone,
and the MBone architecture of today and tomorrow.

MBone Sessions

One of the most popular sessions on the MBone is the audio/video multicast of NASA's
shuttle missions. Other interesting and sometimes rather bizarre multimedia content is
often broadcast over the MBone. For example, individuals have set up pet-cams to
broadcast video of their pets. On one occasion, an engineer set up a cat-cam at home and

kept the workstation at his office tuned in to this video multicast so he could monitor the cat's recovery from its recent surgery.

On another occasion, someone broadcast the live CNN feed of the O. J. Simpson verdict. This multimedia multicast had over 350 members tuned in at one point. Other media events have been multicast over the MBone. In 1994, a Rolling Stones concert was multicast over the MBone from the DEC Systems Research Center. The interesting thing was that about a half-hour before the concert began, the rock group Severe Tire Damage (several members of which were Internet engineers) began transmitting audio and video of their band performing live music. The band timed their show so that they finished as the Rolling Stones concert was beginning, thereby "opening" for the Rolling Stones via the MBone.

Besides the popular NASA shuttle missions and the occasional rock concert, sessions from various conventions and seminars are frequently multicast over the MBone. During a period when I was unable to travel (while I was recovering from minor knee surgery), I tuned in to the Internet Engineering Task Force (IETF) audio and video multicast from my home by way of my Cisco 1600 router and ISDN line that connects me to Cisco's corporate network. This allowed me to keep up with some of the key IETF sessions (which just happened to have to do with IP multicasting) that I was interested in attending.

These sorts of events have been largely responsible for the growing demand for MBone connectivity by more and more Internet users. Although some of the examples that I have given are more for fun than anything else (would you believe that at one time someone was multicasting video of several different lava lamps), commercial and private multicasting over the MBone is rapidly becoming part of the new Internet experience.

History of the MBone

In the early 1990s, several members of the research community complained to the Defense Advanced Research Projects Agency (DARPA)—the governing body of the Internet at that time—that the Internet had become a production network and was therefore no longer available for research and experimentation with new network technologies. As a result, the U.S. government formed the DARPA Testbed Network (DARTNet) to give the researchers a playground network on which they could test and evaluate new tools and technologies without affecting the production Internet.

DARTNet was initially composed of T1 lines connecting various sites including Xerox PARC, Lawrence Berkley Labs, SRI, ISI, BBN, MIT, and the University of Delaware. These sites used Sun SPARCstations running *routed* as the unicast routing daemon as well as *mrouted* as the DVMRP multicast routing daemon. Therefore, DARTNet had native IP multicast support between all sites. Weekly audio conferences between researchers located at the various DARTNet sites around the United States were soon normal practice.

In early 1992, the IETF made plans to hold their next meeting in March in San Diego, California. Unfortunately, one of the DARTNet researchers was not going to be able to travel to San Diego to participate in the IETF and expressed her disappointment to her coworkers. Several DARTNet researchers, including Steve Deering and Steve Casner, decided to audio multicast the IETF proceedings (which not only allowed their colleague to participate in the IETF sessions from the DARTNet network, but also allowed the researchers to further test the concepts of IP multicasting over the Internet).

Steve Deering and Steve Casner volunteered to arrange for the audio to be fed into a borrowed Sun SPARCstation at the San Diego IETF. To get the multicast audio back into DARTNet, a DVMRP tunnel was configured between the SPARCstation at the IETF and the DARTNet backbone. Invitations to participate in this IETF audio multicast were also sent out ahead of time to various Internet research organizations in the United States, Australia, Sweden, and England, along with information on how to configure a Sun SPARCstation with a DVMRP tunnel through the Internet back to the DARTNet backbone. Several sites responded to the invitation and setup DVMRP tunnels to the DARTNet backbone. The result was the first audio multicast of the IETF to several locations on the Internet around the world.

NOTE During one of the plenary sessions at the IETF, Steve Deering and Steve Casner arranged for the audio output of the SPARCstation to be piped into the public address system in the room. The attendees of the plenary session were informed that the session was being audio multicast over the Internet to several locations throughout the United States, Australia, Sweden, and England. At one point in his presentation, the plenary speaker posed a question to the multicast audience. Immediately, the voice of one of the multicast participants in Australia came through as clear as a bell over the public address system (there was much less congestion on the Internet in those days), and the participant proceeded to answer the speaker's question! Multimedia conferencing by way of IP multicast over the Internet had come of age.

At the end of the March 1992 IETF, the DVMRP tunnels to DARTNet were torn down and life on DARTNet generally returned to normal. The audio multicast had been so successful, however, that plans were made to multicast both audio and video from the next IETF convention. Invitations were again sent out to even more sites on the Internet, and DVMRP tunnels were again built from these sites back to the DARTNet backbone. Like the March IETF multicast from San Diego, the Washington, D.C., IETF held that summer was also successfully audio and video multicast to participants all over the world.

People were, by now, beginning to see the power of IP multicasting. The network administrators at DARTNet and the other participating sites decided to leave the DVMRP tunnels in place for on-going multimedia conferencing over the Internet. These initial tunnel sites, coupled with DARTNet serving as the initial multicast core network, were soon dubbed the MBone.

Today's MBone Architecture

From the initial handful of sites connected to the DARTNet multicast core (via DVMRP tunnels and Sun SPARCstations running mrouted) in March 1992, the MBone has grown steadily. Figure 1-7 shows the average number of routes advertised in the MBone over the last 5 to 6 years.

Figure 1-7   *MBone Growth*

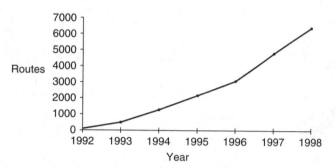

When this book was written, the average number of DVMRP routes being advertised in the MBone was rapidly approaching 7000. Although this number is a significant increase over the 100 or so routes in the early 1990s, keep in mind that the total number of unicast routing prefixes being advertised in the Internet at the same time was on the order of 50,000. Clearly, we have a long way to go before the entire Internet supports IP multicasting.

Although the number of routes in the MBone have increased significantly, the basic architecture of today's MBone has not changed substantially since it was built in 1992. With just a few exceptions, DVMRP routes are still being exchanged between MBone routers over a network of DVMRP tunnels. Unfortunately, DVMRP was never designed to be an inter-domain multicast routing protocol nor will it scale to the size of the Internet. (For one thing, being a distance vector-based routing protocol, DVMRP has a hop-count maximum of 32. The diameter of the Internet is certainly greater than 32!) Clearly, either a new protocol, a new MBone architecture, or both will be necessary to make Internet multicast traffic as ubiquitous as Internet unicast traffic.

Since the initial MBone was created in 1992, using UNIX hosts running mrouted as MBone routers, the percentage of MBone routers running mrouted has slowly been decreasing. Table 1-1 shows statistics (taken at the time this book was written) on the version of the router code and the number of hosts (routers) running that particular version. In general, version numbers greater than or equal to 10.0 are Cisco routers exchanging DVMRP routes, while version numbers less than 10.0 are mrouted UNIX-based hosts. This table clearly shows that more than 50 percent of the MBone has migrated to commercial-based router platforms.

Table 1-1   *MBone Router Versions*

Version	Hosts	Percent
11.2PMS	929	26.5
11.1PMS	928	26.5
3.8PGM	719	20.5
3.255PGM	235	6.7
11.0PMS	205	5.9
11.3PMS	129	3.7
3.8PGMS	92	2.6
3.38PGM	45	1.3
11.1PM	41	1.2
11.2PM	36	1.0
11.3PM	17	0.5
11.0PM	11	0.3
3.255PGMS	2	0.1
10.3pim	32	0.9
3.6PGM	24	0.7
10.2pim	8	0.2
11.0Mpim	3	0.1
10.3	9	0.3
2.2	8	0.2
10.2	7	0.2
3.3	7	0.2
1.0	6	0.2
3.4	4	0.1
2.0	4	0.1
3.5PGM	1	0.0
3.1	1	0.0
Total	3503	

Tomorrow's MBone Architecture

As this book is being written, much work is underway to design new protocols and architectures to permit IP multicasting to be extended to all points on the Internet. New inter-domain multicast routing protocols and forwarding algorithms are being developed to give Internet service providers (ISPs) the control that they need over multicast peering and traffic management in order for them to offer a reliable multicast service that doesn't significantly impact their existing unicast service. Chapter 17 takes a look at some of this work in progress.

In addition to new inter-domain multicast routing protocols, dynamic multicast address allocation may also be necessary to support new multicast architectures and to carefully manage the limited IP multicast address space. (See Chapter 17 for a brief look at these techniques.)

Not only must the technical issues of inter-domain multicast routing be solved, but the ISPs that make up the lion's share of today's Internet must develop the financial and billing models to offer IP multicast as a service to their customers. Should the sender pay a premium for the ability to source multicast traffic (as in the previous ACME example), or should the customer who wants to receive the multicast content pay? Looking down the road to a day when many-to-many multimedia conferences over the Internet are a normal everyday occurrence, it's likely that both parties will need to pay. Again, defining the financial and business models is nearly as complex a process as solving the routing issues and will have to be addressed.

Summary

Although IP multicasting has been around since the early 1990s, its power is only now beginning to be realized. Corporations are seeing the benefits in bandwidth utilization and the capability to deliver content to large numbers of receivers at a time. Internet service providers are also seeing benefits in offering IP multicast as a service to their customers, many of whom are willing to pay for this service. The MBone itself has enjoyed rapid growth in the last few years, and indications are that this trend will continue, although how the technology will evolve to scale to the numbers of networks in the Internet today is unclear.

Having said all of this, IP multicasting is still a new and emerging technology that has its own set of problems, as do all new technologies. There is still much work to be done before IP multicast capabilities are available to all members of the Internet. Finally, networks must be carefully designed, using some new design philosophies, to support IP multicasting without experiencing a myriad of problems. A primary goal of this book is to provide the reader with the necessary information to make good design choices as they change their unicast-only networks of today into multicast-enabled networks of tomorrow.

CHAPTER 2

Multicast Basics

RFC 1112—"IP Multicast Dead Sea Scrolls." No, that's not RFC 1112's real title, but it is what I affectionately call it, particularly when I'm teaching a beginner's class on IP multicasting. The real title of this RFC (which is not nearly as much fun to use as "IP Multicast Dead Sea Scrolls") is "Host Extensions for IP Multicasting." This RFC was written by Dr. Steve Deering and describes and standardizes some of his work on the IP host mechanisms necessary to provide IP multicast capability. The reason I like the name "IP Multicast Dead Sea Scrolls" is that this RFC was the first widely accepted definition of how to do multicasting in an IP network—at least from the IP host perspective. The RFC includes topics such as IP multicast addresses, sending and receiving IP multicast packets, and the first version of the Internet Group Management Protocol (IGMP).

This chapter translates the writings on multicast addresses and multicast Media Access Control (MAC) addresses found in the "IP Multicast Dead Sea Scrolls" (RFC 1112) from RFC-speak into language that I hope is easier to understand.

NOTE The name "IP Multicast Dead Sea Scrolls" is used here only in jest and is not meant to be disparaging. I have referred to RFC 1112 in this manner in conversations with Dr. Deering, and he seemed to appreciate the humor.

This chapter also discusses the important concepts of multicast distribution trees and multicast forwarding. Chapter 3, "Internet Group Management Protocol," covers the remaining topics in RFC 1112, "IGMP" (both versions 1 and 2).

Multicast Addresses

Unlike unicast IP addresses that uniquely identify a single IP host, multicast IP addresses specify an arbitrary group of IP hosts that have joined the group and wish to receive traffic sent to this group. This section explores the format of IP multicast addresses and how these addresses are assigned.

IP Class D Addresses

IP multicast addresses have been assigned to the old class D address space by the Internet Assigned Number Authority (IANA). Addresses in this space are denoted with a binary 1110 prefix in the first 4 bits of the first octet, as shown in Figure 2-1. Thus, IP multicast addresses span a range from 224.0.0.0 through 239.255.255.255.

Figure 2-1   *Multicast Address Format*

Class D Addresses

Octet 1	Octet 2	Octet 3	Octet 4
1110xxxx	xxxxxxxx	xxxxxxxx	xxxxxxxx

NOTE   The use of classful IP addresses has been eliminated with the adoption of classless inter-domain routing (CIDR), which ignores the old class A, B, and C fixed network address boundaries and uses a network prefix/mask instead. This has allowed the allocation of the limited IP address space more efficiently as the popularity of the Internet has increased. It is still common, however, to hear people refer to the IP multicast address space as class D addresses.

Assigned Multicast Addresses

The IANA controls the assignment of IP multicast addresses. Before you run off to the IANA to request a block of the IP multicast address space for your company to use, you need to understand that this address space is a limited resource. Therefore, the IANA is very reluctant to assign any IP multicast addresses unless there is a very good justification to do so. The IANA will certainly not assign an arbitrary block of IP multicast addresses to you! Additionally, the IANA generally does not assign individual IP multicast addresses to new application programs without a really good technical justification. Instead, they tend to assign individual IP multicast addresses for use by specific network protocols. This means that the entire Internet must share the remaining unassigned range of IP multicast addresses in some dynamic, cooperative method. This situation allows multicast addresses to be dynamically allocated or *leased* (as in the Dynamic Host Configuration Protocol [DHCP] model) when needed and then released for use by others when the address is no longer used. The next couple of sections discuss some of the IP multicast addresses that have been reserved for use by specific protocols.

Currently, the most widely used method for dynamic IP multicast address allocation is the Session Directory program (SDR), which is detailed in Chapter 4, "Multimedia Multicast Applications." The techniques used by SDR to avoid IP multicast address collisions, however, were not designed to scale to the thousands of multicast groups that will be active in the future. At the time that this book is being written, a great deal of work is being done in the Internet Engineering Task Force (IETF) either to modify SDR so that it scales well or to define and implement some new form of dynamic multicast address allocation.

NOTE   Not only is it considered by the Internet community to be rather selfish to expect your newly developed application to be assigned its own hard-coded, reserved multicast address, it's also generally not in your best interest to design your application to operate this way. Rather, it is better to design your multicast application so that it can be passed an IP multicast address and port number as parameters at startup time. This makes the application much more flexible and ensures that it will continue to be useful as new dynamic multicast address allocation methods are developed in the future.

Link-Local Multicast Addresses

The IANA has reserved the range of 224.0.0.0 through 224.0.0.255 for use by network protocols on a local network segment. Packets with an address in this range are local in scope, are not forwarded by IP routers (regardless of their time-to-live [TTL] values), and therefore go no farther than the local network. Routers that do happen to forward these multicasts off of the local subnet are referred to affectionately by network administrators as *broken routers*.

Table 2-1 is a partial list of reserved multicast addresses taken directly from the IANA database. The table lists the reserved link-local addresses, the network protocol function to which they have been assigned, and the person that requested the address or the RFC associated with the protocol.

Table 2-1   *Link-Local Multicast Addresses*

Address	Usage	Reference
224.0.0.1	All Hosts	[RFC 1112, JBP]
224.0.0.2	All Multicast Routers	[JBP]
224.0.0.3	Unassigned	[JBP]
224.0.0.4	DVMRP Routers	[RFC 1075, JBP]
224.0.0.5	OSPF Routers	[RFC 1583, JXM1]
224.0.0.6	OSPF Designated Routers	[RFC 1583, JXM1]
224.0.0.7	ST Routers	[RFC 1190, KS14]
224.0.0.8	ST Hosts	[RFC 1190, KS14]
224.0.0.9	RIP2 Routers	[RFC 1723, SM11]
224.0.0.10	IGRP Routers	[Farinacci]

Table 2-1   *Link-Local Multicast Addresses (Continued)*

Address	Usage	Reference
224.0.0.11	Mobile-Agents	[Bill Simpson]
224.0.0.12	DHCP Server/Relay Agent	[RFC 1884]
224.0.0.13	All PIM Routers	[Farinacci]
224.0.0.14	RSVP-Encapsulation	[Braden]
224.0.0.15	All CBT Routers	[Ballardie]
224.0.0.16	Designated-SBM	[Baker]
224.0.0.17	All SBMS	[Baker]
224.0.0.18	VRRP	[Hinden]
224.0.0.19 to 224.0.0.255	Unassigned	[JBP]

For example, the IP multicast address of 224.0.0.1 has been assigned the meaning of All
Hosts, and 224.0.0.2 has been assigned the meaning of All Multicast Routers. Both of these
multicast addresses are used extensively by IGMP, which multicast hosts use to communicate
their desire to join a multicast group to a locally connected router (see Chapter 3).

The Open Shortest-Path Forwarding (OSPF) routing protocol, for example, employs local
subnet multicast addresses. If you use OSPF in your network, you may have seen packets
addressed to the 224.0.0.5 and 224.0.0.6 multicast address on your networks. These
addresses permit OSPF routers to communicate important OSPF data to All OSPF Routers
or All OSPF Designated Routers respectively.

Other Reserved Addresses

The IANA typically assigns single multicast address requests for network protocols or
network applications out of the 224.0.1.xxx address range. Multicast routers will forward
these multicast addresses, unlike multicast addresses in the 224.0.0.xxx address range,
which are local in scope and are never forwarded by routers.

Table 2-2 is a partial list of these single multicast address assignments.

Table 2-2   *Other Reserved Multicast Addresses*

Address	Usage	Reference
224.0.1.0	VMTP Managers Group	[RFC 1045, DRC3]
224.0.1.1	NTP-Network Time Protocol	[RFC 1119, DLM1]
224.0.1.2	SGI-Dogfight	[AXC]
224.0.1.3	Rwhod	[SXD]

Table 2-2   *Other Reserved Multicast Addresses (Continued)*

Address	Usage	Reference
224.0.1.6	NSS-Name Service Server	[BXS2]
224.0.1.8	SUN NIS+ Information Service	[CXM3]
224.0.1.20	Any Private Experiment	[JBP]
224.0.1.21	DVMRP on MOSPF	[John Moy]
224.0.1.32	Mtrace	[Casner]
224.0.1.33	RSVP-encap-1	[Braden]
224.0.1.34	RSVP-encap-2	[Braden]
224.0.1.39	Cisco-RP-Announce	[Farinacci]
224.0.1.40	Cisco-RP-Discovery	[Farinacci]
224.0.1.52	Mbone-VCR-Directory	[Holfelder]
224.0.1.78	Tibco Multicast1	[Shum]
224.0.1.79	Tibco Multicast2	[Shum]
224.0.1.80 to 224.0.1.255	Unassigned	[JBP]

Administratively Scoped Multicast Addresses

In addition to the multicast address ranges previously described, the IANA has reserved the range of 239.0.0.0 through 239.255.255.255 as administratively scoped addresses for use in private multicast domains. These addresses are similar in nature to the reserved IP unicast ranges, such as 10.0.0.0/8, defined in RFC 1918 and the IANA will not assign them to any other group or protocol. Therefore, in theory, network administrators are free to use multicast addresses in this range inside a domain without fear of conflicting with others elsewhere on the Internet. The use of administratively scoped addresses also helps to conserve the limited multicast address space because they can be reused in different regions of the network. In reality, network administrators must configure their multicast routers to ensure that multicast traffic in this address range doesn't cross into or out of their multicast domain. See the "Administratively Scoped Boundaries" section later in this chapter for more information.

Multicast MAC Addresses

The original Ethernet specification (now standardized by the IEEE) made provisions for the transmission of broadcast and/or multicast packets. As shown in Figure 2-2, Bit 0 of Octet 0 in an IEEE MAC address indicates whether the destination address is a broadcast/multicast address or a unicast address.

Figure 2-2   *IEEE 802.3 MAC Address Format*

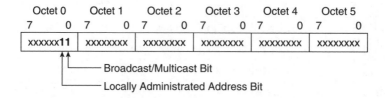

If this bit is set, then the MAC frame is destined for either an arbitrary group of hosts or all hosts on the network (if the MAC destination address is the broadcast address, 0xFFFF.FFFF.FFFF). IP multicasting at Layer 2 makes use of this capability to transmit IP multicast packets to a group of hosts on a LAN segment.

The following sections examine how Layer 3 IP multicast addresses are mapped into IEEE MAC addresses for Ethernet, FDDI, and Token Ring LANs.

Ethernet Multicast MAC Address Mapping

In the case of Ethernet, IP multicast frames all use MAC layer addresses beginning with the 24-bit prefix of 0x0100.5Exx.xxxx. Unfortunately, only half of these MAC addresses are available for use by IP multicast. This leaves 23 bits of MAC address space for mapping Layer 3 IP multicast addresses into Layer 2 MAC addresses. Since all Layer 3 IP multicast addresses have the first 4 of the 32 bits set to 0x1110, this leaves 28 bits of meaningful IP multicast address information. These 28 bits must map into only 23 bits of the available MAC address. This mapping is shown graphically in Figure 2-3.

Figure 2-3   *IP Multicast to Ethernet/FDDI MAC Address Mapping*

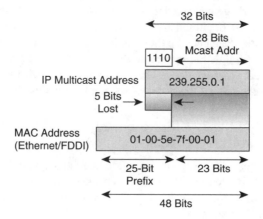

Just 23 Bits?

There's an interesting story as to why only 23 bits worth of MAC address space was allocated for IP multicast. Back in the early 1990s, Steve Deering was bringing some of his research work on IP multicasting to fruition, and he wanted the IEEE to assign 16 consecutive Organizational Unique Identifiers (OUIs) for use as IP multicast MAC addresses. Because one OUI contains 24 bits worth of address space, 16 consecutive OUI's would supply a full 28 bits worth of MAC address space and would permit a one-to-one mapping of Layer 3 IP multicast addresses to MAC addresses. Unfortunately, the going price for an OUI at the time was $1000 and Steve's manager, the late Jon Postel, was unable to justify the $16,000 necessary to purchase the full 28 bits worth of MAC addresses. Instead, Jon was willing to spend $1000 to purchase one   OUI out of his budget and give half of the addresses (23 bits worth) to Steve for use in his IP multicast research.

Performance Impact of MAC Address Mapping

Because all 28 bits of the Layer 3 IP multicast address information cannot be mapped into the available 23 bits of MAC address space, 5 bits of address information are lost in the mapping process. This results in 2^5 or 32:1 address ambiguity when a Layer 3 IP multicast address is mapped to a Layer 2 IEEE MAC address. This means that each IEEE IP multicast MAC address can represent 32 IP multicast addresses, as shown in Figure 2-4.

Figure 2-4   *MAC Address Ambiguities*

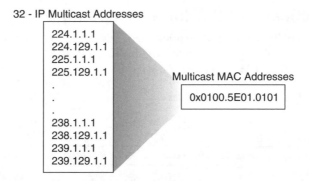

It should be obvious that this 32:1 address ambiguity can cause some problems. For example, a host that wants to receive multicast group 224.1.1.1 will program the hardware registers in the network interface card (NIC) to interrupt the CPU when a frame with a destination multicast MAC address of 0x0100.5E00.0101 is received. Unfortunately, this same multicast MAC address is also used for 31 other IP multicast groups. If any of these 31 other groups are also active on the local LAN, the host's CPU will receive interrupts any time a frame is received for any of these other groups. The CPU will have to examine the

IP portion of each received frame to determine whether it is the desired group, that is, 224.1.1.1. This can have an impact on the host's available CPU power if the amount of "spurious" group traffic is high enough.

In addition to having a possible negative impact on hosts' CPU power, this ambiguity can also cause problems when trying to constrain multicast flooding in Layer 2 LAN switches based solely on these multicast MAC addresses. This problem is addressed in detail in Chapter 14, "Multicast over Campus Networks."

FDDI Multicast MAC Address Mapping

Because FDDI MAC addresses and IEEE MAC addresses conform to the same format, the mapping of IP multicast addresses to FDDI MAC addresses uses the same method as Ethernet (as shown in Figure 2-3) with one minor difference. The low-order bits of FDDI octets are transmitted first; whereas the high-order bits of Ethernet octets are transmitted first. These two bit orderings are referred to as *little-endian* and *big-endian* ordering because either the big end or the little end of the octet is transmitted first. The big-endian Ethernet format is also referred to as the *canonical* form of an IEEE MAC address.

All other aspects of IP address to FDDI MAC address mapping are identical to the Ethernet case. If you are using a network sniffer or similar device to look at multicast frames on a FDDI ring, however, the bit order is going to be reversed. Therefore, the 0x0100.5Exx.xxxx IP multicast MAC prefix becomes 0x8000.7axx.xxxx on a FDDI ring.

Token Ring Multicast MAC Address Mapping

The format of Token Ring destination MAC addresses, as described by IBM, is shown in Figure 2-5. As you can see from this figure, Token Ring MAC addresses differ from canonical, Ethernet MAC address format.

Figure 2-5   *Token Ring Destination MAC Addresses*

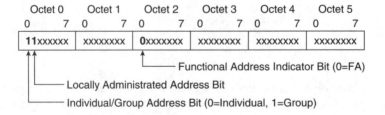

Like FDDI, the low-order bits of Token Ring octets are transmitted first; whereas Ethernet octets transmit high-order bits first. Notice that Bit 0 of Octet 0 has the same basic broadcast/multicast definition as the Ethernet MAC address as shown in Figure 2-5, though IBM refers to this bit as the *Group Address Bit*. Likewise, the *Locally Administrative Bit* is also Bit 1 of Octet 0 as in the Ethernet MAC address. The Token Ring bits are transmitted in the reverse order of the Ethernet bits.

Token Ring Functional Addresses

Unlike IEEE MAC addresses, Token Ring uses the concept of bit-specific functional addresses, which are addressed to a group of nodes on the ring. These functional addresses are denoted by Bit 0 of Octet 2 being cleared, as shown in Figure 2-6.

Figure 2-6 *Token Ring Functional Addresses*

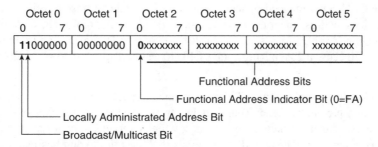

Functional addresses are always multicast to a group address (indicated by Bit 0 in Octet 0 being set) and always are administrated locally (indicated by Bit 1 in Octet 0 being set). Each functional address bit (bits 1 to 7 in Octet 2 as well as all bits in Octets 3, 4, and 5) indicates a special MAC level function such as active monitor or ring error monitor. Nodes on the ring use masks to identify these functions.

For example, a node on the ring could be assigned both the active monitor (0xC000.0000.0001) and the ring error monitor (0xC000.0000.0002) functions. This node then programs its NIC with a mask of 0xC000.0000.0003 so that the NIC interrupts the node's CPU whenever one of these group functional addresses is received.

Many Token Ring NICs do not have the capability to be programmed to interrupt the CPU when an arbitrary multicast MAC address is received. Therefore, the only alternative is to use the all-ones (0xffff.ffff.ffff) broadcast MAC address or a functional address for IP multicast to MAC address mapping as shown in Figure 2-7.

Figure 2-7   *Token Ring Multicast Address Mapping*

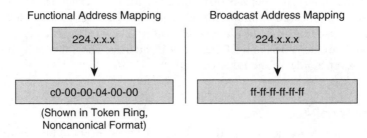

Performance Impact of Token Ring Mapping

The CPU performance impact on a Token Ring node because of this extremely poor multicast address mapping method can be quite considerable. The address ambiguity has now gone from 2^5 or 32:1 to 2^{28} or 268,435,456:1. This means all multicast traffic on the ring will cause a Token Ring node's CPU to be interrupted for every multicast packet on the ring!

In addition to causing this CPU performance impact, the all-into-one mapping scheme virtually precludes Token Ring switches from constraining multicast flooding at the MAC layer. As a result, Token Ring switches, which operate solely at Layer 2, are powerless to prevent any Token Ring node that joins a multicast group and begins receiving multicast traffic from affecting every other node on the ring.

NOTE   IS managers and network administrators who are faced with a growing demand for multimedia or other multicast-based applications on their Token Ring networks should carefully consider the downside of using multicast over Token Ring networks. If possible, you should consider changing to a switched Ethernet environment in these cases.

Multicast Distribution Trees

To understand the IP multicast model, you must have a good working knowledge of multicast distribution trees. In the unicast model, traffic is routed through the network along a single path from the source to the destination host. In the multicast model, however, the source is sending traffic to an arbitrary group of hosts that are represented by a multicast group address.

To deliver multicast traffic to all receivers, multicast distribution trees are used to describe the path that the IP multicast traffic takes through the network. The two basic types of multicast distribution trees are *source trees* and *shared trees*, which are described in the next two sections.

Source Trees

The simplest form of a multicast distribution tree is a source tree whose root is the source of the multicast traffic and whose branches form a spanning tree through the network to the receivers. Because this tree uses the shortest path through the network, it also is referred to frequently as a shortest path tree (SPT).

Figure 2-8 shows an example of an SPT for group 224.1.1.1 rooted at the source, Host A, and connecting two receivers, Hosts B and C.

Figure 2-8   *Host A Shortest Path Tree*

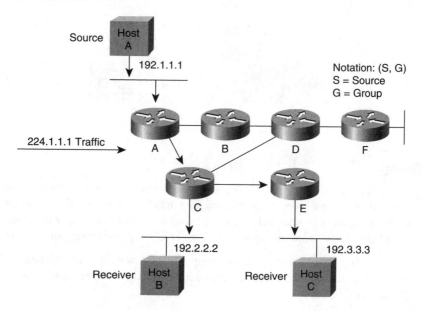

The special notation of *(S, G)*, pronounced "S comma G", enumerates an SPT where *S* is the IP address of the source and *G* is the multicast group address. Using this notation, the SPT for the example in Figure 2-8 would be written as (192.1.1.1, 224.1.1.1).

Notice that this notation implies that a separate SPT exists for every individual source sending to each group, which is precisely what happens. Therefore, if Host B is also sending traffic to group 224.1.1.1 and Hosts A and C are receivers, then a separate (S, G) SPT would exist with a notation of (192.2.2.2, 224.1.1.1) as shown in Figure 2-9.

Figure 2-9   *Host B Shortest Path Tree*

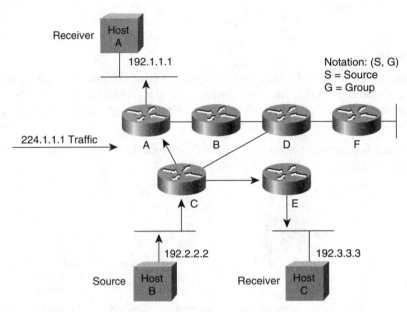

Shared Trees

Unlike source trees that have their roots at the source, shared trees use a single common root placed at some chosen point in the network. Depending on the multicast routing protocol, this root is often called a *rendezvous point* (RP) or *core,* which lends itself to shared trees' other common names: *RP trees (RPT)* or *core-based* trees *(CBT).*

Figure 2-10 shows a shared tree for group 224.2.2.2 with the root located at Router D. When using a shared tree, sources must send their traffic to the root for the traffic to reach all receivers.

Figure 2-10   *Shared Distribution Tree*

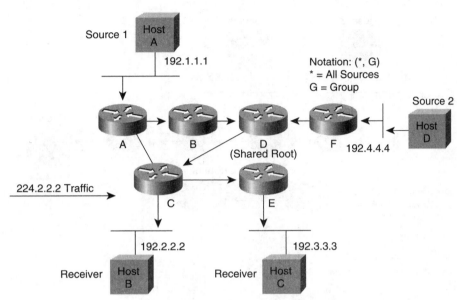

In this example, multicast group traffic from source Hosts A and D travels to the root (Router D) and then down the shared tree to two receivers, Hosts B and C. Because all sources in the multicast group use a common shared tree, a wildcard notation written as *(*, G)*, pronounced "star comma G", represents the tree. In this case, * means all sources, and the *G* represents the multicast group. Therefore, the shared tree shown in Figure 2-10 would be written, (*, 224.2.2.2).

Bidirectional Shared Trees

Shared trees can also be subdivided into two types: unidirectional and bidirectional. In the bidirectional case, multicast traffic may flow up and down the shared tree to reach all receivers. Figure 2-11 shows an example of a bidirectional shared tree.

Figure 2-11 *Bidirectional Shared Tree*

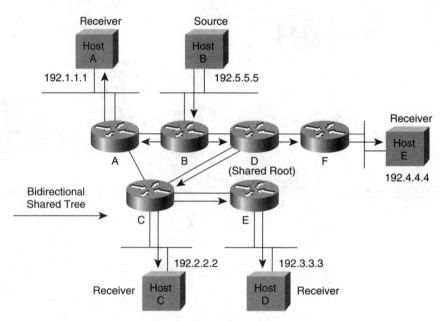

Notice that multicast traffic from Host B is being forwarded by its first-hop router up the tree toward the root of the shared tree as well as down the tree toward the other receivers (in this case, Host A).

Unidirectional Shared Trees

Unidirectional shared trees, on the other hand, only permit multicast traffic to flow down the shared tree from the root to the receivers. Consequently, sources of multicast traffic must use some other means to first get the traffic to the root so that it can be forwarded down the shared tree.

One method that can be used is to have the root join an SPT rooted at the source to pull the traffic to the root for forwarding down the shared tree. Figure 2-12 shows a unidirectional shared tree where the root has joined the SPT to source Host B to pull Host B's multicast traffic to the root. When the root receives the traffic, it is forwarded down the shared tree to the other receivers. Protocol Independent Multicast (PIM) uses this method to get source multicast traffic to the root or RP.

Figure 2-12   *Unidirectional Shared Tree Using SPTs to Get Traffic to the Root*

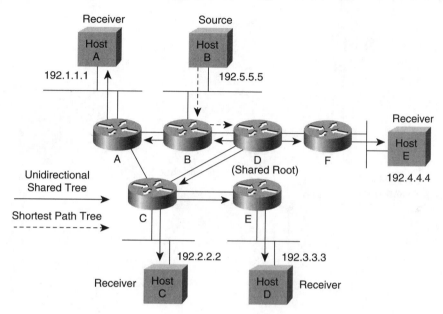

Another method that gets source multicast traffic to the root is for the first-hop router (Router B) to unicast the traffic directly to the root. The CBT multicast routing protocol uses this method when a source-only host wants to send multicast traffic to the group, as depicted in Figure 2-13. Host A is a source-only host that has not joined the multicast group and is therefore not on a branch of the bidirectional shared tree.

Figure 2-13 *CBT Bidirectional Shared Tree Using Unicast to Get Traffic to the Root*

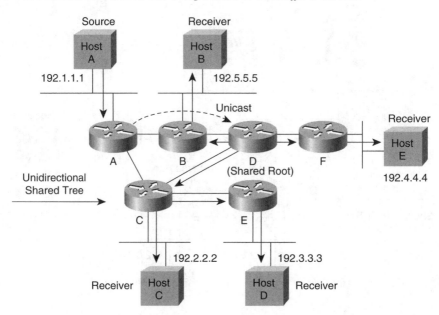

In this example, Host A is the source, and Host B is now a receiver. Router B is encapsulating the multicast traffic received from Host A and unicasting it directly to the root via an IP-IP tunnel. The root de-encapsulates the packet and sends it down the shared tree.

Multicast Forwarding

In the unicast model, routers forward traffic through the network along a single path from the source to the destination host whose IP address appears in the destination address field of the IP packet. Each router along the way makes a unicast forwarding decision, using the destination IP address in the packet, by looking up the destination address in the unicast route table and then forwarding the packet to the next hop via the indicated interface toward the destination.

In the multicast model, the source is sending traffic to an arbitrary group of hosts represented by a multicast group address in the destination address field of the IP packet. In contrast to the unicast model, the multicast router cannot base its forwarding decision on the destination address in the packet; these routers typically have to forward the multicast packet out multiple interfaces for it to reach all receivers. This requirement makes the multicast forwarding process more complex than the one used for unicast forwarding.

This section examines the concept of Reverse Path Forwarding (RPF), which is the basis of the multicast forwarding process in most multicast routing protocols. This section also presents information on multicast forwarding caches, TTL thresholds, and administratively scoped boundaries.

Reverse Path Forwarding

Virtually all IP multicast routing protocols make use of some form of RPF or incoming interface check as the primary mechanism to determine whether to forward or drop an incoming multicast packet. When a multicast packet arrives at a router, the router performs an RPF check on the packet. If the RPF check is successful, the packet is forwarded; otherwise, it is dropped.

For traffic flowing down a source tree, the RPF check mechanism works as follows:

1 The router examines the source address of the arriving multicast packet to determine whether the packet arrived via an interface that is on the reverse path back to the source.

2 If the packet arrives on the interface leading back to the source, the RPF check is successful and the packet is forwarded.

3 If the RPF check fails, the packet is discarded.

How a multicast router determines which interface is on the reverse path back to the source depends on the routing protocol in use. In some cases, the multicast routing protocol maintains a separate multicast routing table and uses it for this RPF check. A good example of this is the Distance Vector Multicast Routing Protocol (DVMRP), which is discussed in Chapter 5, "Distance Vector Multicast Routing Protocol." In other cases, the multicast protocol uses the existing unicast routing table to determine the interface that is on the reverse path back to the source. PIM and CBT are examples of multicast protocols that typically use the unicast routing table to perform the RPF check. PIM and CBT are not limited to using just the unicast routing table for the RPF check, however. They also can use reachability information from a DVMRP router table or a Multicast Border Gateway Protocol (MBGP) route table, or they can statically configure RPF information. The PIM and CBT protocols also are explored in detail in later chapters.

Figure 2-14 illustrates the RPF check process. This example uses a separate multicast routing table, although the concept is the same if the unicast routing table or some other reachability table is used.

Figure 2-14 *RPF Check Fails*

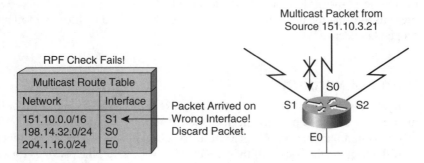

A multicast packet from source 151.10.3.21 is received on interface S0. A check of the multicast routing table shows that the interface on the reverse path back to the source is S1, not S0. Therefore, the RPF check fails, and the packet is discarded.

Figure 2-15 is another example of a multicast packet from source 151.10.3.21 arriving at the router, this time via interface S1.

Figure 2-15 *RPF Check Succeeds*

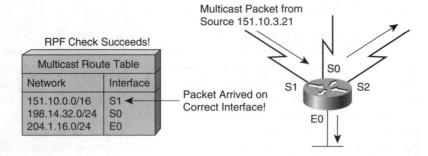

In this case, the RPF check succeeds as interface S1 is on the reverse path back to the source, and therefore the packet is forwarded to all interfaces on the outgoing interface list. (Notice that the outgoing interfaces don't have to necessarily include all interfaces on the router.)

Multicast Forwarding Cache

The section "Multicast Distribution Trees," earlier in this chapter, discussed the concept of building multicast distribution trees that are used to forward multicast traffic through the network to all receivers. From the router's point of view, each SPT or shared tree can be represented in a *multicast forwarding cache* entry (sometimes referred to as a *multicast route table* entry) as an incoming interface associated with zero or more outgoing interfaces. Note that bidirectional shared trees modify this process slightly, as they don't make a distinction between incoming and outgoing interfaces because traffic can flow up and down the tree.

Performing the RPF check on every incoming multicast packet results in a substantial performance penalty on the router. Therefore, it is common for a multicast router to determine the RPF interface when the multicast forwarding cache is created. The RPF interface then becomes the incoming interface of the multicast forwarding cache entry. If a change occurs in the routing table used by the RPF check process, the RPF interface must be recomputed and the multicast forwarding cache entry updated to reflect this information. Note that outgoing interfaces are determined in various ways depending on the multicast routing protocol in use.

Example 2-1 shows a Cisco multicast routing table entry.

Example 2-1   *Cisco Multicast Routing Table Entry*

```
(151.10.3.21/32, 224.2.127.254), 00:04:15/00:01:10, flags: T
  Incoming interface: Serial1, RPF nbr 171.68.0.91
  Outgoing interface list:
    Serial2, Forward/Sparse, 00:04:15/00:02:17
    Ethernet0, Forward/Sparse, 00:04:15/00:02:13
```

This *(S, G)* entry describes the (151.10.3.21/32, 224.2.127.254) SPT as seen by the router in Figure 2-14 and Figure 2-15.

From this information you can see that the entry has an incoming interface, **Serial1**, and two outgoing interfaces, **Serial2** and **Ethernet0**. Don't let all the other nomenclature in this example bother you. It will be detailed in Chapter 10, "Using PIM Dense Mode," and Chapter 11, "Using PIM Sparse Mode." For now, concern yourself only with the concept of incoming and outgoing interfaces.

TTL Thresholds

As you recall, each time an IP multicast packet is forwarded by a router, the TTL value in the IP header is decremented by one. If the TTL of a packet is decremented to zero, the router drops the packet.

TTL thresholds may be applied to individual interfaces of a multicast router to prevent multicast packets with a TTL less than the TTL threshold from being forwarded out the interface. For example, Figure 2-16 shows a multicast router with various TTL thresholds applied to its interfaces.

Figure 2-16   *TTL Thresholds*

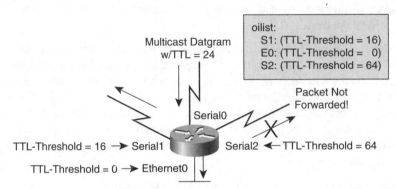

In this example, a multicast packet arrives via **Serial0** with its current TTL value at 24. Assuming that the RPF check succeeds and that interfaces **Serial1**, **Serial2,** and **Ethernet0** are all in the outgoing interface list, the packet therefore normally would be forwarded out these interfaces. Because some TTL thresholds have been applied to these interfaces, however, the router must make sure that the packet's TTL value, which is now down to 23, is greater than or equal to the interface's TTL threshold before forwarding the packet out the interface.

As you can see in this example, the packet is forwarded out interfaces **Serial1** and **Ethernet0**. Note that a TTL threshold of zero means that there is no TTL threshold on this interface. The packet's TTL value of 23 was below the TTL threshold value on interface **Serial2,** however, and therefore the packet was not forwarded out this interface.

TTL thresholds provide a simple method to prevent the forwarding of multicast traffic beyond the boundary of a site or region based on the TTL field in a multicast packet. This technique is referred to as *TTL scoping*. Multicast applications that must keep their traffic inside of a site or region transmit their multicast traffic with an initial TTL value so as not to cross the TTL threshold boundaries.

Figure 2-17 shows an example of TTL threshold boundaries being used to limit the forwarding of multicast traffic. Company ABC has set a TTL threshold of 128 on all router interfaces at the perimeter of its network.

Figure 2-17   *TTL Threshold Boundaries*

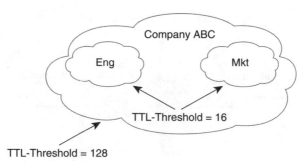

Multicast applications that want to constrain their traffic to within Company ABC's network need to transmit multicast packets with an initial TTL value set to 127. Furthermore, the engineering and marketing departments have set a TTL threshold of 16 at the perimeter of their networks. Therefore, multicast applications running inside of these networks can prevent their multicast transmissions from leaving their respective networks.

Table 2-3 shows the typical initial TTL values and router interface TTL thresholds for various TTL boundaries.

Table 2-3   *Typical TTL Boundary Values*

TTL Scope	Initial TTL Value	TTL Threshold
Local net	1	N/A
Site	15	16
Region	63	64
World	127	128

Administratively Scoped Boundaries

Like TTL thresholds, administratively scoped boundaries may also be used to limit the forwarding of multicast traffic outside of a domain or subdomain. This approach uses a special range of multicast addresses, called *administratively scoped* addresses, as the boundary mechanism. If we configure an administratively scoped boundary on a router's interface, multicast traffic whose multicast group addresses fall in this range will not be allowed to enter or exit this interface, thereby providing a firewall for multicast traffic in this address range.

Figure 2-18 depicts the administratively scoped boundary mechanism at work. Here an administratively scoped boundary is set for the multicast address range 239.0.0.0 through 239.255.255.255 on interface Serial0. This mechanism effectively sets up a firewall that multicast packets in this range cannot cross.

Figure 2-18 *Administrative Boundary Mechanism*

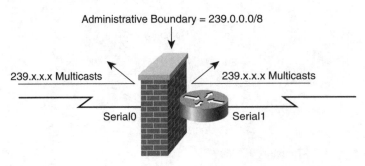

Administrative Boundary = 239.0.0.0/8

239.x.x.x Multicasts   239.x.x.x Multicasts

Serial0   Serial1

Recall from the "Administratively Scoped Multicast Addresses" section in this chapter that administratively scoped multicast addresses fall into the range of 239.0.0.0 through 239.255.255.255 and are considered to be locally assigned. That is, they are not used on the Internet. The administratively scoped boundary mechanism allows for the enforcement of this convention and prevents multicast traffic that falls in this range from entering or leaving the network.

Figure 2-19 is an example of the use of administratively scoped boundaries. Here, Company ABC has used different ranges of administrative addresses to prevent the forwarding of multicast traffic outside of specific boundaries.

Figure 2-19 *Administratively Scoped Boundaries*

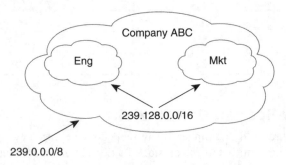

Company ABC

Eng   Mkt

239.128.0.0/16

239.0.0.0/8

In this example, Company ABC has configured an administratively scoped boundary of 239.0.0.0/8 on all router interfaces at the perimeter of its network. This boundary prevents any multicast traffic in the range of 239.0.0.0 through 239.255.255.255 from entering or leaving the network. Similarly, the engineering and marketing departments have configured an administratively scoped boundary of 239.128.0.0/16 around the perimeter of their networks. This boundary prevents multicast traffic in the range of 239.128.0.0 through 239.128.255.255 from entering or leaving their respective networks. It also means that the multicast address range 239.128.0.0 through 239.128.255.255 is being used independently by both the engineering and marketing departments. This reuse of multicast address space permits multicast addresses to be used more efficiently inside of Company ABC.

Multicast Routing Protocol Categories

The current multicast protocols can be subdivided into three basic categories:

- Dense mode protocols (DVMRP and PIM-DM)
- Sparse mode protocols (PIM-SM and CBT)
- Link-state protocols (MOSPF)

Some protocols, such as PIM, are capable of operating in either dense or sparse mode depending on how the router is configured. It is also possible to configure Cisco PIM routers to make the sparse/dense decision dynamically on a multicast group basis.

Dense Mode Protocols

Dense mode protocols such as DVMRP and PIM DM employ only SPTs to deliver (S, G) multicast traffic using a *push* principle. The push principle assumes that every subnet in the network has at least one receiver of the (S, G) multicast traffic, and therefore the traffic is pushed or flooded to all points in the network. This process is analogous to a radio or TV broadcast that is transmitted over the air to all homes within the coverage area. Receivers simply need to tune in to the broadcast to receive the program.

Flood and Prune Behavior

Unlike broadcasting radio waves over the air, however, flooding multicast traffic to every point in the network comes with an associated cost (bandwidth, router CPU, and so on). Therefore, to avoid the unnecessary consumption of valuable network resources, routers send Prune messages back up the source distribution tree to shut off unwanted multicast traffic. The result is that branches without receivers are *pruned* off the distribution tree, leaving only branches that contain receivers.

In Figure 2-20, Router B is responding to unwanted multicast traffic with a Prune message.

Figure 2-20   *Pruning a Dense Mode Flow*

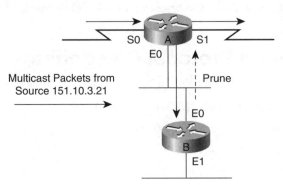

When Router A receives the Prune message for the (S, G) multicast traffic stream on an outgoing interface (in this example, Ethernet0), the router places that interface into Pruned state and stops forwarding the (S, G) traffic out the interface. The interface in this example is connected to a multi-access network, and we are assuming that no other downstream routers on this interface still want to receive the traffic. The method used to determine whether other routers on a multi-access interface need to continue to receive multicast traffic depends on the protocol in use. The details of how each protocol handles this situation are covered in the individual protocol chapters later in the book.

Prunes have a timeout value associated with them such that, when they time out, they cause the router to put the interface back into forward state and to start flooding multicast traffic out this interface again.

Example 2-2 shows the Cisco multicast route table entry for Router A in Figure 2-20.

Example 2-2   *Cisco Multicast Route Table Entry for Router A*

```
(151.10.3.21/32, 224.2.127.254), 00:04:15/00:01:10, flags: T
 Incoming interface: Serial0, RPF nbr 171.68.0.91
 Outgoing interface list:
   Serial1, Forward/Dense, 00:04:15/00:00:00
   Ethernet0, Prune/Dense, 00:00:25/00:02:35
```

Notice that interface Ethernet0 is in prune state (denoted by the **Prune/Dense** indicator) and that no group 224.2.127.254 traffic (from source 151.10.3.21) is being forwarded out this interface. The example also shows that the Prune will timeout in 2 minutes and 35 seconds (as indicated by the last timer value on the line). When the prune times out, the state of this interface will return to **Forward/Dense** and traffic will once again begin flowing out this interface. Assuming that the downstream router (Router B in this case) still has no need to receive the multicast traffic, it again sends a Prune to shut off the unwanted traffic.

The timeout values used for Prunes depend on the multicast routing protocol in use but typically range from 2 to 3 minutes. This periodic flood and Prune behavior is characteristic of dense mode protocols, such as DVMRP and PIM-DM.

Grafting

Most dense mode protocols rapidly can graft a previously pruned branch back onto the distribution tree. This capability is demonstrated, for example, when a new receiver on a previously pruned branch of the tree joins the multicast group. In this case, the router detects the new receiver and immediately sends a Graft message up the distribution tree toward the source. When the upstream router receives the Graft message, the router immediately puts the interface on which the Graft was received into forward state so that the multicast traffic begins flowing down to the receiver.

Figure 2-21 shows the Graft process. In this example, the source, Host E, is transmitting multicast traffic down the SPT (denoted by the solid arrows) to receivers Host A, B, and C.

Figure 2-21   *Dense Mode Grafting*

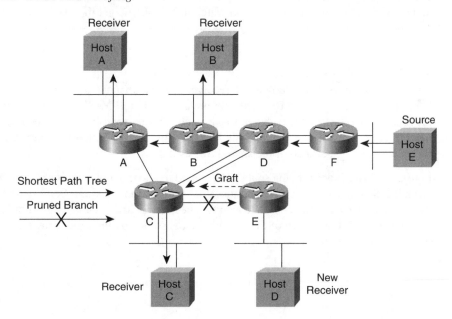

Router E previously has pruned its link to Router C, as it initially had no directly connected receivers. At this point in the example, Host D joins the multicast group as a new receiver. This action prompts Router E to send a Graft message up the SPT to Router C to immediately restart the flow of multicast traffic. By using this Graft process, Router E can avoid having to wait for the previous Prune to time out, thereby reducing the join latency as seen by Host D.

Sparse Mode Protocols

Sparse mode protocols make use of shared trees and occasionally, as in the case of PIM-SM, SPTs to distribute multicast traffic to multicast receivers in the network. Instead of using a push model, however, sparse mode protocols make use of a pull model in which multicast traffic is pulled down to the receivers in the network. The pull model therefore assumes that multicast traffic is not wanted unless it is requested specifically using an explicit Join mechanism. Using the TV analogy again, this model is like a pay-per-view event that is not sent to the receiver unless specifically requested.

NOTE   I realize that I'm stretching the cable TV, pay-per-view model a bit here because, in reality, you are always able to receive the program. When you request a pay-per-view movie, the cable company sends your cable TV box some sort of authorization code that enables you to unscramble the program so you can watch it. I think you get the idea, however.

Shared Tree Join Messages

To pull the multicast traffic down to a receiver in a sparse mode network, a shared tree branch must be constructed from the root node (the RP in PIM-SM or the core in CBT) to the receiver. To construct this shared tree branch, a router sends a shared tree Join message toward the root of the shared tree. This Join message travels router by router toward the root, constructing a branch of the shared tree as it goes.

Figure 2-22 shows Joins being sent up the shared tree to the root. In this example, Router E has a locally connected receiver and therefore sends a Join message (represented by the dashed arrow) toward the root via Router C. The message travels hop by hop until it reaches the root and builds a branch of the shared tree (as shown by the solid arrows).

Figure 2-22   *Shared Tree Join Message*

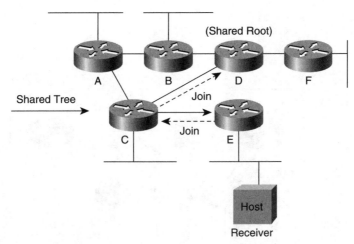

In some cases (PIM-SM, for example), SPT Join messages may also be sent in the direction of the source to construct an SPT from an individual multicast source to receivers in the network. SPTs allow routers that have directly connected receivers to cut through the network and bypass the root node so that multicast traffic from a source can be received via a more direct path.

Figure 2-23 depicts an SPT being built using Join messages sent toward a specific multicast source. In this example, Router E sends an SPT Join message (shown by dashed arrows) toward the source via Router C. The SPT Join travels hop by hop until it reaches Router A, building the SPT (shown by solid arrows) as it goes.

Figure 2-23 *SPT Join Messages*

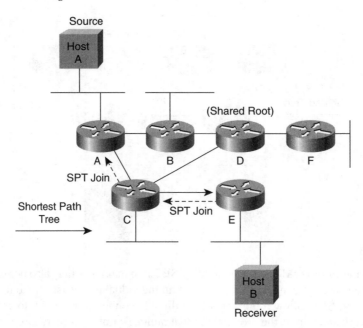

It is important to note that if the branches of distribution trees in a sparse mode network (either shared trees or SPTs) are not refreshed, they will time out and be deleted, thereby stopping traffic flow down the branch of the shared tree. To avoid this problem, the branches of sparse mode distribution trees are maintained by some form of periodic Join refresh mechanism that the routers send along the branch. Some protocols (PIM-SM, for example) handle the refresh by resending the Join message up the tree to refresh the branch periodically.

Prune Messages

In sparse mode, Prune messages are sent up the distribution tree when multicast group traffic is no long desired. This action permits branches of the shared tree or SPT that were created via explicit Joins messages to be torn down when they are no longer needed. For example, if a leaf router detects that it no longer has any directly connected hosts (or downstream multicast routers) for a particular multicast group, the router sends a Prune message up the distribution tree to shut off the flow of unwanted multicast group traffic. Sending Prune messages, instead of waiting for the branch of the sparse mode distribution tree to time out, greatly improves leave latency in the network.

Figure 2-24 shows this process in action. Host A has just left the multicast group; therefore, Router A no longer needs the traffic flowing down the shared tree (indicated by the solid arrows) and sends a Prune message up the shared tree toward the RP. This message prunes the link between Router A and Router B from the shared tree and stops the now unnecessary multicast traffic flow to Router A.

Figure 2-24 *Sparse Mode Prune*

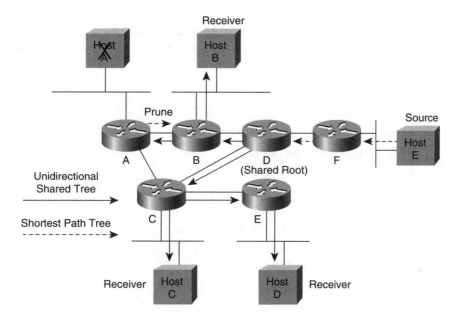

Link-State Protocols

Link-state protocols such as MOSPF function much like dense mode protocols in that they both use SPTs to distribute multicast traffic to the receivers in the network. Link-state protocols, however, don't use the flood and Prune mechanism that is used in DVMRP or PIM-DM. Instead, they flood special multicast, link-state information that identifies the whereabouts of group members (that is, receivers) in the network. All routers in the network use this group membership information to build shortest path trees from each source to all receivers in the group. (MOSPF is covered in more detail in Chapter 9, "Multicast Open Shortest Path First.")

Summary

This chapter covers some of the most basic concepts of IP multicast including multicast addressing at both Layer 2 and Layer 3, types of distribution trees, and multicast forwarding. These topics are the foundation upon which a good understanding of IP multicast is built. Taking the time to learn these fundamentals thoroughly and to build this foundation becomes increasingly important as more complex topics are introduced in later chapters.

The next chapter covers another basic IP multicast building block, IGMP, in detail. IGMP provides the necessary group membership signaling between hosts and routers.

CHAPTER 3

Internet Group Management Protocol

The Internet Group Management Protocol (IGMP) grew out of the Host Membership Protocol from Dr. Steve Deering's doctoral thesis, and the first version, IGMPv1, was defined in RFC 1112 (the "IP Multicast Dead Sea Scrolls" referred to in Chapter 2, "Multicast Basics"). The most recent version, IGMPv2, was ratified in November 1997 as a standard by the Internet Engineering Task Force (IETF) and is covered in RFC 2236.

IGMP messages are used primarily by multicast hosts to signal their local multicast router when they wish to join a specific multicast group and begin receiving group traffic. Hosts may also (with some extensions defined in IGMPv2) signal to the local multicast router that they wish to leave an IP multicast group and, therefore, are no longer interested in receiving the multicast group traffic.

NOTE As you will learn later, IGMP is a rather overloaded protocol. IGMP messages are used for several purposes other than the original Host Membership model defined in RFC 1112. Several multicast routing protocols, such as Distance Vector Multicast Routing Protocol (DVMRP) and Protocol Independent Multicast (PIM) version 1, make use of special IGMP message types to transmit their routing control information. Other multicast control and diagnostic functions (such as mtrace), which are totally unrelated to the Host Membership model, also use a special IGMP message type to accomplish their task, and others are being proposed still. All of this activity results in what I call the "YAPIOI" category of protocols, yet another protocol inside of IGMP.

Using the information obtained via IGMP, routers maintain a list of multicast group memberships on a per interface basis. A multicast group membership is active on an interface if at least one host on that interface has signaled its desire, via IGMP, to receive the multicast group traffic.

This chapter examines the IGMP protocol—versions 1 and 2—in great detail so that you can become better acquainted with its operational aspects. This chapter also takes a quick peek at what IGMP version 3 (in draft proposal stage as this book is being written) may someday offer in terms of new capabilities.

IGMP Version 1

Why bother learning IGMPv1 if IGMPv2 is now the standard? The reason is simple: most IP stacks in today's hosts still use IGMPv1. The pervasive Microsoft Windows 95 operating system includes built-in support for IP multicast, but unless you download an upgraded version of Microsoft's Winsock DLL, you will be running IGMPv1. On the other hand, if you have upgraded to Windows 98, it contains full support for IGMPv2. The same is true for many UNIX implementations. Unless you install a patch or are running the very latest version of the UNIX operating system, you very possibly will be using IGMPv1. Because you are likely to be dealing with older versions of these platforms that support only IGMPv1, you need to understand how it works and know its limitations.

This section focuses on the details of IGMPv1, including

- IGMPv1 Message Format
- The IGMPv1 Query Process
- IGMPv1 Report Suppression Mechanism
- IGMPv1 Query Router
- The IGMPv1 Join Process
- The IGMPv1 Leave Process

IGMPv1 Message Format

IGMP messages are transmitted inside IP datagrams and denoted by an IP protocol number of 2. IGMP messages are transmitted with the IP time-to-live (TTL) field set to 1 and, therefore, are local in scope and not forwarded by routers. Figure 3-1 shows the format of an IGMPv1 message.

Figure 3-1   *IGMPv1 Message Format*

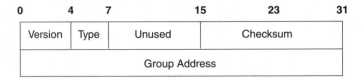

The following sections define the fields, as depicted in Figure 3-1, that make up an IGMPv1 message.

Version Field

The Version field contains the IGMP version identification and is therefore set to 1. This field has been eliminated in version 2, as noted in the "IGMP Version 2" section later in this chapter. A predecessor to IGMP version 1, whose version number is 0, is described in RFC 988.

Type Field

In version 1 of IGMP, the following two message types are used between hosts and routers:

* Membership Query
* Membership Report

Checksum Field

The Checksum field is a 16-bit, one's complement of the one's complement sum of the IGMP message. The Checksum field is zeroed when making the checksum computation.

Group Address Field

The Group Address field contains the multicast group address when a Membership Report is being sent. This field is zero when used in the Membership Query and should be ignored by hosts.

The IGMPv1 Query-Response Process

IGMP primarily uses a Query-Response model that allows the multicast router to determine which multicast groups are active (that is, have one or more hosts interested in a multicast group) on the local subnet. Figure 3-2 shows the Query-Response process in operation.

Figure 3-2   *IGMPv1 Query-Response Process*

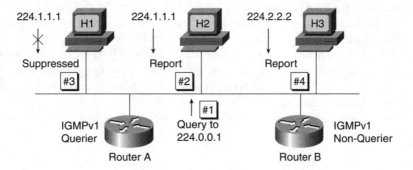

In this example, Hosts H1 and H2 each want to receive multicast traffic for group 224.1.1.1. Furthermore, Host H3 wants to receive multicast traffic for group 224.2.2.2. Router A is the IGMP Querier for the subnet and is responsible for performing the queries. Router B is a non-querier and simply listens and records the hosts' responses.

The IGMPv1 Query-Response mechanism for this example works as follows:

1 Router A (the IGMP Querier) periodically (the default is every 60 seconds) multicasts an IGMPv1 Membership Query to the All-Hosts multicast group (224.0.0.1) on the local subnet. All hosts must listen to this group as long as they have enabled multicast so that these queries can be received.

2 All hosts receive the IGMPv1 Membership Query, and one host (in this example it's H2) responds first by multicasting an IGMPv1 Membership Report to the multicast group, 224.1.1.1, of which the host is a member. This report informs the routers on the subnet that a host is interested in receiving multicast traffic for group 224.1.1.1.

3 Because Host H1 is listening to multicast group 224.1.1.1, it hears the IGMPv1 Membership Report that was multicast by Host H2. Host H1, therefore, suppresses the sending of its report for group 224.1.1.1 because H2 already has informed the routers on the subnet that there is at least one host interested in receiving multicast traffic for group 224.1.1.1. This Report Suppression mechanism helps reduce the amount of traffic on the local network.

4 Host H3 has also received the IGMPv1 Membership Query, and it responds by multicasting an IGMPv1 Membership Report to the multicast group 224.2.2.2, of which it is a member. This report informs the routers on the subnet that a host is interested in receiving multicast traffic for group 224.2.2.2.

As a result of this Query-Response exchange, Router A now knows that there are active receivers for multicast groups 224.1.1.1 and 224.2.2.2 on the local subnet. In addition, Router B has been eavesdropping on the whole process and also knows the same information.

NOTE   Because of the Report Suppression mechanism, routers cannot keep track of the individual hosts joined to a multicast group on a subnet. Therefore, they only keep track of the multicast groups that are active on a subnet. Furthermore, even if the router could keep track of all active members, doing so would not be desirable because it would prevent IGMP from scaling on subnets with large numbers of hosts. Finally, it is not necessary for the router to keep track of each individual member host because traffic is forwarded on a group address and interface basis.

Report Suppression Mechanism

The IGMP Report Suppression Mechanism helps to reduce the amount of IGMP traffic on a subnet to the minimum necessary to maintain a multicast group state. The following describes this mechanism in more detail:

1 When a host receives an IGMP Membership Query, the host starts a countdown report-timer for each multicast group it has joined. Each report-timer is initialized to a random value between zero and the maximum response interval. The default is 10 seconds.

2 If a report-timer expires, the host multicasts an IGMP Membership report for the active multicast group associated with the report-timer.

3 If the host hears another host send an IGMP Membership Report, it cancels its report-timer associated with the received Membership Report, thereby suppressing the sending of a Membership Report for the group.

IGMPv1 Querier

If multiple multicast routers are on a subnet, having more than one of them send IGMPv1 Queries is a waste of bandwidth. In this case, an IGMPv1 Querier, a router responsible for sending all IGMPv1 Queries on a subnet, becomes essential. Unfortunately, RFC 1112 does not specify how that IGMPv1 Querier is elected. Instead, IGMPv1 relies on the Layer 3 IP Multicast Routing protocol (PIM, DVMRP, and so on) to resolve this conflict by electing a Designated Router for the subnet.

NOTE   Notice that there is a distinct difference between the IGMP Querier and the Designated Router. The multicast routing protocol selects the Designated Router to handle certain multicast forwarding duties on the subnet. Exactly how the Designated Router is elected depends on the multicast protocol in use. RFC 1112 assumed that this Designated Router would also perform the tasks of sending IGMP Query messages. These two functions were later separated in IGMPv2, which is described later in this chapter.

The IGMPv1 Join Process

To reduce the join latency (particularly when a host is the first to join a multicast group on a subnet), it is not necessary to wait for the next Membership Query before sending a Membership Report to join a multicast group. Therefore, when a host wants to join a multicast group, the host immediately will send one or more unsolicited Membership Reports for the multicast group it desires to join.

It's important to note that a host only uses IGMP to signal to the local multicast router that it wants to start or stop receiving IP multicast traffic. It is not necessary for the host to join the group just to send multicast traffic to the group. Therefore, send-only multicast applications only need to begin sending traffic addressed to the multicast group to trigger the local multicast router to start forwarding the multicast traffic to receivers elsewhere in the network.

Figure 3-3 illustrates this unsolicited join process. Here, Host H3 wants to receive traffic for multicast group 224.3.3.3.

Figure 3-3 *IGMPv1 Join Process*

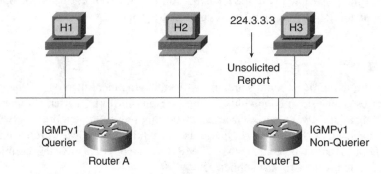

Instead of waiting for the next Membership Query from Router A, it immediately multicasts an unsolicited IGMPv1 Membership Report to group 224.3.3.3 to inform the routers on the subnet of its desire to join this group.

NOTE You occasionally may hear someone use the phrase, "sending an IGMP Join to a router." Although there is no such thing as an IGMP Join packet, the phrase is used frequently in normal multicast conversations to signify that an unsolicited IGMP Membership Report was sent to initiate a *Join* of a multicast group.

The IGMPv1 Leave Process

Unfortunately, IGMPv1 has a rather simple-minded method for hosts to leave a multicast group; they just quietly go away. There is no Leave Group message in IGMPv1 to notify the routers on the subnet that a host no longer wants to receive the multicast traffic from a specific group. The host simply stops processing traffic for the multicast group and ceases responding to IGMP Queries with IGMP Membership Reports for the group.

As a result, the only way IGMPv1 routers know that there are no longer any active receivers for a particular multicast group on a subnet is when the routers stop getting Membership Reports. To facilitate this process, IGMPv1 routers associate a countdown timer with an IGMP group on a subnet. When a Membership Report is received for the group on the subnet, the timer is reset. For IGMPv1 routers, this timeout interval is typically three times the Query Interval, or 3 minutes. This timeout interval means that the router may continue to forward multicast traffic onto the subnet for up to 3 minutes after all hosts have left the multicast group. This worst-case timing scenario is shown in Figure 3-4.

Figure 3-4   *IGMPv1 Leave Group Timing*

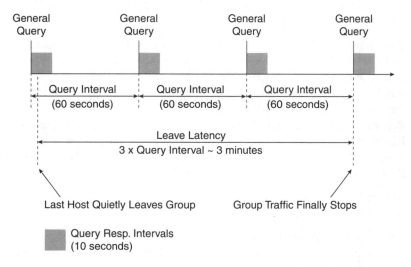

This 3-minute leave latency can cause problems sometimes. Assume for the moment that company ABC is sourcing five different channels of high-rate training videos from a central, video-training server via five different multicast groups. Assume also that the bandwidth available to each remote field office in ABC's network has been sized to support two active training-video streams at a time.

If a user at one of these remote sites is unsure which "channel" (multicast group) contains which training video, the user may simply "channel surf" to locate the desired training video. This action would result in the user's workstation joining and leaving each multicast group as the user surfs the multicast groups for the desired video. In the worst-case scenario, the user may have joined five of the multicast groups and left four of them in rapid succession while surfing. As far as the user is concerned, he or she is now receiving the correct training video (albeit with lots of errors due to some serious congestion problems). Because the IGMPv1 leave latency can be as high as 3 minutes, however, the router will be forwarding all five high-rate video streams onto the subnet for up to 3 minutes.

If some method had been available for the user's workstation to signal the router that it had left the other four groups, this leave latency could be shortened substantially and the probability of this problem occurring reduced. This was one of the primary reasons for developing IGMP version 2.

IGMP Version 2

In November 1997, IGMPv2 was ratified by the IETF as a standard in RFC 2236 that also serves as an update to RFC 1112, which defined IGMPv1 in an appendix. IGMPv2 was developed primarily to address some of the shortcomings of IGMPv1 that were discovered over time and through practical experience.

The Query and Membership Report messages in IGMPv2 are identical to the IGMPv1 messages with two exceptions. The first difference is that IGMPv2 Query messages are broken into two categories: General Queries, which perform the same function as the old IGMPv1 Queries, and Group-Specific Queries, which are queries directed to a single group. The second difference is that IGMPv1 Membership Reports and IGMPv2 Membership Reports have different IGMP Type codes. The (General) Query-Response process in IGMPv2, however, is the same as IGMPv1. Because the process is identical in both versions, this section does not repeat the earlier information. (Refer to the "IGMPv1 Query-Response Process" section of this chapter for more details.)

IGMPv2 includes several new features that are discussed in the sections that follow. Here is a quick summary of the key features added to IGMPv2:

- **Querier election process**—Provides the capability for IGMPv2 routers to elect the Query Router without having to rely on the multicast routing protocol to perform this process.
- **Maximum Response Time field**—A new field in Query messages permits the Query Router to specify the maximum Query-Response time. This field permits the tuning of the Query-Response process to control response burstiness and to fine-tune leave latencies.
- **Group-Specific Query messages**—Permits the Query Router to perform the query operation on a specific group instead of all groups.
- **Leave Group messages**—Provides hosts with a method of notifying routers on the network that they wish to leave the group.

The last two features enable hosts and routers to reduce the leave latency, which was such a problem in IGMPv1, from minutes down to a few seconds.

IGMPv2 Message Format

The format of IGMPv2 messages is shown in Figure 3-5. Notice that the Type field has been merged with IGMPv1's Version field and now occupies a full octet. The values assigned to the various message types have been chosen carefully to provide backward compatibility with IGMPv1.

Figure 3-5 *IGMPv2 Message Format*

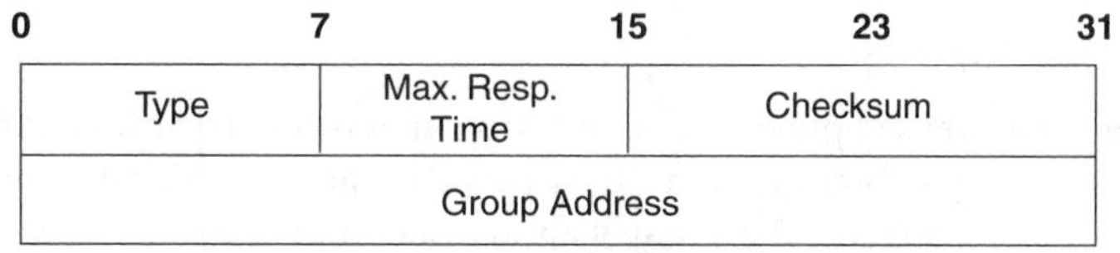

0	7	15	23	31
Type	Max. Resp. Time	Checksum		
Group Address				

For example, the IGMPv1 Membership Query message contains a 0x1 in the 4-bit Version field and 0x1 in the 4-bit Type field. Together they combine to form an 8-bit value of 0x11, which is identical to the IGMPv2 Type code for a Membership Query. The IGMPv2 Type code for a version 1 Membership Report likewise was carefully chosen to provide compatibility between IGMPv1 and IGMPv2. This enables IGMPv2 hosts and routers to recognize IGMPv1 messages when other IGMPv1 hosts or routers are on the network.

The following sections define the fields, as depicted in Figure 3-5, that make up an IGMPv2 message.

Type Field

In version 2 of IGMP, the following four message types are used between hosts and routers:

- Membership Query (Type code = 0x11)

  There are two subtypes of Membership Query messages:

  — **General Query**—Used to determine which multicast groups are active in the same fashion as IGMPv1 does. A General Query is denoted by an all-zeros Group Address field.

  — **Group-Specific Query**—Used to determine whether a specific multicast group has any remaining members. A Group-Specific Query contains the address of the group being queried.

- Version 1 Membership Report (Type code = 0x12)

  This message type is provided solely for backward compatibility with IGMPv1.

- Version 2 Membership Report (Type code = 0x16)
- Leave Group (Type code = 0x17)

Maximum Response Time Field

This field was unused previously in IGMPv1 messages. The Maximum Response Time field is used only in Membership Query messages and specifies the maximum time in units of 1/10 of a second that a host may wait to respond to a Query message. The default value for this field is 100 (10 seconds).

Hosts use the Maximum Response Time value in this field as the upper limit for the random setting of their group report-timers, which are used by the Report Suppression mechanism. The value in this field may be tuned to control either the burstiness of membership responses or leave latency.

Checksum Field

The Checksum field is a 16-bit, one's complement of the one's complement sum of the IGMP message. The Checksum field is zeroed when making the checksum computation.

Group Address Field

When a General Query is sent, the Group Address field is set to zero to differentiate it from a Group-Specific Query, which contains the multicast group of the group being queried.

When a Membership Report or Leave Group message is sent, this field is set to the target multicast group address.

Query-Response Tuning

Instead of an IGMPv2 host using a statically configured value for the Query-Response Interval, the Maximum Response Time field was added to the IGMPv2 Query message. The Maximum Response Time field permits the response time to be configured on the IGMP

Querier, which informs all hosts of the upper limit on the delay of their responses to the query by placing the delay value in this field.

Tuning the Maximum Response Time value controls the burstiness of the response process. This feature can be important when large numbers of groups are active on a subnet and you want to spread the responses over a longer period of time. For example, Figure 3-6 depicts a timing diagram showing General Queries and Responses for IGMPv2 default timer settings for a subnet with 18 active groups spread across 18 different hosts.

Figure 3-6   *IGMPv2 Query-Response Tuning*

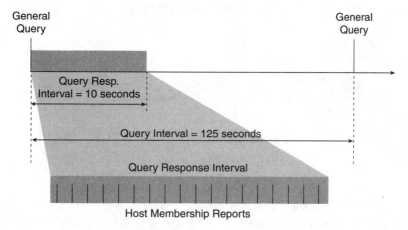

As you can see from this example, the 18 reports tend to be spread across the entire Query-Response Interval. This tendency is due to the random selection of the report-timer values by the hosts in their Report Suppression process. This distribution is affected by the randomness of the host's random-number algorithm in their IGMPv2 implementation. The responses, however, generally are spread across most of the Query-Response Interval.

By increasing the Maximum Response Time value, as shown in Figure 3-7, the period over which hosts may spread their responses to the General Query increases, thereby decreasing the burstiness of the responses.

Figure 3-7 *Decreasing Response Burstiness*

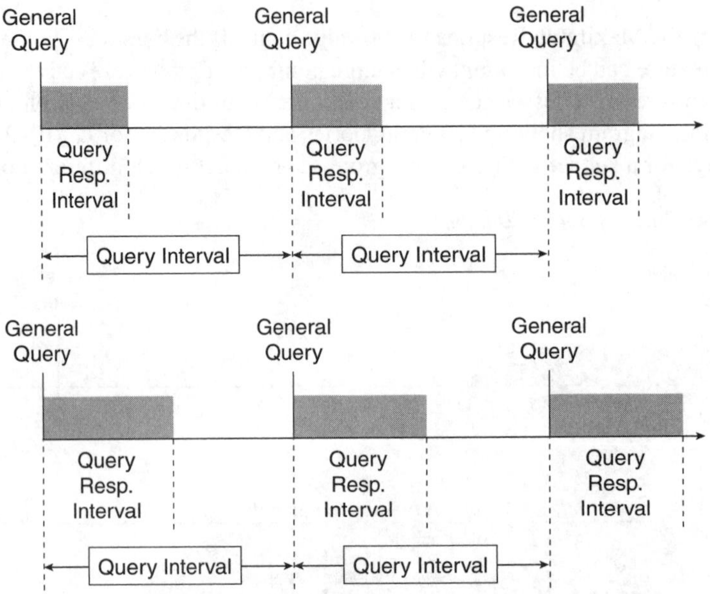

Reducing this burstiness comes with some penalties. Increasing the Query Response Interval by using a larger Maximum Response Time value also increases the leave latency because the Query Router must now wait longer to make sure that there are no more hosts for the group on the subnet. Therefore, your network design must strike a balance between burstiness and leave latency.

NOTE   I remember an important government project that was pushing what today's IP multicast technology is capable of doing. This network typically would have the number of active groups on a subnet in the thousands! Therefore, when the Query Router sent an IGMP General Query, the hosts on the subnet generated thousands of reports. Needless to say, careful tuning of the Query and Query-Response Intervals was crucial to making IP multicast technology work properly on this busy multicast network.

IGMPv2 Leave Group Messages

IGMPv2 defines a new Leave Group message type that hosts should send when they leave the group. The RFC says, "When a host leaves a multicast group, if it was the last host to respond to a query with a Membership Report for that group, it should send a Leave Group message to the all-routers multicast group (224.0.0.2)."

The RFC goes on to say that "a host may always send a Leave Group message when it leaves a group." Unfortunately, the wording in this part of the RFC is *may* and not *must*. This subtle distinction is important when using IGMP Snooping or Cisco Group Management Protocol (CGMP) to optimize LAN switches to constrain multicast flooding. If a host does not always send a Leave Group message, then these optimization techniques quickly can break down because there is no mechanism to report that the individual host has left the group, and multicast traffic for this group need not be forwarded out this port on the switch.

Fortunately, most IGMPv2 implementations (including most UNIX systems as well as Microsoft Windows 98 and NT V5.0) appear to find it easier to implement the Leave Group processing by always sending a Leave Group message when the host leaves the group. Checking whether the host was the last to respond to a query for the group takes considerably more code.

IGMPv2 Group-Specific Query Messages

The other new message type in IGMPv2 is the Group-Specific Query, which is sent by the IGMP Query Router, and whose purpose is exactly what its name implies—that is, to query a single group instead of all groups. In a Group-Specific Query, the Group Address field contains the target group being queried. IGMPv2 hosts that receive this message respond in the same manner as they do to a General Query.

In addition to the Group Address field containing the target group address, another difference between Group-Specific Queries and General Queries is that Group-Specific Queries further reduce Leave Group latency by using a much smaller value of Maximum Response Time. The default is 1 second.

IGMPv2 Leave Process

Without an efficient Leave process, as is the case in IGMPv1, the router continues to forward multicast traffic onto the local subnet for several minutes after the last host leaves the group. The addition of the Leave Group and Group-Specific IGMPv2 messages, coupled with the Maximum Response Time field, permit IGMPv2 to reduce the leave latency to only a few seconds. This situation is a significant improvement over IGMPv1, which has a worst-case leave latency of 3 minutes (assuming the default IGMPv1 timer values are in use).

Figure 3-8 depicts IGMPv2's new Leave process. In this example, Hosts H2 and H3 are currently members of multicast group 224.1.1.1, although Host H2 wants to leave the group.

Figure 3-8 *IGMPv2 Leave Process—Host H2 Leaves*

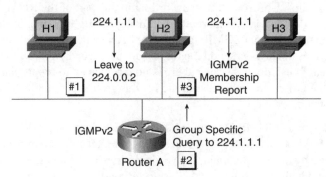

The sequence of events for Host H2 to leave the group is as follows:

1 Host H2 multicasts an IGMPv2 Leave Group message to the All-Routers (224.0.0.2) multicast group to inform all routers on the subnet that it is leaving the group.

2 Router A (assumed to be the IGMP Query Router in this example) hears the Leave Group message from Host H2. However, because routers keep a list only of the group memberships that are active on a subnet—not individual hosts that are members—Router A sends a Group-Specific Query to determine whether any hosts remain for group 224.1.1.1. Note that the Group-Specific Query is multicast to the target group (that is, 224.1.1.1). Therefore, only hosts that are members of this group will respond.

3 Host H3 is still a member of group 224.1.1.1 and, therefore, hears the Group-Specific Query and responds to the query with an IGMPv2 Membership Report to inform the routers on the subnet that a member of this group is still present. Notice that the Report Suppression mechanism is used here, just as in the General Query case, to avoid an implosion of responses when multiple members of the group are on the subnet.

Host H3 is now the last remaining member of group 224.1.1.1. Now, assume that Host H3 also wants to leave the group, as shown in Figure 3-9.

Figure 3-9 *IGMPv2 Leave Process—H3 Leaves*

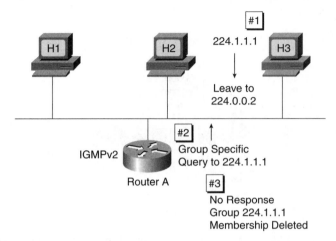

The following sequence of events occurs when Host H3 leaves the group:

1   Host H3 multicasts an IGMPv2 Leave Group message to the All-Routers (224.0.0.2) multicast group to inform all routers on the subnet that it is leaving the group.

2   Again, Router A hears the Leave Group message (this time from Host H3) and sends a Group-Specific Query to determine whether any hosts remain for group 224.1.1.1.

3   There are now no remaining members of group 224.1.1.1 on the subnet; therefore, no hosts respond to the Group-Specific Query. Getting no response, Router A waits a Last Member Query Interval (the default is 1 second) and sends another Group-Specific Query to which there is still no response. (The default number of tries is two.) At this point, Router A times out the group and stops forwarding its traffic onto the subnet.

Figure 3-10 depicts how the new mechanisms in IGMPv2 have reduced the leave latency.

Figure 3-10   *IGMPv2 Leave Group Timing*

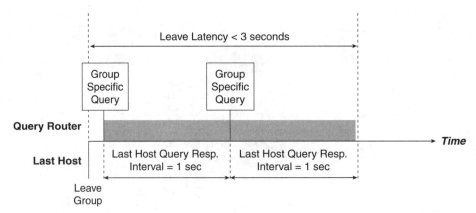

Instead of a total leave latency of roughly two complete query intervals, or 3 minutes, the leave latency is now less than 3 seconds.

Querier Election Process

Another important feature added in version 2 of IGMP is the Querier Election process. Instead of depending on the upper-layer multicast routing protocol, IGMPv2 uses the IP addresses in General Query messages to elect the IGMP Query Router via the following procedure:

1   When IGMPv2 routers start, they each multicast an IGMPv2 General Query message to the All-Multicast-Systems group (224.0.0.1) with their interface address in the Source IP Address field of the message.

2   When an IGMPv2 router receives a General Query message, the router compares the source IP address in the message with its own interface address. The router with the lowest IP address on the subnet is elected the IGMP Querier.

3   All non-querier routers start a querier timer that is reset whenever a General Query message is received from the IGMP Querier. The default duration of this timer is two times the Query Interval, or 250 seconds. If the querier timer expires, it is assumed that the IGMP Querier has gone down, and the election process is run again to elect a new IGMP Querier.

Early IGMPv2 Implementations

Although IGMPv2 was ratified only recently by the IETF, early implementations based on the IETF working drafts have been around for some time. Not surprisingly, some minor differences exist between the final specification and these early implementations. Some of the last minute changes/additions to the IGMPv2 specification are

- **Query Interval timer**—This timer was changed to 125 seconds. Early implementations used a value of 60 seconds. This discrepancy can cause a problem when a router with an early implementation is operating on the same LAN as a router that is the IGMP Querier and is IGMPv2 compliant. In this case, the early implementation router may believe erroneously that the IGMP Querier (the IGMPv2-compliant router) has gone down because the General Queries are 125 seconds apart.

- **Router Alert option**—This IP packet header option was added late in the definition to address some IGMP security issues. Early implementations of IGMPv2 running in hosts may not send IGMP messages with the Router Alert option in the IP header. The omission can cause a problem if an IGMPv2-compliant router is configured to ignore IGMP messages without the Router Alert option.

IGMPv1—IGMPv2 Interoperability

Version 2 of IGMP is designed to be as backward compatible with version 1 as possible. To accomplish this, some special interoperability rules are defined in RFC 2236. The next few sections examine interoperability scenarios:

- **V2 Host/v1 Routers**—Defines how a version 2 host must behave in the presence of an older version 1 router on the same LAN.

- **V1 Host/v2 Routers**—Defines how a version 2 router must behave in the presence of an older version 1 host on the same LAN.

- **Mixed v1 and v2 Routers**—Defines how a version 2 router must behave in the presence of an older version 1 router on the same LAN.

V2 Host/V1 Routers Interoperability

Version 1 routers see an IGMPv2 report as an invalid IGMP message type and ignore it. Therefore, to maintain proper group membership, a version 2 host must send IGMPv1 reports when a version 1 router is active as the IGMP Querier. Figure 3-11 shows a version 2 host on a LAN with an IGMPv1 Query Router.

Figure 3-11   *IGMPv2 Host and IGMPv1 Router Interaction*

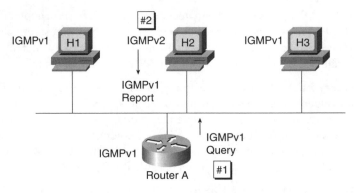

When a version 2 host detects that the IGMP Querier is a version 1 router, it must always respond with IGMPv1 Reports. A version 2 host may also suppress sending Leave Group messages in this situation.

Version 2 hosts can detect the difference between IGMPv1 and IGMPv2 Queries by examining the octet corresponding to the Maximum Response Time field. In IGMPv1 Queries, this field is zero (and is interpreted as 100, or 10 seconds, by version 2 hosts), whereas in IGMPv2 Queries it contains a nonzero Maximum Response Time value. When an IGMPv1 Query is heard, the host marks the interface as an IGMPv1 interface and ceases sending IGMPv2 messages.

To maintain this interface state, the version 2 host starts a 400-second version 1 router present countdown timer whenever an IGMPv1 Query is received on the interface. This timer is reset (back to 400 seconds) when another IGMPv1 Query is received. If the version 1 router present countdown timer expires, the interface is marked back to an IGMPv2 interface and IGMPv2 messages may once again be sent.

RULE   A version 2 host must allow its Membership Reports to be suppressed by either IGMPv1 or IGMPv2 Membership Reports.

In order to maintain the proper operation of the Report Suppression mechanism, version 2 hosts also must be prepared to receive either IGMPv1 or IGMPv2 Reports from other hosts on the LAN and to suppress their reports in the normal fashion.

V1 Host / V2 Routers

Figure 3-12 shows a version 1 host on a LAN with a version 2 IGMP Query Router. Version 1 hosts respond in the normal fashion to either IGMPv1 or IGMPv2 Queries because IGMPv2 Queries have essentially the same format. Only the second octet differs in an IGMPv2 message and is ignored by a version 1 host.

Figure 3-12 *IGMPv1 Host and IGMPv2 Router Interaction*

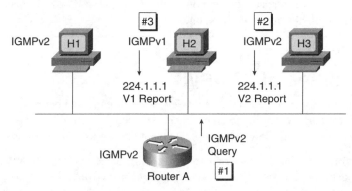

As a result, if a version 2 router is the IGMP Querier and there are version 1 hosts on the LAN that are also members of a group, then IGMPv1 Reports for that group are always received. This situation exists because IGMPv2 Reports do not trigger Report Suppression in version 1 hosts. Version 1 hosts do not understand IGMPv2 Reports and, therefore, ignore them. Thus, in some situations, as shown in Figure 3-12, both an IGMPv1 Report and an IGMPv2 Report are received in response to a General Query.

RULE

Version 2 routers must set a version 1 host present countdown timer associated with the group reported to note that there is a version 1 host on the LAN that is a member of this group. This timer should be the same as the Group Membership Interval.

While version 1 hosts are present for a particular group, routers must ignore any Leave Group messages received for the group.

If the IGMP Query Router were to process Leave Group messages, it would respond by sending a Group-Specific Query to the group in the Leave Group message; however, version 1 hosts ignore this message as an invalid IGMPv1 message type. If the version 1 host is the last member of the group, then there is no response to the Group-Specific Query and the version 2 routers on the subnet incorrectly time out this group. For this reason, the IGMPv2 Leave process is suspended for a group whenever a version 1 host is a member of the group.

Mixed V1 and V2 Routers Interoperability

The initial draft implementations of IGMPv2 made several attempts at automatic detection of IGMPv1 routers and dynamic IGMPv1 mode configuration. None of these methods were reliable, however, which led to another rule.

RULE   If any version 1 routers are present on a subnet, the use of IGMPv1 must be administratively configured on all routers in the subnet.

The Possibilities of IGMPv3

Before IGMP version 2 even was ratified, work already had begun on version 3. Although it is far too early to begin implementing code based on the IGMPv3 specification, it is worth looking at one of the key enhancements this new version of IGMP promises to provide.

A common problem, particularly in multimedia conferencing, is that when a host joins a multicast group, it is basically requesting that traffic from all sources in the group be delivered to the host's subnet. Although several sources may be actively sending traffic to the group, a host actually may want to receive traffic from just one source.

For example, assume that a multimedia audio conference is in session and a speaker is delivering a lecture. What happens if one member of the conference begins to "jam" the session maliciously by talking or sending music? This scenario is a growing possibility as multicast multimedia conferences on the Internet come under attack by a small segment of the Internet community that interferes by jamming the conference with unwanted audio. Most audio multimedia conferencing tools have a widget that allows the user to "mute" any of the other members, thereby silencing the audio of this malicious user. Unfortunately, this measure does not stop the flow of the unwanted traffic from being delivered to the host's subnet. This malicious behavior can take the form of a denial of service attack when the jammer's traffic stream exceeds or congests the traffic flow to the host's subnet.

IGMPv3 may provide a key that will help to solve this problem by giving conference members more control over the sources they want to receive via the network. Version 3 of IGMP extends the Join/Leave mechanism beyond multicast groups to permit joins and leaves to be issued for specific source/group pairs via IGMPv3 (S, G) Join/Leave messages (as shown in Figure 3-13).

Figure 3-13 *IGMPv3 (S, G) Join/Leaves*

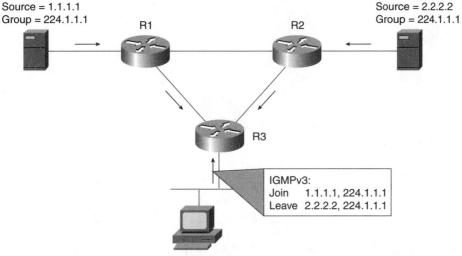

Source = 1.1.1.1
Group = 224.1.1.1

Source = 2.2.2.2
Group = 224.1.1.1

R1   R2

R3

IGMPv3:
Join   1.1.1.1, 224.1.1.1
Leave 2.2.2.2, 224.1.1.1

H1 - Member of 224.1.1.1

In this example, two sources, 1.1.1.1 and 2.2.2.2 are both multicasting to group 224.1.1.1. Host H1 wants to receive traffic addressed to this group from Source 1.1.1.1 but not from Source 2.2.2.2. To do so, H1 sends an IGMPv3 message containing a list of (S, G)s that it wishes to join and a list of (S, G)s that it wishes to leave. Router R3 can now use this information to prune traffic from Source 2.2.2.2 so that only Source 1.1.1.1 traffic is being delivered to R3. For more information on IGMPv3, see http://www.ietf.org/internet-drafts/ draft-ietf-idmr-igmp-v3-00.txt.

Summary

In this chapter, you've seen how IGMP is used as the basic signaling mechanism to inform the routers on a subnet of a host's desire to become a member of a particular multicast group. IGMPv2 extended this signaling mechanism to allow hosts to signal when they no longer wanted to belong to a multicast group. This extension to the protocol significantly has reduced the leave latency that, in turn, allows routers and switches to respond quickly and shut off the flow of unnecessary multicast traffic to parts of the networks where it is no longer needed.

Finally, it is important to remember that IGMP is the only mechanism a host can use to signal routers of its desire to receive multicast traffic for a specific group. Hosts are neither aware of, nor should they be concerned with, which routing protocol is in use by the routers in the network. Instead, the routers in the network are responsible for knowing and understanding the multicast routing protocol in use and for making sure that the multicast traffic is delivered to the members of the group throughout the network.

CHAPTER 4

Multimedia Multicast Applications

For many people, the first thing the term *IP multicast* brings to mind is video conferencing. Therefore, it is very likely that your first exposure to a multicast application will be one of the many exciting multimedia applications used for video and audio conferencing. Because these multimedia conferencing applications are so popular, taking a closer look at some of them makes sense.

This chapter starts by exploring some of the underlying protocols used by multimedia conferencing applications. The first two—Real-Time Protocol (RTP) and its companion protocol, Real-Time Control Protocol (RTCP)—are used to encapsulate the multimedia conference audio and video data streams and to monitor the delivery of the data to the end-stations in the conference. Next, this chapter examines the Session Announcement Protocol (SAP) and the Session Description Protocol (SDP). Conference-directory applications use these protocols to announce and to learn about the existence of the multimedia conference session in the network. Finally, this chapter looks at the popular MBone multimedia conferencing applications that provide video and audio conferencing as well as some limited data sharing.

Real-Time Protocol

RTP is a network layer protocol, documented in RFC 1889, that permits applications to transmit various types of real-time payloads such as audio, video, or other data that has real-time characteristics. RTP typically rides on top of User Datagram Protocol (UDP) and can be used over either unicast or multicast data streams. The protocol also provides payload type identification, sequence numbering, and timestamping, as well as a mechanism to monitor the delivery of the data.

RTP itself does not provide any guaranteed delivery mechanisms and normally relies on the lower-layer protocol to perform this function. Because it frequently rides on top of IP and UDP (as is the case for most multicast multimedia applications), however, RTP depends on the application to deal with the problems of lost datagrams and out-of-order delivery. These conditions can be detected by the use of the Sequence Number field in the RTP header.

RTP consists of two components:

- The RTP component, which carries the real-time data.
- The RTP Control Protocol (RTCP) component, which provides information about the participants of a session and monitors the delivery of data by using some simple quality-of-service measurements, such as packet loss and jitter.

The next section provides an audio conference example to describe the properties of RTP further.

Using RTP and RTCP to Audio Conference: An Example

Multimedia multicast applications typically allocate a multicast group address and two ports: one for the RTP data stream (in this case audio) and the other for the RTCP control stream. In most cases, the control port is numerically one higher than the data port.

The incoming audio signal is sampled in small, fixed time slots (for example, 40 ms) by the audio application. The audio from these time slots then is encoded using one of several audio-encoding schemes (pulse code modulation [PCM], adaptive differential pulse code modulation [ADPCM], linear predicative coding [LPC], and so on), and the encoded data is placed inside of an RTP packet. The header of the RTP packet contains a sequence number and a timestamp as well as an indication of the encoding scheme used.

NOTE   The Robust Audio Tool (RAT) is an audio conferencing application that uses multiple encoding methods to provide some redundancy to the audio data stream. The RTP packet contains an audio sample encoded using a primary encoding scheme followed by one or more audio samples encoded using some secondary encoding scheme. The audio samples that follow the primary sample are delayed slightly so that they can be used as an alternative if the primary data in a previous RTP packet is lost or corrupted.

When the audio application receives an RTP packet, the sequence number and timestamp in the RTP header are used to recover the sender's timing information and determine how many packets have been lost. The encoded audio data sample in the RTP packet then is placed in a *play-out* buffer with previously received audio samples. The audio samples are placed in the play-out buffer in contiguous order based on their sequence number and timestamp so that when they are decoded and played out to the speaker, the original audio is recovered.

The play-out buffer also serves as a de-jitter buffer. Congestion on the network can lead to variable interpacket arrival times that result in choppy audio playback. By using a larger play-out buffer and then delaying the play out of the data until the buffer is nearly full, variations in jitter can be smoothed out and choppy audio playback avoided. The downside of using a large play-out buffer is that it introduces delay in the audio stream. The delay is not a problem for one-way audio broadcasts, but it can become a problem if the application is an interactive audio conferencing tool.

Because it is useful to know who is participating in the conference and how well they are receiving the transmission, the audio application periodically multicasts a receiver report (RR) in an RTCP packet on the control port. These receiver reports contain the user's name and information on the number of packets lost and the interarrival jitter for each source in the conference. Senders can use this information to determine how well their transmissions are being received by each receiver and, in some cases, change to some other encoding method to try to improve the reception. RTCP is described in more detail in the next section.

Senders also periodically multicast *sender reports (SRs)* in RTCP packets to the same control port. These sender reports contain the same information as receiver reports but also include a 20-byte sender information section that contains timestamps, bytes sent, and packets sent on the data port. Members of the group can use this information to compute *round-trip time (RTT)* information and other statistics on the traffic flow.

RTP Control Protocol

All RTP-based applications use RTCP periodically to transmit session control information to all participants of the conference to accomplish the following functions:

1 Provide feedback on the quality of data reception and, in many cases, modify encoding schemes to improve overall reception quality. Third-party applications can also use this information to diagnose delivery problems and to determine areas of the network that are suffering poor reception quality.

2 Uniquely identify each transport layer source in the conference by the use of a *canonical name (CNAME)*. This CNAME may be used to associate several data streams from a given participant as part of a single multimedia session. This is important if you are trying to synchronize audio and video data streams.

3 Transmit RTCP packets so the total number of participants can be determined. This is required of all participants in order to accomplish functions 1 and 2. The information is necessary so that the rate at which RTCP control data is transmitted can be adjusted to some small percentage of the total session bandwidth.

4 Distribute information (username, location, and so on) that identifies the participants in the session in a user-friendly manner. This information normally is displayed in the user interface of the application.

If you are using RTP over IP multicast, functions 1, 2, and 3 are mandatory to allow the application to scale to a large number of participants. The fact that many of the popular multimedia multicast applications use the RTP model has the following very important implication on multicast network design:

> *Every end-station in an RTP-based multimedia multicast session is a source of multicast traffic!*

Even if the end-station is tuned in only to the video broadcast of the company meeting and actually is not sending any audio or video data, it still is multicasting periodic RTCP packets and, therefore, is a multicast source and receiver. Because the end-station is sending multicast traffic also (albeit at a low rate), this traffic is likely to cause a multicast state to be instantiated in some or all routers in the network, depending on the multicast routing protocol in use. The additional state generated by these so-called receiving end-stations should be (and more often is not) considered when doing multicast network design, because some multicast protocols do not scale well with large numbers of senders.

Session Announcement Protocol

The Session Announcement Protocol (SAP) is an announcement protocol for multicast conference sessions and was developed by the Multiparty Multimedia Session Control (MMUSIC) working group of the Internet Engineering Task Force (IETF). The current version of SAP (SAPv1) is described in IETF draft, draft-ietf-mmusic-sap-00.txt.

SAP clients announce their conference sessions periodically by multicasting SAP packets containing session information to an appropriate well-known multicast address and port. The session information inside the packet uses the Session Description Protocol (SDP), which is described in the "Session Description Protocol" section of this chapter. When privacy is desired, the SDP information may be encrypted optionally to avoid its being read by unauthorized parties.

This section continues with a discussion on SAP announcements and their bandwidth limitations.

SAP Announcements

The well-known multicast address and port used to multicast a SAP announcement depends on the multicast scope mechanism in effect at the SAP client. The scope of a multicast session is based either on the session's time-to-live (TTL) value or on an administrative address range that falls within the 239.0.0.0 through 239.255.255.255 multicast address range.

If TTL-scoped announcements are in use, the well-known address is 224.2.127.254 and the UDP port is 9875. TTL-scoped session announcements always are multicast with the same TTL with which the session is multicast.

If administrative-scoped announcements are in use, then a reserved address within the administratively scoped zone (usually the highest address) is used along with a well-known port. Therefore, SAP clients may need to listen to several multicast groups to receive all announcements when administrative-scoped announcements are in use.

NOTE	Because of the complexities of administratively scoped zone discovery, administrative-scoped announcements are seldom used.

SAP Bandwidth Limits

SAP announcements are rate limited so that the amount of network bandwidth consumed does not grow without bound. When TTL-scoped announcements are in use, the rate at which SAP announcements are multicast depends on the TTL scope of the session and the total number of announcements being sent by other SAP clients in the network. Table 4-1 lists the bandwidth limits for each TTL scope as documented in the SAP specification. A SAP client limits the rate of its announcements so that total bandwidth consumed by all announcements in the network of a particular TTL scope do not exceed these limits.

Table 4-1   *TTL-Scoped Bandwith Limits*

TTL	Bandwidth
1 to 15	2 kbps
16 to 63	1 kbps
64 to 127	1 kbps
128 to 255	200 bps

Therefore, as the numbers of session announcements in the network grow, the less frequently a SAP client announces its sessions.

When administratively scoped announcements are in use, the total bandwidth for all announcement traffic within an administratively scoped zone is recommended to be no more than 500 bps.

Session Description Protocol

The Session Description Protocol (SDP) is the companion protocol to SAP and is used to encode the actual session information. SDP was also developed in the Multiparty Multimedia Session Control (MMUSIC) working group of the IETF and is defined currently in the IETF draft document, draft-ietf-mmusic-sdp-*xx*.txt.

This section continues with a description of SDP's message format, an overview of its information description types, and a sample SDP session description.

SDP Message Format

The word *Protocol* in Session Description Protocol is somewhat misleading. SDP is not really a transport protocol in the same sense as SAP. SDP is actually an ASCII-text-based format specification that uses a number of lines of text to describe a session. Each line of text in a SDP announcement has the form

```
type=value
```

where **type** is a SDP *Description Type* that is always exactly one case-significant character. **value** is a structured text string whose format depends on **type** and typically is made up of several fields delimited by a single space character or a free-format string. SDP Description Types are described in more detail in the next section.

Each SDP session description starts with a session-level section denoted by a **v=** line as the first line. The session-level section describes the session in general and is applicable to all media streams in the session. This section is followed by zero or more media-level sections, each beginning with an **m=** line. These media-level sections provide detailed information about a single media stream in the session.

SDP Information Description Types

A complete description of all the SDP description types is beyond the scope of this book. If you really want to break apart a SDP message to see what the fields mean, then I encourage you to refer to the IETF draft document that defines SDP. Although SDP session descriptions are in textual form, they are not very easy to read—unless, of course, you are a serious geek like I am, in which case you may find them fascinating reading. It is useful, however, to understand at least the sort of information that can be carried in a SDP session description.

Table 4-2 lists the session description types used in the session-level section of a SDP session description. The information types in the session-level section must appear in the order shown in Table 4-2. Types shown in boldface on the table are mandatory; all others are optional.

Table 4-2 *SDP Session Description Types*

Type	Description
v=	**Protocol version**
o=	**Owner/creator and session ID**
s=	**Session name**
i=	Session information
u=	URL of description
e=	E-mail address
p=	Phone number
c=	Connection information (option if included in all media)
b=	Bandwidth information
t=	**Time the session is active**
r=	Repeat times
z=	Time zone adjustments
k=	Encryption key
a=	Zero or more attribute lines

Following the session-level section are zero or more media-level sections, each describing one of the media streams in the session. The media description types used in these media-level sections are shown in Table 4-3 and must appear in the order as shown. Types shown in boldface on the table are mandatory; all others are optional. The attribute (**a=**) information type is used primarily to extend SDP so that it may carry information specific to a particular media tool.

Table 4-3 *SDP Media Description Types*

Type	Description
m=	**Media name and transport address**
c=	Connection information (option if included at session-level)
b=	Bandwidth information
k=	Encryption key
a=	Zero or more attribute lines

Sample SDP Session Description

To satisfy the curiosity of readers who want to see a SDP session description, I have included one from the SDP specification in Example 4-1. (If you unexpectedly find reading this example really interesting, I suspect you may have a latent geek tendency.)

Example 4-1 *Sample SDP Session Description*

```
v=0
o=mhandley 2890844526 2890842807 IN IP4 126.16.64.4
s=SDP Seminar
i=A Seminar on the session description protocol
u=http://www.cs.ucl.ac.uk/staff/M.Handley/sdp.03.ps
e=mjh@isi.edu (Mark Handley)
c=IN IP4 224.2.17.12/127
t=2873397496 2873404696
a=recvonly
m=audio 49170 RTP/AVP 0
m=video 51372 RTP/AVP 31
m=application 32416 udp wb
a=orient:portrait
```

Some of the fields in Example 4-1 have fairly obvious meanings (well, at least they are to me because I am definitely a geek). For example:

- **s=SDP Seminar** is the session name and **i=A Seminar on the session description protocol** is the session description.

- The **c=IN IP4 224.2.17.12/127** line states that all media streams in the session are transmitting on multicast group 224.2.17.12 with a TTL of 127 using Internet protocol IP version 4.

- **m=audio 49170 RTP/AVP 0** states that the audio media stream is using port 49170 to transmit RTP encapsulated audio data whose encoding format is described by RTP Audio/Video profile 0.

- The **m=video 51372 RTP/AVP 0** line states that the video media stream is using port 51372 to transmit video data whose encoding format is described by RTP Audio/Video profile 31.

MBone Multimedia Conferencing Applications

Without a doubt, the most widely used multimedia conferencing applications are the MBone freeware applications that provide audio, video, and electronic whiteboard and session directory services. Your introduction to IP multicast applications is likely to be with one or more of these multimedia conferencing applications.

These applications initially were developed to run on UNIX platforms, and versions are available that run on most popular UNIX workstations including SunOS, Solaris, HP-UX, FreeBSD, Linux, and several others. Several of the applications also have been ported (with varying degrees of success) to run on Microsoft Windows 95 and NT platforms.

You can download these applications from several sites on the World Wide Web. One of my favorites is the Multimedia Conferencing Applications Archive located at http://www.video.ja.net/mice/index.html.

The next few sections briefly introduce the following popular MBone conferencing applications:

- SDR—Session Directory Tool
- VAT—MBone Multimedia Audio Tool
- VIC—MBone Multimedia Video Tool
- WB—Shared Whiteboard Tool

SDR—Session Directory Tool

Before you can join a multimedia session, you need to know what multicast group address and port are being used for the session. It would also be nice to know when the session is going to be active and what sort of applications (audio, video, and so forth) are necessary to run on your workstation to participate. The MBone Session Directory tool (SDR) was developed to help accomplish this task. The R in SDR stands for revised. The original Session Directory tool (SD), which was written by Lawrence Berkley Labs, is now obsolete.

SDR is a multicast application that listens for SAP packets on a well-known IP multicast group (for example, 224.2.127.254). These SAP packets contain a session description, the time the session is active, its IP multicast group addresses, media format, contact person, and other information about the advertised multimedia session. The information inside the SAP packet is formatted using the ASCII-text-based SDP described in the "Session Description Protocol" section earlier in this chapter.

The following sections describe SDR's Session Announcement window, information caching, launching applications with SDR, and SDR's media plug-ins.

SDR Session Announcement Window

Figure 4-1 shows SDR's Session Announcement window. Each line corresponds to a multimedia session announcement that SDR received in a SAP packet. As these packets are received, SDR updates this window by adding the multimedia session name to the list. SDR, therefore, permits you to learn what multimedia sessions are being *announced* in the network.

Figure 4-1   *SDR's Session Announcement Window*

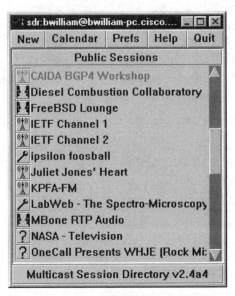

NOTE   Note that I've said *announced* here, as it is possible to run multicast applications that are not announced by SDR. By announcing a session using SDR, however, the session creator simplifies the task of joining the session for others. It's not uncommon for IP multicast beginners to misunderstand how SDR works. They frequently seem to think that SDR magically detects any and all IP multicast traffic in the network and displays this information on the screen. The reality is that if someone doesn't announce a multicast session by sending SAP multicast packets to SDR's well-known multicast group address, then SDR has no idea the multicast session exists. By the same token, just because a session is listed in SDR's main window doesn't mean it is actually active in the network.

SDP Information Caching

As you recall from the "Session Announcement Protocol" section earlier in this chapter, SAP packets (containing SDP information) are sent periodically by the SAP client responsible for announcing the multimedia session. The rate at which a SAP client repeats an announcement primarily depends on the total number of announcements being sent in the network. Therefore, the greater the number of announcements in the network (which equates to the number of lines in the SDR Session Announcement window), the less frequently an announcement is repeated. Unfortunately, this means it may take anywhere from minutes to hours for a newly activated SDR application to hear all announcements and to build a complete listing of the multimedia sessions in the network.

To avoid this problem, when the SDR program exits, it creates SDP cache files, each containing the information from a single received SDP session description packet. When SDR is next activated, it reads these SDP cache files as part of the initialization process and prepopulates its multimedia session listing with the information from these SDP cache files. This step eliminates the wait time to relearn the current multimedia sessions being advertised on the network.

Launching Applications via SDR

Now that you have learned which sessions are advertised from the Session Announcement window, you may opt to launch the appropriate IP multicast application(s) associated with the media stream(s) that make up the multimedia session.

By clicking on a multimedia session title in the SDR main window, a Session Information window such as the one shown in Figure 4-2 is opened. In this example, the NASA Television multimedia session was clicked. Now, you can see the session information that was contained in the SAP announcement packet received by SDR.

Figure 4-2 *Session Information Window*

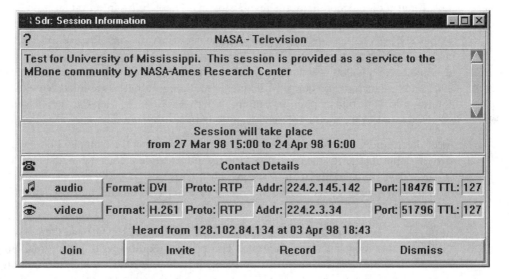

At the top of the window is a description of this multimedia session along with scheduling information to let you know when the session is active. Additional contact information about the multimedia session creator such as name, e-mail address, and phone number can be obtained by clicking the Contact Details bar in the center of the window. Although not shown in this example, a More Information button may be displayed next to the Contact Details button. This button is displayed when the session creator supplies a URL where the user may obtain additional information about the session via the World Wide Web.

NOTE	SDR comes with a built-in, albeit limited, Web browser that is launched when you click the More Information button. If the user has another Web browser installed on the workstation, SDR may be configured to launch this browser instead.

In the bottom portion of the Session Information window is a list of the media types in use by this multimedia session, along with information regarding the IP multicast group address, port number, TTL, and media encoding format. In this example, both an audio and video media stream are associated with this session. We can join all media streams in the multimedia session by clicking the Join button at the lower-left corner of the window. This will launch the multicast applications associated with each media stream. You can also click the individual Audio and/or Video media buttons to launch only the applications associated with these media streams.

SDR's Media Plug-Ins

SDR uses *plug-in configuration files* to map various media streams to one or more media tools for encoding/decoding of the media streams. These "plug-in" configuration files also define the necessary switches that go along with the media encoding formats and attributes so that SDR can launch the media tool with the necessary options. For example, when you click on the Video button in the NASA Television channel example, SDR searches its list of plug-ins for a match based on media type, protocol, and encoding format. In this case, SDR finds a match on the built-in VIC media tool plug-in that has a **video rtp h261** definition. If SDR finds a plug-in configuration match on more than one media tool, SDR asks you to select the media tool you want to launch.

After determining which media tool to launch, SDR formats the command line with the switches appropriate for the encoding formats and so on, launches the media tool, and passes it the command line with all the switches. This step typically is done via the EXEC call in a UNIX environment. Other operating system environments may use slightly different techniques.

Application developers may extend SDR's list of media stream types and their associated applications to support new applications. This process requires writing additional plug-in configuration files that define media, protocol, encoding formats, switch information, and so on and then placing the files in SDR's plug-in subdirectory. The details of writing plug-in configuration files for new media tools are beyond the scope of this book. Details on this process, however, may be found under SDR's Help option.

VAT—MBone Multimedia Audio Tool

VAT, which is the MBone's popular multimedia audio tool, provides a many-to-many audio conference capability. Figure 4-3 shows an example of the main VAT conference window.

Figure 4-3   *VAT Conference Window*

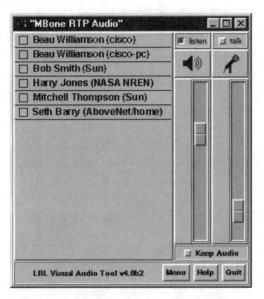

On the left side of the window is a listing of all of the members of the audio conference. When one of the members begins to speak, the small square to the left of the member's name is filled in with a black square and the audio is heard on the workstation's speaker. You may mute an individual member by clicking the box to the left of the member's name, or you can mute the entire conference by deselecting the Listen button above the speaker icon.

The two sliders on the right side of the window control the speaker gain and the microphone gain. Immediately to the left of these sliders are bar-graph–style volume unit (VU) meters that indicate the levels of the incoming and outgoing audio signals. (Note: Because no audio is being sent or received in the example shown in Figure 4-3, the bar graph segments are not visible.)

The right mouse button is used as your push-to-talk button and functions as long as the mouse pointer is anywhere inside the VAT window. You should adjust your microphone gain so that the bar graph only occasionally peaks into the red portion of the scale as you talk.

Clicking on the Menu button at the bottom of the window brings up the Options Menu window shown in Figure 4-4. This menu allows you to control various aspects of VAT's operation.

Figure 4-4   *VAT Options Menu*

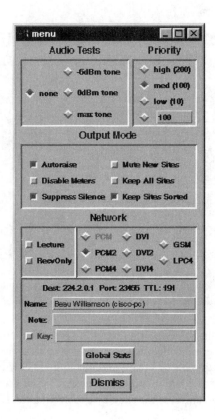

VAT Audio Encoding Formats

Using the center Network section of the menu shown in Figure 4-4, you can select different audio encoding modes, depending on your bandwidth and desired audio quality. This setting controls your transmitted audio only. VAT automatically determines the coding method used on all incoming audio and decodes it properly. The available encoding formats are listed in decreasing order of bandwidth and audio quality in Table 4-4.

Table 4-4   *VAT Audio Encoding Methods*

Mode	BW	Encoding Method
PCM	78 kb/s	8-bit mu-law encoded 8 kHz PCM (20-ms frames)
PCM2	71 kb/s	8-bit mu-law encoded 8 kHz PCM (40-ms frames)
PCM4	68 kb/s	8-bit mu-law encoded 8 kHz PCM (80-ms frames)
DVI	46 kb/s	Intel DVI ADPCM (20-ms frames)
DVI2	39 kb/s	Intel DVI ADPCM (40-ms frames)
DVI4	36 kb/s	Intel DVI ADPCM (80-ms frames)
GSM	17 kb/s	GSM (80-ms frames)
LPC4	9 kb/s	Linear Predictive Coder (80-ms frames)

In the example shown in Figure 4-4, the selected mode is PCM2, which instructs VAT to encode the audio using PCM 8-bit mu-law using an 8-kHz clock and 40-ms samples.

VAT Audio Playback Modes

VAT has two playback modes that can be selected in the Network section of the menu window: Conference mode and Lecture mode. These options control how dynamically VAT adjusts the size of the playout buffer that is used to de-jitter the arriving audio data packets. In Conference mode, which is selected if the Lecture button on the menu is not pressed, VAT vigorously attempts to keep the size of the playout buffer small in order to reduce delay. Excessive delay can be annoying in an interactive conference in which multiple speakers are active. On the other hand, if only a single speaker is talking, such as in the case of an audio broadcast, delay is not really an issue. In these cases, keeping the playout buffer too small can result in choppy audio when packets arrive too late. Selecting Lecture mode tells VAT to reduce the size of the playout buffer much more gradually in response to decreasing interarrival times of audio data.

NOTE   The RecvOnly button that appears directly under the Lecture button on the VAT Options menu (Figure 4-4) simply disables the microphone and prevents accidental transmission of any audio.

VIC—MBone Multimedia Video Tool

VIC is the MBone multimedia video tool that provides many-to-many video conferencing capabilities. Figure 4-5 presents an example of VIC showing multiple video streams being received on the popular Places all over the world session. Notice that the VIC tool is capable of receiving and displaying all the video sources in the session simultaneously.

Figure 4-5   *VIC MBone Multimedia Video Tool*

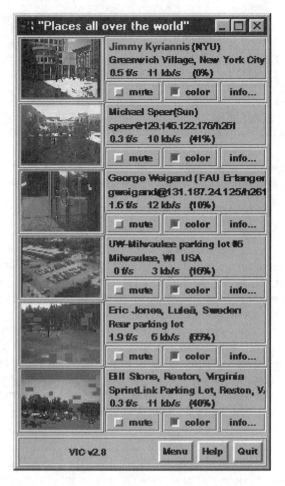

Places all over the world is a just-for-fun session where various participants send low-rate video of their part of the world. Senders are requested to keep their video transmission rates below 10 kb/s so that excessive network bandwidth is not consumed. The window to the right of each image is a sender information block, which gives some basic information about the sender.

In this example, the sender's name and location are shown along with the current frame rate (0.5 f/s) and transmission rate (11 kb/s). The value shown in the parentheses is the current loss rate and indicates how well the video stream is being received. You can obtain even more information about this video source by clicking the Info button in the lower-right corner of the sender information block. The Info pull-down menu is shown in Figure 4-6.

Figure 4-6 *Info Pull-Down Menu*

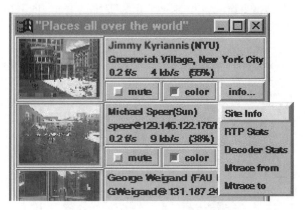

Selecting Site Info on the pull-down menu displays the Site Info window as shown in Figure 4-7.

Figure 4-7 *VIC Site Information Window*

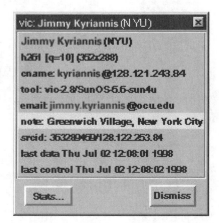

This window gives additional information about the video source including the encoding method (h261), image size (352x288 pixels), tools (VIC-2.8 running on a SunOS-5.6 UNIX platform), e-mail address of the sender, and so on. The last two lines reflect the last time that an RTP packet was received and the last time an RTCP packet was received from this source. These are updated periodically.

You can also obtain additional RTP statistics on the data stream by using the Stats button at the bottom of this window or by selecting RTP Stats from the Info pull-down menu shown previously in Figure 4-6.

Figure 4-8 is an example of the RTP Statistics displayed using either of these two methods. This information can be very useful when attempting to debug a video-quality problem.

Figure 4-8 *RTP Statistics Display*

vic: Jimmy Kyriannis (NYU)			
Jimmy Kyriannis (NYU)			
RTP Statistics			
	EWA	**Delta**	**Total**
Kilobits	2.0	0.0	8030
Frames	0.1	0.0	255
Packets	0.3	0.0	1165
Missing	0.1	0.0	354
Misordered	0.0	0.0	0
Runts	0.0	0.0	0
Dups	0.0	0.0	3
Bad-S-Len	0.0	0.0	0
Bad-S-Ver	0.0	0.0	0
Bad-S-Opt	0.0	0.0	0
Bad-Sdes	0.0	0.0	0
Bad-Bye	0.0	0.0	0
Playout			0ms

Dismiss

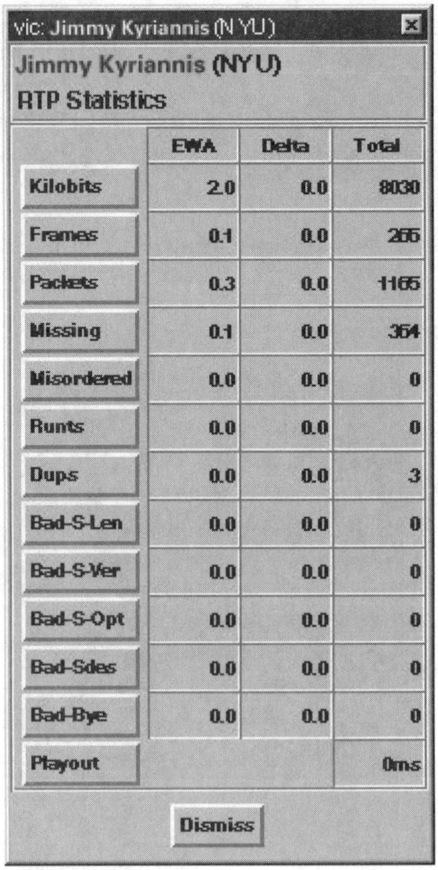

Displaying Video

Viewing the images in the main VIC window is difficult because of their small size. By clicking on the desired thumbnail image in VIC's main window, however, you can launch another window that contains this video, as shown in Figure 4-9. The Size button at the bottom of this window allows you to select several different display sizes and window formats.

Figure 4-9 *Expanded VIC Source Window*

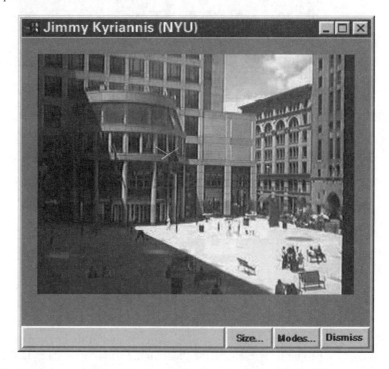

Clicking on the Modes button at the bottom of the window displays the Modes pull-down menu shown in Figure 4-10.

Figure 4-10   *VIC Modes Pull-Down Menu*

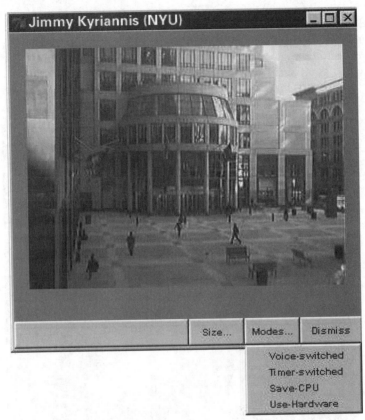

This menu allows you to enable the voice-switched and/or timer-switched display modes. If voice-switched mode is enabled, the video in the window switches to the speaker, using cues that it receives from VAT. If the timer-switched mode is enabled, the video in the window cycles through all unmuted video sources in the session. The other two options on this menu have to do with the use of hardware video decoders and are beyond the scope of this book.

Transmitting Video

If you are lucky enough to have a camera to source your own video, you need to call up VIC's Menu window, shown in Figure 4-11, to set some transmission parameters before you start transmitting.

Figure 4-11 *VIC's Menu Window*

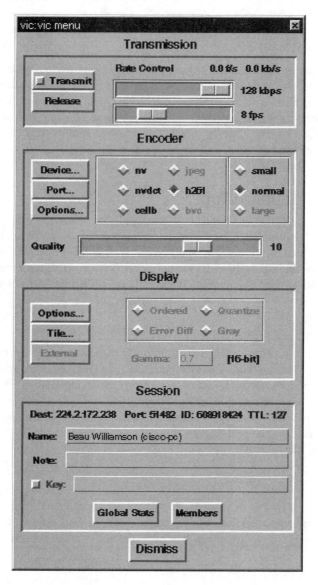

At the top of the window are the control sliders that limit transmission bandwidth and frame rate. You want to adjust these to ensure that you don't consume too much network bandwidth. In the Places all over the world session example, senders should adjust these sliders to ensure that their video doesn't exceed 10 kbps, thereby minimizing the total bandwidth consumed by all video sources in the multicast session.

Immediately below the Transmission section is the Encoder section that allows you to select the video encoding methods and options. The most common video encoding is h261, which is a video compression method designed primarily for video conferencing over low-rate (less than 128 kbps) lines.

The Encoder section also has a Quality slider you can use to modify further the amount of bandwidth the transmitted video uses at the expense of image quality. For example, when transmitting h261 encoded video, reducing the Quality value results in a decrease in image resolution and a decrease in the bandwidth consumed for a given frame rate. Increasing the Quality value has the opposite effect. The remaining items on the menu are not discussed here, as they are beyond the scope of this book.

WB—Shared Whiteboard Tool

Just as its name implies, Whiteboard (the application name is simply wb) is an electronic whiteboard that members of the multicast session may share. Whiteboard differs from the other multimedia conferencing applications already discussed in this chapter in that it uses a reliable multicast protocol to guarantee data delivery to all participants. If the delivery of data was not guaranteed, all participants in the session might not see the same thing on their whiteboards.

NOTE   Audio and video data, especially for interactive conferences, must be delivered to all participants at a constant rate. The amount of time it takes to retransmit a missed audio or video packet is much too long for the retransmitted audio data to arrive in time. Therefore, audio and video data streams usually are not transmitted over a guaranteed transport mechanism. Whiteboard data, on the other hand, does not lose its significance if its delivery is a second or two late. Therefore, it is reasonable to employ some form of retransmission method to guarantee data delivery.

Figure 4-12 shows an example of the Whiteboard application. Users can make use of several graphics tools (shown in the menu along the right edge of the display) to draw on the whiteboard, including the typing of text directly on the whiteboard.

Figure 4-12 *WB—The Electronic Whiteboard*

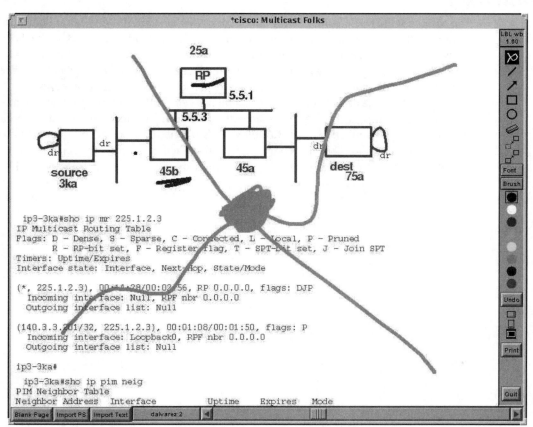

Buttons along the bottom-left corner of the whiteboard permit users to import text or PostScript files or create a new blank whiteboard page. When a user creates a new whiteboard page, previous pages are not lost. Instead, the slider in the lower corner allows users to switch between whiteboard pages in the session. Immediately to the left of the slider is the name of the participant who created the currently displayed whiteboard page along with a page number.

Summary

The MBone multimedia conferencing applications described in this chapter are powerful communication tools that can run over multicast-enabled networks. It's unfortunate that so many newcomers to IP multicast networking think of video conferencing as the primary reason to implement an IP multicast network. The reality is that video frequently provides very little value to most conferences and usually consumes considerable amounts of bandwidth. After the novelty of video conferencing wears off, many people find that an audio-only conference using VAT, coupled with an electronic whiteboard, generally is more productive and cost-effective than a full-blown video conference. As other multicast-based data-sharing applications become commonplace, these audio plus data-sharing conferences probably will become the long-awaited killer application that causes the demand for IP multicast networks to take off.

PART II

Multicast Routing Protocol Overview

This part is entirely devoted to providing an overview of the most popular intra-domain multicast routing protocols that are either currently in use or, as in the case of Core-Based Trees (CBTs), at least well defined by the IETF. Although some of these protocols have been used for inter-domain multicast routing, this part focuses only on their use for intra-domain multicast routing.

Chapter 5 is a fairly in-depth discussion of the first widely used multicast routing protocol, Distance Vector Multicast Routing Protocol (DVMRP). This protocol is covered in great detail because a sound understanding of DVMRP is necessary to fully comprehend later chapters in the book that address interconnecting Cisco routers to DVMRP networks.

Chapters 6 and 7 provide details on the two modes of operation of the Protocol Independent Multicast (PIM) routing protocol. Chapter 6 presents the details of PIM dense mode (PIM-DM) protocol operation, while Chapter 7 covers the details of PIM sparse mode (PIM-SM) protocol operation. These two PIM protocols (PIM-SM in particular) are the primary focus of this book. These two chapters are the key to understanding IP multicast in a Cisco network.

Chapter 8 presents a brief overview of CBTs. While this protocol is not deployed to any significant degree, it has been the subject of much work in the IETF and is presented to provide a somewhat complete treatise on the topic of multicast routing protocols.

Chapter 9 presents the details of Multicast Open Shortest Path First (MOSPF), which is really a multicast routing extension to the existing OSPF unicast routing protocol.

While the chapters in this part are not intended to cover every protocol to the same extent, you should have sufficient information to make an informed decision as to which protocol best suits your networking needs.

CHAPTER 5

Distance Vector Multicast Routing Protocol

Distance Vector Multicast Routing Protocol (DVMRP) was the first true multicast routing protocol to see widespread use. Based on Steve Deering's seminal work, DVMRP is similar in many ways to Routing Information Protocol (RIP) with some minor variations added to support multicast.

Some key characteristics of DVMRP are

- Distance vector based (similar to RIP)
- Periodic route updates (every 60 seconds)
- Infinity = 32 hops (versus 16 for RIP)
- Poison Reverse has special meaning
- Classless (that is, route updates include masks)

Currently, not all router vendors implement the same multicast routing protocols. However, most vendors support DVMRP to some degree; hence, it has become the Esperanto of multicast routing protocols and can be used between virtually all routers. As a result, this chapter explores DVMRP in a little more depth than comparable chapters explore their respective protocols. This information is presented simply to lay a firm foundation for later chapters on Cisco's Protocol Independent Multicast (PIM)-DVMRP interoperability features. This chapter offers comprehensive information on the following topics: DVMRP Neighbor Discovery, route tables, exchanging DVMRP Route Reports, source distribution trees, multicast forwarding, pruning, grafting, and scalability.

DVMRP Neighbor Discovery

DVMRP Neighbor Discovery, as you will soon discover (sorry about the pun) is important because DVMRP routers must maintain a database of DVMRP adjacencies with other DVMRP routers. This is especially true when DVMRP is operating over multiaccess networks, such as Ethernet, FDDI, and so forth, because the network can have many DVMRP routers. As you will see later in this chapter, the normal operation of a DVMRP router requires it to know its DVMRP neighbors on each interface.

To accomplish this, DVMRP Probe messages are periodically multicast to the All DVMRP Router group address (224.0.0.4). Figure 5-1 shows the DVMRP Neighbor Discovery mechanism in action between two DVMRP routers connected to a common Ethernet network.

Figure 5-1   *DVMRP Neighbor Discovery*

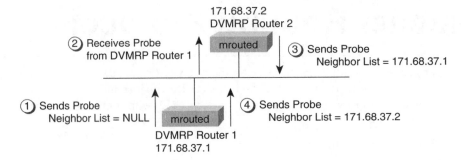

Here's an explanation of the DVMRP Neighbor Discovery mechanism depicted in Figure 5-1:

1 Router 1 sends a Probe packet first. Because Router 1 has not yet heard any other Probes from other routers, the Neighbor List in the Probe packet is empty.

2 Router 2 hears the Probe sent by Router 1 and adds the IP address of Router 1 to its internal list of DVMRP neighbors on this interface.

3 Router 2 then sends a Probe of its own with the IP address of Router 1 in the Neighbor List.

4 Router 1 hears the Probe sent by Router 2 and adds the IP address of Router 2 to its internal list of DVMRP neighbors on this interface. At the next Probe interval, Router 1 sends a Probe with the IP address of Router 2 in the Neighbor List.

When a DVMRP router receives a Probe with its own IP address listed in the Neighbor List, the router knows that a two-way adjacency has been successfully formed between itself and the neighbor that sent the Probe.

DVMRP Route Table

In DVMRP, source network routing information is exchanged in the same basic manner as it is in RIP. That is to say, periodic (every 60 seconds) Route Report messages are sent between DVMRP neighbors. These Route Reports contain entries that advertise a source network (with a mask) and a hop-count that is used as the routing metric.

The routing information stored in the DVMRP routing table is separate from the unicast routing table and is used to

- Build source distribution trees

- Perform multicast forwarding (that is, Reverse Path Forwarding [RPF] checks)

These tasks are discussed in the sections "DVMRP Source Distribution Trees" and "DVMRP Multicast Forwarding" later in this chapter.

Example 5-1 shows a DVMRP route table in a Cisco router.

Example 5-1   *DVMRP Route Table*

```
DVMRP Routing Table - 8 entries
130.1.0.0/16 [0/3] uptime 00:19:03, expires 00:02:13
    via 135.1.22.98, Tunnel0, [version mrouted 3.8] [flags: GPM]
135.1.0.0/16 [0/3] uptime 00:19:03, expires 00:02:13
    via 135.1.22.98, Tunnel0, [version mrouted 3.8] [flags: GPM]
135.1.22.0/24 [0/2] uptime 00:19:03, expires 00:02:13
    via 135.1.22.98, Tunnel0, [version mrouted 3.8] [flags: GPM]
171.69.0.0/16 [0/3] uptime 00:19:03, expires 00:02:13
    via 135.1.22.98, Tunnel0, [version mrouted 3.8] [flags: GPM]
172.21.27.0/24 [0/3] uptime 00:19:04, expires 00:02:12
    via 135.1.22.98, Tunnel0, [version mrouted 3.8] [flags: GPM]
172.21.32.0/24 [0/2] uptime 00:19:04, expires 00:02:12
    via 135.1.22.98, Tunnel0, [version mrouted 3.8] [flags: GPM]
172.21.33.0/24 [0/3] uptime 00:19:04, expires 00:02:12
    via 135.1.22.98, Tunnel0, [version mrouted 3.8] [flags: GPM]
172.21.120.0/24 [0/3] uptime 00:19:04, expires 00:02:12
    via 135.1.22.98, Tunnel0, [version mrouted 3.8] [flags: GPM]
```

Here's an explanation of the first entry:

- **130.1.0.0/16** indicates that there is a DVMRP route for source network 130.1.0.0 with a 16-bit mask.

- **[0/3]** indicates that the administrative distance is 0 and the DVMRP metric is 3 hops.

- **uptime 00:19:03** indicates that this route has been active for 19 hours and 3 seconds.

- **expires 00:02:13** indicates that the route will expire in 2 minutes and 13 seconds unless another Route Report is received to refresh this route.

- **via 135.1.22.98, Tunnel0** indicates the IP address of the next hop and the interface in the direction of the source network.

- **[version mrouted 3.8] [flags: GPM]** provides information about the DVMRP neighbor that sent this route information.

Exchanging DVMRP Route Reports

As stated previously, DVMRP Route Reports are periodically exchanged in a manner similar to the way RIP unicast routing protocol information is exchanged. The key difference is that DVMRP routes are advertised with a subnet mask, making the protocol effectively a classless protocol. This section takes a closer look at the DVMRP Route Report exchange mechanism.

Figure 5-2 shows a portion of a multicast network consisting of two DVMRP routers (in this case, two UNIX workstations running the mrouted DVMRP routing process) connected via a common Ethernet.

Figure 5-2 *DVMRP Route Exchange—Initial State*

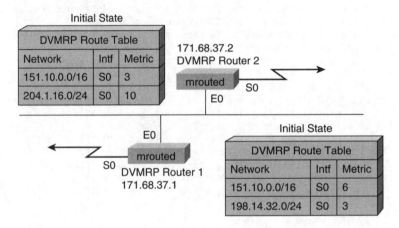

The contents of their DVMRP route tables reflect DVMRP routes that have been learned via their Serial links and are shown before any Route Reports have been exchanged over the Ethernet. Notice that both routers have an entry for the 151.10.0.0/16 network.

Assume that Router 2 sends its route report first as shown by Step 1 in Figure 5-3.

Figure 5-3   *DVMRP Route Exchange—Steps 1 and 2*

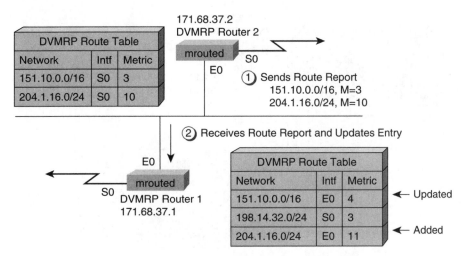

This Route Report, containing two route advertisements, is received by Router 1 (Step 2), which responds by adding a new entry for network 204.1.16.0/24 to its DVMRP route table. Additionally, because Router 2 has a better metric to network 151.10.0.0, Router 1 also updates its existing entry for network 151.10.0.0 with the new metric (4) and next hop interface (E0).

NOTE   Notice that just as in RIP, the metrics of incoming route advertisements are incremented by the cost, typically 1 hop, of the incoming interface.

Now, Router 1 responds by sending its own Route Report (Step 3) to Router 2 as shown in Figure 5-4.

Figure 5-4   *DVMRP Route Exchange—Step 3*

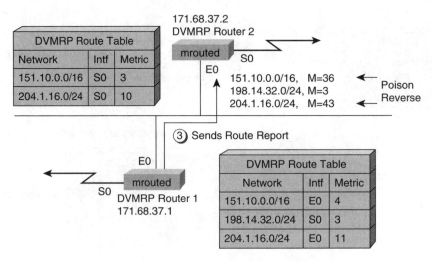

Notice that Router 1 Poison Reverses the two routes that it has received via interface E0 by adding infinity (32) to the current metric. This change informs Router 2 that Router 1 is a child (that is, Router 1 is downstream of Router 2) and that Router 1 expects to receive multicast traffic from these source networks from Router 2.

NOTE   Poison Reverse is used differently in DVMRP than in most unicast distance vector routing protocols that use Poison Reverse to advertise the unreachability of a particular route. In unicast routing protocols such as RIP, a Poison Reverse route is indicated by advertising the route with a metric of infinity (for instance, infinity = 16 in RIP). When a neighboring router receives this advertisement, the router can mark this route as unreachable via this neighbor. In DVMRP, however, Poison Reverse signals to a router's upstream DVMRP neighbor that this router is downstream in the multicast distribution tree.

Router 2 receives this Route Report and updates its own DVMRP route table by adding a new entry for network 198.14.32.0/24 as shown by Step 4 in Figure 5-5.

Figure 5-5   *DVMRP Route Exchange—Steps 4 and 5*

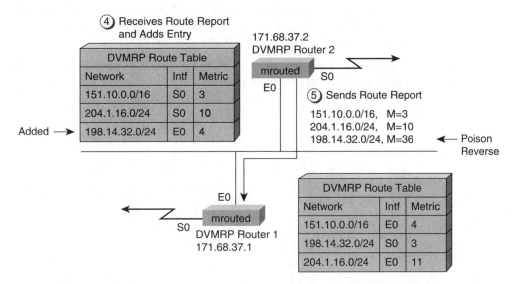

In Step 5 (also shown in Figure 5-5), Router 2 sends another route report and Poison Reverses the 198.14.32.0/24 route that it received from Router 1 by adding infinity (32) to the current metric. This change informs Router 1 that Router 2 is a child (downstream) and expects to receive multicast traffic from source network 198.14.32.0/ 24 from Router 1.

DVMRP Truncated Broadcast Trees

DVMRP is a dense mode protocol that uses *source distribution trees*, also known as *shortest path trees (SPTs)*, to forward multicast traffic. DVMRP source distribution trees are built by the DVMRP routers from *truncated broadcast trees,* which are based on the metrics in the routers' DVMRP route tables. To build a truncated broadcast tree, routers signal their upstream router (the neighbor advertising the best metric to a source network) that they are downstream by advertising a special Poison Reverse route metric for the source network back to the upstream router.

RULE   When sending a Route Report to the upstream DVMRP router for source network X, Poison Reverse the route by adding infinity (32) to the current metric for Network X and advertising it back to the upstream neighbor.

These Poison Reverse route advertisements tell the upstream (parent) router to forward any multicast traffic from the source network out this interface so that the downstream child router can receive it. Basically, the downstream router is telling the upstream router to "put me on the truncated broadcast tree for this source network."

The following should help to clarify the situation. Figure 5-6 shows a sample DVMRP truncated broadcast tree being built for Network S.

Figure 5-6 *DVMRP Truncated Broadcast Tree*

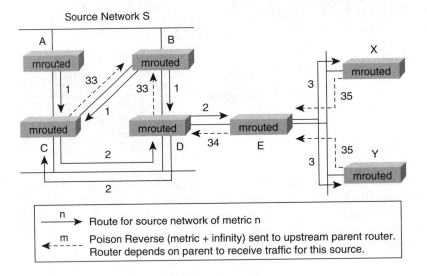

In this example, both Routers A and B advertise a route to Network S (shown by the solid arrows) with a metric (hop-count) of 1 to Routers C and D. Because Router D is downstream of Router B for Network S, Router D adds infinity (32) to the received metric to Poison Reverse the route advertisement (shown by the dashed arrows) to Network S and returns the route advertisement to Router B. This informs Router B that Router D is a child router and that the link to D should be placed in the outgoing interface list (that is, on the truncated broadcast tree) for Network S.

Likewise, Router C receives advertisements with a metric of 1 from both Routers A and B. Using the lowest IP address as the tiebreaker, Router C selects Router B as its parent (that is, upstream) router toward Network S and sends a Poison Reverse (shown by the dashed arrow) to Router B. As a result, Router B places the link to Router C in the outgoing interface list that describes the truncated broadcast tree for Network S.

Routers C and D now both advertise a route to Network S out their common Ethernet. To avoid the delivery of duplicate packets, the router with the best metric to Network S is elected as the *designated forwarder* that is responsible for forwarding multicast packets from Network S to hosts on the Ethernet. In this case, the metrics are equal, so again, the lowest IP address is used as the tiebreaker, which results in Router D being the designated forwarder.

Route advertisements (solid arrows) continue to propagate away from Network S through Routers D and E on down to Routers X and Y as shown in Figure 5-6. At each point, the upstream router is sent a Poison Reverse advertisement (dashed arrows) to tell it to put the interface in the outgoing interface list for Network S. In the end, a truncated broadcast tree for Source Network S has been built as depicted by the solid arrows in Figure 5-7.

Figure 5-7 *Resulting Truncated Broadcast Tree for Network S*

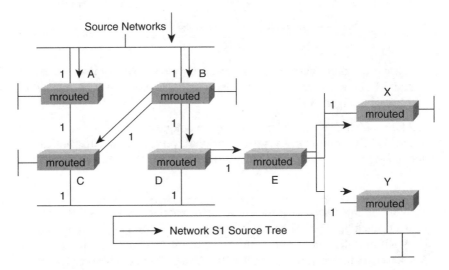

Truncated broadcast trees (such as the one shown in Figure 5-7) describe the distribution tree that is used to deliver multicast traffic from a specific source network to all other locations in the network regardless of whether there are any group members in the network. When a source begins to transmit, the multicast data is flooded down the truncated broadcast tree to all points in the network. DVMRP routers then prune this flow where the traffic is unwanted. (Pruning is described in more detail in the "DVMRP Pruning" section later in this chapter.)

The preceding example kept things simple by showing only the advertisements and the resulting truncated broadcast tree for Network S. In fact, each source network is associated with a truncated broadcast tree. Figure 5-8 shows the truncated broadcast tree that is built for Source Network S1.

Figure 5-8 *Truncated Broadcast Tree for Network S1*

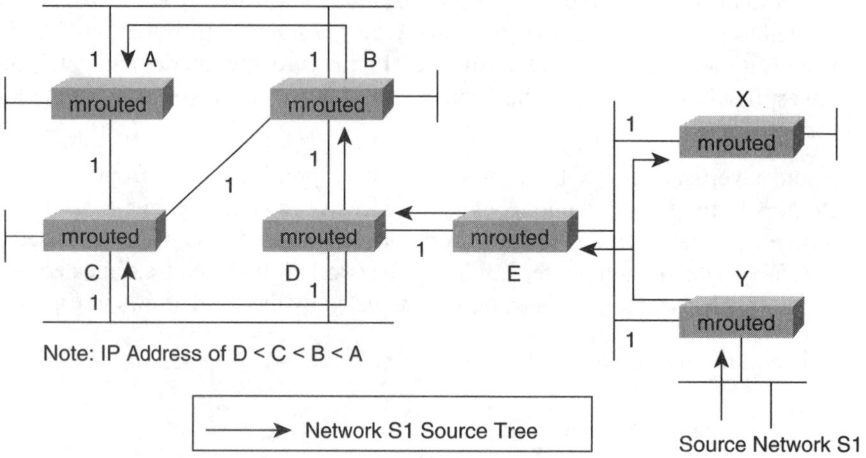

Because each source network has its own truncated broadcast tree, the example in Figure 5-8 shows a completely different tree that is rooted at Source Network S1 than the tree shown in Figure 5-7.

The key point here is that every subnet has a unique truncated broadcast tree that is defined by the DVMRP route metrics and the Poison Reverse mechanism. Multicast data is initially flooded over these truncated broadcast trees to reach all routers in the network.

NOTE   To avoid getting flamed by readers who have experience with DVMRP, let me point out that I have taken a little liberty here with my description of how distribution trees are built in DVMRP. In reality, until some multicast source in Network S begins transmitting traffic, no forwarding data structures (other than the DVMRP route table) are created for Network S in the router. However, as soon as the first packet is received from some multicast source, say S_i, an (S_i, G) entry is created in the multicast forwarding table (assuming that the RPF check succeeds). At this point, the outgoing interface list in the (S_i, G) entry is populated based on the Poison Reverse information for Network S in the DVMRP route table, thereby creating the distribution tree. This on-demand state creation mechanism saves considerable memory in the routers.

DVMRP Multicast Forwarding

Because multicast routing is upside-down routing (that is, you are interested in where the packet came from versus where it is going), the information in the DVMRP routing table is used to determine whether an incoming multicast packet was received on the correct interface. If not, the packet is discarded to prevent multicast loops. Again, forwarding based on the incoming interface is referred to as *Reverse Path Forwarding (RPF)*, and the test to ensure a packet arrived on the correct interface is called the *RPF check*.

An example of an RPF check where a multicast packet arrives on the wrong interface is shown in Figure 5-9.

Figure 5-9 *DVMRP RPF Check Failure*

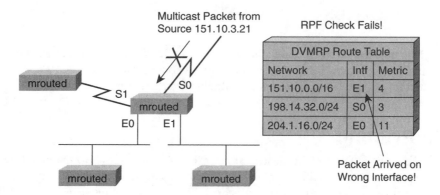

In this example, a multicast packet has arrived from source 151.10.3.21 via interface S0. However, based on the 151.10.0.0/16 entry in the DVMRP route table, multicast traffic from this source should be arriving via interface E1(not S0). The RPF check, therefore, fails, and the multicast packet is quietly discarded.

NOTE   Under normal, stable DVMRP operation, packets would not arrive on the wrong interface because the upstream router would not have forwarded the packet unless the downstream router Poison Reversed the route in the first place. However, there are cases such as immediately after a network topology change when DVMRP routing has not yet converged across all routers (remember, this is distance vector based routing) where this can occur.

Figure 5-10, on the other hand, shows a successful RPF check. Here, a packet is received from multicast source 198.14.32.10 via interface S0.

Figure 5-10   *DVMRP RPF Check Succeeds*

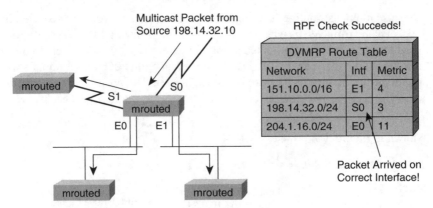

This time the DVMRP route table entry 198.14.32.0/24 indicates that S0 is the correct interface for traffic arriving from this source network. Therefore, the RPF check succeeds, and the packet is forwarded out all outgoing interfaces for this source.

DVMRP Pruning

The section "DVMRP Truncated Broadcast Trees" describes how the initial truncated broadcast trees are built using DVMRP Route Reports. This process occurs even if there are no active receivers on the distribution tree. Like most dense mode protocols, DVMRP uses a *Flood-and-Prune* mechanism to initially deliver multicast traffic to all routers in the network. In the case of DVMRP, the traffic is flooded down a truncated broadcast tree to any possible receivers.

However, to conserve precious network resources, you need to shut off (or prune) the traffic flow down branches of the truncated broadcast tree where there are no receivers. Therefore, leaf routers without any directly connected receivers send DVMRP Prune messages up the truncated broadcast tree to stop the flow of unwanted multicast traffic and *prune* the unwanted branches of the truncated broadcast tree. What remains after DVMRP Pruning is a source distribution tree or SPT for this specific source.

Unfortunately, because DVMRP is a Flood-and-Prune protocol, the source distribution tree that results from DVMRP Pruning reverts to a truncated broadcast tree as soon as the Prunes time out. (Typically, DVMRP Prunes are good for only 2 minutes, after which they expire and traffic is again flooded.) Like PIM-DM, this Flood-and-Prune behavior can also result in the (S, G) state being created in the DVMRP routers in the network, even when there are few receivers.

NOTE   The truncated broadcast tree itself is not pruned as a result of the DVMRP Prunes because it is described by the contents of the DVMRP route table entries across all the routers in the network. These DVMRP route table entries are not modified by DVMRP Prune messages. Instead, the information received in a DVMRP Prune message (which is normally a Prune for a specific (S, G) traffic flow) is stored in a separate data structure in the router. This information is used to modify the flow of (S, G) traffic down the truncated broadcast tree.

Figure 5-11 shows the network with an active Source S_i, sending to multicast Group G.

Figure 5-11   *DVMRP Pruning—Initial Flooding*

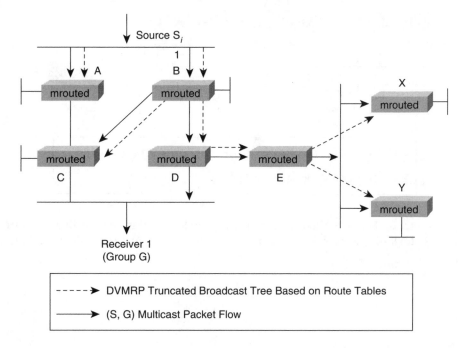

Receiver 1 has joined Group G to receive traffic from S_i. The solid arrows in the diagram show the initial flow of (S_i, G) traffic down the truncated broadcast tree (dashed arrows) before any pruning occurs.

In Figure 5-12, Router C is not the designated forwarder for the Ethernet where Receiver 1 is attached and is therefore a leaf node that has no other directly connected receivers.

Figure 5-12 *DVMRP Pruning—Step 1*

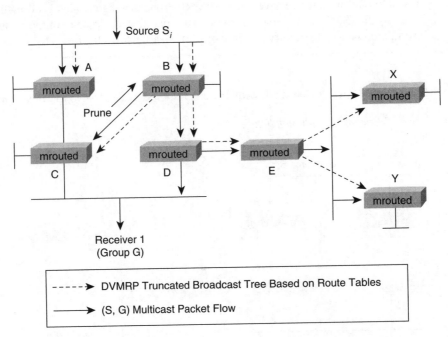

Router C, therefore, sends a Prune message to Router B to stop the flow of unnecessary (S_i, G) traffic. Router B then responds by pruning the link to C as shown in Figure 5-13.

Figure 5-13 *DVMRP Pruning—Step 2*

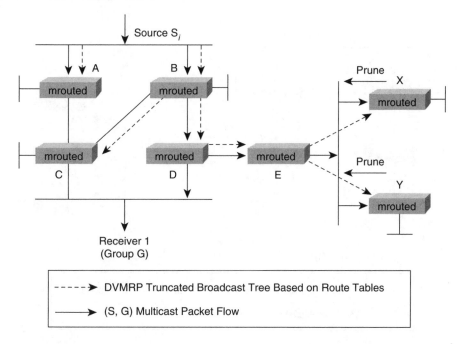

At this point, both Routers X and Y are also leaf nodes without any directly connected receivers and also send Prune messages up the truncated broadcast tree to Router E. Router E is aware (via DVMRP Probes) that it has only two DVMRP neighbors (Routers X and Y) on this interface. Because both neighbor routers on this interface have sent Router E a Prune message for (S_i, G) traffic, Router E knows it can now prune this interface. In Figure 5-14, the removal of the solid arrow from Router E toward Routers X and Y indicates this condition.

Figure 5-14   *DVMRP Pruning—Step 3*

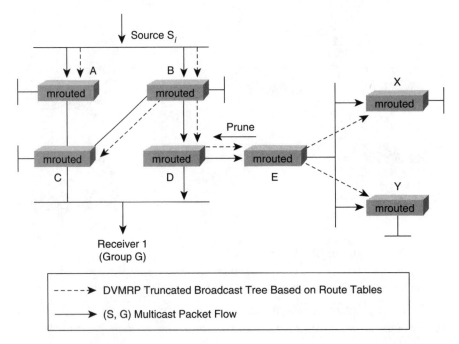

Finally, Router E has pruned all (S$_i$, G) traffic from its downstream interfaces, and it too sends a Prune message up the distribution tree to Router D (see Figure 5-14). Router D responds by pruning the link to Router E, which results in the final pruned state in the network, as seen in Figure 5-15.

Figure 5-15 *DVMRP Pruning—Final Pruned State*

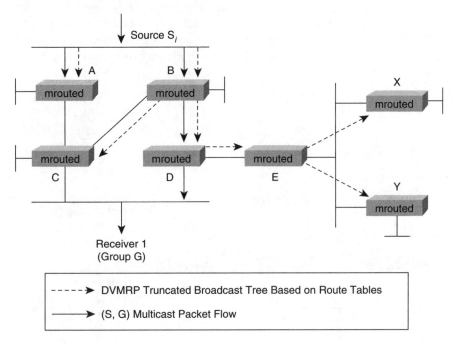

DVMRP Grafting

DVMRP supports a reliable Graft mechanism that grafts back previously pruned branches of a tree. Without this mechanism, the join latency for new hosts in the group might be severely affected because the pruned state in the upstream routers would have to time out before multicast traffic could begin to flow. Depending on the number of routers along the pruned branch and the timeout values in use, several minutes might elapse before the host begins to receive the multicast traffic. By using a Graft mechanism, DVMRP reduces this join latency to a few milliseconds.

Unlike the Prune mechanism, which is unreliable, the Graft mechanism is made reliable by the use of Graft-Ack messages. These messages are returned by the upstream router in response to received Graft messages. This step prevents the loss of a Graft message because of congestion, which would cause the Graft process to fail.

Continuing with the sample network from the earlier section on pruning, take a look at an example of the Graft mechanism in action. Figure 5-16 shows the network immediately after Receiver 2 on Router Y joins the multicast group. Because Router Y still has state for (S_i, G), which indicates that the router was pruned, it knows that it must send a Graft message (indicated by the small solid arrow in Figure 5-16) upstream to Router E to reestablish the flow of traffic.

Figure 5-16   *DVMRP Grafting—Initial State*

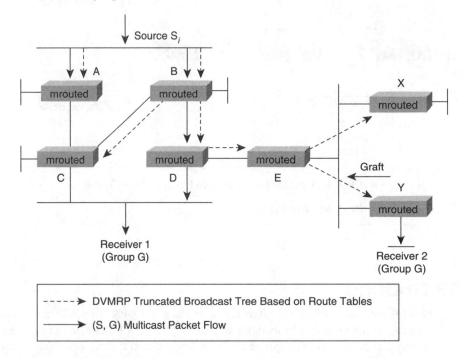

When Router E receives the Graft message, Router E changes the interface state from pruned to forwarding and acknowledges the Graft from Router Y by sending back a Graft-Ack message (refer to Figure 5-17).

Figure 5-17 *DVMRP Grafting—Step 1*

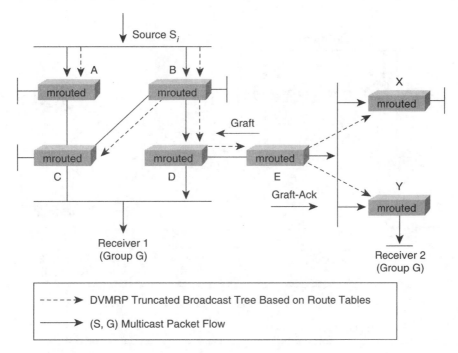

However, because Router E also has previously pruned the (S_i, G) source, it must also send a Graft message upstream to Router D to restart the flow of multicast traffic.

Finally, when Router D receives the Graft from Router E, it returns a Graft-Ack message and changes the interface state from pruned to forwarding. This completes the grafting of the previously pruned branch and starts the flow of multicast traffic down to Receiver 2 as shown in Figure 5-18.

Figure 5-18 *DVMRP Grafting—Step 2*

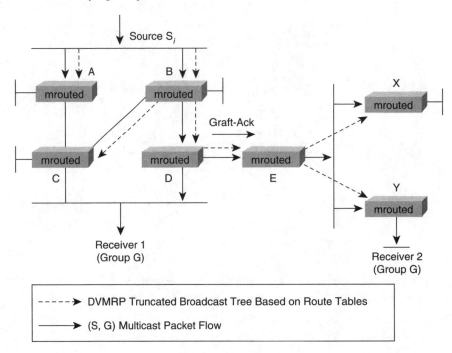

DVMRP Truncated Broadcast Tree Based on Route Tables

------►

(S, G) Multicast Packet Flow

————►

DVMRP Scalability

Although DVMRP has been deployed in the MBone and in other intra-domain multicast networks, some rather severe scalability issues prevent it from being used in large-scale multicast environments.

Because DVMRP uses hop-count as a metric with an infinity (unreachable) value of 32 hops, it clearly cannot be used in a network with a diameter larger than 31 hops without extensive tunneling. For this reason (as well as several others), DVMRP cannot be used as the multicast protocol that interconnects the entire Internet. (Anyone out there believe that the Internet has a diameter less than 32 hops? No, of course you don't!)

Historically, as new areas of the Internet have desired to connect to the MBone, tunneling through large non-multicast portions of the Internet has been necessary. Thus, an extensively tunneled MBone has grown somewhat haphazardly through the use of—despite heroic attempts to the contrary—a rather arbitrary collection of tunnels that interconnect only a small portion of the overall Internet.

In addition to the issue of the diameter of the Internet, DVMRP has all the limitations of a distance vector protocol, including slow convergence and a periodic route update mechanism that cannot handle the nearly 50,000 prefixes active in the Internet. (Can you imagine DVMRP trying to send out 50,000 route updates every 60 seconds?) Clearly, if IP multicast is to become ubiquitous throughout the Internet, a multicast routing protocol other than DVMRP is necessary for use in the backbone.

Summary

Today's multicast network engineers should consider using DVMRP in their networks in much the same way as RIP is used for unicast networks. Virtually all IP networks of any size have been designed around other, more efficient unicast routing protocols such as Open Shortest Path First (OSPF), Enhanced Interior Gateway Routing Protocol (EIGRP), Intermediate System-to-Intermediate System (IS-IS), and Border Gateway Protocol (BGP).

Without a very compelling reason, such as to provide backward compatibility, most network engineers wouldn't even think about deploying a unicast network based on RIP. Multicast networks should be no different. DVMRP should be employed in new network designs only when necessary to interface with existing DVMRP infrastructures—and then only until the network can be migrated to some other more efficient multicast protocol.

CHAPTER 6

PIM Dense Mode

Protocol Independent Multicast (PIM) gets its name from the fact that it is IP routing protocol independent. That is, regardless of which unicast routing protocol(s) is (are) used to populate the unicast routing table (including static routes), PIM uses this information to perform multicast forwarding; hence, it is *protocol independent*. Although we tend to refer to PIM as a *multicast routing protocol*, it actually uses the existing unicast routing table to perform the Reverse Path Forwarding (RPF) check function instead of maintaining a separate multicast route table. Because PIM doesn't have to maintain its own routing table, it doesn't send and/or receive multicast route updates like other protocols, such as Multicast Open Shortest Path First (MOSPF) or Distance Vector Multicast Routing Protocol (DVMRP). By not having to send multicast route updates, PIM's overhead is significantly reduced in comparison to other multicast protocols.

NOTE   Cisco Systems' PIM implementation also permits the RPF check function to use other sources of routing information, such as a DVMRP route table, static multicast routes called *mroutes,* and most recently, special multicast Border Gateway Protocol (BGP) routes. These capabilities are discussed in more detail in later chapters.

Some key characteristics of PIM dense mode (PIM-DM) are

- Protocol independent (uses unicast route table for RPF check)
- No separate multicast routing protocol (à la DVMRP)
- Flood-and-prune behavior (3-minute cycle)
- Classless (as long as classless unicast routing is in use)

Although PIM can be configured to operate in either sparse or dense mode, this chapter provides a brief overview of PIM-DM operation including information on neighbor discovery, source trees, multicast forwarding, pruning, asserts, grafting, and scalability. A more detailed discussion of PIM-DM configuration appears in Chapter 10, "Using PIM Dense Mode." (A brief overview of PIM sparse mode is given in Chapter 7, "PIM Sparse Mode," with a more detailed discussion on its configuration in Chapter 11, "Using PIM Sparse Mode.")

PIM Neighbor Discovery

Like DVMRP, PIM uses a Neighbor Discovery mechanism to establish PIM neighbor adjacencies. To establish these adjacencies, every Hello-Period (default: 30 seconds) a PIM multicast router multicasts a PIM Hello message to the *All-PIM-Routers* (224.0.0.13) multicast address on each of its multicast-enabled interfaces.

NOTE	In PIMv1, these PIM Hello messages were sometimes called *PIM Query messages*. Like all PIMv1 packets, these packets are multicast to the 224.0.0.2 *All Routers* multicast group address and ride inside of Internet Group Membership Protocol (IGMP) packets that have special type codes. On the other hand, PIMv2 has its own assigned protocol number (103) and, therefore, does not ride inside of IGMP packets.

PIM Hello Messages

PIM Hello messages contain a Holdtime value, which tells the receiver when to expire the neighbor adjacency associated with the sender if no further PIM Hello messages are received. The value that is sent in the Holdtime field is typically three times the sender's PIM Hello-Period, or 90 seconds if the default interval of 30 seconds is used.

Keeping track of adjacent PIM-DM routers is very important to building and maintaining PIM-DM source distribution trees as explained in the section "PIM-DM Source Distribution Trees" later in this chapter.

PIM-DM Designated Router

In addition to establishing PIM Neighbor adjacencies, PIM Hello messages are also used to elect the Designated Router (DR) for a multi-access network. PIM routers make note (via PIM Hello messages) of the router on the network with the highest IP address. This PIM router becomes the DR for the network.

NOTE	The DR is primarily used in sparse mode networks and has little meaning in dense mode networks. The only exception to this rule is when IGMPv1 is in use on an interface. In this case, the PIM-DR also functions as the IGMP Query Router since IGMPv1 does not have a Query Router election mechanism.

When more than one router exists on a LAN segment, the network engineer often has a need to force the DR election so that a specific router on the segment is elected as DR. Unfortunately, sometimes it is either inconvenient or impossible to renumber the IP address of the routers to accomplish this goal. A recently proposed enhancement to the PIM protocol will add a new *DR-Priority option* to PIMv2 Hello messages that will be used in the PIM DR election process. The DR-Priority option will allow the network engineer to specify the DR priority of each router on the LAN segment (default priority = 1) so that the router with the highest priority will be elected as the DR. If all routers on the LAN segment have the same priority, then the highest IP address is again used as the tiebreaker.

NOTE   Routers indicate that they support the new *DR-Priority* feature by the inclusion of the DR-Priority option in the PIMv2 Hello message that they transmit. Routers that do not support this option will not send Hello messages with this option (duh!). When PIMv2 routers receive a Hello message without the *DR-Priority* option (or when the message has priority of zero), the receiver knows that the sender of the Hello does not support *DR-Priority* and that DR election on the LAN segment should be based on IP address alone.

On Cisco routers, PIM neighbor adjacencies as well as the elected DRs can be displayed using the **show ip pim neighbor** IOS command. Example 6-1 shows some sample output of a **show ip pim neighbor** command on a Cisco router.

Example 6-1   *show ip pim neighbor Command Output*

```
wan-gw8>show ip pim neighbor
PIM Neighbor Table
Neighbor Address   Interface      Uptime     Expires   Mode
153.68.0.70        FastEthernet0  2w1d       00:01:24  Dense
153.68.0.91        FastEthernet0  2w6d       00:01:01  Dense (DR)
153.68.0.82        FastEthernet0  7w0d       00:01:14  Dense
153.68.0.86        FastEthernet0  7w0d       00:01:13  Dense
153.68.0.80        FastEthernet0  7w0d       00:01:02  Dense
153.68.28.70       Serial2.31     22:47:11   00:01:16  Dense
153.68.28.50       Serial2.33     22:47:22   00:01:08  Dense
153.68.27.74       Serial2.36     22:47:07   00:01:21  Dense
153.68.28.170      Serial0.70     1d04h      00:01:06  Dense
153.68.27.2        Serial1.51     1w4d       00:01:25  Dense
153.68.28.110      Serial3.56     1d04h      00:01:20  Dense
153.68.28.58       Serial3.102    12:53:25   00:01:03  Dense
```

In Example 6-1, router **wan-gw8** has several neighbors on interface **FastEthernet0**. Notice that neighbor 153.68.0.91 is the DR on this FastEthernet segment and has been up for 2 weeks and 6 days (as indicated by **2w6d** in the **Uptime** column). Furthermore, the adjacency with this neighbor expires in 1 minute and 1 second if router **wan-gw8** doesn't receive any further PIM Hellos from this neighbor (for example, if the neighbor router went down or connectivity to it was lost). In this case, a new DR would be elected for the FastEthernet segment.

PIM-DM Source Distribution Trees

Because PIM-DM is a dense-mode protocol, source distribution or shortest path trees (SPTs) are used as the sole means of distributing multicast traffic to receivers in the network. These source distribution trees are built on the fly, using the flood-and-prune mechanism as soon as a multicast source begins transmitting.

Unlike DVMRP, which uses its own multicast routing table and a special Poison Reverse mechanism to initially construct a minimal spanning distribution tree, PIM-DM uses its PIM neighbor information to construct a similar source distribution tree. In PIM-DM, neighbors are initially considered to be on the SPT, with the incoming interface being the interface in the direction of the source (based on the unicast routing table) and all other PIM-DM neighbors being downstream for this source. This initial form of SPT is referred to as a *Broadcast Tree* because a router sends the multicast traffic to all neighbors in a broadcastlike fashion. (In contrast, DVMRP routers use Truncated Broadcast Trees to initially flood multicast traffic to all downstream routers.)

NOTE   This is a slight modification of a technique called *Reverse Path Flooding* where incoming traffic that passes the RPF check is flooded out all other interfaces. The difference here is that the flooding occurs only out interfaces where at least one PIM-DM neighbor has been detected or that have a directly connected receiver(s).

Figure 6-1 shows an example of the initial flooding of multicast traffic in a PIM-DM network down a Broadcast Tree.

Figure 6-1   *PIM-DM Distribution Tree (Initial Flooding)*

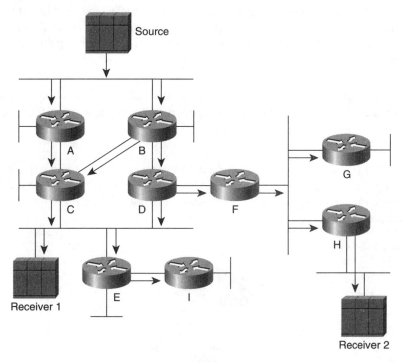

Here, you see a multicast source transmitting data that is picked up by Routers A and B and flooded to their downstream PIM-DM neighbors Routers C and D. Keep in mind that you are looking at the *initial* flow of traffic before any pruning takes place because of redundant paths (such as the two incoming paths to Router C) or duplicate forwarders (such as Routers C and D on their common Ethernet).

This tree is trimmed back to a minimal spanning tree of all PIM-DM routers after all pruning has occurred.

PIM-DM Multicast Forwarding

When a PIM-DM router initially receives a multicast packet, the packet undergoes an RPF check to ensure that it arrived on the correct interface in the direction of the source. In PIM, this RPF check is performed by using the information in the unicast routing table. The PIM-DM router searches the unicast routing table for the longest match of the source IP address in the packet and uses this information to determine the incoming interface for multicast traffic from this source. If multiple entries for the source network exist in the unicast routing table (which would occur if there are equal cost paths to a network), the router chooses only one interface. This implies the following important rule regarding not only PIM but also IP multicast in general.

RULE   A router can have only ONE incoming interface for any entry in its multicast routing table.

In PIM (either dense mode or sparse mode), when multiple entries exist in the unicast routing table, the entry with the *highest* next-hop IP address is used for the RPF check and hence the incoming interface. For example, consider Router R4 in the network shown in Figure 6-2.

Figure 6-2   *Sample Network*

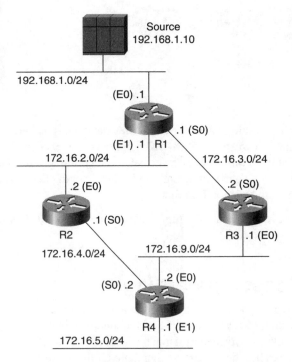

The routing information in Router R4 for the 192.168.1.0 source network is shown in the routing table in Example 6-2.

Example 6-2 *Routing Table for R4*

```
R4>sh ip route
. . .
Gateway of last resort is not set

      172.16.0.0/24 is subnetted, 10 subnets
D        172.16.8.0 [90/2195456] via 172.16.4.1, 20:02:31, Serial0
C        172.16.9.0 is directly connected, Ethernet0
D        172.16.10.0 [90/2195456] via 172.16.9.1, 20:02:31, Ethernet0
C        172.16.4.0 is directly connected, Serial0
C        172.16.5.0 is directly connected, Ethernet1
D        172.16.6.0 [90/2707456] via 172.16.4.1, 20:02:31, Serial0
D        172.16.7.0 [90/2195456] via 172.16.4.1, 20:02:31, Serial0
D        172.16.1.0 [90/2707456] via 172.16.9.1, 00:00:13, Ethernet0
D        172.16.2.0 [90/2221056] via 172.16.9.1, 00:00:13, Ethernet0
D        172.16.3.0 [90/2195456] via 172.16.9.1, 00:00:18, Ethernet0
D     192.168.1.0/24 [90/2733056] via 172.16.4.1, 00:00:14, Serial0
                     [90/2733056] via 172.16.9.1, 00:00:14, Ethernet0
D     192.168.100.0/24 [90/2835456] via 172.16.4.1, 00:00:14, Serial0
                        [90/2835456] via 172.16.9.1, 00:00:14, Ethernet0
```

Notice that there are two equal cost paths in the unicast routing table for source network 192.168.1.0. However, using the rule regarding only having one incoming interface for multicast, the path **via 172.16.9.1, 00:00:14, Ethernet0** is used as the RPF or incoming interface. You can confirm this outcome by using the **show ip rpf** command, which produces the output shown in Example 6-3.

Example 6-3 *RPF Information for Source 192.168.1.10*

```
R4>sh ip rpf 192.168.1.10
RPF information for ? (192.168.1.10)
  RPF interface: Ethernet0
  RPF neighbor: R3 (172.16.9.1)
  RPF route/mask: 192.168.1.0/255.255.255.0
  RPF type: unicast
```

Here, the RPF information for multicast source 192.168.1.10 is via interface Ethernet0 through the RPF neighbor R3 (172.16.9.1).

PIM-DM Pruning

PIM-DM sends Prune messages under the following conditions:

- Traffic arriving on non-RPF point-to-point interfaces
- Leaf router and no directly connected receivers
- Non-Leaf router on a point-to-point link that has received a Prune from its neighbor
- Non-Leaf router on a LAN segment (with no directly connected receivers) that has received a Prune from a neighbor on the LAN segment *and* another neighbor on the LAN segment does not override the Prune

Figure 6-3 continues the PIM-DM network example that was introduced in Figure 6-1. In Figure 6-3, Router C is sending a Prune message to Router B as a result of traffic arriving on the non-RPF interface for the source. In this example, assume that the metric to the source network is better via the link between Router A and C than it is between Router B and C.

Figure 6-3 *PIM-DM Pruning of Non-RPF Interface*

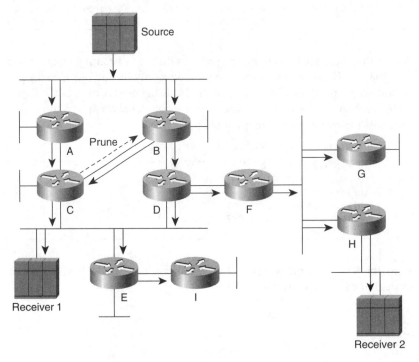

In the next step, shown in Figure 6-4, Router B has responded to the Prune by pruning its link to C. Additionally, Router I is a Leaf router without any directly connected receivers, so it now sends a Prune to Router E.

Figure 6-4 *PIM-DM Pruning—Step 1*

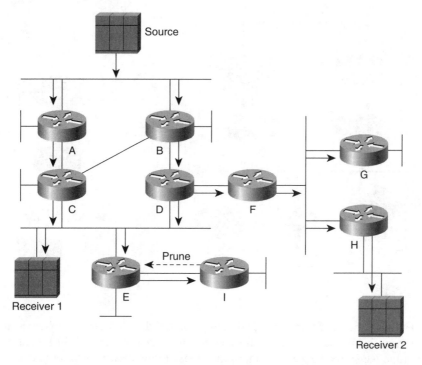

Router E now responds by pruning its link to Router I (see Figure 6-5), and because Router E has no directly connected receivers and all downstream links are pruned, it too sends a Prune message to Routers C and D.

Figure 6-5 *PIM-DM Pruning—Step 2*

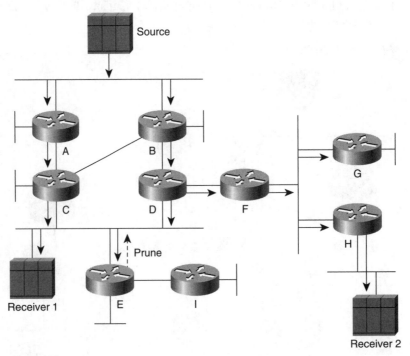

However, because Receiver 1 is directly connected to the same interface, Routers C and D ignore this Prune. (As long as the source continues sending, Router E continues to send Prune messages. However, it rate-limits these Prune messages to roughly every 3 minutes because the interface is a multi-access network. This action avoids an explosion of Prune messages that would consume bandwidth on this network segment.)

Prune Override

The Prune mechanism on multi-access networks operates differently in PIM than it does in DVMRP. Whereas DVMRP keeps track of its neighbors on an interface and records the fact that a neighbor has sent a Prune, PIM-DM does not. Instead, PIM expects to receive overriding Joins from downstream neighbors that wish to continue receiving traffic in response to Prunes by other neighbors on the same interface.

NOTE   Using a legislative analogy, you could say that a PIM router lets its downstream neighbors all vote on a proposed "Prune bill" that will prune a multicast source from the subnet.

Each router has the ability to veto the bill by using a Join message. However, PIM doesn't bother to count the votes; it just listens for a few seconds to see whether there is a veto to the proposed Prune bill on the subnet floor. Hearing none, PIM "passes" the bill and prunes the interface.

DVMRP, on the other hand, operates by *counting* all Prune votes on the subnet floor. There is no time limit on voting, and routers can change their vote (like most wishy-washy politicians) at any time by using a DVMRP Graft message. Only when the vote to prune becomes unanimous with no abstentions does DVMRP pass the bill and prune the source.

Finally, because DVMRP and PIM-DM are both flood-and-prune protocols, any Prune legislation that is passed has a limited life and must be brought back to the senate (subnet) floor to be voted on again every 2 to 3 minutes.

Routers G and H, shown in Figure 6-6, are good examples of this mechanism at work.

Figure 6-6   *PIM Prune Override*

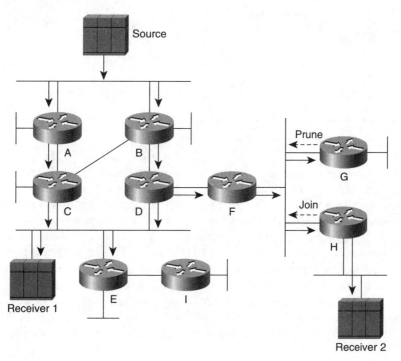

Router G is a leaf node without any directly connected receivers, so it sends a Prune message on the Ethernet to Router F. However, because Prune messages are multicast to the All-PIM-Router (224.0.0.13) group address, Router H overhears the Prune message sent to Router E. Because H *does* have a directly connected receiver, H sends a PIM Join message to override the Prune sent by Router G.

Prune Delay Accumulation

To make pruning work properly, a 3-second *Prune-delay* timer is started when a PIM router receives a Prune message on a multi-access network. If no overriding Join message is received to cancel this timer, the Prune takes place when the timer expires. You need to be mindful of this multi-access prune delay when designing PIM networks. In some situations, this delay can accumulate when unwanted multicast traffic is flowing across multiple multi-access networks.

Figure 6-7 shows an example of this type of delay and how it can affect Prune latency.

Figure 6-7   *PIM Prune-Delay Accumulation*

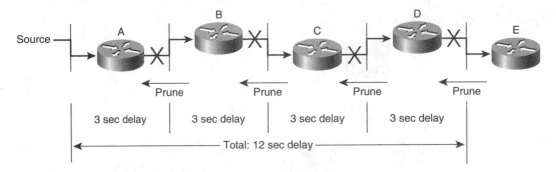

This example shows a string of routers connected to each other via multi-access (for instance, Ethernet) networks. Now a multicast source begins transmitting traffic that is flooded all the way down to Router E. However, Router E is a leaf node without any directly connected receivers, so it sends a Prune message back upstream to Router D. Router D must wait the normal 3-second multi-access network Prune-delay time to see whether an overriding Join comes from another PIM router on the network. At the end of this delay period, Router D prunes the interface and (because it has no directly connected receivers and all downstream interfaces are pruned) sends its own Prune message upstream to Router C. This process continues until Router A receives the Prune and has waited the 3-second Prune-delay period for a total Prune delay of 12 seconds. Because PIM Prunes have a lifetime of 3 minutes, this process occurs again when the Prune at Router A times out.

PIM-DM Asserts

Going back to the network example (shown in Figure 6-6), source traffic is now flowing only to points in the network where receivers are present. That leaves one final issue: the duplicate traffic being delivered by Routers C and D onto the Ethernet where Receiver 1 is connected.

To address this issue and shut off all but one flow of multicast to this network, PIM uses an Assert mechanism to elect a "forwarder" for a particular multicast source. The Assert mechanism is triggered by the following rule.

RULE   If a router receives a multicast packet via an interface in the outgoing interface list associated with a multicast source, send a PIM Assert message out the interface to resolve which router will continue forwarding this traffic.

When the Assert mechanism is triggered on an interface, a PIM router sends a PIM Assert message containing its metric to the source. All PIM routers on the network examine the metric in the PIM Assert message to determine which router has the best metric back to the multicast source. The router with the best metric continues to forward traffic from this source onto the network while all other PIM routers prune their interface. If there is a tie in the metrics, the router addresses are used as the tiebreaker and the highest IP address wins.

Figure 6-8 shows the PIM Assert mechanism in action.

Figure 6-8   *PIM Assert Mechanism*

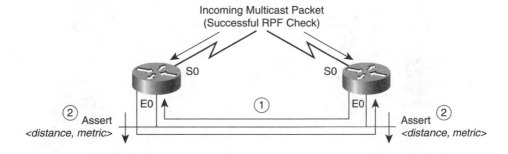

Here's a description of the two-step PIM Assert mechanism in Figure 6-8:

Step 1   Both routers begin receiving traffic from the same source through their serial interface and forward it onto the common Ethernet network. As a result, each router receives a packet from the multicast source via an interface (in this case, Ethernet0) that is on its outgoing interface list. This action triggers both routers to send PIM Assert messages to resolve who should be the forwarder.

Step 2   The routers send and receive PIM Assert messages that contain the administrative distance (used as the high-order portion of the compared value) and the routing protocol metric for the source (used as the low-order portion of the compared value). The values in the PIM Assert messages are compared and the lowest value (that is, has the best metric to the source when both administrative distance and route metric are considered) wins the Assert battle. The loser(s) stop sending the source traffic onto the network by pruning their interface(s) for this source traffic.

Returning to the sample network (see Figure 6-9), Routers C and D are sending PIM Assert messages in response to receiving a multicast packet from the source via their outgoing interface (the Ethernet network).

Figure 6-9   *PIM Assert Example*

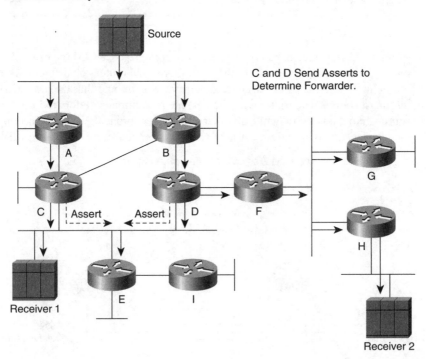

Assuming that Routers C and D have the same metrics and that C has a higher IP address, C wins the Assert battle and continues to forward traffic onto the Ethernet while Router D prunes its interface, as shown in Figure 6-10.

Figure 6-10   *PIM Network—After Assert*

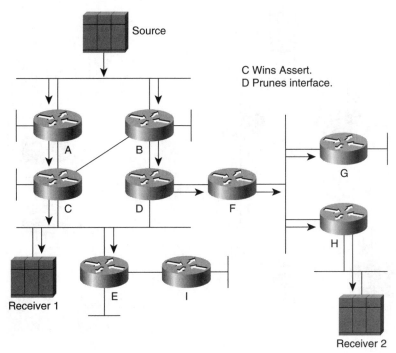

PIM-DM Grafting

PIM-DM also has a capability to graft back previously pruned branches of a distribution tree so that restarting the flow of multicast traffic can be accomplished with minimum delay. Figure 6-11 shows the network example with a third receiver now joined to the multicast group off Router I.

Figure 6-11 *PIM-DM Grafting—Step 1*

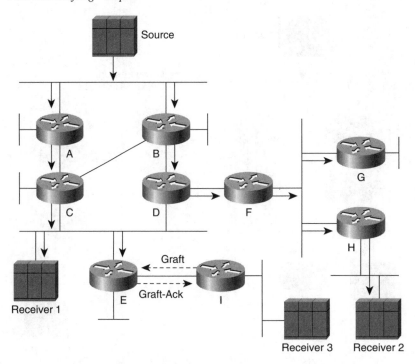

When Router I receives the IGMP Membership Report from Receiver 3, Router I knows that it must send a Graft message to Router E to restart the flow of multicast traffic. (It knows this because it still has multicast state, albeit pruned, for the source.) When Router E receives the Graft message from Router I, it responds by sending back a Graft-Ack message.

Because Router E had previously sent a Prune for this source (although it was ignored because Receiver 1 is directly connected to this network), it too sends a Graft message to Router C, which immediately responds by sending a Graft-Ack message, as shown in Figure 6-12. At this point, multicast traffic begins to flow through Router E and Router I to Receiver 3.

Figure 6-12 *PIM-DM Grafting—Step 2*

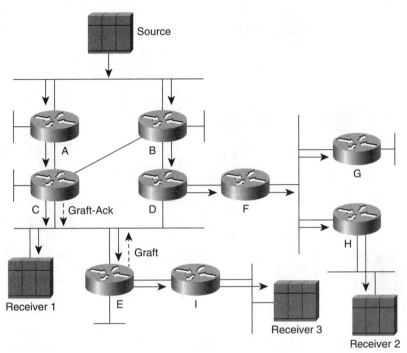

Future PIM-DM Enhancement—State-Refresh

As this book was going to press, the Internet Engineering Task Force (IETF) was completing work on an extension to the PIM-DM protocol specification that would all but eliminate the periodic flood-and-prune behavior of PIM-DM. This extension is called *State-Refresh* and basically does what the name implies: It refreshes downstream state so that the pruned branches of the Broadcast Tree do not time out.

State-Refresh is accomplished by first-hop routers periodically sending an (S, G) State-Refresh message down the original Broadcast Tree as long as Source *S* is still sending traffic to Group *G*.

Figure 6-13 shows an example of (S, G) State-Refresh messages being sent hop by hop in a network whose (S, G) Broadcast Tree has been pruned back by the PIM-DM Prune and Assert mechanisms described in the previous sections.

Figure 6-13 *State Refresh*

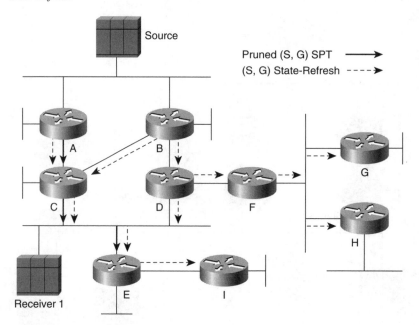

In this example, only Receiver 1 is an active member of Group *G* and is receiving traffic from Source *S* along the path shown by the solid arrows. To refresh the state of this tree and prevent the pruned interfaces from timing out, the first-hop routers, Routers A and B, are both periodically sending (S, G) State-Refresh messages, as shown by the dashed arrows in the drawing. When these messages reach the routers along the original (S, G) Broadcast Tree, they reset the prune timers in their (S, G) outgoing interface list. This prevents the pruned interfaces (indicated in the drawing by the solid arrows) from timing out and causing (S, G) traffic to again be flooded everywhere in the network.

The new State-Refresh mechanism provides an additional benefit that may not be immediately obvious. It also refreshes interfaces that were pruned as a result of the Assert process. This is accomplished by including the same basic route metric information in the State-Refresh message that is passed in Assert messages. This further reduces PIM-DM overhead because it eliminates the need to periodically rerun the Assert mechanism to prune off redundant paths.

PIM-DM Scalability

If the unicast network is well designed and makes good use of hierarchical IP Address assignment and route aggregation, PIM-DM has the potential to scale much better than DVMRP scales. The reason is that PIM uses the underlying unicast routing table in the routers to perform its RPF checks and, unlike DVMRP, does not send separate multicast routing updates. However, PIM-DM has the same basic flood-and-prune behavior as DVMRP and, therefore, can suffer from the periodic flooding of unwanted traffic through the dense mode domain. The proposed *State-Refresh* extension to the PIM specification (although still not implemented when this book went to press) will prevent prune state from timing out and avoid the periodic flooding of unwanted traffic.

Summary

PIM-DM is best used in high-speed networks where the bandwidth consumed by periodic flooding is not an issue. Using PIM-DM for general-purpose multicast on networks that employ medium- to low-speed WAN links is generally not desirable. Even when the State-Refresh extension becomes a reality, PIM-DM will still create (S, G) state in every router in the network. In networks that have large numbers of active sources and groups, the amount of multicast routing state that must be maintained in the routers in the network can become an issue. Furthermore, networks that have large numbers of sources, such as financial networks, or in which RTP-based multimedia applications are used, tend to suffer from bursty source problems.

NOTE   Most of the sources in these networks tend to send a single multicast packet every few minutes. The State-Refresh enhancement will not help in these scenarios because the (S, G) state in the first-hop routers will time out if the time interval between packets sent by the source is greater than 3 minutes. Because of these factors, most PIM multicast network engineers are opting for PIM sparse mode, which requires less state in the routers and does not suffer from a flood-and-prune behavior.

CHAPTER 7

PIM Sparse Mode

Protocol Independent Multicast sparse mode (PIM-SM), like PIM dense mode (PIM-DM), uses the unicast routing table to perform the Reverse Path Forwarding (RPF) check function instead of maintaining a separate multicast route table. Therefore, regardless of which unicast routing protocol(s) is (are) used to populate the unicast routing table (including static routes), PIM-SM uses this information to perform multicast forwarding; hence, it too is protocol independent.

Some key characteristics of PIM-SM are

- Protocol independent (uses unicast route table for RPF check)
- No separate multicast routing protocol (à la Distance Vector Multicast Routing Protocol [DVMRP])
- Explicit Join behavior
- Classless (as long as classless unicast routing is in use)

This chapter provides an overview of the basic mechanisms used by PIM-SM, which include

- Explicit Join model
- Shared trees
- Shortest path trees (SPT)
- Source registration
- Designated Router (DR)
- SPT switchover
- State-Refresh
- Rendezvous point (RP) discovery

In addition, some of the mechanisms that are used in PIM-DM (covered in Chapter 6, "PIM Dense Mode") are also used by PIM-SM. These include

- PIM Neighbor Discovery
- PIM Asserts

This chapter does not repeat these topics. However, the reader is encouraged to review these topics before proceeding with this chapter. Finally, it's important to keep in mind that this chapter is strictly an overview of PIM-SM and covers only the basics. The details of the mechanisms, state rules, and so forth are covered in Chapter 11, "Using PIM Sparse Mode."

Explicit Join Model

Just as its name implies, PIM-SM conforms to the sparse mode model where multicast traffic is only sent to locations of the network that specifically request it. In PIM-SM, this is accomplished via PIM Joins, which are sent hop by hop toward the root node of tree. (The root node of a tree in PIM-SM is the RP in the case of a shared tree or the first-hop router that is directly connected to the multicast source in the case of a SPT.) As this Join travels up the tree, routers along the path set up multicast forwarding state so that the requested multicast traffic will be forwarded back down the tree.

Likewise, when multicast traffic is no longer needed, a router sends a PIM Prune up the tree toward the root node to prune off the unnecessary traffic. As this PIM Prune travels hop by hop up the tree, each router updates its forwarding state appropriately. This update often results in the deletion of the forwarding state associated with a multicast group or source.

The key point here is that in the Explicit Join model, forwarding state in the routers is set up as a result of these Joins. This is a substantial departure from flood-and-prune protocols such as PIM-DM where router forwarding state is set up by the arrival of multicast data.

PIM-SM Shared Trees

PIM-SM operation centers around a single, unidirectional shared tree whose root node is called the rendezvous point (RP). These shared trees are sometimes called RP trees because they are rooted at the RP. (Shared trees or RP trees are frequently known as RPTs so as to avoid confusion with source trees, which are also known as shortest path trees; hence, the acronym SPTs.)

Last-hop routers (routers that have a directly connected receiver for the multicast group) that need to receive the traffic from a specific multicast group, join this shared tree. When the last-hop router no longer needs the traffic of a specific multicast group (that is, when there are no longer any directly connected receivers for the multicast group), the router prunes itself from the shared tree.

Because PIM-SM uses a unidirectional shared tree where traffic can only flow down the tree, sources must register with the RP to get their multicast traffic to flow down the shared tree (via the RP). This registration process actually triggers an SPT Join by the RP toward the Source when there are active receivers for the group in the network. (SPT Joins are described in more detail in the section, "PIM-SM Shortest Path Trees," and registers are described in more detail in the "Source Registration" section.)

Shared Tree Joins

Figure 7-1 shows the first step of a Shared Tree Join in a sample PIM-SM. In this step, a single host (Receiver 1) has just joined multicast Group G via an Internet Group Membership Protocol (IGMP) Membership Report.

Figure 7-1   *PIM Shared Tree Joins—Step 1*

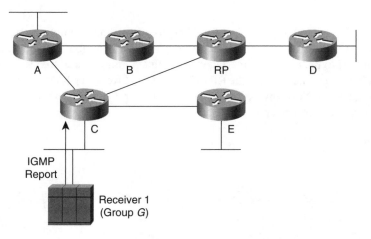

Because Receiver 1 is the first host to join the multicast group in the example, Router C had to create a (*, G) state entry in its multicast routing table for this multicast group. Router C then places the Ethernet interface in the outgoing interface list of the (*, G) entry as shown by the solid arrow in Figure 7-2. Because Router C had to create a new (*, G) state entry, it must also send a PIM (*, G) Join (indicated by the dashed arrow in Figure 7-2) toward the RP to join the shared tree. (Router C uses its unicast routing table to determine the interface toward the RP.)

Figure 7-2 *PIM Shared Tree Join—Step 2*

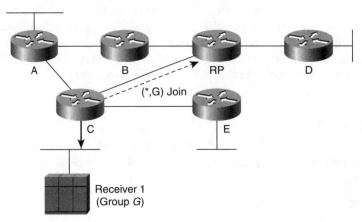

The RP receives the (*, G) Join, and because it too had no previous state for multicast Group G, creates a (*, G) state entry in its multicast routing table and adds the link to Router C to the outgoing interface list. At this point, a shared tree for multicast Group G has been constructed from the RP to Router C and Receiver 1, as shown by the solid arrows in Figure 7-3. Now, any traffic for multicast Group G that reaches the RP can flow down the shared tree to Receiver 1.

Figure 7-3 *Shared Tree Joins—Step 3*

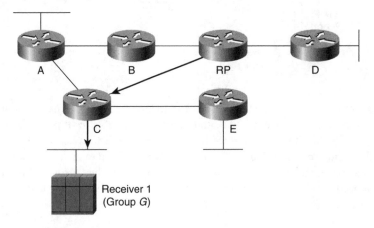

Let's continue the example and assume that another host (Receiver 2) joins the multicast group as shown in Figure 7-4. Again, the host has signaled its desire to join multicast Group G by using an IGMP Membership Report that was received by Router E.

Figure 7-4   *Shared Tree Joins—Step 4*

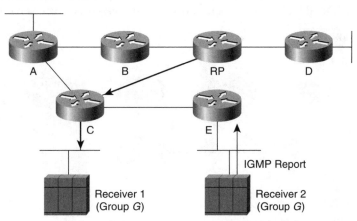

Because Router E didn't have any state for multicast Group G, it creates a (*, G) state entry in its multicast routing table and adds the Ethernet interface to its outgoing interface list (shown by the solid arrow in Figure 7-5). Because Router E had to create a new (*, G) entry, it sends a (*, G) Join (indicated by the dashed arrow in Figure 7-5) toward the RP to join the shared tree for Group G.

Figure 7-5   *Shared Tree Joins—Step 5*

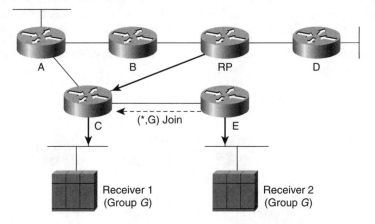

When Router C receives the (*, G) Join from Router E, it finds that it already has (*, G) state for Group G (that is, it's already on the shared tree for this group). As a result, Router C simply adds the link to Router E to the outgoing interface list in its (*, G) entry.

Figure 7-6 shows the resulting shared tree (indicated by the solid arrows) that includes Routers C and E along with their directly connected hosts (Receiver 1 and Receiver 2).

Figure 7-6 *Shared Tree Joins—Step 6*

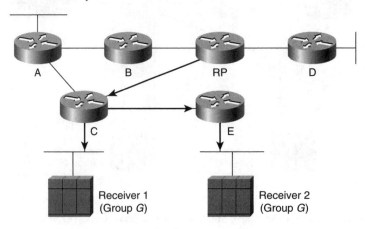

Shared Tree Prunes

Because PIM-SM uses the Explicit Join model to build distribution trees as needed, it also uses Prunes to tear down the trees when they are no longer needed. (We could just stop sending periodic Joins to refresh the tree and allow the tree branches to time out. However, that isn't a very efficient usage of network resources.)

As an example, assume that Receiver 2 leaves multicast Group G by sending an IGMP Leave message (shown in Figure 7-7).

Figure 7-7 *Shared Tree Prunes—Step 1*

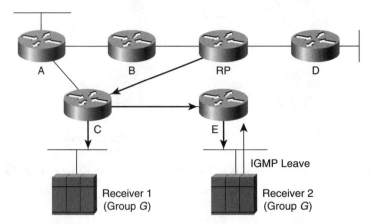

Because Receiver 2 was the only host joined to the group on Router E's Ethernet interface, this interface is removed from the outgoing interface list in its (*, G) entry. (This is represented by the removal of the arrow on Router E's Ethernet in Figure 7-8.) When the interface is removed, the outgoing interface list for this (*, G) entry is null (empty), which indicates that Router E no longer needs the traffic for this group. Router E responds to the fact that its outgoing interface list is now null by sending a (*, G) Prune (shown in Figure 7-8) toward the RP to prune itself off the shared tree.

Figure 7-8   *Shared Tree Prunes—Step 2*

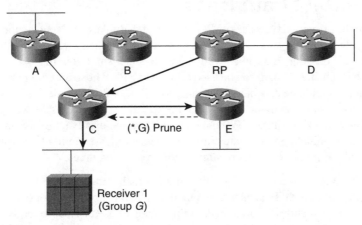

When Router C receives this Prune, it removes the link to Router E from the outgoing interface list of the (*, G) entry (as indicated by the removal of the arrow between Router C and Router E in Figure 7-9). However, because Router C still has a directly connected host for the group (Receiver 1), the outgoing interface list for the (*, G) entry is not null (empty). Therefore, Router C must remain on the shared tree, and a Prune is not sent up the shared tree toward the RP.

Figure 7-9   *Shared Tree Prunes—Step 3*

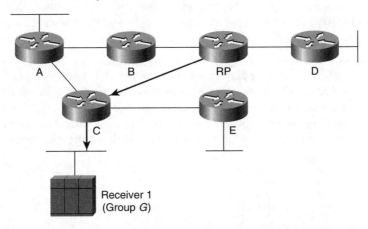

NOTE	The prune examples in this section did not cover the situation in which a (*, G) prune is being sent on a multi-access network (such as an Ethernet segment) with several other PIM-SM routers still joined to the same shared tree. However, the same Prune Override mechanism that was described in Chapter 6 on PIM-DM is also used in PIM-SM by the other routers on the network to prevent the shared tree from being pruned prematurely.

PIM-SM Shortest Path Trees

One of the primary advantages of PIM-SM is that, unlike other sparse mode protocols (such as core-based trees), it doesn't limit us to receiving multicast traffic only via the shared tree. Just as it is possible to use the Explicit Join mechanism to join the shared tree, whose root is the RP, this mechanism can be used to join the SPT whose root is a particular source. The advantage should be obvious. By joining the SPT, multicast traffic is routed directly to the receivers without having to go through the RP, thereby reducing network latency and possible congestion at the RP. On the other hand, the disadvantage is that routers must create and maintain (S, G) state entries in their multicast routing tables along the (S, G) SPT. This action, of course, consumes more router resources.

Still, the overall amount of (S, G) information maintained by the routers in a PIM-SM network that uses SPTs is generally much less than is necessary for dense mode protocols. The reason is that the Flood-and-Prune mechanism used by dense mode protocols results in all routers in the network maintaining (S, G) state entries in their multicast routing tables for all active sources. This is true even if there are no active receivers for the groups to which the sources are transmitting. By joining SPTs in PIM-SM, we gain the advantage of an optimal distribution tree without suffering from the overhead and inefficiencies associated with other dense mode protocols such as PIM-DM, DVMRP, and Multicast Open Shortest Path First (MOSPF). (By now, you are probably beginning to understand why PIM-SM is generally recommended over other dense mode protocols.)

This leads to an obvious question: If using SPTs in PIM-SM is so desirable, why join the shared tree in the first place? The problem is that without the shared tree to deliver the first few multicast packets from a source, routers have no way of knowing that a source is active.

NOTE	Several methods (including the use of dynamic Domain Name System [DNS] entries) have been proposed to tell routers which sources are currently active for which groups. Using this information, a router could immediately and directly join the SPT of all active sources in the group. This would eliminate the need for a shared tree and its associated Core or RP. Unfortunately, none of the methods proposed to date have met with much acceptance in the Internet community.

The sections that follow present the basic concepts of building SPTs using (S, G) Joins and Prunes. Keep in mind that the goal here is to understand the basic concepts of joining the SPT. The details as to why and when PIM-SM routers actually join the SPT are discussed later.

Shortest Path Tree Joins

As you recall from the section "Shared Tree Joins," routers send a (*, G) Join toward the RP to join the shared tree and receive multicast traffic for Group G. However, by sending an (S, G) Join toward Source S, a router can just as easily join the SPT for Source S and receive multicast traffic being sent by S to Group G.

Figure 7-10 shows an example of an (S, G) Join being sent toward an active source to join the SPT. (The solid arrows in the drawing indicate the path of the SPT down which traffic from Source S_1 flows.) In this example, Receiver 1 has already joined Group G (indicated by the solid arrow from Router E).

Figure 7-10 *SPT Join—Step 1*

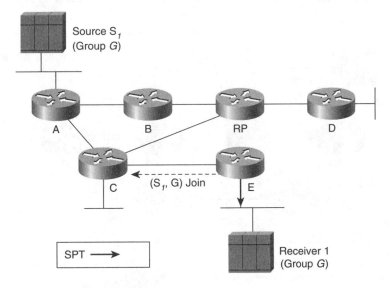

For the sake of this example, assume that Router E somehow magically knows that Source S_1 is active for Group G.

NOTE   In reality, Router E would have learned that Source S_1 is active because it would have received a packet from the source via the shared tree. However, to make the point that PIM SPTs are independent from shared trees (and to simplify this example), we are going to ignore this minor detail and concentrate on the fact that a router can explicitly join a SPT just as a router can join the shared tree.

Because Router E wants to join the SPT for Source S_1, it sends an (S_1, G) Join toward the source. Router E determines the correct interface to send this Join out by calculating the RPF interface toward Source S_1. (The RPF interface calculation uses the unicast routing table, which in turn indicates that Router C is the next-hop router to Source S_1.)

When Router C receives the (S_1, G) Join, it creates an (S_1, G) entry in its multicast forwarding table and adds the interface on which the Join was received to the entry's outgoing interface list (indicated by the solid arrow from Router C to Router E in Figure 7-11). Because Router C had to create state for (S_1, G), it also sends an (S_1, G) Join (as shown by the dashed arrow in Figure 7-11) toward the source.

Figure 7-11   *SPT Join—Step 2*

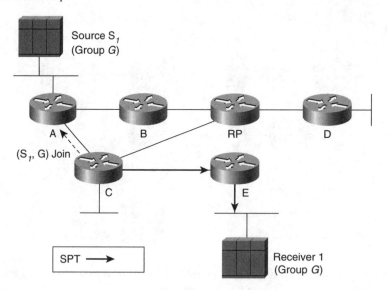

Finally, when Router A receives the (S_1, G) Join, it adds the link to Router C to the outgoing interface list of its existing (S_1, G) entry as shown by the solid arrow in Figure 7-12. (Router A is referred to as the first hop router for Source S_1 and would have already created an (S_1, G) entry as soon as it received the first packet from the source.)

Figure 7-12   *SPT Join—Step 3*

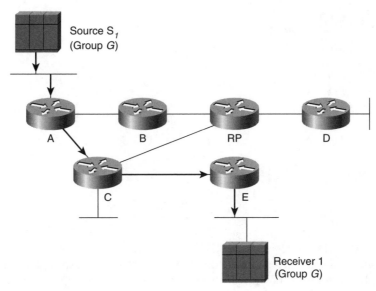

Shortest Path Tree Prunes

SPTs can be pruned by using (S_1, G) Prunes in the same manner that shared trees were pruned by using $(*, G)$ Prunes.

NOTE   Again, the prune examples in this section do not cover the situation where an (S, G) prune is being sent on a multi-access network (such as an Ethernet segment) with several other PIM-SM routers still joined to the same SPT. However, the same Prune Override mechanism that was described in Chapter 6 on PIM-DM is also used in PIM-SM by the other routers on the network to prevent the SPT from being pruned prematurely.

Continuing with the SPT example, assume that Router E no longer has a directly connected receiver for Group G and therefore has no further need for (S_1, G) traffic. Therefore, Router E sends an (S_1, G) Prune toward Source S_1 (as shown by the dashed arrow in Figure 7-13).

Figure 7-13   *SPT Prunes—Step 1*

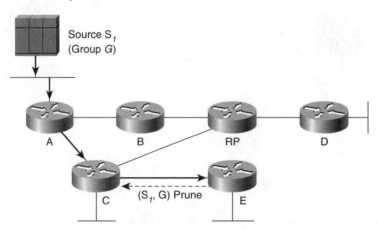

When Router C receives the (S_1, G) Prune from Router E, it removes the interface on which the message was received from the outgoing interface list of its (S_1, G) entry (indicated by the absence of the solid arrow between Routers C and E in Figure 7-14). This results in Router C's (S_1, G) entry having an empty outgoing interface list. Because the outgoing interface list is now empty, Router C has to send an (S_1, G) Prune toward the source S_1 (as shown by the dashed arrow in Figure 7-14).

Figure 7-14   *SPT Prunes—Step 2*

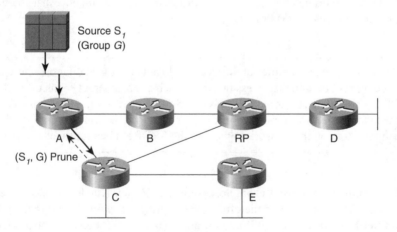

When Router A receives the (S_1, G) Prune from Router C, it removes the interface on which it received the Prune from the outgoing interface list of its (S_1, G) entry (indicated by the absence of the solid arrow between Routers A and C in Figure 7-15). However, because Router A is the first-hop router for Source S_1 (in other words, it is directly connected to the source), no further action is taken. (Router A simply continues to drop any packets from Source S_1 because the outgoing interface list in Router A's (S_1, G) entry is empty.)

Figure 7-15 *SPT Prunes—Step 3*

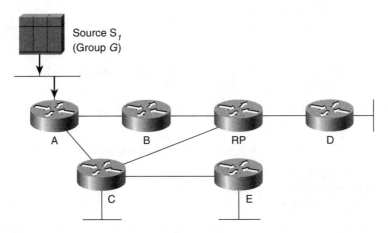

NOTE   To avoid being flamed by readers who are experienced PIM-SM users, I should point out that the previous SPT examples have been radically simplified to make the concepts of SPTs in PIM-SM easier to understand. Again, the key point here is that the PIM-SM explicit Join/Prune mechanism can be used to Join/Prune SPTs as well as shared trees. This capability becomes important in later sections on source registering and SPT switchover.

PIM Join/Prune Messages

Although we have been referring to PIM Prunes and Joins as if they were two individual message types, the reality is that there is only a single PIM Join/Prune message type. (See Appendix A, "PIM Packet Formats," for a detailed description of the format of PIM Join/Prune messages.) Each PIM Join/Prune message contains both a Join list and a Prune list, either one of which may be empty, depending on the information being conveyed up the distribution tree. By including multiple entries in the Join and/or Prune lists, a router may Join/Prune multiple sources and/or groups with a single PIM Join/Prune message. This greatly improves the efficiency of the periodic refresh mechanism because typically only a single message is necessary to refresh an upstream router's state.

The entries in the Join and Prune lists of PIM Join/Prune messages share a common format, containing (among other things) the following information:

- **Multicast source address**—IP address of the multicast source to Join/Prune. (If the Wildcard flag is set, this is the address of the RP.)
- **Multicast group address**—Class D multicast group address to Join/Prune.
- **WC bit (Wildcard flag)**—This entry is a shared tree (*, G) Join/Prune message.
- **RP bit (RP Tree flag)**—This Join/Prune information is applicable to and should be forwarded up the shared tree.

By manipulating the preceding information in each Join/Prune list entry, various requests may be signaled to an upstream router.

For example, a PIM Join/Prune message with an entry in the Join list of

Source address = 192.16.10.1
Group address = 224.1.1.1
Flags = WC, RP

indicates that this item is a (*, G) (denoted by the WC and RP flags being set) Join for Group 224.1.1.1 whose RP is 192.16.10.1.

A PIM Join/Prune message with an entry in the Prune list of

Source address = 191.1.2.1
Group address = 239.255.1.1
Flags = none

indicates that this is an (S, G) (denoted by the WC and RP flags being clear) Prune for source 191.1.2.1, Group 239.255.1.1.

NOTE   The reason that this information on the Join/Prune message contents is presented here is that it (particularly the part about the RP flag) will be important when we discuss pruning specific source traffic flows from the shared tree in the "Shortest Path Tree Switchover" section.

PIM-SM State-Refresh

To prevent a stale PIM-SM forwarding state from getting stuck in the routers, it is given a finite lifetime (3 minutes), after which it is deleted. (For example, if an upstream router loses a Prune because of congestion, the associated forwarding state could remain in the router for a long time.) The lifetime is established by associating a 3-minute expiration timer with each (*, G) and (S, G) state entry in the multicast routing table. When these timers expire, the state entry is deleted. As a result, downstream routers must periodically refresh this forwarding state to prevent it from timing out and being deleted. To do so, routers send PIM Join/Prune messages to the appropriate upstream neighbor once a minute. When the upstream neighbor receives the PIM Join/Prune message, it refreshes its existing multicast forwarding state and resets the 3-minute expiration timers.

Routers refresh shared trees by periodically (once a minute) sending (*, G) Joins to the upstream neighbor in the direction of the RP. Additionally, routers refresh SPTs by periodically (once a minute) sending (S, G) Joins to the upstream neighbor in the direction of the source.

These periodic (*, G) and (S, G) Joins are sent by routers as long as they have a nonempty outgoing interface list in their associated (*, G) and (S, G) entries (or a directly connected host for multicast Group G). If these periodic Joins were not sent, multicast state for G would eventually time out (after 3 minutes) and the distribution tree associated with the (*, G) and/or (S, G) multicast routing entry would be torn down.

NOTE   I find that this periodic refresh mechanism is one of the most frequently overlooked aspects of PIM-SM when students are initially learning PIM-SM fundamentals. This results in confusion regarding the maintenance of certain timers in the multicast forwarding table as well as confusion when this periodic Join message traffic is observed during debugging sessions.

Source Registration

In the section "PIM-SM Shared Trees," you learned how routers use (*, G) Joins to join the shared tree for multicast Group G. However, because PIM-SM uses a unidirectional shared tree, multicast traffic can only flow down this tree. Therefore, multicast sources must somehow get their traffic to the RP so that the traffic can flow down the shared tree. PIM-SM accomplishes this by having the RP join the SPT back to the source so it can receive the source's traffic. First, however, the RP must somehow be notified that the source exists. PIM-SM makes use of PIM Register and Register-Stop messages to implement a source registration process to accomplish this task.

NOTE   A common misconception is that a source must register before any receivers can join the shared tree. However, receivers can join the shared tree, even though there are currently no active sources. But when a source does become active, the RP then joins the SPT to the source and begins forwarding this traffic down the shared tree. By the same token, sources can register first even if there are no active receivers in the network. Later, when a receiver does join the group, the RP Joins the SPT toward all sources in the group and begins forwarding the group traffic down the shared tree. These scenarios are covered in more detail in Chapter 11.

The following sections discuss the mechanics of the source registration process that makes use of *PIM Register* and *PIM Register-Stop* messages. This process notifies an RP of an active source in the network and delivers the initial multicast packets to the RP to be forwarded down the shared tree. At the end of this section, a detailed, step-by-step example shows this process in action.

PIM Register Messages

PIM Register messages are sent by first-hop DRs (that is, a DR that is directly connected to a multicast source) to the RP. The purpose of the PIM Register message is twofold:

1 Notify the RP that Source S_1 is actively sending to Group G.

2 Deliver the initial multicast packet(s) sent by Source S_1 (each encapsulated inside of a single PIM Register message) to the RP for delivery down the shared tree.

Therefore, when a multicast source begins to transmit, the DR (to which the source is directly connected) receives the multicast packets sent by the source and creates an (S, G) state entry in its multicast routing table. In addition, because the source is directly connected (to the DR), the DR encapsulates each multicast packet in a separate PIM Register message and unicasts it to the RP. (How the DR learns the IP address of the RP is discussed in the "RP Discovery" section.)

NOTE   Unlike the other PIM messages that are multicast on a local segment and travel hop by hop through the network, PIM Register messages and their close cousins, PIM Register-Stop messages (discussed in the next subsection) are unicast between the first-hop router and the RP.

When an RP receives a PIM Register message, it first de-encapsulates the message so it can examine the multicast packet inside. If the packet is for an active multicast group (that is, shared tree Joins for the group have been received), the RP forwards the packet down the shared tree. The RP then joins the SPT for Source S_1 so that it can receive (S_1, G) traffic natively instead of it being sent encapsulated inside of PIM Register messages. If, on the other hand, there is no active shared tree for the group, the RP simply discards the multicast packets and does not send a Join toward the source.

Does Anyone Know a Multicast Source?

Every time I describe the PIM Register process to students learning PIM-SM, I can't help but use an analogy of an elementary school class. Remember back when you were in elementary school, and a few kids in class always seemed to have the answer to the teacher's question and were dying to be called on? Their response to these questions would be to throw their hand high into the air while blurting out, "Oh, oh, me, me, ME!" (This was generally accompanied by painful facial expressions that were a result of attempts to raise their hand higher than anyone else in class, sometimes nearly to the point of dislocating a shoulder.) Now imagine that the teacher has just asked, "Who has multicast traffic for me?" I like to think of PIM Register messages as the "Oh, oh, me, me, ME!" message sent by first-hop DRs that are trying to notify the teacher (the RP) that they have multicast traffic. Of course, in PIM-SM first-hop DRs (just like many elementary students) don't wait to be called on before blurting out their "Oh, oh, me, me, ME!" Register messages.

PIM Register-Stop Messages

The RP unicasts PIM Register-Stop messages to the first-hop DR, instructing it to stop sending (S_1, G) Register messages under any of the following conditions:

- When the RP begins receiving multicast traffic from Source S_1 via the (S_1, G) SPT between the source and the RP.

- If the RP has no need for the traffic because there is no active shared tree for the group.

When a first-hop DR receives a Register-Stop message, the router knows that the RP has received the Register message and one of the two conditions above has been met. In either case, the first-hop DR terminates the Register process and stops encapsulating (S_1, G) packets in PIM Register messages.

Source Registration Example

Refer back to the point in the network example (see Figure 7-6) where two receivers have joined multicast Group G (as a result of receiving IGMP Membership Reports from directly connected hosts). At this point, Routers C and E have successfully joined the shared tree back to the RP. Let's now assume that multicast Source S_1 begins sending multicast traffic to Group G, as shown in Figure 7-16.

Figure 7-16 *Source Registration—Step 1*

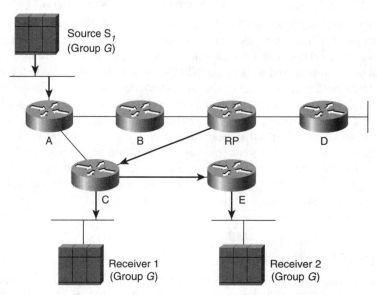

Because Router A is the first-hop DR, it responds to the incoming multicast traffic from Source S_1 by encapsulating the multicast packets in a PIM Register message and unicasting them (as shown by the dashed arrow in Figure 7-17) to the RP. (Note that Register messages are not sent hop by hop like other PIM messages, but are sent directly to the RP as a normal unicast packet.)

Figure 7-17 *Source Registration—Step 2*

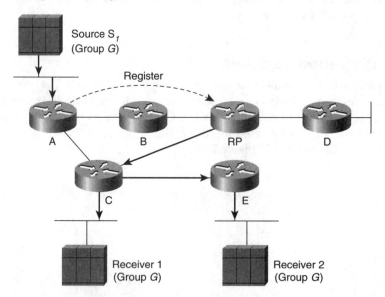

When the RP receives the Register message, the RP de-encapsulates the message and sees that the packet is addressed to multicast Group G. The RP also sees that an active shared tree with a nonempty outgoing interface list exists and therefore sends the de-encapsulated packet down the shared tree (depicted by the solid arrows in Figure 7-17). Furthermore, because an active shared tree exists for this group (with a nonempty outgoing interface list), the RP sends an (S_1, G) Join back toward Source S_1 to join the SPT and to pull the (S_1, G) traffic down to the RP. The (S_1, G) Join travels hop by hop back to the first-hop DR, Router A (see Figure 7-18).

Figure 7-18   *Source Registration—Step 3*

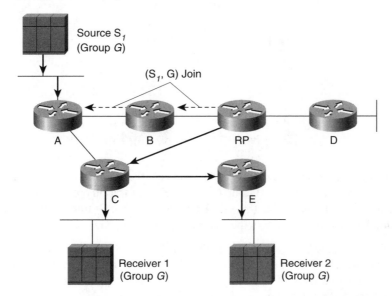

When the (S_1, G) Join reaches Router A, an (S_1, G) SPT has been built from Router A to the RP (indicated by the solid arrows from Router A to the RP in Figure 7-18). Now the (S_1, G) traffic begins to flow to the RP via this newly created (S_1, G) SPT.

At this point, the RP no longer needs to continue to receive the (S_1, G) traffic encapsulated in Register messages, so the RP unicasts a Register-Stop message back to the first-hop DR (Router A), as shown in Figure 7-19.

Figure 7-19 *Source Registration—Step 4*

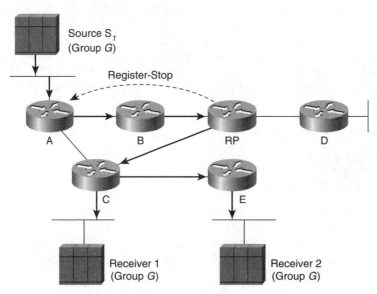

Let's continue with the example and assume another multicast source, S_2, connected to Router D begins sending to Group G. The same registration process would occur and would result in the RP joining the (S_2, G) SPT to pull the (S_2, G) traffic down to the RP so that it could be forwarded on down the shared tree for Group G.

At this point, the RP has joined both the (S_1, G) and (S_2, G) SPTs, (as seen in Figure 7-20) for the two active sources for Group G. This traffic is being forwarded down the $(*, G)$ shared tree to Receivers 1 and 2. Now, the paths are complete between the sources and the receivers, and multicast traffic is flowing properly.

Figure 7-20   *Source Registration—Step 5*

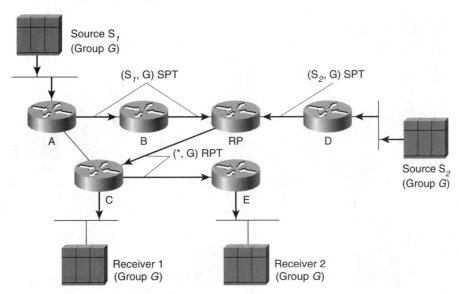

Shortest Path Tree Switchover

PIM-SM enables a last hop DR (that is, a DR with directly connected hosts that have joined a multicast group) to switch from the shared tree to the SPT for a specific source. This step is usually accomplished by specifying an SPT-Threshold in terms of bandwidth. If this threshold is exceeded, the last-hop DR joins the SPT. (Cisco routers have this threshold set to zero by default, which means that the SPT is joined as soon the first multicast packet from a source has been received via the shared tree.)

SPT Switchover Example

Let's return to the network example at the point where there are two receivers and two active sources (refer to Figure 7-20). Because Router C is a last-hop DR, it has the option of switching to the SPT's for Source S_1 and Source S_2. (For now, we are concentrating on Source S_1 because it is the more interesting case.) To accomplish this, Router C would send an (S_1, G) Join toward Source S_1, as shown by the dashed arrow in Figure 7-21.

Figure 7-21   *SPT Switchover—Step 1*

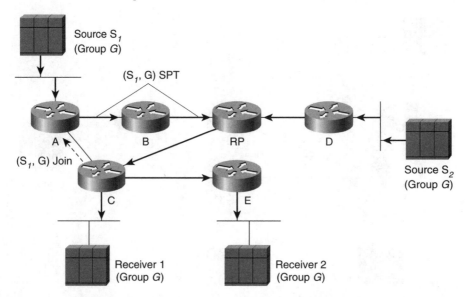

When Router A receives this Join, it adds the interface over which the Join was received to the outgoing interface list of the (S_1, G) entry in its multicast forwarding table. This effectively adds the link from Router A to Router C to the (S_1, G) SPT, as indicated in Figure 7-22. At this point, (S_1, G) multicast traffic can flow directly to Router C via the (S_1, G) SPT.

NOTE   Normally, Group SPT-Thresholds are configured consistently on all routers in the network. If this situation occurred in our example, Router E would also initiate a switch to the SPT by sending an (S, G) Join to the upstream router toward the source that, in this case, would be Router C. However, to keep the example simple, we only examined the case where Router C initiated the switch. Finally, remember that the routers, not the receivers, initiate the switchover to the SPT.

Figure 7-22   *SPT Switchover—Step 2*

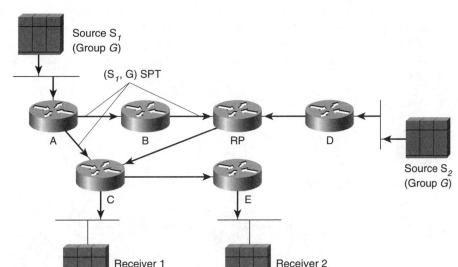

You have probably noticed that there are now two paths over which (S_1, G) multicast traffic can flow to reach Router C: the shared tree and the SPT. This would result in duplicate packets being delivered to Router C and is a waste of network bandwidth. So, we need to tell the RP to prune the (S_1, G) multicast traffic from the shared tree, which is precisely the topic of our next section.

Pruning Sources from the Shared Tree

When encountering the situation shown in Figure 7-22, in which source traffic is flowing down the shared tree that is also receiving via the SPT, a special type of Prune is used to tell the RP to prune this source's traffic from the shared tree. This special prune is referred to as an *(S, G) RP-bit Prune* because it has the RP flag set in the Prune list entry. As you recall from the section "PIM Join/Prune Messages," the RP flag (also referred to as the RP-bit) indicates that this message is applicable to the shared tree and should be forwarded up the shared tree toward the RP. Setting this flag/bit in an (S_1, G) Prune and sending it up the shared tree tells the routers along the shared tree to prune Source S_1 multicast traffic from the shared tree.

Referring to Figure 7-23, Router C sends an (S_1, G) RP-bit Prune up the shared tree toward the RP to prune S_1 multicast traffic from the shared tree. After receiving this special prune, the RP updates its multicast forwarding state so that (S_1, G) traffic is not forwarded down the link to Router C. However, because this link was the only interface on the shared tree that had (S_1, G) traffic flowing down it, the RP no longer has any need for the (S_1, G) traffic either.

Figure 7-23   *Pruning Sources from the Shared Tree—Step 1*

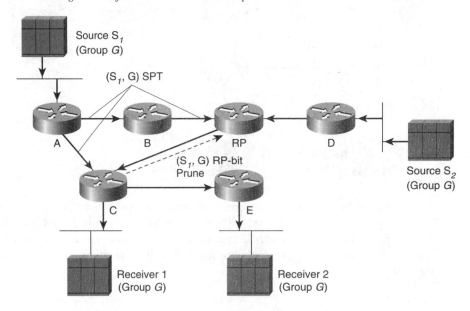

To shut off the now unneeded flow of (S_1, G) traffic, the RP sends an (S_1, G) Prune back toward Source S_1. This Prune (shown by the dashed arrows in Figure 7-24) travels hop by hop through Router B until it reaches the first-hop router, Router A.

Figure 7-24 *Pruning Sources from the Shared Tree—Step 2*

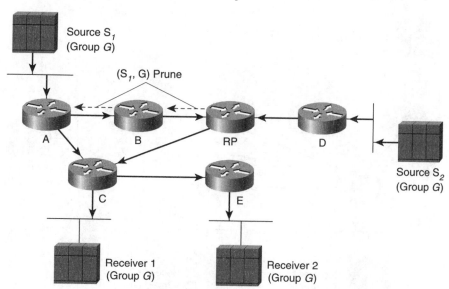

Figure 7-25 shows the result. Now, the (S_1, G) SPT has been pruned, leaving only the link between Router A and Router C. Note that Router E is still receiving (S_1, G) traffic from Router C (indicated by the solid arrow from C to E), although Router E is not aware that its upstream neighbor (Router C) has switched over to the SPT for Source S_1.

Figure 7-25 *Pruning Sources from the Shared Tree—Step 3*

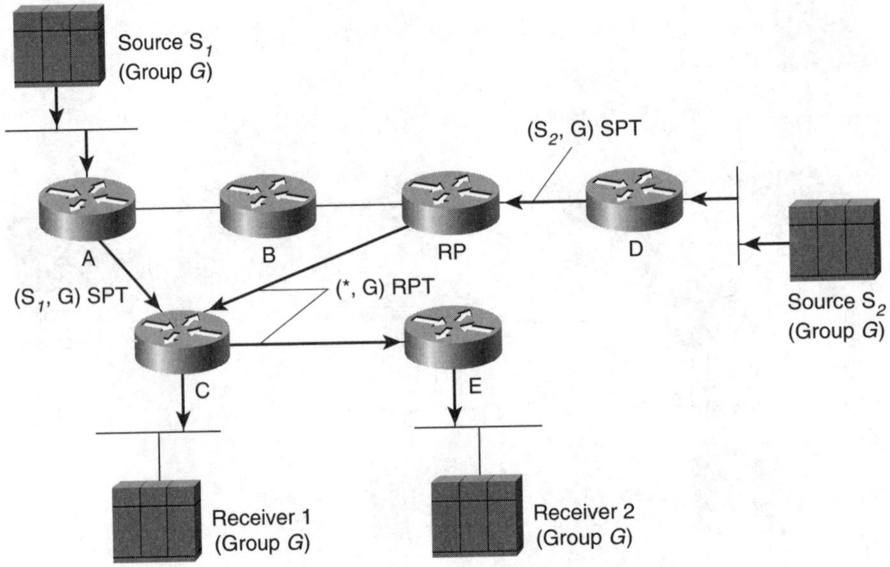

Also note in Figure 7-25 that (S_2, G) traffic is still flowing to the RP and down the shared tree to reach Receiver 1 and Receiver 2.

PIM-SM Designated Router

As discussed in Chapter 6, PIM elects a DR on each multi-access network (for example an Ethernet segment) using PIM Hello messages. In PIM-DM, the DR had meaning only if IGMPv1 was in use on the multi-access network because IGMPv1 does not have an IGMP Querier Election mechanism. In that case, the elected DR also functions as the IGMP Querier. However, in PIM-SM, the role of the DR is much more important, as you will see shortly.

The Role of the Designated Router

Consider the network example shown in Figure 7-26, in which two PIM-SM routers are connected to a common multi-access network with an active receiver for Group G. Because the Explicit Join model is used, only the DR (in this case, Router A) should send Joins to the RP to construct the shared tree for Group G. If both routers are permitted to send (*, G) Joins to the RP, parallel paths would be created and Host A would receive duplicate multicast traffic.

Figure 7-26   *PIM-SM Designated Router*

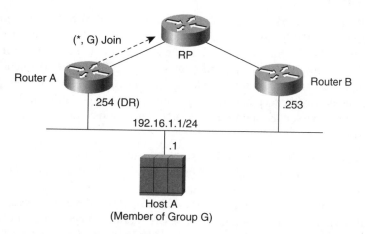

By the same token, if Host A begins to source multicast traffic to the group, the DR (Router A) is the router responsible for sending Register messages to the RP. Again, if both routers were permitted to send Register messages, the RP would receive duplicate multicast packets.

Designated Router Failover

When more than one router is connected to a LAN segment, PIM-SM provides not only a method to elect the DR but also a way to detect the failure of the current DR. If the current DR (Router A) shown in Figure 7-26 were to fail, Router B would detect this situation when its neighbor adjacency with Router A timed out. Now, a new DR election takes place, and Router B becomes the active DR for the network.

In this case, Router B is already aware that an active receiver (Host A) exists on the network because it has been hearing IGMP Membership Reports from the host. As a result, Router B already has IGMP state for Group G on this interface, which would cause B to send a Join to the RP as soon as it was elected the new DR. This step re-establishes traffic flow down a new branch of the shared tree via Router B. Additionally, if Host A were sourcing traffic, Router B would initiate a new Register process immediately after receiving the next multicast packet from Host A. This action would trigger the RP to join the SPT to Host A via a new branch through Router B.

RP Discovery

For PIM-SM to work properly, all routers within the PIM-SM domain must know the address of the RP. In small networks that use a single RP for all multicast groups, manually specifying the IP address of the RP in the configuration of each router might be possible. However, if the size of the network grows or if the RP changes frequently, manual configuration of every router becomes an administration nightmare. This problem is further compounded by the fact that different multicast groups use different RPs in other locations in the domain to either optimize the shared tree or spread the RP workload across multiple routers.

PIMv2 defines a *Bootstrap* mechanism that permits all PIM-SM routers within a domain to dynamically learn all *Group-to-RP* mappings and avoid the manual RP configuration problem. In addition, Cisco's PIM implementation has another mechanism, *Auto-RP*, which can accomplish the same thing. (Cisco's Auto-RP was developed before the PIMv2 specification was written so that existing Cisco PIM-SM networks could dynamically learn *Group-to-RP* mappings.) Both of these mechanisms are discussed in Chapter 12, "PIM Rendezvous Points."

PIM-SM Suitability/Scalability

Because PIM-SM uses the Explicit Join model, multicast traffic is better constrained to only those portions of the network where it is actually desired. Therefore, PIM-SM does not suffer from the inefficiencies found in flood-and-prune protocols such as DVMRP and PIM-DM. As a result, PIM-SM is better suited to multicast networks that have potential members at the end of WAN links.

In addition to the obvious advantages of the Explicit Join model, PIM-SM enables network engineers to use SPTs to reduce the network latency commonly associated with the use of shared trees. The decision to use or not use SPTs can be made on a group-by-group basis. For example, a low-rate, many-to-many multicast application (such as SDR) running over a star-topology network may not warrant the use of SPTs. In this case, the use of Infinity as the group's SPT-Threshold could force all group traffic to remain on the shared tree. This ability to control the use of SPTs gives network engineers greater control over the amount of state created in the routers in the network. Ultimately, the amount of state in the routers in the network is one of the primary factors that affects the scalability of any multicast routing protocol.

PIM-SM is arguably the best choice for an intra-domain multicast routing protocol for most general-purpose multicast networks. The possible exceptions are dedicated, special purpose networks that are designed to run very specific network applications under the complete control of the network administrators. (In these cases, PIM-SM may still be the best choice, although other protocols could possibly be made to work adequately given the tight controls that the network administrators have over the network and its applications.)

Summary

This chapter has presented an overview of the fundamentals of PIM-SM. The key points of PIM-SM are the use of an Explicit Join model to build shared trees and SPTs. In addition, because traffic only flows down the shared tree in traditional PIM-SM, there must be some way to get traffic from a source to the RP. This task is accomplished by the RP joining the SPT toward the source. However, first the RP must be made aware that the source exists, which requires the PIM Register mechanism. The final point, and possibly the most overlooked aspect of PIM-SM, is that routers with directly connected receivers usually immediately join the SPT to a newly detected source and bypass the RP.

CHAPTER 8

Core-Based Trees

The Core-Based Tree (CBT) multicast routing protocol is truly a work-in-progress and has been so for several years. The original version, CBTv1, was superseded by CBTv2 (defined in RFC 2189) which is, unfortunately, not backward compatible with CBTv1. However, because CBTv1 was never really implemented in any production networks to speak of, backward compatibility is not an issue. CBTv2 has also not really seen any significant deployment to date, which is probably good, because a new draft specification for CBTv3 is already out that supersedes and is not backward compatible with CBTv2.

This chapter provides a brief discussion of the concepts and mechanisms used by version 2 of the CBT multicast routing protocol. The coverage includes a brief overview followed by more details on the following CBTv2 topics:

- Joining the CBT shared tree
- Pruning the CBT shared tree
- CBT state maintenance
- CBT Designated Router
- Core Discovery

Finally, a very short discussion of some of the changes proposed in version 3 of the CBT protocol is followed by an examination of the scalability and suitability to the use of CBT in today's multicast network.

CBT Overview

The original designers of CBT were concerned with the scalability of multicast as the number of active groups in the network grows. Therefore, a primary goal of CBT is the reduction of multicast state in the routers in the network to $O(G)$ (pronounced "order G"). To accomplish this goal, CBT was designed as a sparse mode protocol (similar in many ways to Protocol Independent Multicast Sparse Mode [PIM-SM]) that uses only *bidirectional* shared trees to deliver multicast group traffic to portions of the network that have specifically joined the group. These bidirectional shared trees are rooted at a *Core* router, (hence the name, Core-Based Trees) and permit multicast traffic to flow in both directions, up or down the tree. The bidirectional nature of these trees means that routers already on the shared tree do not have to perform any special tasks to forward locally sourced multicast traffic to the Core. Instead, the first-hop CBT router can simply send the traffic up the tree. Each router on the tree simply forwards the traffic out all interfaces on the tree other than the interface on which the packet was received.

Figure 8-1 is an example of a CBT that has several member hosts, M1 to M7, joined to the tree. In this example, member M3 is also a source of multicast traffic to the group. Because it is both a member and a source, M3 is called a *member source*.

Figure 8-1 *Traffic Flow on CBTs*

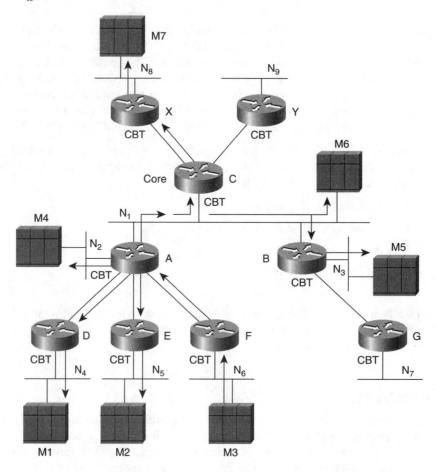

Notice that the traffic sent by M3 flows both up and down the shared tree as shown by the arrows in Figure 8-1. The bidirectional nature of CBT means that no special processing is necessary to get the traffic to the Core so that it can flow down the other branches of the CBT to other members. The key benefit here is that there is also no need for additional forwarding state in the routers for member senders.

NOTE   Note that PIM-SM differs from CBT in that source traffic cannot flow *up* the shared tree because it is *unidirectional*. Instead, PIM-SM uses shortest path trees (SPTs) between the rendezvous point (RP) and the source to get the traffic to the RP so it can be forwarded *down* the shared tree.

Unfortunately, routers that have nonmember sources attached (that is, routers that are not on the shared tree) still must send any traffic sent by these locally attached nonmember sources to the Core via an IP-in-IP tunnel so that the traffic can flow down the tree to the receivers. Unlike PIM-SM, CBT does not have a way to eliminate the encapsulation of this traffic short of the nonmember source joining the group.

Finally, because CBT has the notion of a shared tree only to minimize state in the routers, it does not support SPTs. As a result, CBT does not have the capability to cut over to SPTs. Although this approach does achieve the goal of reducing the amount of multicast state in the routers (by maintaining only (*, G) state entries in the multicast routing table) traffic can suffer from increased latency. This increase can occur because of suboptimal Core placement, which can cause multicast traffic to take a less than optimum path across the network.

Figure 8-2 shows how multicast traffic can take a suboptimal path to reach certain receivers in the network.

Figure 8-2 *Suboptimal Traffic Flow*

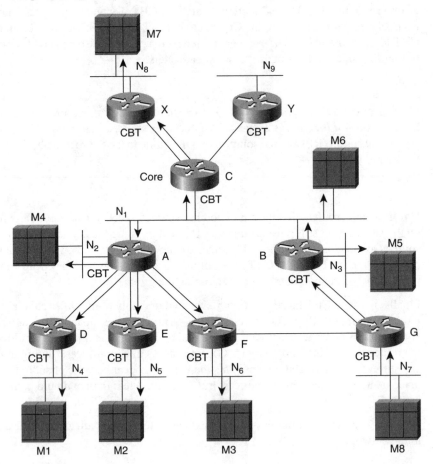

In this example, member M8 has caused Router G to join the CBT via the path through Router B. In addition, M8 is also sourcing multicast traffic onto network N_7 which is being forwarded up the shared tree to the Core. Member M3 is receiving this traffic flow via the path through Routers G-B-A-F. However, in this example, Router G has a direct link to Router F which would be a more optimal path for the traffic flow from M8 to M3. Unfortunately, CBT does not provide a capability for Router F to join the SPT for source M8 and, therefore, latency is increased.

Now that the basic concepts of how traffic flows in a CBT network have been presented, the next sections provide a basic explanation of how the shared tree is constructed and maintained.

Joining the Shared Tree

When a CBT router receives an Internet Group Membership Protocol (IGMP) Membership Report from a locally connected host, the router initiates the CBT Join process by sending a CBT Join-Request message to the next-hop router in the direction of the Core. (Much like PIM-SM, CBT calculates the next-hop router in the direction of the Core by using the information in the unicast routing table. Therefore, CBT is also considered to be *protocol independent*.)

NOTE   CBT Join-Request, like most CBT messages, are multicast with a Time To Live (TTL) of 1 to the *All-CBT-Routers* multicast group (224.0.0.15) whenever the link supports multicast. If the link does not support multicast, the Join-Request is unicast to the next-hop router in the direction of the Core. In addition, CBT has been assigned its own protocol number (7) and, therefore, all CBT packets are transmitted using this protocol.

The CBT routers in the network forward the Join-Request message hop by hop toward the Core until the message reaches either the Core or a CBT router that is already on the shared tree. At this point, the Core (or the "on tree" router) sends back a Join-Ack message in response to the Join-Request to confirm the join. Only when the Join-Ack is received is the branch of the shared tree successfully established and multicast traffic permitted to flow up/down the branch.

The CBT router that originated the Join-Request is also responsible for retransmission of the Join-Request if no corresponding Join-Ack is received within the Retransmit Interval (RTX-INTERVAL), which is typically 5 seconds. If the retransmission of several Join-Requests fails to produce a corresponding Join-Ack within the 17.5 second (typical) JOIN-TIMEOUT interval (which is always 3.5 times the RTX-INTERVAL per the CBT specification), the join process is aborted with an error condition and retriggered by the next incoming IGMP Membership Report from the locally attached host.

Transient State

As a Join-Request threads its way through the network on the way to the Core (or an "on tree" router), each router along the path sets up a transient Join state entry, which contains the following:

```
(group, incoming interface, {outgoing interface list})
```

These transient Join state entries permit routers to forward Join-Ack messages in the reverse path back down the tree to the originator(s) of the Join-Request. When a CBT router receives a Join-Ack message, the *<group, arrival interface>* of the message must match the *<group, incoming interface>* of a transient Join state entry. If there is no match, the Join-Ack is ignored. If there is a match, the matching transient Join state router is converted to a Forwarding Cache entry and the Join-Ack forwarded out the outgoing interface(s) indicated in the transient Join state entry. If a corresponding Join-Ack is not received within the TRANSIENT-TIMEOUT interval (which is specified in the CBT spec as 1.5 times the RTX-INTERVAL, or roughly 7.5 seconds), the associated transient Join state entry is deleted.

Forwarding Cache

After transient Join state is confirmed by the receipt of a corresponding Join-Ack message, the information in the transient state is converted into a multicast forwarding cache entry and the original transient Join state is deleted.

Multicast forwarding cache entries are indexed by group and contain a list of interfaces over which Joins have been successfully confirmed. Although forwarding cache entries do not maintain the notion of an "incoming" or "outgoing" interface, the upstream, or parent, interface in the direction of the Core is noted. The remaining interfaces in the list are considered to be child interfaces, which implies that forwarding cache entries have the following format:

```
(group, parent interface, {child interface list})
```

NOTE   It is also worth noting that the *parent interface* and the *child interface list* are mutually exclusive. That is to say, the parent interface never appears in the child interface list.

When transient Join state is converted to a forwarding cache entry, the forwarding cache is searched for an existing entry for the group. If one is not found, a new forwarding cache entry for the group is created and the incoming interface in the transient Join state entry becomes the upstream or parent interface in the forwarding cache entry. In either case, all outgoing interfaces in the transient Join state entry are added to the list of child interfaces in the forwarding cache entry. The resulting multicast forwarding cache entry is then used to forward subsequent group multicast traffic up and down the tree.

Multicast Forwarding

When a multicast packet arrives, the destination group address in the packet's IP header is used as the index into the forwarding cache. If a matching forwarding cache entry is found and the packet arrives on one of the interfaces in the interface list, the packet is forwarded out all remaining interfaces in the interface list. If a match is not found or if the arriving interface is not listed in the forwarding entry's interface list, the packet is simply discarded.

Notice that CBT does not use Reverse Path Forwarding (RPF) checks on arriving multicast packets. Because traffic can flow both up and down the shared tree, RPF checks are not applicable. As a result, great care must be taken in the design of the CBT shared tree maintenance algorithms to ensure that no multicast route loops are ever generated.

Nonmember Sending

Up to now, our discussion of CBT has focused on the forwarding of multicast group traffic sent by members of the group who by definition are on the shared tree. In general, this is the norm because many of the popular multicast applications (particularly multimedia conferencing applications that use the Real-Time Protocol [RTP] model) fall into the category of "sender is receiver." However, the basic multicast host model described in RFC 1112 (our "IP Multicast Dead Sea Scrolls") does not require a sender to be a member of the group to which it is sending.

CBT handles the case of nonmember senders by using an IP-in-IP tunnel to forward this traffic to the Core. Figure 8-3 shows a nonmember (S1) sending to the group. Because Router G is not on the tree, it must encapsulate the traffic and send it to the Core in the IP-in-IP tunnel shown. When the IP-in-IP encapsulated traffic reaches the Core at the other end of the tunnel, it is de-encapsulated and forwarded down the shared tree to all of the receivers as shown in Figure 8-3.

Figure 8-3 *Nonmember Sending*

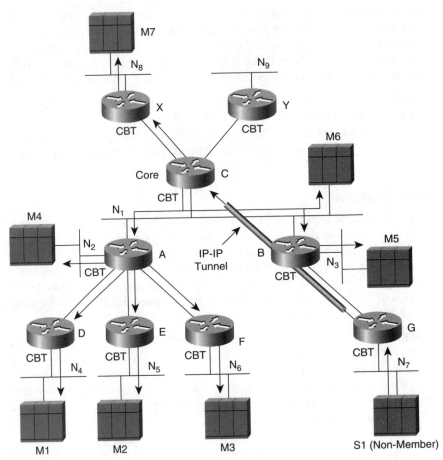

In the current version of CBT (version 2) defined in RFC 2189, there was no way to convert this IP-in-IP tunnel over to a branch of the shared tree. Furthermore, if there is no member of the group to which the nonmember is sending, CBTv2 has no means to tell the router at the end of the tunnel to stop sending this unwanted group traffic. This is obviously a key deficiency in CBTv2, particularly if the send-only source is physically many hops away from the core because unnecessary bandwidth is consumed on each link along this path.

To overcome this deficiency, the newer CBTv3 draft specification permits the CBT router to send a special, unidirectional Join to the Core to establish a one-way branch of the tree. When established, this one-way branch permits native (nonencapsulated) nonmember traffic to flow up the tree toward the Core so that it can be forwarded to other members on the tree. However, because this is a one-way branch, unnecessary group traffic does not flow down branch in the direction of the nonmember sender.

CBT State Maintenance

Because CBT uses the Explicit Join model, the branches of the CBT must be refreshed periodically. The periodic refresh mechanism used in CBT is based on sending *keepalive* messages on the upstream link to the parent and listening for a corresponding response. These keepalive messages allow a child router to monitor the reachability of its parent and to take action to repair the tree should connectivity be lost. The keepalive messages used to accomplish the above are the CBT *Echo-Request* and *Echo-Response* messages, which are described in the next sections.

Echo-Request Messages

As long as a CBT router has a forwarding cache entry whose child interface list is not NULL, it periodically (every ECHO-INTERVAL, which is typically 60 seconds) sends an Echo-Request message on the parent link. The Echo-Request message contains no group information itself. Instead, it is a request for the parent router to report back (via Echo-Response message) all active groups on this network.

CBT uses an Echo-Request suppression mechanism so that only one child router sends an Echo-Request when multiple child routers exist on a broadcast-capable, multi-access network. When a CBT router receives an Echo-Request on its parent interface, it restarts its ECHO-INTERVAL timer and suppresses the sending of its own Echo-Request. This suppression mechanism helps to reduce Echo-Request traffic because only one needs to be sent upstream every ECHO-INTERVAL period.

Echo-Response Messages

A router that receives an Echo-Request message over one of its child interfaces responds by sending back an Echo-Response message that contains a list of all groups for which the interface is a child. When this response is received, each child router scans this group information and refreshes its matching forwarding entries. Forwarding cache entries that are not refreshed in this manner eventually (in GROUP-EXPIRE-TIME seconds, which, per the CBT spec, is 1.5 x ECHO-INTERVAL or roughly 90 seconds) time out and are deleted. Following this deletion, the router sends a Quit-Notification message (detailed in the section "Pruning the Shared Tree") for the group upstream and a Flush-Tree message (discussed in the next section) for the group downstream to completely tear down this branch of the tree.

Flush-Tree Messages

As the name implies, Flush-Tree messages are used to tear down downstream branches of a tree whenever the integrity of a branch has been compromised because of loss of connectivity upstream. If a router loses connectivity with its parent, Flush-Tree messages for the group are sent down all child interfaces. When the routers downstream receive the Flush-Tree message for a group, the message is forwarded on all child interfaces and the associated forwarding cache entry is deleted. The net result is to completely delete all branches of the tree from the originating router down. Any routers that were on these deleted branches and that had directly attached members retrigger the Join process, which causes a new branch to be constructed.

Pruning the Shared Tree

A CBT may be pruned in basically the same manner as PIM-SM shared trees (as described in Chapter 7, "PIM Sparse Mode") and for basically the same reasons. When the last directly connected member leaves the group on a Leaf router, the multicast group traffic no longer needs to continue to flow down the tree. One option would be to just stop sending Echo-Requests to refresh the parent router's state for the tree and allow the branch to time out. However, this step would take a finite period of time during which network resources are being consumed to deliver unwanted multicast traffic. Therefore, the CBT Leaf router sends a form of a Prune message up the tree to immediately stop the flow of the traffic.

The notion of pruning in CBT is implemented by the use of Quit-Notification messages, which CBT routers send upstream toward the Core. Routers send Quit-Notification messages whenever the child interface list of a forwarding cache entry becomes NULL. Unlike Join-Request messages, Quit-Notification messages are not acknowledged. Instead, they are simply repeated (the number of repeats is specified in the CBT specification by the MAX-RTX parameter), spaced apart by HOLDTIME seconds (typically 3 seconds) to reduce the possibility of the message being lost by its parent.

When a CBT router receives a Quit-Notification message on a child interface that is a point-to-point link, it simply deletes the child interface from the forwarding cache entry. On the other hand, if a CBT router receives a Quit-Notification message on a child interface that is a broadcast capable, multi-access network (such as an Ethernet segment), other child CBT routers may possibly exist on the interface. If the parent just deletes the child interface from the forwarding cache entry, one of the other downstream routers on the interface could be starved of group traffic that it still wishes to receive.

To avoid this situation, CBT uses a Prune Override mechanism similar to PIM. When a CBT router receives a Quit-Notification message on a child interface that is a broadcast, multi-access network, it starts a child-deletion-timer. This child-deletion-timer is specified in the CBT spec as 1.5 times HOLDTIME (which is a generic response interval defined in CBT to be 3 seconds) or roughly 4.5 seconds. This delay gives other CBT routers on the subnet the opportunity to override the Quit-Notification by sending a Join-Request.

During this child-deletion delay, if the parent router receives a Join-Request, the child-deletion-timer is canceled and the child interface is not deleted. However, if the child-deletion-timer expires, then no other downstream, on-tree router is present and the child interface can be deleted from the forwarding cache entry.

NOTE   To avoid multiple sibling routers from all sending an overriding Join-Request at the same time, each schedules the Join-Request to be sent between 0 and HOLDTIME seconds. If, during this time, a Join-Request from a sibling is heard, the scheduled Join-Request transmission is canceled.

In addition, the new draft CBTv3 specification changes this pruning procedure such that the other child routers use group-specific Echo-Request messages to override the Quit-Notification message and prevent the link from being pruned from the shared tree.

CBT Designated Router

CBT also elects a Designated Router (DR) on multi-access, broadcast-capable subnets in a manner similar to PIM-SM. This section covers some of the basic functions of the CBT DR. Like PIM DRs, CBT DRs must be elected on multi-access networks, such as Ethernet segments. In addition, CBT DRs perform a function called *Join brokering*, which is unique to CBT. Both of these topics are discussed next.

CBT Hello Protocol

CBT's Hello protocol is used solely to elect the CBT DR on a multi-access, broadcast-capable subnet. This differs from the PIM Hello protocol that is used not only to elect the PIM DR but also to establish and maintain PIM neighbor adjacencies. (PIM DRs and the PIM Hello protocol are covered in the "PIM Neighbor Discovery" section in Chapter 6, "PIM Dense Mode.")

To elect the DR, CBT routers periodically (typically every 60 seconds) multicast Hello messages to the All-CBT-Router group with a TTL of 1. These Hello messages contain a preference value of from 1 to 255 (the default is usually 255) where 1 is considered to be most eligible to be elected as the CBT DR. These preference values can be configured on a per interface basis by the network administrator so that the election of the CBT DR can be controlled. If two or more CBT routers advertise the same preference value in their Hello messages, the IP address of the advertising router is used as the tiebreaker and the lowest IP addressed router wins.

Once a router has been elected the DR, it continues to advertise itself as the elected DR by setting the preference value to zero in the CBT Hello message. Furthermore, Hello messages have a suppressing effect on other routers whose preference is worse (higher) than the preference being advertised. In other words, a router that receives a Hello message with a better preference does not send a Hello message of its own. The net effect is that once a CBT DR is elected, it continues to send CBT Hellos (with a preference of zero) while all other routers on the subnet suppress the sending of Hello messages. (For this reason, CBT Hellos can not be used to maintain CBT neighbor information.)

Given that the elected CBT DR is sending Hellos with a preference value of zero (regardless of its originally configured preference), one would expect that DR preemption would not be possible. However, a new CBT-DR election process is triggered by the arrival of a new CBT router on the network. (In the animal kingdom, this event is similar to a younger male lion challenging the current male leader for dominance of the lion pride.) When a CBT router comes up, it *always* immediately transmits two CBT Hello messages with its configured preference value. This unsolicited transmission of a CBT Hello message with a nonzero preference triggers a new DR election process. Routers with a better preference (lower) respond by transmitting a Hello with their better preference value. Routers configured with a lower preference suppress sending their Hello messages. (The routers know they can't win anyway, so why bother losing any fur trying to be king of the jungle.) In the end, if the preference value of the new router is better (lower) than the configured value of the current CBT DR, the new router assumes the role of the CBT DR.

DR Join Brokering

The CBT DR is considered the *join broker* for all Joins crossing the multi-access, broadcast-capable subnet and determines how the Join-Request is to be routed off the subnet based on its routing viewpoint. (All routers on the subnet don't necessarily share the same routing viewpoint. Without a single CBT DR to make the join-routing decision, conflicts in routing information could result in tree loops.) When a CBT DR receives a Join-Request message from a downstream router, the best path to the Core may be through one of the other routers on the same subnet. In this case, the CBT DR unicasts the Join-Request directly to this router, thereby making it the upstream router for the group. As a result of the Join brokering performed by the CBT DR, the upstream router for the group may be some other router on the subnet than the CBT DR.

Finally, the CBT DR is also the router responsible for initiating the Join process as a result of any directly connected member hosts on the multi-access, broadcast-capable subnet. In this case, it would originate the Join-Request message itself.

Core Router Discovery

For CBT to work properly, all routers within the CBT domain must know the address of the Core router. In small networks that use a single Core for all multicast groups, manually specifying the core in the configuration of each router might be possible. However, if the size of the network grows or the core changes frequently, manual configuration of every router becomes an administration nightmare. This problem is further compounded by the fact that different multicast groups use different cores in other locations in the domain to optimize the trees. CBT uses the same Bootstrap mechanism used in PIMv2 to permit all CBT routers within a domain to dynamically learn all <core, group> mappings and avoid the manual core configuration problem. (This PIMv2 Bootstrap router mechanism is described in detail in Chapter 12, "PIM Rendezvous Points," in the section titled, oddly enough, "PIMv2 Bootstrap Router Mechanism.")

CBT Version 3

When this book was being written, version 3 of CBT had been published in initial, Internet Engineering Task Force (IETF) draft form. CBTv3 is primarily concerned with extensions that permit it to better handle inter-domain multicast by the use of CBT border routers (BRs). Compared to its predecessors, version 3 requires significantly more state information in the routers so that this BR function can be implemented efficiently.

For example, CBTv2 needed to maintain (*, G) state information only in the form of its forwarding cache entries. (As you recall, minimizing router state to O(G) is one of the stated advantages of CBT.) However, CBTv3 defines new (*, Core) and (S, G) states in order to support pruning of multicast traffic flowing into, out of, or across the domain through the BRs. This, in turn, has resulted in a fairly substantial change and extension to the CBT packet formats that are not backward compatible with CBTv2.

CBT Suitability/Scalability

Compared to protocols that support SPTs, CBT's biggest advantage is that it is more efficient in terms of the amount of multicast state it creates in the routers. In networks with large numbers of sources and groups, CBT's ability to minimize multicast state to O(G) is very appealing. However, this efficiency results in a lack of support for SPTs (which some may argue is a plus) when network latency is an issue. Furthermore, the simple (*, G) state model that is maintained in CBTv2 does not handle nonmember senders or inter-domain border routers particularly well. To remedy this, work on CBTv3 is (at the time this book was written) underway. CBTv3 is a substantially more complex protocol that departs from the simple bidirectional (*, G)-state-only model and introduces new (*, Core) and (S, G) states as well as the concept of *unidirectional* branches of the CBT. It could be argued that these extensions can potentially cause the amount of state in a CBT domain to approach the amount of state in a similar PIM-SM domain.

Summary

This chapter has provided a brief overview of the mechanisms of version 2 of the CBT multicast routing protocol, which is based on the use of a bidirectional, shared tree rooted at a Core router in the network. Because CBTv2 supports only traffic forwarding along this shared tree and does not support the notion of SPTs, the amount of state that must be maintained is considerably reduced. Although the overall idea of minimizing router state is quite attractive, CBT continues as a work-in-progress with little or no actual network implementations.

CHAPTER 9

Multicast Open Shortest Path First

OSPFv2 (currently defined in RFC 2328) is a link-state unicast routing protocol that uses a two-tier, network hierarchy. At the top of the hierarchy is Area 0, sometimes called the backbone area, to which all other areas in the second tier must connect, either physically or through a virtual link. Open Shortest Path First (OSPF) is hierarchical because all interarea traffic must flow through the backbone area, Area 0. Inside each OSPF area, routers flood link-state information that describes the network topology within the area, and each router maintains a copy of this information in its area database. Each time the topology changes, new link-state information is flooded throughout the area so that all routers get an updated picture of the topology. Using the topology information in the area databases, each router (using itself as the root) constructs a lowest cost, spanning tree of the networks within the area via a special Dijkstra algorithm. This lowest cost, spanning tree is then used to build a unicast forwarding table. Special area border routers (ABRs) connect second-tier areas to Area 0 and maintain separate area databases for each area it connects (including Area 0) so that it can forward traffic across the area boundaries.

NOTE

I realize that my "Tiny Guide to OSPF" in the preceding paragraph is an extremely high-level description of OSPF. Therefore, if you are unfamiliar with OSPF, you may want to do some additional reading on OSPF basic concepts before proceeding. Another Cisco Press book, *OSPF Network Design Solutions*, by Thomas M. Thomas, ISBN 1578700469, can provide you with additional information on the OSPF protocol and OSPF network design. If you don't have at least a little background on OSPF, you may find the remainder of this chapter to be nothing more than an excellent cure for insomnia because it assumes at least some basic OSPF knowledge.

Multicast Open Shortest Path First (MOSPF), defined in RFC 1584, "Multicast Extensions to OSPF" is, as the RFC title implies, an extension to the OSPFv2 unicast routing protocol. MOSPF provides additional OSPF data format definitions and operating specifications based, in part, on the "Link-State Multicast Routing" section of Steve Deering's seminal work published in 1991. These extensions to the OSPF protocol permit multicast traffic to be forwarded within an OSPF unicast network using shortest path trees (SPTs) by either a partial or full set of MOSPF routers. (An MOSPF router is one that supports the multicast extensions to OSPF and has been configured to function as an MOSPF router. All routers in the OSPF network need not be running MOSPF extensions for multicast traffic to be forwarded. However, routers that are configured to function as MOSPF routers perform multicast routing in addition to performing normal OSPF routing.)

This chapter provides a brief overview of the concepts and mechanisms of MOSPF including the following topics:

- MOSPF intra-area multicast routing
- MOSPF interarea multicast routing
- MOSPF inter-AS multicast routing

Finally, a brief discussion of MOSPF's suitability and scalability is presented.

MOSPF Intra-Area Multicast Routing

The fundamental concept of MOSPF intra-area multicast routing is based on the following assumption stated in the OSPF specification, *RFC 2328*: "If all routers within an area know which network segments have multicast group members, they can use the Dijkstra algorithm to construct Shortest-Path Trees for any (source-network, group) pair in the area." Using these SPTs, a router can then perform a Reverse Path Forwarding (RPF) check on incoming multicast packets and (if the check succeeds) determine which of its remaining interfaces (if any) are on the tree and should therefore receive copies of the multicast packet.

Group Membership Link-State Advertisements

The biggest addition to the OSPF data formats needed to support multicast is the definition of a new link-state advertisement (LSA) that is used to flood information about group membership throughout the area. Each group membership LSA contains the following basic information:

- Multicast group address (link-state ID)
- Advertising router ID
- List of the router interfaces (identified by IP address) that have members for this group

Group membership LSAs are flooded throughout the OSPF area and are maintained in the MOSPF router's local group database in the same fashion as router and network LSAs. Group membership LSAs are also similar to network LSAs in that only the Designated Router (DR) originates group membership LSAs on behalf of the multi-access network.

For example, assume that Router C (shown in Figure 9-1) is the OSPF DR for network N_1. Because there is a member on network N_1, Router C originates a group membership LSA for Group G that contains the IP address of its interface on network N_1. This LSA is flooded throughout the area and informs all MOSPF routers that a member of Group G exists on Network N_1.

Figure 9-1   *MOSPF Area Containing Sources and Members for Multicast Group G*

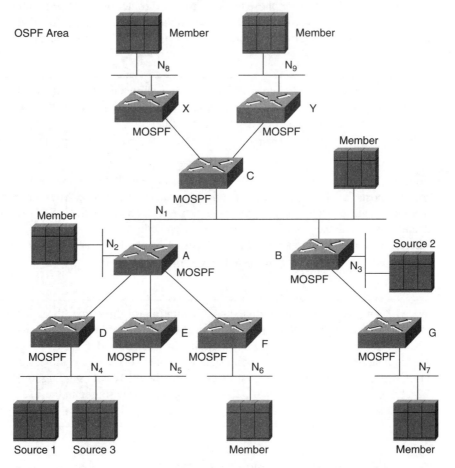

Because it is possible to mix OSPF and MOSPF routers in a network, an MOSPF router needs to be elected as the DR on any multi-access network. This can be accomplished by setting the OSPF router priority to zero on all non-MOSPF routers on the multi-access network. (If an OSPF-only router (that is, a non-MOSPF router) were to be elected as DR for a multi-access network, group membership LSAs would not be originated for this network and multicast traffic forwarding would not function correctly.)

Intra-Area Shortest Path Trees

After the databases in all area routers have synchronized, the combination of group membership LSAs along with router and network LSAs provides each MOSPF router with the information necessary to construct intra-area SPTs for any (source-network, group) pair within the area. To construct these trees, an MOSPF router uses a Dijkstra algorithm to construct a single multicast SPT that is rooted at the source-network. Note that the Dijkstra algorithm must be run for each (source-network, group) SPT to be created.

NOTE	This same computationally intensive Dijkstra algorithm is used to construct the unicast shortest path first (SPF) tree used for intra-area unicast routing by OSPF. However, in this case the unicast SPF tree is rooted at the local router.

Figure 9-1 is an example of an OSPF area that has three multicast sources and several active member hosts for Group G located at various points in the network. After the area database has synchronized, each router has the capability to construct the (S, G) SPTs for Sources 1, 2, and 3. Note that these SPTs are *source-subnet* specific and not individual source specific. Therefore, although there are multiple sources on Network N_3 for Group G, only a single (N_3, G) *source-network* SPT needs to be constructed.

NOTE	We will continue to use the shorthand (S, G) notation for these trees throughout this chapter, even though the S refers to *source-subnet* instead of individual source. In real practice, we avoid this ambiguity by extending this notation to (S/m, G) where S is the source IP address, m is the network mask length, and G is the group address. For example, (172.16.1.1/32, 224.1.1.1) denotes a *specific* source (172.16.1.1) sending to group 224.1.1.1, whereas (172.16.0.0/16, 224.1.1.1) refers to *any* source in the 172.16.0.0/16 network sending to group 224.1.1.1.

Part A of Figure 9-2 shows the resulting MOSPF (N_4, G) SPT, which is rooted at source-network N_4 and contains Sources 1 and 3. Part B of Figure 9-2 shows the resulting (N_3, G) SPT, which is rooted at source-network N_3 where Source 2 resides.

Figure 9-2   *Resulting MOSPF SPTs for Networks N_3 and N_4*

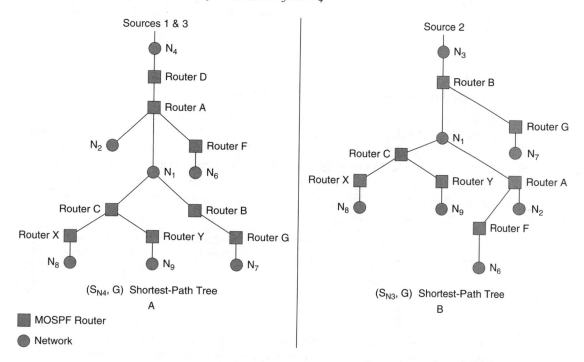

These SPTs are used as the basis for forwarding multicast traffic inside the area as long as the group membership information remains static. If there are any changes to group membership or if the network topology changes (say because of a flapping link), the SPTs must be recalculated with the Dijkstra algorithm.

MOSPF Forwarding Cache

The Dijkstra algorithm is very computationally intensive and would place the MOSPF router under too much strain if it had to compute every source-network SPT in the network in advance of the receipt of any multicast traffic. Therefore, to reduce the number of Dijkstra computations to *O(S)* (pronounced "order S"), MOSPF uses an on-demand scheme where an MOSPF router does not compute the (S, G) SPT until the first multicast packet from a source in network S is received for group G. The MOSPF router then uses the results of this (S, G) SPT calculation to populate its MOSPF forwarding cache for use in forwarding (S, G) traffic.

Entries in the MOSPF forwarding cache are organized by group address and source-network address. Each entry in the forwarding cache contains the following basic information:

- Upstream neighbor
- Incoming interface
- Outgoing interfaces

Table 9-1 shows the MOSPF forwarding cache in Router A for the network example shown in Figure 9-1. These entries were populated using the information from the (S_N, G) SPTs (shown in Figure 9-2) that were calculated by Router A as soon as the first packet was received from sources in networks N_3 and N_4. (The upstream neighbor address is not required for multicast forwarding. It is simply maintained as part of the data structure. Future versions of MOSPF may use this information to accomplish other functions.)

Table 9-1   *MOSPF Forwarding Cache in Router A*

Group	Source-Network	Upstream Neighbor	Incoming Interfaces	Outgoing Interfaces
G	N_3	Router B	N_1	N_2
G	N_4	Router D	N_{A-D}	N_1, N_2, N_{A-F}

Although the use of on-demand SPT calculations and an MOSPF forwarding cache help to reduce the demands on the MOSPF router under steady state network conditions, they don't provide much relief when the topology of the area changes. Each time the topology changes, all MOSPF routers within the area must invalidate their entire MOSPF forwarding caches. Consequently, the Dijkstra algorithm must be rerun to build new forwarding-cache entries for any incoming multicast packets. (Note that topology changes outside the area do not cause the Dijkstra algorithm to run.)

Given the potential for a flapping WAN link in a remote part of an OSPF area to cause all MOSPF routers to rerun the Dijkstra algorithm for all active (source-network, group) pairs, it is even more crucial for network engineers to pay close attention to OSPF area design. As the number of source networks and active groups within an area increase, a point may finally be reached at which the network becomes unconditionally unstable and is unable to recover from a single topology change.

In addition, because topology changes invalidate the entire cache, all forwarding-cache entries associated with a group must be invalidated if there are any changes to the group membership LSAs stored in the local group database. This, in turn, results in the Dijkstra algorithm having to be rerun for all active sources in the group. Therefore, rapidly changing group membership can result in a substantial increase in router CPU workload in networks where hosts frequently join and leave multicast groups.

Although flooding group membership information within the area, and then having to run the Dijkstra algorithm, has its disadvantages, it does have one advantage that most multicast protocols don't have. The advantage is that because MOSPF routers have a complete knowledge of all group members inside of the area, they therefore know the diameter of the group membership. This can be useful as routers can simply discard a multicast packet if it has an insufficiently large enough Time To Live (TTL) to reach the closest member in the area. Therefore, a multicast packet can be dropped early on in the path instead of traveling multiple hops only to be dropped because of a zero TTL before reaching a group member.

MOSPF Interarea Multicast Routing

Up to this point, we have been concerned with how MOSPF routes multicast traffic inside a single OSPF area. This section, however, examines the mechanisms that MOSPF employs to forward multicast packets between OSPF areas. This occurs when a multicast source is in one area while one or more receivers reside in a different area(s).

The way that MOSPF handles interarea multicast routing is in many ways similar to OSPF's handling of unicast. In OSPF, routers that connect a second-tier area to the backbone area are called area border routers (ABRs) and are responsible for forwarding routing information (primarily in the form of OSPF summary LSAs) and unicast traffic between the two areas. ABRs do not pass router or network LSAs between the areas; therefore, the topology of one area is not seen by a bordering area. (Only OSPF summary LSAs, which summarize the networks inside an area, and external-AS LSAs, which summarize external network connections made inside the area, are exchanged across ABRs.)

Multicast Area Border Routers

To support interarea multicast, RFC 1584 defines interarea multicast forwarders, which are a subset of the OSPF ABRs in the network and are configured to perform multicast-related tasks such as

- Summarizing group membership into Area 0
- Forwarding multicast packets between areas

Given these tasks and their similarity to the unicast-related tasks performed by ABRs, I prefer to call these routers multicast area border routers (MABRs) and do so for the remainder of this chapter. (Why the protocol authors didn't use this term is a mystery to me, as it seems to be a more descriptive term than interarea multicast forwarder.)

Interarea Group Membership Summary

For multicast traffic to flow down the OSPF hierarchy (that is, from the backbone area to the other second-tier areas), backbone area routers must know which MABRs are connected to areas that have active group members. To facilitate this, MABRs summarize the group membership information in their non-backbone area and flood this information into the backbone area via group membership LSAs. However, unlike unicast OSPF summary LSAs that are flooded symmetrically across area borders, the group membership summary is asymmetric and flows from only non-backbone areas into the backbone area as shown in Figure 9-3.

Figure 9-3 *Group Membership Summary into the Backbone*

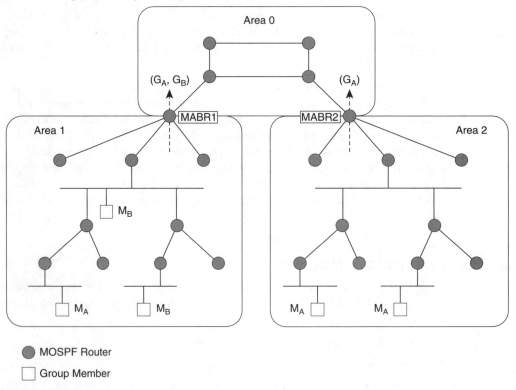

In this example, Area 1 contains one member of group A (M_A) and two members of Group B (M_B). This group membership is summarized by MABR1 and flooded into the backbone area (Area 0) via group membership LSAs (indicated by the dashed arrow). Area 2 contains two members of Group A and this information is summarized and flooded into the backbone area by MABR2. (Notice that group membership information does not flow back out across the MABRs and therefore routers in the two non-backbone areas are unaware of the other's group membership status.)

Figure 9-4 now shows two active sources, S_1 and S_2, that are sending to multicast Groups B and A, respectively. The group membership information that was flooded into the backbone area by MABRs 1 and 2 inform the routers in the backbone area to include the MABRs in any SPTs associated with these groups. As a result, the (S_1, B) SPT (dashed arrows) and the (S_2, A) SPT (dotted arrows) are constructed in the backbone area and permit Group A and Group B traffic to be forwarded into Areas 1 and 2 as appropriate.

Figure 9-4   *Resulting SPTs in the Backbone Area*

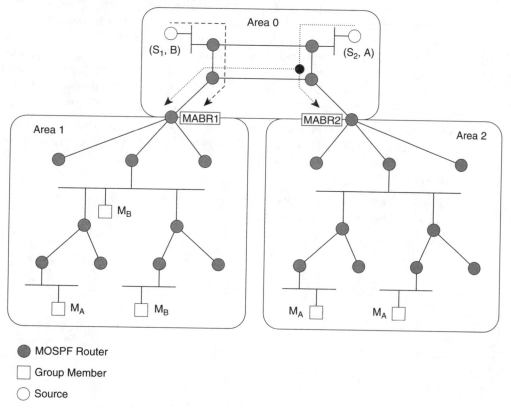

At this point, intra-area SPTs in the two areas are built in the normal fashion with the MABRs as the root of the tree. (In other words, the MABRs appear to be the source of the traffic to all the routers inside the area.)

Wildcard Multicast Receivers

The preceding example works fine when multicast sources reside in the backbone area and we are trying to get traffic into a non-backbone area. However, rarely do all sources of multicast traffic reside in the backbone area. (The reason is that most Real-Time Protocol (RTP) based multicast applications—VIC and VAT, for example—multicast RTP Control Protocol (RTCP) send control traffic to the group even if they are not sending any audio/video content. Therefore, even a receive-only VAT client in a non-backbone area is a constant source of multicast traffic.) Obviously, if a multicast source exists in a non-backbone area and there are receivers outside of the area, some other method must be used to get the traffic out of the area.

MOSPF handles this situation by defining a new wildcard multicast receiver flag (W-bit, meaning wildcard) in the *rtype* field of router LSA packets. (Refer to the OSPF specification for more details on the format of the fields in router LSA packets.) The W-bit indicates that the advertising router wishes to receive all multicast traffic and therefore is a wildcard multicast receiver. Therefore, when a router must calculate a new SPT for an incoming multicast packet, it searches through its local area database for router LSAs that have the W-bit set and treats these routers as if they were members of the destination group.

All MABRs set the W-bit in router LSAs that they originate into non-backbone areas. This has the effect of pulling all multicast traffic originated by sources inside the non-backbone area to the MABR. The MABR can then forward this traffic into the backbone area as necessary.

Figure 9-5 depicts the same network used in the previous example, but with the sources (S_1, B) and (S_2, A) now in the non-backbone areas.

Figure 9-5   *Sources in Non-Backbone Areas*

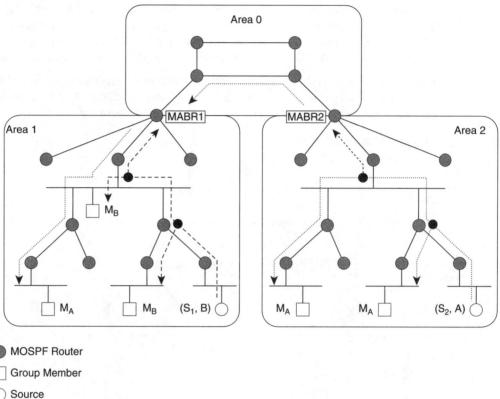

Consider source (S_2, A) now in Area 2. The normal intra-area (S_2, A) SPT (dotted arrows) is constructed as usual. However, because MABR2 is a wildcard multicast receiver (it sets the W-bit in Router LSAs originated into Area 2), the (S_2, A) SPT is extended to include MABR2. Furthermore, because MABR1 is originating summarized group membership LSAs for groups A and B into the backbone area, (see Figure 9-3), all routers in the backbone (including MABR2) construct an (S_2, A) SPT that includes MABR1. This backbone SPT permits (S_2, A) traffic to flow across the backbone to MABR1 and into Area 1 (as shown by the dotted arrows).

In the case of source (S_1, B) in Area 1, a normal intra-area (S_1, B) SPT (dashed arrows) is constructed and allows traffic to flow to members inside Area 1. Like MABR2 in Area 2, MABR1 is a wildcard multicast receiver in Area 1 that causes it to be included in the (S_1, B) SPT. However, because there is no members of Group B inside the backbone area (other than MABR1 itself), MABR1 simply discards any Group B multicast traffic that it receives.

Unfortunately, the wildcard receiver concept can result in unnecessary multicast traffic flow inside a non-backbone area. Consider the situation shown in Figure 9-6 in which the previous sources are active, but there are no receivers in the network.

Figure 9-6   *Non-Backbone Source-Only Network*

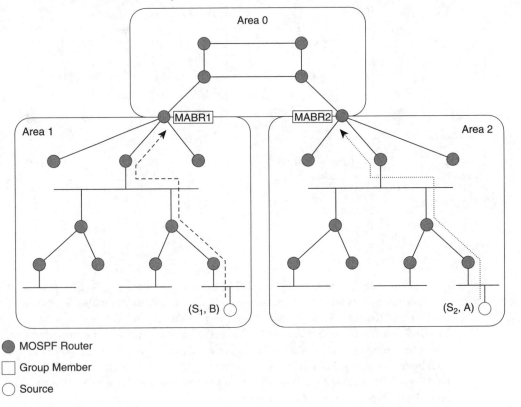

In this situation, network resources are unnecessarily consumed by routing multicast traffic across the area to the MABR. Therefore, network engineers should watch for sources that have the potential for high-rate, low membership group traffic and try to move them close to the area borders. Unfortunately, it is not always possible to move or control the location of these sources. In such cases, the only solution is to sufficiently overprovision the bandwidth in the MOSPF network to accommodate the worst-case scenario.

MOSPF Inter-AS Multicast Routing

This section takes a brief look at the mechanisms that MOSPF provides for inter-AS multicast routing. In the case of unicast traffic, OSPF uses autonomous system border routers (ASBR) to forward multicast traffic into and out of the OSPF domain. Although common practice is to place ASBRs in the backbone area, it is not a requirement. ASBRs may reside in non-backbone areas when network topology and interconnectivity dictates.

In OSPF, an ASBR originates an external LSA for each external network for which it has a route. (Frequently, only the default route is injected into the OSPF domain.) These external LSAs are flooded throughout the OSPF domain (with the exception areas configured as stub areas) and permit routers within the domain to compute the best exit for unicast traffic destined for these external networks.

Multicast Autonomous System Border Routers

The MOSPF specification, RFC 1584, also defines Inter-AS Multicast Forwarders that are responsible for forwarding multicast traffic into and out of the MOSPF domain. It is assumed Inter-AS Multicast Forwarders are also running some other multicast routing protocol that permits multicast distribution trees to cross the border into and out of the external AS.

NOTE   Historically, the *other* multicast routing protocol has typically been Distance Vector Multicast Routing Protocol (DVMRP). However, this will change in the near future as other more scalable protocols are developed that are better suited for use as an inter-domain multicast routing protocol. (Refer to the section titled "Issues in Inter-Domain Multicast Routing" in Chapter 17, "Inter-Domain Multicast Routing," for a brief overview.)

Although the term is not used in RFC 1584, it seems only natural to refer to these routers as Multicast AS Border Routers (MASBRs) because that is what their functionality implies.

MASBRs are configured as wildcard multicast forwarders and signal this to other routers in the area by originating a router LSA with the W-bit set in the *rtype* field. This causes all multicast traffic inside the area to flow to the MASBR so that it can be forwarded out to the external AS as appropriate.

Figure 9-7 shows an example of two active multicast sources, (S_1, B) and (S_2, A), whose traffic is being pulled into the backbone areas by MABRs 1 and 2. This traffic travels on across the backbone to the MASBR for forwarding out to the external AS (shown by the dashed and dotted lines). Note that all multicast traffic sourced inside the MOSPF domain is pulled to the MASBR regardless of whether the external AS has any receivers for the traffic or not.

Figure 9-7 *Multicast Traffic Flowing out of the MOSPF Domain*

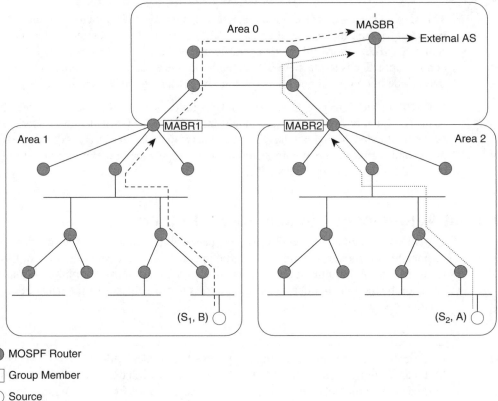

● MOSPF Router
☐ Group Member
○ Source

Figure 9-8 shows an example of multicast traffic flowing into the MOSPF from sources (S_1, B) and (S_2, A) that are now in the external AS. Because the MABRs are forwarding summarized group membership information into the backbone area, the routers in the backbone construct (S_1, B) and (S_2, A) SPTs that forward this traffic to the MABRs as shown. (Note that as far as the routers in the backbone are concerned, the roots of these SPTs appear to be the MASBR). When the traffic reaches the MABRs, it is forwarded into the non-backbone areas (as shown by the dashed and dotted arrows in Figure 9-8).

Figure 9-8 *Multicast Traffic Flowing into the MOSPF Domain*

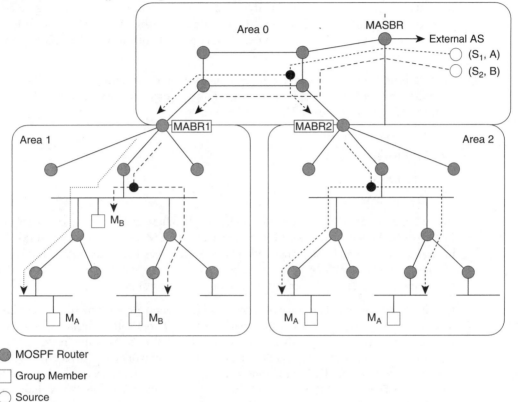

Although it is possible to configure an MASBR in one of the non-backbone areas, placing it in the backbone area is typically better. Doing so allows incoming multicast traffic to be efficiently pruned because an MASBR in the backbone is aware of the total group membership in the OSPF domain. The MASBR placed in a non-backbone area would not have this information.

MOSPF Suitability/Scalability

The biggest advantage to MOSPF is that it shares OSPF's capability to respond rapidly to changes in network topology because it uses link-state routing methods to compute multicast distribution trees. This capability, however, comes at the huge expense of rapidly increasing router CPU resources as the number of (source-network, group) pairs in the network increase. This, in turn, directly translates into an increase in the number of Dijkstra computations in each router. Highly dynamic networks (where group membership and/or the network topology changes frequently because of unstable WAN links) also suffer from an increased number of Dijkstra computations required to reconstruct the (source-network, group) SPTs in the area.

MOSPF is probably best suited for special-purpose multicast networks where the network administrators have absolute rigid control over very crucial factors that affect the performance and scalability of MOSPF, such as

- Location of sources
- Number of sources
- Number of groups
- Group membership

Because most of these factors are often *not* under absolute rigid control of today's corporate IS networks, the long-term suitability and scalability of MOSPF in these networks should be carefully questioned. (Some network administrators may insist that they do have this sort of control in their corporate IS network, but I would argue that they need to do a reality check to make sure they are not suffering from delusions of grandeur.)

Finally, the reason that these variables are generally not under absolute rigid control is that it is usually impossible to completely control the set of applications installed on every PC in the network. (For example, there is little to stop users from installing freeware MBone multimedia conferencing tools on their laptops, PCs, and workstations. Attempting to control this with access lists in the routers can quickly become a network administration nightmare.) Therefore, MOSPF is probably truly suited only for a small percentage of all general-purpose IP networks in use today.

NOTE   Some may argue that a more significant number of MOSPF networks are already deployed, and therefore they are more suitable for general-purpose IP networks than I have lead the reader to believe. However, I would challenge those people. In my opinion, the MOSPF networks that are deployed today are composed of very limited numbers of multicast sources. (I believe this assumption to be reasonable because any compelling multicast applications are quite new.) Given this and in light of some of the scalability issues raised in this chapter around Dijkstra computations in the routers, it is my opinion that the general-purpose IP networks that have deployed MOSPF networks are potential accidents waiting to happen. As more hosts in these networks begin to source multicast traffic, the computational demands of the Dijkstra algorithm will very likely overwhelm the routers. Of course, two age-old caveats apply here: "Your mileage may vary" and "Y'all be careful now, ya hear!"

Summary

This chapter has provided a very brief overview of the MOSPF extension to OSPFv2 that permits multicast traffic to be routed in an OSPF unicast network. The basic concept employed by MOSPF for intra-area multicast routing is the flooding of group membership information throughout the area, using a special group membership LSA. When the MOSPF routers know where all members are in the area, SPTs can be constructed for each source-subnet, using the same Dijkstra algorithm that is used for OSPF unicast routing.

In the case of interarea multicast routing, the group membership in each area is summarized and injected into Area 0 by the MABRs. These MABRs also function as wildcard receivers, which automatically join all active multicast groups so that all multicast traffic can be injected into Area 0 for forwarding to other areas as well as other external autonomous systems.

Finally, the scalability of MOSPF in networks with large numbers of multicast source-subnets has been a topic of many a heated debate. Although MOSPF is currently deployed in some production networks, it is still too early to tell whether these networks will continue to scale up as more multicast applications come online.

Implementing Cisco Multicast Networks

This part is dedicated to the detailed design, implementation, and debugging of IP multicast networks using Cisco routers.

Chapters 10 and 11 present the basic configuration tasks and operations of Cisco routers using PIM Dense Mode (PIM-DM) and PIM Sparse Mode (PIM-SM), respectively. These chapters provide details on the multicast routing state that is used in Cisco routers to describe multicast distribution trees, as well as forward multicast traffic. The basic rules that govern the creation and maintenance of these state entries are presented to help the reader understand exactly how a Cisco router will behave. These chapters provide detailed, step-by-step network scenarios with explanations of how the rules are applied. At each critical step, examples of the resulting state in the Cisco router are displayed to further promote the understanding of the PIM mechanisms at work.

Chapter 12 addresses the topic of PIM rendezvous points (RPs). In this chapter, the details of the Auto-RP and Bootstrap router mechanisms are presented along with information on how these features can be configured and used in Cisco routers.

Chapter 13 addresses the topic of connecting Cisco PIM routers to DVMRP networks in considerable depth.

CHAPTER 10

Using PIM Dense Mode

This chapter builds on the basic information about Protocol Independent Multicast (PIM) dense mode (or PIM-DM) mechanisms covered in Chapter 6, "PIM Dense Mode," and explores these mechanisms in considerable detail, using Cisco's implementation as an example. To accomplish this, the mechanisms of PIM-DM mode are reviewed step by step, using sample networks under typical situations. Each step examines the interim state that is created in a Cisco router and provides the tools necessary to interpret the output of various **show** commands. Furthermore, some of the basic rules that Cisco routers use to create and maintain multicast forwarding state will be covered. Use these rules to predict what the router will do under various circumstances. This knowledge is important when trying to troubleshoot PIM-DM networks.

Configuring PIM-DM

Configuring PIM-DM (or PIM sparse mode [PIM-SM] for that matter) is really quite straightforward. On each router in the network, IP multicast routing must be enabled by using the following global command (which was first introduced in IOS version 10.1):

```
ip multicast-routing
```

Then, it is best to enable PIM-DM on every interface in every router in the network, using the following interface command:

```
ip pim dense-mode
```

The reason for turning on multicast on every interface is that IP multicast routing is upside-down routing that forwards (or does not forward) multicast packets based on where the packets came from (source IP address) as opposed to where they are going (multicast group address). Consequently, the control mechanism over multicast traffic paths is not quite the same as the control mechanism over unicast routing.

NOTE   In actuality, the recommended method for enabling multicast on an interface is the use of
the **ip pim sparse-dense-mode** command. This command allows the router to use either
dense or sparse mode, depending on the existence of rendezvous point (RP) information for
each multicast group. This makes it much easier to switch the entire network from dense
mode to sparse mode (or vice versa) as needed.

Not turning on multicast routing on every interface is a common mistake when network
administrators are first enabling multicast routing. Failure to enable multicast on every
interface often results in Reverse Path Forwarding (RPF) failures. As you recall from
Chapter 2, "Multicast Basics," and Chapter 6, the RPF interface for a particular source of
multicast traffic is the interface that would be used if the router were to send traffic to this
particular source.

For example, Figure 10-1 shows two routers within a network with parallel but unequal cost
links.

Figure 10-1   *Failure to Enable Multicast on Every Interface*

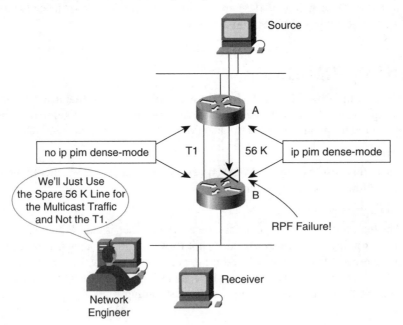

Our friendly network engineer has decided to enable **ip pim dense-mode** only on the spare 56 K line so that the multicast traffic doesn't affect the unicast traffic. Unfortunately, this results in an RPF failure for the traffic arriving over the 56 K link. Why? Because the unicast routing table will show that the best metric to the Source is via the T1 link and, therefore, PIM will compute the T1 as the RPF interface (also referred to as the incoming interface) for multicast traffic arriving from the Source. However, because multicast was enabled only on the 56 K link, the multicast traffic is arriving only on the non-RPF interface and is therefore dropped by Router B.

If this sort of network topology is necessary, it is possible to force Router B to perform an RPF to the 56 K link using static mroutes or Distance Vector Multicast Routing Protocol (DVMRP) routes. However, this can quickly get out of hand and become an administration nightmare if used on a large-scale basis throughout the network. (We discuss the use of static mroutes and DVMRP routing for traffic engineering purposes in Chapter 16.)

PIM-DM State Rules

Although configuring PIM-DM is relatively easy, it is another thing completely to understand what the router does in response to arriving multicast traffic, Prunes, grafts, and so on. Therefore, a good working knowledge of some of the basic state rules that a Cisco router employs to create and maintain multicast forwarding state is extremely valuable. This is particularly useful when trying to debug multicast problems in your network.

In Cisco routers, multicast forwarding state takes the form of (*, G) and (S, G) entries in the multicast routing table, or mroute table. This information can be displayed in a Cisco router by using the **show ip mroute** command. (See Example 10-1, in the section titled "PIM-DM State Entries" for an example of this information.)

The following section explains some of the basic state maintenance rules used in PIM-DM. In some cases, these rules are generic to both PIM-DM and PIM-SM (albeit sometimes for different reasons) and are labeled as general rules. The rules that are only applicable to dense mode are labeled as such.

NOTE	Let me point out that I am giving only the basic state rules (not a complete set of all the rules) so you have a basic understanding of how a Cisco router creates and maintains state. The reason I'm not giving you all the state rules is that, if I tried to explain them at one time, it would probably make your brain explode and that is not my goal. (I have heard a rumor, however, that the U.S. military once explored using the complete set of state rules as an offensive weapon that would cause its enemy's brains to explode. I believe that this plan was abandoned because a suitable delivery vehicle could not be found.)

PIM-DM (*, G) State Rules

Although not specifically required by the PIM-DM specification, Cisco's implementation automatically creates parent (*, G) state whenever (S, G) state is created. The primary reason is that all (S, G) data structures in Cisco's implementation of PIM are linked to a parent (*, G) data structure. The additional memory consumed as a result of maintaining these (*, G) entries in PIM-DM is minimal and is offset by gains in various internal optimizations in PIM. This leads to the first PIM general rule.

General Rule 1

Whenever it is necessary to create an (S, G) entry and a corresponding parent (*, G) entry does not exist, a new (*, G) entry is automatically created first.

Dense mode (*, G) entries are not used for multicast forwarding. They mainly function to maintain information pertaining to the group as a whole. For example, (*, G) entries denote the mode in which the group is operating (in this case dense mode) and, in dense mode, also reflect the interfaces where other PIM neighbors or directly connected members of the group exist. This information is used to initially populate the outgoing interface list (OIL) of any newly created (S, G) entries for the group. This leads to the first dense mode rule.

Dense Mode Rule 1

The outgoing interface list of a dense mode (*, G) entry reflects the interfaces where (1) other PIM-DM neighbors exist or (2) directly connected members of the group exist.

PIM-DM (S, G) State Rules

In PIM-DM, the arrival of multicast traffic creates (S, G) entries. (Again, if a parent (*, G) entry doesn't exist, it is first created and its outgoing interface list is populated as described in the previous section.)

The incoming interface for the (S, G) entry is computed by calculating the RPF interface for Source S. The RPF interface is calculated by using the following rule.

General Rule 2

The RPF interface is computed as the interface with the lowest cost path (based on administrative distance/metric) to the IP address of the source (or in the case of a sparse mode (*, G) entry, the RP). If multiple interfaces have the same cost, the interface with the highest IP address is chosen as the tiebreaker.

The default behavior is to take the lowest cost path to the source that is indicated in the unicast routing table. However, it is possible to RPF to a different interface using other sources of information, such as the Multicast Border Gateway Protocol (MBGP) table, DVMRP route table, or the static mroute table. Each table has its own administrative distance that can effect the RPF calculation. (MBGP is discussed briefly in Chapter 17, "Inter-Domain Multicast Routing." Additionally, the DVMRP route table is introduced in Chapter 13, "Connecting to DVMRP Networks," and static mroutes are described in Chapter 16, "Multicast Traffic Engineering.")

NOTE   Just as in the case of Cisco unicast routing, multicast RPF calculations use administrative distances when a route is learned from more than one routing source. This would occur when multiple routing protocols run in the router or when static routes are defined. The value of the administrative distance (often times simply referred to as distance) of each route is used as the high-order portion of the cost comparison when multiple routes for the same network are encountered. In this case, the route with the lowest distance is selected.

Table 10-1 shows the default administrative distances for the various sources of RPF data.

Table 10-1   *Administrative Distance*

Table	Default Distance
Unicast	(Distance of route)
iMBGP[1]	200
eMBGP[2]	20
DVMRP	0
Static mroutes	0

1.   Routes learned from internal MBGP peers

2.   Routes learned from external MBGP peers

It is important to note that static mroutes are preferred over other sources if the administrative distances are equivalent. Also, if multiple matching routes are found within a table, the longest matching route is used. This does not occur across tables! For example, if there is a 151.10.0.0/16 route in the DVMRP route table (assuming a default DVMRP distance of zero) and a matching 151.10.1.0/24 router in the unicast route table, the DVMRP route is used, even though the unicast route has a longer match. However, if the DVMRP route table has both a 151.10.0.0/16 and a 151.10.1.0/24 route entry, then the 151.10.1.0/24 route is used because it is from the same table.

When the (S, G) entry is created, its outgoing interface list is initially populated with a copy of the outgoing interface list from its parent (*, G) entry. (Because the outgoing interface list of the parent, dense mode (*, G) entry contains a list of all PIM neighbors or directly connected members, this copy operation results in traffic initially being forwarded in a flood-and-prune manner via the newly created (S, G) entry.) This leads to General Rule 3.

General Rule 3

When a new (S, G) entry is created, its outgoing interface list is initially populated with a copy of the outgoing interface list from its parent (*, G) entry.

However, it is quite likely that the incoming interface of an (S, G) entry was also in the copy of the outgoing interface list of the parent (*, G) entry. If you were to stop at this point, the incoming interface would also appear in the outgoing interface list for this (S, G) entry. This is a big no-no as it would lead to a multicast routing loop. Therefore, every time the RPF interface for an (S, G) entry is calculated, a check is made to determine whether the interface also exists in the outgoing interface list. If it does, the interface is removed from the outgoing interface list. The next general rule summarized this process.

General Rule 4

The incoming interface (RPF interface) of a multicast forwarding entry must never appear in its outgoing interface list.

PIM-DM State Maintenance Rules

When a multicast packet arrives and an appropriate PIM-DM state is created, the state entries are updated periodically as a result of various events.

The most common maintenance event is the periodic recalculation of the RPF interface (incoming interface) for all entries in the multicast forwarding table. The recalculation is done so that multicast routing can converge after a change in the network topology.

General Rule 5

The RPF interface (that is, the incoming interface) of every multicast state entry is recalculated every 5 seconds and the outgoing interface list is adjusted appropriately based on General Rule 4 (to prevent the incoming interface from appearing in the outgoing interface list).

Additionally, when a dense mode (S, G) entry is created, the status of each interface in the outgoing interface list is marked **Forward/Dense** to initially flood traffic out all outgoing interfaces in dense mode. Pruning one of these interfaces (as a result of receiving a Prune from a downstream neighbor for this (S, G) traffic) does not delete the interface from the outgoing interface list. Instead, it is marked **Prune/Dense,** and a 3-minute Prune timer is started. When this 3-minute Prune timer expires, the interface is returned to **Forward/ Dense** state and traffic begins flooding out this interface again.

Dense Mode Rule 2

Outgoing interfaces in dense mode (S, G) entries are not removed as a result of Prunes. Instead, they are marked as **Prune/Dense** and left in the outgoing interface list.

Finally, the interfaces in the outgoing interface list of all (S, G) entries are kept synchronized (within the constraints of General Rule 4) with the interfaces in the outgoing interface of the parent (*, G) entry. This allows any additions or deletions of PIM neighbors or directly connected group members, which is reflected by changes in the outgoing interface list of the dense mode (*, G) entry, to be reflected in the corresponding (S, G) entries. General Rule 6 summarizes this process.

General Rule 6

Additions or deletions to the outgoing interface list of a (*, G) entry are replicated (within the constraints of General Rule 4) to all associated (S, G) entries for the group.

General Rule 6 typically comes into play when a new PIM-DM neighbor is detected on another interface. This interface is first added to the outgoing interface list of the (*, G) entry according to Dense Mode Rule 1. Next, the new interface is added to the outgoing interface lists of the associated (S, G) entries according to General Rule 6 so that traffic will be flooded to this new neighbor.

By applying both the general and dense mode rules presented above, you can predict how a Cisco router will behave under typical dense mode operating conditions. If the whys and hows of the above rules seem a bit unclear at the moment, don't worry. The sections beginning with "PIM-DM Flooding" step through some typical dense mode scenarios and show how these rules result in changes in multicast forwarding state in the router and how these changes accomplish the desired multicast forwarding behavior. After reviewing these examples, what the rules accomplish will be much clearer.

PIM-DM State Entries

Before diving into some detailed examples of PIM-DM operation, it is important to have a good understanding of the PIM-DM state information that is displayed by the **show ip mroute** command. This information is frequently the source of much confusion for new multicast users and yet is one of the most important bits of information gained from the router when debugging a multicast problem. This section looks at some sample output from this command for dense mode state and examines it line by line. Defining the flags that are displayed with each entry and explaining what they mean will help you understand these entries. This is the subject of the next section.

PIM-DM State Flags

Each entry in the mroute table displays one or more state flags in the Flag field at the end of the first line of the entry. Table 10-2 explains the state flags that appear in the Flag field of dense mode entries. Understanding when these state flags are set and cleared and what they mean is a big step toward understanding mroute state.

Table 10-2 *PIM-DM State Flags*

D	Dense mode flag	The meaning of this flag should be pretty obvious. It indicates that the multicast group is a dense mode group. (Note: The D flag appears only on (*, G) entries.
C	Connected flag	The C flag appears on both (*, G) and (S, G) entries and indicates that there is a directly connected member for this multicast group (that is, a receiver).
L	Local flag	The L flag appears on both (* G) and (S, G) entries and indicates that the router itself is a member of this group. Hence, the router will process all multicast traffic sent to this group at process level.
		A good example of a group that the router itself would join is the PIM RP-Discovery (224.0.1.40) group that is used to distribute Auto-RP information.
P	Pruned flag	The P flag indicates that the outgoing interface list is either Null or all interfaces in the outgoing interface list are in the Prune state. This flag results in a Prune being sent to the upstream (RPF) neighbor for this (S, G) entry.

Table 10-2 *PIM-DM State Flags (Continued)*

T	Shortest path tree (SPT) flag	The T flag (or SPT flag) appears only on (S, G) entries and indicates that this traffic is being forwarded via the (S, G) entry (that is, the SPT). This flag is set whenever the first (S, G) packet is received corresponding to this mroute table entry (therefore, in dense mode the T flag is always set on (S, G) entries).
J	Join SPT flag	For dense mode groups, the J flag appears only on the (*, G) entry and is simply used internally to tell PIM that an (S, G) state should be automatically created for any arriving (S, G) traffic. (This flag can be ignored for dense mode groups.)

PIM-DM State Example

Now that the various flags that can be encountered in a dense mode entry have been defined, consider Example 10-1, which shows the sample output of a **show ip mroute** command.

Example 10-1 *Sample Output of **show ip mroute** Command*

```
(*, 224.2.127.254), 00:00:10/00:00:00, RP 0.0.0.0, flags: D
  Incoming interface: Null, RPF nbr 0.0.0.0
  Outgoing interface list:
    Serial0, Forward/Dense, 00:00:10/00:00:00
    Serial1, Forward/Dense, 00:00:10/00:00:00
    Serial3, Forward/Dense, 00:00:10/00:00:00

(128.9.160.43/32, 224.2.127.254), 00:00:10/00:02:50, flags: T
  Incoming interface: Serial0, RPF nbr 198.92.1.129
  Outgoing interface list:
    Serial1, Forward/Dense, 00:00:10/00:00:00
    Serial3, Prune/Dense, 00:00:10/00:02:50
```

The first line of the (*, G) entry shown in Example 10-1

```
(*, 224.2.127.254), 00:00:10/00:00:00, RP 0.0.0.0, flags: D
```

provides general information about the (*, G) entry in the multicast forwarding table (also referred to as the mroute table) and is broken down in Table 10-3.

Table 10-3 *General Information on (*, G) Entry in Example 10-1*

(*, 224.2.127.254)	Indicates that this is the (*, G) entry for multicast group 224.2.127.254.
00:00:10/00:00:00	Uptime/expire timer counters. The uptime timer shows that this entry has been up for 10 seconds, but that the expire timer is not running. (This situation is normal for (*, G) dense mode entries that have associated (S, G) entries. When all the (S, G) entries are deleted, this timer will start. At that point, if the timer expires, the (*, G) will be deleted.) Expire timers usually count down from 3 minutes. When the expiration time is reached, the state entry is deleted.
RP 0.0.0.0	Indicates the IP address of the RP. Because this is a dense mode group, there is no RP and, therefore, 0.0.0.0 is displayed.
flags: D	Indicates that this group is a dense mode group. (Note: The S (Sparse) and D flags are shown only on the (*, G) entries.)

The second line of the (*, G) entry in Example 10-1 reads as follows:

```
Incoming interface: Null, RPF nbr 0.0.0.0
```

This line, which gives RPF information about the entry, including the incoming interface and the upstream RPF neighbor, is broken down in Table 10-4.

Table 10-4 *RPF Information on (*,G) Entry in Example 10-1*

Incoming interface: Null	Indicates the incoming interface. However, because this entry is a dense mode (*, G) entry, this information is not used. Dense mode forwards using (S, G) entries instead of (*, G) entries. Therefore, the incoming interface is shown as Null.
RPF nbr 0.0.0.0	Indicates the IP address of the upstream (RPF) neighbor for this multicast traffic. Again, because you don't forward on dense mode (*, G) entries, this information is always 0.0.0.0.

The next few lines of the (*, G) entry in Example 10-1 are repeated here:

```
Outgoing interface list:
    Serial0, Forward/Dense, 00:00:10/00:00:00
    Serial1, Forward/Dense, 00:00:10/00:00:00
    Serial3, Forward/Dense, 00:00:10/00:00:00
```

These lines display the outgoing interface list for the entry. The outgoing interface list of dense mode (*, G) entries reflects any interfaces having a PIM neighbor or a directly connected member of the group. This information is used to initially populate the outgoing interface list of any (S, G) entries for Group G. The entries in this list are broken down in Table 10-5.

Table 10-5   *Outgoing Interface List for (*, G) Entry in Example 10-1*

Serial0	Indicates the outgoing interface.
Forward/dense	Indicates the forwarding state and mode of the interface. Because this entry is in the outgoing interface list of a dense mode (*, G) entry, it always reflects forward and dense mode.
00:00:10/00:00:00	Uptime/expire timer for this interface. The uptime indicates how long this interface has been in its current state (forward or Prune). The expire timer in this example is not running because forwarding dense mode interfaces never time out. (It's also not running because it's in the outgoing interface list of a dense mode (*, G) entry and is not used for forwarding.)

Here's the next line of Example 10-1 output:

```
(128.9.160.43/32, 224.2.127.254), 00:00:10/00:02:50, flags: T
```

This line provides general information about an (S, G) entry in the multicast forwarding table (also referred to as the mroute table) and is broken down in Table 10-6.

Table 10-6   *General Mroute Information for (S, G) Entry in Example 10-1*

(128.9.160.43/32, 224.2.127.254)	Indicates that this is the (S, G) entry for IP multicast source 128.9.160.43 (the /32 is a mask) sending to multicast group 224.2.127.254.
00:00:10/00:02:49	Uptime/expire timer counters. The uptime shows that this entry has been up for 10 seconds. The expire timer is running and is counting down from 3 minutes. Because this is an (S, G) entry, the timer will be reset back to 3 minutes every time the router forwards an (S, G) packet. If the expiration timer reaches zero, the router assumes that the source has stopped sending to the group and the state entry is deleted.
flags: T (SPT)	Indicates that multicast traffic for this source/group is being forwarded using this entry. (In other words, the (S, G) traffic is being forwarded on the shortest path tree.)

The second line of the (S, G) entry is

```
Incoming interface: Serial0, RPF nbr 198.92.1.129
```

This line gives RPF information about the entry including the incoming interface and the upstream RPF neighbor. This information is broken down in Table 10-7.

Table 10-7   *RPF Information on (S, G) Entry in Example 10-1*

Incoming interface: Serial0	Indicates that Serial0 is the incoming (RPF) interface for this (S, G) traffic.
RPF nbr 198.92.1.239	Indicates the IP address of the upstream (RPF) neighbor in the direction of the source is 198.92.1.239.

The remaining lines in the (S, G) entry in Example 10-1 are as follows:

```
Outgoing interface list:
    Serial1, Forward/Dense, 00:00:10/00:00:00
    Serial3, Prune/Dense, 00:00:10/00:02:50
```

These lines display the outgoing interface list for the (S, G) entry. The entries in this list are broken down in Table 10-8.

Table 10-8   *Outgoing Interface List for (S, G) Entry in Example 10-1*

Serial3	Indicates the outgoing interface.
Prune/Dense	Indicates the forwarding state and mode of the interface. Dense mode (S, G) outgoing interface list entries reflect either **Forward/Dense** or **Prune/Dense** depending on whether the interface has been pruned or not.
00:00:10/00:02:50	Uptime/expire timer for this interface. The uptime indicates how long this interface has been in its current state (forward or Prune).
	If the current state of the interface is **Forward/Dense,** the expire timer will not be running because forwarding dense mode interfaces never time out (that is, they continue to forward until they are pruned).
	If the current state of the interface is **Prune/Dense,** the expire timer reflects how long before the Prune expires and this dense mode interface will begin to flood traffic out the interface again. This Prune expiration timer is a countdown timer that begins counting down from 3 minutes whenever the interface is pruned.

PIM Forwarding

When the appropriate mroute table entries have been set up in the router, multicast traffic can be forwarded. This is accomplished as follows:

- Whenever a multicast packet is received, a search for the longest match of the mroute table is performed using the source address (S) and group address (G) of the incoming packet. This longest match search will first try to match an (S, G) entry in the table and use it. If no matching (S, G) entry exists, it will try to find a matching (*, G) entry and use it.

NOTE   Note that dense mode uses only source trees that correspond to (S, G) entries in the mroute table, and, therefore, dense mode multicast traffic is only forwarded using the (S, G) entries. Therefore, if a matching (S, G) entry doesn't exist when a multicast packet for a dense mode group arrives, an (S, G) entry is created based on the rules given in the section "PIM-DM State Rules" earlier in the chapter.

- When a matching entry is found (or created), an RPF check is performed on the incoming packet. This is accomplished by comparing the incoming interface in the matching mroute table entry with the packet's actual incoming interface. If the packet didn't arrive via the incoming interface, the packet is dropped.

    Note   Maintaining incoming interface information in the mroute table entries reduces processing overhead considerably because all that is necessary is a simple check to see whether the arrival interface matches the incoming interface. If this information was not maintained, the router would have to scan the unicast routing table each time a multicast packet arrived to perform the RPF check function. This process would have a significant impact on performance. Instead, the incoming interface information in each mroute entry is recalculated once every 5 seconds to account for any topology changes in the network.

- If the packet arrived via the correct interface (that is, the RPF check succeeded), the packet is forwarded out all unpruned interfaces in the outgoing interface list.

PIM-DM Flooding

This section examines in detail the initial PIM-DM flooding process and the multicast forwarding state that is set up in the router.

Figure 10-2 depicts a portion of a sample PIM-DM network. In this example, assume that no multicast traffic has been flowing up to this point. Now, let's assume that Router A begins receiving multicast packets from a new multicast source (128.9.160.43) for group 224.2.127.254 via Serial0.

Figure 10-2   *PIM-DM Initial Flooding*

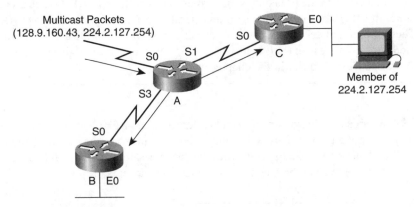

Because you are using PIM-DM, these packets are initially flooded to all PIM neighbors. To make this happen, Router A responds to the arrival of the first of these multicast packets by creating a new (S, G) entry and its parent (*, G) entry (based on General Rule 1). This information is derived by issuing the **show ip mroute** command 10 seconds after the initial packet arrives (see Example 10-2). Notice the uptime timer values on the entries.

Example 10-2   *Initial State in Router A*

```
rtr-a>show ip mroute
IP Multicast Routing Table
Flags: D - Dense, S - Sparse, C - Connected, L - Local, P - Pruned
       R - RP-bit set, F - Register flag, T - SPT-bit set, J - Join SPT
Timers: Uptime/Expires
Interface state: Interface, Next-Hop or VCD, State/Mode

(*, 224.2.127.254), 00:00:10/00:00:00, RP 0.0.0.0, flags: D
  Incoming interface: Null, RPF nbr 0.0.0.0
  Outgoing interface list:
    Serial0, Forward/Dense, 00:00:10/00:00:00
    Serial1, Forward/Dense, 00:00:10/00:00:00
    Serial3, Forward/Dense, 00:00:10/00:00:00

(128.9.160.43/32, 224.2.127.254), 00:00:10/00:02:49, flags: T
  Incoming interface: Serial0, RPF nbr 198.92.1.129
  Outgoing interface list:
    Serial1, Forward/Dense, 00:00:10/00:00:00
    Serial3, Forward/Dense, 00:00:10/00:00:00
```

Notice that Router A has automatically created the parent (*, G) entry, (*, 224.2.127.254), and populated its outgoing interface list with interfaces Serial0, Serial1, and Serial3 (based on Dense Mode Rule 1). These are the interfaces on Router A that have PIM neighbors. Note that the PIM neighbor connected to Router A's Serial0 interface is not shown.

The (S, G) entry, (128.9.160.43/32, 224.2.127.254), shown in Example 10-2 has its incoming interface computed as Serial0, with an RPF neighbor set to 198.92.1.129 (this neighbor is not shown in Figure 10-2), using the RPF calculation stated in General Rule 2. The (S, G) entry has also had its outgoing interface list initially populated from a copy of the interfaces in the (*, G) outgoing interface list (based on Dense Mode Rule 1). Finally, Serial0 (the incoming interface) was removed from the outgoing interface list (based on General Rule 4) so that the incoming interface does not appear in the outgoing interface list and cause a route loop.

Notice that all interfaces in the (S, G) outgoing interface list are in **Forward/Dense** state and their expiration timers are not running in order to flood traffic out all interfaces until a Prune is received.

PIM-DM Pruning

Continuing with the example shown in Figure 10-2, notice that Router B is a leaf node (that is, it has no downstream neighbors) for this (S, G) multicast traffic and also has no directly connected members for group G. This is reflected in the output of the **show ip mroute** command shown in Example 10-3.

Example 10-3 *Initial State in Router B*

```
rtr-b>show ip mroute
IP Multicast Routing Table
Flags: D - Dense, S - Sparse, C - Connected, L - Local, P - Pruned
       R - RP-bit set, F - Register flag, T - SPT-bit set, J - Join SPT
Timers: Uptime/Expires
Interface state: Interface, Next-Hop or VCD, State/Mode

 (*, 224.2.127.254), 00:00:12/00:00:00, RP 0.0.0.0, flags: D
  Incoming interface: Null, RPF nbr 0.0.0.0
  Outgoing interface list:
    Serial0, Forward/Dense, 00:00:12/00:00:00

(128.9.160.43/32, 224.2.127.254), 00:00:12/00:02:48, flags: PT
  Incoming interface: Serial0, RPF nbr 198.92.2.1
  Outgoing interface list: Null
```

Once again, the arrival of the first (S, G) multicast packet caused Router B to create the (S, G) and (* G) entries (based on General Rule 1). Notice that the Flags field of the (*, G) entry indicates that this is a dense mode group, and because the (*, G) entry is not used to forward multicast traffic in dense mode, the entry reflects a **Null** incoming interface. In addition, the outgoing interface list of the (*, G) contains a single entry, **Serial0**, which is the interface that connects to its PIM neighbor, Router A.

The incoming interface of the (S, G) entry has been computed as Serial0 (based on General Rule 2) with an RPF neighbor of 198.92.2.1, which is the IP address of Serial3 on Router A.

The outgoing interface list was initially populated with interfaces from the (* G) outgoing interface list, that is, Serial0. However, applying General Rule 4 and removing the incoming interface from the outgoing interface list leaves a **Null** outgoing interface list in the (S, G) entry as shown in the output of the initial state in Router B above.

Because the outgoing interface list is **Null**, Router B sets the **P** flag in the (S, G) entry and sends an (S, G) Prune (shown in Figure 10-3) upstream to Router A to shut off the flow of unnecessary (S, G) multicast traffic.

Figure 10-3 *PIM-DM Pruning*

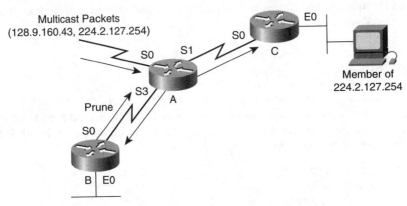

When Router A receives the Prune, the router responds by pruning interface Serial3. (Remember that there is no Prune delay on point-to-point links. Therefore, Serial3 was immediately pruned by Router A.) This results in the mroute state shown in Example 10-4.

Example 10-4 *State in Router A After Pruning*

```
rtr-a>show ip mroute
IP Multicast Routing Table
Flags: D - Dense, S - Sparse, C - Connected, L - Local, P - Pruned
       R - RP-bit set, F - Register flag, T - SPT-bit set, J - Join SPT
Timers: Uptime/Expires
Interface state: Interface, Next-Hop or VCD, State/Mode

 (*, 224.2.127.254), 00:04:10/00:00:00, RP 0.0.0.0, flags: D
  Incoming interface: Null, RPF nbr 0.0.0.0
  Outgoing interface list:
    Serial0, Forward/Dense, 00:04:10/00:00:00
    Serial1, Forward/Dense, 00:04:10/00:00:00
    Serial3, Forward/Dense, 00:04:10/00:00:00

 (128.9.160.43/32, 224.2.127.254), 00:04:10/00:02:39, flags: T
  Incoming interface: Serial0, RPF nbr 198.92.1.129
  Outgoing interface list:
    Serial1, Forward/Dense, 00:04:10/00:00:00
    Serial3, Prune/Dense, 00:01:29/00:01:31
```

Notice that interface Serial3 in the outgoing interface list of the (S, G) entry (shown in boldface) is now in **Prune/Dense** state and that the interface timers are now reflecting Prune information. The Prune timeout information of **00:01:29/00:01:31** indicates that interface Serial3 was pruned 1 minute and 29 seconds ago and that the prune will expire in 1 minute and 31 seconds. When the expiration timer counts down to zero, the interface will be placed in **Forward/Dense** state, which will result in (S, G) traffic again being flooded out Serial3 to Router B. This cycle will continually repeat itself every 3 minutes while source S is still sending Group G traffic, thereby causing Router B to send a Prune to Router A again.

Normally, when a packet is received on a non-RPF interface, the router will send a Prune in an attempt to try to get the upstream router to prune its interface and stop sending the traffic. If, for some reason, the upstream router ignores this prune and keeps sending, you don't want to send a prune for every packet received on this non-RPF interface. To avoid this, the sending of Prunes is *rate limited*.

For example, suppose for the moment that a configuration error or some other routing anomaly causes Router A to begin receiving (S, G) traffic via a point-to-point, non-RPF interface, say, Serial1, as shown in Figure 10-4.

Figure 10-4   *Rate-Limited Prunes*

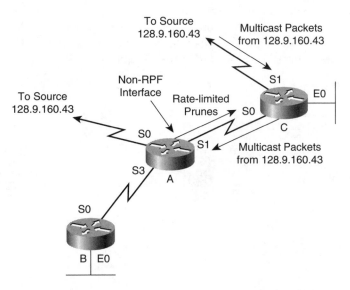

This could be caused by Router C being configured with the **ip igmp static-group <group>** command on interface Serial0 that forces the router to forward group traffic out this interface as if there were a directly connected member on the interface. (I don't know why you would intentionally do this other than to demonstrate rate-limited Prunes, but stranger things have been known to happen.)

If this occurs, Router A will respond to the arrival of packets over the non-RPF interface by sending rate-limited Prunes back out the interface in an attempt to shut off the flow of (S, G) traffic. Note that if there was not a (S, G) state before, Router A would automatically create the state with a Null outgoing interface list and continue to send back rate-limited Prunes.

NOTE   Rate-limited pruning of packets arriving on non-RPF interfaces occurs only on point-to-point interfaces. In the case of multi-access networks such as Ethernet, Prunes are not sent in response to packets arriving on non-RPF interfaces. Instead, the packets are simply discarded.

Dense Mode Grafting

Let's assume that Router B has a directly connected host Join Group G as shown in Figure 10-5. Now, Router B needs to get the flow of (S, G) traffic started as quickly as possible to deliver it to Router B's directly connected member. If Router B just simply waits until the upstream Prune state on Router A times out, the result could be a worst-case delay of 3 minutes before traffic is received. Fortunately, because Router B still has (S, G) state, it is aware that this source is active and can respond by sending a Graft message to its upstream neighbor to quickly restart the flow of multicast traffic. (The upstream neighbor is indicated in the RPF nbr field of the (S, G) entry.)

Figure 10-5   *PIM-DM Grafting*

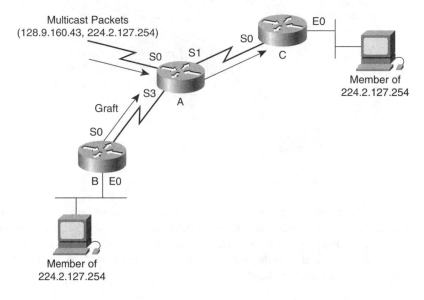

The router output in Example 10-5 shows the updated state in Router B after the directly connected member has joined the group.

Example 10-5 *State in Router B After the Graft*

```
rtr-b>show ip mroute
IP Multicast Routing Table
Flags: D - Dense, S - Sparse, C - Connected, L - Local, P - Pruned
       R - RP-bit set, F - Register flag, T - SPT-bit set, J - Join SPT
Timers: Uptime/Expires
Interface state: Interface, Next-Hop or VCD, State/Mode

 (*, 224.2.127.254), 00:04:10/00:00:00, RP 0.0.0.0, flags: D
  Incoming interface: Null, RPF nbr 0.0.0.0
  Outgoing interface list:
    Serial0, Forward/Dense, 00:04:10/00:00:00
    Ethernet0, Forward/Dense, 00:04:10/00:00:00

(128.9.160.43/32, 224.2.127.254), 00:04:10/00:02:39, flags: CT
  Incoming interface: Serial0, RPF nbr 198.92.2.1
  Outgoing interface list:
    Ethernet0, Forward/Dense, 00:00:26/00:00:00
```

Notice that the **C** flag has been set in the (S, G) entry, which indicates that Router B has a directly connected member for this traffic. Also, the (S, G) outgoing interface is no longer **Null** as it now includes **Ethernet0**. This interface was added to the outgoing interface list as a result of a directly connected member joining the group roughly 26 seconds ago. (The uptime counter value of **00:00:26** in the Ethernet0 entry of the (S, G) outgoing interface list reflects this situation.) Example 10-6 displays the state in Router A after it has received and processed the Graft from Router B.

Example 10-6 *State in Router A After the Graft*

```
rtr-a>show ip mroute
IP Multicast Routing Table
Flags: D - Dense, S - Sparse, C - Connected, L - Local, P - Pruned
       R - RP-bit set, F - Register flag, T - SPT-bit set, J - Join SPT
Timers: Uptime/Expires
Interface state: Interface, Next-Hop or VCD, State/Mode

 (*, 224.2.127.254), 00:04:10/00:00:00, RP 0.0.0.0, flags: D
 Incoming interface: Null, RPF nbr 0.0.0.0
 Outgoing interface list:
    Serial0, Forward/Dense, 00:04:10/00:00:00
    Serial1, Forward/Dense, 00:04:10/00:00:00
    Serial3, Forward/Dense, 00:04:10/00:00:00

(128.9.160.43/32, 224.2.127.254), 00:04:10/00:02:39, flags: T
  Incoming interface: Serial0, RPF nbr 198.92.1.129
  Outgoing interface list:
    Serial1, Forward/Dense, 00:04:10/00:00:00
    Serial3, Forward/Dense, 00:00:26/00:00:00
```

Notice that the state of interface Serial3 in the (S, G) outgoing interface list was updated to **Forward/Dense** as a result of the Graft that was received approximately 26 seconds ago. The uptime counter value of **00:00:26** in the Serial3 entry in the (S, G) outgoing interface list reflects this situation.

At this point, the flow of traffic to Router B has been restored as shown in Figure 10-6 as a result of **Serial3** being grafted back onto the SPT.

Figure 10-6   *PIM-DM Network After Graft*

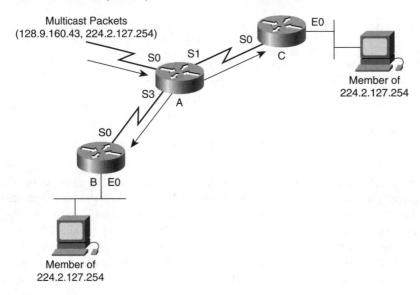

New PIM Neighbor Adjacencies

If multicast traffic is already flowing when a new PIM neighbor adjacency is established, it may be necessary to modify the dense mode forwarding state so that this new neighbor is immediately included in the flooding of the currently active multicast stream.

If the new neighbor is on a newly activated point-to-point link, the router will add this interface to the outgoing interface list of all dense mode (*, G) entries and synchronize the outgoing interface lists of all (S, G) entries to match their parent (*, G). For example, let's assume that multicast traffic is already flowing as indicated by the arrows in the dense mode network shown in Figure 10-7 and that the link from Router A to Router D is not yet up.

Figure 10-7 *New PIM Neighbor on a Point-to-Point Link*

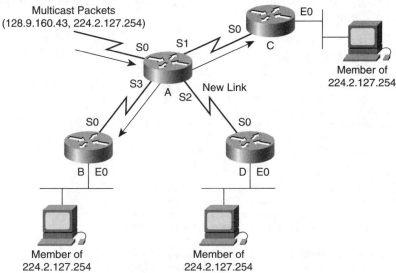

At this point, the state in Router A would be as shown in Example 10-7.

Example 10-7 *State in Router A Before New Link Is Activated*

```
rtr-a>show ip mroute
IP Multicast Routing Table
Flags: D - Dense, S - Sparse, C - Connected, L - Local, P - Pruned
       R - RP-bit set, F - Register flag, T - SPT-bit set, J - Join SPT
Timers: Uptime/Expires
Interface state: Interface, Next-Hop or VCD, State/Mode

 (*, 224.2.127.254), 00:04:10/00:00:00, RP 0.0.0.0, flags: D
  Incoming interface: Null, RPF nbr 0.0.0.0
  Outgoing interface list:
    Serial0, Forward/Dense, 00:04:10/00:00:00
    Serial1, Forward/Dense, 00:04:10/00:00:00
    Serial3, Forward/Dense, 00:04:10/00:00:00

(128.9.160.43/32, 224.2.127.254), 00:04:10/00:02:39, flags: T
  Incoming interface: Serial0, RPF nbr 198.92.1.129
  Outgoing interface list:
    Serial1, Forward/Dense, 00:04:10/00:00:00
    Serial3, Forward/Dense, 00:04:10/00:00:00
```

However, as soon as the new link has come up and an adjacency with dense mode Router D is established, the state in Router A is updated so that flooding to Router D begins to occur immediately (see Example 10-8).

Example 10-8   *State in Router A After New Link*

```
rtr-a>show ip mroute
IP Multicast Routing Table
Flags: D - Dense, S - Sparse, C - Connected, L - Local, P - Pruned
       R - RP-bit set, F - Register flag, T - SPT-bit set, J - Join SPT
Timers: Uptime/Expires
Interface state: Interface, Next-Hop or VCD, State/Mode

 (*, 224.2.127.254), 00:04:10/00:00:00, RP 0.0.0.0, flags: D
   Incoming interface: Null, RPF nbr 0.0.0.0
   Outgoing interface list:
     Serial0, Forward/Dense, 00:04:10/00:00:00
     Serial1, Forward/Dense, 00:04:10/00:00:00
     Serial3, Forward/Dense, 00:04:10/00:00:00
     Serial2, Forward/Dense, 00:00:05/00:00:00

 (128.9.160.43/32, 224.2.127.254), 00:04:10/00:02:39, flags: T
   Incoming interface: Serial0, RPF nbr 198.92.1.129
   Outgoing interface list:
     Serial1, Forward/Dense, 00:04:10/00:00:00
     Serial3, Forward/Dense, 00:04:10/00:00:00
     Serial2, Forward/Dense, 00:00:05/00:00:00
```

Notice in that interface **Serial2** was added to the outgoing interface list of the (*, G). This is a direct result of Dense Mode Rule 1, which causes the outgoing interface list of a dense mode (*, G) entry to always list those interfaces having directly connected members or PIM-DM neighbors. In addition, note that **Serial2** has been added to the outgoing interface list of the (S, G) entry. This results in traffic being forwarded to Router D out interface **Serial2**. The addition of **Serial2** to the (S, G) outgoing interface list is a result of General Rule 6, which keeps the outgoing interface list of (S, G) entries in sync with any additions or deletions to the outgoing interface list of their parent (*, G) entry.

Figure 10-8 shows a slightly different situation where the new adjacency (Router C) is being established on a multi-access network (Ethernet) with other existing dense mode neighbors (Router A and Router B).

Figure 10-8 *New PIM Neighbor on a Multi-access Network*

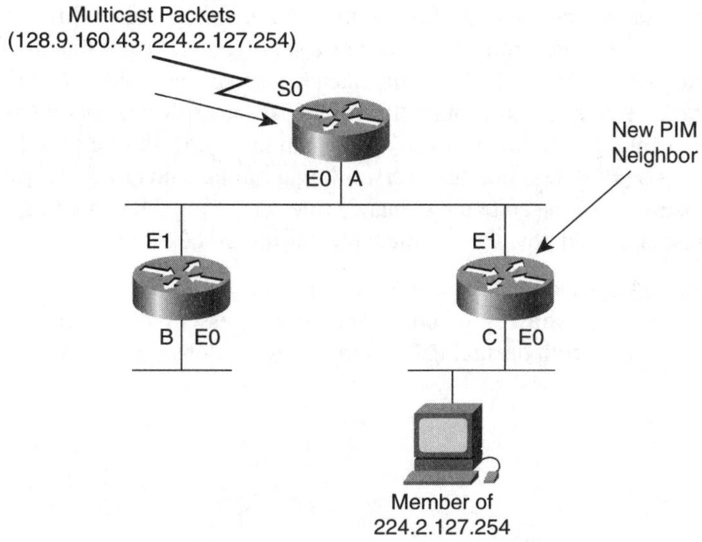

In this case, interface Ethernet0 on Router A will already be in all the appropriate outgoing interface lists and the new neighbor, Router C, will simply begin receiving the traffic that is already being flooded to the other neighbors on the network. Wait a minute! What if all of the existing neighbors (in this case Router B) on the network had already pruned this traffic flow? The new neighbor would not begin receiving the multicast traffic until the prune times out as much as 3 minutes later! Worse, Router C doesn't even know to send a Graft message upstream to restart the traffic flow because it is unaware that this multicast traffic stream even exists! (Remember that in dense mode, state is not created until traffic arrives.)

These new neighbor situations cause the addition of another rule for dense mode.

Dense Mode Rule 3

When a new PIM neighbor is added to the list of PIM neighbors on an interface, the interface is reset to **Forward/Dense** state in all PIM-DM (S, G) outgoing interface lists.

By applying this rule to dense mode groups whenever a new PIM neighbor is detected, the flooding of multicast traffic to the new neighbor can be initiated with a minimum delay. This allows the new neighbor to immediately create state for this multicast traffic flow and prune it if it is unwanted.

Summary

This chapter presented a set of dense mode rules that govern PIM-DM multicast state maintenance in Cisco routers, as well as a set of general rules that apply not only to PIM-DM but also to PIM-SM state maintenance. In addition to these rules, the format of the mroute table entries that contain this multicast state information in Cisco routers was presented along with the necessary information on how to interpret them. Finally, the examples on PIM-DM flooding, forwarding, pruning, and grafting presented in this chapter demonstrate how the state maintenance rules are applied under common PIM-DM circumstances and how the mroute table entries are effected.

A working knowledge of these rules and how they come into play and an understanding of the output from a **show ip mroute** command are essential tools for multicast network engineers faced with designing, implementing, or debugging a PIM-DM network.

CHAPTER 11

Using PIM Sparse Mode

This chapter continues building on the knowledge base of Protocol Independent Multicast (PIM) sparse mode (or PIM-SM) mechanisms introduced in Chapter 7, "PIM Sparse Mode." The use of numerous network examples and an examination of the state that is created in a Cisco router using PIM-SM supplement the detailed exploration of these mechanisms. This state is analyzed and explained in a step-by-step fashion, using the output of **show ip mroute** commands taken from the Cisco routers in the sample networks. Furthermore, the chapter covers the basic rules that Cisco routers use to create and maintain sparse mode multicast forwarding state. These rules enable you to predict what a Cisco router will do under various circumstances in PIM-SM networks. This knowledge is critical when trying to troubleshoot PIM-SM networks.

NOTE   Several of the concepts that were presented in Chapter 10, "Using PIM Dense Mode," such as the PIM forwarding rules, are also applicable to PIM-SM. Therefore, it would be a good idea to read Chapter 10 if you haven't done so already.

Configuring PIM-SM

PIM-SM is only slightly more complicated to configure than PIM-DM. All you need is knowledge of three configuration commands, and you can have sparse mode up and running. As in PIM-DM, you need to enable PIM on each router in the network by using the following global command:

```
ip multicast-routing
```

Next, enable PIM-SM on every interface in every router in the network by using the following interface command:

```
ip pim sparse-mode
```

The final step is to configure each of the routers in the network with the IP address of the rendezvous point (RP), using this global command:

```
ip pim rp-address <address>
```

This command tells the router where to send the (*, G) joins when it needs to join the shared tree in sparse mode. The use of Cisco's Auto-RP and PIMv2's Bootstrap mechanism are discussed in Chapter 12, "PIM Rendezvous Points." These are two features that enable Cisco routers in the network to dynamically learn the address of the RP without having to manually configure this information on every router in the network.

NOTE

The recommended method for enabling multicast on an interface is the use of the **ip pim sparse-dense-mode** command. This allows the router to use either dense or sparse mode, depending on the existence of RP information for each multicast group, and makes it much easier to switch the entire network from dense mode to sparse mode (or vice versa) as needed. Sparse-dense mode also allows the use of Auto-RP without having to configure every router in the network with Bootstrap RP information to get Auto-RP data to flow through the network via multicast. (We discuss Auto-RP in more detail in Chapter 12.)

PIM-SM State Rules

The preceding section established that configuring PIM-SM is only marginally more complex than configuring PIM-DM. That is to say, it is simple. If, on the other hand, you need to understand what a PIM-SM router in the network will do in response to directly connected hosts joining a group or the arriving multicast traffic, Joins, or Prunes, then this is where you, as a network administrator, are going to earn your pay. Having a solid working knowledge of basic PIM-SM state rules employed by a Cisco router is going to be crucial, particularly when trying to debug PIM-SM problems in your network.

The following section explains the key PIM-SM state maintenance rules just as Chapter 10 did for PIM-DM. As you recall, several of the general rules that were presented in that chapter also apply to PIM-SM. Just so you don't have to keep flipping back and forth between this chapter and the previous chapter to locate a specific rule, here is a list of the general rules that were presented in Chapter 10.

- **General Rule 1**—Whenever it is necessary to create an (S, G) entry and a corresponding parent (*, G) entry does not exist, a new (*, G) entry is automatically created first.

- **General Rule 2**—The Reverse Path Forwarding (RPF) interface is computed as the interface with the lowest cost path (based on administrative distance/metric) to the IP address of the source (or in the case of a sparse mode (*, G) entry, the RP). If multiple interfaces have the same cost, the interface with the highest IP address is chosen as the tiebreaker.

- **General Rule 3**—When a new (S, G) entry is created, it's outgoing interface list (OIL) is initially populated with a copy of the outgoing interface list from it's parent (*, G) entry.

- **General Rule 4**—The incoming interface of a multicast forwarding entry must never appear in its outgoing interface list.

- **General Rule 5**—The RPF interface (that is, incoming interface or IIF) of every multicast state entry is recalculated every 5 seconds, and the outgoing interface list is adjusted appropriately based on General Rule 4 (to prevent the incoming interface from appearing in the outgoing interface list).

- **General Rule 6**—Additions or deletions to the outgoing interface list of a (*, G) entry are replicated (within the constraints of General Rule 4) to all associated (S, G) entries for the group.

NOTE   Let me reiterate that I am giving you only the key state rules and not a complete set of all rules and their exceptions so you have a basic understanding of how a Cisco router creates and maintains sparse mode state.

PIM-SM (*, G) State Rules

Unlike dense mode, sparse mode (*, G) entries are used for forwarding multicast traffic. Each PIM-SM (*, G) entry in the mroute table defines the incoming and outgoing interfaces that the router uses to forward Group G traffic down the shared tree. In PIM-SM, (*, G) state is typically (although there are some exceptions) created only on demand, either as a result of directly connected host joining the group or in response to the receipt of a (*, G) Join from a downstream router.

This situation leads to the first PIM-SM state rule.

PIM-SM Rule 1

A sparse mode (*, G) entry is created as a result of an Explicit Join operation.

The initial creation of sparse mode (*, G) state can be caused by the receipt of either a (*, G) Join from a downstream PIM neighbor or an Internet Group Membership Protocol (IGMP) Membership Report from a directly connected host desiring to join Group G.

Because traffic flows down a shared tree from the RP, the incoming interface for a sparse mode (*, G) entry is computed differently than an incoming interface for an (S, G) entry. In the case of a sparse mode (*, G) entry, the IP address of the RP is used to calculate the RPF interface. This establishes a second PIM-SM rule.

PIM-SM Rule 2

The incoming interface of a sparse mode (*, G) entry always points up the shared tree toward the RP.

PIM-SM (S, G) State Rules

In PIM-SM, (S, G) entries are typically created on demand by the receipt of an Explicit (S, G) Join. (They can also be created as a result of an (S, G) Prune, but we will save this discussion for later.) An (S, G) Join is sent when a router wants to receive (S, G) traffic via the shortest path tree (SPT). (S, G) state may also be created when a last-hop router switches over to the SPT. This would occur on a router that has a directly connected member of the group and the traffic rate flowing down the shared tree exceeds the SPT-Threshold for the group.

This leads to the next PIM-SM state rule:

PIM-SM Rule 3

A sparse mode (S, G) entry is created under the following conditions:

- Receipt of an (S, G) Join/Prune message

- On a last-hop router when it switches to the SPT

- Unexpected arrival of (S, G) traffic when no (*, G) state exists

- At the RP when a Register message is received

Notice that the first item in PIM-SM Rule 3 is virtually identical to PIM-SM Rule 1 for (*, G) state entries. I could have generalized PIM-SM Rule 1 to cover both cases; however, I find that people tend to forget that the PIM-SM SPTs are also created (and hence (S, G) state created) by using the same basic Explicit Join mechanism as the shared tree. Therefore, I have stated this rule separately to emphasis the point.

PIM-SM Outgoing Interface Rules

The outgoing interface lists of (*, G) and (S, G) entries are handled a little differently in sparse mode than they were in dense mode. In sparse mode, an interface is added or removed from the outgoing interface list as a result of Explicit Joins or Prunes.

This leads to the following rule governing outgoing interfaces:

PIM-SM Rule 4

An interface is added to the outgoing interface list of a sparse mode (*, G) or (S, G) entry in either of the following conditions:

- When an appropriate (*, G) or (S, G) Join is received via this interface
- When a directly connected member of the group exists on the interface

---

As an example, if a (*, G) Join is received from a downstream neighbor over an interface, that interface is added to the outgoing interface of the (*, G) entry. (Note: This event may also result in the addition of this interface to the outgoing interface lists of all child (S, G) entries for the group, based on General Rule 6 which keeps the (S, G) outgoing interfaces in sync with the parent (*, G) entry.)

Let's take a look at an example for an (S, G) Join. Assume that a router receives an (S, G) Join from a downstream neighbor via some interface. In this case, the interface is added to the outgoing interface list of the (S, G) entry only—the (S, G) Join is specific to SPT for Source S and Group G and is not applicable to the shared tree that the (*, G) entry controls.

The removal of interfaces from the outgoing interface list of sparse mode (*, G) and (S, G) entries are governed by PIM-SM Rule 5.

PIM-SM Rule 5

An interface is removed from the outgoing interface list of a sparse mode (*, G) or (S, G) entry in either of the following situations:

- When an appropriate (*, G) or (S, G) Prune (that is not overridden) is received via this interface (and where there is no directly connected member)
- When the interface's expiration timer counts down to zero

Notice that this situation is different from dense mode where you leave the pruned interface in the outgoing interface list and change its state to **Prune/Dense**. Therefore, you should never see an interface in a sparse mode outgoing interface list whose state is marked as **Prune/Sparse**. (If you do, it's a bug!)

PIM-SM Rule 4 and PIM-SM Rule 5 basically mean that the outgoing interface list of a sparse mode (*, G) or (S, G) entry always reflects the interfaces in which (1) a downstream PIM-SM neighbor has joined the tree or (2) a directly connected member of the group exists.

PIM-SM Outgoing Interface Timers

Interface expiration timers of interfaces in sparse mode outgoing interface lists are also handled differently than similar elements are handled in dense mode. Whenever an interface is added to an outgoing interface list of a sparse mode (*, G) or (S, G) entry, the expiration timer is initialized to 3 minutes and begins to start counting down to zero. Thus, if nothing else happens to reset this count (back to 3 minutes), the interface would be removed from the outgoing interface list according to the second item in PIM-SM Rule 5.

PIM-SM State Maintenance Rules

After all sparse mode state has been created through Explicit Joins and/or Prunes, the state entries are updated periodically as a result of various events. The most important event is the periodic recalculation of the RPF interface (incoming interface) for all entries in the multicast forwarding table. This topic was discussed in Chapter 10 and is described by General Rule 5. The recalculation of RPF interface information is necessary so that multicast routing can converge after a change in the network topology.

To prevent interfaces from being removed prematurely from the outgoing interface list, the reset of interface expiration timers are governed by PIM-SM Rule 6.

PIM-SM Rule 6

The expiration timer of an interface is reset to 3 minutes as a result of either of the following conditions:

- An appropriate (*, G) or (S, G) Join is received via this interface.

- An IGMP Membership Report is received from a directly connected member on this interface.

Because downstream neighbors periodically (once a minute) refresh state by sending (*, G) and (S, G) Joins, the first part of PIM-SM Rule 6 will keep the interface's expiration timer from reaching zero. This behavior can best be observed by periodically issuing a **show ip mroute** command and watching the interface expiration timers. The expiration timers will continuously count down from 3 minutes to 2 minutes (roughly) and then be reset back up to 3 minutes.

Special PIM-SM (S, G)RP-Bit State Rules

Chapter 7 discussed the capability of PIM-SM last-hop routers to switch from the shared tree to a source's SPT to cut through the network and reduce latency. When the last-hop router has switched to the (S, G) SPT for (S, G) traffic, that router no longer needs to receive the same (S, G) traffic down the shared tree.

To stop the flow of this redundant (S, G) traffic down the shared tree, a router with (S, G) state will send a special (S, G) Prune with the RP-bit set up the shared tree. Because the RP-bit is set in this (S, G) Prune, this message as an (S, G)RP-bit Prune.

Setting the RP-bit in an (S, G) Prune indicates to the receiving router that the prune is applicable to the shared tree (otherwise known as the RP Tree, hence the name RP-bit). The receiving router therefore interprets this message as a request to prune the specified (S, G) traffic from this branch of the shared tree.

Sending (S, G)RP-Bit Prunes

As you recall from the overview of PIM-SM presented in Chapter 7, there are times when a router wishes to prune a specific source's traffic from the shared tree. This would occur when a router has joined the SPT for the source and no longer wants to receive the source's traffic via the shared tree. This prune is accomplished by sending an (S, G)RP-bit Prune up the shared tree. However, to avoid sending conflicting (S, G) Join and (S, G)RP-bit Prunes out the same interface, the following rule, PIM-SM Rule 7, is applied.

PIM-SM Rule 7

Routers will send an (S, G)RP-bit Prune up the shared tree when the RPF neighbor for the (S, G) entry is different from the RPF neighbor of the (*, G) entry.

The preceding rule basically means that the (S, G)RP-bit Prune will originate at the point where the shared tree and the SPT diverge. In many cases, the origination of the (S, G)RP-bit Prune will occur at the last-hop router that joined the (S, G) SPT. (The example in Figure 11-1 shows this situation.) However, this is not true when the shared tree and the SPT are congruent at the last-hop router. (An example is shown later in SPT-Switchover.)

Receiving (S, G)RP-Bit Prunes

When a router receives an (S, G)RP-bit Prune from a downstream neighbor, it does the following:

1 Creates an (S, G) state entry (if it doesn't already exist).

2 Sets the RP-bit in the (S, G) entry (denoted by the R flag).

3 Populates the outgoing interface list of the (S, G) entry with a copy of the interfaces from the parent (*, G) entry based on General Rule 3.

4 Removes (that is, prunes) the interface from which the (S, G)RP-bit Prune was received from the outgoing interface list.

5 (Re)computes the RPF information (incoming interface and RPF neighbor) of the (S, G) entry based on the RP address instead of the source address.

The reason that the last step is performed may not be immediately obvious and deserves additional discussion. Because the RP-bit signifies that this (S, G) forwarding state is applicable to the shared tree, the incoming interface of the (S, G) entry must point up the shared tree toward the RP instead of toward Source S. This leads to the PIM-SM Rule 8 that controls the calculation of the RPF interface for sparse mode (S, G) entries.

PIM-SM Rule 8

The RPF interface (that is, the incoming interface) of a sparse mode (S, G) entry is calculated by using the IP address of the source except when the RP-bit is set, in which case the IP address of the RP is used.

After this rule (along with General Rule 4, which prevents the incoming interface from appearing in the outgoing interface list) has been applied, the resulting (S, G)RP-bit entry will control the forwarding/pruning of (S, G) traffic flowing down the shared tree.

The reason that the (S, G)RP-bit entry will control the flow of (S, G) traffic down the shared tree is that the incoming interface of the (S, G) entry is now pointing up the shared tree as a result of the RP-bit being set and PIM-SM Rule 8 being applied. Additionally, the interface that the (S, G)RP-bit Prune was received on is removed from the outgoing interface list of the (S, G) entry because this was, after all, a Prune.

Figure 11-1 shows an example of two routers, Router B and Router C, both receiving (S, G) traffic down the shared tree.

Figure 11-1 *Traffic Flow Before (S, G)RP-Bit Prune*

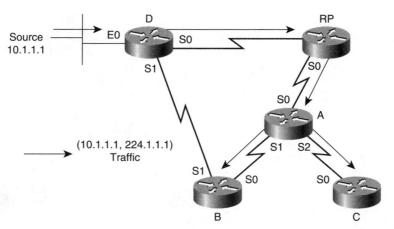

Example 11-1 shows the initial state in Router A.

Example 11-1 *Initial State in Router A Before (S, G)RP-Bit Prune*

```
rtr-a>show ip mroute
IP Multicast Routing Table
Flags: D - Dense, S - Sparse, C - Connected, L - Local, P - Pruned
       R - RP-bit set, F - Register flag, T - SPT-bit set, J - Join SPT
Timers: Uptime/Expires
Interface state: Interface, Next-Hop or VCD, State/Mode

 (*, 224.1.1.1), 00:00:12/00:00:00, RP 10.1.5.1, flags: S
  Incoming interface: Serial0, RPF nbr 198.92.2.1
  Outgoing interface list:
    Serial1, Forward/Sparse, 00:00:12/00:02:48
    Serial2, Forward/Sparse, 00:04:28/00:02:32
```

Assume that Router B joins the SPT to Source S via Router D and sends an (S, G)RP-bit Prune to Router A, which stops the redundant flow of (S, G) traffic down the shared tree as shown in Figure 11-2.

Figure 11-2   *Traffic Flow After (S, G) RP-Bit Prune*

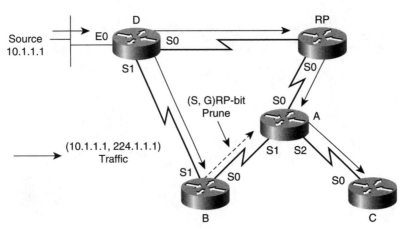

When Router A receives the (S, G)RP-bit Prune, it creates an (S, G) entry based on the rules presented earlier in this section. The state in Router A is shown in Example 11-2.

Example 11-2   *State in Router A After the (S, G)RP-Bit Prune*

```
rtr-a>show ip mroute
IP Multicast Routing Table
Flags: D - Dense, S - Sparse, C - Connected, L - Local, P - Pruned
       R - RP-bit set, F - Register flag, T - SPT-bit set, J - Join SPT
Timers: Uptime/Expires
Interface state: Interface, Next-Hop or VCD, State/Mode

 (*, 224.1.1.1), 00:04:35/00:00:00, RP 10.1.5.1, flags: S
  Incoming interface: Serial0, RPF nbr 198.92.2.1
  Outgoing interface list:
    Serial1, Forward/Sparse, 00:00:19/00:02:41
    Serial2, Forward/Sparse, 00:04:35/00:02:25

(10.1.1.1/32, 224.1.1.1), 00:00:07/00:02:43, flags: RT
  Incoming interface: Serial0, RPF nbr 198.92.2.1
  Outgoing interface list:
    Serial2, Forward/Sparse, 00:00:07/00:02:53
```

Now, when a (10.1.1.1, 224.1.1.1) packet arrives at Router A via the shared tree, Router A will search its mroute table for a matching entry. Finding the matching (S, G) entry, Router A will use it (because an existing (S, G) entry is always used) to forward the packet. Router A then checks the incoming interface information in the (10.1.1.1, 224.1.1.1) entry to see whether the arriving packet passes the RPF check. Because the RP-bit (denoted by the **R** flag in the (S, G) entry) is set, the incoming interface (Serial0) points up the shared tree toward the RP instead of toward the source (via Serial1) as a result of the application of PIM-SM Rule 8. Because the packet is flowing down the shared tree and, therefore, arrives via Serial0, the RPF check succeeds and Router A will then forward the packet out all interfaces in the outgoing interface list.

Hopefully, you noticed that interface Serial1 is not in the outgoing interface list of the (10.1.1.1, 224.1.1.1) entry. The interface is missing because it was removed by the (S, G)RP-bit Prune. The result is that the (S, G) traffic is pruned from the leg of the shared tree that runs from Router A to Router B.

NOTE   If the preceding (S, G)RP-bit Prune mechanism is perfectly clear to you at this point, give yourself a major pat on the back, as you have just learned one of the more difficult concepts of PIM-SM. However, if it is not clear, don't despair. We will return to this process in the section on SPT-Switchover later in this chapter.

PIM-SM State Entries

Having a solid understanding of the PIM state information that is displayed by the **show ip mroute** command is even more important in sparse mode than in dense mode. This section looks at a sample output from this command for a sparse mode group and examines it line by line.

Consider the sample output of a **show ip mroute** command shown in Example 11-3.

Example 11-3   *Sample Output for **show ip mroute** Command*

```
(*, 224.2.127.254), 00:03:10/00:00:00, RP 10.1.5.1, flags: S
  Incoming interface: Serial0, RPF nbr 198.92.1.129
  Outgoing interface list:
    Serial1, Forward/Sparse, 00:03:10/00:02:50
    Serial3, Forward/Sparse, 00:03:10/00:02:50

(128.9.160.43/32, 224.2.127.254), 00:00:40/00:02:20, flags: T
  Incoming interface: Serial1, RPF nbr 198.92.2.1
  Outgoing interface list:
    Serial3, Forward/Sparse, 00:00:40/00:02:20
```

The first line in Example 11-3 contains general information about the (*, G) entry in the multicast forwarding table (also referred to as the mroute table) and is broken down in Table 11-1.

Table 11-1 *General Information on (*, G) Entry for Example 11-3*

(*, 224.2.127.254)	Indicates that this is the (*, G) entry for multicast group 224.2.127.254.
00:03:10/00:00:00	Uptime/expire timer counters. The uptime shows that this entry has been up for 3 minutes and 10 seconds, whereas the expire timer is not running. (This condition is normal for (*, G) sparse mode entries when a child (S, G) entry exists.) Expire timers usually count down from 3 minutes. When the expiration time is reached, the state entry is deleted.
RP 10.1.5.1	Indicates the IP address of the RP.
flags: S	Indicates that this group is a sparse mode group. (Note: The S (Sparse) and D flags are shown only on (*, G) entries.)

The second line in Example 11-3 provides RPF information about the entry including the incoming interface (also referred to as the RPF interface) and the upstream RPF neighbor and is broken down in Table 11-2.

Table 11-2 *RPF Information on (*, G) Entry for Example 11-3*

Incoming interface: Serial0	Indicates that the incoming interface for traffic flowing down the shared tree is Serial0. (Note: Because the RP is the root of the shared tree, the incoming interface is always the Null interface when this command is executed on the RP.)
RPF nbr 198.92.1.129	Indicates the IP address of the upstream (RPF) neighbor for this multicast traffic.

The next few lines of the (*, G) entry in Example 11-3 are shown here:

```
Outgoing interface list:
    Serial1, Forward/Sparse, 00:03:10/00:02:50
    Serial3, Forward/Sparse, 00:03:10/00:02:50
```

These lines display the outgoing interface list for the entry. The outgoing interface list of sparse mode (*, G) entries reflects downstream interfaces on the shared tree. This information is used to initially populate the outgoing interface list of any (S, G) entries for Group G. The entries in this list are broken down in Table 11-3.

Table 11-3 *Outgoing Interface List Information on (*, G) Entry for Example 11-3*

Serial1	Indicates the outgoing interface.
Forward/Sparse	Indicates the forwarding state and mode of the interface.
00:03:10/00:02:50	Uptime/expire timer for this interface. The uptime indicates how long this interface has been in forward state. The expire timer indicates that this interface will expire in 2 minutes and 50 seconds at which time it will be removed from the outgoing interface list.

Here's the next line of Example 11-3:

```
(128.9.160.43/32, 224.2.127.254), 00:00:40/00:02:20, flags: T
```

This line gives you general information about an (S, G) entry in the multicast forwarding table (also referred to as the mroute table) and is broken down in Table 11-4.

Table 11-4 *General Mroute Information for (S, G) Entry in Example 11-3*

(128.9.160.43/32, 224.2.127.254)	The (S, G) entry for IP multicast source 128.9.160.43 (the /32 is a mask) sending to multicast group 224.2.127.254.
00:00:40/00:02:20	Uptime/expire timer counters. The uptime shows that this entry has been up for 40 seconds. The expire timer is running and is counting down from 3 minutes. Because this is an (S, G) entry, this timer will be reset back to 3 minutes every time the router forwards an (S, G) packet. (In this case, a packet was received roughly 7 seconds ago.) If the expiration timer reaches zero, the router assumes that the source has stopped sending to the group and the state entry is deleted.
flags: T	Indicates that multicast traffic for this source/group is being forwarded using this entry. (In other words, the (S, G) traffic is being forwarded on the SPT.)

The second line of the (S, G) entry is

```
Incoming interface: Serial1, RPF nbr 198.92.2.1
```

This line gives you RPF information about the entry including the incoming interface (also referred to as the RPF interface) and the upstream RPF neighbor and is broken down in Table 11-5.

Table 11-5 *RPF Information on (S, G) Entry in Example 11-3*

Incoming interface: Serial1	Indicates that Serial1 is the incoming (RPF) interface for the (S, G) traffic flowing down the SPT.
RPF nbr 198.92.2.1	Indicates the IP address of the upstream (RPF) neighbor for this multicast traffic is 198.92.2.1.

The remaining lines in the (S, G) entry in Example 11-3 are as follows:

```
Outgoing interface list:
    Serial3, Forward/Sparse, 00:00:40/00:02:20
```

These lines display the outgoing interface list for the (S, G) entry. The entries in this list are broken down in Table 11-6.

Table 11-6   *Outgoing Interface List for (S, G) Entry in Example 11-3*

Serial3	Indicates the outgoing interface.
Forward/Sparse	Indicates the forwarding state and mode of the interface.
00:00:40/00:02:20	Uptime/expire timer counters. The uptime shows that this entry has been up for 40 seconds. The expire timer is running and is counting down from 3 minutes. The expire timer will be reset back to 3 minutes every time an (S, G) Join is received from a downstream neighbor via this interface. (In this case, an (S, G) Join was received roughly 40 seconds ago.) The expire timer can also be reset by the existence of directly connected members on this interface.

PIM-SM State Flags

In the PIM-SM state entries in Example 11-3, you saw the Flag field on each entry and encountered just a few of the possible sparse mode flags. Table 11-7 explains the State flags that can be found in the Flag field of sparse mode entries. After you have a good understanding of when these State flags are set and cleared and what they mean, you will have come a long way toward understanding mroute state.

Table 11-7   *PIM-SM State Flags*

S	Sparse mode flag	The meaning of this flag should be pretty obvious. The S flag indicates that the multicast group is a sparse mode group. (Note: The S flag appears only on (*, G) entries.)
C	Connected flag	The C flag appears on both (*, G) and (S, G) entries and indicates that there is a directly connected member for this multicast group.
L	Local flag	The L flag appears on both (* G) and (S, G) entries and indicates that the router itself is a member of this group. Therefore, the router will process all multicast traffic sent to this group at process level. A good example of a group that the router itself would join is the PIM RP-Discovery (224.0.1.40) group that distributes Auto-RP information.
P	Pruned flag	The P flag indicates that the outgoing interface list is Null. This condition causes a Prune to be sent to the upstream (RPF) neighbor for this (*, G) or (S, G) entry.
T	SPT flag	The T flag (or SPT flag) appears only on (S, G) entries and indicates that this traffic is being forwarded via the (S, G) entry (that is, the SPT). This flag is set whenever the first (S, G) packet is received corresponding to this mroute table entry.
X	Proxy-Join timer flag	The X flag appears only on (S, G) entries and indicates that the Proxy-Join timer is running. (This flag was introduced in IOS 12.0 and is discussed in the section titled "Proxy-Join Timer" later in the chapter.)

Table 11-7 *PIM-SM State Flags (Continued)*

J	Join SPT flag (*, G)	For sparse mode (*, G) entries, the J flag is set whenever the rate of traffic flowing down the shared tree exceeds the SPT-Threshold. (This calculation is done once a second.) When the J flag has been set on the (*, G) entry, the next (S, G) packet received down the shared tree will cause source S to be cut over to the SPT. (This switchover occurs only if the C flag is also set.)
J	Join SPT flag (S, G)	The J flag is set on sparse mode (S, G) entries to indicate that this source was previously cut over to the SPT. This flag tells PIM to check the traffic rate flowing down the SPT against the SPT-Threshold to see whether this source should be switched back to the shared tree. (This calculation is only done once a minute to prevent a flip-flop condition.)
F	Register flag	The F flag is used on (S, G) entries to indicate that we must send Register messages for this traffic. (How we got F out of "Register" is a mystery to me.)
		The F flag is typically set on an (S, G) entry when a multicast source S is directly connected to the router sending traffic to Group G.
R	RP-bit flag (S, G) only	The R flag is the RP-bit flag and indicates that the information in the (S, G) entry is applicable to the shared tree. (The shared tree is sometimes called the RP Tree, hence the name, "RP-bit".) (S, G)RP-bit entries are used to prune redundant (S, G) traffic from the shared tree after a downstream router has joined the SPT for Source S.
		(Note: When the RP-bit is set, the (S, G) incoming interface is switched to point toward the RP instead of the source, S. This is done so that the RPF check will succeed for (S, G) traffic flowing down the shared tree.)

Joining the Shared Tree

Now that you have a good understanding of the basic sparse mode state rules and also how to interpret the sparse mode mroute state information, let's now take a closer look at the various mechanisms used by PIM-SM, beginning with joining the shared tree.

The example in Figure 11-3 depicts the sequence of events that take place when a host (Rcvr A) joins a multicast group, thereby triggering the local Designated Router (DR) (in this case, Router B) to join the shared tree for the group.

Figure 11-3   *Joining the Shared Tree*

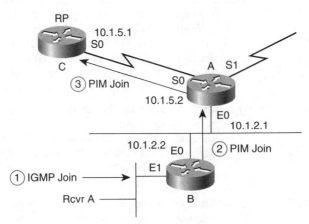

Host Rcvr A signals its desire to join multicast group 224.1.1.1 by multicasting an IGMP Membership Report to 224.1.1.1 (step 1). We frequently refer to this action as sending an "IGMP Join" although, technical speaking, we are actually sending an IGMP Membership Report. It's just easier to say "IGMP Join," and everyone knows what we mean.

When the DR, Router B, receives this IGMP Join for group 224.1.1.1, the DR scans its mroute table for a (*, G) entry for this group. Because there has been no previous activity for this group, Router B does not find a (*, 224.1.1.1) entry and therefore must create a new (*, G) entry. The result is that the state shown in Example 11-4 is created in Router B.

Example 11-4   *State in Router B After Receiving the IGMP Join from Rcvr A*

```
rtr-b>show ip mroute
IP Multicast Routing Table
Flags: D - Dense, S - Sparse, C - Connected, L - Local, P - Pruned
       R - RP-bit set, F - Register flag, T - SPT-bit set, J - Join SPT
Timers: Uptime/Expires
Interface state: Interface, Next-Hop or VCD, State/Mode

(*, 224.1.1.1), 00:00:05/00:02:59, RP 10.1.5.1, flags: SC
  Incoming interface: Ethernet0, RPF nbr 10.1.2.1
  Outgoing interface list:
  Ethernet1, Forward/Sparse, 00:00:05/00:02:55
```

The output of the **show ip mroute** command in Example 11-4 shows a single (*, G) entry for group 224.1.1.1. The first line of this entry indicates that it was created (based on PIM-SM Rule 1) roughly 5 seconds ago. In this case, the entry was created as a result of the receipt of the IGMP Join from Rcvr A. The entry will expire in roughly 3 minutes and the RP for this group is 10.1.5.1 (Router C). Finally, because there is a directly connected member (Rcvr A) for this group, the C flag has been set on this (*, G) entry.

The second line shows the incoming (RPF) interface for this (*, G) entry to be Ethernet0. This RPF information was computed using PIM-SM Rule 2 and General Rule 2, which dictate the address to use (source or RP) in the RPF calculation and how to calculate the RPF information. In this case, the RPF information in the second line points up the shared tree toward the RP through RPF neighbor 10.1.2.1, which is Router A.

The remaining lines of the entry show the outgoing interface list, and it contains a single entry for Ethernet1, which was added as a result of PIM-SM Rule 4, which controls the population of outgoing interfaces. In this case, Ethernet1 was added to the outgoing interface list as the indirect result of the receipt of an IGMP Join from Rcvr A via Ethernet1.

Technically speaking, Ethernet1 was added to the outgoing interface list because the IGMP Membership Cache contains an entry indicating that there is at least one directly connected member of this group on this interface. You can verify this by using the **show ip igmp group** command to show the contents of the IGMP Membership Cache, as shown in Example 11-5.

Example 11-5 *Results of the **show ip igmp group** Command*

```
rtr-b>show ip igmp group
IGMP Connected Group Membership
Group Address    Interface         Uptime    Expires    Last Reporter
224.1.1.1        Ethernet1         00:0010   00:01:39   171.70.144.21
```

Notice that the output of this command shows only the **Last Reporter** for this group on this interface. The router does not need to keep track of all members of the group on the interface; in fact, all the router needs to know is whether at least one member of the group is still active on this interface. (This example only has a single member active on the interface, so presumably it is the address of Rcvr A.)

Finally, successive **show ip mroute** commands would show that the interface expire timer for Ethernet1 in the outgoing interface list was periodically being reset back to 3 minutes. In this case, the timer is being reset because an entry for this group exists on this interface in the IGMP Membership Cache.

Let's continue with the next step of the "joining the shared tree" example shown in Figure 11-3. Because Router B created a new (*, G) entry, it sends a triggered (*, G) Join up the shared tree to its RPF neighbor, Router A (step 2). The Join is actually multicast on Ethernet0 and is heard by all PIM neighbors on the network. However, the address of the RPF neighbor, in this case 10.1.2.1, is contained in the Join, which informs Router A that the Join is addressed to it.

When Router A receives this (*, G) Join, A too must create a new (*, G) entry for group 224.1.1.1 in the same fashion (and by applying the same rules) as did Router B. This results in the following state in Router A (see Example 11-6), which was obtained using the **show ip mroute** command.

Example 11-6 *State in Router A After Processing (*, G) Join from Router B*

```
rtr-a>show ip mroute
IP Multicast Routing Table
Flags: D - Dense, S - Sparse, C - Connected, L - Local, P - Pruned
       R - RP-bit set, F - Register flag, T - SPT-bit set, J - Join SPT
Timers: Uptime/Expires
Interface state: Interface, Next-Hop or VCD, State/Mode

 (*, 224.1.1.1), 00:01:10/00:02:59, RP 10.1.5.1, flags: S
  Incoming interface: Serial0, RPF nbr 10.1.4.1
  Outgoing interface list:
    Ethernet0, Forward/Sparse, 00:01:10/00:02:50
```

In this case, Serial0 is the incoming interface and Ethernet0 was added to the outgoing interface list as a result of the receipt of the (*, G) Join from downstream neighbor, Router B.

Pay particular attention to the fact that the C flag is *not* set in the (*, 224.1.1.1) entry in Router A. Why? Because in this example, Router A does not have any directly connected members of group 224.1.1.1. However, if a host on Ethernet0, for example, were to join the group at some point, then the C flag would also be set in the (*, 224.1.1.1) entry on Router A. (We can use the **show ip igmp group** command to verify that there is or isn't a directly connected member for this group.)

Once again, if you do successive **show ip mroute** commands, you will see that the interface expire timer on Ethernet0 in the outgoing interface list is periodically being reset back to 3 minutes. This time, however, the interface expire timer is being reset by the receipt of (*, G) Joins sent periodically (once a minute) by Router B to refresh this branch of shared tree.

Refer back to Figure 11-3 for the final step of the example. Because Router A also had to create a new (*, G) entry, A sends a triggered (*, G) Join up the shared tree to its RPF neighbor, Router C (step 3). In this case, the RPF neighbor *is* the RP.

When the RP receives the (*, G) Join from Router A, it responds by creating a (*, G) entry in its mroute table, as shown by the output of a **show ip mroute** command listed in Example 11-7.

Example 11-7 *State in the RP After Processing the (*, G) Join from Router A*

```
rtr-c>show ip mroute
IP Multicast Routing Table
Flags: D - Dense, S - Sparse, C - Connected, L - Local, P - Pruned
       R - RP-bit set, F - Register flag, T - SPT-bit set, J - Join SPT
Timers: Uptime/Expires
Interface state: Interface, Next-Hop or VCD, State/Mode

 (*, 224.1.1.1), 00:03:14/00:02:59, RP 10.1.5.1, flags: S
  Incoming interface: Null, RPF nbr 0.0.0.0,
  Outgoing interface list:
    Serial0, Forward/Sparse, 00:03:14/00:02:45
```

Here again, Router C applied the same rules to the creation of the (*, G) state as did Router B and Router A. This process caused Serial0 (the interface by which the (*, G) Join was received) to be placed in the entry's outgoing interface list. If you again do successive **show ip mroute** commands, you will see that the interface expire timer on Serial0 is also being reset by the receipt the periodic (*, G) Joins from Router A that are arriving roughly once a minute.

Notice that the incoming interface in the (*, G) entry on the RP is a bit different from the other routers. The incoming interface is Null, and the RPF neighbor is 0.0.0.0 (that is, there is no RPF neighbor). This occurs simply because the RP is the "root" of the shared tree, and, therefore, both the incoming interface and the RPF neighbor are meaningless. A good analogy to this situation would be to stand at the North Pole. Now take 10 steps to the north. You can't! Just as you can't travel any further up the shared tree than the RP.

At this point, you have successfully set up state in all the routers shown in Figure 11-3, which effectively builds a branch of the shared tree for group 224.1.1.1. This branch starts at the RP (Router C) and extends through Router A on down to Router B where the directly connected member, "Rcvr A", resides. Any multicast traffic arriving at the RP (the next section explains how traffic gets to the RP) is forwarded down this branch and received by Rcvr A.

PIM Register Process

Now that you have examined the details of how mroute state is set up to build the shared tree from the RP down to the receivers, you need to understand how multicast traffic gets to the RP in the first place.

Recall from Chapter 7 that PIM-SM uses a unidirectional shared tree where multicast traffic can only flow *down* the branches from the RP. To get multicast traffic to the RP, first-hop routers (routers with directly connected sources) use a Register process to basically notify the RP of the existence of a source of multicast traffic. The RP processes the Register messages sent by the first-hop router and then joins the SPT to the source to "pull" the multicast traffic flow to the RP. This traffic is then delivered down the shared tree to the receivers.

Naturally, the preceding description is a simplified version of the PIM Register process. The next few sections look at this process in considerable detail, again using several sample networks and the output of **show ip mroute** commands to explain the process.

We will break the PIM Register process into three scenarios and examine each in detail. These scenarios are

- Receivers join the shared tree first
- Sources register first
- Receivers along the SPT between source and RP join the group

Receivers Join First

Figure 11-3 showed how mroute state is built all the way up the shared tree to and including the RP when a receiver joins the multicast group. Let's assume that process has already taken place and two branches of the shared tree have been built before any sources begin sending.

Figure 11-4 shows a portion of the network that includes the RP with two branches of the shared tree already built on Serial0 and Serial1.

Figure 11-4 *Initial Network with Two Branches of the Shared Tree*

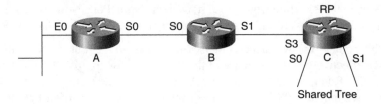

If we look at the state in the RP before any source begins sending, we would see the state shown in Example 11-8.

Example 11-8 *State in the RP with Two Branches of the Shared Tree*

```
rtr-c>show ip mroute
IP Multicast Routing Table
Flags: D - Dense, S - Sparse, C - Connected, L - Local, P - Pruned
       R - RP-bit set, F - Register flag, T - SPT-bit set, J - Join SPT
Timers: Uptime/Expires
Interface state: Interface, Next-Hop or VCD, State/Mode

 (*, 224.1.1.1), 00:03:14/00:02:59, RP 10.1.5.1, flags: S
  Incoming interface: Null, RPF nbr 0.0.0.0,
  Outgoing interface list:
    Serial0, Forward/Sparse, 00:01:36/00:02:24
    Serial1, Forward/Sparse, 00:03:14/00:02:45
```

The other two routers in the example, Router A and Router B, initially do not have any state because they have not had any directly connected hosts either join the group or begin sending to the group. If you do a **show ip mroute** command for the sample group 224.1.1.1 on these routers at this point, you would see the output shown in Example 11-9.

Example 11-9   *Initial State in Router A and Router B*

```
rtr-a>show ip mroute 224.1.1.1

Group 224.1.1.1 not found.


rtr-b>show ip mroute 224.1.1.1

Group 224.1.1.1 not found.
```

Now that the stage is set, let's activate a multicast source for group 224.1.1.1 and see what happens. Figures 11-5 through 11-8 reflect the following eight steps that are involved in the Register process when the receiver joins first:

Step 1   Source begins sending Group G traffic.

Step 2   Router A encapsulates packets in Register messages; unicasts to RP.

Step 3   Router C (RP) de-encapsulates packets; forwards down shared tree.

Step 4   RP sends (S, G) Join toward source; builds SPT.

Step 5   RP begins receiving (S, G) traffic down SPT.

Step 6   RP sends Register Stop to Router A.

Step 7   Router A stops encapsulating traffic in Register messages.

Step 8   (S, G) traffic is flowing down a single path (SPT) to RP.

These eight steps are detailed in the following sections.

Receivers Join First: Registering Steps 1–3

Figure 11-5 shows the first three steps of the Register process in action. Let's examine what happens at each step.

Figure 11-5   *Registering Steps 1–3 (Receivers Join First)*

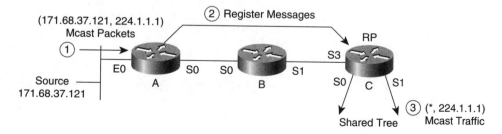

A multicast source (171.68.37.121) begins sending to group 224.1.1.1. Notice that the source did not bother to join the multicast group first. This would have caused Router A to join the shared tree and would complicate the example. Therefore, assume that the source is a send-only multicast source so that you can focus on the state created by the Register process.

When Router A receives the first multicast packet from the source, it searches for a match in its mroute table. In this case, it has neither a matching (S, G) entry nor a matching (*, G) entry. Therefore, to process the incoming multicast packet, Router A must create an (S, G) entry. This step automatically causes a (*, G) entry to also get created based on General Rule 1 that requires a parent (*, G) to exist for any (S, G) entries.

Router A now checks the IP address of the source and sees that it is an address within the subnet defined on Ethernet0 (Step 1). In other words, the source is directly connected to Router A. Therefore, Router A begins encapsulating the packets from the source in Register messages and unicasting them to the RP.

When the RP receives these Register messages, it de-encapsulates them and examines the destination address of the multicast packet inside (Step 2). In this case, the RP finds that the destination is multicast group 224.1.1.1 for which it has a (*, G) entry. The RP then forwards the multicast packet out all interfaces in the outgoing interface list. This action results in the packet being sent down the shared tree via interfaces Serial0 and Serial1.

If you type quick enough, you can catch this transitory state in Router A with an **show ip mroute** command. The output is shown in Example 11-10.

Example 11-10   *State in Router A While Registering*

```
rtr-a>show ip mroute
IP Multicast Routing Table
Flags: D - Dense, S - Sparse, C - Connected, L - Local, P - Pruned
       R - RP-bit set, F - Register flag, T - SPT-bit set, J - Join SPT
Timers: Uptime/Expires
Interface state: Interface, Next-Hop or VCD, State/Mode

(*, 224.1.1.1), 00:00:03/00:02:56, RP 10.1.5.1, flags: SP
  Incoming interface: Serial0, RPF nbr 171.68.28.191,
  Outgoing interface list: Null

(171.68.37.121/32, 224.1.1.1), 00:00:03/00:02:57, flags: FPT
  Incoming interface: Ethernet0, RPF nbr 0.0.0.0, Registering
  Outgoing interface list: Null
```

Let's stop here and take the above output apart line by line and make sure what is happening is clear.

The first entry is, of course, the (*, G) entry for group 224.1.1.1. The first line of this entry shows that the RP is 10.1.5.1 (Router C), the group is a sparse mode group (S flag), and the entry is pruned (P flag) because the outgoing interface list is Null. The second line shows that the incoming interface is pointing toward the RP via Serial0 and that the RPF neighbor (upstream in the direction of the RP) is 171.68.28.191 (Router B). The fact that this (*, G) entry is "pruned" (that is, the outgoing interface list is Null) frequently confuses Cisco multicast neophytes. Let me explain.

The (*, G) entry controls the forwarding of group multicast traffic *down* the shared tree, where there are directly connected members of the group or other downstream routers that have joined the group. Because there are neither at this point (remember, the source did not join the multicast group), the outgoing interface list of the (*, G) entry is Null and therefore the P flag is set. This would not be the case if the source had also joined the multicast group before it began sending. However, because I want to focus just on the Register process, I specifically used an example of a send-only host here.

The second entry in the output of the **show ip mroute** command is the (S, G) entry for the source, 171.68.37.121, which is sending to group 224.1.1.1. The first line of this entry shows that the source sent the first packet roughly 3 seconds ago and that this entry will expire and be deleted in roughly 2 minutes in 57 seconds. (Note: (S, G) entry expire timers are reset back to 3 minutes each time a multicast packet is forwarded using the entry.) The Flags field indicates that Register messages must be sent(F flag) for this (S, G) traffic (that is, because S is a directly connected source). The flags also indicate that at least one packet has been forwarded using this entry (T flag) and that the entry is pruned (P flag) because the outgoing interface list is Null.

The second line of the entry shows the incoming interface for this traffic is Ethernet0 and, because this is a directly connected source (that is, it is on the subnet connected to Ethernet0), the RPF neighbor is 0.0.0.0. In other words, no RPF neighbor exists for this source because it is directly connected to Router A.

Again, the fact that the outgoing interface list is Null (hence, the P flag being set) might seem to be an error. However, this condition is currently correct because the outgoing interface list of an (S, G) entry reflects interfaces where there are directly connected members of the group or downstream neighbors that have joined the SPT for this source. Once more, neither of these two conditions has been met, and therefore the outgoing interface list of the (S, G) entry is Null.

Receivers Join First: Registering Step 4

Figure 11-6 shows Step 4 in the receiver-joins-first example of the Register process.

Figure 11-6   *Registering Step 4 (Receivers Join First)*

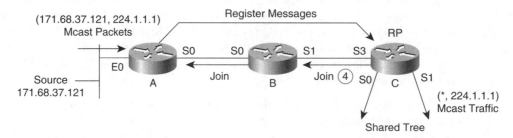

Because the RP has (*, 224.1.1.1) state whose outgoing interface list is not Null, the RP sends an (S, G) Join toward the first-hop router (Router A) so that Router A can join the SPT and "pull" multicast traffic from source 171.68.37.121 sending to group 224.1.1.1 via native multicast. The (S, G) Join travels hop by hop through Router B and on to Router A, setting up an SPT between the source and the RP.

If we could freeze time at this moment and type the **show ip mroute** command on all the routers, we would see the output shown in Examples 11-11, 11-12, and 11-13.

Example 11-11   *State in RP (Router C) Immediately After (S, G) Join*

```
rtr-c>show ip mroute 224.1.1.1
IP Multicast Routing Table
Flags: D - Dense, S - Sparse, C - Connected, L - Local, P - Pruned
       R - RP-bit set, F - Register flag, T - SPT-bit set, J - Join SPT
Timers: Uptime/Expires
Interface state: Interface, Next-Hop or VCD, State/Mode

(*, 224.1.1.1), 00:09:21/00:02:38, RP 10.1.5.1, flags: S
  Incoming interface: Null, RPF nbr 0.0.0.0,
  Outgoing interface list:
    Serial0, Forward/Sparse, 00:09:21/00:02:38
    Serial1, Forward/Sparse, 00:03:14/00:02:46

(171.68.37.121, 224.1.1.1, 00:00:01/00:02:59, flags: T
  Incoming interface: Serial3, RPF nbr 171.68.28.139,
  Outgoing interface list:
    Serial0, Forward/Sparse, 00:00:01/00:02:59
    Serial1, Forward/Sparse, 00:00:01/00:02:59
```

Example 11-12 *State in Router B Immediately After (S, G) Join*

```
rtr-b>show ip mroute 224.1.1.1
IP Multicast Routing Table
Flags: D - Dense, S - Sparse, C - Connected, L - Local, P - Pruned
       R - RP-bit set, F - Register flag, T - SPT-bit set, J - Join SPT
Timers: Uptime/Expires
Interface state: Interface, Next-Hop or VCD, State/Mode

(*, 224.1.1.1), 00:00:01/00:02:59, RP 10.1.5.1, flags: SP
  Incoming interface: Serial1, RPF nbr 171.68.28.140,
  Outgoing interface list: Null

(171.68.37.121/32, 224.1.1.1), 00:00:01/00:02:59, flags: T
  Incoming interface: Serial0, RPF nbr 171.68.28.190
  Outgoing interface list:
    Serial1, Forward/Sparse, 00:00:01/00:02:59
```

Example 11-13 *State in Router A Immediately After (S, G) Join*

```
rtr-a>show ip mroute
IP Multicast Routing Table
Flags: D - Dense, S - Sparse, C - Connected, L - Local, P - Pruned
       R - RP-bit set, F - Register flag, T - SPT-bit set, J - Join SPT
Timers: Uptime/Expires
Interface state: Interface, Next-Hop or VCD, State/Mode

 (*, 224.1.1.1), 00:00:02/00:02:59, RP 10.1.5.1, flags: SP
  Incoming interface: Serial0, RPF nbr 171.68.28.191,
  Outgoing interface list: Null

(171.68.37.121/32, 224.1.1.1), 00:00:2/00:02:58, flags: FT
  Incoming interface: Ethernet0, RPF nbr 0.0.0.0, Registering
  Outgoing interface list:
    Serial0, Forward/Sparse, 00:00:01/00:02:59
```

Working backwards from the RP toward Router A, Example 11-11 shows that the RP has created a new (S, G) entry as a result of sending the (S, G) join. Pay particular attention to the fact that the outgoing interface list of the (S, G) was populated with a copy of the outgoing interface list from the parent (*, G) entry according to General Rule 3. The incoming interface points toward the source through RPF neighbor 171.68.28.139 (Router B) via interface Serial3, based on PIM-SM Rule 8 and General Rule 2.

Example 11-13 shows that Router A has received the (S, G) Join (via Router B) and has added Serial0 to the outgoing interface list of the (S, G) entry. This step caused the P flag to be reset because the outgoing interface list is no longer Null.

Example 11-12 shows that Router B has created (*, G) and (S, G) state as a result of the (S, G) Join received from the RP. Notice that the (*, G) entry on Router B is also pruned (P flag is set) because the outgoing interface list is Null. This state is normal given the current conditions for the same reason seen on Router A earlier. That is, Router B has no directly connected members or downstream neighbors that have joined the shared tree. Therefore, the (*, G) entry is pruned.

The (S, G) entry, on the other hand, has an incoming interface that points toward the source via RPF neighbor 171.68.28.190 (Router A) via Serial0. The outgoing interface list contains Serial1, which is the interface by which the (S, G) Join from the RP was received. The combination of the incoming interface and outgoing interface list on the (S, G) entry in Router B allows traffic from the source to flow down the SPT, through Router B on its way to the RP.

Finally, Example 11-13 shows that Router A has added interface Serial0 to the outgoing interface list of its (S, G) entry as a result of the (S, G) Join received from Router B via Serial0. Now that the outgoing interface list is no longer Null, the P flag is reset in the (S, G) entry.

Because we were somehow able to type the **show ip mroute** command at this frozen instant in time, we were able to catch Router A still indicating **Registering** on the (S, G) entry. However, in actual practice, this event usually happens so fast that you can't catch the router in this state.

Receivers Join First: Registering Steps 5 and 6

Figure 11-7 shows Steps 5 and 6 in the receivers-join-first registering example.

Figure 11-7   *Registering Steps 5 and 6 (Receivers Join First)*

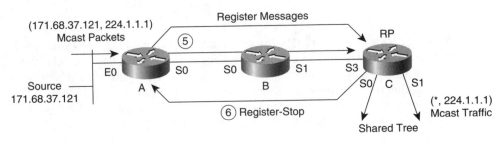

The RP now begins receiving (S, G) traffic natively via the newly created SPT (Step 5).

The next time the RP receives an (S, G) Register message, the RP sees that it is now receiving (S, G) traffic successfully via the SPT (indicated by the T flag being set in the (S, G) entry) and responds by sending back an (S, G) Register-Stop message (Step 6).

Receivers Join First: Registering Steps 7 and 8

Figure 11-8 depicts the final two steps in the receivers-join-first registering example.

Figure 11-8 *Registering Steps 7 and 8 (Receivers Join First)*

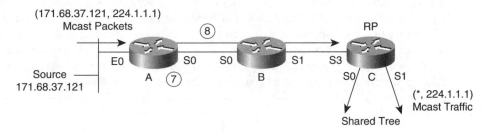

When Router A receives the (S, G) Register-Stop message from the RP, it stops sending multicast packets from the source encapsulated in Register messages and updates its (S, G) state entry by clearing the Registering indicator (Step 7).

The Register process is now complete, and (S, G) traffic is flowing to the RP only via the SPT (Step 8). From the RP, this traffic is then forwarded down the branches of the shared tree to the receivers.

Now that the entire process has completed, the state in Routers C and B will be the same as the output shown in Examples 11-11 and 11-12, respectively. The exception is the output of Router A, which is shown in Example 11-14.

Example 11-14 *State in Router A After Register*

```
rtr-a>show ip mroute
IP Multicast Routing Table
Flags: D - Dense, S - Sparse, C - Connected, L - Local, P - Pruned
       R - RP-bit set, F - Register flag, T - SPT-bit set, J - Join SPT
Timers: Uptime/Expires
Interface state: Interface, Next-Hop or VCD, State/Mode

 (*, 224.1.1.1), 00:00:03/00:02:59, RP 10.1.5.1, flags: SP
  Incoming interface: Serial0, RPF nbr 171.68.28.191,
  Outgoing interface list: Null

(171.68.37.121/32, 224.1.1.1), 00:00:3/00:02:58, flags: FT
  Incoming interface: Ethernet0, RPF nbr 0.0.0.0
  Outgoing interface list:
    Serial0, Forward/Sparse, 00:00:03/00:02:57
```

The difference between Examples 11-14 and 11-13 may not be obvious. However, if you look closely, you'll notice that the **Registering** indicator on the second line of the (S, G) entry is now gone. This change indicates that Router A is no longer sending Register messages to the RP for this (S, G) traffic.

NOTE	Occasionally, a first-hop router can appear to get stuck in the Registering state where the word *Registering* continuously appears in the (S, G) entry. This is an indication of a problem in the network. This problem most often occurs when not all interfaces in the network (between the first-hop router and the RP) have been enabled for multicast. At other times, some sort of reachability problem in the network can cause this problem. Finally, this condition can sometimes occur if the first-hop router has been configured with a static RP address via the **ip pim rp-address** command and another router between it and the RP is configured with an **ip pim accept-rp** command that denies this RP address as a valid RP. (The **ip pim accept-rp** command is discussed in more detail in Chapter 12.)

Source Registers First

In the previous sections, it was assumed that receivers would join the multicast group (hence create branches of the shared tree) first. Frequently, however, the multicast source may begin sending traffic before any receivers join the group.

In this case, the Register process works pretty much the same way, except the RP doesn't bother to join the SPT to the source until a receiver has joined the group and caused a branch of the shared tree to be created.

Using the same network example, but this time assuming that there are no receivers joined to the group (and hence no branches of the shared tree have been created), would have the state in the routers shown in Example 11-15.

Example 11-15 *State in Routers Before Register*

```
rtr-a>show ip mroute 224.1.1.1

Group 224.1.1.1 not found.




rtr-b>show ip mroute 224.1.1.1

Group 224.1.1.1 not found.




rtr-c>show ip mroute 224.1.1.1

Group 224.1.1.1 not found.
```

Figures 11-9 through 11-13 shows the following nine steps of the Register process when a source registers before any receivers join the group.

Step 1 Source begins sending Group G traffic.

Step 2 Router A encapsulates the packets in Registers; unicasts to RP.

Step 3 Router C (RP) has no receivers on shared tree; discards packet.

Step 4 RP sends Register-Stop to Router A.

Step 5 Router A stops encapsulating traffic in Register messages; drops further packets from source.

Step 6 Router C receives (*, G) Join from a receiver on shared tree.

Step 7 RP sends (S, G) Joins for all known sources in group.

Step 8 RP begins receiving (S, G) traffic down SPT.

Step 9 RP forwards (S, G) traffic down shared tree to receivers.

These steps are detailed in the following sections.

Source Registers First: Steps 1–3

Figure 11-9 shows the first three steps in the Register process when a source registers before any receivers join the group.

Figure 11-9 *Registering Steps 1–3 (Source Registers First)*

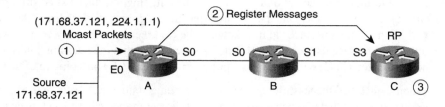

Our multicast source (171.68.37.121) begins sending to group 224.1.1.1 (Step 1).

Router A now checks the IP address of the source and sees that it is an address within the subnet defined on Ethernet0. In other words, the source is directly connected to Router A. This causes Router A to begin encapsulating the packets from the source in Register messages and unicasting them to the RP (Step 2).

When the RP receives these Register messages, it de-encapsulates them and examines the destination address of the multicast packet inside. In this case, the RP finds that the destination is multicast group 224.1.1.1 for which the RP does not have any state (because no one has joined the shared tree yet) and creates an (S, G) entry according to the fourth item in PIM-SM Rule 3. However, according to General Rule 1, an (S, G) entry cannot exist without a parent (*, G) entry and, therefore, the RP creates a (*, G) entry for group 224.1.1.1 with a Null outgoing interface list first.

If we were again able to freeze time at this point and issue a **show ip mroute** command on the RP, its mroute state would resemble Example 11-16.

Example 11-16   *State in RP (Router C) After Register*

```
rtr-c>show ip mroute
IP Multicast Routing Table
Flags: D - Dense, S - Sparse, C - Connected, L - Local, P - Pruned
       R - RP-bit set, F - Register flag, T - SPT-bit set, J - Join SPT
Timers: Uptime/Expires
Interface state: Interface, Next-Hop or VCD, State/Mode

(*, 224.1.1.1), 00:01:15/00:01:45, RP 10.1.5.1, flags: SP
  Incoming interface: Null, RPF nbr 0.0.0.0,
  Outgoing interface list: Null

(171.68.37.121/32, 224.1.1.1, 00:01:15/00:01:45, flags: PT
  Incoming interface: Serial3, RPF nbr 171.68.28.139,
  Outgoing interface list: Null
```

Because the (*, G) entry was initially created in response to the receipt of a Register and not as a result of the receipt of a (*, G) Join, the outgoing interface list is Null. Put another way, because no one has joined the shared tree, the outgoing interface list of the (*, G) entry will not have any interfaces in it. Likewise, the (S, G) entry is initially created with a Null outgoing interface list per General Rule 3, which states that the outgoing interface list of a newly created (S, G) entry receives a copy of its parent (* G) outgoing interface list.

When the RP has successfully created the preceding state, the RP attempts to forward the multicast packet that was encapsulated in the Register message based on this newly created state. However, in this instance the matching (S, G) entry has a Null outgoing interface list, and the RP therefore discards the packet (Step 3).

Issuing a **show ip mroute** command on Router A (while time was still frozen), its mroute state would resemble Example 11-17.

Example 11-17 *State in Router A While Registering*

```
rtr-a>show ip mroute
IP Multicast Routing Table
Flags: D - Dense, S - Sparse, C - Connected, L - Local, P - Pruned
       R - RP-bit set, F - Register flag, T - SPT-bit set, J - Join SPT
Timers: Uptime/Expires
Interface state: Interface, Next-Hop or VCD, State/Mode

(*, 224.1.1.1), 00:00:03/00:02:56, RP 10.1.5.1, flags: SP
  Incoming interface: Serial0, RPF nbr 171.68.28.191,
  Outgoing interface list: Null

(171.68.37.121/32, 224.1.1.1), 00:00:03/00:02:57, flags: FPT
  Incoming interface: Ethernet0, RPF nbr 0.0.0.0, Registering
  Outgoing interface list: Null
```

This state is identical to what was seen at this point in time in the preceding example when receivers joined the shared tree first. That is, Router A has created an (S, G) entry as a result of the multicast packets being received from the directly connected source, and Router A is still sending Register messages to the RP at this moment. The **FPT** flags are set, which indicates

- Source S is directly connected and the Register process must be used to notify the RP of this source (**F** flag).

- The outgoing interface list is Null (**P** flag) because no one has joined the SPT for this source at this point in time.

- Traffic is being received (**T** flag) from this source.

Source Registers First: Step 4

Figure 11-10 shows the next step in the Register example.

Figure 11-10 *Registering Step 4 (Source Registers First)*

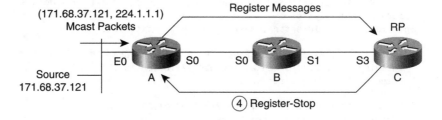

Because the (S, G) entry in the RP is pruned (that is, a Null outgoing interface list causes the P flag to be set), it has no current need for any (S, G) traffic. The RP therefore sends an (S, G) Register-Stop message to the first-hop router (Router A) to shut off the flow of encapsulated (S, G) packets (Step 4).

Notice that the RP did not send an (S, G) Join as it does when there are branches of the shared tree. However, the RP did create state for this particular (S, G) source, which will become important later.

Source Registers First: Step 5

Figure 11-11 shows Step 5 in the source registers first example.

Figure 11-11 *Registering Step 5 (Source Registers First)*

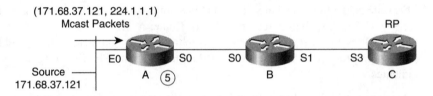

When Router A receives the (S, G) Register-Stop message from the RP, it stops sending multicast packets from the source encapsulated in Register messages and updates its (S, G) state entry by clearing the **Registering** indicator (Step 5). Furthermore, because the outgoing interface list is still Null, any future packets received from the source will be discarded.

Example 11-18 shows the current state in Router A.

Example 11-18 *State in Router A After Register*

```
rtr-a>show ip mroute 224.1.1.1
IP Multicast Routing Table
Flags: D - Dense, S - Sparse, C - Connected, L - Local, P - Pruned
       R - RP-bit set, F - Register flag, T - SPT-bit set, J - Join SPT
Timers: Uptime/Expires
Interface state: Interface, Next-Hop or VCD, State/Mode

(*, 224.1.1.1), 00:01:28/00:02:59, RP 10.1.5.1, flags: SP
  Incoming interface: Serial0, RPF nbr 171.68.28.191,
  Outgoing interface list: Null

(171.68.37.121/32, 224.1.1.1), 00:01:28/00:01:32, flags: FPT
  Incoming interface: Ethernet0, RPF nbr 0.0.0.0
  Outgoing interface list: Null
```

The important change is that the **Registering** indicator in the (S, G) entry has been cleared and that the outgoing interface list is still Null. This is why Router A will now drop any further packets received from the source, 171.68.37.121.

NOTE You should also be aware that the (S, G) entry expire timer will continue to count down to zero at which time the (S, G) entry will be deleted. If source 171.68.37.121 is still active and sending multicast packets to group 224.1.1.1, the (S, G) entry will get recreated when Router A receives the next packet and the Register, Register-Stop sequence will be repeated. This process will continue to occur every 3 minutes until either the source stops sending or a receiver joins the shared tree.

Now let's continue with the example (refer to Figure 11-12) and see what happens when receivers join the group and cause branches of the shared tree to be created.

Figure 11-12 *Registering Steps 6–7 (Source Registers First)*

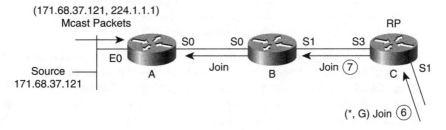

Assume that a receiver somewhere else in the network joins the multicast group, which triggers its local DR to send a (*, G) Join up the shared tree toward the RP (Step 6).

When the RP receives the (*, G) Join via Serial1, the RP applies PIM-SM Rule 4, which causes the interface by which the Join was received to be added to the outgoing interface list of the (*, G) entry. Next, General Rule 6 is applied, which causes interface Serial1 to be added to the outgoing interface list of all (S, G) entries associated with the parent (*, G) entry. The resulting state in the RP is shown in Example 11-19.

Example 11-19   *State in RP (Router C) After Receivers Join the Shared Tree*

```
rtr-c>show ip mroute
IP Multicast Routing Table
Flags: D - Dense, S - Sparse, C - Connected, L - Local, P - Pruned
       R - RP-bit set, F - Register flag, T - SPT-bit set, J - Join SPT
Timers: Uptime/Expires
Interface state: Interface, Next-Hop or VCD, State/Mode

(*, 224.1.1.1), 00:02:32/00:02:59, RP 10.1.5.1, flags: S
  Incoming interface: Null, RPF nbr 0.0.0.0,
  Outgoing interface list:
    Serial1, Forward/Sparse, 00:00:03/00:02:57

(171.68.37.121/32, 224.1.1.1, 00:02:32/00:02:57, flags: T
  Incoming interface: Serial3, RPF nbr 171.68.28.139,
  Outgoing interface list:
    Serial1, Forward/Sparse, 00:00:03/00:02:57
```

The key changes are the addition of Serial1 to both outgoing interface lists, which also result in the clearing of the P flag on both entries. Now, the RP is ready to forward any (171.68.37.121, 224.1.1.1) traffic that it receives via Serial3 down the shared tree. However, the router must first tell all first-hop routers (in this case just Router A) to start sending traffic to the RP. This leads to Step 7 (Figure 11-12).

When the (*, G) entry on the RP switches from pruned to not pruned (denoted by the clearing of the P flag), it triggers a Batch-Join process that sends an (S, G) Join toward all sources that the RP knows are active for group G (Step 7). The Batch-Join builds the SPTs from the sources to the RP and restarts the flow of all (S, G) traffic to the RP so that the traffic can be forwarded down the shared tree. Now you see why the RP keeps (S, G) state for all active sources when the shared tree had no branches. By keeping this state in the RP, the Batch-Join process (that was triggered by the (*, G) Join) can send an (S, G) Join for each child (S, G) entry under the parent (*, G) entry.

As the (S, G) Join is sent hop by hop toward the source to restart the flow of traffic to the RP, state is created on all intervening routers along the path (Router B in the example). When the (S, G) Join reaches the first-hop router (Router A here), Router A adds the interface on which it received the (S, G) Join to the outgoing interface list of its (S, G) entry. This step results in the final state on Router B and Router A shown in Example 11-20 and Example 11-21, respectively.

Example 11-20   *State in Router B After Receiving the (S, G) Join*

```
rtr-b>show ip mroute 224.1.1.1
IP Multicast Routing Table
Flags: D - Dense, S - Sparse, C - Connected, L - Local, P - Pruned
       R - RP-bit set, F - Register flag, T - SPT-bit set, J - Join SPT
Timers: Uptime/Expires
Interface state: Interface, Next-Hop or VCD, State/Mode

(*, 224.1.1.1), 00:00:03/00:02:59, RP 10.1.5.1, flags: SP
  Incoming interface: Serial1, RPF nbr 171.68.28.140,
  Outgoing interface list: Null

(171.68.37.121/32, 224.1.1.1), 00:00:03/00:02:59, flags: T
  Incoming interface: Serial0, RPF nbr 171.68.28.190
  Outgoing interface list:
    Serial1, Forward/Sparse, 00:00:03/00:02:57
```

Example 11-21   *State in Router A After Receiving the (S, G) Join*

```
rtr-a>show ip mroute
IP Multicast Routing Table
Flags: D - Dense, S - Sparse, C - Connected, L - Local, P - Pruned
       R - RP-bit set, F - Register flag, T - SPT-bit set, J - Join SPT
Timers: Uptime/Expires
Interface state: Interface, Next-Hop or VCD, State/Mode

 (*, 224.1.1.1), 00:00:03/00:02:59, RP 10.1.5.1, flags: SP
  Incoming interface: Serial0, RPF nbr 171.68.28.191,
  Outgoing interface list: Null

(171.68.37.121/32, 224.1.1.1), 00:00:3/00:02:58, flags: FT
  Incoming interface: Ethernet0, RPF nbr 0.0.0.0
  Outgoing interface list:
    Serial0, Forward/Sparse, 00:00:03/00:02:57
```

Source Registers First: Step 8 and 9

Figure 11-13 depicts the final steps in the source-registers-first example.

Figure 11-13   *Registering Steps 8 and 9 (Source Registers First)*

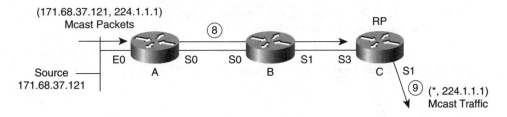

Once the state in Examples 11-20 and 11-21 is set up, (171.68.37.121, 244.1.1.1) traffic begins to flow down the SPT to the RP (Step 8). When this traffic reaches the RP, it is forwarded down the shared tree according to the interfaces in the outgoing interface list of the (S, G) entry (Step 9). Remember, routers always forward based on a matching (S, G) entry if one exists. Thus, when adding an interface to the (*, G) outgoing interface list, also add it to all the child (S, G) entries.

Receivers Along the SPT

Another common misconception of PIM-SM is that when a router that is somewhere along the (S, G) SPT between the source and the RP joins the group, (S, G) traffic must first flow to the RP and then turn around and come back down. This is not the case.

Consider the network example that was shown in Figure 11-13. Traffic is flowing down the SPT from Router A to the RP (Router C). Example 11-22 shows the current state in Router B.

Example 11-22 *State in Router B Before Local Host Joins*

```
rtr-b>show ip mroute 224.1.1.1
IP Multicast Routing Table
Flags: D - Dense, S - Sparse, C - Connected, L - Local, P - Pruned
       R - RP-bit set, F - Register flag, T - SPT-bit set, J - Join SPT
Timers: Uptime/Expires
Interface state: Interface, Next-Hop or VCD, State/Mode

 (*, 224.1.1.1), 00:04:28/00:01:32, RP 10.1.5.1, flags: SP
   Incoming interface: Serial1, RPF nbr 171.68.28.140,
   Outgoing interface list: Null

(171.68.37.121/32, 224.1.1.1), 00:04:28/00:01:32, flags: T
   Incoming interface: Serial0, RPF nbr 171.68.28.190
   Outgoing interface list:
     Serial1, Forward/Sparse, 00:04:28/00:01:32
```

Because there are no directly connected members of group 224.1.1.1 and because no downstream neighbors have joined the shared tree, the (*, G) entry has a Null outgoing interface list and is therefore pruned (indicated by the P flag).

The (S, G) entry, on the other hand, is not pruned and is being used to forward (S, G) traffic through Router B and down the SPT to the RP.

Figure 11-14 shows what happens if a directly connected host on Router B joins the group, which, in turn, causes Router B to join the shared tree.

Figure 11-14   *Host Joins Along the SPT*

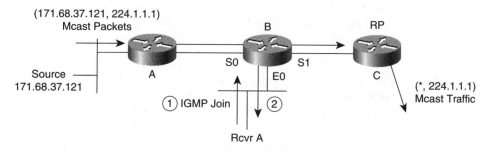

Host Rcvr A signals its desire to join multicast group 224.1.1.1 by sending an IGMP Membership Report (Step 1).

When Router B receives the IGMP Membership Report (or IGMP Join as we often call it), it adds an entry to its IGMP Membership Cache to indicate that a member of this group exists on this interface. Since this member is the first member to join group 224.1.1.1, Router B updates its mroute entries for the group and sends a (*, G) Join up the shared tree toward the RP (Step 2).

The state in Router B after Rcvr A joins the group is shown in Example 11-23.

Example 11-23   *State in Router B After Rcvr A Joins the Group*

```
rtr-b>show ip mroute 224.1.1.1
IP Multicast Routing Table
Flags: D - Dense, S - Sparse, C - Connected, L - Local, P - Pruned
       R - RP-bit set, F - Register flag, T - SPT-bit set, J - Join SPT
Timers: Uptime/Expires
Interface state: Interface, Next-Hop or VCD, State/Mode

 (*, 224.1.1.1), 00:04:28/00:01:32, RP 10.1.5.1, flags: SC
  Incoming interface: Serial1, RPF nbr 171.68.28.140,
  Outgoing interface list:
    Ethernet0, Forward/Sparse, 00:00:30/00:02:30

(171.68.37.121/32, 224.1.1.1), 00:04:28/00:01:32, flags: CT
  Incoming interface: Serial0, RPF nbr 171.68.28.190
  Outgoing interface list:
    Serial1, Forward/Sparse, 00:04:28/00:01:32
    Ethernet0, Forward/Sparse, 00:00:30/00:02:30
```

Example 11-23 shows that Router B has added interface Ethernet0 (where it now has a directly connected member of the group) to the outgoing interface list of the (*, G) entry based on PIM-SM Rule 4. Next, General Rule 6 was applied, which caused Ethernet0 to be added to all (S, G) entries under the (*, G) entry.

Before moving on, let's apply the PIM forwarding rules to the (S, G) traffic that is flowing through Router B on its way to the RP and see what happens. When Router B receives a multicast packet from source 171.68.37.121 sent to group 224.1.1.1, Router B searches its mroute forwarding table, finds a matching (S, G) entry, and uses that entry to forward the packet as follows:

- Using the matching (S, G) entry, Router B performs an RPF check to determine whether the packet arrived on the correct interface. In this case, the RPF check succeeds because the packet arrived on the incoming interface, Serial0. (If the packet had not arrived via Serial0, it would fail the RPF check and be discarded.)

- Because the RPF check succeeded, Router B forwards the packet out all interfaces in the outgoing interface list. Because Router B is using the matching (S, G) entry, the packet is forwarded on toward the RP out interface Serial1 and out interface Ethernet0 to the directly connected member, Rcvr A.

In other words, any (S, G) traffic flowing to the RP will be "picked off" as it passes through Router B and forwarded out all interfaces in the (S, G) outgoing interface list. Or, look at this situation another way: Router B was already on the (S, G) SPT and therefore receives this traffic via a more direct path.

Hopefully, you are already beginning to wonder about the (*, G) Join that Router B sent to the RP. Won't that cause duplicate (S, G) traffic to flow back down the shared tree to Router B? The simple answer is no. Here's what happens.

The state in the RP that results from the receipt of the (*, G) Join is shown in Example 11-24.

Example 11-24 *State in RP (Router C) After Receiving (*, G) Join from Router B*

```
rtr-c>show ip mroute
IP Multicast Routing Table
Flags: D - Dense, S - Sparse, C - Connected, L - Local, P - Pruned
       R - RP-bit set, F - Register flag, T - SPT-bit set, J - Join SPT
Timers: Uptime/Expires
Interface state: Interface, Next-Hop or VCD, State/Mode

(*, 224.1.1.1), 00:06:23/00:02:59, RP 10.1.5.1, flags: S
  Incoming interface: Null, RPF nbr 0.0.0.0,
  Outgoing interface list:
    Serial1, Forward/Sparse, 00:06:23/00:02:37
    Serial3, Forward/Sparse, 00:00:03/00:02:57

(171.68.37.121/32, 224.1.1.1, 00:06:23/00:02:57, flags: T
  Incoming interface: Serial3, RPF nbr 171.68.28.139,
  Outgoing interface list:
    Serial1, Forward/Sparse, 00:06:23/00:02:37
```

When the RP received the (*, G) Join from Router B, the RP added interface Serial3 (on which the (*, G) Join was received) to the outgoing interface list based on PIM-SM Rule 4. The RP then applied General Rule 6 and added interface Serial3 to the outgoing interface list of all associated (S, G) entries under the (*, G) entry. Finally, General Rule 4, which states that the incoming interface cannot appear in the outgoing interface, was applied to the (S, G) entries. This action resulted in the removal of interface Serial3 from the outgoing interface list of the (S, G) entry.

Now when a multicast packet sent by source 171.68.37.121 to group 224.1.1.1 arrives at the RP, it searches its mroute forwarding table and finds the matching (S, G) entry (171.68.37.121/32, 224.1.1.1) and uses it to forward the packet. (Remember, routers always forward based on the (S, G) entry if one exists.) The RP then performs an RPF check and finds that the packet arrived on the correct incoming interface, Serial3. Still using the (S, G) entry, the RP forwards the packet out all interfaces in the (S, G) outgoing interface list. In this case, only Serial1 is in the outgoing interface list as a result of the application of General Rule 4.

The combination of the above rules results in state being built in the RP that prevents the (S, G) traffic from flowing back down the same path it came in on. This effectively prevents duplicate (S, G) traffic from flowing back to Router B in the example.

SPT-Switchover

Chapter 7 introduced the capability of PIM-SM to switch from the shared tree to the SPT of a multicast source when the traffic rate exceeds a predetermined threshold. Cisco's implementation of PIM-SM refers to this predetermined threshold as the "SPT-Threshold" and defaults to zero kilobits per second. In other words, the default action is for a last-hop router to immediately join the SPT when a new source is detected.

Exceeding the SPT-Threshold

Just exactly how the Cisco PIM implementation detects when the SPT-Threshold has been exceeded and by which source is often an element of confusion for newcomers to Cisco PIM-SM. The common assumption is that a last-hop router (that is, a router that has the C flag set in the (*, G) entry) keeps track of the individual traffic rates of all sources sending down the shared tree. This assumption is, in fact, not true, as it would basically require the last-hop router to maintain (S, G) state for all sources in the group. This would defeat the purpose of shared trees, which is to minimize (S, G) state in the router. Instead, Cisco routers use a clever optimization that effectively accomplishes the same goal, which is to switch to the SPT for the high-rate sources in the group but without having to maintain traffic rate statistics for each individual source. This optimization is accomplished by performing the two tasks in Step 1:

Step 1

— Once each second, compute the total traffic rate flowing down shared tree.

— If this rate exceeds the SPT-Threshold, then set the "Join SPT" ("J") flag in the (*, G) entry.

Now, examining the J flag in the (*, G) entry can show whether the traffic rate flowing down the shared tree (that is, being forwarded via the (*, G) entry) is exceeding the SPT-Threshold or not. This action leads to Step 2, which triggers a switch to the SPT that is executed the next time a packet is received via the shared tree. When this packet arrives, its source address is the SPT tree that is joined.

Step 2   If the J flag is set in (*, G), then

— Join the SPT for (S_i, G)

— Mark (S_i, G) entry with J flag

— Clear J flag in (*,G)

The preceding optimization tends to result in the last-hop router switching over to the SPT for the high-rate source that is sending down the shared tree. This change occurs because the next packet received down the shared tree will probably be a high-rate source that is sending above the SPT-Threshold. Even if the next packet is not a high-rate source, the switchback mechanism, which is discussed later in this section, will result in this low-rate source being switched back to the shared tree.

SPT-Switchover Process

Let's now examine the process of switching to the SPT in more detail and also consider the state that is built in the routers when this switch occurs.

Figure 11-15 depicts a sample network with (S_i, G) traffic flowing down the shared tree to Rcvr A prior to the switchover to the SPT.

Figure 11-15   *Traffic Flow Before SPT-Switchover*

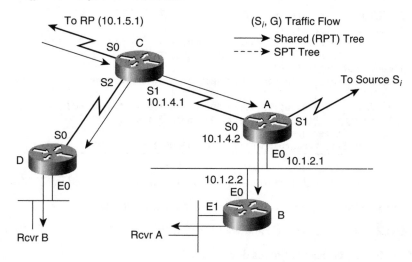

Examples 11-25, 11-26, and 11-27 show the state in each of the three routers along the shared tree before switching to the SPT.

Example 11-25   *State in Router C Before SPT-Switchover*

```
rtr-c>show ip mroute 224.1.1.1
IP Multicast Routing Table
Flags: D - Dense, S - Sparse, C - Connected, L - Local, P - Pruned
       R - RP-bit set, F - Register flag, T - SPT-bit set, J - Join SPT
Timers: Uptime/Expires
Interface state: Interface, Next-Hop or VCD, State/Mode

 (*, 224.1.1.1), 00:03:21/00:02:59, RP 10.1.5.1, flags: S
  Incoming interface: Serial0, RPF nbr 10.1.5.1,
  Outgoing interface list:
    Serial1, Forward/Sparse, 00:01:43/00:02:11
    Serial2, Forward/Sparse, 00:03:21/00:02:39
```

Example 11-26   *State in Router A Before SPT-Switchover*

```
rtr-a>show ip mroute 224.1.1.1
IP Multicast Routing Table
Flags: D - Dense, S - Sparse, C - Connected, L - Local, P - Pruned
       R - RP-bit set, F - Register flag, T - SPT-bit set, J - Join SPT
Timers: Uptime/Expires
Interface state: Interface, Next-Hop or VCD, State/Mode

 (*, 224.1.1.1), 00:01:43/00:02:59, RP 10.1.5.1, flags: S
  Incoming interface: Serial0, RPF nbr 10.1.4.1,
  Outgoing interface list:
    Ethernet0, Forward/Sparse, 00:01:43/00:02:11
```

Example 11-27   *State in Router B Before SPT-Switchover*

```
rtr-b>show ip mroute 224.1.1.1
IP Multicast Routing Table
Flags: D - Dense, S - Sparse, C - Connected, L - Local, P - Pruned
       R - RP-bit set, F - Register flag, T - SPT-bit set, J - Join SPT
Timers: Uptime/Expires
Interface state: Interface, Next-Hop or VCD, State/Mode

 (*, 224.1.1.1), 00:01:43/00:02:59, RP 10.1.5.1, flags: SCJ
  Incoming interface: Ethernet0, RPF nbr 10.1.4.2,
  Outgoing interface list:
    Ethernet1, Forward/Sparse, 00:01:43/00:02:11
```

Figure 11-16 through Figure 11-19 detail the nine steps involved in SPT-Switchover:

Step 1   Group G rate exceeds SPT-Threshold at Router B.

Step 2   Set J flag in (*, G) and wait for next (S_i, G) packet.

Step 3   (S_i, G) packet arrives down shared tree.

Step 4   Clear J flag in (*, G).

Step 5   Send (S_i, G) toward S_i.

Step 6   SPT and RPT diverge; Router A forwards (S_i, G) Join toward S_i.

Step 7   Router A triggers an (S_i, G)RP-bit Prune toward RP.

Step 8   (S_i, G) traffic begins flowing down SPT tree.

Step 9   Unnecessary (S_i, G) traffic is pruned from the shared tree.

SPT-Switchover: Steps 1 and 2

Continuing with the example, Figure 11-16 shows the first two steps of SPT-Switchover.

Figure 11-16 *SPT-Switchover Steps 1 and 2*

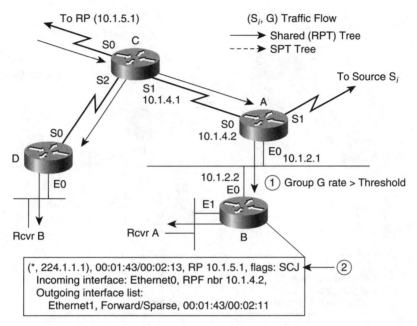

Let's assume that the total rate of traffic flowing down the shared tree exceeds the SPT-Threshold at Router B (Step 1).

As a result of this traffic rate, Router B sets the Join SPT (J) flag in the (*, G) entry for the group to indicate that a switch to the SPT is in order (Step 2). Consequently, the next (S, G) packet received will cause a switch to the SPT for this source.

SPT-Switchover: Steps 3, 4, and 5

Figure 11-17 depicts the next steps of the switchover example.

Figure 11-17   *SPT-Switchover Steps 3, 4, and 5*

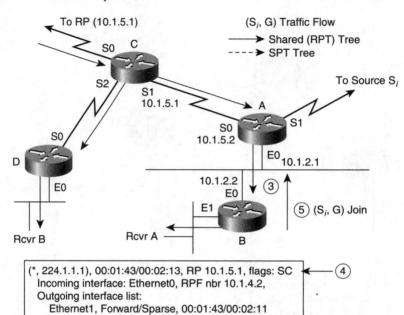

Let's now assume that we receive an (S_i, G) packet down the shared tree (Step 3). Router B then checks the $(*, G)$ entry and sees that the J flag is set, which indicates that a switch to the SPT-Threshold is in order.

Router B then temporarily resets the J flag until the next measurement interval (Step 4). This action prevents more than one source from being switched to the SPT until the 1-second measurement interval is run again *after* switching this source to the SPT.

Router B then creates (S_i, G) state and sends an (S_i, G) Join toward the source to join the SPT for this source (Step 5). This Join travels hop by hop toward the source and builds an SPT.

SPT-Switchover: Steps 6 and 7

Figure 11-18 presents Step 6 and Step 7 of the switchover example.

Figure 11-18 *SPT-Switchover Steps 6 and 7*

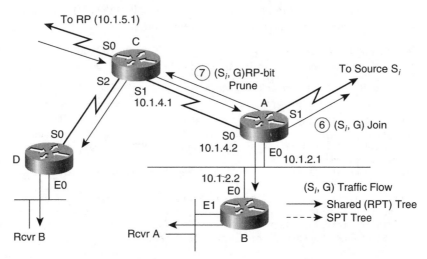

Example 11-28 shows the resulting state in Router B at this time.

Example 11-28 *State in Router B After the SPT-Switchover*

```
rtr-b>show ip mroute 224.1.1.1
IP Multicast Routing Table
Flags: D - Dense, S - Sparse, C - Connected, L - Local, P - Pruned
       R - RP-bit set, F - Register flag, T - SPT-bit set, J - Join SPT
Timers: Uptime/Expires
Interface state: Interface, Next-Hop or VCD, State/Mode

 (*, 224.1.1.1), 00:01:49/00:02:59, RP 10.1.5.1, flags: SC
  Incoming interface: Ethernet0, RPF nbr 10.1.2.1,
  Outgoing interface list:
    Ethernet1, Forward/Sparse, 00:01:49/00:02:05

(171.68.37.121/32, 224.1.1.1), 00:00:05/00:02:56, flags: CJT
  Incoming interface: Ethernet0, RPF nbr 10.1.2.1
  Outgoing interface list:
    Ethernet1, Forward/Sparse, 00:00:05/00:02:55
```

Notice that the J flag is currently reset in the (*, G) entry. This flag will again be set after the next 1-second measurement interval has completed and the rate of traffic flowing down the shared tree is still above the SPT-Threshold. (Note: If the default SPT-Threshold of 0 kbps is in effect, the J flag will appear to always be set. The only time that this flag would be reset is if you just happen to catch the (*, G) entry immediately after an SPT-Switchover but before the next 1-second measurement interval has completed. In practice, this moment is very difficult to catch.)

Additionally, notice that an (S_i, G) entry has been created in Router B and that the J flag has been set to indicate that the state was created as a result of the SPT-Switchover mechanism. We will consider the significance of this event shortly.

When Router A receives the (S_i, G) Join, A also joins the SPT and creates an (S_i, G) entry in its mroute table as shown in Example 11-29.

Example 11-29 *State in Router A After the SPT-Switchover*

```
rtr-a>show ip mroute 224.1.1.1
IP Multicast Routing Table
Flags: D - Dense, S - Sparse, C - Connected, L - Local, P - Pruned
       R - RP-bit set, F - Register flag, T - SPT-bit set, J - Join SPT
Timers: Uptime/Expires
Interface state: Interface, Next-Hop or VCD, State/Mode

 (*, 224.1.1.1), 00:02:16/00:02:59, RP 10.1.5.1, flags: S
  Incoming interface: Serial0, RPF nbr 10.1.4.1,
  Outgoing interface list:
    Ethernet0, Forward/Sparse, 00:02:16/00:02:11

(171.68.37.121/32, 224.1.1.1), 00:00:27/00:02:56, flags: T
  Incoming interface: Serial1, RPF nbr 10.1.9.2
  Outgoing interface list:
    Ethernet0, Forward/Sparse, 00:00:27/00:02:33
```

The newly created (S_i, G) entry shown in Example 11-29 has its incoming interface pointing toward the source, S_i, via interface Serial1 and has an outgoing interface of Ethernet0. This entry allows (S_i, G) traffic flowing down the SPT to be forwarded to Router B. Again, refer to Figure 11-18.

Because Router A created the new (S_i, G) entry, it triggers an (S_i, G) Join in the direction of the Source S_i out interface Serial1 (Step 6). This continues the process of building the SPT back to the source.

Router A now detects that the paths of the shared tree and SPT diverge at this point and triggers an (S_i, G)RP-bit Prune out Serial0 up the shared tree toward the RP to Router C (Step 7). This was a direct result of PIM-SM Rule 7, which governs the sending of (S, G)RP-bit Prunes. Note that Router B did not trigger an (S_i, G)RP-bit Prune as a result of PIM-SM Rule 7 because the incoming interfaces of the (S_i, G) and $(*, G)$ entries did match.

SPT-Switchover: Steps 8 and 9

Figure 11-19 depicts the final steps in the switchover process.

Figure 11-19 *SPT-Switchover Steps 8 and 9*

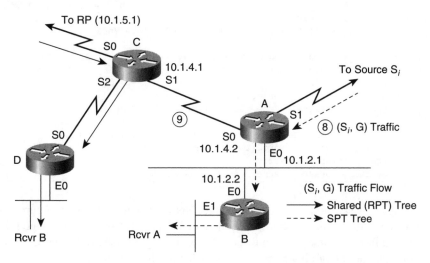

The (S_i, G) Join travels hop by hop to the first-hop router for Source S_i, building the SPT back down to Router B via Router A. After this is accomplished, (S_i, G) traffic begins flowing to Router B via the SPT (Step 8; shown by the dashed arrows in Figure 11-19.)

The (S_i, G)RP-bit Prune is sent up the shared tree to Router C (Step 9).

When Router C receives the (S_i, G)RP-bit Prune, it responds by creating an (S_i, G) entry in its mroute table and populates its outgoing interface list with a copy of the interfaces from the $(*, G)$ entry (based on General Rule 3). However, because the (S_i, G)RP-bit Prune was received via interface Serial1, this interface is pruned (removed) from the outgoing interface list, leaving only Serial2. Furthermore, because the RP-bit was set in the Prune, Router C sets the RP-bit (denoted by the R flag) in the (S_i, G) entry and applies PIM-SM Rule 8. This step causes the incoming interface of the (S_i, G) entry *to be pointed toward the RP instead toward of the source*. This finally results in the state being instantiated in Router C as shown in Example 11-30.

Example 11-30   *State in Router C After SPT-Switchover*

```
rtr-c>show ip mroute 224.1.1.1
IP Multicast Routing Table
Flags: D - Dense, S - Sparse, C - Connected, L - Local, P - Pruned
       R - RP-bit set, F - Register flag, T - SPT-bit set, J - Join SPT
Timers: Uptime/Expires
Interface state: Interface, Next-Hop or VCD, State/Mode

 (*, 224.1.1.1), 00:03:54/00:02:59, RP 10.1.5.1, flags: S
  Incoming interface: Serial0, RPF nbr 10.1.5.1,
  Outgoing interface list:
    Serial1, Forward/Sparse, 00:01:43/00:02:11
    Serial2, Forward/Sparse, 00:03:54/00:02:06

(171.68.37.121/32, 224.1.1.1), 00:00:25/00:02:53, flags: R
  Incoming interface: Serial0, RPF nbr 10.1.5.1
  Outgoing interface list:
    Serial2, Forward/Sparse, 00:00:25/00:02:35
```

Things now start to get a bit complicated. Notice that at Router C in Figure 11-19 (S_i, G) traffic is still flowing to Router D (indicated by the solid arrows), although it has been pruned from the link going to Router A. Examining the state in Router C at this point and applying the forwarding rules can show what has happened.

As traffic from (S_i, G) arrives at Router C, a scan of the mroute table is performed and an exact (S_i, G) match is found for (171.68.37.121/32, 224.1.1.1). Using the information in this entry, Router C first performs an RPF check to make sure that the traffic is arriving on the correct interface.

The RPF check succeeds because the traffic is arriving via Serial0 and the incoming interface information in the (S_i, G) entry is

```
 Incoming interface: Serial0, RPF nbr 10.1.5.1
```

Router C then forwards the multicast packet out all the non-pruned interfaces in the outgoing interface list, which for the (S_i, G) entry is

```
Outgoing interface list:
    Serial2, Forward/Sparse, 00:00:25/00:02:35
```

This results in (S_i, G) traffic being forwarded only to Router D, as shown in Figure 11-19.

The purpose of (S_i, G)RP-bit entries should now be quite clear. By applying the rules in the manner described above to create (S_i, G)RP-bit entries, redundant (S_i, G) traffic can be pruned from the shared tree.

SPT-Switchback Process

Once an (S, G) entry has been created as a result of the SPT-Switchover process (such as the (171.68.37.121/32, 224.1.1.1) entry shown in Example 11-28), it is now possible for the router to begin collecting actual traffic statistics on the (S, G) flow. (This is because Cisco routers keep traffic statistic counters for each (S, G) flow in special fields in the (S, G) mroute table data structure.) As you recall, when an (S, G) entry is created as a result of the SPT-Switchover process, the J flag is set in the (S, G) entry. When the J flag is set on an (S, G) entry, the Cisco router will periodically (once per minute) check the (S, G) traffic flow rate to see if it has fallen below the SPT-Threshold. If the rate has dropped below the SPT-Threshold, the router will switch the (S, G) flow back to the shared tree and prune off the flow of traffic down the SPT.

Pruning

The Prune mechanism for PIM-SM networks is performed in the same basic manner as in PIM-DM networks. That is, a Prune is sent up the distribution tree to stop the flow of unwanted multicast traffic. However, unlike PIM-DM networks, which use only source trees, PIM-SM networks use both source trees and shared trees.

The following sections provide detailed explanations of the PIM-SM Prune mechanisms for both the shared tree case and the source tree case.

Pruning the Shared Tree

Pruning multicast traffic from the shared tree is a straightforward process. When multicast traffic flowing down the shared tree is no longer wanted (that is, when the router is a leaf node and the last directly connected member leaves the group), the router simply sends a (*, G) Prune to its upstream neighbor on the shared tree. When the upstream neighbor receives the (*, G) Prune via one of its interfaces, it removes that interface from the outgoing interface list. If this results in the outgoing interface list becoming Null, the (*, G) entry is marked as *pruned* (with the P flag) and another (*, G) Prune is sent on up the shared tree. This continues until the (*, G) Prune reaches the RP or some other router up the shared tree that still has other interfaces in its outgoing interface list after performing the Prune operation.

Figure 11-20 is an example of a portion of an active shared tree prior to pruning.

Figure 11-20 *Shared Tree Before Pruning*

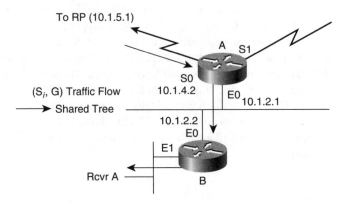

Notice that a single receiver (Rcvr A) is a member of the group and that multicast traffic is flowing down the shared tree (shown by the solid arrows) through Router A and Router B. This example assumes that the routers have been configured with an SPT-Threshold of infinity, which prevents Router B from joining the SPT of any active sources. Executing a **show ip mroute** command on these two routers shows the state information for the active group 224.1.1.1 as listed in Examples 11-31 and 11-32.

Example 11-31 *State in Router B Before Shared Tree Pruning*

```
rtr-b>show ip mroute 224.1.1.1
IP Multicast Routing Table
Flags: D - Dense, S - Sparse, C - Connected, L - Local, P - Pruned
       R - RP-bit set, F - Register flag, T - SPT-bit set, J - Join SPT
Timers: Uptime/Expires
Interface state: Interface, Next-Hop or VCD, State/Mode

 (*, 224.1.1.1), 00:01:43/00:02:59, RP 10.1.5.1, flags: SC
  Incoming interface: Ethernet0, RPF nbr 10.1.2.1,
  Outgoing interface list:
    Ethernet1, Forward/Sparse, 00:01:43/00:02:11
```

Example 11-32 *State in Router A Before Shared Tree Pruning*

```
rtr-a>show ip mroute 224.1.1.1
IP Multicast Routing Table
Flags: D - Dense, S - Sparse, C - Connected, L - Local, P - Pruned
       R - RP-bit set, F - Register flag, T - SPT-bit set, J - Join SPT
Timers: Uptime/Expires
Interface state: Interface, Next-Hop or VCD, State/Mode

 (*, 224.1.1.1), 00:01:43/00:02:59, RP 10.1.5.1, flags: S
  Incoming interface: Serial0, RPF nbr 10.1.4.1,
  Outgoing interface list:
    Ethernet0, Forward/Sparse, 00:01:43/00:02:11
```

Because the shared tree is being used exclusively to deliver traffic, only (*, G) entries exist in the two routers.

The shared tree Prune process is depicted in Figures 11-21 and 11-22 with six steps:

Step 1   Router B is a leaf router; last host Rcvr A leaves group G.

Step 2   Router B removes E1 from (*, G) and any (S_i, G) outgoing interface lists.

Step 3   Router B (*, G) outgoing interface list is now empty; sends (*, G) Prune toward RP.

Step 4   Router A receives Prune; removes E0 from (*, G) outgoing interface list.

Step 5   Router A (*, G) outgoing interface list is now empty; send (*, G) Prune toward RP.

Step 6   Pruning continues back toward RP.

Pruning the Shared Tree: Steps 1–3

Figure 11-21 shows the first three steps of the Prune process that is initiated when the last member (Rcvr A in this example) leaves the group.

Figure 11-21   *Pruning the Shared Tree Steps 1–3*

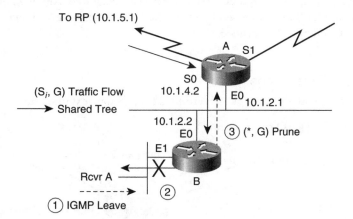

Rcvr A sends an IGMP Leave Group message, signaling Router B that it is leaving the multicast group (Step 1). Because Rcvr A is the last member of group 224.1.1.1 on interface Ethernet1, Router B removes the 224.1.1.1 IGMP Group Membership Cache entry for Ethernet1. (Note: The normal IGMP leave processing is not shown in this example.)

As a result of the removal of the 224.1.1.1 IGMP group Membership Cache entry, Router B removes interface Ethernet1 from the (*, G) outgoing interface list (Step 2).

The state in Router B that results from Ethernet1 being removed from the outgoing interface list is shown in Example 11-33.

Example 11-33   *State in Router B After Last Member (Rcvr A) Leaves Group*

```
rtr-b>show ip mroute 224.1.1.1
IP Multicast Routing Table
Flags: D - Dense, S - Sparse, C - Connected, L - Local, P - Pruned
       R - RP-bit set, F - Register flag, T - SPT-bit set, J - Join SPT
Timers: Uptime/Expires
Interface state: Interface, Next-Hop or VCD, State/Mode

 (*, 224.1.1.1), 00:03:17/00:02:47, RP 10.1.5.1, flags: SCP
  Incoming interface: Ethernet0, RPF nbr 10.1.2.1,
  Outgoing interface list: Null
```

Notice that the (*, G) expiration timer (00:02:47) is now counting down (it had been stopped previously as there were non-pruned interfaces in the outgoing interface list) and will expire in 2 minutes and 47 seconds. When the expiration timer reaches a count of zero, the (*, G) entry will be deleted.

Because the outgoing interface list on Router B is now Null, the P flag is set and a (*, G) Prune is sent up the shared tree to Router A (Step 3). (Note: Although not shown in Figure 11-21, Router B also stops sending periodic (*, G) Joins to refresh the shared tree because the (*, G) entry is now pruned.)

Pruning the Shared Tree: Steps 4–6

Continuing with the example, Figure 11-22 shows the next three steps in the Prune process.

Figure 11-22   *Pruning the Shared Tree Steps 4–6*

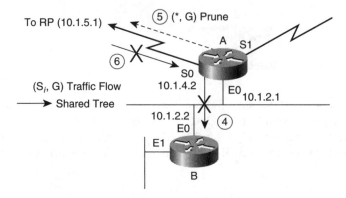

When Router A receives the (*, G) Prune from Router B via Ethernet0, it schedules the interface to be pruned after a 3-second delay (Step 4). The 3-second delay is to wait and see whether another router on the multi-access network wishes to override the Prune with a Join. At the end of this 3-second delay, Router A removes interface Ethernet0 from the outgoing interface list of the (*, G) entry.

The removal of Ethernet0 from the outgoing interface list of the (*, G) entry in Router A results in the state shown in Example 11-34.

Example 11-34 *State in Router A After Receiving the (*, G) Prune*

```
rtr-a>show ip mroute 224.1.1.1
IP Multicast Routing Table
Flags: D - Dense, S - Sparse, C - Connected, L - Local, P - Pruned
       R - RP-bit set, F - Register flag, T - SPT-bit set, J - Join SPT
Timers: Uptime/Expires
Interface state: Interface, Next-Hop or VCD, State/Mode

 (*, 224.1.1.1), 00:03:23/00:02:32, RP 10.1.5.1, flags: SP
  Incoming interface: Serial0, RPF nbr 10.1.4.1,
  Outgoing interface list: Null
```

Again, notice that the (*, G) expiration timer (00:02:32) on this entry is also now counting down and will expire in 2 minutes and 32 seconds, at which time the entry will be deleted. The expiration timer had previously been stopped because the outgoing interface list contained non-pruned interfaces.

At this point, the outgoing interface list of the (*, G) entry in Router A is also Null. This triggers Router A to also send a (*, G) Prune up the shared tree and to mark the entry as pruned with the P flag (Step 5).

Step 4 and Step 5 of the Prune process continue back up the shared tree until the RP is reached or a router is reached whose outgoing interface list does not become Null as a result of the Prune (Step 6). In other words, a router is reached that still has other active branches of the shared tree.

Pruning the Source Tree

Pruning is slightly more interesting when traffic is flowing down the SPT instead of the shared tree. The method is basically the same as for shared tree pruning. That is, (*, G) Prunes are sent up the shared tree, which removes the appropriate interfaces from the outgoing interface list of both the (*, G) and all its (S, G) entries. Again, if the outgoing interface list of a (*, G) entry becomes Null, it is marked as pruned (with the P flag), a (*, G) Prune is sent on up the shared tree, and the entry is allowed to time out. The same basic process is applied to any (S, G) entries whose outgoing interface list becomes Null. However, no (S, G) Prunes are sent up the SPT. Instead, the (S, G) entries are allowed to time out.

Figure 11-23 is an example where the last-hop router (Router B in this case) has switched to the SPT to receive traffic from some source, S_i. In this example, Router B (which has a directly connected member of group 224.1.1.1) has switched to the SPT (depicted by the dashed arrows) to receive multicast traffic from source 171.68.37.121. (This example assumes that the SPT-Threshold for the group was left at its default value of zero.)

Figure 11-23 *SPT Before Pruning*

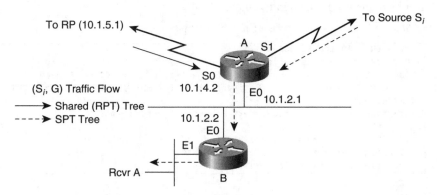

Executing a **show ip mroute** command on the two routers in this figure produces the state information for the active group 224.1.1.1 as listed in Examples 11-35 and 11-36.

Example 11-35 *State in Router B Before Source Tree Pruning*

```
rtr-b>show ip mroute 224.1.1.1
IP Multicast Routing Table
Flags: D - Dense, S - Sparse, C - Connected, L - Local, P - Pruned
       R - RP-bit set, F - Register flag, T - SPT-bit set, J - Join SPT
Timers: Uptime/Expires
Interface state: Interface, Next-Hop or VCD, State/Mode

 (*, 224.1.1.1), 00:01:43/00:02:59, RP 10.1.5.1, flags: SCJ
  Incoming interface: Ethernet0, RPF nbr 10.1.2.1,
  Outgoing interface list:
    Ethernet1, Forward/Sparse, 00:01:43/00:02:11

(171.68.37.121/32, 224.1.1.1), 00:01:38/00:02:53, flags: CJT
  Incoming interface: Ethernet0, RPF nbr 10.1.2.1
  Outgoing interface list:
    Ethernet1, Forward/Sparse, 00:01:38/00:02:22
```

Example 11-36 *State in Router A Before Source Tree Pruning*

```
rtr-a>show ip mroute 224.1.1.1
IP Multicast Routing Table
Flags: D - Dense, S - Sparse, C - Connected, L - Local, P - Pruned
       R - RP-bit set, F - Register flag, T - SPT-bit set, J - Join SPT
Timers: Uptime/Expires
Interface state: Interface, Next-Hop or VCD, State/Mode

 (*, 224.1.1.1), 00:01:43/00:02:59, RP 10.1.5.1, flags: SJ
  Incoming interface: Serial0, RPF nbr 10.1.4.1,
  Outgoing interface list:
    Ethernet0, Forward/Sparse, 00:01:43/00:02:11

(171.68.37.121/32, 224.1.1.1), 00:01:32/00:02:53, flags: T
  Incoming interface: Serial1, RPF nbr 10.1.9.2
  Outgoing interface list:
    Ethernet0, Forward/Sparse, 00:01:32/00:02:28
```

The state in Router B (Example 11-35) shows that a directly connected receiver (denoted by the C flag in the (*, G) entry) exists for the multicast group. In addition, because the SPT-Threshold is set to its default value of zero, any traffic flowing down the shared tree results in the J flag being set in the (*, G) entry, which indicates that SPT-Threshold is being exceeded. The combination of these two conditions caused Router B to create the (S_i, G) entry shown in Example 11-35 and to join the SPT.

Also, notice that in the case of Router A, the shared tree and the SPT paths diverge. The incoming interface for the shared tree (represented by the (*, G) entry) is interface Serial0, whereas the incoming interface for the SPT (represented by the (S_i, G) entry) is interface Serial1.

Pruning the source tree requires eight steps. These are depicted in Figures 11-24 and 11-25 and are summarized as follows:

Step 1 Router B is a leaf router; last host, Rcvr A, leaves group G.

Step 2 Router B removes E1 (*, G) and any (S_i, G) outgoing interface lists.

Step 3 Router B (*, G) outgoing interface list is now empty; sends (*, G) Prune toward RP.

Step 4 Router B stops sending periodic (S, G) Joins.

Step 5 Router A receives Prune; removes E0 from (*, G) outgoing interface list.

Step 6 Router A (*, G) outgoing interface list now empty; sends (*, G) Prune toward RP.

Step 7 (S_i, G) state times out; (S_i, G) Prune sent toward S_i.

Step 8 (S_i, G) traffic ceases flowing down SPT.

These steps are detailed in the following sections.

Source Tree Pruning: Steps 1–3

Figure 11-24 shows the first three steps of the prune process when an SPT is active.

Figure 11-24   *Source Tree Pruning Steps 1–3*

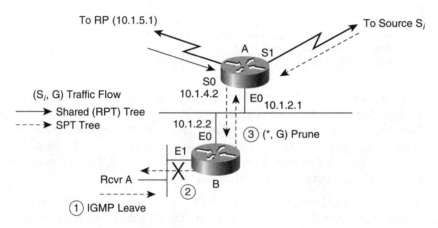

Rcvr A sends an IGMP Leave Group message, signaling Router B that it is leaving the multicast group (step 1). Because Rcvr A is the last member of group 224.1.1.1 on interface Ethernet1, Router B will remove the 224.1.1.1 IGMP Group Membership Cache entry for Ethernet1. (Note: The normal IGMP leave processing is not shown in this example.)

As a result of the removal of the 224.1.1.1 IGMP group Membership Cache entry, Router B removes interface Ethernet1 from the outgoing interface list of the (*, G) entry (Step 2). In addition, Ethernet1 is also removed from all (S, G) entries under the (*, G), based on General Rule 6 that keeps the (S, G) outgoing interface lists in sync with the (*, G) entry.

After Ethernet1 has been removed from the outgoing interface lists of the (*, G) and all (S, G) entries, the state in Router B is as shown in Example 11-37.

Example 11-37 *State in Router B After Last Member (Rcvr A) Leaves Group*

```
rtr-b>show ip mroute 224.1.1.1
IP Multicast Routing Table
Flags: D - Dense, S - Sparse, C - Connected, L - Local, P - Pruned
       R - RP-bit set, F - Register flag, T - SPT-bit set, J - Join SPT
Timers: Uptime/Expires
Interface state: Interface, Next-Hop or VCD, State/Mode

 (*, 224.1.1.1), 00:03:21/00:02:59, RP 10.1.5.1, flags: SJP
  Incoming interface: Ethernet0, RPF nbr 10.1.2.1,
  Outgoing interface list: Null

(171.68.37.121/32, 224.1.1.1), 00:03:18/00:02:32, flags: PJT
  Incoming interface: Ethernet0, RPF nbr 10.1.2.1
  Outgoing interface list: Null
```

Because the outgoing interface list on the (*, G) entry is now Null, the P flag is set and a (*, G) Prune is sent up the shared tree to Router A (Step 3).

Notice that because the outgoing interface list in the (S, G) entry is now Null, the P flag is set, indicating that the (S, G) entry is pruned and is therefore no longer being used to forward data. At this point, the (S, G) entry's expiration timer (00:02:32) continues to count down and will not be reset by the arrival of further data. Therefore, the entry will expire and be deleted in 2 minutes and 32 seconds.

Also, it is very important to note that the expiration timer on the (*, G) entry (00:02:59) will not begin counting down until all (S, G) entries under the (*, G) expire and are deleted. (In this example, the expiration timer in the (*, G) entry will begin to count down after the single (S_i, G) entry has expired and is deleted. Subsequently, when the expiration timer of the (*, G) counts down to zero, it too will be deleted.)

Source Tree Pruning: Step 4

Continuing with the example, Figure 11-25 shows the next step in the Prune process.

Figure 11-25 *Source Tree Pruning Step 4*

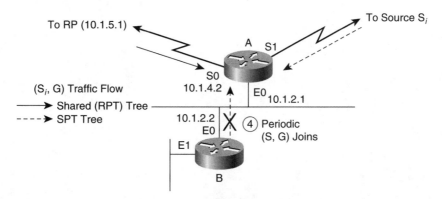

Because the (S_i, G) entry is now pruned, Router B stops sending periodic (S_i, G) Joins to refresh the SPT (Step 4). Router B also stops sending periodic $(*, G)$ Joins to refresh the shared tree. The important thing here is that an (S_i, G) Prune is not sent up the SPT as a direct result of the (S_i, G) outgoing interface transitioning to Null.

Source Tree Pruning: Steps 5 and 6

Figure 11-26 shows the final steps in the Prune process.

Figure 11-26 *Source Tree Pruning Steps 5 and 6*

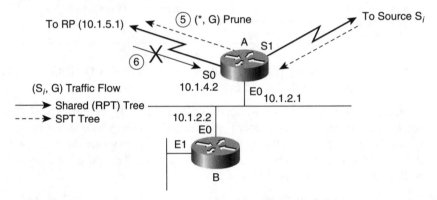

When Router A receives the $(*, G)$ Prune from Router B via Ethernet0, it schedules the interface to be pruned after a 3-second delay. The 3-second delay is to wait and see whether another router on the multi-access network wishes to override the Prune with a Join. At the end of this 3-second delay, Router A removes interface Ethernet0 from the outgoing interface list of the $(*, G)$ entry as well as from all associated (S, G) entries.

After Ethernet0 has been removed from the outgoing interface list of the $(*, G)$ entry and from all (S, G) entries under the $(*, G)$, the state in Router A is shown in Example 11-38.

Example 11-38 *State in Router A After Receiving the (*, G) Prune*

```
rtr-a>show ip mroute 224.1.1.1
IP Multicast Routing Table
Flags: D - Dense, S - Sparse, C - Connected, L - Local, P - Pruned
       R - RP-bit set, F - Register flag, T - SPT-bit set, J - Join SPT
Timers: Uptime/Expires
Interface state: Interface, Next-Hop or VCD, State/Mode

 (*, 224.1.1.1), 00:03:25/00:02:59, RP 10.1.5.1, flags: SJP
  Incoming interface: Serial0, RPF nbr 10.1.4.1,
  Outgoing interface list: Null

(171.68.37.121/32, 224.1.1.1), 00:03:20/00:02:21, flags: PT
  Incoming interface: Serial1, RPF nbr 10.1.9.2
  Outgoing interface list: Null
```

Again note that because the outgoing interface list in the (S_i, G) entry is now Null, the P flag is indicating that the entry is *pruned*. As a result, the expiration timer in the (S_i, G) entry continues to count down and is no longer reset by the arrival of (S_i, G) traffic. The expiration timer in the (*, G) entry will begin counting down after the last (S, G) entry has been deleted (in this case, after 2 minutes and 21 seconds have elapsed and the sole (S_i, G) entry has expired and has been deleted).

The outgoing interface list of the (*, G) entry in Router A has now transitioned to Null, and the (*, G) entry has been marked *pruned*. This triggers Router A to also send a (*, G) Prune up the shared tree (step 5). When this (*, G) Prune reaches the next router in the direction of the RP, the shared tree to Router A is pruned (Step 6).

Step 5 and Step 6 of the Prune process continue back up the shared tree until the RP is reached or a router is reached whose outgoing interface list does not become Null as a result of the Prune. In other words, a router is reached that still has other active branches of the shared tree.

Source Tree Pruning: Steps 7 and 8

At this point, (*, G) Prunes have been sent to stop the flow of Group G traffic down the shared tree; however, no (S_i, G) Prunes were sent to stop the flow of traffic down the SPT. Instead of triggering an (S_i, G) Prune when the outgoing interface list transitioned to Null, (S_i, G) Prunes are triggered by the arrival of (S_i, G) data packets.

Figure 11-27   *Source Tree Pruning Steps 7 and 8*

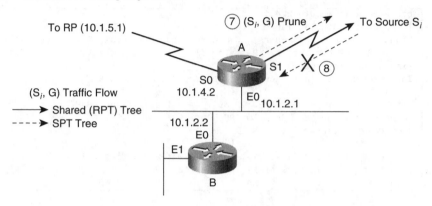

This situation is shown in Figure 11-27. Both Router A and Router B now have (S_i, G) entries with the P flag set (because their outgoing interface lists are both Null). However, because no (S_i, G) Prunes have been sent up the SPT, data from the source continues to arrive at Router A via Serial1. (We're assuming the source is still sending.) Because the P flag is set on the (S_i, G) entry, Router A responds to the arrival of an (S_i, G) data packet by sending an (S_i, G) Prune toward the source (Step 7).

When the router upstream of Router A (toward the source) receives this (S_i, G) Prune, the upstream router responds by removing the interface on which it received the Prune from the outgoing interface list of its (S_i, G) entry. This step prunes the flow of (S_i, G) traffic to Router A (Step 8).

NOTE	The reason that (S, G) Prunes are triggered only by the arrival of data is to optimize the amount of control traffic sent in the network. Specifically, this means that bandwidth is not wasted sending (S, G) Prunes for bursty or other low-rate sources in the network. If on the other hand, the source is still sending, the next arriving packet will trigger an immediate (S, G) Prune to shut off the flow of traffic.

PIM-SM Special Cases

The previous sections have covered most of the basic scenarios of sparse mode operation. However, some other interesting cases deserve special attention because they do occur more frequently than one would initially expect. Specifically, unexpected data arrival and "RP on a stick" are the most common special cases and are presented in the following sections.

Unexpected Data Arrival

In the previous sections on PIM-SM, the primary recurring theme is that state is created as a result of an explicit Join (or sometimes Prune) mechanism. However, one of the most overlooked scenarios is that state also can be created in a PIM-SM network in response to the arrival of unexpected (S, G) traffic, when no state for Group G existed previously. Figure 11-28 shows an example of this situation.

Figure 11-28   *State Creation by the Arrival of Data in a Sparse Mode Network*

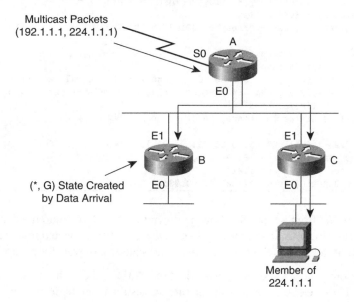

In this case, Router C has a directly connected member of group 224.1.1.1 and has joined the shared tree via Router A. This causes (*, G) state to be created in both Router A and Router C, as shown in Example 11-39.

Example 11-39 *State in Router A and Router C After Unexpected Data Arrival*

```
rtr-a>show ip mroute 224.1.1.1
IP Multicast Routing Table
Flags: D - Dense, S - Sparse, C - Connected, L - Local, P - Pruned
       R - RP-bit set, F - Register flag, T - SPT-bit set, J - Join SPT
Timers: Uptime/Expires
Interface state: Interface, Next-Hop or VCD, State/Mode

 (*, 224.1.1.1), 00:03:25/00:02:59, RP 10.1.5.1, flags: S
  Incoming interface: Serial0, RPF nbr 10.1.4.1,
  Outgoing interface list:
    Ethernet0, Forward/Sparse, 00:03:25/00:02:35

rtr-c>show ip mroute 224.1.1.1
IP Multicast Routing Table
Flags: D - Dense, S - Sparse, C - Connected, L - Local, P - Pruned
       R - RP-bit set, F - Register flag, T - SPT-bit set, J - Join SPT
Timers: Uptime/Expires
Interface state: Interface, Next-Hop or VCD, State/Mode

 (*, 224.1.1.1), 00:03:30/00:02:59, RP 10.1.5.1, flags: SC
  Incoming interface: Ethernet1, RPF nbr 10.1.2.1,
  Outgoing interface list:
    Ethernet0, Forward/Sparse, 00:03:30/00:02:31
```

Now, traffic from Source S is flowing down the shared tree onto the common Ethernet segment. However, Router B does not have a directly connected member and prior to the arrival of the unwanted (S, G) traffic has no state whatsoever for group 224.1.1.1.

Therefore, when Router B receives the first (S, G) packet, it automatically creates a (*, G) entry. However, because there are neither downstream neighbors nor any directly connected members for Group G, the outgoing interface lists of the (*, G) entry is Null.

The current state in Router B is shown in Example 11-40.

Example 11-40 *State in Router B After Unexpected Data Arrival*

```
rtr-b>show ip mroute 224.1.1.1
IP Multicast Routing Table
Flags: D - Dense, S - Sparse, C - Connected, L - Local, P - Pruned
       R - RP-bit set, F - Register flag, T - SPT-bit set, J - Join SPT
Timers: Uptime/Expires
Interface state: Interface, Next-Hop or VCD, State/Mode

 (*, 224.1.1.1), 00:00:05/00:02:59, RP 10.1.5.1, flags: SP
  Incoming interface: Ethernet1, RPF nbr 10.1.2.1,
  Outgoing interface list: Null
```

Because there is nothing going on to reset the expiration timers of these entries, this state will time out after 3 minutes and be deleted. If (S, G) traffic is still being forwarded on the common Ethernet segment, Router B will again recreate this state when it receives another (S, G) packet.

At first glance, for Router B to create state for this unwanted traffic may seem to be a waste of time. However, the existence of this state actually *improves* the overall performance of Router B, albeit at the slight expense of additional memory usage. The reason that performance is improved is that the preceding state tells the router that it can immediately drop this incoming traffic. If multicast fast switching is enabled on this incoming interface (via the **ip mroute-cache command**), the packet can be dropped in the fast-switching code path. (Note: This process is referred to as the *fast dropping* of packets. One can think of this as fast switching to the bit bucket.)

If, on the other hand, no state were created, the router would not know what to do with these unwanted packets. Instead, each time an unwanted packet arrived, the router would have to switch to *process level* to determine how to handle the packet. Because any work done at process level in the router is expensive in terms of CPU horsepower, this change would severely degrade the router's performance. Therefore, by creating this *Null* forwarding state when the first packet arrives, the router can quickly make a forwarding decision and discard the packet with a minimum amount of processing.

RP on a Stick

The RP-on-a-stick scenario (sometimes referred to as the "one-legged RP") results when the incoming interface of an (S, G) entry at the RP is also the only outgoing interface on the shared tree for Group G. General Rule 4, which prevents the incoming interface from appearing in the outgoing interface list, often results in forwarding state in the RP that confuses the newcomer to PIM multicast networks.

The RP-on-a-stick scenario occurs more frequently than one might initially think. Even if the RP is not a dedicated router with a single interface, changes in the location of sources and group membership in the network can result in this phenomenon. For example, the potential for this scenario exists whenever the RP is placed on a backbone, multi-access network with other PIM-SM routers. Figure 11-29 is a simplified example of how RP on a stick can happen.

Figure 11-29   *RP on a Stick*

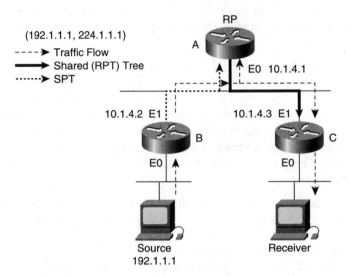

In this example, Router A is the RP connected to a common backbone Ethernet segment along with Router B and Router C. A branch of the shared tree for group 224.1.1.1 (shown by the heavy solid arrow in Figure 11-29) extends from the RP to Router C behind which a receiver for the group exists. The source (192.1.1.1) behind Router B is transmitting multicast traffic to the RP via the SPT shown by the heavy dashed arrow. However, because the SPT and the shared tree share this common Ethernet segment, the traffic flow is across the common backbone to Router C as shown by the thin dashed arrow. The state in Router B and Router C in this example is shown in Example 11-41.

Example 11-41   *State for Router B and Router C in RP on a Stick*

```
rtr-c>show ip mroute 224.1.1.1
IP Multicast Routing Table
Flags: D - Dense, S - Sparse, C - Connected, L - Local, P - Pruned
       R - RP-bit set, F - Register flag, T - SPT-bit set, J - Join SPT
Timers: Uptime/Expires
Interface state: Interface, Next-Hop or VCD, State/Mode

 (*, 224.1.1.1), 00:03:20/00:02:59, RP 10.1.4.1, flags: SCJ
  Incoming interface: Ethernet1, RPF nbr 10.1.4.1,
  Outgoing interface list:
    Ethernet0, Forward/Sparse, 00:03:20/00:02:40

(192.1.1.1/32, 224.1.1.1), 00:01:25/00:02:21, flags: CJ
  Incoming interface: Ethernet1, RPF nbr 10.1.4.2
  Outgoing interface list:
    Ethernet0, Forward/Sparse, 00:01:25/00:02:35
```

Example 11-41 *State for Router B and Router C in RP on a Stick (Continued)*

```
rtr-b>show ip mroute 224.1.1.1
IP Multicast Routing Table
Flags: D - Dense, S - Sparse, C - Connected, L - Local, P - Pruned
       R - RP-bit set, F - Register flag, T - SPT-bit set, J - Join SPT
Timers: Uptime/Expires
Interface state: Interface, Next-Hop or VCD, State/Mode

 (*, 224.1.1.1), 00:01:25/00:02:59, RP 10.1.4.1, flags: SP
  Incoming interface: Ethernet1, RPF nbr 10.1.4.1,
  Outgoing interface list: Null

(192.1.1.1/32, 224.1.1.1), 00:01:25/00:02:21, flags: FT
  Incoming interface: Ethernet0, RPF nbr 0.0.0.0
  Outgoing interface list:
    Ethernet1, Forward/Sparse, 00:01:25/00:02:35
```

This is expected in any last-hop router (Router C in this example) and any first-hop router (Router B in this example). Unfortunately, a common mistake when first encountering this topology is to assume that the traffic is first flowing to the RP and then back out the same interface to Router C. However, if we examine the state in the RP, we find the output shown in Example 11-42.

Example 11-42 *State for RP in RP on a Stick*

```
rtr-a>show ip mroute 224.1.1.1
IP Multicast Routing Table
Flags: D - Dense, S - Sparse, C - Connected, L - Local, P - Pruned
       R - RP-bit set, F - Register flag, T - SPT-bit set, J - Join SPT
Timers: Uptime/Expires
Interface state: Interface, Next-Hop or VCD, State/Mode

 (*, 224.1.1.1), 00:03:20/00:02:59, RP 10.1.4.1, flags: S
  Incoming interface: Null, RPF nbr 0.0.0.0,
  Outgoing interface list:
    Ethernet0, Forward/Sparse, 00:03:20/00:02:40

(192.1.1.1/32, 224.1.1.1), 00:01:25/00:02:35, flags: PT
  Incoming interface: Ethernet0, RPF nbr 10.1.4.2
  Outgoing interface list: Null
```

Notice that the outgoing interface list of the (S, G) entry is Null, which means that the RP is actually dropping this multicast traffic and not forwarding at all. (Assuming that multicast fast switching is enabled on interface Ethernet0, the RP will be fast dropping this traffic.) Instead, the multicast traffic is flowing directly across the backbone Ethernet segment from Router B to Router C, which is the desired behavior in this case.

The state in the RP may seem counterintuitive at first but can be explained by applying the PIM-SM state rules covered earlier in this chapter:

1 From the state shown in Example 11-2, you know that the receiver joined the shared tree first—approximately 3 minutes and 20 seconds ago, based on the timer values in the Router A and Router C state. This process caused the branch of the shared tree to be created, and the state in the RP at that instant would have been as shown in Example 11-43.

Example 11-43 *State for RP as Shared Tree Is Created*

```
rtr-a>show ip mroute 224.1.1.1
IP Multicast Routing Table
Flags: D - Dense, S - Sparse, C - Connected, L - Local, P - Pruned
       R - RP-bit set, F - Register flag, T - SPT-bit set, J - Join SPT
Timers: Uptime/Expires
Interface state: Interface, Next-Hop or VCD, State/Mode

 (*, 224.1.1.1), 00:00:10/00:02:59, RP 10.1.4.1, flags: S
  Incoming interface: Null, RPF nbr 0.0.0.0,
  Outgoing interface list:
    Ethernet0, Forward/Sparse, 00:00:10/00:02:50
```

2 When the source began sending a few minutes later, Router B would have performed the normal Register operation with the RP and the RP would have responded by creating (S, G) state and joining the SPT toward the source. The RP would have applied General Rule 3, which initially populated the outgoing interface list of the (S, G) entry with a copy of the interfaces in the outgoing interface list of the (*, G). If it were somehow possible to actually capture the state in the RP at this precise instant, the state would be as shown in Example 11-44.

Example 11-44 *State for RP*

```
rtr-a>show ip mroute 224.1.1.1
IP Multicast Routing Table
Flags: D - Dense, S - Sparse, C - Connected, L - Local, P - Pruned
       R - RP-bit set, F - Register flag, T - SPT-bit set, J - Join SPT
Timers: Uptime/Expires
Interface state: Interface, Next-Hop or VCD, State/Mode

 (*, 224.1.1.1), 00:03:20/00:02:59, RP 10.1.4.1, flags: S
  Incoming interface: Null, RPF nbr 0.0.0.0,
  Outgoing interface list:
    Ethernet0, Forward/Sparse, 00:03:20/00:02:40

(192.1.1.1/32, 224.1.1.1), 00:00:00/00:02:59, flags: PT
  Incoming interface: Ethernet0, RPF nbr 10.1.4.2
  Outgoing interface list:
    Ethernet0, Forward/Sparse, 00:00:00/00:02:59
```

NOTE	Don't bother trying to catch the router with the above state because it isn't possible to ever see this sort of display. I have shown this internal intermediate step only to make the overall process clear. If you do ever catch a Cisco router in this state, it's a bug!

3 Notice that the incoming interface in the (S, G) preceding entry also appears in the outgoing interface list, which would have caused a route loop. However, before proceeding further, the RP also applies General Rule 4 (that is, the incoming interface cannot also appear in the outgoing interface list) and removes Ethernet0 from the outgoing interface list. This results in the final desired state of Example 11-45.

Example 11-45 *Final State for RP*

```
rtr-a>show ip mroute 224.1.1.1
IP Multicast Routing Table
Flags: D - Dense, S - Sparse, C - Connected, L - Local, P - Pruned
       R - RP-bit set, F - Register flag, T - SPT-bit set, J - Join SPT
Timers: Uptime/Expires
Interface state: Interface, Next-Hop or VCD, State/Mode

 (*, 224.1.1.1), 00:03:20/00:02:59, RP 10.1.4.1, flags: S
  Incoming interface: Null, RPF nbr 0.0.0.0,
  Outgoing interface list:
    Ethernet0, Forward/Sparse, 00:03:20/00:02:40

(192.1.1.1/32, 224.1.1.1), 00:01:25/00:02:35, flags: PT
  Incoming interface: Ethernet0, RPF nbr 10.1.4.2
  Outgoing interface list: Null
```

Now comes the really tricky part! (You thought things were getting complex. Just wait.) Notice that the expiration timer in the (S, G) entry above would normally count down to zero because it is pruned and no longer being used to forward this traffic. This, in turn, would cause the entry to be deleted when the timer reached zero. Additionally, because the (S, G) entry is marked *pruned* (denoted by the P flag), the RP would normally stop sending periodic (S, G) Joins to refresh the SPT from the first-hop router to the RP. However, if Router B stops receiving these (S, G) Joins, its (S, G) entry expiration timer would eventually time out and the (S, G) entry would be deleted. If this were allowed to happen, (S, G) traffic would cease to flow to the backbone segment while the receiver behind Router C is still active.

Turnaround Router

As it turns out, the RP-on-a-stick scenario is actually a degenerate case of the more general scenario called the *turnaround router*. The turnaround-router scenario occurs when the path of the SPT and the path of the shared tree merge at some point in the network. The router at which these two paths merge (yet are flowing in opposite directions) is the turnaround router. Therefore, the turnaround router is *upstream* of receivers on the shared tree and *downstream* of the source on the SPT.

Figure 11-30 repeats the basic RP-on-a-stick example in Figure 11-29 but with the RP now moved one hop farther away from the source and receiver by way of Router X. Notice that Router X is the turnaround router because the paths of the SPT and the shared tree first merge on the common Ethernet backbone at Router X.

Figure 11-30 *Unnecessary Traffic Flowing to the RP Prior to IOS 12.0*

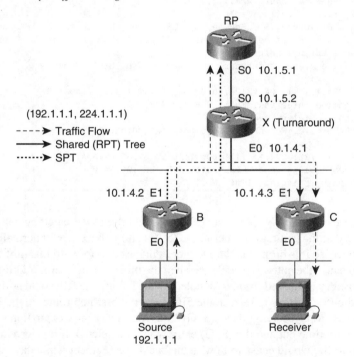

Note that the flow of traffic (indicated by the thin dashed arrows) is flowing not only across the common backbone from Router B to Router C but also through Router X all the way to the RP where it is being dropped. (It is dropped because in this scenario there are no other branches of the shared tree.) This unnecessary flow of traffic back to the RP is clearly a waste of network bandwidth and is undesirable. What is needed is a way to have the (S, G) traffic flow stop at the turnaround router and not continue on up toward the RP where it is unneeded. To stop the traffic flow this way, the turnaround router must assume the task of originating periodic proxy (S, G) Joins toward the source instead of the RP.

Proxy-Join Timer

With IOS release 12.0, Cisco routers introduced Proxy-Join timers (on (S, G) entries) to implement the turnaround router concept. When an (S, G) Proxy-Join timer is running (which is indicated by a new **X** flag in the (S, G) entry), the router is the turnaround router and it must periodically send *proxy* (S, G) Joins toward source S on behalf of the RP. In addition, the router must not send (S, G) Prunes toward the source (because doing so would conflict with the proxy (S, G) Joins), even though the outgoing interface list in the (S, G) entry is Null. Thus, the (S, G) state that exists along the path between the first-hop router and the turnaround router remains refreshed as long as the source is active and receivers exist.

NOTE	Remember, the normal procedure when the outgoing interface list in an (S, G) entry is Null is to send (S, G) *Prunes*, not (S, G) Joins, toward the source. This procedure is reversed when the Proxy-Join timer is running.

The trick is to have the routers detect the special conditions that indicate that they have become the turnaround router and to start the Proxy-Join timer. A few simple rules control the starting and stopping of the Proxy-Join timer. However, before getting to these rules, let's do a quick review of PIM Join/Prune messages and establish some additional terminology to describe (*, G) Joins.

Atomic and Nonatomic (*, G) Joins

Recall from the discussion of SPT-Switchover that (S, G)RP-bit Prunes are sent up the shared tree to prune off sources whose traffic is being received directly via the SPT along a different path. (As you know by now, the RP-bit indicates that the information is applicable to the shared tree and, therefore, (S, G)RP-bit Prunes are sent up the shared tree and not the SPT.) These (S, G)RP-bit Prunes must continue to be sent periodically along with the associated (*, G) Join to refresh state along the shared tree. When these periodic Joins are sent up the shared tree, both the (*, G) Join and any associated (S, G)RP-bit Prunes are all sent inside of the same PIM Join/Prune message. This leads to the following two new categories of (*, G) Joins:

- **Atomic (*, G) Joins**—These are Join/Prune messages that contain both the (*, G) Join along with all associated (S, G)RP-bit Prunes for Group G.

- **Nonatomic (*, G) Joins**—These are Join/Prune messages that contain only the (*, G) Join without any associated (S, G)RP-bit Prunes for Group G.

Now that you are armed with some better terminology to describe (*, G) Joins, you can state some simple rules for starting and stopping the Proxy-Join timer.

Proxy-Join Timer Rules

A Proxy-Join timer is associated only with the (S, G) state entries in the Cisco mroute table. Three rules govern the start and stop of this timer.

Proxy-Join Timer Rule 1

The Proxy-Join timer for an (S, G) entry is (re)started under the following conditions:

- A nonatomic (*, G) Join is received on the incoming interface of the (S, G) entry from other than the RPF neighbor toward Source S.

- In the RP when an (S, G) entry is created as a result of the receipt of a Register message and the (*, G) entry has a non-Null outgoing interface list.

Proxy-Join Timer Rule 2

Proxy-Join timers are not stopped by any direct event. Instead, they are simply allowed to time out if not restarted by the receipt of a nonatomic (*, G) Join.

Whenever a Proxy-Join timer for an (S, G) entry is running, the X flag is displayed in the Flags field of the (S, G) entry in the mroute table, as shown in Example 11-46.

Example 11-46 *Mroute Table*

```
rtr-x>show ip mroute 224.1.1.1
IP Multicast Routing Table
Flags: D - Dense, S - Sparse, C - Connected, L - Local, P - Pruned
       R - RP-bit set, F - Register flag, T - SPT-bit set, J - Join SPT
Timers: Uptime/Expires
Interface state: Interface, Next-Hop or VCD, State/Mode

 (*, 224.1.1.1), 00:03:20/00:02:59, RP 10.1.4.1, flags: S
  Incoming interface: Null, RPF nbr 0.0.0.0,
  Outgoing interface list:
    Ethernet0, Forward/Sparse, 00:03:20/00:02:40

(192.1.1.1/32, 224.1.1.1), 00:01:25/00:02:35, flags: PXT
  Incoming interface: Ethernet0, RPF nbr 10.1.4.2
  Outgoing interface list: Null
```

In this example, the Proxy-Join timer is running on the (192.1.1.1/32, 224.1.1.1) entry in Router X. This modifies the periodic Join/Prune behavior of Router X for this (S, G) entry as described in the following rule:

Proxy-Join Timer Rule 3

While the Proxy-Join timer is running on an (S, G) entry, the router will perform the following steps:

- Send periodic (S, G) Joins toward Source S

- Suppress sending (S, G) Prunes toward Source S

NOTE   As I did for the other general rules and PIM-SM rules, I have simplified the Proxy-Join timer rules for clarity. There are minor exceptions to the preceding rules, such as the stopping of a Proxy timer when the RP interface changes on an (S, G) entry. In general, the rules presented here are sufficient to convey the function and use of Proxy-Join timers.

Proxy-Join Example

Let's step through a highly simplified example of the turnaround router scenario, using the sample network shown in Figure 11-30.

1 The RP starts its Proxy-Join timer upon receiving the first (S, G) Register message (according to the second part of Proxy-Join Timer Rule 1) from the first-hop router (Router B in this example).

2 Because the (S, G) Proxy-Join timer is running, the RP begins sending periodic (S, G) Joins toward the source according to Proxy-Join Timer Rule 3. This, in turn, builds the initial (S, G) SPT from the source to the RP and creates (S, G) in all the routers along the path.

3 (S, G) traffic begins flowing to the RP. Notice that Proxy-Join Timer Rule 3 also prevents the RP from sending (S, G) Prunes toward the source, even though its (S, G) outgoing interface list is Null.

4 When traffic is flowing, Router X receives a nonatomic (*, G) Join from Router C on the incoming interface of the (S, G) entry. Because Router C is not the RPF neighbor toward the source, the first part of Proxy-Join Timer Rule 1 comes into play and causes Router X to start its (S, G) Proxy-Join timer.

5 Router X has now become the turnaround router (because its (S, G) Proxy-Join timer is running) and begins sending periodic (S, G) Joins toward the source.

6 Router X begins sending periodic atomic (*, G) Joins toward the RP as a result of PIM-SM Rule 7, which states that (S, G)RP-bit Prunes will be sent when the (S, G) and (*, G) RPF neighbors are different. (In other words, the periodic (*, G) Joins sent by Router X will contain (S, G)RP-bit Prunes and therefore, by definition, be atomic.)

7 The RP is receiving atomic (*, G) Joins (which do not restart its (S, G) Proxy-Join timer), and the (S, G) Proxy-Join timer in the RP is allowed to expire.

8 When the (S, G) Proxy-Join timer expires, the RP stops sending (S, G) Joins toward the source.

9 Because Router X is no longer getting (S, G) Joins from the RP via Serial0, this interface eventually times out and is removed from the (S, G) outgoing interface list on Router X. This step stops the flow of unnecessary (S, G) traffic to the RP.

Make careful note of the fact that (other than when the turnaround router is the RP) the turnaround-router function occurs only when SPT-Thresholds of infinity are in use, that is, when routers with directly connected members are not joining the SPT to the source.

The reason that the function doesn't work when a router joins the SPT is that atomic (*, G) Joins are generated instead of nonatomic (*, G) Joins. Therefore, the upstream router does not start its Proxy-Join timer and become the turnaround router.

For example, if Router C in Figure 11-30 had joined the SPT toward the source, it would begin sending atomic (*, G) Joins to Router X (based on PIM-SM Rule 7, which states that (S, G)RP-bit Prunes are to be sent when the RPF neighbor of the (*, G) and (S, G) are different). Therefore, Router X would *not* start its (S, G) Proxy-Join timer because Proxy-Join Timer Rule 1 (which governs the starting of the Proxy-Join timer) would not have been met.

Summary

The configuration of PIM-SM requires only three simple commands on each router in the network. (The next chapter addresses the use of Auto-RP, which eliminates the need to manually configure an RP address on each router in the network. Auto-RP reduces the required number of commands on each router in the network to only two.) Although turning on PIM-SM is quite straightforward and easy for a network administrator, it is another thing entirely to understand how PIM-SM creates and maintains forwarding state in the routers. This chapter defined several PIM-SM rules in addition to the six general rules that were introduced in the preceding chapter. Together, these rules define the basic behavior of PIM-SM routers and can be used by network engineers to understand and troubleshoot the mroute state information in Cisco routers.

CHAPTER 12

PIM Rendezvous Points

Newcomers to IP multicast often view the design, configuration, and placement of Protocol Independent Multicast (PIM) rendezvous points (RPs) as a complex task that only persons possessing IP multicast guru status can accomplish. As an IP multicast consultant, I'm constantly asked the question, "Where should I place the RP?" Most of the time, I answer, "Wherever it's convenient." I don't give this simple reply to be flippant but because (usually) the people who ask this question are building basic PIM sparse mode (PIM-SM) networks that don't require any fancy RP engineering.

The goal of this chapter is to provide you with the information necessary to understand how the various RP configuration methods work, as well as to provide guidance in the engineering of RPs to accomplish various special tasks such as providing redundancy in the case of an RP failure. To accomplish this goal, this chapter starts off by covering the two primary methods that Cisco routers can use to dynamically discover the identity of the RP in the PIM-SM network. These two methods are

- Cisco's Auto-RP
- PIMv2 Bootstrap router

In both cases, details of the configuration, tuning, and underlying protocol mechanisms employed by these two RP discovery methods are presented. Following these two topics is a section that covers the placement and tuning of RPs in a PIM-SM network.

Auto-RP

Early versions of Cisco PIM-SM required each router in the network to be manually configured with the address of the RP, using the following configuration command:

```
ip pim rp-address address [group-list acl]
```

Initially, this method was sufficient for simple PIM-SM networks that used a single, static RP for all multicast groups. However, even in these initial networks, it was sometimes necessary to change the IP address of the RP (for example to another interface on the same router) or to reassign the RP task to another router in the network. This process required the network administrator to update the configuration of each router in the network to reflect this change. During the update process, the RP address would at some point be inconsistent across the routers in the network. This frequently caused multicast outages that lasted until the network administrator was able to complete the update process. Additionally, the manual update process was prone to human error as a result of mistyped commands or even routers that were inadvertently not updated.

PIMv2's Bootstrap router feature, with the capability for all PIMv2 routers in the network to *learn* the IP address of the RP(s), promised to provide a solution to this problem. However, PIMv2 was still in draft form at that time and was a long way from being implemented. Obviously, some other method of dynamically updating all the routers in the network was needed that could be implemented within the framework of a PIMv1 network.

Overview of Auto-RP

Beginning with IOS version 11.1(6), Cisco introduced support for a new feature, called Auto-RP, that eliminated the need to manually configure RP information in every router in the network. The concept of Auto-RP is both simple and elegant. Use IP multicast to distribute Group-to-RP information to all routers in the network.

For this to work, all Cisco PIM routers in the network learn about the active Group-to-RP mapping by automatically joining the *Cisco-RP-Discovery* (224.0.1.40) well-known IP multicast group in order to receive Group-to-RP mapping information. This RP mapping information is multicast to this well-known group by a Cisco router configured as a Mapping Agent. (Note: Multiple Mapping Agents can be configured to provide redundancy in the case of a failure.)

Mapping Agents also use IP multicast to learn which routers in the network are possible candidate RP's by joining the well-known *Cisco-RP-Announce* (224.0.1.39) multicast group to receive candidate RP announcements. Candidate RPs announce their intention to be the RP for a particular group or group range by multicasting *RP-Announce* messages to the Cisco-RP-Announce multicast group.

Candidate RPs multicast these RP-Announce messages every RP_ANNOUNCE_INTERVAL seconds (the default is 60 seconds). Each RP-Announce message contains a *holdtime* in seconds that tells the Mapping Agent(s) how long the candidate RP announcement is valid. This holdtime is set to 3 times the RP_ANNOUNCE_INTERVAL (the default is 180 seconds).

Mapping Agents listen to these candidate RP announcements and use the information contained in them to create entries in their Group-to-RP mapping caches. Only one mapping cache entry is created for any Group-to-RP range received even if multiple candidate RPs are sending RP announcements for the same range. As the RP-Announce messages arrive, a Mapping Agent selects the RP for a given multicast group address range(s) based on the candidate RPs' IP address. The highest candidate RP IP address is selected, and the Mapping Agent stores this RP address in the Group-to-RP mapping cache entry.

Mapping Agents multicast the contents of their Group-to-RP mapping cache in RP-Discovery messages every RP_DISCOVERY_INTERVAL seconds (the default is 60 seconds). Like RP-Announce messages, RP-Discovery messages contain a holdtime in seconds that tells the routers in the network how long the Group-to-RP mapping is valid. This holdtime is set to three times the RP_DISCOVERY_INTERVAL (the default is 180 seconds). If a router fails to receive RP-Discovery messages and the Group-to-RP mapping information expires, the router switches to a statically configured RP that was defined with the **ip pim rp-address** command. If no statically configured RP exists, the router switches the group(s) to dense mode.

Figure 12-1 depicts the Auto-RP mechanism in action. In this example, routers B and C are both candidate RPs and are multicasting their RP candidate announcements (shown by the dotted arrows) to the Cisco-RP-Announce multicast group, 224.0.1.39.

Figure 12-1 *Basic Auto-RP Mechanism*

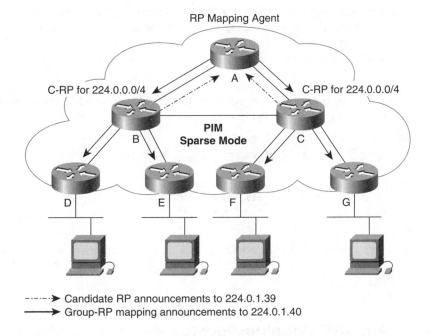

Router A, the Mapping Agent, receives these candidate announcements and selects the router with the highest IP address as the active RP. Router A then multicasts this selected Group-to-RP mapping information to all routers in the network via the Cisco-RP-Discovery multicast group, 224.0.1.40. Finally, all routers in the network automatically join the Cisco-RP-Discovery multicast group when they start up and therefore receive the Group-to-RP mapping information.

Configuring Auto-RP Candidate RPs

One or more routers in a PIM-SM network may be configured as candidate RPs by using the following command:

```
ip pim send-rp-announce interface scope ttl [group-list acl]
```

When this global configuration command is added to a router's configuration, the router begins to multicast RP-Announce messages to the Cisco-RP-Announce multicast group (224.0.1.39) with a Time To Live (TTL) of *ttl*. Each RP-Announce message contains the IP address of the specified interface (often a loopback interface) along with the group range(s) (using an group/mask format) that were specified in the optional **group-list** access control list. The group range specified in this **group-list** clause indicates the groups for which the router is willing to be RP.

NOTE   If the optional **group-list** clause is omitted, the group range advertised is 224.0.0.0/4. This range corresponds to all IP multicast group addresses, which indicates that the router is willing to serve as the RP for all groups.

A router may be configured to serve as candidate RP for more than one group range by carefully crafting the access list in the router configuration as shown in Example 12-1.

Example 12-1   *Access List Configuration for Candidate RP*

```
ip pim send-rp-announce loopback0 scope 16 group-list 10

access-list 10 permit 239.254.0.0 0.0.255.255
access-list 10 permit 239.255.0.0 0.0.255.255
access-list 10 permit 224.0.0.0 7.255.255.255
```

The router configuration in Example 12-1 configures the router to advertise itself as candidate RP for group range 239.254.0.0–239.255.255.255 and 224.0.0.0–231.255.255.255.

Configuring Auto-RP Mapping Agents

The function of Mapping Agent can be assigned to one or more routers in the network using the following global configuration command:

```
ip pim send-rp-discovery scope ttl
```

This command directs the router to begin serving as RP Mapping Agent by

1 Joining the Cisco-RP-Announce multicast group (224.0.1.39).

2 Caching the received RP-Announce messages from the candidate RPs in the network.

3 Selecting the RP(s) using the highest IP address in the RP-Announce messages for a given group range(s). (Note: The interface specified in the **ip pim send-rp-announce** command on the candidate RP router determines this address.)

4 Periodically (every 60 seconds) multicasting the selected RP information to all routers in the network via the Cisco-RP-Discovery multicast group (224.0.1.40), using the TTL that was specified by the *scope* clause in the **ip pim send-rp-discovery** configuration command.

Using Multiple Mapping Agents for Redundancy

It is not uncommon for network designers to configure more than one Mapping Agent in a network so that, if one agent fails, a second continues to operate. However, network engineers often misunderstand how multiple Mapping Agents interact and frequently attribute more complexity to this interaction than actually exists.

In actual practice, each Mapping Agent functions independently, multicasting identical Group-to-RP mapping information in RP-Discovery messages to all routers in the network. Therefore, if two Mapping Agents are in the network, let's call them Mapping Agent A and Mapping Agent B, each router in the network receives two RP-Discovery messages every RP_DISCOVERY_INTERVAL seconds: one from Mapping Agent A and one from Mapping Agent B.

Receiving Group-to-RP mapping data from two Mapping Agents is not a problem because both agents transmit identical mapping information. (They hear the same set of RP announcements from candidate RPs and apply the same selection algorithm of highest IP address to pick the active RP.) All routers in the network create a single set of Group-to-RP mapping cache entries despite receiving redundant sets of information from multiple Mapping Agents. The only noticeable effect is that the entries in the router's Group-to-RP mapping cache indicate a different source (that is, different Mapping Agents) of the Group-to-RP mapping information, depending on the exact instant that the cache is examined. This flip-flopping of the source of the Group-to-RP mapping information in the routers is insignificant and should not concern network administrators.

The real advantage of having all Mapping Agents operate simultaneously is that it eliminates the need to maintain a master-slave relationship between the Mapping Agents and eliminates a complex *failover* protocol that could go wrong. Instead, by having all Mapping Agents operating simultaneously, if one Mapping Agent goes "off the air," the other(s) are still operating and providing identical Group-to-RP mapping information to the network.

Auto-RP Discovery messages are transmitted unreliably because the protocol has no provision to detect missed packets and no way to request retransmission. A side effect of using multiple Mapping Agents for redundancy is a slight increase in the reliability of the delivery of Group-to-Mapping information because the Mapping Agents are transmitting redundant information.

Using Multiple RPs for Redundancy

Using Auto-RP, network administrators may configure more than one RP for any particular group range. The most common example is when a secondary RP is configured in case the primary RP for the network fails. This can be accomplished with the following configuration commands:

1 Router A configuration (primary RP):

```
Interface loopback0
ip address 192.168.100.2 255.255.255.255

ip pim send-rp-announce loopback0 scope 16
```

2 Router B configuration (secondary RP):

```
Interface loopback0
ip address 192.168.100.1 255.255.255.255

ip pim send-rp-announce loopback0 scope 16
```

In this example, both Routers A and B are candidate RPs for the entire range of group addresses. (Note the absence of a **group-list** clause.) Because Router A is configured with a higher RP address than Router B, Router A will serve as the primary RP. However, if Router A fails, Router B will take over the function of RP for all groups.

The Birth of Sparse-Dense Mode

Using IP multicast as the basic method of distributing RP information to all routers in the network introduces a classic chicken-and-egg problem. If the network is configured in sparse mode and all routers are expected to learn the RP information via the RP-Discovery multicast group, 224.0.1.40, how do they join the (*, 224.0.1.40) shared tree if they don't know the IP address of the RP? Furthermore, how can they learn the IP address of the RP if they don't join the shared tree?

One solution to this problem is to configure every router in the network with a dedicated RP that serves the (*, 224.0.1.40) shared tree. This could be accomplished by adding the following router configuration commands to every router in the network:

```
ip pim rp-address x.x.x.x group-list 10

access-list 10 permit 224.0.1.40
access-list 10 deny all
```

The preceding commands would cause all routers to use IP address $x.x.x.x$ as the RP for the RP-Discovery multicast group (224.0.1.40). As soon as a router boots up, it would join this group and begin receiving dynamic Group-to-RP information from the Mapping Agent(s) via this group.

The downsides to this approach should be obvious. What if router *x.x.x.x* fails? Furthermore, one of the primary goals of Auto-RP is to avoid having to configure static RP information on every router in the network. Therefore, this solution is suboptimal, and some other method is clearly desired. One possibility is to assume that the RP-Discovery (224.0.1.40) and RP-Announce (224.0.1.39) multicast groups are always operated as dense mode groups. This approach would allow the Auto-RP information to flow throughout the network in dense mode while all the other groups could operate in sparse mode.

In the end, the solution was to define a new PIM interface mode called *sparse-dense mode,* using the following router interface configuration command:

```
ip pim sparse-dense-mode
```

This command causes the router to make the decision to use sparse mode on an interface based on whether the router has RP information for the group in question. If a particular group maps to an entry in the router's Group-to-RP mapping cache, then that group is treated as a sparse mode group on that interface. On the other hand, if the group doesn't map to an entry in the router's Group-to-RP mapping cache, then the group is treated as a dense mode group on that interface.

Sparse-dense mode not only allows the Auto-RP mechanism to work (by assuming the two Auto-RP groups are in dense mode by default) but also provides another significant advantage. If sparse-dense mode is configured on all interfaces on all routers in the network, the network administrator can control which groups are sparse and which are dense by modifying the configuration on a single router!

For example, refer to the following configuration on the router that is functioning as sole candidate RP for the network:

```
ip pim send-rp-announce loopback0 scope 16 group-list 10

access-list 10 permit 224.1.1.1
```

This configuration results in this router serving as the RP for group 224.1.1.1 and no other! Because this router is the sole candidate RP in the network, only group 224.1.1.1 will operate in sparse mode; all other multicast groups will operate in dense mode. This might be very useful when you are transitioning the network from dense mode to sparse mode and desire to verify proper sparse mode operation on a single test multicast group or group range. When the test has been completed and the network administrator is satisfied that sparse mode is operating correctly, the network can be completely switched to sparse mode by simply modifying the configuration in the candidate RP(s) to reflect the following:

```
ip pim send-rp-announce loopback0 scope 16
```

The absence of the **group-list** clause in the preceding command results in this router advertising itself as a candidate RP for all multicast groups.

NOTE	The use of sparse-dense mode is now the recommended method of enabling PIM on any interface because the combination of sparse-dense mode and Auto-RP enables the network administrator to use either dense mode or sparse mode in the network depending on how the candidate RPs (if any) are configured. Using sparse-dense mode, a network administrator can start off with a dense mode network and later switch to a sparse mode network without having to change PIM modes on every interface in the network.

A Simple Auto-RP Configuration

Figure 12-2 shows a network that has been configured to run PIM-SM, using the Auto-RP feature to distribute Group-to-Mapping information. In this example, Router C is configured as the RP for all multicast groups in the network.

Figure 12-2   *A Simple Auto-RP Configuration*

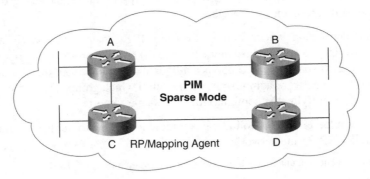

The commands shown in Table 12-1 are sufficient to enable PIM-SM on these routers and configure Router C as the RP.

Table 12-1   *Commands for Enabling PIM-SM and Assigning an RP*

On each router	**ip multicast-routing**
On each interface	**ip pim sparse-dense mode**
On Router C (RP)	**ip pim send-rp-announce ethernet0 scope 16** **ip pim send-rp-discovery scope 16**

Notice that Router C is configured as both a candidate RP and a Mapping Agent. This practice is fairly common.

Once this has been configured, you can confirm that everything is working correctly by examining the Group-to-RP mapping cache on the routers in the network using the **show ip pim rp mapping** command. Example 12-2 shows the expected Group-to-RP information on one of the routers obtained with this command.

Example 12-2 *Output for **show ip pim rp mapping** on Rtr-D*

```
Rtr-D# show ip pim rp mapping
PIM Group-to-RP Mappings

Group(s) 224.0.0.0/4, uptime: 00:01:20, expires: 00:02:38
    RP 172.16.2.1 (Rtr-C), PIMv1
    Info source: 172.16.2.1 (Rtr-C)
```

The output in Example 12-2 indicates that Rtr-C is the current RP for the multicast group range 224.0.0.0–239.255.255.255 (that is, all multicast groups). The output also shows that this information was learned via Auto-RP (indicated by the PIMv1 tag) and that the source of this information was Rtr-C.

Example 12-3 is the output of the same command issued on Rtr-C, which is the RP and the Mapping Agent. Notice that the first two lines of the output indicate that this router is an RP and a Mapping Agent.

Example 12-3 *Output for **show ip pim rp mapping** on Rtr-C*

```
Rtr-C# sh ip pim rp mapping
PIM Group-to-RP Mappings
This system is an RP
This system is an RP-mapping agent

Group(s) 224.0.0.0/4, uptime: 00:23:47, expires: 00:02:01
    RP 172.16.2.1 (Rtr-C), PIMv1
    Info source: 172.16.2.1 (Rtr-C)
```

NOTE   If multiple RPs and Mapping Agents were desired in this network, the two additional commands that were added to Router C's configuration could be also added to another router in the network to define a second candidate RP and Mapping Agent.

RP Failover in Auto-RP Networks

RP Mapping Agents store the information in the received RP-Announce messages in a Group-to-RP mapping cache. Each entry in the Group-to-RP mapping cache has an expiration timer that is initialized to the holdtime values in the received RP-Announce message. Because the originating candidate RP sets the holdtime to three times the RP_ANNOUNCE_INTERVAL, this is the period of time that must elapse before the Mapping Agent deletes the current Group-to-RP Mapping. Then, the Mapping Agent selects a new RP from its Group-to-RP mapping cache and sends out an RP-Discovery message with the updated Group-to-RP mapping.

Prior to IOS version 12.0(5), the RP_ANNOUNCE_INTERVAL was fixed at 60 seconds which, in turn, resulted in RP-Announce holdtimes of 180 seconds, or 3 minutes. Therefore, RP Failover could take as long as 3 minutes from the actual time that the RP router failed.

After IOS version 12.0(5), a new form of the **ip pim send-rp-announce** command was introduced that allowed the RP_ANNOUNCE_INTERVAL to be specified from 1 second up to 65,535 seconds. This new command has the following format:

```
ip pim send-rp-announce interface scope ttl [group-list acl] [interval secs]
```

Network administrators who want shorter RP Failover times can tune this interval to reduce RP Failover times to roughly 3 seconds by specifying a 1-second interval in the preceding command. However, tuning this interval down from the default of 60 seconds to achieve faster RP Failover times comes at the expense of the added multicast traffic in the network due to more frequent RP announcements. In some networks, this added traffic load is worth the shorter RP Failover times.

NOTE   In most cases, the default behavior (that is, SPT-Threshold = 0) of a PIM-SM network is for all last-hop routers to immediately join the SPT and bypass the RP for any new source detected. The net result of this behavior is that the failure of an RP has little effect on the delivery of multicast traffic that is already flowing in the network. Generally, only new sources that just happen to come active during the RP Failover period are affected because the last-hop routers are not yet aware that these sources exist and have not yet joined these sources' SPTs. However, after the RP Failover process completes, the multicast traffic from these new sources begins flowing down the shared tree, which is now rooted at the new RP.

Constraining Auto-RP Messages

When configuring an Auto-RP candidate RP, care must be taken to ensure that the TTL scope specified is sufficiently large so that the RP-Announce messages reach all Auto-RP Mapping Agents in the network.

Figure 12-3 shows an example of what can happen if careful attention is not paid to the *ttl* value specified in the **scope** portion of the **ip pim send-rp-announce** command. In this example, Router C is an Auto-RP candidate RP that has been configured with a TTL scope of 16 hops. This scope is sufficient for the RP-Announce messages to reach the closest Mapping Agent in the network, Router A. Unfortunately, the TTL scope is not large enough to allow RP-Announce messages to travel to the far side of the network (which has a total diameter of 32 hops) and be received by the second Mapping Agent, Router B. This results in inconsistencies in the RP mapping caches of Routers A and B. This inconsistency could cause the two Mapping Agents to select and advertise different RPs for the same group range(s). Because both Mapping Agents are operating simultaneously, the routers in the network could be receiving conflicting RP information, which could, in turn, cause serious problems.

Figure 12-3   *Improper TTL Scope of RP-Announce Messages*

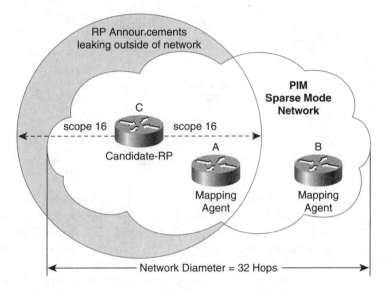

The same attention to TTL scope should also be applied to the RP-Discovery messages to ensure that all routers in the network can receive the Group-to-RP mapping information.

Figure 12-4 shows what can happen if an improper *ttl* value is specified in the **scope** portion of the **ip pim send-rp-discovery** command. In this example, the Mapping Agent (Router A) is configured with a TTL scope that is insufficient for the RP-Discovery messages to make it across the network to Router D. Thus, Router D incorrectly assumes that all multicast groups are to operate in dense mode because D is not in receipt of any Group-to-RP mapping information.

Figure 12-4 *Improper TTL Scope of RP-Discovery Messages*

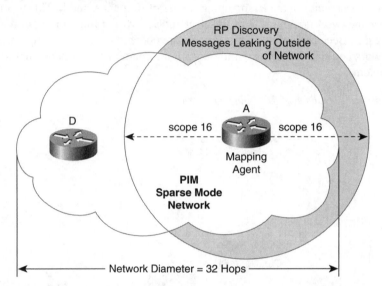

Figures 12-3 and 12-4 also illustrate another potential problem that can occur if steps are not taken to prevent RP-Announce and/or RP-Discovery messages from leaking outside the PIM-SM network into an adjacent network. In Figure 12-3, Router C is less than 16 hops away from the nearest boundary of the PIM-SM network, which is resulting in RP-Announce messages being leaked into the adjacent network on the left. Trying to solve this problem by further reducing the TTL scope only makes things worse because it is quite possible that the RP-Announce messages won't even make it to Router A.

Likewise, in Figure 12-4, Router A is less than 16 hops away from the nearest boundary of the PIM-SM network. This results in RP-Discovery messages leaking into the adjacent network to the right. Again, reducing TTL scope only makes things worse because then even fewer routers in the network (besides Router D) will receive critical Group-to-RP mapping information.

One of the best ways to handle this situation is to configure the TTL scope to the maximum diameter (in hops) of the network. This configuration ensures that the RP-Announce and RP-Discovery messages will be multicast with a TTL sufficiently large to reach all points in the network.

Multicast boundaries are also used to prevent RP-Announce and RP-Discovery messages from traveling beyond the boundaries of the network. For example, if interface Serial0 is an external interfaces on a boundary router, the commands shown in Example 12-4 would prevent RP-Announce and RP-Discovery messages (which are multicast to groups 224.0.1.39 and 224.0.1.40) from crossing into or out of the network.

Example 12-4 *Commands to Block RP-Announce and RP-Discovery Messages*

```
Interface Serial0
ip multicast boundary 10

access-list 10 deny 224.0.1.39
access-list 10 deny 224.0.1.40
access-list 10 deny 239.0.0.0 0.255.255.255
access-list 10 permit 224.0.0.0 15.255.255.255
```

Notice that the access list is also preventing administratively scoped multicast traffic (239.0.0.0–239.255.255.255) from crossing into or out of the network.

Using a multicast boundary in this manner has the added benefit of preventing any RP-Announce or RP-Discovery packets originated by routers outside the network from leaking into the network and causing problems.

For example, consider what would happen if an RP-Announce message sent by a candidate RP from outside of the network leaked into the network and reached one or more internal Mapping Agents. In this situation, the Mapping Agents may select this bogus outside candidate RP if its IP address is higher than the IP address of the valid internal candidate RPs. The Mapping Agents would then advertise this bogus RP to all routers in the network that would, in turn, attempt to use this bogus outside router as the RP.

In addition, consider what would happen if bogus RP-Discovery packets were to leak into the internal network. Unless for some strange coincidence the Group-to-RP mapping information in these bogus RP-Discovery messages is identical to the information advertised by the valid internal Mapping Agents, the routers that receive these message would flip-flop between the valid internal RP and the bogus external RP.

Preventing Candidate RP Spoofing

Keeping all routers in the network updated with the correct Group-to-RP mapping information is critical to maintaining proper PIM-SM operation. Network administrators may wish to add router configuration commands to the Mapping Agents to prevent a maliciously configured router from masquerading as a candidate RP and causing problems. This is accomplished by the use of the following global configuration command on each Mapping Agent in the network:

```
ip pim rp-announce-filter rp-list acl [group-list acl]
```

This command configures an incoming filter for RP-Announce messages on a Mapping Agent. If this command is not configured on a Mapping Agent, all incoming RP Announce messages are accepted by default. The **rp-list** *acl* clause configures an access-list of candidate RP addresses that, if permitted, will be accepted for the group ranges supplied in the optional **group-list** *acl* clause. If this clause is omitted, the filter applies to all multicast groups. If more than one Mapping Agent is to be used, the filters must be consistent across all Mapping Agents so that no conflicts occur in the Group-to-RP mapping information.

Example 12-5 is a sample router configuration on an Auto-RP Mapping Agent that is used to prevent candidate RP announcements from being accepted from unauthorized candidate RP routers.

Example 12-5 *Router Configuration on Auto-RP Mapping Agent*

```
ip pim rp-announce-filter rp-list 10 group-list 20
access-list 10 permit host 172.16.5.1
access-list 10 permit host 172.16.2.1

access-list 20 deny 239.0.0.0 0.0.255.255
access-list 20 permit 224.0.0.0 15.255.255.255
```

In this example, the Mapping Agent will accept candidate RP announcements only from two routers, 172.16.5.1 and 172.16.2.1. Additionally, the Mapping Agent will accept candidate RP announcements from these two routers only for multicast groups that fall in the group range of 224.0.0.0–238.255.255.255. The Mapping Agent will not accept candidate RP announcements from any other routers in the network. Furthermore, the Mapping Agent will not accept candidate RP announcements from 172.16.5.1 and 172.16.2.1 if the announcements are for any groups in the 239.0.0.0–239.255.255.255 range. (Note: This range is the administratively scoped address range.)

PIMv2 Bootstrap Router Mechanism

While Cisco charged ahead and developed the Auto-RP feature for its routers, the company continued to work with the multicast working groups within the Internet Engineering Task Force (IETF) to define PIMv2, which was eventually published in RFC 2117 and recently updated by RFC 2362. PIMv2 provides yet another method to distribute Group-to-RP mapping information to all PIM routers in the network. This method is frequently referred to as simply the *Bootstrap router method* because it relies on a router to flood *Bootstrap* messages containing Group-to-RP mapping information to all routers in the network.

This section covers the basic mechanisms of the Bootstrap router method including an overview of the protocol, candidate RPs (C-RPs), candidate Bootstrap routers (C-BSRs), and the BSR election mechanism.

Overview of PIMv2 Bootstrap Router

Beginning with IOS version 11.3, Cisco introduced support for PIMv2 along with its associated Bootstrap router (BSR) capability. Like Auto-RP, the PIMv2 Bootstrap router mechanism eliminates the need to manually configure RP information in every router in the network. However, instead of using IP multicast to distribute Group-to-RP mapping information, BSR uses hop-by-hop flooding of special BSR messages (sent by the currently elected BSR) to distribute all Group-to-RP mapping information to all routers in the network.

Just as in Auto-RP, more than one router may be configured to be a C-RP for a group to provide redundancy. However, unlike Auto-RP, C-RPs send their C-RP advertisements directly to the currently elected BSR via unicast. C-RPs send these C-RP advertisement messages every C-RP-ADV-PERIOD seconds (the default is 60 seconds). Each C-RP advertisement contains an *RP-holdtime* in seconds that tells the BSR how long the C-RP advertisement is valid. The advertising C-RP router sets this RP-holdtime to 2.5 times the C-RP-ADV-PERIOD (the default is 150 seconds).

The combination of hop-by-hop flooding of BSR messages and unicasting C-RP advertisements to the BSR completely eliminates the need for multicast in order for the BSR mechanism to function. Eliminating this dependency on multicast avoids the chicken-and-egg problem that was encountered by Auto-RP where the RP had to be known by all routers in the network before RP information could be delivered to all routers in the network.

BSR messages are periodically flooded out all interfaces by the currently elected BSR every 60 seconds. However, unlike Auto-RP, BSR messages contain the set of all known Group-to-RP C-RP advertisements that have been received from the C-RPs in the network. This set of C-RP advertisements is referred to as the *candidate RP-set*, or *RP-set* for short. Every router in the network then runs the same hashing algorithm on the RP-set to select the currently active RP for a given group or group range. Because every router in the network receives an identical RP-set and runs an identical hashing algorithm, all routers will select an identical RP. If for some reason the current RP fails, all routers in the network can quickly and easily select a new RP from the RP-set and continue operation.

To provide some measure of redundancy in the network against BSR failure, multiple C-BSRs may be configured. The current BSR is elected as part of the normal operation of BSR message flooding throughout the network in a fashion similar to how the Root Bridge is elected by LAN Bridges. To force certain C-BSRs to be preferred over others in the election mechanism, some C-BSRs may be configured with a higher BSR priority than other C-BSRs. This approach allows the network administrator to determine the primary BSR and backup BSRs should the primary fail. However, should all C-BSRs fail, routers will cease to receive periodic BSR messages and their Group-to-RP mapping information will eventually expire. In this case, a Cisco router will switch to a statically configured RP that was defined with the **ip pim rp-address** command. If no statically configured RP is available, the router will switch the group(s) to dense mode.

A direct side effect of the hop-by-hop BSR election mechanism is that all routers in the network automatically learn the IP address of the currently elected BSR. This is how C-RPs learn which router to unicast their C-RP advertisements.

Figure 12-5 shows the PIMv2 BSR mechanism in action. In this example, Routers B and C are both candidate RPs and are sending their PIMv2 C-RP advertisements (shown by the dashed arrows) directly to the BSR router via unicast. Router A has previously been elected as the BSR and receives and stores all the PIMv2 C-RP advertisements in its local RP-set cache.

Figure 12-5 *Basic PIMv2 BSR Mechanism*

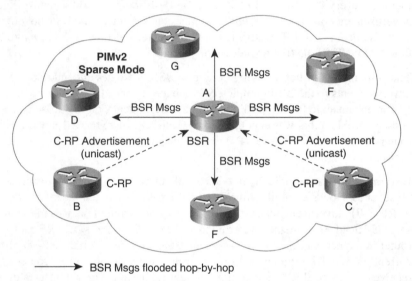

Router A periodically transmits the contents of its local RP-set cache in BSR messages (shown by the solid arrows) out all interfaces. These BSR messages are flooded hop by hop throughout the network to all routers. The routers in the network then store the RP-set information contained in the BSR messages in their local RP-set cache and select the current RP(s) by the use of a common RP hashing algorithm.

NOTE   Cisco network administrators who have migrated to PIMv2 are not required to use PIMv2 BSR. Networks that comprise all Cisco routers running PIMv2 may optionally be configured to use Auto-RP instead of the PIMv2 BSR mechanism. This allows network administrators to leverage some of the features and functionality of Auto-RP in their PIMv2 network. However, for the network to function properly, it should not contain any non-Cisco routers because they do not support Auto-RP and hence will not operate properly in an Auto-RP environment.

Configuring PIMv2 Candidate RPs

One or more routers in a PIM-SM network may be configured as C-RPs by using the following command:

```
ip pim rp-candidate interface [group-list acl]
```

When this global configuration command is added to a router's configuration, the router begins to unicast PIMv2 C-RP advertisements to the currently elected BSR. Each C-RP advertisement contains the IP address of the specified interface (often a loopback interface) along with the group range(s) (using an group/mask format) that were specified in the optional **group-list** access-control list.

NOTE	Like Auto-RP, if the optional **group-list** clause is omitted, the group range advertised is 224.0.0.0/4. This range corresponds to all IP multicast group addresses, which indicates that the router is willing to serve as the RP for all groups.

A router may be configured to serve as candidate RP for more than one group range by carefully crafting the access-list in the router configuration as shown in Example 12-6.

Example 12-6 *Configuring a Router as a Candidate RP*

```
ip pim rp-candidate loopback0 group-list 10

access-list 10 permit 239.254.0.0 0.0.255.255
access-list 10 permit 239.255.0.0 0.0.255.255
access-list 10 permit 224.0.0.0 7.255.255.255
```

The preceding PIMv2 router configuration causes the router to advertise itself as PIMv2 C-RP for group ranges 239.254.0.0–239.255.255.255 and 224.0.0.0–231.255.255.255.

Configuring PIMv2 Candidate BSRs

The function of BSR can be assigned to one or more candidate BSR (C-BSR) routers in the network by using the following global configuration command:

```
ip pim bsr-candidate interface hash-mask-length [priority]
```

This command directs the router to begin serving as a candidate BSR and participate in the BSR election process. (The BSR election process is covered in detail in the next section.) If the router is elected as the BSR, it begins to periodically (every 60 seconds) flood BSR messages out all interfaces that have another PIMv2 neighbor. These BSR messages contain the following information:

1 A unicast RP address that corresponds to the IP address of the **interface** specified in the **bsr-candidate** command.

2 The RP hash mask length specified in the **hash-mask-length** field of the **bsr-candidate** command.

3 The BSR priority specified in the optional **priority** field of the **bsr-candidate** command. (If this field is omitted, the BSR messages will contain a BSR priority of 0 by default.)

4 The complete candidate RP-set learned from all C-RPs via C-RP advertisement messages.

Using Multiple C-RPs for Redundancy & RP Load Balancing

Network administrators may configure a PIMv2 network with more than one C-RP for any particular group range. Examples 12-7 and 12-8 show configurations for two routers configured as candidate RPs for a specific group range.

Example 12-7 *Candidate RP: Router A Configuration*

```
Interface loopback0
ip address 192.168.100.1 255.255.255.255

ip pim rp-candidate loopback0 group-list 10

access-list 10 permit 239.254.0.0 0.0.255.255
```

Example 12-8 *Candidate RP: Router B Configuration*

```
Interface loopback0
ip address 192.168.100.2 255.255.255.255

ip pim rp-candidate loopback0 group-list 10

access-list 10 permit 239.254.0.0 0.0.255.255
```

Both Routers A and B are C-RPs for the group range of 239.254.0.0–239.254.255.255. However, at this point the Auto-RP and PIMv2 BSR mechanisms differ significantly. In Auto-RP either Router A or Router B is selected as the RP for the entire group range. However, in PIMv2 BSR, Routers A and B share the RP workload for multicast groups in this range. For example, let's assume that the network currently has N active multicast groups in this group range. Router A would be the active RP for half of the groups while Router B would be the active RP for the other half. (Notice that only one router is functioning as the active RP for a specific group at any moment.) The mechanism used to distribute the RP workload across all C-RPs is the RP hashing algorithm and is described in the next section.

RP Selection—The RP Hash Algorithm

All PIMv2 routers use the same RP hashing algorithm to select an RP for a given group. The hashing algorithm takes as input variables, a C-RP address C_i, a group address G, and a hash mask M, and then returns a hash value. The router runs the hashing algorithm on all C-RP addresses in the RP-set whose advertised group range matches the target group. From this set of C-RPs, the one with the lowest hash value is selected as the active RP for target group G. If for some reason two C-RPs result in the same hash value, the tie is broken in favor of the C-RP with the highest IP address.

The hash mask M, that is used in the hash algorithm is taken from the *Hash Mask Length* field that contains the BSR messages and that was specified in the **ip pim bsr-candidate** router configuration command. By modifying the mask, it is possible to control the number of consecutive group addresses that *hash* to the same C-RP address. For example, if M=0xFFFFFFFC, four consecutive groups will hash (that is, map) to a single C-RP address. This may be important when separate multicast groups are carrying related data and it is desirable for all of these related groups to share a common router as RP.

As a simple example, let's assume there are two candidate-RPs, Router A and Router B, for group range 239.0.0.0–239.255.255.255 (that is, the entire administratively scoped multicast group range). Furthermore, let's assume that the BSR is advertising a hash mask length of 30, meaning that the mask is 0xFFFFFFFC. This mask will result in four consecutive groups hashing to the same router. Given that there are two C-RPs and that the first address in the range (239.0.0.0) hashes to Router A, then Router A will also be assigned as RP for the next three consecutive group addresses, 239.0.0.1, 239.0.0.2, and 239.0.0.3. Assuming that the hash algorithm is evenly distributed, Router A will be assigned as RP for half of the groups in the 239.0.0.0–239.255.255.255 range and Router B will be assigned as RP for the other half.

Using Multiple C-BSRs for Redundancy

Network administrators who want to use PIMv2 BSR will typically want to configure more than one router as C-BSR to provide some redundancy to the BSR function. The PIMv2 BSR mechanism differs significantly from the operation of Mapping Agents in Cisco's Auto-RP feature. In the case of PIMv2 BSR, only a single BSR is active in the network at a time. The currently active BSR is elected from the set of all C-BSR routers in the network, using the BSR election mechanism. In addition, all C-RP routers in the network must be informed of the results of the BSR election so that they know how to send their C-RP advertisements to the current BSR.

The following sections cover the BSR election mechanism and the BSR message-flooding mechanism used in PIMv2 networks. Both of these mechanism are key to the automatic distribution of Group-to-RP mapping information when PIMv2 BSR is used in the network.

BSR Election

The BSR is elected from the set of "candidate" routers in the domain that have been configured to function as BSR. The election mechanism is similar to the *Root Bridge* election mechanism used in bridged LANs. BSR election is based on the router's BSR priority contained in the BSR messages that are sent hop by hop through the network. This election mechanism allows another C-BSR to be elected as BSR should the active BSR fail. A simplified version of the BSR election mechanism follows.

1 Initially, a C-BSR sets its Bootstrap timer to the Bootstrap timeout value (150 seconds) and enters the *C-BSR* state, waiting to receive BSR messages from the current BSR.

2 If the router receives a preferred BSR message (that is, the message contains either a higher BSR priority than the router's BSR priority or the same BSR priority but with a higher BSR IP address), the message is accepted, the Bootstrap timer is reset to the Bootstrap timeout value. The message is then forwarded out all other interfaces. If the message is not a preferred BSR message, it is simply discarded.

3 If the Bootstrap timer expires, the C-BSR enters the *Elected-BSR* state and assumes that it is now the BSR. While in the Elected-BSR state, the router periodically (every 60 seconds) sends its own BSR message containing its priority and the RP-set out all interfaces.

4 If the router is in the Elected-BSR state and it receives a preferred BSR message, the router transitions back to the C-BSR state. It then returns to Step 1 and starts the process again.

NOTE   It's important to note that the election mechanism causes the current BSR to be *preempted* (after a short delay) by a newly activated C-BSR that has a higher BSR priority than the current BSR. The delay in this preemption is a result of the new C-BSR waiting one Bootstrap timeout period (150 seconds) before transitioning to the Elected-BSR state.

The BSR receives all the PIMv2 C-RP advertisement messages that are sent by the C-RP routers and stores this information in its local C-RP-set cache. The BSR then periodically advertises the contents of its local RP-set cache in BSR messages to all other routers in the PIM-SM domain. These BSR messages travel hop by hop throughout the entire PIM-SM domain, using the BSR message-flooding algorithm that is described in the next section.

BSR Message Flooding

BSR messages are multicast to the ALL-PIM-Routers (224.0.0.13) multicast group with a TTL of 1. Neighboring PIMv2 routers receive the BSR message and remulticast it out all other interfaces (except the one on which it was received), again with a TTL of 1. In this way, BSR messages travel hop by hop throughout the entire PIM-SM domain.

Because BSR messages contain the IP address of the current BSR, the flooding mechanism also permits all C-RPs to automatically learn which router has been elected BSR. This is especially important if a router is also functioning as a C-RP because it must know the IP address of the BSR to unicast its C-RP advertisements to the BSR.

The BSR message-flooding logic in non-candidate BSRs helps in the election of the preferred C-BSR (that is, the C-BSR with the highest priority) as the current BSR. A simplified version of the message-flooding logic follows.

1 Initially, a non-candidate BSR router sets its Bootstrap timer to the Bootstrap timeout value (150 seconds), enters the *Accept-Any* state, and waits to receive the first BSR message. (Receipt of BSR messages causes the Bootstrap timer to be reset to the Bootstrap timeout value.)

2 If a non-candidate BSR router is in the Accept-Any state and a BSR message is received, the router accepts and saves this information as the current BSR. It then forwards this BSR message out all other interfaces and transitions to the Accept-Preferred state.

3 If a non-candidate BSR router is in the Accept-Preferred state and it receives a BSR message, the router will accept (as new BSR) and forward the message only if the new BSR is preferred (that is, has a higher priority) over the current. If it is not preferred, the received BSR message is discarded.

4 If a non-candidate BSR router's Bootstrap timer ever expires, the router transitions back to the Accept-Any state and starts the process over, beginning with Step 1 above.

RP Failover in PIMv2 BSR Networks

The process of RP Failover in networks that are using the PIMv2 BSR mechanism to distribute Group-to-RP information is somewhat simpler than is the process for Auto-RP. This is a direct result of the fact that all routers in a network maintain the complete RP-set of PIMv2 C-RP advertisements in their Group-to-RP mapping cache. Furthermore, each entry also contains a holdtime that specifies how long the C-RP advertisement is valid.

Each PIMv2 C-RP entry in the Group-to-RP mapping cache has an expiration timer that is initialized to the holdtime value that was contained in the associated C-RP entry of the received BSR message. Because the originating PIMv2 C-RP sets the holdtime to 2.5 times the C-RP-ADV-PERIOD, this value defaults to a holdtime of 150 seconds and is the period of time that must elapse before the router will delete the PIMv2 C-RP entry from the Group-to-RP mapping cache. Deleting this entry triggers a new computation of the hash values of RPs for any active groups. Therefore, if the deleted PIMv2 C-RP entry had been the active RP for a group, a new RP will have been selected by the router and new (*, G) Join messages sent as appropriate.

In older versions of IOS, the C-RP_ADV-PERIOD was fixed at 60 seconds that, in turn, resulted in fixed C-RP holdtimes of 150 seconds or 2.5 minutes. Thus RP Failover could take as long as 2.5 minutes from the actual time that the RP router failed.

In more recent versions of IOS, a new form of the **ip pim rp-candidate** command was introduced that allowed the C-RP_ADV-PERIOD to be specified from 1 second up to 65,535 seconds. This new command has the following format:

```
ip pim rp-candidate interface [group-list acl] [interval secs]
```

Network administrators who want shorter RP Failover times can tune this interval to reduce RP Failover times down to roughly 2.5 seconds by specifying a 1-second interval in the preceding command. However, tuning this interval down from the default of 60 seconds to achieve faster RP Failover times comes at the expense of the added traffic from the C-RP router to the BSR. In some networks, this added traffic load is worth the shorter RP Failover times.

Constraining BSR Messages

As IP multicast becomes more widespread, the chances of one PIMv2 domain bordering on another PIMv2 domain is increasing. Because these two domains probably do *not* share the same set of RPs, BSRs, C-RPs, and C-BSRs, some way is needed to constrain PIMv2 BSR messages from flowing into or out of the domain. If these messages are allowed to *leak* across the domain borders, the normal BSR election in the bordering domains would be adversely affected and a single BSR would be elected across all bordering domains. Even worse, C-RP advertisements from the bordering domains would be co-mingled in the BSR messages, which would result in the selection of RPs in the wrong domain.

In Cisco routers, constraint of BSR messages may be accomplished by the use of the **ip pim border** interface command. This command should be placed on all interfaces that connect to other bordering PIM domains. This command instructs the router to neither send nor receive PIMv2 BSR messages on this interface. The command effectively stops the flow of BSR messages across the domain border and keeps the PIMv2 domains operating independently.

Figure 12-6 shows an example of a PIMv2 network that is using the BSR mechanism to distribute Group-to-RP mapping information to routers inside the domain. In this example, the BSR router is periodically sending BSR messages out all interfaces. The PIMv2 routers in the network flood these messages hop by hop throughout the entire PIMv2 domain. However, border routers A and B have been configured with the **ip pim border** interface command on their external interfaces, which prevents the flow of BSR messages both into and out of the network.

Figure 12-6 *Constraining PIMv2 BSR Messages*

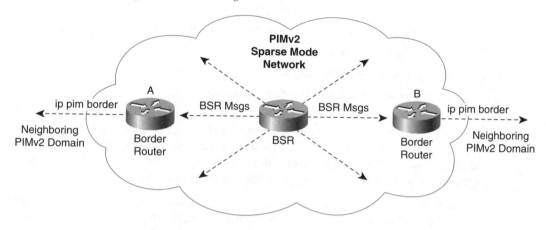

NOTE   The **ip pim border** command effects only the flow of PIMv2 BSR messages on the interface. It does *not* affect the normal flow of other PIM messages (for example, Joins and Prunes), nor does it block the flow of multicast traffic. It's not uncommon for network administrators to make the mistake of thinking that they can use this command to provide a hard boundary that blocks all multicast traffic.

RP Placement and Tuning

Regardless of the method that one selects for RP configuration, at times a network administrator may want to tune the distribution and usage of RPs in the network. For example, the administrator might want to force certain groups to remain in either sparse mode or dense mode or provide some additional bulletproofing of the network against attack from malicious users. These topics, as well as the subject of RP placement, are discussed in the sections that follow.

Selecting RP Placement

"Where do I put my RP?" is a question that I am frequently asked by network administrators who are putting sparse mode into production on their networks. My typical response is a tried and true Cisco answer: It depends. This answer is not really intended to be flippant (although I must personally admit to deriving some pleasure when I use this answer). The problem is that many variables can effect the decision to place an RP in one location as opposed to another. Most network administrators tend to be concerned about the following factors:

- The location of the multicast receivers
- The amount of traffic that will flow through the RP
- The location of the multicast senders
- The need to reduce traffic latency
- RP redundancy and Failover requirements

The bad news is that this list can go on and on. The really bad news is that it is beyond the scope of this book to provide a comprehensive set of guidelines on RP placement. However, the good news is that, for most networks, most of these variables are nonissues as a result of the following often overlooked default behavior of Cisco routers in PIM sparse mode networks: Last-hop routers immediately join the SPT for any new sources!

The default SPT-Threshold on a Cisco router is zero, which forces it to immediately join the SPT toward the source S upon receiving the first multicast packet from this source. Because of this default behavior, the only function that the RP must perform in many networks is to serve as a meeting place for multicast receivers and senders (almost like a multicast dating service for multicast routers). Once a last-hop router has joined the SPT to the source, the (S, G) traffic is frequently no longer flowing through the RP. This situation is particularly true where network administrators have installed a dedicated router to serve this function.

Resource Demands on RPs

Just because all traffic is flowing through the network on SPTs and the RP is not having to replicate and forward multicast traffic does not mean that there are *no* resource demands on the RP. RP routers must still have sufficient memory to store all (*, G) and (S, G) mroute table entries for all groups for which it is serving as RP. Furthermore, the RP must have sufficient CPU horsepower to maintain these state entries and send, receive, and process the periodic Joins and Prunes necessary to keep all of this state alive.

Memory Demands

The primary memory resource demand on a multicast router is the storage of (*, G) and (S, G) state entries in the mroute table. Table 12-3 lists the memory requirements to store (*, G) and (S, G) entries in the Cisco mroute table.

Table 12-2 *Mroute Table Memory Requirements*

(*, G) entry	260 bytes + outgoing interface list overhead
(S, G) entry	212 bytes + outgoing interface list overhead
Outgoing interface list overhead	80 bytes per outgoing interface list entry

Assuming that you have the information regarding the average number of active multicast groups, senders, and the average number of interfaces in each outgoing interface list, you can use this information to calculate average memory demands in a router.

For example, let's assume that you are designing a network for an enterprise that will be using multicast for multimedia conferencing. Estimates are that an average of five multimedia sessions will be active at any time, each using an average of two multicast groups (one for audio and one for video), for a total of 10 active multicast groups each requiring a (*, G) entry. The average number of participants has been estimated to be six participants per session. This information translates into six (S, G) entries per group or a total of 60 (S, G) entries (10 groups times 6 sources per group). Finally, the typical fan out (that is, the typical number of interfaces in any outgoing interface list) on each router is expected to be three. This translates in the following calculations:

Therefore, the total amount of memory needed to store the (*, G) entries is

<# of (, G)s>* $(260 + (<\# \text{ of OIL entries}> \times 80)) = 10 (260 + (3 \times 80)) = 5000$ bytes

Therefore, the total amount of memory needed to store the (S, G) entries is

<# of (S, G)s> $(212 + (<\# \text{ of OIL entries}> \times 80)) = 60 (212 + (3 \times 80)) = 27,120$ bytes

Thus, the average amount of memory used by the mroute table will be 32,120 bytes, which should be well within the capabilities of most Cisco routers.

CPU Demands

Although giving specific values of the CPU loading associated with running PIM-SM is impossible, the primary CPU demands on any PIM-SM router may be summarized as follows:

- **Packet replication**—Packet replication is by far the biggest CPU demand on a PIM-SM router and depends on the number of entries in the outgoing interface list. The more entries in the list, the more the CPU load on the router. However, because by default Cisco PIM-SM networks use SPTs, the RP is generally bypassed and is not concerned with this load.

- **RPF recalculation**—RPF recalculation is typically the next biggest CPU demand on a PIM-SM router and depends on the number of entries in the mroute table. To converge the multicast network after any topology change, every 5 seconds a Cisco router recalculates the RPF information on every entry in the mroute table. The CPU impact of this recalculation depends, to a great extent, on the size and complexity of the unicast routing table as it is scanned to perform each RPF calculation.

- **State maintenance**—State maintenance has the least CPU impact CPU of any of the PIM-SM tasks performed on the router. This process consists of sending and receiving periodic PIM Join/Prune and PIM Hello messages to/from the router's PIM neighbors to refresh mroute table state as well as PIM neighbor adjacency. The Join/Prune messages are sent roughly once per minute, whereas PIM Hellos are typically sent every 30 seconds. The CPU load of this is task on the router is general very low.

In addition to the preceding tasks performed by every PIM router, RPs must also perform the following tasks that result in additional CPU loads:

- **Register processing**—Arriving PIM Register messages result in the RP's processing the Register message at process level. This action would result in a fairly significant CPU load on the RP except that it has to process only a few of these Registers (generally only one) when a source first starts transmitting. In this case, the RP immediately joins the SPT to the source to receive the traffic natively and then sends a Register-Stop message to shut off further Register messages. As a result, the CPU load of Register processing on the RP is typically insignificant.

Summary of RP Load Factors

The memory and CPU demands on the RP presented in the previous sections may seem like a lot. However, except for extremely large multicast networks in which the RP must maintain thousands of state entries, most midsize Cisco routers are quite capable of handling this load without any problems. Even a low-end Cisco router can be used as an RP in some cases when the maximum number of state entries in the mroute table is kept under 100 and careful attention is paid to memory usage.

The bottom line is that many network administrators do not need to be overly concerned about the placement of the RP(s) in their network. Simply place it on a midsize router at a convenient location in the network. Again, the bad news is that issues other than traffic flow that can be important to the RP placement decision are too numerous to address here, particularly because no two networks are the same. (In some cases, the same network isn't even the same from day to day as traffic flow and other aspects of network operation change on a daily basis.) However, the good news is that once you have read this book, you will understand the internal mechanisms of PIM multicast networks and can intelligently address and consider those variables that are important to the placement of RPs in your network.

Forcing Groups to Remain in Dense Mode

In some cases, the network administrator may wish to ensure that certain groups always operate in dense mode. The following global configuration command does the job:

```
ip pim accept-rp {rp-address | Auto-rp} [group-list acl]
```

This command is effectively used as an address filter to accept or reject a particular IP address as being a valid RP address for a specific group. (The various forms of this configuration command are discussed in more detail in the next section, "Using **ip pim accept-rp** Commands.") Depending on how it is used, this command can be configured on all routers in the network or, in some special cases, in just the RP.

The router applies this RP validation process when making the following three decisions:

1 Determining group mode (sparse/dense) when a (*, G) entry is being created in the multicast routing table as a direct result of a local host joining the group.

2 Accepting or rejecting an incoming (*, G) Join that has been sent by a downstream router. (The RP address to be validated is contained in the (*, G) Join message.)

3 Accepting or rejecting an incoming PIM Register message from a Designated Router.

In the first case, the router first searches the Group-to-RP mapping cache for a matching entry for the group. If there is a matching entry, the router applies the **ip pim accept-rp** filter(s) to the RP address in the matching entry. If the filter permits this address, it is a valid RP address and the new group is created in sparse mode; otherwise, the new group is created in dense mode. The graphic in Figure 12-7 represents this first case. In the upper portion of the figure, the router has just received an Internet Group Membership Protocol (IGMP) Join for group G. Because the router does not have a (*, G) state entry in its multicast routing table, it must create one. However, it needs to determine whether the (*, G) entry should be created in sparse mode or dense mode.

Figure 12-7 *Accept RP Filter Application—Case 1*

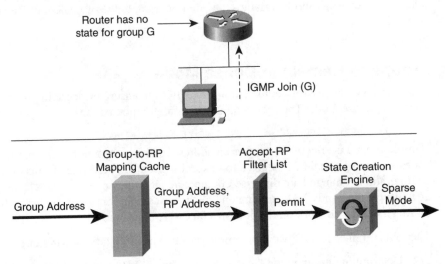

Figure 12-7 shows how the **ip pim accept-rp** filters fit into this decision process. Initially, group address G is used to search the Group-to-RP mapping cache. If a matching RP address is found, the combination of group address and RP address is run through the **ip pim accept-rp** filter. If the filter permits this Group/RP address combination, an RP address is passed to the multicast state creation engine, which causes a (*, G) sparse mode entry to be created. If on the other hand, either no RP address is found in the Group-to-RP mapping cache or the **ip pim accept-rp** filter denies the Group/RP address combination, the (*, G) entry is created in dense mode.

In the second case, the router applies the **ip pim accept-rp** filter(s) to the RP address contained in the incoming (*, G) Join message. If the filter permits this address, the (*, G) Join will be processed; otherwise, it is ignored. This can be used to stop (*, G) Joins from being propagated, which, in turn, prevents misconfigured downstream routers from generating sparse mode state in the network for groups that should be operating in dense mode.

Figure 12-8 shows an example of this second case of **ip pim accept-rp** filters being applied.

Figure 12-8   *Accept RP Filter Application—Case 2*

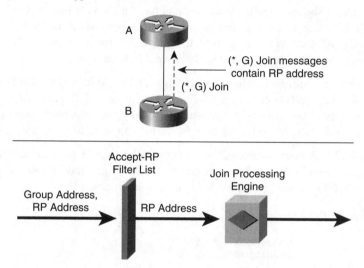

Router A has just received a (*, G) Join from a downstream PIM neighbor. However, before processing the message, the group address G and the RP address (both of which are contained in the body of the (*, G) Join message) are run through the **ip pim accept-rp** filter. If the filter permits this Group/RP combination, then the incoming (*, G) Join message is processed; otherwise, it is ignored.

NOTE   This situation brings up an important point about RPs that is often missed. There is a common misconception that if the router isn't somehow configured to be the RP of a group, that router will never become the RP. What actually happens is that when a router sends a (*, G) Join, it searches the Group-to-RP mapping cache to find the address of the RP (subject to case 1 of the Accept RP filter application), puts this address in a field in the (*, G) Join, and sends the address toward the RP. The other routers in the network forward the (*, G) Join hop by hop toward the router whose address is specified in this field. When the router whose address is in this field receives the (*, G) Join message, it sees its own address in this field and assumes that it must be the RP for the group. Therefore, a router always assumes the duties of RP for a group (subject to case 2 of the Accept RP filter application) any time it receives an incoming (*, G) Join that contains the address of one of its multicast-enabled interfaces in this field.

In the third case, a router will apply the **ip pim accept-rp** filter(s) to incoming PIM Register messages. (The router will use the destination IP address of the received Register message as the RP address.) If the **ip pim accept-rp** filter permits this address, (that is, the address is a valid RP address for the group), then the router functions as the RP for this group and processes the Register message in the normal fashion.

However, if the filter identifies this address as an invalid RP address for the group, the router immediately sends back a Register-Stop message to the DR and does not process the Register message further. This prevents misconfigured DRs from erroneously creating sparse mode state on an RP for groups that are supposed to be operating in dense mode.

Figure 12-9 shows a graphic of this process. In the upper portion of the figure, Router A has just received a PIM-Register message (via unicast) from first-hop Router B who is directly connected to a multicast source S that is sending to group G.

Figure 12-9 *Accept RP Filter Application—Case 3*

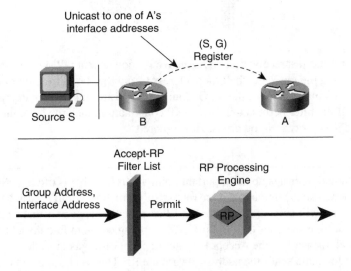

When Router A receives the PIM Register message addressed to one of its interfaces (which is often a loopback interface), it runs the Group address and the IP address of the interface through the **ip pim accept-rp** filter. If the filter permits this group address and IP address, the router processes the Register message as the RP for the group in the normal fashion. If the **ip pim accept-rp** filter denies this group address/IP address combination, then the router immediately sends back a PIM Register-Stop message and ignores the PIM Register. Subsequently, any network routers that believe this router to be the RP for this group will be unable to register successfully with the RP. This condition, in turn, would effectively prevent multicast traffic from sources connected to these routers from reaching the RP.

The primary use of the second and third cases of the Accept RP filter is to prevent routers in the network from inadvertently assuming the duties of the RP. By configuring

```
ip pim accept-rp Auto-rp
```

on every router in the network, only the router that has been elected as RP for the group will receive and process (*, G) Joins and PIM Register messages. This is an extra bit of network insurance against configuration mistakes elsewhere in the network.

Using **ip pim accept-rp** Commands

Multiple **ip pim accept-rp** filters may be defined in a router configuration to control which RPs are valid for which groups. If a **ip pim accept-rp** filter (more than one can be defined) matches the RP address and the specified **group-list** *acl* permits this group, then the RP is valid. However, if all **ip pim accept-rp** filters that match the RP address have a group-list that denies this group, then the RP address is invalid. If the optional **group-list** *acl* clause is not specified, it is assumed to mean **permit any**, which matches all groups.

The **ip pim accept-rp** command has the following three basic forms:

```
ip pim accept-rp rp-address [group-list acl]
ip pim accept-rp Auto-rp [group-list acl]
ip pim accept-rp 0.0.0.0 [group-list acl]
```

The first form may appear multiple times in a router configuration and specifies a single RP address. The second form specifies that the target RP address must be in the Group-to-RP mapping cache. (Specifically, the target address must be listed in the Group-to-RP mapping cache as the current RP for the group, and the group cannot be either of the two Cisco Auto-RP multicast groups 224.0.1.39 or 224.0.1.40.) The last form is a special *wildcard* RP address form of the first command that matches any RP address.

| NOTE | Both the **Auto-rp** and the **0.0.0.0** (wildcard) forms of the **ip pim accept-rp** command may each appear only once in a router configuration. If you attempt to enter additional versions of these two commands, the last version entered will supercede the previously entered version. |

The router maintains the list of the **ip pim accept-rp** commands in the order in which they are given in the previous section. When the router attempts to validate an RP address for a group, the router searches the list from top to bottom looking for an RP address match on the first field. If a match is found and the matching entry is not the Auto-RP entry, the search terminates and the specified group-list is applied to the group address. If the specified group-list permits this group, the RP address is accepted as a valid RP for the group. If the specified group-list denies this group, the RP address is rejected as a valid RP for the group.

If, on the other hand, the matching entry is an Auto-RP entry, and the specified group-list permits this group, the search terminates and the RP address is accepted as a valid RP for the group. However, if the group-list ACL on an Auto-RP entry denies the group, the wildcard RP entry is tried (if one exists), its group-list ACL is applied, and the RP is either accepted or rejected for the group, depending on the whether the group is permitted or denied, respectively. Finally, if the end of the list is reached without encountering a matching RP address that permits the group, the RP address is rejected as an invalid RP for the group.

NOTE   Notice that the "continue search on deny" behavior for Auto-RP entries is the opposite of most ACLs, which terminate the search whenever they encounter either a specific deny or permit condition. This can be a source of confusion when an **ip pim accept-rp Auto-rp** command is used with a **ip pim accept-rp 0.0.0.0** command because a specific deny condition in the Auto-RP group-list ACL does not necessarily cause the search to terminate.

Example 12-9 is a set of **ip pim accept-rp** commands that demonstrate the interaction of the various forms of the command.

Example 12-9   *ip pim accept-rp Commands*

```
ip pim accept-rp 172.16.8.2
ip pim accept-rp Auto-rp group-list 10
ip pim accept-rp 0.0.0.0 group-list 12

access-list 10 deny 224.1.1.0 0.0.0.255
access-list 10 permit any

access-list 12 deny 224.1.2.0 0.0.0.255
access-list 12 permit any
```

NOTE   The configuration in Example 12-9 is a horribly contrived example that should not serve as a model on how to use this feature in real networks. For example, the normal practice for using the **Auto-rp** form of this command is to not use a group-list, which implies the acceptance of any RP in the Group-to-RP mapping cache.

The first **accept-rp** command instructs the router to accept 172.16.8.2 as a valid RP address for any group. (The missing group-list ACL implies a permit any.) The second command (**Auto-rp**) would normally instruct the router that RPs defined in the Group-to-RP mapping cache (which are learned via Auto-RP or the PIMv2 Bootstrap router) are valid for any group except the group range 224.1.1.0–224.1.1.255. However, in this case, the third command (wildcard RP) overrides the deny clause for this group range in the Auto-RP group-list (access-list 10) because of the permit any in its group-list (access-list 12). The wildcard RP entry also specifically denies group range 224.1.2.0–224.1.2.255.

Depending on the actual goals of the preceding configuration, it would probably be better to remove the **Auto-rp** command altogether and use the configuration in Example 12-10 instead.

Example 12-10 *Removing the **Auto-rp** Command*

```
ip pim accept-rp 172.16.8.2
ip pim accept-rp 0.0.0.0 group-list 12

access-list 12 deny 224.1.1.0 0.0.0.255
access-list 12 deny 224.1.2.0 0.0.0.255
access-list 12 permit any
```

In this case, 172.16.8.2 is still accepted as a valid RP address for all groups. All other RPs (whether they are in the Group-to-RP mapping cache or not) will be accepted for all groups except for group ranges 224.1.1.0–224.1.1.255 and 224.1.2.0–224.1.2.255.

In the end, administrators who want to force a group range to always remain in dense mode throughout the network will want to simplify the preceding example into a single wildcard RP **accept-rp** command with an appropriate group-list ACL that is configured on all routers in the network. For example, the configuration in Example 12-11 (when placed on all routers in the network) forces group range 224.1.0.0–224.1.255.255 to always operate in dense mode.

Example 12-11 *Configuration for Dense Mode Operation*

```
ip pim accept-rp 0.0.0.0 group-list 10

access-list 10 deny 224.1.0.0 0.0.255.255
access-list 10 permit any
```

NOTE   It is not necessary to configure a deny clause for the *Cisco-Discovery* (224.0.1.40) and *Cisco-Announce* (224.0.1.39) multicast groups on access-lists used with the **ip pim accept-rp Auto-rp** command. A **deny** is automatically assumed for these two multicast groups so as to not interfere with normal dense mode flooding of Auto-RP information.

Using Negative Auto-RP Announcements

Beginning with IOS version 12.0(1.1), the Auto-RP function was extended to allow C-RPs to send *negative RP announcements* to advertise group ranges that are to remain in dense mode.

Negative RP announcements may be specified via the use of a **deny** clause in the access-list as shown in Example 12-12.

Example 12-12   *Using* ***deny*** *in the Access List*

```
ip pim send-rp-announce loopback0 scope 16 group-list 10

access-list 10 permit 224.0.0.0 15.255.255.255
access-list 10 deny 225.1.1.0 0.0.0.255
```

In this example, the C-RP router is sending a positive RP announcement for the multicast group range 224.0.0.0–2239.255.255.255 and a negative RP announcement for group range 225.1.1.0–225.1.1.255. This forces multicast groups 225.1.1.x to remain in dense mode.

When a Mapping Agent receives a negative RP announcement, it overrides any positive announcements that were received from other C-RPs for the same group range. Specifically, the Mapping Agent forwards any negative RP announcements that it receives on to the routers in the network via RP-Discovery messages (along with the currently selected positive RP announcements). When the routers in the network receive these negative RP announcements from the Mapping Agent(s), the routers respond by treating multicast groups in this group range as dense mode groups.

NOTE   Prior to IOS release 12.0(1.1), the **deny** clause was sometimes used to make the access-list more readable by specifically noting which groups were not to be advertised in the C-RP announcements. (This was not really necessary because the **ip pim send-rp-announce** command assumed the **deny all others** clause.) These **deny** clauses should be removed so that an upgrade to IOS release 12.0 (1.1) or later will not cause unexpected behavior.

Forcing Groups to Remain in Sparse Mode

The default behavior for PIM is to fall back into dense mode for any groups that no longer have a valid, working RP. The idea is that when all C-RPs for a group are down, the network will continue to deliver multicast traffic, using dense mode's less efficient flood-and-prune behavior.

However, in some cases, network administrators may prefer that multicast traffic simply cease flowing if all C-RPs fail, instead of using dense mode to flood the traffic throughout the network. Stopping the flow of multicast traffic can be accomplished by defining a "last ditch" static RP address in all routers in the network by using the **ip pim rp-address** command.

If, for some reason, all C-RPs fail, the Group-to-RP mapping cache will eventually time out and will not contain an RP. Not finding an entry in the Group-to-RP mapping cache, the router will then fall back to a statically configured last-ditch RP if one exists.

As an example, assume that the network administrator has configured the network to use Auto-RP and has defined primary and secondary C-RPs (let's say 172.16.8.1 and 172.16.9.1, respectively) for redundancy. In addition, the network administrator has added the commands shown in Example 12-13 to all routers in the network to define a last-ditch RP.

Example 12-13   *Defining a Last-Ditch RP*

```
ip pim rp-address 172.16.9.1 10

access-list 10 deny 224.0.1.39
access-list 10 deny 224.0.1.40
access-list 10 permit any
```

Notice that the RP address happens to be the address of the secondary C-RP and that an access-list has been used to prevent the Cisco-Discovery (224.0.1.40) and the Cisco-Announce (224.0.1.39) groups from accidentally operating in sparse mode, using 172.16.9.1 as the RP for these two Auto-RP groups.

After Example 12-13 has been configured on all routers in the network and the contents of the Group-to-RP mapping cache are displayed during normal network operation, you would see the output shown in Example 12-14.

Example 12-14   *Output from Group-to-RP Mapping Cache*

```
Rtr-X# show ip pim rp mapping
PIM Group-to-RP Mappings

Group(s) 224.0.0.0/4, uptime: 2w4d, expires: 00:02:12
    RP 172.16.8.1 (Rtr-A), PIMv1
    Info source: 172.16.8.1 (Rtr-A)
Acl: 10, Static
    RP: 172.16.9.1 (Rtr-B)
```

Now, if both C-RPs fail, the information in the Group-to-RP mapping cache that was learned via Auto-RP (denoted by the PIMv1 in the example), would time out, leaving the output shown in Example 12-15.

Example 12-15   *Output After Timeout of Group-to-RP Mapping Cache*

```
Rtr-X# show ip pim rp mapping
PIM Group-to-RP Mappings

Acl: 10, Static
    RP: 172.16.9.1 (Rtr-B)
```

Now, the only entry in the Group-to-RP mapping cache is the static last-ditch RP, which also happens to be the address of the failed secondary RP. Even though the last RP has failed, the routers in the network continue to use the statically defined RP address as a last-ditch RP, which prevents the network from reverting to dense mode.

Summary

The primary focus of this chapter was to acquaint you with the details of Auto-RP and PIMv2 BSR features, both of which are methods that can be employed to permit PIM routers to dynamically discover the identity of the RP for a specific multicast group. Both methods have advantages and disadvantages. To date, Cisco's Auto-RP feature seems to be the most widely deployed method primarily because it was the first method available to PIM-SM engineers. Having said that, Chapter 16, "Multicast Traffic Engineering," will show that Auto-RP has a clear advantage when trying to configure administratively scoped zones to control the flow of multicast traffic.

In addition to introducing the details of configuring, tuning, and engineering Auto-RP and BSR networks, this chapter also covered the topics of RP placement and RP loading. The key points here are that RP placement is often much less critical than most network engineers initially think because the default behavior of Cisco routers is to cut over to the SPT as soon as a new source of multicast traffic is detected. This typically reduces the engineering requirements of the RP to one of multicast state maintenance. In this case, the key issue is to determine whether the RP has sufficient memory and CPU to maintain an mroute table that includes (S, G) entries for every source in every group for which the RP is responsible.

CHAPTER 13

Connecting to DVMRP Networks

Up to this point in the book, it has been assumed that the network engineer has the luxury of designing and implementing the multicast network using only Cisco routers running PIM. Although this situation may occur in a new network or existing networks composed entirely of Cisco routers, the network engineer must often deal with other legacy routing equipment that are unable to run Protocol Independent Multicast (PIM).

Assuming that it is desirable to have multicast traffic flow into and out of these legacy, non-PIM portions of the network, the network engineer must carefully design the network to accomplish this goal. Although designing the network to allow unicast traffic to flow across dissimilar unicast routing protocol boundaries is a fairly simply matter, the upside-down nature of IP multicast routing complicates this task. Furthermore, because most router vendors implement only a small subset of the total spectrum of multicast routing protocols (Cisco is no exception), it is sometimes necessary to use a third multicast routing protocol as the common boundary routing protocol. Typically, the common IP multicast routing protocol that all router vendors have the capability to either run or interoperate with is Distance Vector Multicast Routing Protocol (DVMRP).

This chapter explores the use of Cisco's DVMRP interoperability features to permit a Cisco router to serve as a PIM-DVMRP gateway. The topics include DVMRP interoperability, controlling DVMRP route exchanges, network connection examples, and debugging tips.

Cisco DVMRP Interoperability

Network administrators frequently have the mistaken idea that Cisco routers can be configured to run DVMRP instead of PIM. Although Cisco routers can't run DVMRP per se, they can be used as a PIM-DVMRP gateways and interoperate with DVMRP routers. This subtle distinction is sometimes the source of problems when a network administrator assumes that the Cisco router that is configured for DVMRP interoperability is going to behave in the same fashion as a DVMRP router.

The two key areas (when this book was written) in which Cisco routers do not behave in the same fashion as a DVMRP router are as follows:

* Cisco routers do not maintain router state for each individual DVMRP router on a multi-access network.

* Cisco routers do send triggered DVMRP route updates, which are sent at the next update period.

The first of these two places some limitations on the operation of DVMRP interoperability across multi-access links, such as Ethernet, and is explored in detail later in the chapter. The second item could possibly effect the convergence time of DVMRP routing if the PIM network is used as a transient network for DVMRP routing. However, unless you are an ISP, your PIM network probably will not be a transient network and, therefore, this won't be an issue.

NOTE   On the other hand, if you are an ISP with numerous DVMRP network connections, the best way to handle this problem is to convert these DVMRP networks to stub networks and to simply inject the default DVMRP route (0.0.0.0) into these stub networks.

The remainder of this section covers the details of Cisco's DVMRP interoperability and provides you with the necessary information to understand the interactions between a Cisco router and a connected DVMRP router. After you have a solid working knowledge of these interactions, it should be much easier to understand what actually happens when you connect a Cisco router running PIM with a DVMRP router.

NOTE   The following sections assume a solid understanding of the details of the DVMRP protocol. If you are unfamiliar with these details or feel that your level of understanding of DVMRP is a little rusty, you may wish to review Chapter 5, "Distance Vector Multicast Routing Protocol," before proceeding.

Enabling DVMRP Interoperability

If you have ever searched the Cisco Command Reference manual looking for the command to enable DVMRP interoperation on an interface, you already know that such a command doesn't exist. The reason is quite simple: To provide for the unexpected introduction of a DVMRP router in the network, DVMRP interoperability is activated automatically when a Cisco router hears a DVMRP Probe message on a multicast enabled interface.

Figure 13-1 shows a Cisco router with multicast enabled on both of its interfaces. In this example, a DVMRP router (in this case, a UNIX workstation running the *mrouted* DVMRP multicast routing daemon) is active on Ethernet0. As soon as the DVMRP router sends a DVMRP Probe message on this Ethernet segment, the Cisco router hears it. This causes the Cisco router to mark Ethernet0 as having a DVMRP neighbor active on the segment, which automatically enables DVMRP interoperability.

Figure 13-1   *Automatic Detection of DVMRP Routers*

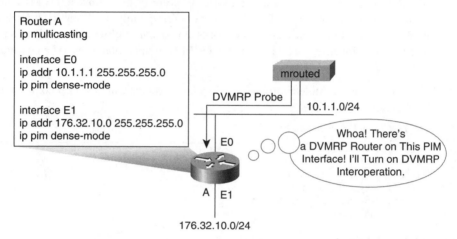

It's important to note that the Cisco router does not respond to the DVMRP Probe from this DVMRP neighbor with a DVMRP Probe message of its own. If it did, other Cisco routers on the network might confuse Router A with another non-Cisco, DVMRP router that would alter the basic PIM-DVMRP interaction. You will see why this can be a problem later in this section.

PIM-DVMRP Interaction

Understanding the PIM-DVMRP interactions that occur across the boundary between a Cisco router and a DVMRP router is the key to implementing PIM-DVMRP gateways in a Cisco network. Because the idea was to simply provide a PIM-DVMRP gateway function in Cisco routers, the initial types of interactions that took place across this boundary were extremely simple. However, over the years, the type of interactions across this boundary between a Cisco router and a DVMRP router have grown and expanded in scope until today's Cisco routers perform nearly all the functions of a DVMRP router. (Note that I said *nearly all*. Some notable exceptions still need to be kept in mind, particularly when you are using an older version of Cisco IOS that doesn't have some of the newer, enhanced interactions.)

The next two sections, "Interaction over Point-to-Point Links" and "Interaction over Multi-Access Links," describe the PIM-DVMRP interactions built in to the current release (which was version 12.0 at the time that this book was written) of IOS. The interactions that were available in older versions of IOS are described in a later section.

Interaction over Point-to-Point Links

DVMRP tunnels are the most common forms of point-to-point links in DVMRP networks. As you recall from Chapter 5, DVMRP networks frequently use DVMRP tunnels to interconnect two multicast-enabled networks across non-multicast networks. To provide this same functionality, Cisco IOS allows DVMRP tunnel interfaces to be configured on Cisco routers.

Example 13-1 is a sample configuration of a Cisco router that has been configured with a DVMRP tunnel interface.

Example 13-1 *DVMRP Tunnel Configuration*

```
interface Tunnel0
  ip unnumbered Ethernet0
  ip pim sparse-dense-mode
  tunnel source Ethernet0
  tunnel destination 192.168.1.10
  tunnel mode DVMRP

interface Ethernet0
  ip address 172.16.2.1 255.255.255.0
  ip pim sparse-dense-mode
```

In this sample configuration, the actual IP address of the tunnel on the Cisco router is assigned by the use of the **ip unnumbered Ethernet0** command, which causes the tunnel to appear to have the same IP address as the Ethernet 0.

The **tunnel mode DVMRP** command forces the tunnel to use IP-in-IP encapsulation (which is standard DVMRP tunnel encapsulation). Any packets sent through the tunnel will be encapsulated in an outer IP header. The **tunnel source Ethernet0** command specifies the source address of this outer IP header (which results in a tunnel endpoint source address of 172.16.2.1), and the **tunnel destination 192.168.1.10** command specifies the destination IP address of the outer IP header. This destination address is the tunnel endpoint address of the remote DVMRP router to which the tunnel is connected.

Figure 13-2 shows the PIM-DVMRP interactions that take place across the DVMRP tunnel that was configured in Example 13-1.

Figure 13-2   *PIM-DVMRP Interaction over Point-to-Point Links*

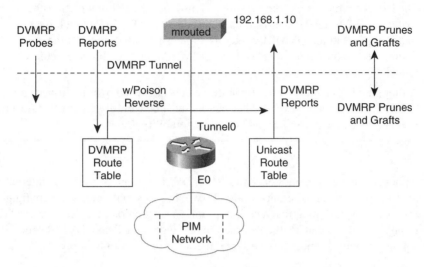

As Figure 13-2 shows, the Cisco router is performing nearly all the interactions a normal DVMRP router would over a tunnel. The only major exception to normal DVMRP router interaction is that the Cisco router does not send DVMRP Probes (which is important when the connection is a multi-access network, as discussed in the next section); however, virtually all other interactions are implemented. In most DVMRP router implementations, the failure to send DVMRP Probes has no impact on the proper operation of the DVMRP router and is not an issue.

For example, both DVMRP Prunes and Grafts are supported and are exchanged across the boundary when appropriate for normal DVMRP routing. Additionally, the Cisco router receives DVMRP routes into a local DVMRP routing table and Poison-Reverses source routes for multicast sources that it expects to receive via the DVMRP router.

The Cisco router also sends a subset of routes from its own unicast routing table to the DVMRP router. This permits the DVMRP router to properly perform Reverse Path Forwarding (RPF) to the tunnel for multicast sources in the PIM network. (Again, if this seems a bit confusing, you may wish to review the details of the DVMRP protocol discussed in Chapter 5.)

Finally, the actual subset of unicast routes that the Cisco router sends in DVMRP Reports depends on several factors. These details are covered in the section titled "DVMRP Route Exchanges" later in this chapter. For now, it is sufficient to understand that the Cisco router *advertises* a portion of the routes in the PIM network to the DVMRP router via DVMRP Route Reports.

The key point here is worth repeating. The set of DVMRP interactions between a Cisco router and a DVMRP router is at its fullest across a DVMRP tunnel. As a result, the Cisco router appears to the DVMRP router as another DVMRP router at the end of the tunnel. Therefore, the maximum level of PIM-DVMRP interoperability is achieved via DVMRP tunnels.

Although this maximum interoperability can be achieved over multi-access networks such as Ethernet segments, several other factors must be carefully controlled (discussed in the next section) to achieve this level of interoperability.

Although this section has concentrated on DVMRP tunnels, the same interaction rules apply to other forms of point-to-point links, such as serial links when configured properly. For example, assuming that a common link encapsulation method were used (PPP, Frame Relay, and so on) that enabled a Cisco router and a non-Cisco, DVMRP router to establish a point-to-point connection, the same interaction rules would apply.

Interaction over Multi-Access Links

As discussed previously, multi-access interfaces (Ethernet, Fast Ethernet, FDDI, and so on) that are multicast enabled will automatically activate DVMRP interoperability when a DVMRP Probe is received from a DVMRP router via the interface.

Example 13-2 is a sample configuration of a Cisco router that has been configured with Ethernet interfaces: one (Ethernet0) connected to the local PIM multicast network, and the other (Ethernet1) connected to a LAN segment with an active DVMRP router.

Example 13-2   *Ethernet Interfaces Configuration*

```
interface Ethernet0
 ip address 172.16.2.1 255.255.255.0
 ip pim sparse-dense-mode

interface Ethernet1
 ip address 192.168.10.1 255.255.255.0
 ip pim sparse-dense-mode
```

Notice that there is really nothing special about the way that these two interfaces are configured. They each have multicast enabled via the **ip pim sparse-dense-mode** command. No other special DVMRP related commands are really required because the router automatically enables DVMRP interoperability on Ethernet1 immediately upon hearing a DVMRP Probe message from the DVMRP router on that LAN segment.

Figure 13-3 shows DVMRP interactions that take place between a Cisco router and a DVMRP router across a multi-access interface (such as an Ethernet LAN segment) similar to the one described in Example 13-2.

Figure 13-3 *PIM-DVMRP Interaction over Multi-Access Links*

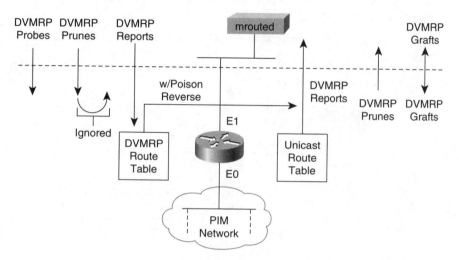

If you do a quick comparison between this set of interactions and those shown in Figure 13-2, you will see that they are nearly identical. Therefore, just as it did in the point-to-point link case, the Cisco router closely approximates the operation of a DVMRP router. The one exception is that the Cisco router no longer processes DVMRP Prunes that are received over a multi-access link. Consequently, if the DVMRP router attempts to prune some (S, G) multicast stream that is flowing out of the PIM cloud across to Ethernet1, the Cisco router will ignore it and continue to forward the unwanted multicast stream. This leads to the following important note that is worth emphasizing.

NOTE   *Cisco routers do not process DVMRP Prunes received across multi-access links.* (They will, however, send DVMRP Prunes as depicted in Figure 13-2). If full support for DVMRP Pruning is desired, a DVMRP tunnel (or some other point-to-point link) must be used.

The reason that DVMRP Pruning is not supported across multi-access links is a direct result of the fact that Cisco routers do not maintain state on each individual DVMRP router on a multi-access link. However, as described in Chapter 5, DVMRP routers expect their upstream neighbor to maintain *pruning state* on all DVMRP routers on the multi-access network and to prune the traffic only when all child DVMRP routers on the network have sent prunes for the traffic. This is in stark contrast to the PIM dense mode (PIM-DM) pruning operation. In the case of PIM-DM, the upstream PIM-DM router expects a downstream router to override a PIM Prune, sent by a sibling PIM router, with a PIM Join. This eliminates the need for upstream PIM routers to maintain pruning state on each downstream PIM router.

Figure 13-4 shows what happens when a Cisco router receives a DVMRP Prune on a multi-access link.

Figure 13-4   *Pruning Problem on Multi-Access Links*

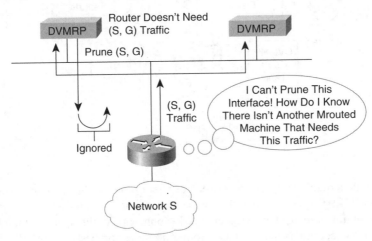

In this example, an (S, G) DVMRP Prune was received from the DVMRP router on the left side of the drawing. However, the Cisco router does not keep track of individual DVMRP routers on the multi-access network and, therefore, can't maintain Prune state for each router on the multi-access network DVMRP router. As a result, it can't be sure that another DVMRP router on the network has not pruned this (S, G) traffic and continues to forward traffic to the multi-access network.

NOTE   Cisco has received numerous requests to add support for DVMRP Pruning across multi-access links. It is quite possible that by the time this book is published, this feature will have been added to a later version of Cisco IOS. Readers are encouraged to check the status of this via the Cisco Systems Web page at http://www.cisco.com/.

Solving Pruning Problems on Multi-Access Links

The pruning problem described in the preceding section is usually not an issue when establishing an inter-domain DVMRP multicast connection because DVMRP tunnels are typically used. However, this is frequently not the case when a network administrator is enabling IP multicast in an existing network consisting of both Cisco and non-Cisco, DVMRP-only routers. In this case, the configuration shown in Figure 13-4 can be encountered. To handle this situation and provide DVMRP Pruning between the DVMRP routers and the Cisco router(s), DVMRP tunnels must be used.

Figure 13-5 shows the use of DVMRP tunnels to solve the pruning problem. In the example, two DVMRP tunnels have been configured between the Cisco router and the two DVMRP routers. Notice also that multicast has been disabled on Ethernet1 on the Cisco and the Ethernet interfaces on the two DVMRP routers. Multicast traffic now flows via the two DVMRP tunnels and not directly over the Ethernet segment.

Figure 13-5   *Solving the Pruning Problem on Multi-Access Links*

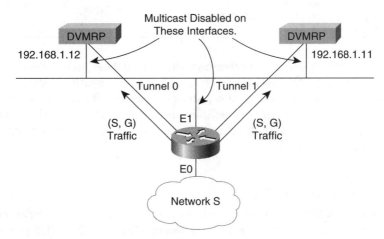

Example 13-3 is the configuration that would be used in the Cisco router to avoid this pruning problem on a multi-access network such as an Ethernet.

Example 13-3 *DVMRP Tunnel Configuration (Bypass Ethernet)*

```
interface Tunnel1
 ip unnumbered Ethernet0
 ip pim sparse-dense-mode
 tunnel source Ethernet0
 tunnel destination 192.168.1.11
 tunnel mode DVMRP

interface Tunnel0
 ip unnumbered Ethernet0
 ip pim sparse-dense-mode
 tunnel source Ethernet0
 tunnel destination 192.168.1.12
 tunnel mode DVMRP

interface Ethernet1
 ip address 192.168.10.1 255.255.255.0

interface Ethernet0
 ip address 172.16.2.1 255.255.255.0
 ip pim sparse-dense-mode
```

Notice that the **ip pim sparse-dense-mode** command has been removed from the configuration of **Ethernet1** to disable multicast on this interface. Although this solves the pruning problem, this modification also increases the traffic across the Ethernet LAN by a factor equal to the number of tunnels. In this case, two tunnels have been configured which means the same multicast packet must be sent across the Ethernet segment twice, once for each tunnel configured.

DVMRP Interaction in Older IOS Versions

The Cisco DVMRP interoperability feature has seen quite a bit of enhancement since it was first introduced. Although the more recent releases of Cisco IOS provide DVMRP interoperability that results in the Cisco router being able to almost completely emulate operation of a DVMRP router, it's still important to understand the DVMRP interoperability of older IOS releases. This knowledge is particularly important because old Cisco routers in use today are running IOS releases as old as version 8.1. Therefore, it is not unthinkable for a network administrator to need to deal with a Cisco router running, say, version 11.1 of Cisco IOS where the DVMRP interoperability feature set is considerably less robust than it's current versions.

The initial attempts at DVMRP interoperability in Cisco IOS used a simple Internet Group Membership Protocol (IGMP) hack that spoofed a locally attached DVMRP router into thinking that a host on the network had joined a particular multicast group.

Figure 13-6 shows the PIM-DVMRP interactions that take place across non-tunnel interfaces in IOS versions prior to 11.2(13). If you compare this diagram to the one shown in Figure 13-3, you will notice some similarities in the interactions across this interface (that is, DVMRP Prunes are ignored) as well as several major differences.

Figure 13-6   *PIM-DVMRP Interaction over Non-Tunnels Prior to IOS 11.2(13)*

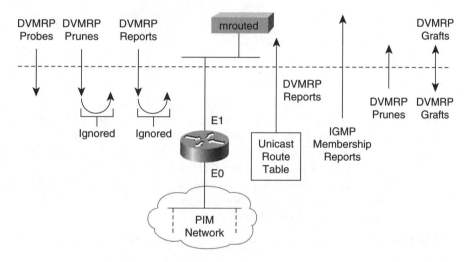

Probably the most noticeable difference is that the Cisco router does not Poison Reverse any incoming DVMRP Route Reports and does not accept any DVMRP Route Reports for storage into a DVMRP route table. The Cisco router does, however, advertise a portion of the routes in its unicast route table to the DVMRP router via DVMRP Route Reports. This permits the DVMRP router to perform RPF correctly for any incoming multicast traffic from sources in the PIM network. Secondly, and this is a key difference, instead of sending Poison Reverse routes to trigger the DVMRP router to forward multicast traffic from sources in the DVMRP network, the Cisco router sends IGMP Membership Reports for any groups that appear in its multicast routing table.

This simple DVMRP interoperability mechanism worked pretty well in PIM-DM networks where every multicast receiver was also a sender but had problems under other conditions.

For example, consider the situation shown Figure 13-7.

Figure 13-7   *Problem with Old PIM-DVMRP Interaction Prior to IOS 11.2(13)*

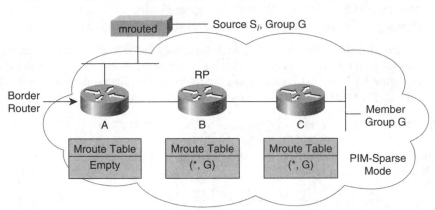

Here, a PIM sparse mode (PIM-SM) network has a member of Group G attached to Router C. This causes PIM Joins to be sent to the rendezvous point (RP), Router B, and (*, G) entries to be created in the mroute tables of both Routers B and C. However, Router A (the Border Router) does not have any entry for Group G in its mroute table and, therefore, does not send any IGMP Membership Reports to the DVMRP router. Because Router A is not sending IGMP Membership Reports for Group G (and is not sending Poison Reverse routes for Network S in the DVMRP network), the DVMRP router will not forward any S_i traffic across the Ethernet to Router A.

The DVMRP router doesn't forward this traffic for the following reasons:

- It doesn't see a downstream child DVMRP router, which would be indicated by the receipt of a Poison Reverse route for Network S.

- It doesn't see any local members of Group G on the Ethernet, which would be indicated by the receipt of an IGMP Membership Report for Group G.

Forcing DVMRP Route Exchanges

To overcome the problem with the IGMP hack in the older versions of Cisco IOS described earlier, it is necessary to force the Cisco routers to exchange DVMRP routing information and to send Poison Reverse routes back to the DVMRP router as necessary. This can be accomplished by the following Cisco interface configuration command:

```
ip dvmrp unicast-routing
```

NOTE	In my opinion, the **ip dvmrp unicast-routing** command is one of the more misunderstood IOS configuration commands. Upon seeing this command for the first time, many people think that it enables the routing of unicast traffic using DVMRP routes and ask, "Why would I want to route my unicast traffic using DVMRP routing information?" To avoid this confusion, I tell people that whenever they see this command in a configuration, they should mentally translate it to **ip dvmrp exchange-routes** because it is basically telling the Cisco router to send and receive DVMRP routes.

When the **ip dvmrp unicast-routing** command is configured on a non-tunnel interface (such as the one shown previously in Figure 13-6), it modifies the PIM-DVMRP interactions.

Figure 13-8 shows the new modified set of interactions that result when this command is added.

Figure 13-8 *Using **ip dvmrp unicast-routing** to Solve Interaction Problems*

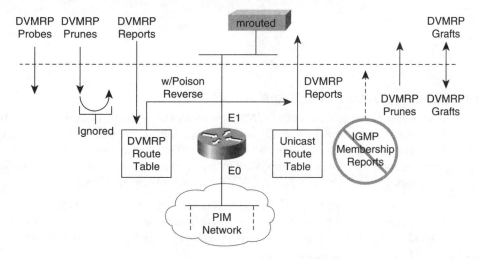

The first thing to notice is that the addition of the ip **dvmrp unicast-routing** command prevents the sending of IGMP Membership Reports (the IGMP hack). Instead, the Cisco router is now sending and receiving DVMRP Route Reports with Poison Reverse as appropriate. (Notice also that the problem with DVMRP Prunes is still there, which means that it would probably be better to just disable IP multicast from the Ethernet and configure a DVMRP tunnel between the Cisco and DVMRP routers.)

Now that the Cisco router is sending DVMRP route information including Poison Reverse to the DVMRP router (as shown in Figure 13-9), traffic from source S_i will flow across the Ethernet to Border Router A. This results in (S, G) state being created in Router A and a PIM Register message being sent to the RP as if the source was directly connected to Router A.

Figure 13-9 *Results of Using **ip dvmrp unicast-routing** to Solve Interaction Problems*

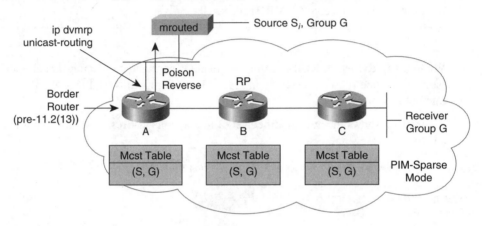

Accepting/Rejecting DVMRP Neighbors

In some cases, the existence of a DVMRP router on a network interface may cause DVMRP interoperability to be automatically enabled when it is not desired. Although there is no interface configuration command to disable the automatic nature of DVMRP interoperability, it can be accomplished by using a form of the **ip dvmrp accept-filter** command to effectively ignore any DVMRP routers on the interface.

For example, assume that a network administrator wants to prevent DVMRP interoperability from being automatically activated on an Ethernet interface where known DVMRP routers exist. The router configuration in Example 13-4 accomplishes this goal.

Example 13-4 *Non-DVMRP Interoperability Configuration*

```
Interface Ethernet0
 ip address 172.36.10.1 255.255.255.0
 ip dvmrp accept-filter 0 neighbor-list 10

access-list 10 deny all
```

Example 13-4 works because the **ip dvmrp accept-filter** is also applied to any incoming DVMRP Probe messages before they are processed. Because the access list specified in the **neighbor-list** clause in the preceding example is **deny all**, no DVMRP Probe messages (or DVMRP Route Reports, for that matter) are accepted on this interface and hence DVMRP interoperability will not be automatically enabled.

NOTE   The use of **access-list 0** in the **accept-filter** clause in Example 13-4 is an implied **accept any**. Because **access-list 10** will reject all DVMRP messages, the use of **access-list 0** has no effect and simply avoids the need to define a separate access-list. (The **ip dvmrp accept-filter** command is discussed in greater detail in the section "Controlling DVMRP Route Acceptance.")

Rejecting Non-Pruners

Believe it or not, early versions of DVMRP did not support the concept of pruning. This feature was added in a later version but not until may sites had already implemented the non-pruning version. As the MBone grew, the lack of DVMRP Pruning was causing a large amount of bandwidth to be wasted in the MBone. To fix this problem, key Internet administrators made a collective effort to encourage all sites to migrate to the newer version of DVMRP that supported pruning. A deadline was proposed that would require all DVMRP routers to be upgraded to support DVMRP Pruning. Routers that were not upgraded would have their tunnels disconnected to stop the wasted bandwidth caused by the lack of DVMRP Pruning support.

To assist with the automation of this task, Cisco implemented a special command to automatically reject DVMRP routers that were non-Prune as DVMRP neighbor routers. The format of this command is

```
ip dvmrp reject-non-pruners
```

This command instructs the Cisco router not to peer with a DVMRP neighbor on this interface if the neighbor doesn't support DVMRP Pruning/Grafting. If a DVMRP Probe or Report message is received without the Prune-Capable flag set, a syslog message is logged and the DVMRP message is discarded. This command is off by default, and therefore all DVMRP neighbors are accepted, regardless of capability (or lack thereof).

DVMRP Route Exchanges

Most of the figures in the previous sections on PIM-DVMRP interaction indicate that the actual unicast routes advertised by the Cisco router to the DVMRP router depend on several factors. This section covers the various special Cisco configuration commands (frequently

referred to as nerd knobs by network engineers) that allow the network administrator to
tune the advertisement of DVMRP routes by the Cisco router. These nerd knobs are
discussed in the sections that follow and cover the following:

- Advertising connect routes (default behavior)
- Classful route summarization
- Controlling DVMRP route advertisements

A sample router is used throughout this section to make these topics easier to understand.
As each modification is made to the configuration of the Cisco router in the example, refer
back to this example and see how the modification affects the DVMRP routes being
advertised by the Cisco router.

Figure 13-10 shows this sample network consisting of a Cisco router that has been
configured with a DVMRP tunnel to a DVMRP router. This Cisco router is connected to a
large enterprise network (not shown) via the two interfaces, Ethernet0 and Ethernet1.
Notice also that the DVMRP tunnel has been configured with **ip unnumbered Ethernet0**,
which causes the tunnel to share the IP address of Ethernet0 as if the 176.32.10.1 address
were its own IP address. This configuration will become important later.

Figure 13-10   *Example DVMRP Route Exchange Network*

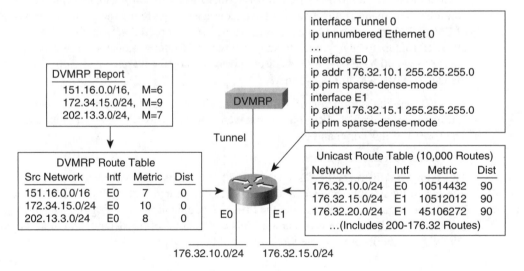

As you can see from the diagram, the design of this rather large enterprise network has
resulted in a unicast routing table of 10,000 entries. Of these 10,000 route entries, 200 are
unsummarized routes in the 176.32.0.0/16 Class B network.

NOTE	I realize that an enterprise network that results in a route table with 10,000 entries is probably an indication of a poor design that is suffering from a lack of any significant route summarization. I hope that you haven't had to assume responsibility for the administration of such a network because it can be a real headache to manage. However, this example allows us to focus on the effects of various configuration changes on the advertisement of routes to the DVMRP router.

Continuing with the example, it is clear that the DVMRP router is advertising the following three routes in the DVMRP network (not shown) to the Cisco router:

- 151.16.0.0/16   Metric: 6 hops
- 172.34.15.0/24   Metric: 9 hops
- 202.13.3.0/24   Metric: 7 hops

The Cisco router stores these DVMRP routes in a separate DVMRP route table for use by the router's multicast forwarding mechanism to RPF check multicast packets arriving over the DVMRP tunnel. In addition, the metrics of the DVMRP routes received by the Cisco router are automatically incremented by a metric offset of 1 hop to reflect the cost of the link. (This automatic metric offset can also be controlled by using other Cisco configuration commands if it is desirable to increment incoming DVMRP route metrics by some value other than 1 hop.)

Advertising Connected Routes (Default Behavior)

By default, a Cisco router advertises only connected unicast routes (that is, only routes to subnets that are directly connected to the router) from its unicast routing table in DVMRP Route Reports. Furthermore, these routes undergo normal DVMRP classful route summarization. This process depends on whether the route being advertised falls into the same classful network as the interface over which it is being advertised. This topic is discussed in more detail shortly.

Figure 13-11 shows an example of this default behavior. First, observe that the DVMRP Report sent by the Cisco router contains the three original routes received from the DVMRP router that have been Poison Reversed by adding 32 (infinity) to the DVMRP metric. Following these Poison Reverse routes are the two other routes (shown in shaded text) that are advertisements for the two directly connected networks, 176.32.10.0/24 and 176.32.15.0/24, that were taken from the unicast routing table. These two routes are advertised with a DVMRP metric of 1 hop by default. This value can be also be modified by the use of special Cisco configuration commands.

Figure 13-11 *Only Connected Unicast Routes Are Advertised by Default*

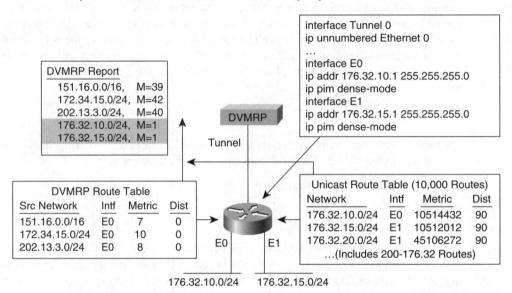

Again, the important thing to remember is that the default behavior of a Cisco router is to advertise only connected unicast routes in DVMRP Route Reports. In this case, only the two Ethernet segments fall into this category and, therefore, only these two entries in the unicast route table are advertised. As a result, the DVMRP router will be able to Poison Reverse only these two routes and hence will be able to RPF properly only for multicast traffic sent by sources on these two Ethernet segments. Any other multicast sources in the network behind the Cisco router not on these two Ethernet segments will not RPF check properly on the DVMRP router and will be discarded. (The next few sections describe how the Cisco router can be configured to advertise something other than just the connected routes.)

Classful Summarization of DVMRP Routes

As mentioned in the preceding section, Cisco routers perform normal classful summarization of DVMRP routes. In the example shown in Figure 13-11, the two directly connected subnets, 176.32.10.0/24 and 176.32.15.0/24, fell into the same Class B network (176.32.0.0/16) as the tunnel interface. In this case, the DVMRP tunnel shares the same IP address as Ethernet0, specifically 176.32.10.1. As a result, classful summarization of these routes was not performed.

Figure 13-12 depicts a new configuration where the IP address of the DVMRP tunnel does *not* fall into the same Class B network as the two directly connected subnets: 176.32.10.0/24 and 176.32.15.0/24.

Figure 13-12 *Classful Summarization of Unicast Routes*

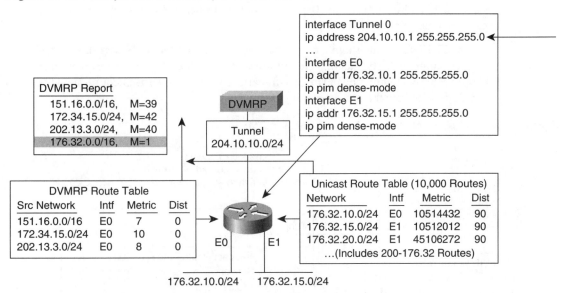

In this example, the configuration of Tunnel0 has been modified and given its own IP address of 204.10.10.1 by the use of the **ip address 204.10.10.1 255.255.255.0** command. As a result, notice that the DVMRP Report now contains only the Class B, summarized route (shown in shaded text) of the two directly connected networks. This configuration, in turn, not only allows the DVMRP router to Poison Reverse the entire Class B network but also allows any incoming multicast traffic from sources in the 176.32.0.0/16 network to RPF correctly.

This configuration allows the DVMRP router to receive all multicast sources in the 176.32.0.0 network but also uses up additional IP addresses in the 204.10.10.0 range. In some cases, the use of additional IP address space to address the DVMRP tunnel is not an option. Obviously, what is needed is some way to force classful summarization to occur without having to waste additional IP addresses.

Beginning with Cisco IOS version 11.2(5), the following interface command was added:

```
ip dvmrp summary-address <address> <mask>
```

This command instructs the Cisco router to advertise the summary address (indicated by the address/mask pair specified in the command) to be advertised in place of any route that falls in this address range. In other words, the summary address is sent in a DVMRP Route Report if the unicast routing table contains at least one route in this range. If the unicast route table does not contain any routes within this range, the summary address is not advertised in a DVMRP Report.

By using this new command, the DVMRP tunnel in the example can still be configured to share the IP address of Ethernet 0 using the **ip unnumbered Ethernet0** command and still perform route summarization.

Figure 13-13 shows the sample network reconfigured with the **ip dvmrp summary-address** command. The diagram clearly shows that (besides the Poison Reverse routes) the Cisco router is sending only a single summarized Class B advertisement for network 176.32.0.0/16 from the unicast routing table.

Figure 13-13   *Forcing DVMRP Route Summarization (11.2(5))*

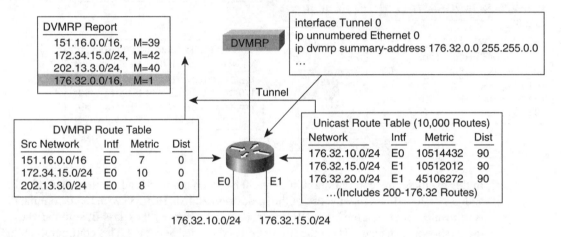

Controlling DVMRP Route Advertisement

The examples in the two preceding sections have focused on the advertisement and summarization of the 176.32.10.0/24 and 176.32.15.0/24 connected routes. However, the network in the example has considerably more than these two routes (or their Class B summarization of 176.32.0.0/16).

To get the Cisco router to go beyond its default behavior of advertising connected routes only requires the **ip dvmrp metric** interface configuration command. This command specifies which routes in the unicast routing table the router is to advertise in DVMRP Route Reports on this interface.

The most basic form of the **ip dvmrp metric** command is

```
ip dvmrp metric <metric> [list <access-list>]
```

This command instructs the Cisco router to advertise routes from the unicast route table that match the qualifying **<access-list>** as DVMRP routes with a metric of **<metric>**. It is important to remember that if the option list **<access-list>** clause is omitted, all routes in the unicast routing table are advertised. In some cases, advertising the entire unicast routing table to the neighboring DVMRP router may be very undesirable, especially when the unicast routing table contains many routes and no summarization is used to cut down the number of routes advertised. In some cases, this process not only is undesirable but also can prove to be deadly to neighboring DVMRP routers.

Figure 13-14 depicts what can happen if the **list <access-list>** clause is accidentally omitted from the **ip dvmrp metric** command. In this example, all 10,000 routes from the unicast routing table are being advertised in DVMRP Route Reports to the DVMRP router.

Figure 13-14   *The Deadly **ip dvmrp metric n** Command*

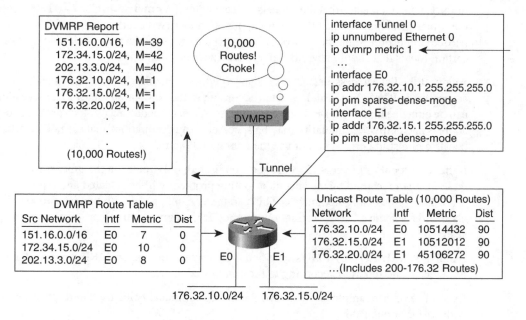

NOTE	As the use of multicast in audio and video multimedia sessions grew in popularity, more and more administrators connected their networks to the MBone. Unfortunately, failure to supply an access control list (ACL) on the **ip dvmrp metric** command was a common mistake. This error resulted in a huge jump in the total number of DVMRP routes being advertised into the MBone and was often made worse by a lack of any summarization. In addition, this configuration error often caused other DVMRP route instabilities because DVMRP route loops were often formed as a result of incorrect route redistribution.

For most network administrators, the basic form of the **ip dvmrp metric** command presented in the previous example (along with an **ip dvmrp summary-address** command) is often all that is necessary. Frequently, however, a finer granularity of control over the DVMRP routes being advertised is necessary. In this case, the **ip dvmrp metric** command may be used multiple times on an interface; additional qualifying clauses may also be used. The complete format of this command is

```
ip dvmrp metric <metric> [list <access-list>]
                        {[<protocol> <process-id> | [dvmrp]}
```

The acceptable **<metric>** value is between 0 and 32. If a **<metric>** value of 32 is specified, the routes (specified by the other clauses) are advertised as having a metric of DVMRP infinity, which indicates that the route is unreachable. If a **<metric>** value of 0 is specified, the routes (specified by the other clauses) are not advertised at all. A value of 0 is particularly useful when the network administrator wants to block the advertisement of certain routes that should never be advertised under any condition.

Again, if the **list <access-list>** clause is specified, only the destinations that match the access-list will be selected and reported according to the configured metric. The access-list can be either a simple or an extended access-list. When extended access-lists are used, both address and netmask granularity may be specified. Any destinations that are not advertised because of a split horizon do not use the configured metric.

If the **<protocol> <process-id>** clause is configured, only routes in the unicast routing table that were learned by the specified routing protocol will be selected and reported according to the configured metric. This parameter can be used with the list **<access-list>** clause so a selective list of destinations learned from a given routing protocol may be selected.

Finally, if the **dvmrp** keyword is specified, only routes from the DVMRP routing table will be selected and reported according to the configured metric.

Example 13-5 is a sample of the **ip dvmrp metric** command being used multiple times and with various options.

Example 13-5 *ip dvmrp metric Command Options*

```
ip dvmrp metric 1 list 10
ip dvmrp metric 2 ospf 1
ip dvmrp metric 0 dvmrp

access-list 10 permit 172.36.0.0 0.0.255.255
```

In this example, the first command specifies that any routes that fall in the range of 172.36.0.0–172.36.255.255 should be advertised with a DVMRP metric of 1. The second command specifies that any route in the unicast routing table learned by the Open Shortest Path First (OSPF) routing protocol (with a process ID of 1) should be advertised with a DVMRP metric of 2. Finally, the third command specifies that any routes that are learned via DVMRP (and hence reside in the DVMRP routing table) should not be advertised.

The **ip dvmrp metric 0 dvmrp** form of this command can also be used to prevent a PIM network from inadvertently becoming a transient network when it is multihomed to a DVMRP network.

Figure 13-15 shows an example of a PIM network that is multihomed to a DVMRP network. By configuring the **ip dvmrp metric 0 dvmrp** command on both DVMRP tunnels, DVMRP routes learned from one DVMRP router will not be advertised again to the other DVMRP router. This prevents multicast traffic sent by sources in the DVMRP cloud from flowing through the Cisco router and back into the DVMRP cloud.

Figure 13-15   *Avoiding Becoming a DVMRP Transient Network*

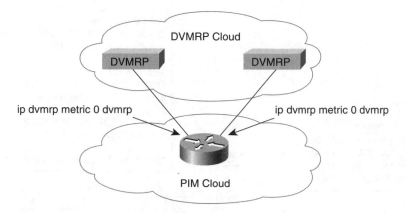

Disabling Automatic Classful Summarization

Earlier in the chapter, it was implied that classful summarization of DVMRP routing information is always the desired behavior; in fact, classful summarization may not always be the desired behavior. In some special cases providing the neighboring DVMRP router with all subnet information enables the network administrator to better control the flow of multicast traffic in the DVMRP network. One such case might occur if the PIM network is connected to the DVMRP cloud at several points and more specific (that is, unsummarized) routes are being injected into the DVMRP network to advertise better paths to individual subnets inside the PIM cloud.

Prior to IOS release 11.2(5), the network administrator had no control over the automatic classful summarization mechanism in cases such as the example shown in Figure 13-12 and could not disable this feature. However, beginning with IOS release 11.2(5), the following interface configuration command provides control over this mechanism:

```
[no] ip dvmrp auto-summary
```

By default, this command is in effect and is not displayed in the Cisco interface configuration. Only if the **no ip dvmrp auto-summary** form is configured does the command appear in the configuration on the interface.

As an example, assume the network administrator wishes to advertise all 200 of the 176.32.0.0 subnets from the unicast routing table to the DVMRP router using the configuration shown in Figure 13-16. Notice that instead of advertising all 200 of the 176.32.0.0 subnets, the automatic classful summarization mechanism has resulted in only a single summarized route being advertised.

Figure 13-16 *Unwanted Classful Summarization*

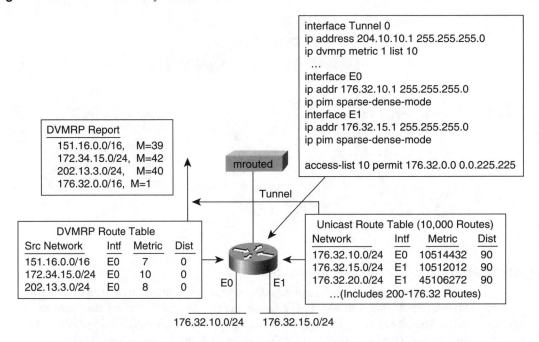

Figure 13-17 shows the effects of the use of the **no ip dvmrp auto-summary** command (shown in boldface on the figure). Now, all two hundred 176.32.0.0 subnets are being advertised to the DVMRP router as the network administrator had desired.

Figure 13-17 *Disabling DVMRP Auto-Summarization*

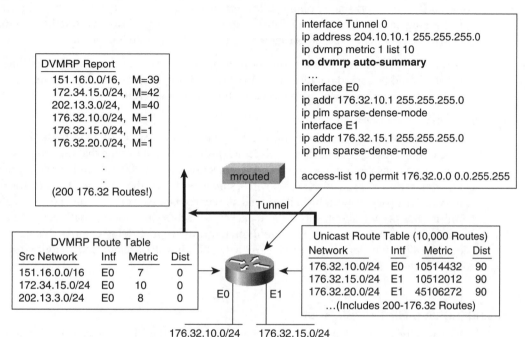

NOTE   Disabling summarization is normally not desirable, particularly if there is only a single connect between the DVMRP and PIM networks as shown in Figure 13-17. However, if the PIM network is connected to the DVMRP network at multiple points (separated by some distance), injecting more specific routes into the DVMRP network at each connection point might be desirable. This would provide for more efficient routing of multicast traffic flowing from the PIM network to the DVMRP network.

Pacing DVMRP Route Reports

When it came time to send the periodic DVMRP Route Reports, early versions of IOS would simply send the DVMRP Report packets all at once. If the number of DVMRP routes being advertised was quite large (as might be the case at a core router in the MBone), the number of DVMRP Report packets needed to send all the routes could be rather large. This would result in a huge burst of DVMRP Report packets being sent at the start of the

DVMRP Report interval. Unfortunately, many DVMRP routers (especially those consisting of a small UNIX workstation running the *mrouted* process) could not buffer this huge burst of incoming packets, and some DVMRP Reports were dropped. Route instabilities in the DVMRP network could occur as routes timed out and went into holddown.

To avoid this problem (and better comply with the DVMRP specification, which says these packets should be spread out over the entire DVMRP Report period), the following configuration command was added to Cisco IOS in version 11.2(5):

```
ip dvmrp output-report-delay <delay-time> [<burst>]
```

This command configures an interpacket delay between DVMRP Route Reports. The **<delay-time>** value (specified in milliseconds) is the amount of time that the router waits between the transmission a set of **<burst>** number of report packets. For example, assume that **<delay-time>** is specified as 200 with a **<burst>** of 2. At the periodic DVMRP Report interval, if six packets must be built to send all reports, two packets are sent, a delay of 200 milliseconds occurs, and then two more packets are sent. This process continues until all report packets have been sent. If the **ip dvmrp output-report-delay** command is not configured (on IOS versions after 11.2(5)), a default **<burst>** size of 2 and a **<delay-time>** of 100 milliseconds is assumed.

Advertising the DVMRP Default Route

Occasionally, a network administrator may wish to have the Cisco router advertise the DVMRP *default route* (network 0.0.0.0) to the DVMRP neighbors on an interface. The DVMRP default route functions in the same way as a unicast default route. That is, it is a wildcard route that matches any network not matched by a more specific route. However, in this case, the DVMRP default route computes the RPF information for any multicast sources that don't match a more specific route.

Advertising the DVMRP default route may be accomplished by the use of the **ip dvmrp default-information** interface command, which has the following format:

```
ip dvmrp default-information {originate ¦ only}
```

This command causes the DVMRP default route (network 0.0.0.0) to be advertised to DVMRP neighbors on this interface. When the keyword **only** is used, *only* the DVMRP default route is advertised on the interface. All other DVMRP routes are suppressed and are not advertised on the interface. When the keyword **originate** is used, other more specific DVMRP routes will be advertised (depending on the normal DVMRP advertisement rules) in addition to the DVMRP default route.

Controlling DVMRP Route Acceptance

Up to this point, the discussion of DVMRP Route Report control has considered the sending of DVMRP Route Reports. Cisco IOS also provides control over the *receiving* of DVMRP Route Reports through the use of the **ip dvmrp accept-filter** command, which has the following format:

```
ip dvmrp accept-filter <access-list> [neighbor-list <neighbor-acl>]
                                     [<distance>]
```

This command configures an acceptance filter for incoming DVMRP Route Reports on the interface. Any routes received in DVMRP Reports from neighbors that match the optional **<neighbor-acl>** and that also match the **<access-list>** are stored in the DVMRP routing table. If the **<distance>** value is specified in the command, the routes are stored in the DVMRP route table with their Administrative Distance (which is often just referred to simply as *distance*) set to **<distance>**.

If the optional **neighbor-list** clause is not specified, the **<access-list>** is applied to routes received from any DVMRP neighbor. In addition, if the **<distance>** value is not specified, the accepted routes are stored with their distance set to the default DVMRP distance (which is normally 0 unless modified by the **ip dvmrp distance** global command).

The **ip dvmrp accept-filter** command is often used to avoid DVMRP route loops that can be introduced when more than one connection exists between the PIM network and the DVMRP network. In some cases, unicast routes from the PIM network can be injected into the DVMRP cloud as DVMRP routes. These routes may reenter the PIM network at the other PIM-DVMRP connection as DVMRP routes, which have a better distance than the original unicast routes. This could cause the PIM border routers to RPF incorrectly to the DVMRP networks for sources that actually reside inside the PIM network.

NOTE   The Administrative Distance of a route in the DVMRP routing table is compared to the Administrative Distance of the same route in the unicast routing table. The route with the lower Administrative Distance (taken either from the unicast routing table or from the DVMRP routing table) takes precedence when computing the RPF interface for a source of a multicast packet. If both Administrative Distances are equal, the DVMRP route is preferred.

Adjusting the Default DVMRP Distance

As discussed in the preceding section, Cisco routers assign a default distance of 0 to all routes in the DVMRP route table. However, the **ip dvmrp accept-filter** command can be used to override the default distance of 0 when it is desirable to use some other distance value as the default for DVMRP routes. DVMRP routes that match the access-list specified in the **ip dvmrp accept-filter** command are assigned the distance value specified by the optional **<distance>** value.

The 11.2 version of IOS introduced a command that modifies the default DVMRP distance to some value other than 0. The format of this global configuration command is

```
ip dvmrp distance <admin-distance>
```

This command instructs the Cisco router to set the default Administrative Distance for *all* received DVMRP routes to **<admin-distance>** instead of 0. (The **ip dvmrp accept-filter** command may override this value when specified on an interface.)

Tuning the Administrative Distance of DVMRP routes affects not only the RPF calculation on incoming multicast traffic but also the advertisement of DVMRP routes to other DVMRP routers. For example, setting the Administrative Distance of the DVMRP routes higher than the Administrative Distance of the unicast routes causes the original unicast routes to continue to be advertised using their appropriate DVMRP metric. On the other hand, if the Administrative Distance of the DVMRP routes is left at 0 and hence those routes are preferred over the unicast routes, the DVMRP routes and their received DVMRP metrics (suitably incremented) will be reflected back to other DVMRP neighbors.

Offsetting DVMRP Metrics

In networks where DVMRP routes are used extensively, it is sometimes desirable to artificially manipulate DVMRP routing metrics to achieve the desired flow of traffic. On Cisco routers, this may be accomplished via the use of the ip dvmrp metric-offset interface command. The full format of this command is as follows:

```
ip dvmrp metric-offset [in ¦ out] <increment>
```

This command instructs the Cisco router to add the value of **<increment>** to the metric of an incoming or outgoing DVMRP route advertisement. When the **in** (or no keyword) is supplied), the **<increment>** is added to incoming DVMRP Reports. (This value is also reported in replies to *mrinfo* requests.) When the out keyword is supplied, the **<increment>** is added to outgoing DVMRP Reports for routes from the DVMRP routing table. This is similar to the metric keyword in mrouted configuration files used on UNIX workstations that are functioning as DVMRP routers. If the **ip dvmrp metric-offset** command is not configured on an interface, the default increment value for incoming routes is 1 and the default increment value for outgoing routes is 0.

Special MBone Features

As the size of the MBone grew, the number of DVMRP routes being advertised began to grow exponentially. Because DVMRP is a periodic update, distance vector protocol, this exponential growth began to affect the overall performance of the MBone. In some cases, misconfiguration of key routers resulted in enormous spikes in the number of DVMRP routes being advertised, which often precipitated serious throughput problems.

In an attempt to provide some extra bulletproofing against sudden spikes of bogus routes being injected into the MBone, Cisco added two new features that are automatically configured whenever **ip multicast-routing** is configured on a router. These two features are

- DVMRP route limits
- DVMRP route-hog Notification

DVMRP Route Limits

As more and more network administrators connected their networks to the MBone, the frequency of Cisco routers being misconfigured with **ip dvmrp metric** commands without an access-list to limit the routes injected into the MBone rose dramatically. This configuration error was sometimes compounded by the fact the Cisco routers injecting their entire unicast route table were running External Border Gateway Protocol (BGP) and had a unicast routing table that consisted of every route prefix in the Internet, which was about 45,000 route prefixes. Of course, normal DVMRP classful summarization would reduce this number somewhat, but the end result was still the same: MBone meltdown. (MBone meltdown was a vivid reminder that DVMRP would have to be phased out at some point and a new method found to distribute multicast routing information into the Internet. Fortunately, BGP4+—sometimes called Multicast BGP (MBGP)—appears to be capable of taking over this task.)

As a result of an increasing number of misconfiguration incidents, the **ip dvmrp route-limit** command was added by Cisco in IOS release 11.0. As of this release, all Cisco routers automatically configure this command whenever **ip multicast-routing** is enabled.

The format of this global configuration command is

```
ip dvmrp route-limit <route-count>
```

This command instructs the Cisco router to limit the number of DVMRP routes advertised over an interface to **<route-count>** and effectively limits the number of routes that can be injected into a DVMRP cloud. The default **<route-count>** value, 7000, is entered when the router auto-configures this command. However, this value can be modified as desired. The **no** version of this command removes the route limit and allows any number of DVMRP routes to be advertised.

DVMRP Route-Hog Notification

Although the use of automatic DVMRP route limits prevents network administrators from accidentally injecting too many routes into a DVMRP network, it would also be nice if administrators could receive proactive notification when some other network was injecting too many routes.

A command introduced in IOS release 10.2 provides this proactive notification. Beginning with this release, the ip routehog-notification command is automatically configured on the router whenever ip multicast-routing is enabled.

The format of this global configuration command is

```
ip dvmrp routehog-notification <route-count>
```

This command configures a threshold value of **<route-count>** number of routes that the Cisco router can receive on an interface within an approximate 1-minute interval. If this threshold is exceeded, a syslog message warns that a route surge may be occurring within the MBone. This syslog message is typically used to quickly detect when someone has misconfigured a router to inject a large number of routes into the MBone. The Cisco router automatically configures the default value of 10,000 routes whenever **ip multicast-routing** is enabled. However, this value may be adjusted by specifically configuring a different value. (This feature may also be disabled by specifically configuring the no form of this command.)

NOTE   A running count of the number of DVMRP routes received on an interface during a 1-minute interval may be displayed by using the **show ip igmp interface** command. When the route-hog notification threshold is being exceeded, an "*** ALERT ***" string is appended to the line.

PIM-DVMRP Boundary Issues

So far, this chapter has primarily been concerned with the details of the interactions and route exchanges that take place between a DVMRP network and a PIM network at the border router. However, more than just configuring the border router to interoperate and exchange DVMRP routes with its DVMRP neighbor must be considered when interconnecting PIM and DVMRP networks.

Frequently, the mere act of creating a DVMRP tunnel into the PIM network can create RPF problems in the routers inside the PIM network for multicast traffic that originated in the DVMRP cloud. By default, PIM routers make use of their unicast routing table to perform RPF calculations. As a result, the arrival of multicast traffic from outside the network via a DVMRP tunnel at some arbitrary point in the PIM network introduces a *unicast-multicast congruency issue.*

In addition, the basic nature of the tree-building mechanisms in PIM-SM and DVMRP are diametrically opposed. Specifically, the dense mode behavior of DVMRP uses a *push* methodology in which traffic is pushed out to all points in the network and then pruned back where it is not wanted. On the other hand, PIM-SM uses a *pull* methodology in which traffic is pulled down to only those points in the network where the traffic has been expressly requested. (This problem between PIM-SM and DVMRP is not a unique situation. In fact, it exists any time two networks, one using a sparse mode protocol and the other a dense mode protocol, are interconnected. This includes PIM-SM to PIM-DM network interconnections as well.)

In the sections that follow, the unicast-multicast congruency and the PIM-SM boundary problems are explored in detail. In both cases, several examples along with possible solutions and their side effects are presented.

Unicast-Multicast Congruency

The introduction of a separate DVMRP routing table in the Cisco router opens another source of RPF check data to the multicast forwarding algorithm in addition to the normal source, which is the unicast routing table. This can result in incongruent multicast and unicast network topologies. (This Ph.D. talk simply means that unicast and multicast traffic flows via different paths through the network.) Although this incongruency is sometimes intentional, quite often it is not and can cause RPF failures at other points in the network.

Consider for a moment the network hierarchy shown in Figure 13-18.

Figure 13-18 *DVMRP Tunnel Problem*

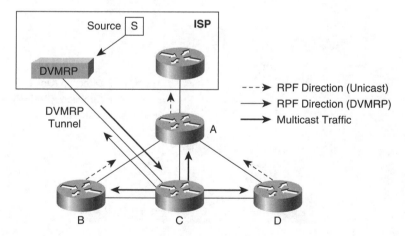

In this example, a tunnel has been run to a DVMRP router somewhere in the ISP's network to obtain multicast traffic from sources in the Internet. However, instead of terminating the DVMRP tunnel on the Internet access router (Router A), the tunnel has been terminated on a less critical router further down the hierarchy (Router C). This happens quite often because network administrators are typically loath to introduce configuration changes to the crucial Internet access router that is providing the network's Internet connectivity.

Notice that traffic from multicast Source S is flowing down the DVMRP tunnel to Router C. Because Router C is receiving DVMRP routes from the DVMRP router via the tunnel, it uses this information to compute its RPF direction (shown by the thin solid arrow) for Source S. Because the RPF information correctly points up the tunnel, Router C forwards the multicast traffic to the other routers in the network. However, these routers do not have any DVMRP routing information and therefore default to using their unicast routing table to compute their RPF direction (shown by the dashed, thin arrows) for Source S. Unfortunately, multicast traffic from Source S is arriving on the wrong interface at these routers and is therefore dropped because of the RPF check failure.

This is a classic example of incongruent multicast and unicast networks. Only hosts directly attached to Router C in this example are able to receive multicast traffic from Source S. All other hosts in the network are unable to receive this traffic.

Solution 1: Making the Networks Congruent

The best solution to this problem is to make the unicast and multicast networks congruent by moving the endpoint of the tunnel to Router A, as shown in Figure 13-19.

Figure 13-19 *Solution 1: Terminate Tunnel at Top of Hierarchy*

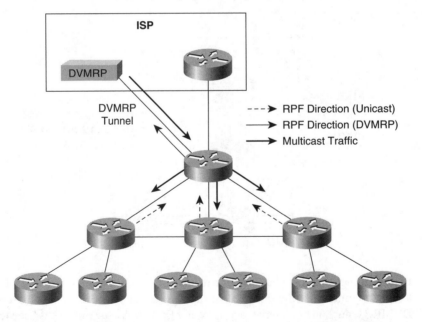

Terminating the tunnel at the very top of the hierarchy (where the network connects to the Internet or other outside network) forces the topologies to be physically congruent. Observe that Routers B, C, and D still compute their RPF information by using the unicast routing information (shown by the dashed arrows) for multicast traffic from sources outside the network. However, now that the multicast traffic is flowing along the same path as unicast traffic (shown by the solid arrows), the RPF checks succeed and traffic is forwarded farther down the hierarchy.

Solution 2: Using DVMRP Routes

The obvious down side to solution 1 is that it was necessary to modify the configuration of Router A. If one of the goals is to (at least initially) avoid making changes to Router A's configuration and to keep it out of the multicast forwarding business, then this solution is not acceptable (even though it is often the best solution in the long run). Therefore, another solution must be found that avoids the RPF problem of physically incongruent networks.

One way to avoid physically incongruent networks is to provide Routers B, C, and D with DVMRP routing information so that they can compute their RPF interfaces (for multicast traffic from sources outside of the network) using DVMRP routes instead of unicast routes. This can be accomplished by enabling **ip dvmrp unicast-routing** on all interconnecting links between Routers A, B, C, and D.

Adding the **ip dvmrp unicast-routing** command to the on the interfaces on Router C instructs the router to begin exchanging DVMRP Route Reports on these interfaces. This step, in turn, causes the DVMRP routes that were learned via the DVMRP tunnel to be advertised to Routers A, B, and D. If the **ip dvmrp unicast-routing** command is also added to the same set of interfaces on these routers, they will begin accepting the DVMRP routes and using those routes to compute RPF information for multicast sources outside the network.

Figure 13-20 shows what happens when **ip dvmrp unicast-routing** is enabled on all the links between Routers A, B, C, and D. Notice that Routers A, B, and D are now computing their RPF information using DVMRP routes (shown by the thin solid arrows) and will now accept and forward this traffic to other parts of the network.

Figure 13-20 *Solution 2: Use **ip dvmrp unicast-routing***

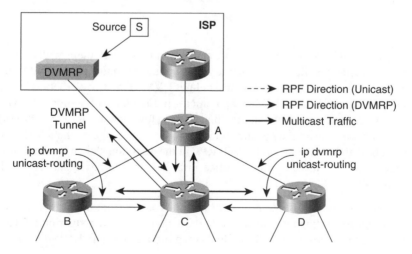

The one potential problem with simply adding **ip dvmrp unicast-routing** to the interfaces between these routers is that, according to the DVMRP interaction rules described earlier, each router will also advertise a subset of its unicast routing table in DVMRP Route Reports. This causes Routers A, B, C, and D to have routes for networks not only outside the local domain in the DVMRP route table but also inside the local domain. Because DVMRP routes are preferred over unicast routes for multicast RPF checking, this condition is likely to cause RPF failures on these routers for multicast traffic from sources inside the network.

Figure 13-21 shows what can happen if unicast-to-DVMRP redistribution occurs inside the network.

Figure 13-21 *DVMRP Route Redistribution Problem*

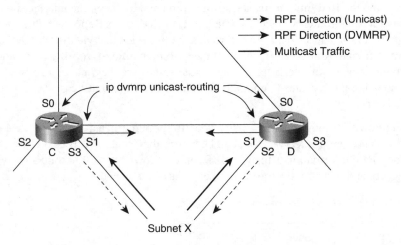

In this example, Routers C and D are exchanging DVMRP routes with each other, using the rules described earlier in this chapter. This includes sending a DVMRP Route Report with an advertisement for subnet X with a default DVMRP metric of 1. Now, both Routers C and D have entries in their DVMRP and unicast routing tables for subnet X, which results in RPF information as shown in the thin arrows. However, because the DVMRP routes have a smaller administrative distance than the unicast routes have, the DVMRP routes are preferred and Routers C and D will RPF in the direction shown by the thin solid arrows in Figure 13-21. This causes any multicast traffic from sources in subnet X to RPF fail at Routers C and D.

The solution to this problem is to prevent the routers from redistributing any routes from their unicast routing table to each other. This type of route redistribution can be prevented by using the appropriate ACLs on **ip dvmrp metric** commands. For example, if the routing protocol used inside the network is OSPF, the configuration in Example 13-6 can be used on Routers C and D to prevent unicast-to-DVRMP redistribution.

Example 13-6 *Preventing Unicast-to-DVMRP Redistribution*

```
interface Serial1
 ip address x.x.x.x y.y.y.y
 ip pim sparse-dense-mode
 ip dvmrp unicast-routing
 ip dvmrp metric 0 ospf 1
```

In the preceding configuration excerpt, the **ip dvmrp metric 0 ospf 1** command instructs the router to not advertise in the unicast routing table any route learned by OSPF in DVMRP Route Reports. However, any routes that are in the DVMRP routing table are advertised. The result is that only those routes learned from outside the network via the DVMRP tunnel will be in the DVMRP route table in Routers C and D.

PIM Sparse Mode Issues

Special problems occur any time a network that uses a sparse mode protocol is connected with a network that uses a dense mode protocol. The reason is that sparse mode protocols (for example, PIM-SM and CBT) rely on a *pull* type of mechanism to get the multicast traffic to members, whereas dense mode protocols (for example PIM-DM and DVMRP) use a *push* type of mechanism.

Figure 13-22 shows a PIM-SM network that is connected to a DVMRP network through Border Router A and a DVMRP tunnel. In this example, the PIM-SM has an active source for Group G, whereas the DVMRP network has a receive-only member for Group G.

Figure 13-22 *Problem: Receive-Only Hosts in DVMRP Cloud*

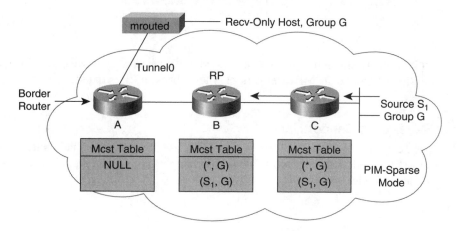

Assuming that the Border Router is not the RP for the group and that it has no directly connected members for Group G, it will not have joined the shared tree. Therefore, traffic from Source S will not make it to the Border Router A, will not be flooded over the tunnel to the DVMRP router, and will not be received by the receive-only host in the DVMRP network.

Solution 1: Terminate Tunnel on RP

Again, the simplest solution to this problem is to move the tunnel endpoint so that the Border Router and the RP are one in the same.

Figure 13-23 shows an example of this solution. Moving the tunnel to the RP guarantees that any traffic from any source in the PIM network will reach the RP and be flooded over the tunnel to the DVMRP router by default.

Figure 13-23 *Solution 1: Terminate Tunnel on RP*

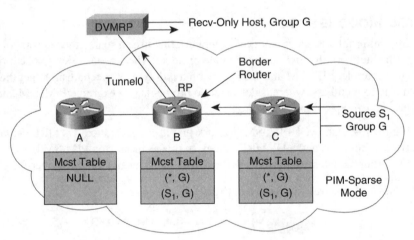

Unfortunately, this solution is not always possible, as is the case when the PIM network is multihomed to the DVMRP network or when a backup RP is in use.

Solution 2: Receiver-Is-Sender Hack

The next solution to this problem is commonly used by networks that tunnel to the older, DVMRP-based MBone network and is based on the assumption that all receivers are senders and vice versa.

Figure 13-24 shows this solution in operation. Because the host in the DVMRP cloud is also a sender, multicast state is created in the Border Router, which (because it is a PIM-DVMRP Border Router) causes the router to join the shared tree for the group.

Figure 13-24   *Solution 2: Receiver-Is-Sender Hack*

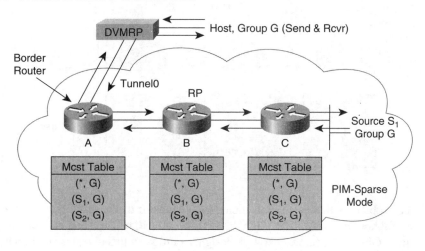

This solution has been used successfully in the past when the lion's share of multicast traffic was based on multimedia conferencing application where every participant in the multicast session transmitted Real-Time Transport Control Protocol (RTCP) packets to the group. However, as more multicast applications are developed, this assumption is not always valid because not all receivers are senders.

Solution 3: Use of Dense Mode Border Network

The last solution to this problem is to extend the dense mode behavior of the DVMRP network all the way to the RP (or RPs) by configuring PIM-DM on all interfaces along all paths between the RP and the Border Router.

Figure 13-25 shows an example of this solution. Notice that the configurations of Router A and the RP have been modified from the initial network so that **ip pim dense-mode** is configured on the link between them. This causes multicast traffic that reaches the RP to be flooded (using PIM-DM operation) over this link to Router A, which, in turn, floods the traffic to the DVMRP router.

Figure 13-25 *Solution 3: Use Dense Mode Between Border and RP*

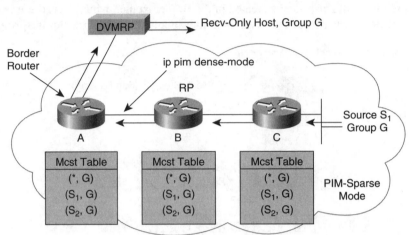

The problem with this solution should be obvious. If the Border Router and the RP are several hops away, the size of the PIM-DM cloud will be large and network efficiency may suffer. Obviously, careful network design should keep this distance small, but sometimes maintaining such a distance is difficult, for example, when a backup RP is utilized in case of a failure of the primary RP, Router B. For the network to continue forwarding multicast traffic to the DVMRP network, this backup RP must also be connected to the Border Router via PIM-DM interfaces. If the backup RP is adjacent to the primary RP (Router B), then this connection can be accomplished easily. However, if the backup RP is geographically quite far away from the primary RP, it may be necessary to use a generic routing encapsulation (GRE) tunnel to logically reduce the number of hops between the Border Router and the backup RP.

DVMRP Network Connection Examples

This section presents some detailed examples of PIM-DVMRP interconnections under a variety of conditions that include single and multihomed DVMRP connections for both PIM-DM and PIM-SM networks. Although the examples are based on connections to the Internet's old DVMRP-based MBone, they can be applied to general PIM-DVMRP network interconnections.

NOTE   When this book was written, several large first-tier Internet service providers (ISPs) had already switched their core multicast networks from a DVMRP-based network to a new, native, multicast network based on PIM-SM, MBGP, and a new protocol, Multicast Source Discovery Protocol (MSDP). As more ISPs make this switch, the dependence on DVMRP to route multicast in the Internet will disappear. Therefore, network administrators who want to obtain multicast connectivity to the Internet should begin making plans to use these newer protocols in lieu of DVMRP tunnels.

Physically Congruent Networks

The issues of unicast and multicast networks that are not physically congruent (there's that fancy word again) were addressed at some length. However, in an attempt to provide a complete coverage of the various forms of PIM-DVMRP interconnectivity, a few examples are also provided here.

Figure 13-26 shows a single-homed, physically congruent network (that is, unicast and multicast traffic flow the same path in and out of the network). This configuration has the DVMRP tunnel terminating on the ISP Customer Premise Equipment (CPE) router (the router that connects the customer's network to the ISP's network) thereby making the network congruent.

Figure 13-26   *Physically Congruent—Single Homed*

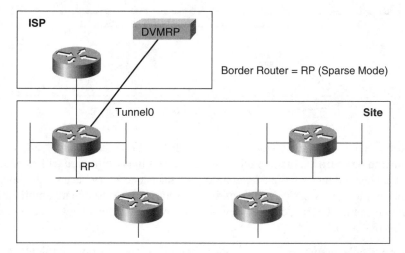

This example is the simplest form of connectivity and can be used for either PIM-DM or PIM-SM networks. (In the case of PIM-SM, the RP, the CPE router, and the router terminating the DVMRP tunnel must be the same router.)

Unfortunately, this configuration does not provide any redundancy should the CPE router fail and is often unacceptable when unicast and multicast Internet connectivity must be maintained.

Figure 13-27 shows a slightly more complex example of a physically congruent, PIM-DM network that is multihomed to the Internet. In this drawing, two separate ISP CPE routers (A and B) are used (often connected to different ISPs for better redundancy), each with a DVMRP tunnel to a DVMRP router somewhere in the ISP's network.

Figure 13-27   *Dense Mode: Multihomed*

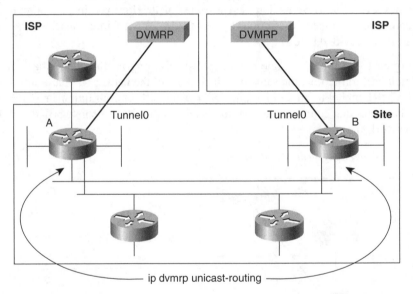

Notice that a separate network connects CPE Routers A and B and that **ip dvmrp unicast-routing** has been enabled on this network so that the two routers will exchange DVMRP routes learned through their separate ISPs. This is necessary because the Internet's unicast and multicast networks are frequently not congruent. Consequently, multicast traffic from a source in the Internet can arrive at one CPE router via the other CPE router by way of the DVMRP tunnel.

For example, assume the normal flow of multicast traffic from a particular source in the Internet into the customer network is via CPE Router B. This traffic is then flooded to CPE Router A via the interconnecting link. Without the exchange of DVMRP information (learned via their respectively DVMRP tunnels), Router A would most likely compute the

RPF interface to the source as its own DVMRP tunnel and would therefore drop this multicast traffic because of an RPF failure. Furthermore, without the exchange of DVMRP routing information between the CPE routers, both CPE routers would Poison Reverse every DVMRP route they received from their DVMRP neighbor at the other end of the tunnel. This behavior would very likely result in duplicate streams of multicast traffic entering the network from every source in the Internet.

Figure 13-28 shows the same network, but this time, instead of PIM-DM, PIM-SM with primary and secondary RPs is in use. The configuration for this network variation is basically identical to the PIM-DM example shown in Figure 13-27 with one minor exception: The interconnecting network between the CPE routers must be configured with **ip pim dense-mode**. The reason was outlined in solution 3 of the section "PIM Sparse Mode," which discussed the use of dense mode between the active RP and the Border Router.

Figure 13-28 *Sparse Mode: Multihomed*

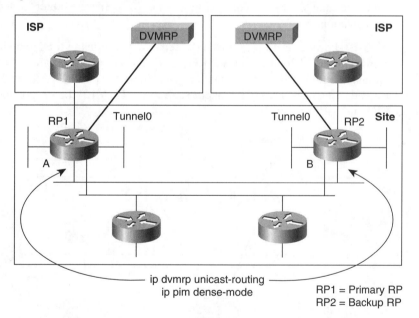

Just exactly why this situation is applicable may not be readily apparent at first glance. Consider the situation where multicast traffic from some source in the Internet is arriving at CPE Router B, which is the backup RP and is therefore not currently acting as the RP for the network. This results in the sparse mode boundary situation described previously and requires the use of dense mode to flood the arriving traffic to CPE Router A so the traffic can be forwarded down the shared tree to any active members for the group.

NOTE	Note that the previous two network examples used an Ethernet segment as the inter-connecting network between the two CPE routers. In reality, these two routers are often geographically very far apart, say, in Los Angles and New York, and not on a local Ethernet segment. In this case, it may be necessary to configure a GRE tunnel running in dense mode between these two routers to logically construct the preceding topology.

Separate MBone Router

Keeping the unicast and multicast networks congruent when connecting to the Internet may not always be possible for a number of reasons. The most common is that, at least initially, many network administrators do not wish to make significant changes to the CPE routers responsible for their Internet connection. Instead, it is often preferable to use a separate router to make the connection to the MBone. Therefore, the remainder of this section presents some sample network configurations that use a separate router for the DVMRP tunnel connection(s).

Figure 13-29 shows an example of a single, separate router being used to connect a PIM-DM network to the MBone via a DVMRP tunnel. The network configuration also shows how optional, multihomed connectivity may be achieved to provide additional redundancy by terminating a second DVMRP tunnel to a different DVMRP router (potentially located in a different ISP's network).

Figure 13-29 *Dense Mode: Single MBone Router*

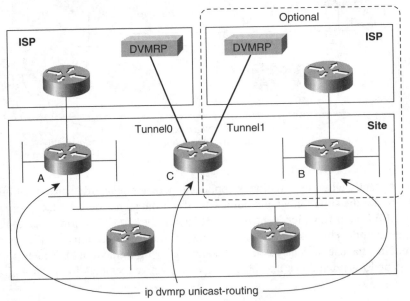

In this network configuration, the MBone router, Router C, is connected to the CPE Routers A and B. Although the diagram shows an Ethernet segment to make the connections from Router C to Routers A and B, these connections could also be accomplished via two point-to-point links. Again, ip dvmrp unicast-routing must be used on these links to redistribute the DVMRP routes received via the DVMRP tunnel(s) by Router C in order for Routers A and B to RPF correctly for multicast traffic from sources in the Internet. If this DVMRP routing information is not redistributed to Routers A and B, they would use their unicast routing table and select the interface that connects them to their ISP as the RPF interface for multicast sources in the Internet. This behavior would result in RPF failures and traffic from these sources would not be forwarded into the customer's network.

Figure 13-30 shows the same network configuration but using PIM-SM, instead of PIM-DM. This configuration is basically identical to the example shown in Figure 13-29 except that the link(s) from Router C to Routers A and B must also have ip pim dense-mode enabled so that traffic is flooded to both the primary and backup RPs, Routers A and B, respectively.

Figure 13-30   *Sparse Mode: Single MBone Router*

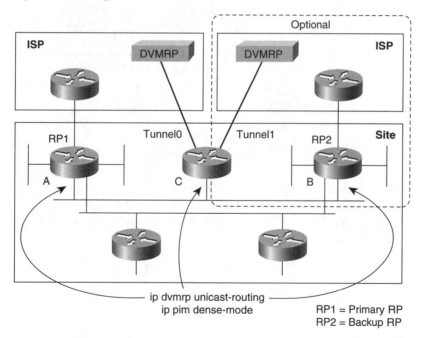

Although the preceding two examples provide a certain amount of redundancy for the delivery of multicast traffic from the Internet, a single point of failure still exists. If Router C were to fail, all multicast traffic would cease to flow into or out of the network.

To provide even more redundancy, two MBone routers (Routers C and D) can be used, each with its own DVMRP tunnel as shown in Figure 13-31. The PIM-DM configuration in this example functions identically to the configuration in Figure 13-29. The only difference is that two separate routers are used for added redundancy.

Figure 13-31 *Dense Mode: Dual Redundant MBone Routers*

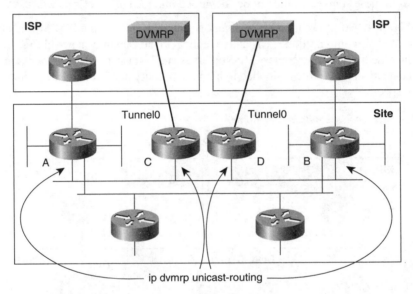

The same approach can be used for a PIM-SM network as shown in the configuration depicted in Figure 13-32. This configuration is also identical to its single router configuration shown in Figure 13-30 and must also have ip pim dense-mode enabled on the links between Routers A, B, C, and D.

Figure 13-32 *Sparse Mode: Dual Redundant MBone Routers*

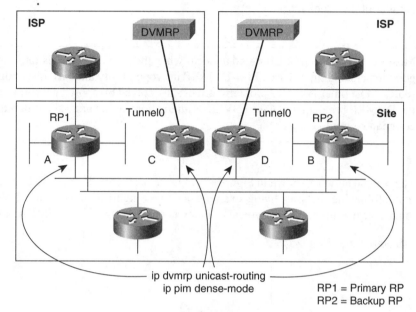

NOTE   In some cases, it may not be possible to use a multi-access network, such as an Ethernet, to interconnect routers A, B, C, and D in the previous two examples (say, if Routers A and C are connected to an ISP in Dallas while Routers B and D, located in Chicago, are connected to a different ISP). In this case, the following set of individual point-to-point links would have to be used: link C-A, link C-B, link D-A, link D-B, and link C-D.

Debugging Tips

This section provides some very basic debugging tips are provided that can be helpful when PIM-DVMRP interoperability is in use. These tips will cover the following areas:

- Verifying DVMRP tunnel status
- Verifying DVMRP route exchange

Obviously, this list of DVMRP debugging topics is not exhaustive, but it catches a large number of the problems.

NOTE   Most PIM-DVMRP problems tend to occur when the network administrator fails to have a good understanding of Cisco PIM-DVMRP interoperability and has misconfigured the router. Most other DVMRP problems are usually solved by applying a solid knowledge of the DVMRP protocol and Cisco DVMRP interactions to the analysis of **debug ip dvmrp** command output.

The sample network shown in Figure 13-33 is the basis for all sample debug output shown in the following sections. In this example, a Cisco router is connected to a DVMRP router via a DVMRP tunnel and is typical of many connections into the DVMRP-based MBone.

Figure 13-33   *Sample Network for Debug Tips*

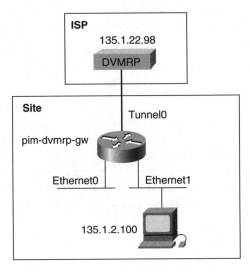

The Cisco router configuration for this tunnel is shown in Example 13-7.

Example 13-7 *VMRP Tunnel Configuration for Figure 13-33*

```
pim-dvmrp-gw:

interface tunnel0
 ip unnumbered ethernet0
 ip pim dense-mode
 tunnel mode dvmrp
 tunnel source ethernet0
 tunnel destination 135.1.22.98

interface ethernet0
 ip address 135.1.3.102 255.255.255.0
 ip pim dense-mode

interface ethernet1
 ip address 135.1.2.102 255.255.255.0
 ip pim dense-mode
```

You may wish to refer to Example 13-7 and the diagram shown in Figure 13-33 while reading the following sections.

Verifying DVMRP Tunnel Status

The first thing to check for is proper connectivity between the Cisco router and the DVMRP router. Because a tunnel is being used, several hops may exist between the routers, which makes checking connectivity a little more difficult.

The most obvious step in checking connectivity would be to use a **show interface** command to check the status of the DVMRP tunnel. The output of this command is shown in Example 13-8.

Example 13-8 *Output for **show interface** of DVMRP Tunnel*

```
pim-dvmrp-gw> show interface tunnel 0
Tunnel0 is up, line protocol is up
  Hardware is Tunnel
  Interface is unnumbered.  Using address of Ethernet0 (135.1.3.102)
  MTU 1500 bytes, BW 9 Kbit, DLY 500000 usec, rely 255/255, load 1/255
  Encapsulation TUNNEL, loopback not set, keepalive set (10 sec)
  Tunnel source 135.1.3.102 (Ethernet0), destination 135.1.22.98
  Tunnel protocol/transport IP/IP (DVMRP), key disabled, sequencing disabled
  Checksumming of packets disabled,  fast tunneling enabled
  Last input 00:00:05, output 00:00:08, output hang never
  Last clearing of "show interface" counters never
  Input queue: 0/75/0 (size/max/drops); Total output drops: 0
```

Notice that the tunnel interface is up and the line protocol is also up. If the output of this command did not show both elements in the **up** status, then further investigation would be necessary. For example, a unicast routing problem might exist between the Cisco and the DVMRP router. Otherwise, the physical interface over which the tunnel flows might have a problem that must be corrected.

Typically, the output of a **show interface** command on the tunnel results in an **up** status on both the interface and the protocol. However, **up** does not necessarily mean that bidirectional DVMRP control traffic flow over the tunnel has been established. The best way to check is by issuing the **mrinfo** command on both the Cisco and the DVMRP routers to determine whether each side sees the other through the tunnel.

Example 13-9 shows the output of an **mrinfo** command issued on the Cisco router.

Example 13-9 *Output for **mrinfo***

```
pim-dvmrp-gw>mrinfo
135.1.3.102 [version cisco 11.2] [flags: PMA]:
  135.1.3.102 -> 0.0.0.0 [1/0/pim/querier/leaf]
  135.1.2.102 -> 135.1.2.2 [1/0/pim/querier]
  135.1.2.102 -> 135.1.2.3 [1/0/pim/querier]
  135.1.3.102 -> 135.1.22.98 [1/0/tunnel/querier]
```

The last line of this output shows the tunnel status as listed in Table 13-1.

Table 13-1 *Description of **mrinfo** Output Line*

135.1.3.102 -> 135.1.22.98	The tunnel from the Cisco router (135.1.3.102) to the DVMRP router (135.1.22.98)
[1/0/tunnel/querier]	Interface status information as follows:
	1—Tunnel metric (1 hop).
	0—TTL Threshold (none).
	tunnel—Indicates a tunnel interface.
	querier—The router is the IGMP querier.

The important thing to notice is the absence of the keyword **down** from the interface status field. (If the tunnel where down, it would be indicated by a **down** keyword in this field.) This field shows that the tunnel is operational from the Cisco end.

Next, you need to perform the same operation from the DVMRP router end. However, it is not necessary to actually log on to the DVMRP router to obtain **mrinfo** output. Instead, the Cisco router can be instructed to obtain this information from the DVMRP router by specifying the IP address of the DVMRP router in the **mrinfo** command as shown in Example 13-10.

Example 13-10   *Output for **mrinfo** with DVMRP Router Address*

```
pim-dvmrp-gw>mrinfo 135.1.22.98
135.1.22.98 [version mrouted 3.8] [flags: GPM]:
  172.21.32.98 -> 172.21.32.191 [1/1]
  172.21.32.98 -> 172.21.32.1 [1/1]
  135.1.22.98 -> 135.1.22.102 [1/1/querier]
  135.1.22.98 -> 135.1.3.102 [1/1/tunnel]
```

Notice that the last line of this output shows the status of the tunnel but this time from the DVMRP router's perspective. Because the **down** keyword is not shown, the tunnel is up in this direction as well. Therefore, there is full tunnel connectivity.

Verifying DVMRP Route Exchanges

When full tunnel connectivity has been established, it is important to check whether the correct DVMRP routes are being exchanged between the Cisco and the DVMRP routers. The quickest way to determine whether DVMRP routes are being received from the DVMRP router is to use the **show ip dvmrp route** command, as shown in Example 13-11.

Example 13-11   *Output for **show ip dvmrp route***

```
pim-dvmrp-gw# show ip dvmrp route
DVMRP Routing Table - 8 entries
130.1.0.0/16 [0/3] uptime 00:19:03, expires 00:02:13
    via 135.1.22.98, Tunnel0, [version mrouted 3.8] [flags: GPM]
135.1.0.0/16 [0/3] uptime 00:19:03, expires 00:02:13
    via 135.1.22.98, Tunnel0, [version mrouted 3.8] [flags: GPM]
135.1.22.0/24 [0/2] uptime 00:19:03, expires 00:02:13
    via 135.1.22.98, Tunnel0, [version mrouted 3.8] [flags: GPM]
171.69.0.0/16 [0/3] uptime 00:19:03, expires 00:02:13
    via 135.1.22.98, Tunnel0, [version mrouted 3.8] [flags: GPM]
172.21.27.0/24 [0/3] uptime 00:19:04, expires 00:02:12
    via 135.1.22.98, Tunnel0, [version mrouted 3.8] [flags: GPM]
172.21.32.0/24 [0/2] uptime 00:19:04, expires 00:02:12
    via 135.1.22.98, Tunnel0, [version mrouted 3.8] [flags: GPM]
172.21.33.0/24 [0/3] uptime 00:19:04, expires 00:02:12
    via 135.1.22.98, Tunnel0, [version mrouted 3.8] [flags: GPM]
172.21.120.0/24 [0/3] uptime 00:19:04, expires 00:02:12
    via 135.1.22.98, Tunnel0, [version mrouted 3.8] [flags: GPM]
```

This output shows that the Cisco router is receiving eight DVMRP routes from the DVMRP router. This list of routes should be compared to what the network administrator expects to be receiving from the DVMRP network.

Taking things a step further, the network administrator can watch the exchange of DVMRP routes between the Cisco and the DVMRP routers by using the **debug ip dvmrp** command as shown in Example 13-12.

Example 13-12   *Output for **debug ip dvmrp***

```
pim-dvmrp-gw# debug ip dvmrp
DVMRP debugging is on
pim-dvmrp-gw#
DVMRP: Aging routes, 0 entries expired
DVMRP: Received Probe on Tunnel0 from 135.1.22.98
DVMRP: Building Report for Tunnel0 224.0.0.4
DVMRP: Send Report on Tunnel0 to 135.1.22.98
DVMRP: 2 unicast, 8 DVMRP routes advertised
DVMRP: Aging routes, 0 entries expired
DVMRP: Received Probe on Tunnel0 from 135.1.22.98
DVMRP: Received Report on Tunnel0 from 135.1.22.98
```

This debug output is extremely useful not only for verifying DVMRP route exchange but also for normal DVMRP protocol operation. Notice that the debug output also includes information on DVMRP Probes received and route aging.

In this case, the important information about the route exchange is highlighted and shows a DVMRP Route Report being built and sent on Tunnel0 and that **2 unicast** and **8 DVMRP routes** were advertised. Thus, the network administrator knows that two routes were taken from the Cisco's unicast route table and advertised and that eight routes were taken from the DVMRP route table and advertised in the DVMRP Route Report.

Unfortunately, exactly which routes were advertised in the route report cannot be identified. To see this information in the debug output, it is necessary to use the **debug ip dvmrp detail** command.

WARNING   The use of the **debug ip dmvrp route detail** command can result in so much output that it can effect the Cisco router's performance. Care should be taken when this command is used, particularly if the network administrator suspects that a large number of routes are being exchanged.

Example 13-13 is a sample of the debug output obtained from the sample network with the **debug ip dvmrp detail** command.

Example 13-13 *Output for debug ip dvmrp detail*

```
pim-dvmrp-gw# debug ip dvmrp detail
DVMRP debugging is on
DVMRP: Building Report for Tunnel0 224.0.0.4
DVMRP: Report 130.1.0.0/16, metric 35, from DVMRP table
DVMRP: Report 135.1.0.0/16, metric 35, from DVMRP table
DVMRP: Report 135.1.22.0/24, metric 34, from DVMRP table
DVMRP: Report 171.69.0.0/16, metric 35, from DVMRP table
DVMRP: Report 172.21.27.0/24, metric 35, from DVMRP table
DVMRP: Report 172.21.32.0/24, metric 34, from DVMRP table
DVMRP: Report 172.21.33.0/24, metric 35, from DVMRP table
DVMRP: Report 172.21.120.0/24, metric 35, from DVMRP table
DVMRP: Report 135.1.2.0/24, metric 1
DVMRP: Report 135.1.3.0/24, metric 1
DVMRP: Send Report on Tunnel0 to 135.1.22.98
DVMRP: 2 unicast, 8 DVMRP routes advertised
```

In this example, the debug output shows every route being advertised in the DVMRP Route Report by the Cisco router. Notice that the first eight routes were taken from the DVMRP route table and all have a metric greater than 32. These routes are the Poison Reverse routes being sent back to the DVMRP router to inform it that the Cisco router is a child router for sources in these networks in the DVMRP cloud. This causes the DVMRP router to forward any multicast traffic from these sources over the tunnel to the Cisco router.

The last two routes in the DVMRP Route Report are the two directly connected networks (135.1.2.0/24 and 135.1.3.0/24) on the Cisco router that are being advertised to the DVMRP router with a metric of 1.

Continuing with the capture of debug output results in the output shown in Example 13-14.

Example 13-14 *Debug Output*

```
DVMRP: Received Report on Tunnel0 from 135.1.22.98
DVMRP: Origin 130.1.0.0/16, metric 2, metric-offset 1, distance 0
DVMRP: Origin 135.1.0.0/16, metric 2, metric-offset 1, distance 0
DVMRP: Origin 171.69.0.0/16, metric 2, metric-offset 1, distance 0
DVMRP: Origin 135.1.2.0/24, metric 34, metric-offset 1, infinity
DVMRP: Origin 135.1.3.0/24, metric 34, metric-offset 1, infinity
DVMRP: Origin 135.1.22.0/24, metric 1, metric-offset 1, distance 0
DVMRP: Origin 172.21.27.0/24, metric 2, metric-offset 1, distance 0
DVMRP: Origin 172.21.32.0/24, metric 1, metric-offset 1, distance 0
DVMRP: Origin 172.21.33.0/24, metric 2, metric-offset 1, distance 0
DVMRP: Origin 172.21.120.0/24, metric 2, metric-offset 1, distance 0
```

This output shows the incoming DVMRP Route Report that the Cisco router is receiving from the DVMRP router. Notice the two advertisements near the middle of the output with a metric of 34. These two advertisements are Poison Reversed routes being sent back by the DVMRP router for the two directly connected networks that were previously advertised by the Cisco router.

The remaining routes in the preceding debug output are being advertised by the DVMRP router. The last field on these lines indicates the administrative distance that the Cisco router has assigned to the DVMRP router. (Notice that the Poison Reverse routes are given an **infinity** distance so that they are not used by the multicast forwarding RPF check mechanism.)

At this point, it should be clear that routes are being properly exchanged between the two routers and that multicast traffic should be able to flow across the tunnel.

Summary

Interconnecting independent multicast domains is generally a complex task, particularly when dissimilar multicast routing mechanisms, such as sparse and dense mode protocols, are used. Interfacing PIM networks to DVMRP networks is no exception to this rule and requires the network administrator to have a solid understanding of both protocols and how they will interact.

This chapter supplies all the basic information that a network administrator needs to understand the details of Cisco's DVMRP interoperability features and where they depart from normal DVMRP functionality. Furthermore, the examples given in this chapter (albeit focused primarily on connecting to the old DVMRP-based MBone) should prove helpful as templates for trouble-free PIM-DVMRP network interconnectivity.

PART V

Multicast at Layer 2

This part addresses the topic of IP multicast over Layer 2 network infrastructures.

Chapter 14 addresses the inefficiencies in campus multicast networks where the use of Layer 2 LAN switches tend to dominate the network design. This chapter describes the problems that are often encountered when trying to constrain the flooding of IP multicast traffic using techniques at Layer 2, such as IGMP Snooping or the proprietary Cisco Group Management Protocol (CGMP).

Chapter 15 covers the issues involved when trying to run PIM over Nonbroadcast, Multiaccess (NBMA) networks, such as Frame Relay or ATM. Several scenarios are presented in a step-by-step fashion to demonstrate the problems associated with routing multicast traffic on this type of network. This chapter also introduces special Cisco router IOS commands and configuration techniques that can be used to work around these issues.

Multicast over Campus Networks

Over the last few years, Layer 2 LAN switching equipment has gone from an expensive, leading-edge technology that was deployed only in the backbone of the network to a relatively mature, cost-effective technology that is now often seen in even the smallest wiring closets. This has led to some rather large LAN switching topologies being built where a number of LAN switches are interconnected via high-speed trunks to form a single, large, switched subnet.

This chapter explores some of the issues with IP multicasting in these LAN switching topologies and takes a look at some of the current and proposed methods for dealing with them.

The Flat Earth Society

The success of LAN switching technology has been so great that some vendors have gone so far as to adopt what is known as the "flat earth" approach to building networks. Members of the Flat Earth Society tend to preach the sermon of "switches good, routers bad" and encourage moving all routing functions to the farthest edges of the network while "flattening" the network address space (hence the name Flat Earth Society). This approach results in a network with hundreds and, in some extreme cases, thousands of nodes in a single subnet. The rational behind this approach was that by moving to high-speed, switched LANs, Ethernet collisions were all but eliminated and there was now little or no need for routing.

NOTE	The "switching good, routing bad" argument has always been a source of amusement to me. Most of the people who preach this gospel apply the term *switching* to either Layer 2 or Layer 3 and will extend this argument by saying, "Layer 3 switching good, routing bad." This statement seems silly because routing is simply switching packets in one port and out another based on the Layer 3 destination address.

Although switched LANs have made the Ethernet collision problem virtually a thing of the past, the flat earth prophets have failed to consider the effects of broadcast/multicast on these enormously flat networks. Some work has been done to address the scaling of multicasting in the switched-LAN environment; however, most of this problem is still best solved by the router.

Characteristics of LAN Switches

As you are probably already aware, the differences between a bridge and a switch are basically speed and number of ports. Like a bridge, a switch forwards an incoming Media Access Control (MAC) frame by looking up the destination MAC address in a MAC address forwarding table to determine out which port the frame should be forwarded. For a switch to populate its forwarding table, the switch must learn the Layer 2 MAC addresses of the stations and the ports to which the stations are connected. The switch learns by examining the source MAC address of frames sent between stations on the LAN and by noting on which port this frame arrived. After a station's MAC address and port have been learned, the MAC address and the port number are stored in the forwarding table.

When LAN switches first began to appear on the market, the main CPU in the switch performed all switching tasks. When the CPU received a frame on one port, it would look up the destination MAC address in the forwarding table and then copy the frame to the specified output port. To speed up the lookup process, most of these early switches stored the forwarding table in some form of content-addressable memory (CAM), which allows the MAC address to be used as the pointer to the desired entry. (This forwarding table is generally referred to as the CAM table.)

As the demand for better performance in these switches grew, the actual switching-decision logic was off-loaded from the main CPU and built into a special Switching Engine that could access the CAM table and switch the frames from input to output port at wire-rate speeds.

Figure 14-1 shows a block diagram of a typical LAN switch that can perform high-speed, wire-rate switching of MAC frames. Typically, a small microprocessor-based CPU in the switch performs network management functions and populates the CAM table with the stations' MAC addresses along with their associated port numbers. The Layer 2 Switching Engine then uses the information in the CAM table to make forwarding decisions. This CPU is usually also connected to a port on the Switching Engine just like any other port in the switch. By populating the CAM table with the MAC address of the switch itself and associating this entry with the port connecting the CPU, incoming frames addressed to the switch (such as Simple Network Management Protocol [SNMP] and Telnet) may be switched to the CPU for processing.

Figure 14-1 *Simple LAN Switch Architecture*

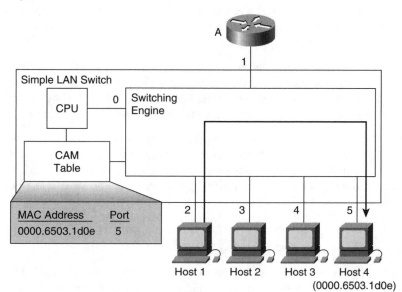

To achieve wire-rate switching speeds, most LAN switches employ a Layer 2 Switching Engine based on special, custom-built application-specific integrated circuits (ASICs). These ASICs can examine the Layer 2, destination MAC address of a frame, look up this MAC address in the CAM table, and switch the frame to the output port indicated by the CAM table entry. Because the logic in these ASICs is implemented in silicon, they are capable of performing this CAM table lookup and Layer 2 switching at speeds that allow wire-rate forwarding of frames through the LAN switch.

In the example in Figure 14-1, Host 1 is sending a frame addressed to Host 4. The CPU has previously learned the MAC address and port number of Host 4 and has populated the CAM table with this information. The Switching Engine then uses this information to switch the frame out Port 5.

Broadcast/Multicast Flooding

If a switch receives a frame with no matching entry in the CAM table, it has no choice but to flood the frame out all other ports on the switch in hopes of getting the frame to the destination. This typically happens in the following situations:

- The destination MAC address has not yet been learned.
- The destination MAC address is a broadcast or multicast address.

The first situation is not a problem because the switch will eventually add the destination MAC address into the CAM table upon "hearing" the destination station transmit a frame. From then on, all transmissions to this station will not be flooded. It is the second of these cases with which to be concerned.

In the second situation, broadcast frames must always be flooded out all ports (other than the incoming port) that are in Forwarding state on the switch. By the same token, there is usually no way for a switch to know on which ports multicast members reside. Therefore, multicast frames must also be flooded out all ports in the same fashion.

It is this shotgun approach to delivering multicast traffic that the flat-earth network engineers have failed to take into account in their approach to network design. Given the growing popularity of multicast-based multimedia applications, networks based on the flat earth theory will suffer as unwanted multicast traffic is flooded to every point in the network.

Constraining Multicast Flooding

As LAN switching technology grew in popularity, attempts were made to place some controls on the flooding of broadcast/multicast frames. The first was to implement broadcast/multicast rate limiting. The idea was to enforce some configurable limit to the amount of bandwidth that broadcast/multicast traffic could consume before frames would be discarded. As it turns out, rate limiting is a really bad idea as the arbitrary dropping of certain types of broadcast frames can result in network instability that in some cases can be bad enough to melt down the network.

For example, bridge protocol data units (BPDUs) are multicast to the special All Bridges multicast MAC address. If enough of these BPDUs are discarded, the network can suffer instabilities as the spanning tree algorithm constantly attempts to converge. As the spanning tree algorithm in the switches tries to converge, more BPDUs may be lost, leading to a network meltdown. Open Shortest Path First (OSPF) Hello messages are another good example of a critical frame that is multicast to the All OSPF Routers multicast MAC address. If enough of these frames are discarded because of broadcast/multicast rate limiting, OSPF adjacencies may be lost, which can result in Layer 3 network instability. (My personal motto is: "Just say no to MAC Layer broadcast/multicast rate limiting.")

The second, saner approach is to extend the CAM table format to allow a list of port numbers to be associated with a MAC address. This approach permits a network administrator to manually enter a MAC layer multicast address into the switch's CAM table along with a list of ports. Now, when the switch receives multicast frames that match this address, the flooding of these frames is constrained to only those ports listed in the CAM table entry. This approach initially worked fine for somewhat static multicast groups, such as the All OSPF Router group, where the members of the group could be configured ahead of time and were not likely to change. Unfortunately, the manual configuration method does not lend itself to dynamic multicast groups, as is the case in IP multicast. Clearly, some other approach was needed to constrain multicast flooding in traditional LAN switch environments.

To date, three methods have been defined to address this problem:

- IGMP Snooping
- Cisco Group Management Protocol (CGMP)
- IEEE's Generic Attribute Resolution Protocol (GARP) (defined in IEEE 802.1p)

Of these three methods, only the first two have seen wide-scale deployment and are discussed in detail in the following sections. IEEE's GARP, on the other hand, is a radically new approach that will require changes to end-station hardware and software to implement.

IGMP Snooping

The most obvious method to constrain the flooding of multicast traffic in LAN switches is IGMP Snooping. Just as its name implies, IGMP Snooping requires the LAN switch to snoop on the IGMP conversation between the host and the router. When the switch hears an IGMP Report from a host for a particular multicast group, the switch adds the host's port number to the associated multicast CAM table entry. When the switch hears an IGMP Leave Group message from a host, it removes the host's port from the CAM table entry.

On the surface, this seems like a simple solution to put into practice. However, depending on the architecture of the switch, implementing IGMP Snooping may be difficult to accomplish without seriously degrading the performance of the switch.

The sections that follow explore the mechanics involved in implementing efficient IGMP Snooping along with the potential performance impact it has on Layer 2 switches lacking special hardware to assist with the IGMP Snooping process. Next, several special scenarios such as send-only sources and the automatic detection and handling of routers by the IGMP Snooping software in the switch are explored.

Joining a Group Using IGMP Snooping

At first glance, you might expect that the additional load IGMP Snooping places on a LAN switch would be minimal. After all, IGMP was designed to minimize its impact on host and router CPU as well as on network bandwidth, right? However, this true statement doesn't necessarily apply to Layer 2 devices such as LAN switches. The reason that it doesn't apply should become apparent shortly.

Figure 14-2 shows an example of a simple Layer 2–only switch (that is, one lacking special Layer 3 hardware to assist with IGMP Snooping) that is doing IGMP Snooping.

Figure 14-2 *Joining a Group with IGMP Snooping—Step 1*

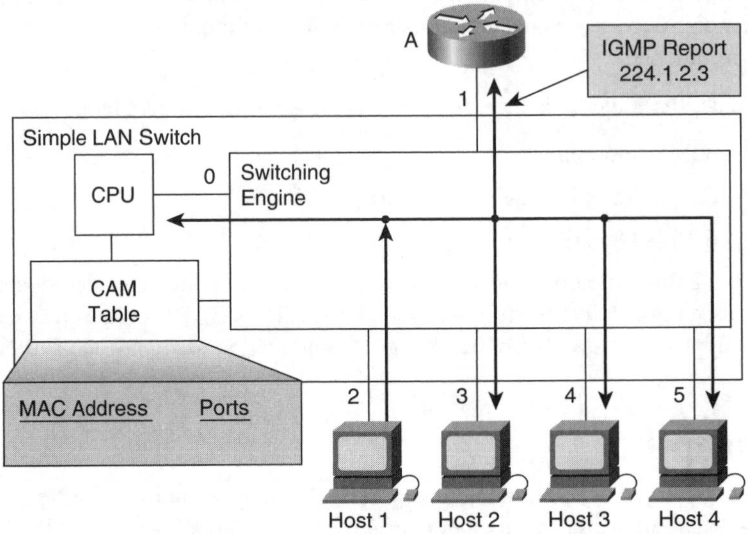

Let's take a look at what typically happens in the switch when a couple of hosts join a multicast group and state is set up in the switch's CAM table to constrain multicast flooding.

1 Host 1 desires to join multicast group 224.1.2.3 and, therefore, multicasts an unsolicited IGMP Membership Report to the group with a MAC destination address of 0x0100.5E01.0203. Because initially there are no entries in the CAM table for this multicast MAC address (see Figure 14-2), the report is flooded to all ports on the switch (including the internal port connected to the switch's CPU).

2 When the CPU receives the IGMP Report multicast by Host 1, the CPU uses the information in the IGMP Report to set up a CAM table entry as shown in Table 14-1 that includes the port numbers of Host 1, the router, and the switch's internal CPU.

Table 14-1 *CAM Table Entry After Host 1 Joins*

Destination Address	Ports
01-00-5E-01-02-03	0, 1, 2

As a result of this CAM table entry, any future multicast frames addressed to multicast MAC address 0x0100.5E01.0203 will be constrained to Ports 0, 1, and 2 and will not be flooded to the other ports on the switch. (The switch's CPU must continue to receive these frames because it must watch for other IGMP messages addressed to this MAC address.)

Let's now assume that Host 4 wants to join the group and sends an unsolicited IGMP Report for the same group. Figure 14-2 now shows Host 4 joining the group by sending an IGMP Membership Report for group 224.1.2.3. The switch forwards the IGMP Membership Report to external ports 1 and 2 based on the CAM table entry shown previously in Table 14-1. (This same CAM table entry can now also be seen in Figure 14-3.)

Figure 14-3 *Joining a Group with IGMP Snooping—Step 2*

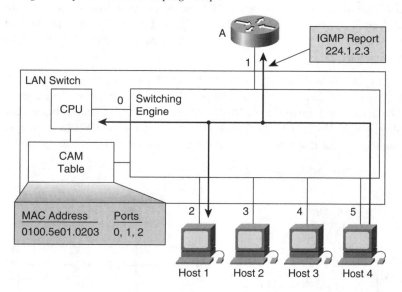

Because the CPU in the switch also received the IGMP Membership Report, it adds the port on which the report was heard (in this case, Port 5) to the CAM table entry for MAC address 0x0100.5E01.0203. This results in the CAM table shown in Table 14-2.

Table 14-2 *CAM Table Entry After Host 4 Joins*

Destination Address	Ports
01-00-5E-01-02-03	0, 1, 2, 5

At this point, any multicast traffic sent with a destination MAC address of 0x0100.5E01.0203 (which corresponds to multicast group 224.1.2.3) will be constrained to only Host 1, Host 4, the router, and the internal CPU. It would certainly seem that this takes care of the steps necessary to cover the join process in IGMP Snooping. However, a potentially serious problem with switches that use this sort of Layer 2–only mechanism is explained in the next section.

Performance Impact of IGMP Snooping

Remember that the CAM table entry shown in Table 14-2 included Port 0 in its port list. This port is included so that the Switching Engine would continue to pass IGMP messages addressed to this group to the switch's internal CPU. (Remember that IGMP Membership Reports are multicast to the target multicast group.) If this weren't done, the CPU would not have heard the IGMP Report from Host 4 when it tried to join the group. Therefore, to continue to receive any future IGMP Reports, the Switching Engine was instructed to send all frames addressed to MAC address 0x0100.5E01.0203 to the internal CPU. At this point, you begin to run into performance problems when trying to implement IGMP Snooping in this manner.

Figure 14-4 now depicts the same LAN switch from the previous example except that Host 1 is now multicasting a 1.5 Mbps MPEG video stream to the target group, 224.1.2.3. This means that the multicast MAC address of the video frames being sent by Host 1 are also 0x0100.5E01.0203. Therefore, the only way for the CPU to intercept any IGMP messages is for it to intercept all multicast traffic addressed to the group!

Figure 14-4 *Multicast Traffic Overloading the Switch's CPU*

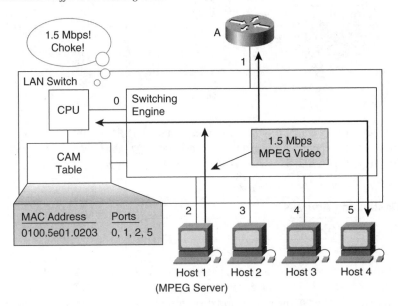

Obviously, the work load of having the CPU examine every multicast frame passing through the switch just to find an occasional IGMP packet will usually result in a drastic reduction in overall switch performance and, in some cases, a catastrophic failure of the switch. Unfortunately, many of today's low-cost, Layer 2–only LAN switches that implement IGMP Snooping suffer from this problem. The switch may perform just fine in a limited demo environment but can begin to fail when the buyer puts it into a production environment. In some cases, this failure takes the form of drops in both the multicast and unicast traffic flows through the switch. In other cases, the Switching Engine continues to forward both the multicast and unicast traffic without any drops, although the internal CPU begins to drop packets because it can't keep up with the incoming traffic stream. These drops at the input of the internal CPU result in missed IGMP packets, which can seriously affect Join and Leave latencies.

To avoid this problem, it is necessary to redesign the Switching Engine in these LAN switches to use new ASICs and CAM tables that can look deeper into the frame and examine Layer 3 information before making a switching decision. Given a switch designed in this fashion, the CAM table can be programmed to only forward frames containing IGMP messages to the CPU for processing.

Figure 14-5 shows a simplified version of the LAN switch after its Switching Engine has been redesigned with new ASICs that are Layer 3 aware. (Too bad it's not really this easy to redesign a switch to be Layer 3 aware. At least it keeps the engineers busy and off the streets.)

Figure 14-5   *Layer 3–Aware Switching Architecture*

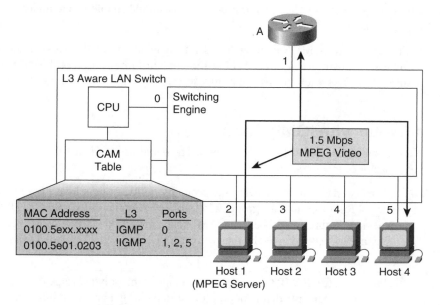

Because the switch is now Layer 3 aware, each entry in the CAM table shown in Figure 14-5 can be loaded with additional Layer 3 information that further modifies the Switching Engine's behavior. As you can see, the 1.5-Mbps MPEG video is no longer interrupting the CPU as it flows through the switch. The rate of traffic being sent to the CPU is now reduced to only a few frames of IGMP traffic per second, which the CPU can handle quite easily.

To understand how this process works, let's examine the two entries that the CPU has loaded into the CAM table shown in Figure 14-5 in more detail.

- The first entry tells the Switching Engine to send IGMP packets only to the switch's CPU.

- The second entry tells the Switching Engine to send frames addressed to the 0x0100.5E01.0203 multicast MAC address that are not IGMP packets (!IGMP = "not IGMP") to the router and the two hosts that have joined the group.

The first entry means that the CPU is effectively intercepting all IGMP packets and not allowing the Switch Engine to forward them to the other ports on the switch. This approach allows the CPU to perform any special processing of IGMP packets necessary and to be in complete control of the IGMP packets that need to be sent to the other devices connected to the switch. (The reason for this will become clear later.)

The process that takes place in the new Layer 3–aware LAN switch when hosts join a group is basically the same as the process in the simple LAN switch example. The key difference is that now the CAM table entry has been loaded with supplemental Layer 3 information so the Switching Engine does not forward multicast data to the CPU. (I'm actually over-simplifying the process here, but this description should enable you to understand the basic mechanisms involved.)

Let's continue the IGMP Snooping discussion, again assuming that Hosts 1 and 4 are group members as shown in Figure 14-5. (The remainder of this section on IGMP Snooping assumes that the switch makes use of this sort of Layer 3–aware architecture.)

Leaving a Group with IGMP Snooping

Now, assume that Host 1 leaves the group. The departure of Host 1 causes the following sequence of events to occur:

1 Host 1 signals that it is leaving the group by multicasting a Leave Group message to the All Routers multicast group, 224.0.0.2 (MAC address 0x0100.5E00.0002) as shown in Figure 14-6. The first CAM table entry shown in Figure 14-6 causes this message to be intercepted by the switch's CPU and not be forwarded to any other ports.

Note	The IGMP Leave Group message is the only message that a host transmits that is not multicast to the target group address. In this one case, a simple Layer 2–only switch can safely employ a CAM table entry that intercepts these IGMP messages because only IGMP Group Leave messages are multicast to the 0x0100.5E00.0002 MAC address. Unfortunately, this doesn't help the switch capture the other 99.99% of host-initiated IGMP messages: the IGMP Membership Reports.

Figure 14-6 *IGMP Snooping: Leaving a Group—Step 1*

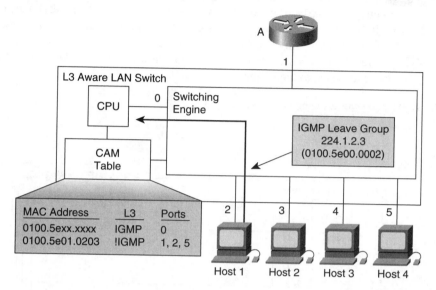

2 The CPU in the switch responds to the Leave Group message by sending an IGMP General Query back out Port 2 (see Figure 14-7) to see whether there are any other hosts that are members of this group on the port. (This could occur when multiple hosts are connected to the switch port via a hub.)

Figure 14-7 *IGMP Snooping: Leaving a Group—Step 2*

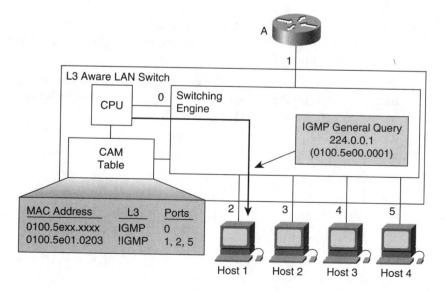

3 If another IGMP Report is received from a host connected to Port 2, then the CPU quietly discards the original Leave Group message from Host 1. If, on the other hand, no IGMP Report is received on this port, (which is the case here), then the CPU deletes the port from the CAM table entry (see the resulting CAM table entry in Figure 14-8). Because other nonrouter ports are still in the CAM table entry, no message is sent to the router.

Figure 14-8   *IGMP Snooping: Leaving the Group—Step 3*

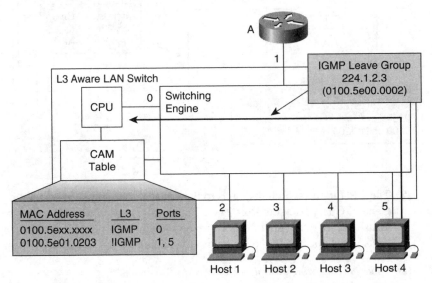

4 Now, let's assume that Host 4 leaves the group and sends an IGMP Leave Group message. Once again, the Leave Group message is intercepted by the switch's CPU, as shown in Figure 14-8.

5 The CPU responds to this Leave Group message by sending another General Query back out Port 5 (see Figure 14-9) to see whether there are any other hosts that are members of this group on the port.

Figure 14-9 *IGMP Snooping: Leaving the Group—Step 4*

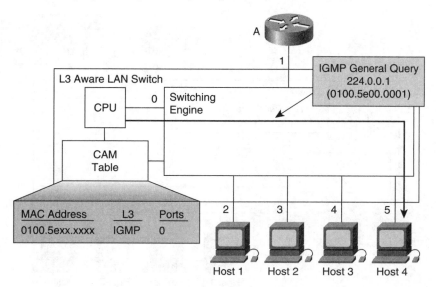

6 Because there are no other hosts on this port in the example, no IGMP Report for this group is received and the switch deletes this port from the CAM table entry. Because this port was the last nonrouter port for the CAM table entry for 0x0100.5E01.0203, the switch's CPU deletes the CAM table entries for this group and forwards the IGMP Leave Group message to the router for normal processing. (See Figure 14-10.)

Figure 14-10 *IGMP Snooping: Leaving the Group—Step 5*

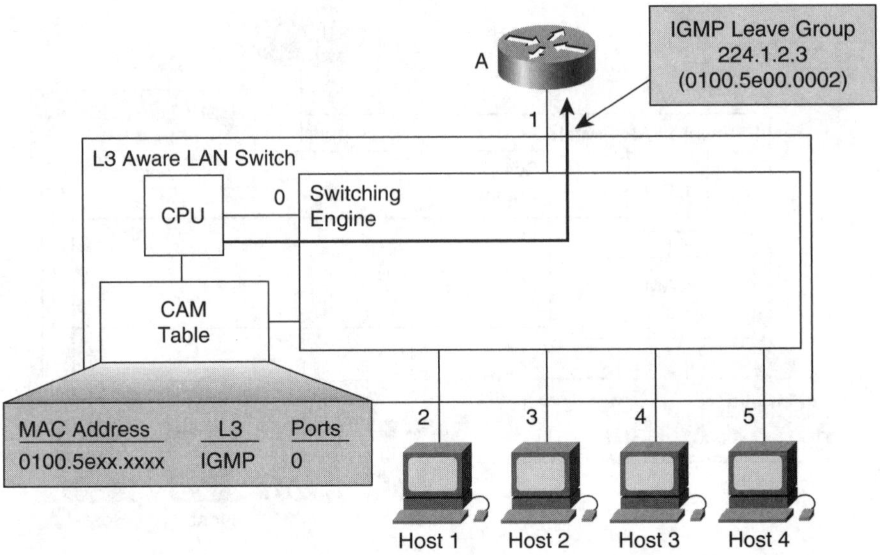

Maintaining the Group with IGMP Snooping

Obviously, the Leave process described in the preceding section assumes that all IGMPv2 hosts always send a Leave Group message when they leave the group. Unfortunately, however, RFC 2236 says that a host *may* always send a Group Leave message (not *must,* as maybe the RFC should have said) when it leaves the group. Because of this minor oversight, you can't always count on receiving a Leave Group message when a host leaves. Furthermore, the host may be running IGMPv1 (which doesn't use Group Leave messages) or the Leave Group message may be lost because of congestion in the switch. Thus, in a worst-case scenario, you must fall back to the group/port state maintenance procedure, using the General Query/Report mechanism to detect when a host has left the group (either because of a lost Leave Group message or because an IGMPv1 host just leaves the group quietly).

Assume that Hosts 1 and 4 have again previously joined multicast group 224.1.2.3, which results in the CAM table entries shown in Figure 14-11 that depicts the group/port membership state maintenance procedure in action.

Figure 14-11 *Maintaining a Group with IGMP Snooping—Step 1*

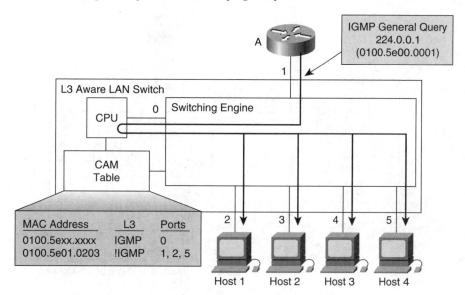

1 Router A periodically multicasts a General Query to the All Hosts group, 224.0.0.1 (MAC address 0x0100.5E00.0001). The switch's CPU intercepts the General Query and retransmits it out all ports on the switch. (See Figure 14-11.)

2 Each host that is a member of the group (in this case, Hosts 1 and 4) sends an IGMP Report in response to the General Query. (See Figure 14-12.) Notice that because the switch's CPU is intercepting all IGMP messages, the hosts do not hear each other's IGMP Report. This effectively overrides the host's report suppression mechanism, forcing each to send an IGMP Report. This is necessary so that the switch's CPU receives an IGMP Report on every port where there is a member of the group so it will maintain those ports in the port list.

Figure 14-12 *Maintaining a Group with IGMP Snooping—Step 2*

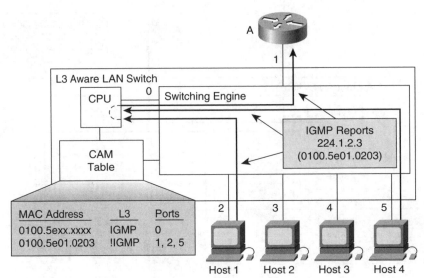

3 To keep the IGMP Group Membership State alive in the router, the LAN switch must forward either one or more (preferably only one) of the IGMP Reports up to Router A.

IGMP Snooping and Send-Only Sources

Multicast sources are not required to join the multicast group to which they are sending and, therefore, do not need to send IGMP Membership Reports. This poses a problem for LAN switches that depend on IGMP Snooping to constrain multicast traffic flooding.

Consider the situation shown in Figure 14-13, where Host 1 is a send-only source that has just started sending a 1.5 Mbps MPEG video stream to multicast group 224.1.2.3 without sending an IGMP Membership Report to the group. Let's also assume that none of the hosts on the switch have joined this multicast group.

Figure 14-13 *IGMP Snooping and Send-Only Sources—Step 1*

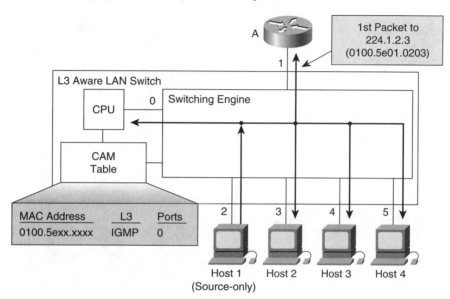

Handling this situation can be a problem for low-cost switches. To detect this situation, the CPU must indiscriminately listen to all multicast frames flowing through the switch. Switches that do not have either sufficient CPU horsepower or the assistance of special hardware ASICs to help reduce the workload on the CPU can suffer drastic performance degradation trying to handle this situation. In many cases, the switch designers simply opt to allow send-only sources to continue to be flooded to all ports in the switch until some host connected to the switch sends an IGMP Membership Report for the group.

The hypothetical Layer 3–aware switch in the example, on the other hand, immediately detects this unconstrained flow of multicast traffic and responds by updating the CAM table with entries, as shown in Figure 14-14, that will constrain this source-only multicast flow to only the router ports. (The way this step is accomplished depends on how the Layer 3 ASICs in the switch are implemented.)

Figure 14-14 *IGMP Snooping and Send-Only Sources—Step 2*

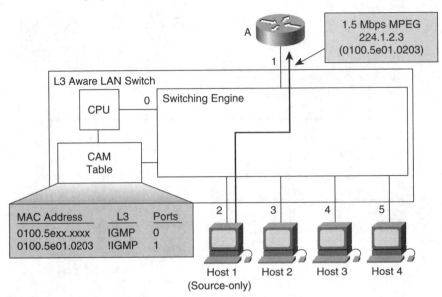

Detecting Routers with IGMP Snooping

You may have noticed in the previous examples that the port connected to Router A was automatically added to the port list in the CAM table entry for the 0x0100.5E01.0203. The reason is that routers must indiscriminately receive all multicast traffic for all groups. This raises an interesting question (which I hope you already noticed): How did the LAN switch know to include Port 1 in the port list of CAM table entry 0x0100.5E01.0203?

One obvious answer is that the switch "overheard" a previous IGMP General Query from Router A and remembers that a router is connected to this port. Presumably, if the port ever transitions to a down state or if the LAN switch fails to hear General Queries on this port after some timeout period, the switch makes the assumption that a router is no longer attached to this port. Unfortunately, these techniques are insufficiently robust to handle all cases.

For example, let's assume that there is more than one router connected to switch. Because only one router may function as the IGMP Querier, the remaining routers connected to the switch will not be sending General Queries in deference to the elected IGMP Querier. In this case, the switch will not be able to detect that other routers are connected to the switch.

The better approach is not only to listen to IGMP Queries to detect routers but also to listen for any special routing protocol packets that can be easily detected to tip off the switch that a router is connected. On Cisco switches that implement IGMP Snooping, this includes packets such as OSPF PIMv1 and PIMv2 Hellos, DVMRP Probes, IGMP Queries, CGMP self-joins, and Hot Standby Router Protocol (HSRP) messages that are sent by routers periodically.

IGMP Snooping Summary

Although the examples in the preceding sections may imply that IGMP Snooping is relatively easy to implement, I should point out that I have presented some of the simplest cases in which only a single router is in use on a single switch with a single host per port. Things get much more complicated when multiple multicast routers are used or when multiple hosts are connected to a single switch port via a shared hub. Additionally, it is not uncommon to interconnect many LAN switches together via high-speed trunks to form a large, LAN switching campus environment, which can complicate the implementation of IGMP Snooping.

Instead of exhaustively addressing every possible case, I will leave the problem of implementing IGMP Snooping to cover such situations as an exercise to the reader. Given your newly acquired knowledge of IGMP, you should be able to formulate a methodology that allows a LAN switch to successfully perform IGMP Snooping to constrain multicast traffic in these complex LAN switch environments.

On the other hand, if you don't have the ambition to tackle such an exercise, ask your LAN switch vendor to supply the nitty-gritty details of how they implemented IGMP Snooping. If the vendor won't supply this information, you may find out the hard way that they have failed to address some of these more complex situations.

Finally, the performance impact of a LAN switch can suffer dramatically when IGMP Snooping is implemented without Layer 3–aware ASICs to augment the CPU's processing of IGMP traffic. The reason is that virtually all IGMP messages transmitted by the hosts are sent with the same destination MAC address as the multicast data itself. The only exceptions are IGMPv2 Group Leave messages, which are transmitted to the 0x0100.5E00.0002 MAC address (corresponding to the All-Routers multicast address, 224.0.0.2).

Although many vendors can (and frequently do) demonstrate that IGMP Snooping works on their low-end LAN switch in a laboratory environment, the wise user will test the LAN switch's IGMP Snooping under a moderate to high multicast traffic load before buying.

Cisco Group Management Protocol

In early 1996, Dino Farinacci and Alex Tweedly of Cisco Systems recognized the need for an alternative solution to the problem of multicast flooding (other than IGMP Snooping). Work was underway on the design of new Layer 3–aware ASICs for the Cisco Catalyst 5000 series switches that would permit efficient IGMP Snooping to be implemented. However, these ASICs wouldn't be ready for use in the Catalyst 5000 switch for some time. Furthermore, use of these ASICs in the low-end Catalyst switches would not be economical, and therefore some other solution was needed to constrain multicast flooding in these low-cost switches.

Together, Dino and Alex designed a new, lightweight protocol that would run in both the router and the Catalyst series of switches and permit Layer 2 group membership information to be communicated from the router to the switch. This information could then be used to instantiate multicast membership state in the CAM table entries to constrain multicast traffic to ports with group members. This new protocol was called the Cisco Group Management Protocol (CGMP) and is now supported on all Cisco routers and most LAN switches.

CGMP Messages

CGMP messages are composed of a type code field followed by a list of Group Destination Address (GDA) and Unicast Source Address (USA) tuples that each identify a host and the group that the host just joined or left.

All CGMP messages are MAC layer multicast to the well-known CGMP multicast MAC address 0x0100.0cdd.dddd. All CGMP-enabled switches listen to this well-known multicast MAC address to receive CGMP messages. Using a multicast MAC address to communicate CGMP messages has the added benefit that they are flooded out all switch ports by default, whether the switch is a CGMP-enabled switch or not. This permits CGMP messages to travel across all interswitch links throughout the entire Layer 2 switching domain and reach all CGMP-enabled switches, even if there are non-CGMP switches in the middle the network.

Because LAN switches operate at Layer 2 and hence understand only MAC addresses, the GDA and the USA fields both contain 48-bit IEEE MAC addresses. The GDA field contains the IP multicast group address translated into its MAC address equivalent (for example, IP multicast group 239.255.1.2 would appear as 0x0100.5e7f.0102), and the USA field contains the MAC level unicast address of the host that sent the original IGMP Report message.

The host MAC address information in the USA field of a CGMP message is used by the CGMP switch to look up the port number associated with the host. Using this port information, the CGMP switch either adds or removes this port to/from the CAM table entry associated with the multicast MAC address in the GDA field.

Table 14-3 lists the various CGMP messages. The first two messages allow the router to inform CGMP switches when a host joins or leaves a group.

In addition to being able to inform the CGMP switch when a host joins or leaves a multicast group, the router uses CGMP messages to tell the switch to perform other special CGMP functions. Special values in the GDA and USA fields, shown in Table 14-3, communicate these special functions.

Table 14-3   *CGMP Messages*

GDA	USA	Join/Leave	Meaning
Mcst MAC	Client MAC	Join	Add port to group
Mcst MAC	Client MAC	Leave	Delete port from group
0000...0000	Router MAC	Join	Assign router port
0000...0000	Router MAC	Leave	Deassign router port
Mcst MAC	0000...0000	Leave	Delete group
0000...0000	0000...0000	Leave	Delete all groups

The third and fourth messages in Table 14-3, Assign/Deassign Router Port, (signified by a zero GDA field and a nonzero USA field) are particularly important. These CGMP messages allow the router to inform CGMP switches that the station whose MAC address appears in the USA field is a router and to either set (via a Join message) or clear (via a Leave message) the associated port as a router port. The LAN switch needs to know which ports have routers connected. It must include these ports in every multicast CAM table entry that is created so that the routers receive all multicast traffic.

The last two Leave messages in Table 14-3, Delete Group and Delete All Groups, are used for special maintenance functions by the router. For example, the Cisco router interface command

```
clear ip cgmp <interface>
```

causes the router to send the Delete All Groups message to the switch, which removes all multicast CAM table entries from the switch. The normal IGMP Query mechanism causes the switch to relearn the multicast group membership state and to repopulate its multicast CAM table through normal CGMP operation.

Joining a Group with CGMP

The basic concept of CGMP is shown in Figure 14-15. When a host joins a multicast group (as shown in part A of Figure 14-15), it multicasts an unsolicited IGMP Membership Report message to the target group (224.1.2.3, in this example). The IGMP Report is passed through the switch to the router for normal IGMP processing. The router (which must have CGMP enabled on this interface) receives this IGMP Report and, in addition to setting up its internal IGMP state for the group, translates the IGMP Report (sometimes loosely referred to as an IGMP Join) into a CGMP Join message.

Figure 14-15   *Basic CGMP Operation*

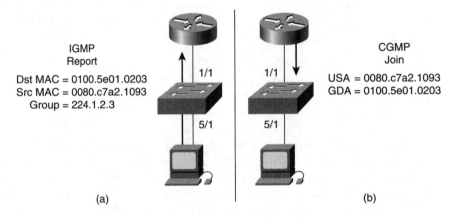

The router accomplishes the translation from IGMP Report to CGMP Join in the follow steps:

1 Copy the destination MAC address, 0x0100.5e01.0203, (which corresponds to IP multicast group 224.1.2.3) from the IGMP Report message into the GDA field of the CGMP Join message.

2 Copy the source MAC address, 0x0080.c7a2.1093, (which is the unicast MAC address of the host that is joining the group) from the IGMP Report into the USA field of the CGMP Join.

Now that the CGMP Join message has been constructed, the router sends the message to the CGMP-enabled switch (Part B of Figure 14-15) via the 0x0100.0cdd.dddd well-known CGMP multicast MAC address.

When the CGMP-enabled switch receives the CGMP Join message, it performs the following steps:

1 Searches the CAM table for an entry for the multicast group specified in the GDA field of the CGMP Join message.

2 If a CAM table entry for this group is not found, the switch creates the entry and adds all router ports to the newly created CAM table entry's port list. (The entry is created so that all routers connected to the switch can receive multicasts addressed to this group.)

3 Searches the CAM table for the entry that matches the unicast MAC address specified in the USA field of the CGMP Join message. Copies the port number from this CAM table entry (the port connected to the Host) to the multicast CAM table entry found/created in the previous steps.

The preceding process results in a multicast CAM table entry, shown in Example 14-1, which is set up in the Cisco Catalyst switch, shown in Figure 14-15.

Example 14-1 *CAM Table Entry for Cisco Catalyst Switch*

```
cat5000 (enable) show cam static
VLAN Dest MAC/Route Des  Destination Ports or VCs
---- ------------------  ------------------------
1       01-00-5e-01-02-03*  1/1,5/1
```

Maintaining the Group with CGMP

Maintaining group membership state in the switch is much easier with CGMP than with IGMP Snooping. Individual ports are removed from the CAM table entry only as a result of receiving a Delete Port message from the router. The CAM table entry expiration timer is reset each time a CGMP Join message is received for the group, which occurs every time the router sends out the General Query. However, there are other times when the switch deletes the CAM table entry and the group membership state must be relearned. Multicast CAM table entries are deleted in the following circumstances:

- Whenever the VLAN spanning tree topology changes. (This change can occur when a port on the VLAN transitions from the Learning state to the Forwarding state.)

- When the router sends a Delete Group or Delete All Group message.

- When a line card in the switch is removed/inserted.

Whenever the multicast CAM table entries are deleted, the switch automatically relearns the group/port membership state through the normal IGMP General Query mechanism. During this relearning period, hosts send IGMP Reports in response to IGMP General Queries from the router. These reports, in turn, are translated into CGMP Joins by the router, which causes the switch to repopulate the entries in its CAM table. (The entire relearning process takes from 1 to 1.5 IGMP Query intervals to complete.)

NOTE   VLAN spanning tree topology changes occur whenever a port on the switch transitions
          from the Learning state to the Forwarding state. This change normally happens when a port
          initially comes up, for example, when the host connected to the port is activated. The VLAN
          spanning tree topology change and hence the relearning of all CAM table entries can be
          avoided by configuring Cisco Catalyst ports that are directly connected to hosts (that is, not
          connected to hubs or other switches) with the "spanning tree port-fast enable" option. This
          option causes the port to transition immediately from the Blocking state to the Forwarding
          state without going through the Learning state. This approach avoids causing a VLAN
          spanning tree topology change every time a host connected to the switch is activated.

Leaving a Group with CGMP

When an IGMPv2 host leaves a group, it normally multicasts an IGMP Leave Group
message to the All Router (224.0.0.2) multicast group. When CGMP is enabled on the
router and the LAN switch, the router can simply translate this Leave Group message into
a CGMP Leave message by using the translation method shown in the Join example in
Figure 14-15. Like IGMP Snooping, this CGMP leave mechanism depends on the host
always sending an IGMPv2 Leave Group message to trigger this process. Unfortunately,
IGMPv2 hosts are not required to always send an IGMP Leave Group message when they
leave the group. Furthermore, there are still a lot of hosts (including Windows 95) that only
run IGMPv1 and therefore do not send IGMP Leave Group messages.

NOTE   Because it was an unfortunate oversight that the IGMPv2 specification (RFC 2236) did not
          require hosts always to send a Leave Group message, the IGMPv2 implementations in the
          TCP/IP stacks on some hosts might not always send IGMP Leave Group messages.
          Fortunately, most of the more popular implementations of IGMPv2 do always send IGMP
          Leave Group messages, including Windows 98 and most of the recent UNIX platforms.
          However, to be safe, check with your vendor to make sure that your implementation always
          sends IGMP Leave Group messages if you expect CGMP or IGMP Snooping to work
          properly on your LAN switches.

CGMP Local Leave Processing

Later versions of CGMP implementations on Cisco Catalyst switches have the capability
to do IGMPv2 leave processing locally in the switch without getting the router involved.

As you will recall from Chapter 3, "Internet Group Management Protocol," IGMPv2 requires all Leave Group messages to be multicast to the All Routers (224.0.0.2) multicast group and not to the multicast group that is being left. This opens the door to having the CGMP-enabled switch do some of the Leave Group processing itself. By tuning in to the 224.0.0.2 multicast group at the MAC level (multicast MAC address 0x0100.5e00.0002), the CPU in the LAN switch can receive and process these IGMP Leave Group messages without having to intercept all multicast data traffic.

Local Leave processing concerns itself with making sure no other listeners remain on the segment/port after a Group Leave message has been received. If a member remains, the deletion of the port is canceled because the flow to that port must continue. If no members respond on that port, the switch then checks whether any members are on other ports of the switch. If a member is found, nothing happens. If no other members exist, however, the switch sends an IGMP Leave Group message to the router sourced from the switch. The router then goes through its processing to make sure no other members exist in the LAN.

Figure 14-16 shows CGMP Local Leave processing on a switch when multiple hosts are connected to the switch port via shared media hubs.

Figure 14-16 *CGMP Local Leaving Processing—Step 1*

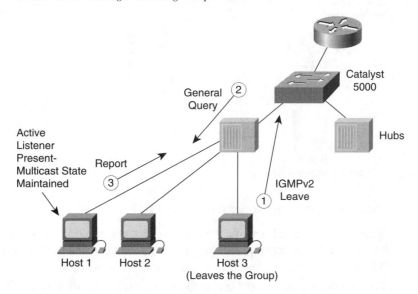

Initially, Hosts 1, 2, and 3 are members of the same multicast group. The following three steps are depicted in Figure 14-16.

 1 Host 3 wants to leave the group and multicasts an IGMPv2 Leave Group message to the All Router (224.0.0.2) multicast group. (This message is locally processed by the switch and not forwarded to the router.)

2 The switch sends an IGMP General Query out the port where the Leave Message was received to determine whether there are any remaining members for the group on this port. (Note that an IGMP General Query was used on the port instead of an IGMPv2 Group-Specific Query so that IGMPv1 hosts will also respond.)

3 Host 1 (in this example) responds with an IGMP Report for the group, which tells the switch that there are still members for the group on this port and that the port should not be removed from the CAM table entry for this group.

Figure 14-17 shows CGMP Local Leave processing when the last host leaves the group.

Figure 14-17 *CGMP Local Leaving Processing—Step 2*

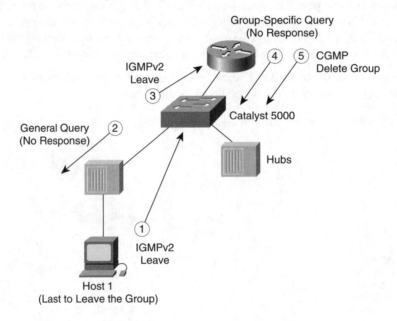

The following five steps are depicted in Figure 14-17.

1 Host 1 signals that it is leaving the group by sending an IGMP Leave Group message. This Leave Group message is intercepted by the switch and not forwarded to the router.

2 The switch sends an IGMP General Query out the port on which it received the Leave Group message.

3 Because no response to the General Query is received, the switch sources its own IGMP Leave Group message to the router.

4 The router receives the Leave Group message and performs the normal IGMP Leave Group processing by multicasting a Group-Specific Query to the multicast group to see whether there are any remaining members of the group.

5 Because no response is received to the Group-Specific Query, the router deletes its IGMP state for the group and sends a CGMP Delete Group message to the switch. This causes the switch to delete the CAM table entry for the group.

Performance Impact of CGMP

The performance impact of implementing CGMP on a switch is very low compared to the impact of IGMP Snooping. The reason is that the switch has to receive and process only low-rate CGMP frames from the router, as opposed to receiving and processing all multicast frames for IGMP Snooping. Therefore, CGMP can be implemented on even low-cost LAN switches, such as the Cisco 1900 and 2800 series switches, without the need for special ASICs that would drive up the cost of the switch.

The performance impact of CGMP on routers is also quite low. In most cases, the additional CPU overhead of CGMP on the router is too small to measure and need not be a concern to network engineers.

CGMP and Send-Only Sources

Unlike IGMP Snooping, CGMP switches do not need to do special processing to efficiently handle the case where a send-only source exists without any other members for the group on the LAN. In this case, it is desirable for the CGMP switch to constrain the source's traffic so that it isn't flooded to all the other hosts on the switch that are not members of the group. The only port on the switch that must receive the source's traffic is the router.

Having a router detect when this occurs is a relatively simple process. For example, if a router is receiving multicast group traffic from a directly connected source on an interface and there is no IGMP membership group state on this interface, then the router knows that there is a send-only source on the interface. In this case, the router responds by sending a CGMP Join message for itself so that the switch will create a new multicast CAM table entry that contains only the router's port in its port list. If the source stops sending traffic to the group, the multicast state in the router eventually times out. This causes the router to send a Delete Group message to the switch to remove the multicast CAM table entry for the group.

Detecting Routers with CGMP

Although Cisco Catalyst switches have a command to manually designate a port as a router port, this step is not necessary when a Cisco router is connected to the switch. CGMP

Assign Router Port messages are automatically sent to the switch by any Cisco router that has CGMP enabled on its interface. This message informs the switch that the port has a router attached and should be included in all newly created multicast CAM table entries.

Cisco routers can also perform this function on the behalf of other DVMRP multicast routers that are connected to the same interface by using the following interface command:

```
ip cgmp proxy
```

This command instructs the Cisco router to send a CGMP proxy Assign Router Port message every time it receives a DVMRP Probe packet on this interface. The proxy Assign Router Port message is sent with the MAC address of the DVMRP router (taken from the DVMRP Probe packet) in the USA field of the message. (Note that this command works only for multicast routers that are running the DVMRP protocol.) Upon hearing this proxy message, the switch assigns the port on which the DVMRP router is connected as a router port. Router port information automatically times in the switch if not periodically refreshed. Therefore, if the DVMRP router goes down, DVMRP Probes will stop being received by the Cisco router, which causes the proxy router information to time out in the switch.

CGMP Summary

Although CGMP is proprietary to Cisco switches and routers, it solves the same basic set of problems as IGMP Snooping. However, unlike IGMP Snooping, which requires expensive, Layer 3–aware ASICs to implement properly, CGMP can be implemented in low-cost switches. (Danger: Marketing pitch immediately ahead.) Therefore, CGMP permits a network engineer to design a LAN switch topology that includes the ability to control multicast flooding all the way to the smallest wiring closet when low-cost Cisco switches are used.

Neither IGMP Snooping nor CGMP is perfect, and each falls far short of solving all the issues of multicast flooding over LAN switch topologies (as explained in the next section). Regardless of which protocol you choose to run in your network, the preceding sections should have provided you with enough good information to allow you to make an intelligent decision regarding their use.

Other LAN Switching Issues

Although IGMP Snooping and CGMP can help control some of the unwanted flows of multicast traffic in LAN switching topologies, this technology doesn't address every problem. Even with IGMP Snooping or CGMP, constraining multicast traffic can be a problem if the network is not properly designed with multicast in mind. Furthermore, when the stations in the network employ outdated multicast support software (that is, IGMPv1), problems can become even worse.

The next few sections address just a few of the more common problems that network engineers must keep in mind when designing a multicast-enabled network. These problems include, but are not limited to, the following:

- IGMPv1 Leave Latency problem
- Interswitch link problem
- Router core switch problem

IGMPv1 Leave Latency Problem

Because IGMPv1 hosts do not send IGMP Leave Group messages when they leave a multicast group, severe Leave Latency problems can occur with CGMP or IGMP Snooping.

Consider the example shown in Figure 14-18, where two IGMPv1 hosts have joined the same multicast group. In this case, the router has already sent CGMP Join messages to the LAN switch, which, in response, has set up a CAM table entry to limit multicast frames addressed to this group to only the ports that are connected to the router and the two hosts.

Figure 14-18 *IGMPv1 Leave Latency Problem*

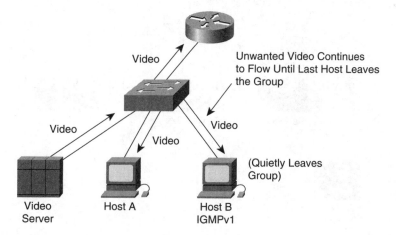

Now, if Host B leaves the group, it just quietly leaves the group without sending an IGMP Leave Group message. This, in turn, results in no CGMP Leave message being sent to the switch to remove the host's port from the CAM table entry. (The same thing would happen with IGMP Snooping. The only difference is that the LAN switch would be looking for the

IGMP Leave Group message itself.) Therefore, the LAN switch continues to flood multicast traffic out the port connecting Host B until the last host has left the multicast group!

At this point, Host B continues to receive unwanted multicast traffic as long as Host A remains joined to the multicast group. Things can get really ugly if Host B is surfing several high-rate, video multicast groups, hoping to find some group containing reruns of the *Three Stooges*. If there are active receivers on the LAN switch for each of the video groups that Host B joins as a result of this "Three Stooges Surfing Safari," then Host B will receive each of these high-rate video streams until the last member of the group leaves.

Interswitch Link Problem

In multiple LAN switch networks, bandwidth can be consumed unnecessarily on the interswitch links as multicast traffic is sent to the routers connected to the switches. In Figure 14-19, current Layer 2 technology (including CGMP and IGMP Snooping) fails to efficiently constrain multicast traffic in this topology.

Figure 14-19 *Interswitch Link Problem*

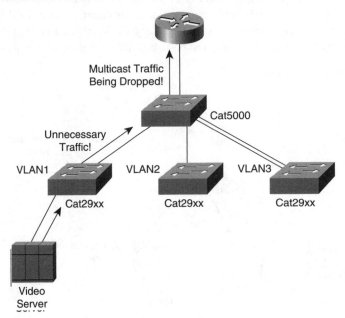

This example shows a commonly used hierarchical LAN switch topology consisting of a central, high-speed LAN switch (such as a Cisco Catalyst 5000 series switch) and several low-cost, satellite switches in the wiring closest with a multicast source connected to one of the switches. A router connected to the central LAN switch provides the connection to the rest of the network and is running CGMP, as are all the switches. Let's further assume that the multicast source is an IP/TV server that is multicasting a 1.5-Mbps MPEG video stream that is currently not being received by any hosts anywhere in the entire network.

Remember, multicast routers must indiscriminately receive all multicast frames from stations on their local LAN in order to

- Receive and process IGMP Membership Reports
- Receive all multicast data so that it may be routed as necessary to other parts of the network

These two requirements result in the 1.5 Mbps video flowing over the interswitch link to the router connected to the central switch. This would occur even if no members of this multicast group were in the network! This is not a problem if inter-switch bandwidth is not an issue. However, in cases where you are paying for this bandwidth, such as when the interswitch links are purchased from a metropolitan-area network (MAN) service provider, then you are just pounding money down a rat hole.

A partial solution to this problem is shown in Figure 14-20. Here, the network has been redesigned so that the multicast sources (such as the IP/TV Server in this example) are connected to the central Catalyst switch.

Figure 14-20 *Partial Interswitch Link Solution*

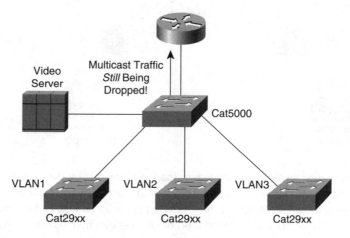

Under this condition, CGMP sets up CAM table entries in the switch that will constrain the flow of the 1.5-Mbps video data to the router only for routing off campus to the rest of the network. Unfortunately, if there are no receivers elsewhere in the network, the data flowing to the router is still wasted bandwidth. This leads to the router core switch problem.

Router Core Switch Problem

Consider the extremely common situation shown in Figure 14-21, in which a switch is used as the core network for several routers in a campus network. Because LAN switches do not participate in the multicast routing protocol, they have no way of knowing whether a router on the core network needs to receive traffic for a multicast group. (After all, multicast routing is really a Layer 3 switching function. If intelligence is put in a switch so that it can perform Layer 3 switching, then what does it effectively become? A Router!)

Figure 14-21   *Router Core Switch Problem*

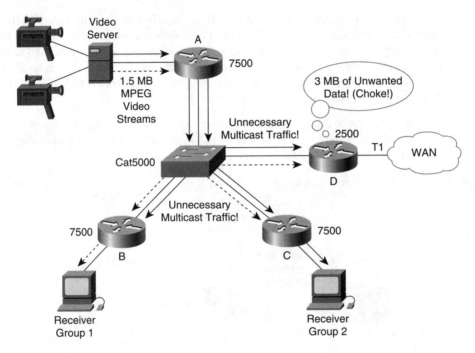

In most cases, this is not a problem as long as all routers on the core network have sufficient performance to "fast drop" all unwanted multicast traffic without becoming overloaded. However, the network design shown in Figure 14-21 includes a low-end Cisco 2500 router (Router D) directly connected to this core network switch to provide WAN connectivity off campus.

Although the campus network equipment is certainly capable of handling all local MPEG video multicast traffic, Router D is receiving all this traffic as well. Even if no members of these video multicast groups are in the WAN, Router D will still be inundated with 3 Mbps of unwanted multicast traffic.

In addition to overloading Router D with unwanted multicast traffic, unnecessary multicast traffic is also flowing to Routers B and C. Again, this situation occurs because routers must always receive any multicast traffic in order for them to route it to other portions of the network. Therefore, even though Router B and Router C need to receive only one of the two multicast video streams (because each router has only a single receiver joined to one of the two video streams), the routers are receiving both.

Figure 14-22 shows a partial solution to this problem. By redesigning the network so that the Router D is not on the same router core network, Router D can use a multicast routing protocol to signal Router A to not send the unwanted multicast traffic. (This can be accomplished using a separate VLAN on the Catalyst 5000 between Router A and Router D without making any wiring changes.)

Figure 14-22   *Partial Route Core Network Solution*

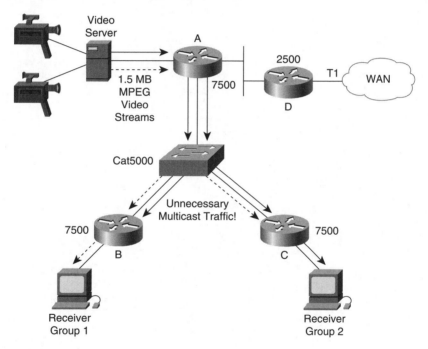

Summary

With the growing popularity of IP multicasting, the old debate of routing versus switching (which is the same thing as bridging) has resurfaced. As IP multicast becomes an important part of companies' network infrastructure, the need to constrain multicast traffic over large LAN switching networks becomes important. Because complete control of the flow of multicast traffic requires today's Layer 3 technologies, the need for more routing in the campus network is once again on the rise. Large flat campus networks, designed by members of the Flat Earth Society, are doomed to suffer increasing wastes of bandwidth over the links between switches. When bandwidth is an issue, network engineers and designers will find that their flat, campus network designs of the past are inadequate to meet future demands for more multimedia applications.

CHAPTER 15

Multicast over NBMA Networks

Nonbroadcast multiaccess (NBMA) networks, such as Frame Relay or ATM, have become a mainstay for wide-area networking in today's corporate networks. These wide-area network solutions provide considerable cost savings over traditional point-to-point circuitry such as T1 and fractional-T1 links. However, some issues must be considered if multicast traffic is to flow efficiently over traditional NBMA networks.

This chapter takes a close look at some of the problems that a network administrator will encounter when trying to use Frame Relay or ATM as a traditional NBMA network over which multicast traffic is to flow. The chapter examines the problems that result from the disparity between the Layer 3 topology and the actual underlying Layer 2 topology of the NBMA network. This disparity manifests itself in problems in router performance and, in some cases, can actually break normal Protocol Independent Multicast (PIM) control mechanisms.

Traditional NBMA Networks

Before proceeding, let's be perfectly clear on what *traditional NBMA network* means. An example of a traditional NBMA network is a Frame Relay or ATM network that connects multiple routers together, such as the network shown in Figure 15-1.

Figure 15-1 *Full Mesh NBMA Network*

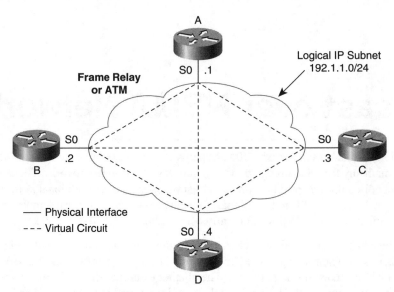

Each router is connected to this network with a single physical interface on which multiple virtual circuits are defined, each connecting to a different router through the Frame Relay or ATM network. When a physical interface on a router has more than a single virtual circuit associated with it, the interface is referred to as a point-to-multipoint (p2mp) interface. In a traditional NBMA network, these p2mp interfaces are configured as a single IP subnet, sometimes referred to as a *logical IP subnet* (LIS), such as the 192.1.1.0/24 network shown in Figure 15-1.

The LIS approach is sometimes preferred over the subinterface approach. LIS makes more efficient use of IP addresses because a larger subnet mask may be used for the LIS and only a single IP address is used for each router interface that connects to the LIS. The subinterface approach, on the other hand, consumes four IP addresses for every logical point-to-point (p2p) circuit configured through the Frame Relay or ATM cloud, even though only two addresses are needed for the circuit. (The smallest IP host mask that can be used is 2 bits long, which results in two host addresses, one broadcast address, and the address of the subnet itself.)

Although the LIS approach is more efficient in its consumption of IP addresses, it does introduce other problems for both unicast and multicast routing. Problems are especially likely if a partial mesh virtual circuit topology is used in which each router is not connected to every other router in the network via a separate virtual circuit.

Figure 15-2 is an example of a partial mesh NBMA network where virtual circuits are configured only between a single central router and all the other remote site routers.

Figure 15-2 *Partial Mesh NBMA Network*

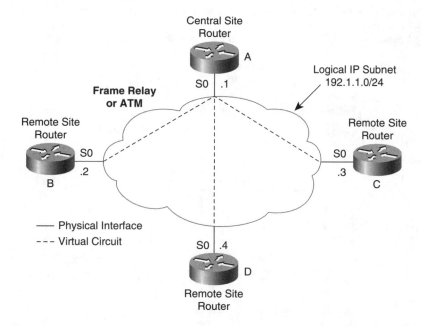

This sort of topology is frequently used as a cost-effective means to connect large numbers of remote site access routers to a central site. It is typically more cost-effective because the Frame Relay or ATM service provider generally charges on a per virtual circuit basis. In addition, this sort of access method permits the number of remote access routers to scale to large numbers. As a result of these two key advantages, partial mesh NBMA networks are much more prevalent than are full mesh NBMA networks.

NOTE   It is important to note that we are not talking about the case where the routers are configured using subinterfaces that implement logical p2p circuits over each virtual circuit in the Frame Relay or ATM network. Such networks operate in basically the same fashion as traditional p2p circuitry and do not suffer from the problems associated with NBMA networks. (Of course, they do still have the same inefficiencies associated with the overhead of Frame Relay or ATM networks, such as control message traffic and additional queuing delays, that physical p2p circuits do not have.)

Multicast over Traditional NBMA Networks

When an NBMA network is configured as a LIS, the network appears to the router to operate (at Layer 3) in the same manner as an Ethernet network. Figure 15-3 shows an example of an NBMA network and how it appears to the router.

Figure 15-3 *A Router's Layer 3 Viewpoint of an NBMA Network*

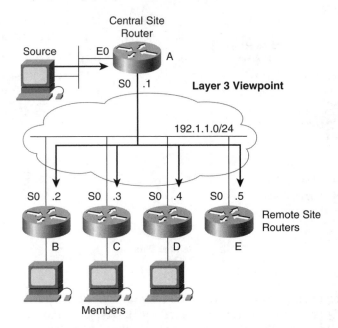

Notice that the network has been configured as the 192.1.1.0/24 LIS to which Router A is connected. Router A's Layer 3 viewpoint of this network is that all other PIM neighbors (Routers B, C, D, and E) are directly connected to the network via a broadcast medium. Therefore, Router A is required to send only a single copy of a multicast packet into the LIS for it to be received by all other routers in the LIS.

Although the network appears to Router A at Layer 3 to be a broadcast medium, the real topology of this NBMA network at Layer 2 is shown in Figure 15-4.

Figure 15-4 *Layer 2 Reality of an NBMA Network*

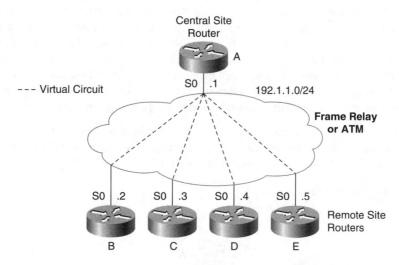

The network shown in Figure 15-4 may or may not be a full mesh network. If the network were a full mesh network, each router would have virtual circuits to each of the other routers in the network. However, in this example only the virtual circuits from Router A to the other routers are shown, whether the network is full mesh or not.

As a result of the realities of the underlying Layer 2 topology, Router A is unable to send just a single copy of a multicast packet to the LIS for all routers in the LIS to receive it. Instead, Router A must use a technique called *pseudobroadcast* to send a copy of the multicast packet over each virtual circuit for each router in the LIS to receive a copy.

Pseudobroadcast

Pseudobroadcast, as its name implies, requires the Layer 2 Frame Relay or ATM driver code in the router to perform the replication of the broadcast or multicast packet that is to be sent to the LIS. Replication must be done to provide the router's Layer 3 functions with the appearance of a broadcast medium. Although this simplifies things for the Layer 3 multicast forwarding code, packet replication in the Frame Relay or ATM interface driver code is typically a very inefficient way of handling broadcast and/or multicast traffic. This is true for Cisco routers as well because pseudobroadcast must be done in the slower process-level switching paths in the router where additional buffers can be allocated to make the actual copies of the packets.

The performance impact of pseudobroadcast on the router for an occasional routing update or routing protocol Hello packet to maintain router adjacencies is generally insignificant. However, this assumes a well-designed network that uses efficient network address aggregation to limit the frequency and size of route updates. (I've seen numerous examples of networks that don't meet this standard, such as in IPX networks where the amount of IPX routing updates and SAP messages resulted in heavy pseudobroadcast activity. This behavior generally caused the Frame Relay broadcast queues to overflow and routing updates to be lost, which, in turn, resulted in network instability.)

Pseudobroadcast not only causes the multicast packet replication rate to suffer but also generally results in unnecessary packet replication. Consider the PIM sparse mode (PIM-SM) NBMA network shown in Figure 15-5.

Figure 15-5 *Layer 3 View of NBMA*

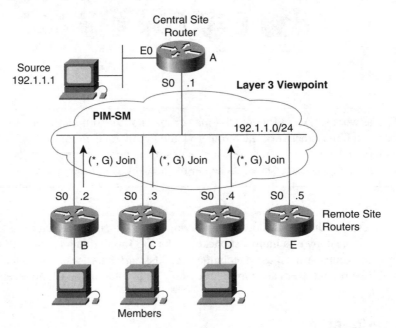

In this example, Routers B, C, and D all have members that are sending (*, G) Joins to the rendezvous point (RP), Router A, to join the multicast group so that they can receive traffic from the source. This results in the state shown in Example 15-1 being created in Router A.

Example 15-1   *State in Router A*

```
(*, 224.1.1.1), 00:00:12/00:02:59, RP 192.1.1.1, flags: SC
  Incoming interface: null, RPF nbr 0.0.0.0
  Outgoing interface list:
    Serial0, Forward/Sparse, 00:00:12/00:02:48

(192.1.1.1/32, 224.1.1.1), 00:00:12/00:02:59 flags: C
  Incoming interface: Ethernet0, RPF nbr 0.0.0.0
  Outgoing interface list:
    Serial0, Forward/Sparse, 00:00:12/00:02:48
```

Notice that, because the network appears to the Layer 3 PIM code as a broadcast medium, the only entry in the outgoing interface list is **Serial0**, which is the interface to the NBMA network. As far as the router's Layer 3 PIM code is concerned, only a single copy of the multicast traffic must be sent out this interface.

Figure 15-6 shows the reality of this situation at Layer 2. In this diagram, Routers B, C, and D are receiving multicast traffic from the source via the pseudobroadcast mechanism.

Figure 15-6   *Layer 2 Reality of NBMA Mode*

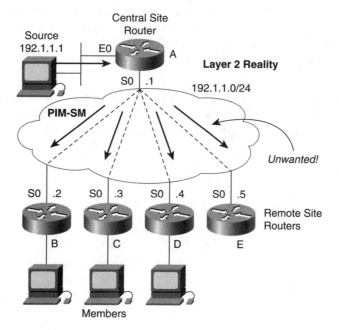

Note, however, that Router E does not have a directly connected host (or downstream router) that is a member of the group. However, because the pseudobroadcast mechanism is *spoofing* the router into thinking (at Layer 3) that the network is a broadcast medium, an additional, unwanted copy of the multicast traffic is being replicated and sent to Router E.

Obviously, the combination of the performance impact of pseudobroadcast on the router and the inefficient use of bandwidth and CPU to replicate unnecessary traffic means that pseudobroadcast is a poor choice for any serious multicast network design. (Moral: Just say no to pseudobroadcast.)

What is needed is some way to make the Layer 3 PIM code aware of the true NBMA topology underneath so that it can efficiently replicate the multicast packets in the PIM fast-switching code path. This concept is the whole idea of *PIM NBMA mode,* which is discussed in a later section.

PIM and Partial Mesh NBMA Networks

Partial mesh NBMA networks (that is, where every router doesn't have a virtual circuit to every other router in the network) pose an additional problem for the proper operation of PIM across the NBMA cloud. The problem is due to the fact that a multicast packet sent by a router into a partial mesh NBMA cloud may not reach all members of the network. Certain mechanisms of PIM operation depend on this and will break if this is not the case. One of the best examples of when these mechanisms fail is PIM dense mode (PIM-DM) Pruning.

Consider the Layer 3 viewpoint of the sample network shown in Figure 15-7. The routers in this example treat the NBMA network as a broadcast network (although the broadcast function is actually accomplished at Layer 2 via pseudobroadcast).

Figure 15-7   *Layer 3 View of PIM-DM Pruning*

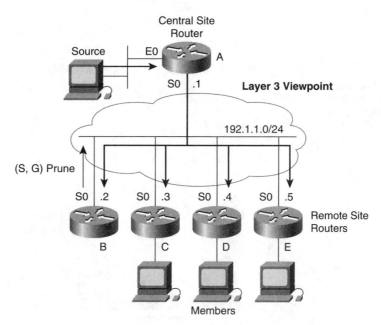

In the example shown, Router B does not have a directly connected host (or downstream router) that is a member of the group and therefore attempts to prune the traffic using the normal dense mode pruning mechanism. In this network, however, a hub-and-spoke topology of virtual circuits has been used instead of a fully meshed network to create the NBMA network.

Figure 15-8 shows the Layer 2 reality of this hub-and-spoke topology. Notice that because Router B only has a single virtual circuit back to the central site router (Router A), the (S, G) Prune is not being received by Routers C, D, and E. Because these routers do not hear the (S, G) Prune sent by Router B, they are unaware that they need to send an (S, G) Join to override the Prune. Hearing no overriding (S, G) Join message from the other routers, Router A dutifully prunes interface **Serial0** after the usual 3-second multi-access network delay that cuts off the flow of traffic to the members of the group.

Figure 15-8   *Layer 2 Reality of PIM-DM Pruning*

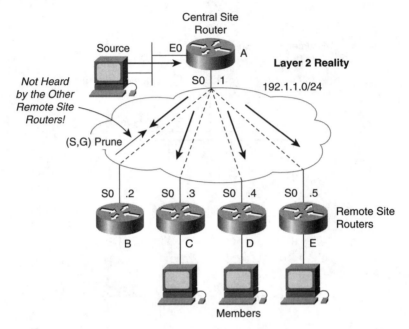

The upshot should be quite obvious. PIM-DM does not work over traditional NBMA networks unless a full mesh topology is used. Even if one does use a full mesh topology of virtual circuits to build the NBMA cloud, the performance impact of pseudobroadcast remains, making PIM-DM a poor choice for NBMA networks.

PIM NBMA Mode

The preceding section pointed out that the normal pruning mechanisms that are so crucial to the proper operation of PIM-DM fail in partial mesh NBMA networks. Unfortunately, PIM-DM is not the only case where the limited broadcast/multicast functionality of a partial mesh network causes problems. Even in PIM-SM, there are cases where this problem causes things to break. Obviously, what is needed is to make the PIM code in the router aware of the actual Layer 2 topology of the NBMA cloud. This can be accomplished if the PIM code in the router treats the NBMA cloud as a collection of p2p circuits instead of a broadcast medium.

Beginning with Internetwork Operating System (IOS) release 11.0, Cisco added special support for NBMA networks that work in conjunction with PIM-SM. The concept is actually quite simple. Whenever the **ip pim nbma-mode** command is added to the router configuration for an interface that is connected to an NBMA network, the PIM code will maintain "next hop" information in the (*, G) and (S, G) outgoing interface list in addition to the interface.

For example, consider the NBMA network shown in Figure 15-4. To configure **Serial0** on Router A for NBMA mode operation, the Frame Relay configuration shown in Example 15-2 might be used.

Example 15-2 *Frame Relay Configuration*

```
interface serial0
 ip address 192.1.1.1 255.255.255
 ip pim sparse-mode
 ip pim nbma-mode
 frame-relay lmi-type ansi
```

Let's assume again that Routers B, C, and D all have directly connected members for the target group but that Router E does not.

Figure 15-9 now shows that (*, G) Joins are being sent to the RP (Router A) for the multicast group just as in the previous examples.

Figure 15-9 *PIM NBMA Mode*

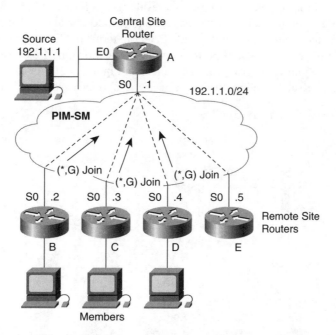

However, because **Serial0** on Router A is configured to use **ip pim nbma-mode**, it will put a separate entry in the outgoing interface list that contains the interface name and the IP address of the router that sent each (*, G) Join. This results in the mroute state in Router A shown in Example 15-3.

Example 15-3 *Mroute State in Router A*

```
(*, 224.1.1.1), 00:01:36/00:02:59, RP 192.1.1.1, flags: SC
  Incoming interface: null, RPF nbr 0.0.0.0
  Outgoing interface list:
    Serial0, 192.1.1.4 Forward/Sparse, 00:01:36/00:02:24
    Serial0, 192.1.1.2 Forward/Sparse, 00:00:54/00:02:06
    Serial0, 192.1.1.3 Forward/Sparse, 00:00:12/00:02:48

(192.1.1.1/32, 224.1.1.1), 00:00:06/00:02:59 flags: C
  Incoming interface: Ethernet0, RPF nbr 0.0.0.0
  Outgoing interface list:
    Serial0, 192.1.1.4 Forward/Sparse, 00:00:06/00:02:48
    Serial0, 192.1.1.2 Forward/Sparse, 00:00:06/00:02:48
    Serial0, 192.1.1.3 Forward/Sparse, 00:00:06/00:02:48
```

Notice that **Serial0** now appears in the outgoing interface lists three times, once each for Routers B, C, and D. Therefore, Router A can now perform efficient multicast packet replication for Routers B, C, and D in the Cisco PIM fast-switching code in the same way as it would for discrete interfaces. As a result, the multicast traffic is not queued to the Frame Relay output as broadcast packets, and pseudobroadcast is not used. The Cisco PIM fast-switching path is not only more efficient in terms of CPU overhead (compared to pseudobroadcast) but also is performing the replication only for those routers that have specifically joined the group, as can be seen in Figure 15-10. As a result, Router E is not receiving any unwanted multicast traffic as it did in the case of pseudobroadcast.

Figure 15-10 *NBMA Mode Details at Layer 2*

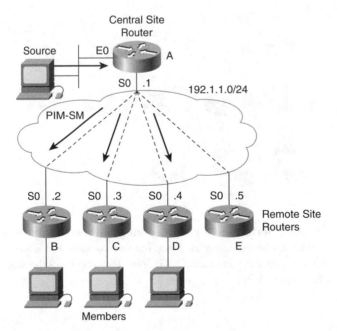

Because NBMA mode causes the router to treat the network as a collection of p2p circuits, the problems caused by a lack of a true broadcast mechanism in a partial mesh NBMA network are eliminated. For example, when a router no longer has a directly connected host (or downstream router) that is a member of the group and sends a (*, G) Prune, its associated entry is simply removed from the outgoing interface list. This does not affect the other routers in the network, because when NBMA mode is in use, a separate entry is maintained for each router that has sent a Join.

NOTE   Depending on how they are configured, Cisco Dialer interfaces also exhibit NBMA characteristics and should be configured with the **ip pim nbma-mode** command.

For example, assume Router B no longer has a directly connected host that is a member of the group. In this case, Router B would send a (*, G) Prune to Router A, which would result in the mroute state entry in Router A shown in Example 15-4.

Example 15-4   *Mroute State in Router A After (*, G) Prune*

```
(*, 224.1.1.1), 00:01:36/00:02:59, RP 192.1.1.1, flags: SC
  Incoming interface: null, RPF nbr 0.0.0.0
  Outgoing interface list:
    Serial0, 192.1.1.4 Forward/Sparse, 00:01:36/00:02:24
    Serial0, 192.1.1.3 Forward/Sparse, 00:00:12/00:02:48

(192.1.1.1/32, 224.1.1.1), 00:00:06/00:02:59 flags: C
  Incoming interface: Ethernet0, RPF nbr 0.0.0.0
  Outgoing interface list:
    Serial0, 192.1.1.4 Forward/Sparse, 00:00:06/00:02:48
    Serial0, 192.1.1.3 Forward/Sparse, 00:00:06/00:02:48
```

Notice that the entry for Router B has been deleted, which immediately stops the flow of traffic to this router and only this router. Traffic flow is maintained to Routers C and D.

NOTE   Although the NBMA mode concepts presented above could be made to work for dense mode, current releases of Cisco IOS support **ip pim nbma-mode** only for sparse mode networks. This may change in a future release of Cisco IOS, but the current thinking is that the combination of **ip pim nbma-mode** and dense mode would result in extremely large outgoing interface lists. The resulting increase in router state in a dense mode network could prove to be problematic.

Auto-RP over NBMA Networks

The lack of a true broadcast/multicast capability in partial mesh NBMA networks also introduces a problem with the proper flooding of Cisco Auto-RP messages. If this problem is not accounted for in the NBMA network design, the proper operation of Auto-RP cannot be guaranteed.

Figure 15-11 shows what can happen if the true Layer 2 topology of the NBMA network is not considered when configuring an Auto-RP Candidate-RP or a Mapping Agent.

Figure 15-11 *PIM-DM Auto-RP Message Flooding Problem*

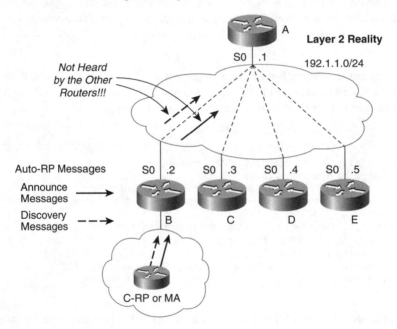

In this example, an Auto-RP Candidate-RP and/or Mapping Agent has been configured in the network behind Router B. In a partial mesh network, Router B does not have virtual circuits to all routers in the NBMA cloud. (Presumably, the configuration is a hub-and-spoke network with Router A serving as the hub.) As a result, Auto-RP messages from the router in the network behind Router B do not reach the other routers in the network. This problem is due to the fact that the Auto-RP groups (224.0.1.39 and 224.0.1.40) are normally flooded in dense mode unless a static RP is configured in all the routers in the network. (Configuring an RP address on every router in the network usually defeats the primary reasons for using Auto-RP.) In this situation (which is the norm), Router A will not forward any Auto-RP Announce or Discovery messages back out Serial0. The result is that inconsistent Group-to-RP mapping information is distributed, which, in turn, will cause problems in the sparse mode network.

The most serious problem that will occur in the preceding example is that critical Auto-RP Discovery messages sent by the Mapping Agent in the network behind Router B will not reach Routers C, D, and E. If only the one Mapping Agent is in the network, Routers C, D, and E will assume the network is operating in dense mode because they are not receiving any Group-to-RP mapping information.

The best way to fix this problem is to enable **ip pim nbma-mode** and move the Mapping Agent function to the central site network but leave the Candidate-RP where it is, as shown in Figure 15-12.

Figure 15-12   *Proper Placement of Mapping Agents*

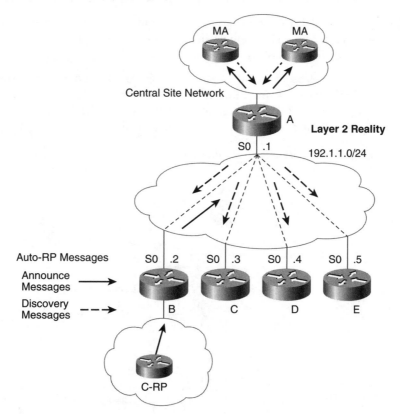

Now, the Auto-RP Discovery messages can reach all routers in the network and the Candidate-RP message can simultaneously reach the Mapping Agent(s). As long as all Mapping Agents are inside the central site network (notice that redundant Mapping Agents are shown in Figure 15-12), Auto-RP should function as desired.

NOTE   For the topology shown in Figure 15-12 to work properly, **ip pim nbma-mode** *must* be used. If this command is not used and the Candidate-RP behind Router B is elected as RP, Router A will not forward (*, G) Joins received from Routers C, D, and E to Router B. The net result is that Routers C, D, and E will not be able to join the shared tree and, therefore, will not be able to receive multicast traffic.

To summarize, the general rule of thumb is that all Auto-RP Mapping Agents should be configured inside the central site network to prevent problems in the Auto-RP mechanisms.

On the other hand, if it is necessary to depart from this design and place an Auto-RP Mapping Agent at one of the remote site networks, it will be necessary to add virtual circuits to the NBMA network.

For example, to place a Mapping Agent in the network behind Router B would require additional virtual circuits from Router B to all other routers in the NBMA network, as shown in Figure 15-13. This configuration allows the Auto-RP Discovery messages to flow properly from Router B to all other routers in the network.

Figure 15-13   *Adding Virtual Circuits to Solve the Problem*

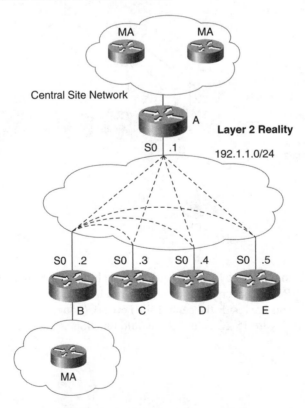

Multicast over ATM NBMA Clouds

ATM networks are often implemented using the same *permanent virtual circuit* (PVC) infrastructure as used in Frame Relay networks. In these cases, the ATM or Frame Relay service provider manually configures the virtual circuit paths through the ATM or Frame Relay network. However, many ATM networks have the capability to also support the creation of *switch virtual circuits* (SVCs) via standard ATM User-Network Interface (UNI) signaling that permits the routers to establish new paths through the ATM fabric on the fly. ATM UNI signaling not only allows p2p virtual circuits to be created, but also supports p2mp virtual circuits as well. These p2mp circuits can be leveraged to substantially increase the efficiency of multicast traffic flow across the ATM network.

This section explores the use of the p2mp SVC capabilities of ATM to improve multicast flow and how to configure a Cisco router to take advantage of these capabilities. In addition, this section examines the output of several **show** commands that can be used to debug the flow of multicast traffic over these p2mp circuits.

ATM Point-to-Multipoint Broadcast Virtual Circuit

Instead of using the highly inefficient method of pseudobroadcast to replicate a broadcast or multicast packet in an ATM NBMA network, it would be nice if there were some way to let the ATM network perform this replication task. In such a setting, the router would have to send only a single broadcast or multicast packet into the ATM fabric, and it would reach all routers in the NBMA network. This can be accomplished by the use of ATM p2mp virtual circuits (VCs) that are dedicated to delivering broadcast or multicast traffic.

Figure 15-14 shows a p2mp broadcast SVC connecting Router A to all other routers in the ATM NBMA network. Router A uses this p2mp VC to deliver all broadcast or multicast traffic to Routers B, C, and D. Although only the p2mp VC from Router A to Routers B, C, and D is shown in the drawing, each router would have its own p2mp VC that connects the router to all other routers in the network. The result is a total of four p2mp VCs in the example shown in Figure 15-14.

Figure 15-14 *ATM Broadcast VC*

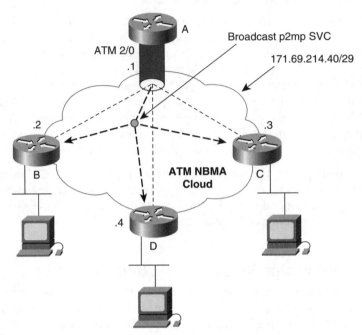

The p2mp broadcast SVC connection may be accomplished by using the **atm multipoint-signaling** interface configuration command. This command instructs the router to signal the ATM fabric (using standard UNI ATM signaling mechanisms) to create a p2mp VC that connects all routers in the network that have the **broadcast** keyword in their static ATM map statement.

For instance, Example 15-5 shows the commands necessary to configure Router A to create a p2mp broadcast VC to the other routers in the network.

Example 15-5 *Commands for p2mp Broadcast VC*

```
interface ATM2/0
  ip address 171.69.214.41 255.255.255.248
  ip pim sparse-dense-mode
  ip ospf network broadcast
  atm nsap-address 47.00918100000000410B0A1981.111111111111.00
  atm pvc 1 0 5 qsaal
  atm pvc 2 0 16 ilmi
  atm multipoint-signaling
  map-group mpvc

map-list mpvc
  ip 171.69.214.41 atm-nsap 47.00918100000000410B0A1981.111111111111.00 broadcast
  ip 171.69.214.42 atm-nsap 47.00918100000000410B0A1981.222222222222.00 broadcast
  ip 171.69.214.43 atm-nsap 47.00918100000000410B0A1981.333333333333.00 broadcast
  ip 171.69.214.44 atm-nsap 47.00918100000000410B0A1981.444444444444.00 broadcast
```

The key configuration items in Example 15-5 are highlighted in boldface. Notice that the **atm multipoint-signaling** command has been added to interface **ATM2/0**. Also notice that the **broadcast** keyword is appended to each of the ATM mapping statements in **map-list mpvc**. The network service access point (NSAP) information in these mapping commands instructs the ATM fabric to add these ATM nodes to the p2mp VC.

NOTE   The obvious downside to using the preceding approach is that a full mesh of SVCs will be created between all routers. However, if this full mesh SVC network is acceptable, the trade-off is reduced workload on the router, as it doesn't have to replicate broadcast packets using pseudobroadcast.

ATM Point-to-Multipoint VC per Group

The use of a special broadcast p2mp VC certainly reduces the packet replication workload on the router, which increases multicast efficiency (at least as far as the router is concerned). However, the network still has inefficiencies that can be eliminated. For example, assume that only Router B has joined a multicast group and Router A is sending this traffic via the broadcast p2mp VC. Although Router A has to send only one packet into the ATM fabric via the broadcast p2mp VC, that unwanted traffic is being delivered to Routers C and D. What we really would like to see is for the ATM fabric to deliver the multicast traffic only to the routers that actually want the traffic!

Extending the ATM switch fabric to be multicast aware would require the ATM switches to somehow snoop in on the PIM control traffic flowing over the ATM NBMA network. This is obviously a non-trivial task and would require all ATM switches to have this feature implemented in order to work. However, it is quite possible to have the routers to instruct the ATM fabric to create separate p2mp VCs that can be used to distribute the multicast traffic to only those routers that have requested it.

Figure 15-15 shows an example of how individual p2mp VCs could be used to efficiently distribute multicast traffic over the ATM NBMA network. In this example, notice that the broadcast p2mp VC is still being used for general broadcast traffic (such as OSPF Hellos or other generic link-local multicast or broadcasts).

Figure 15-15 *ATM P2MP VC per Group*

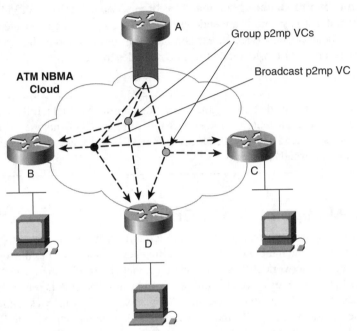

However, now separate group p2mp VCs are in use that map to only the subset of the routers in the network that have joined a specific multicast group. (Again, only the p2mp circuits originating from Router A are shown for clarity.) This allows Router A to send a single multicast packet into the ATM fabric and have this packet reach only the routers that have a need for the traffic. This network represents the maximum multicast efficiency that can be obtained in an ATM network without having the ATM switches be multicast aware.

PIM Multipoint Signaling

The use of group-specific p2mp VCs for multicast traffic delivery is precisely what is accomplished by configuring **ip pim multipoint-signaling** on an ATM interface in a PIM-SM network. This command instructs the router to create and maintain a separate p2mp VC for each group (up to a limit, which is discussed later). Each Join message that the router receives for a group from another router is translated into an *Add-Party* ATM UNI signal to the ATM switch fabric. The process involves searching the ATM mapping information for the IP address of the router that sent the Join and using the associated ATM NSAP address in the mapping statement to instruct the ATM switch fabric which *Party* to add to the p2mp

VC. By the same token, the reverse operation is used when a Prune message is received from a router. This message causes a *Drop-Party* ATM UNI signal to be sent to the ATM fabric to remove the router from the p2mp VC.

Example 15-6 shows PIM Multipoint Signaling being configured on Router A in Figure 15-15.

Example 15-6   *PIM Multipoint Signaling Configuration*

```
interface ATM2/0
  ip address 171.69.214.41 255.255.255.248
  ip pim sparse-dense-mode
  ip pim multipoint-signaling
  ip ospf network broadcast
  atm nsap-address 47.00918100000000410B0A1981.111111111111.00
  atm pvc 1 0 5 qsaal
  atm pvc 2 0 16 ilmi
  atm multipoint-signaling
  map-group mpvc

map-list mpvc
  ip 171.69.214.41 atm-nsap 47.00918100000000410B0A1981.111111111111.00 broadcast
  ip 171.69.214.42 atm-nsap 47.00918100000000410B0A1981.222222222222.00 broadcast
  ip 171.69.214.43 atm-nsap 47.00918100000000410B0A1981.333333333333.00 broadcast
  ip 171.69.214.44 atm-nsap 47.00918100000000410B0A1981.444444444444.00 broadcast
```

Notice that the configuration is identical to Example 15-5 with the exception of the addition of the **ip pim multipoint-signaling** command on interface **ATM2/0**.

Limiting the Number of PIM Multipoint VCs

Unfortunately, the use of individual p2mp VCs by the Cisco router doesn't come free. For example, the number of active multicast groups in the network can grow to the point where the number of p2mp VCs needed exceeds the capabilities of the router. In addition to increased resource demands on the router, the use of p2mp SVC in the ATM network increases the resource demands on the ATM switch fabric. Therefore, to place an upper bound on the resources consumed by PIM Multipoint Signaling, there is a maximum number of VCs that PIM Multipoint Signaling will be allowed to use. This maximum value can be tuned by using the following global command:

```
ip pim vc-count <count>
```

This command configures PIM Multipoint Signaling to limit itself to using a maximum of **count** VCs. If this command is not specified, the default value of **count** is 200 VCs. When the router hits this maximum limit, it will delete an inactive PIM multipoint VC in order to open VCs for new groups.

The determination of whether a VC is inactive or not depends on whether its traffic rate is below the *minimum-vc-rate* in packets per seconds. VCs that fall below this minimum rate are considered eligible for deletion when the *vc-count* limit is reached. The *minimum-vc-rate* can be tuned by using the following global command:

```
ip pim minimum-vc-rate <pps>
```

This command configures the minimum traffic rate in **pps** for PIM multipoint VCs to be considered active. If the maximum number of PIM multipoint VCs is in use and a new VC needs to be created for a new group, the router scans the list of existing PIM multipoint VCs. If a VC is found that has a rate less than or equal to **pps**, it is deleted so that a new VC can be created for the new group. If a VC whose rate is below this minimum is not found, a new VC is not created. If a multicast group does not have its own multipoint VC, the router drops back to using the shared broadcast p2mp VC that delivers packets to all routers in the NBMA network.

If the **ip pim minimum-vc-rate** command is not specified, a default value of 0 **pps** is automatically used. Thus, VCs are allocated on a first come, first served basis until the maximum number of PIM multipoint VCs is reached. At that point, all new groups that are created use the shared broadcast p2mp VC.

Debugging ATM P2MP Virtual Circuits

This section introduces some of the basic commands that monitor and/or debug ATM p2mp virtual circuits that are used for IP multicasting. Using these commands, the network administrator can quickly and easily determine the number, status, and activity of these p2mp circuits.

PIM Show Commands

At the top of the list of show commands is **show ip pim vc**. This command displays a list of all p2mp VCs in use by PIM by group, as shown in Example 15-7.

Example 15-7   *Sample show ip pim vc Output*

```
router-a> show ip pim vc
       IP Multicast ATM VC Status
       ATM0/0 VC count is 5, max is 5
       Group           VCD     Interface     Leaf Count   Rate
       224.0.1.40      21      ATM2/0        3            0 pps
       224.2.2.2       26      ATM2/0        1            3 pps
       224.1.1.1       28      ATM2/0        1            1 pps
       224.4.4.4       32      ATM2/0        2            1 pps
       224.5.5.5       35      ATM2/0        1            2 pps
```

In this example, the multicast group address is displayed along with the virtual circuit descriptor (VCD) number, the ATM interface, the number of leaf nodes in the p2mp circuit, and the traffic rate in packets per second that is flowing over the VC.

In addition to the preceding command, the **show ip mroute** command uses an extended format when ATM p2mp VCs are in use as shown in Example 15-8.

Example 15-8   *Sample show ip mroute Output*

```
router-a> show ip mroute 224.1.1.1

IP Multicast Routing Table
Flags: D - Dense, S - Sparse, C - Connected, L - Local, P - Pruned
       R - RP-bit set, F - Register flag, T - SPT-bit set, J - Join SPT
Timers: Uptime/Expires
Interface state: Interface, Next-Hop or VCD, State/Mode

(*, 224.1.1.1), 00:03:57/00:02:54, RP 130.4.101.1, flags: SJ
  Incoming interface: Null, RPF nbr 0.0.0.0
  Outgoing interface list:
    ATM2/0, VCD 28, Forward/Sparse, 00:03:57/00:02:53
```

Notice that in addition to the interface name, the VCD number of the p2mp VC is included as part of the information in the outgoing interface list. By using this VCD number as a parameter in the **show atm** commands (as described in the next section), you can obtain even more detailed information on the multicast p2mp VC.

ATM Show Commands

The output format of the **show atm vc** command can also be used to display the status of p2mp VCs in use by the router. Example 15-9 is an sample of the output that can be obtained using this command.

Example 15-9   *Sample show atm vc Output*

```
router-a> show atm vc
                                 AAL                    Peak  Avg.  Burst
Interface  VCD  VPI  VCI Type    Encapsulation  Kbps    Kbps  Cells Status
ATM2/0     1    0      5 PVC      AAL5-SAAL      155000  155000   96 ACT
ATM2/0     2    0     16 PVC      AAL5-ILMI      155000  155000   96 ACT
ATM2/0     6    0    124 MSVC-3   AAL5-SNAP      155000  155000   96 ACT
ATM2/0     9    0    125 SVC      AAL5-SNAP      155000  155000   96 ACT
ATM2/0     13   0    126 SVC      AAL5-SNAP      155000  155000   96 ACT
ATM2/0     21   0    127 MSVC     AAL5-SNAP      155000  155000   96 ACT
ATM2/0     26   0    128 MSVC-1   AAL5-SNAP      155000  155000   96 ACT
ATM2/0     28   0    129 MSVC-3   AAL5-SNAP      155000  155000   96 ACT
ATM2/0     32   0    131 SVC      AAL5-SNAP      155000  155000   96 ACT
ATM2/0     32   0    132 MSVC-3   AAL5-SNAP      155000  155000   96 ACT
ATM2/0     35   0    135 MSVC-2   AAL5-SNAP      155000  155000   96 ACT
```

All p2mp VCs listed by this command are indicated with the *Multipoint Switched Virtual Circuit* (**MSVC**) designation in the Type field of the display. Example 15-8 shows that group 224.1.1.1 is using VCD 28 on interface ATM2/0. Locating this interface and VCD in the **show atm vc** display, you see that the Type field contains an indication of **MSVC-3**. This designation indicates that Router A is the root node and that three leaf nodes have been added to the p2mp VC. On the other hand, **ATM2/0, VCD 26** contains a Type field value of **MSVC-1**, which indicates that Router A is again the root node for this p2mp VC and that only one leaf node is connected to the VC. If the Type field contains only the value of **MSVC** (without a dash and number), it indicates that the router is a leaf node on this p2mp VC. In the sample output in Example 15-9, **ATM2/0, VCD 21** is an example where Router A is a leaf node and not the root node of the p2mp VC.

Finally, by supplying the VCD number of a specific ATM VC, even more detail on the p2mp VC can be obtained, as shown in Example 15-10.

Example 15-10   *Sample show atm vc with VCD Number Output*

```
router-a> show atm vc 28

ATM0/0: VCD: 28, VPI: 0, VCI: 129, etype:0x0, AAL5 - LLC/SNAP, Flags: 0x650
PeakRate: 155000, Average Rate: 155000, Burst Cells: 96, VCmode: 0xE000
OAM DISABLED, InARP DISABLED
InPkts: 0, OutPkts: 12, InBytes: 0, OutBytes: 496
InPRoc: 0, OutPRoc: 0, Broadcasts: 12
InFast: 0, OutFast: 0, InAS: 0, OutAS: 0
OAM F5 cells sent: 0, OAM cells received: 0
Status: ACTIVE, TTL: 2, VC owner: IP Multicast (224.1.1.1)
interface = ATM2/0, call locally initiated, call reference = 2
vcnum = 11, vpi = 0, vci = 129, state = Active
 aal5snap vc, multipoint call
Retry count: Current = 0, Max = 10
timer currently inactive, timer value = 00:00:00
Leaf Atm Nsap address: 47.0091810000000002BA08E101.444444444444.02
Leaf Atm Nsap address: 47.0091810000000002BA08E101.333333333333.02
Leaf Atm Nsap address: 47.0091810000000002BA08E101.222222222222.02
```

In Example 15-10, the **VC owner** is listed as **IP Multicast (224.1.1.1)** and indicates that the VC is in use by PIM. In addition, the actual ATM NSAP addresses of the three leaf nodes on the p2mp VC are listed at the end of the display.

Classical IP over ATM Networks

Up to this point, the discussion of ATM NBMA networks has been confined to the special case where the network is used only to interconnect routers into an ATM core network. One way to interconnect nodes routers across an ATM network is to use a *classical IP over ATM* network, which was originally defined in RFC 1577 and has now been superceded by RFC 2225. In these networks, extensive ATM UNI signaling dynamically sets up and tears down p2p SVCs as needed between the nodes in the ATM NBMA network to permit traffic to flow.

However, to resolve IP-to-ATM addressing so that an SVC call can be made, an ATM Address Resolution Protocol (ARP) server must be used. All ATM nodes in the network register their IP/ATM NSAP addresses with the ATM ARP server. When an ATM node wishes to communicate with another node across the classical IP over ATM network, it must query the ATM ARP server for the ATM NSAP address associated with the destination IP address. The ATM node then uses the NSAP address received in the response from the ATM ARP server to place the SVC call to the destination node.

The use of classical IP over ATM networks is not strictly limited to core networks consisting only of routers. Some of the nodes in these NBMA LISs are frequently end stations and not routers. Because the SVCs in a classical IP over ATM network are built on demand, the set of SVCs that interconnect the nodes in the network at any particular instant may or may not be a full mesh. In fact, most implementations tear down an SVC if no traffic has flowed over it for some period of time so that precious ATM resources can be reused. This can increase the chance that the set of SVCs at any particular instant is not a complete, full mesh of all nodes in the NBMA LIS. Because the set of SVCs may not reach all other nodes in the network, any broadcast or multicast traffic sent may not reach all nodes in the network. As a result, RFC 2225 states that broadcast and multicast are not supported across classical IP over ATM.

NOTE   Even if an implementation of classical IP over ATM attempted to establish a full mesh of SVCs to all nodes in the network, it would not have any way to determine which IP addresses in the LIS were valid. You might argue that you could query the ATM ARP server for every address in the network address range to determine the valid nodes in the LIS. Even if you were willing to query every address (which could be a rather large number), there is no guarantee that the ATM ARP server would have a complete mapping at query time. Consequently, to maintain a complete full mesh of all nodes in the LIS, the node would have to query the ATM ARP server for the entire IP address repetitively. Sorry, bad idea.

It's an unfortunate fact that many proponents of bringing ATM to the desktop have built large ATM LISs utilizing classical IP over ATM networks with the idea that they would be in a good position to roll out multimedia applications. Although ATM's (yet to be realized) promise of quality of service (QoS) would be desirable in a multimedia network, the reality is that many of these multimedia applications are IP multicast based. Because classical IP over ATM clearly does not support multicast, these multimedia applications will not work over such networks.

Considerable work is underway to find a workable solution around this limitation. Several other RFCs have defined rather complex techniques to extend classical IP over ATM to support multicast. These include RFC 2022, *Support for Multicast over UNI 3.0/3.1 Based ATM Networks*, and RFC 2149, *Multicast Server Architectures for MARS-Based ATM Multicasting*. Collectively, the methods defined in these RFCs are referred to as *ATM MARS* and are centered around the following basic components:

- **Multicast Address Resolution Server (MARS)**—This device resolves Group-to-End-node mapping by extending the IGMP-based multicast host model to ATM. Nodes that want to join a group must register with the MARS. By the same token, when a node leaves the group, it must notify the MARS so that its NSAP address can be removed from the Group-to-End-node map list.

- **Multicast Content Server (MCS)**—This device distributes actual IP multicast traffic in the same fashion as the broadcast and unknown server (BUS) in ATM LAN Emulation (LANE) delivers all broadcast/unknown traffic. That is to say, all IP multicast traffic is sent to the MCS, which then sends it to the members of the group in the LIS. The MCS may employ either p2p or p2mp VCs to distribute this traffic to end stations. The MCS must also work closely with the MARS to determine the current Group-to-End-node mapping.

- **Mesh of p2mp VCs**—This approach may be used as an alternative to the MCS and requires each end station that wants to transmit to the group to establish and maintain p2mp VCs to the other members of the group. This solution also requires close coordination with the MARS to maintain a current Group-to-End-node mapping.

The preceding extremely high-level description of ATM MARS belies the enormous complexity behind extending the multicast host model of IGMP to an ATM network. Until more work in this highly complex area has been done, Cisco Systems has elected to not implement ATM MARS in its current versions of IOS. It is possible that this decision may change when this technology matures sufficiently.

Summary

This chapter examined how the lack of a native broadcast capability in NBMA networks, such as on Frame Relay, ATM, and Dialer interfaces, creates some interesting issues for proper IP multicast operation. Cisco routers use pseudobroadcast to emulate a native broadcast service on NBMA networks. Although pseudobroadcast is generally sufficient for the occasional routing update, its performance impact is too significant to be used for IP multicasting. As a result, Cisco has introduced PIM NBMA mode for use in PIM-SM networks to provide efficient IP multicast services over NBMA networks.

When the NBMA network is built on an ATM network that supports SVCs and that network is acting as a core network to interconnect Cisco routers, p2mp VCs can be used to achieve improvements in ATM network efficiency using Cisco's PIM Multipoint Signaling feature. This feature provides the maximum IP multicast efficiency that can be obtained across an ATM network and should be the preferred method when an ATM core network is used.

Finally, considerable work is being done to extend the classical IP over ATM model to support IP multicast. However, this technology has yet to see any widespread usage, primarily because of its complexity. Only time will tell whether these extensions to the classical IP over ATM model will become commonplace in networks.

PART V

Advanced Multicast Topics

This final part addresses advanced topics in IP multicasting.

Chapter 16 covers IP multicast traffic engineering and presents a popular multicast topic: limiting the bandwidth consumed by multicast traffic. Two specific techniques to limit bandwidth consumption are presented along with examples on how to configure Cisco routers to make use of these techniques. Chapter 16 also includes a section on controlling the paths of multicast traffic flow through the network. In addition, this chapter presents a special feature that can be used to convert IP broadcast traffic to IP multicast traffic and vice versa.

Chapter 17 is a brief introduction to inter-domain IP multicast routing and presents recently developed protocols that permit multiple, independent PIM-SM domains to be interconnected. This chapter also provides a brief overview of some of the efforts by IETF working groups on new protocols to address inter-domain IP multicast and dynamic multicast group address allocation.

CHAPTER 16

Multicast Traffic Engineering

This chapter considers several topics in multicast traffic engineering that are commonly encountered in IP multicast networks. Certainly, this presentation is not an exhaustive study of issues that you are likely to encounter while designing IP multicast-enabled networks, but I feel certain that these issues are likely to surface sooner than most others.

The topics that are covered in this chapter include

- Bandwidth control
- Path engineering
- Load splitting
- Broadcast-to-multicast conversion

Of these, the first topic, bandwidth control, seems to almost always come up at some point in the initial phases of the network design. Additionally, traffic engineering issues immediately pop up whenever network engineers decide to "just run IP multicast on certain links." Finally, load splitting and broadcast-to-multicast conversions are typically only seen under special situations. However, having a solid understanding of these two issues and their associated solutions is always a good idea.

Controlling Multicast Bandwidth Usage

"I'm not going to enable IP multicast in our network because it might consume too much bandwidth and affect our existing unicast applications." This statement is often heard when network managers are discussing the topic of IP multicast. However, the reality is that the growing popularity of multimedia applications (especially video) is already placing increased bandwidth demands on these managers' networks every day. In many cases, the managers are just not aware of it.

Chapter 1, "Introduction to IP Multicast," points out that many of these applications are using User Datagram Protocol (UDP) based unicast, which results in multiple video streams consuming bandwidth in the network. By this point, it should be clear that the use of IP multicast is actually an excellent way to conserve network bandwidth. Having said that, there are still conditions under which one is prudent to protect the network against the possibility of poorly behaved or improperly used multicast applications from consuming too much bandwidth and causing problems.

This section examines two techniques that can help protect the network from multicast applications that consume too much bandwidth on critical links. These methods are

- Rate-limiting process
- Scoped zones

These two methods are not mutually exclusive and can (and often are) used together to provide increased network bandwidth control over IP multicast traffic.

Bandwidth Control with Rate Limiting

Cisco Systems introduced the capability to rate limit IP multicast traffic back in Internetwork Operating System (IOS) version 11.0 with the use of the **ip multicast rate-limit** interface command. This command has numerous options that limit the flow of incoming or outgoing multicast traffic on a particular interface and is a brute-force method of limiting multicast bandwidth usage. The format of this command is

```
[no] ip multicast rate-limit in ¦ out {[video] ¦ [whiteboard]}
                [group-list <acl>] [source-list <acl>]  [<kbps>]
```

The **ip multicast rate-limit in** form of the command limits the rate at which the specified multicast stream is accepted on the interface to **<kbps>**. The **ip multicast rate-limit out** form of the command limits the rate at which the specified multicast stream can be sent out the interface to **<kbps>**. The router silently discards packets that cause the specified rate to be exceeded. If the **<kbps>** parameter is not specified in the command, the default value of 0 **<kbps>** is assumed, meaning that all packets in the specified stream are discarded. (This value can be used as a filter to block the flow of a particular multicast stream.)

The optional **group-list** and **source-list** clauses fine-tune the rate-limiting command so that it applies to specific groups and sources or to the interface as a whole. If both of these clauses are omitted, the specified rate limiting is applied to the aggregate of all multicast traffic flowing on the interface, regardless of source, group, or number of multicast flows.

If either the **group-list** or **source-list** clause is specified, rate limiting is applied to each individual multicast traffic flow. In addition, multiple iterations of the **ip multicast rate-limit** command may be configured on an interface. This permits a variety of rate-limiting combinations to be specified.

For example, if only the **group-list <acl>** clause is specified, rate limiting is performed on any sources sending to the groups specified in the access control list (ACL). If only the **source-list <acl>** clause is specified, rate limiting is performed on the specific sources listed in the acl, regardless of which groups they are sending. If both clauses are specified, rate limiting is performed only on sources that are sending to the groups matched by the **group-list <acl>** and that match the **source-list <acl>**.

Finally, if the optional keyword **video** or **whiteboard** is specified, then rate limiting is performed on all specified video or whiteboard multicast streams, respectively. The router identifies these multicast streams by the UDP port number used by the respective video or whiteboard media. The UDP port numbers of these media streams are, in turn, obtained by the router as follows:

1 The router's Session Directory Protocol (sdr) cache is searched for multicast sessions that contain video or whiteboard media streams.

2 The multicast group address, along with the UDP port number of the associated media stream, is recorded for use in rate-limiting checks.

NOTE   For video or whiteboard multicast rate limiting to work, the command **ip sdr listen** must be enabled on the router so that the port number can be obtained from the sdr cache. If the group address corresponding to the video or whiteboard multicast stream is not in the router's sdr cache, no rate limiting is done for the group. This situation would occur if **ip sdr listen** is not enabled on the router or if the router is not receiving the sdr announcements for the group.

The use of rate limiting to control bandwidth utilization is a rather brute-force method that doesn't always meet the needs of the network engineer. It requires an arbitrary upper bound to be set on the bandwidth utilization of a link and enforces this limit religiously even if available bandwidth on the link could be used to deliver the traffic.

Aggregate Rate Limiting

Because network engineers generally usually do not know which sources will be sending to which groups in their network, the most common application of rate limiting is to set an absolute upper bound for all multicast traffic being sent on an interface and is referred to as *aggregate rate limiting*. When this form of rate limiting is in use, the total rate of all multicast traffic flowing over the interface is compared to the rate limit. If this rate is being exceeded, the router begins dropping multicast packets.

For example, the router configuration in Example 16-1 could be used to limit the amount of multicast traffic sent on a T1 line to roughly 70% of the total available bandwidth or approximately 1 Mbps.

Example 16-1   *Sample Rate Limiting Configuration*

```
interface serial0
 description "T1 line to Timbuktu"
 ip address 192.1.1.1 255.255.255.252
 ip pim sparse-dense
 ip multicast rate-limit out 1000
```

Note that this configuration does not use either the **group-list** or **source-list** clause, which means that aggregate rate limiting is in use. In other words, the rate limit is applied to the *aggregate* of all multicast traffic flowing out the interface regardless of whether there is one multicast stream or one hundred.

If the network engineer wants to limit the rate of multicast traffic being accepted by an interface, the configuration in Example 16-2 can be used.

Example 16-2   *Configuration to Limit Multicast Traffic*

```
interface ethernet0
  description "Multicast Server LAN Segment"
  ip address 192.100.1.1 255.255.255.0
  ip pim sparse-dense
  ip multicast rate-limit in 3000
```

The preceding configuration would limit the rate of accepted multicast traffic to a total *aggregate* rate of all arriving multicast traffic to 3 Mbps. (Note that the router has no control of how much multicast traffic the servers on this LAN segment send. The router can set limits only on the maximum rate it will accept. If the total aggregate rate of all multicast traffic exceeds the set limit, the router begins dropping multicast packets at this input interface.)

Rate Limiting by Mroute Entry

Rate limiting on an aggregate interface basis is sometimes insufficient to meet certain network needs because this technique sets an upper bound on the total amount of multicast traffic an interface is permitted to carry. In some cases, a network engineer may want to limit each individual multicast stream to a maximum rate. This type of limit can be implemented by rate limiting on an mroute table entry basis instead of on an aggregate interface basis.

When interface rate limiting by mroute entry is in use, the traffic rate value maintained in the individual (*, G) or (S, G) entry (depending on which is being used to forward the traffic) is compared with the list of configured rate limits for the interface. If a matching entry is found, the limit is compared to the traffic rate value in the associated mroute entry. If the rate is less than the configured limit, the multicast packet is forwarded normally; otherwise, it is dropped.

Consider the configuration in Example 16-3 of interface rate limiting by mroute entry:

Example 16-3   *Rate Limiting by Mroute Entry*

```
interface serial0
 description "T1 line to Timbuktu"
 ip address 192.1.1.1 255.255.255.252
 ip pim sparse-dense
 ip multicast rate-limit out group-list 10 50

access-list 10 permit 239.255.0.0 0.0.255.255
```

This configuration limits each individual mroute table entry whose group address falls into the range of 239.255.0.0–239.255.255.255, to a maximum of 50 kbps out interface **serial0**. If four (S, G) mroute table entries happen to match this group and they have **serial0** in their outgoing interface lists, each entry would be permitted to forward up to 50 kbps out **serial0** for a total of 200 kbps.

WARNING   If multicast traffic is being forwarded in a sparse mode network using the (*, G) entry (such as when SPT-Thresholds of infinity have been configured), the rate is applied to the aggregate of all (*, G) traffic flowing over the interface. Consequently, if four active sources for a multicast group are being forwarded via the (*, G) entry, the aggregate rate of all four sources is compared to the specified rate limit. If the aggregate rate exceeds the limit, multicast packets will be dropped. Therefore, if it is important for each individual multicast source to be allowed to transmit traffic up to some specified limit, that SPT-Thresholds of zero (the default) should be used so that individual (S, G) entries are created.

Again, it is possible to configure multiple **ip multicast rate-limit** commands on a single interface. The configuration in Example 16-4 extends the configuration shown Example 16-3 to also define a limit on all multicast traffic transmitted in the 239.192.0.0–239.192.255.255 range.

Example 16-4   *Using Multiple **ip multicast rate-limit** Commands*

```
interface serial0
 description "T1 line to Timbuktu"
 ip address 192.1.1.1 255.255.255.252
 ip pim sparse-dense
 ip multicast rate-limit out group-list 20 1000
 ip multicast rate-limit out group-list 10 50

access-list 10 permit 239.255.0.0 0.0.255.255

access-list 20 permit 239.192.0.0 0.0.255.255
```

Now, each (S, G) multicast traffic flow in the 239.255.0.0–239.255.255.255 range can transmit 50 kbps out **serial0** while each (S, G) multicast traffic flow in the 239.192.0.0–239.192.255.255 range can transmit up to 1 Mbps.

Finally, whereas the previous examples defined individual mroute entry limits for outgoing interfaces by the use of the **out** qualifier, the same limits may be applied to the incoming interface by the use of the **in** qualifier.

Bandwidth Control with Scoped Zones

Another efficient method to control the bandwidth utilization is via the use of scoped zones and IP multicast boundaries. The basic idea behind this approach is to prevent high-rate multicast traffic from traveling outside of regions that are provisioned to handle this rate of multicast traffic.

An example of where this approach is useful is to prevent high-rate multicast from leaving a campus network and traveling over the wide-area network (WAN), as shown in Figure 16-1.

Figure 16-1   *Preventing High-Rate Multicast from Leaving a Campus*

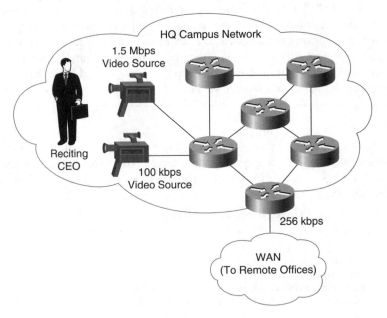

In this example, two video sources of the company's CEO reciting the words to a popular 1960s rock-and-roll tune are being multicast live to the entire company. (Evidentially, this sort of event is popular at some high-tech companies.) Employees located at the headquarters campus can join the high-rate, 1.5-Mbps video multicast session so that they can see and hear the CEO recite with the highest audio and video fidelity. Employees located at remote offices, however, should not join the 1.5-Mbps session because they would overload the WAN link. Instead, employees at these remote sites are expected to join the low-rate, 100-kbps session. However, unless some preventive steps are taken, an employee at a remote office could join the 1.5 Mbps by accident, overload the WAN link, and effectively ruin the show for all the other employees at the remote sites. By using scoped zones and multicast boundaries for high-rate multicast traffic, it is possible to prevent employees at the remote offices from joining the high-rate multicast feeds.

The idea behind bandwidth control using scoped zones is to develop a hierarchy of multicast traffic rates. Each level of the hierarchy defines a range of multicast addresses that can be used to transmit multicast traffic up to some maximum rate within that level of the hierarchy. For example, Table 16-1 shows a simple three-tier hierarchy that could be used to divide multicast traffic rates into three zones with their corresponding rate limits.

Table 16-1   *Simple Three-Tiered Zone Hierarchy*

Zone	Group Range	Rate
Site-Local	239.255.0.0/16	>256 Kbps
Organization-Local	239.192.0.0/10	<= 256 Kbps
Global	224.0.1.0 – 238.255.255.255	<= 128 Kbps

Figure 16-2 shows an example of this hierarchy being applied to the company network. A Site-Local zone would typically be an area where the bandwidth that interconnected all the network segments was plentiful, for example, a site or campus network with Ethernet or better rates.

Figure 16-2 *Bandwidth Control with Scoped Zones*

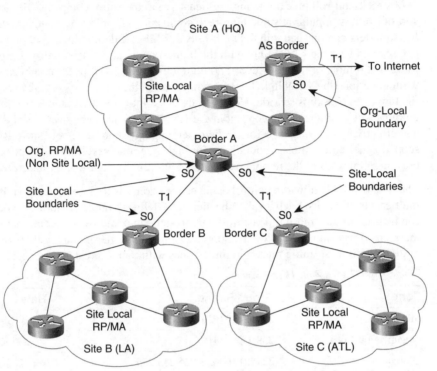

The drawing shows two remote sites (or campuses) in Los Angeles and Atlanta, each connected back to the headquarters (Site A) site via T1 links. Each of these sites is configured as a Site-Local zone with Site-Local boundaries on the T1 links on their respective border routers. Multicast sources in these sites that want to transmit only to receivers inside of their site would use a multicast address in the Site-Local group range. (In this example, this range has been assigned as the 239.255.0.0/16 group range.) By using the Site-Local group range, multicast sources inside the site can safely source traffic at rates above 256 kbps. This traffic would typically include things like MPEG video sources at rates up to 1.5 Mbps or possibly more (depending on the site/campus bandwidth infrastructure). The Site-Local boundaries configured on the border routers prevent any multicast traffic in the 239.255.0.0/16 group range from entering or leaving the site. This multicast boundary prevents the (potentially) high-rate Site-Local multicast traffic from congesting the inter-site T1 links.

<table>
<tr><td>**NOTE**</td><td>The addresses in the Site-Local address range (in this example, the 239.255.0.0/16 range) are allocated independently by all sites in the network. Therefore, two different multicast sessions could be using the same group address at the same time but at different sites. For example, the high-rate session of the CEO reciting the words to a 1960s rock-and-roll number might be using 239.255.1.1 at the Headquarters site (Site A) while, at the LA site (Site B), the same 239.255.1.1 group is being used to multicast reruns of the *Three Stooges*. Because the Site-Local boundaries prevent these multicasts from leaving the site, there is no problem with these two multicast streams becoming merged.</td></tr>
</table>

The next level of the Scoped zone hierarchy would be the Organization-Local zone, which includes all portions of the company's internal network. Multicast sources inside the company's internal network that need to reach other locations in the company would use a multicast address in the Organization-Local group range. (In this example, this range has been assigned as the 239.192.0.0/10 group range.) Sources transmitting in this group range must limit their rates to 256 kbps or less to not overload the T1 rate WAN links between each site. The Organization-Local boundary configured on Border Router A prevents any multicast traffic in the 239.192.0.0/10 group range from congesting the T1 link into the Internet. This boundary also prevents sensitive Organization-Local multicast traffic from leaving the company and entering the Internet.

The last level of the sample hierarchy is the Global zone, which is intended for multicast traffic that is to reach outside of the company's network and travel into the Internet. These sources would use a multicast group address allocated out of the 224.0.1.0–238.255.255.255 range and must limit their rates to 128 kbps so as to not overload the T1 Internet access link shown in the drawing. In addition, hosts inside of the company network are able to receive multicast traffic originated in the Internet.

Configuring Scoped Zones

Several key tasks must be accomplished to configure scoped zones to control multicast bandwidth in a PIM sparse mode (PIM-SM) network. These tasks include

- Configuring Site-Local Multicast Boundaries
- Configuring Organization-Local Multicast Boundaries
- Defining Site-Local RPs and Mapping Agents
- Defining Organization RPs and Mapping Agents

Each task is covered in detail in the following sections. The last two tasks in the list are specific to sparse mode networks and require some careful planning if Auto-RP is in use. Careful planning is required to ensure that RPs and Mapping Agents are properly defined for all group ranges at all sites. (Unfortunately, scoped zones cannot be used with Bootstrap routers (BSRs). The reasons are discussed in "Scoped Zones and BSR.")

The sparse mode network shown in Figure 16-2 is used in the configuration examples that follow. Because the network is to use sparse mode, each site must have its own RP/Mapping Agent for the Site-Local group range. (In this example, the Site Local RP and the Mapping Agent are configured on the same router for simplicity. In actual practice, these functions may be assigned to separate routers if necessary.)

In addition to the Site-Local RPs and Mapping Agents inside each site network, a primary RP must be configured to handle the remaining multicast group ranges (including the Organization-Local group range). The router used for this function can be any router in the network and might even be one of the Site-Local RPs. However, the Organization Mapping Agent(s) for the network cannot be assigned to the same router as the Site-Local Mapping Agent(s) routers. The reason for this restriction is discussed in more detail in the next few sections on configuration.

Configuring Site-Local Boundaries

The first step to building scoped zones is to configure the Site-Local boundary on the three border routers shown in Figure 16-2. This step is accomplished by using the configurations shown in Examples 16-5, 16-6, and 16-7.

Example 16-5 *Configuration of Headquarters Site Border Router A*

```
Interface Serial0
 description "T1 line to Los Angeles (Site B)"
 ip address 192.168.255.1 255.255.255.252
 ip pim sparse-dense
 ip multicast boundary 10
 ip multicast ttl-threshold 16

Interface Serial1
 description "T1 line to Atlanta (Site C)"
 ip address 192.168.255.5 255.255.255.252
 ip pim sparse-dense
 ip multicast boundary 10
 ip multicast ttl-threshold 16

access-list 10 deny 239.255.0.0 0.0.255.255
access-list 10 permit any
```

Example 16-6 *Configuration of Border Router B*

```
Interface Serial0
 description "T1 line to HQ"
 ip address 192.168.255.2 255.255.255.252
 ip multicast boundary 10
 ip multicast ttl-threshold 16

access-list 10 deny 239.255.0.0 0.0.255.255
access-list 10 permit any
```

Example 16-7 *Configuration of Border Router C*

```
Interface Serial0
 description "T1 line to HQ"
 ip address 192.168.255.6 255.255.255.252
 ip multicast boundary 10
 ip multicast ttl-threshold 16

access-list 10 deny 239.255.0.0 0.0.255.255
access-list 10 permit any
```

In these configurations, the **ip multicast boundary** commands block all Site-Local multicast traffic (the 239.255.0.0/16 range) from entering and/or leaving via the site via the border serial interfaces. This multicast boundary also protects the interfaces from becoming congested with potentially high-rate, Site-Local multicast traffic that shouldn't ever leave the site.

In addition to the multicast boundary, the **ip multicast ttl-threshold** command, also defined on the border interfaces, prevents Site-Local Candidate-RP (C-RP) announcements from leaking out of the site. This topic is discussed in more detail when the Site-Local RP/Mapping Agents are defined.

Configuring Organization-Local Boundaries

The next step is to define the Organization-Local boundary on the Autonomous System (AS) border router in the Headquarters site (Site A) as shown in Example 16-8.

Example 16-8 *Configuration of the Headquarters AS Border Router*

```
Interface Serial0
 ip address 10.1.1.1 255.255.255.0
 ip pim sparse-dense
 ip multicast boundary 10
 ip multicast ttl-threshold 128

access-list 10 deny 239.0.0.0 0.0.0.255
access-list 10 deny 224.0.1.39
access-list 10 deny 224.0.1.40
access-list 10 permit any
```

In this configuration, the **ip multicast boundary** command is being used to block all multicast traffic in the 239.0.0.0/8 range from entering and/or leaving the company via the AS border serial interfaces. This command protects the company from the possibility of its internal multicast traffic leaving the network and flowing into the Internet. The **ip multicast ttl-threshold** command also defined on the AS border interface is an optional command that also helps to ensure that sensitive company multicast traffic doesn't leak into the Internet. By using a Time To Live (TTL) value of 127 or less on all internal company multicasts, the **ttl-threshold** of 128 set on this interface also prevents the multicast traffic from leaking into the Internet.

Configuring Site-Local RPs and Mapping Agents

The next step is to configure an RP and a Mapping Agent in each of the three sites for the Site-Local group range as shown in Examples 16-9, 16-10, and 16-11. This step is necessary because the operation of Site-Local multicast at each site is independent of the other sites. The trick here is to configure things so that the candidate RP's Announcement messages and the Mapping Agent's Discovery messages for the Site-Local group range don't leak into a neighboring site. To accomplish this, careful scoping of the TTL values of the candidate RP Announcement messages and Mapping Agent Discovery messages is necessary.

Example 16-9   *Configuration of Site-Local RP/Mapping Agent in Remote Site A*

```
interface Loopback0
 ip address 192.168.10.3 255.255.255.255
 ip pim sparse-dense

ip pim send-rp-discovery scope 15
ip pim send-rp-announce Loopback0 scope 15 group 20

access-list 20 permit 239.255.0.0 0.0.255.255
```

Example 16-10   *Configuration of Site-Local RP/Mapping Agent in Remote Site B*

```
interface Loopback0
 ip address 192.168.10.2 255.255.255.255
 ip pim sparse-dense

ip pim send-rp-discovery scope 15
ip pim send-rp-announce Loopback0 scope 15 group 20

access-list 20 permit 239.255.0.0 0.0.255.255
```

Example 16-11   *Configuration of Site-Local RP/Mapping Agent in Remote Site C*

```
interface Loopback0
 ip address 192.168.10.1 255.255.255.255
 ip pim sparse-dense

ip pim send-rp-discovery scope15
ip pim send-rp-announce Loopback0 scope 15 group 20

access-list 20 permit 239.255.0.0 0.0.255.255
```

Notice in the preceding configurations that a loopback interface has been defined for use as the RP address. The use of loopback interfaces permits careful crafting of which router is the primary RP and which router is the secondary RP for a specific group range.

In these configurations, the **ip pim send-rp-announce** command and its associated access list cause the router to advertise itself as a candidate RP for the Site-Local group range, 239.255.0.0/16. Notice that the TTL scope has been carefully set to 15 hops. This setting, combined with a **ttl-threshold** of 16 set on **Serial0** (see the Border Routers' configurations in the previous section) prevents the Site-Local candidate RP Announcement messages from leaking outside the sites.

The **ip pim send-rp-discovery** command shown in the preceding configurations defines the router as a Mapping Agent. Like the **ip pim send-rp-announce** command, this command is also defined with a TTL scope of 15 to prevent the Site-Local Mapping Agent's Discovery messages (containing Site-Local RP information) from leaking outside the site.

Again, the goal of the configurations shown in this and the preceding sections is to configure an RP at each site that is dedicated to handling Site-Local multicast traffic. Additionally, care must be taken in the configuration of these Site-Local RPs and Mapping Agents so as to avoid interfering with the operation of the Organization-Local RP.

Configuring the Organization RP and Mapping Agent

The final step is to configure an Organization RP(s) and Mapping Agent(s) whose function is to cover all other multicast groups (224.0.0.0–238.255.255.255) not in the Site-Local multicast group range (Example 16-12). Although there is some flexibility in which router(s) in the network to configure as candidates for the Organization RP, the selection and configuration of the Organization Mapping Agent(s) must be carefully crafted so that it never sends Discovery messages that contain any Site-Local RP mapping information. If this were allowed to happen, the Mapping Agent would be sending Site-Local RP information that was valid only for the site in which it resides. However, because the Discovery messages sent by the Organization Mapping Agent reaches all routers in the network, it would contaminate other sites with erroneous Site-Local RP mapping information.

In the example shown in Figure 16-2, Border Router A is used as a combined RP and Mapping Agent for the Organization. (This choice was made to simplify the example. Separate routers could be used to perform these functions.)

Example 16-12   *Configuration of Organization RP/Mapping Agent (on Border Router A)*

```
interface Loopback0
 ip address 192.168.1.3 255.255.255.255

ip pim send-rp-discovery scope 64
ip pim send-rp-announce Loopback0 scope 64 group-list 20
ip pim rp-announce-filter rp-list 10

access-list 10 deny 192.168.10.0 0.0.0.255
access-list 10 permit all

access-list 20 permit 224.0.0.0 7.255.255.255
access-list 20 permit 232.0.0.0 3.255.255.255
access-list 20 permit 236.0.0.0 1.255.255.255
access-list 20 permit 238.0.0.0 0.255.255.255
```

In Example 16-12 the **ip pim send-rp-announce** command is used (along with its associated access-list) to configure the router as a candidate Organization RP for groups 224.0.0.0–238.255.255.255. In this case, the TTL scope has been set to 64 so that RP Announcement messages will be propagated to all routers in the network and not be blocked by the **ttl-thresholds** set on **Serial0** and **Serial1**.

Because this router is also designated as an Organization Mapping Agent, the **ip pim send-rp-discovery** command is also configured. Like the **ip pim send-rp-announce** command, the TTL scope of this command is also set to 64 so that the Mapping Agent's Discovery messages (containing Organization RP mapping information) will be propagated to all routers in the network.

Finally, and probably most important, an **ip pim rp-announce-filter** (as seen in the configuration example above) must be configured on all Organization Mapping Agents so that they will ignore Site-Local candidate RP announcements. This is crucial step because any Site-Local RP mapping information learned by the Organization Mapping Agents is propagated to all routers in the network. This erroneous Site-Local RP information would conflict with Site-Local RP mapping information being sent by each site's own Site-Local RP/Mapping Agent and would cause Site-Local multicast to break. (It would break because routers inside the site would select an RP in another site for Site-Local traffic.)

NOTE   Unfortunately, any hosts whose Designated Router is serving as an Organization Mapping Agent will be unable to send/receive Site-Local traffic. Therefore, this factor should be considered when assigning this task to routers in the network. In the example given, this task was assigned to a Border router that does not have any directly connected hosts. When this book was written, Cisco Systems was researching the addition of new features that will avoid this problem and make scoped zone configuration easier.

Scoped Zones and BSR

All the previous discussion and configuration examples assumed that Auto-RP was in use in a PIMv1 or PIMv2 network. In general, Auto-RP supplies more robust features than BSR does when it comes to addressing scoped zones. In fact, the current definition of BSR (summer 1999) is not capable of handling scoped zones for a variety of reasons. For example, only a single BSR may be elected under the current definition of PIMv2 BSR. In addition, the messages sent from the single BSR are flooded throughout the entire PIM network. Finally, the current candidate RP message format does not have any support to indicate that the candidate is for a scoped zone. Even if this were the case, some way is needed to clearly identify which portion of the network the candidate RP advertisement is valid.

Research is underway in the Internet Engineering Task Force (IETF) to extend the standard BSR mechanism to support scoped zones. However at this time, scoped zones can be accomplished only by using Auto-RP and the methods outlined earlier.

Controlling Multicast Traffic Paths

A common situation that network engineers face requires them to *traffic engineer* the flow of multicast traffic so that it follows specific paths through their network.

Although traffic engineering was relatively simple to accomplish for unicast traffic by carefully adjusting routing metrics, summarizing routes, or using redistributed static routes, the same is not necessarily true for multicast traffic. Multicast routing is *upside-down routing* primarily concerned about the source IP address in the packet (that is, where the traffic came from) and how to calculate the proper Reverse Path Forwarding (RPF) interface, instead of the destination IP address. (Remember, it helps if you stand on your head when trying to understand IP multicast routing because it is upside-down routing.) The upside-down nature of IP multicast routing, traffic engineering of multicast flows a relatively complex undertaking.

This section examines some aspects and issues of traffic engineering of IP multicast, including

- Using alternative sources of RPF information
- GRE tunnels
- Pseudo load-sharing

In addition, a simple example of multicast traffic engineering is presented along with sample configurations.

Alternative Sources of RPF Information

Chapter 10, "Using PIM Dense Mode," points out that the RPF calculation in Cisco's PIM implementation is not necessarily limited to using information in the unicast routing table. Chapter 13, "Connecting to DVMRP Networks," includes several examples in which Distance Vector Multicast Routing Protocol (DVMRP) route table information, instead of information from the unicast routing table, is used for the RPF calculation.

As of Cisco's 12.0S version of IOS, the following are the possible sources of RPF information:

- Unicast Route Table
- MBGP Route Table
- DVMRP Route Table
- Static Mroute Table

These alternative sources of RPF information can be helpful when trying to traffic engineer the flow of IP multicast traffic in networks. Primarily, administrative distance is used to determine exactly which source of information the RPF calculation is based on. The specific rules are as follows:

1 All the preceding sources of RPF data are searched for a match on the source IP address. (Remember that when using shared trees, the RP address is used instead of the source address.)

2 If more than one matching route is found, the route with the lowest administrative distance is used.

3 If the administrative distances are equal, then the following order of preference (listed from most to least preferred) is used: static mroutes, DVMRP routes, Multicast Gateway Border Protocol (MBGP) routes, unicast routes.

4 If multiple entries for a route occur within the same route table, the longest matching route is used.

Traffic Engineering with Static Mroutes

Multicast static routes (called a *static mroute,* or *mroute* for short) are similar to their close cousins, unicast static routes, with the following differences.

Multicast static routes

- Are used to calculate RPF information, not to forward traffic
- Cannot be redistributed

Static mroutes are strictly local to the router on which they are defined; hence the final bullet item. Because PIM does not have its own routing protocol *per se*, there is really no way to distribute static mroutes through out the network. This situation tends to make the use of multicast static mroutes more of an administrative headache than the use of unicast static routes.

Static mroutes are stored in the Cisco router in a separate table called the *static mroute table*. Multicast static routes may be entered into a Cisco router's static mroute table using the **ip mroute** Cisco IOS global configuration command. This command was introduced in IOS version 11.0 and has the following format:

```
[no] ip mroute <source> <mask> [<protocol><as-number>] [route-map <map>]
                        {<rpf-address> | <interface>} [<distance>]
```

This command enters an IP multicast static route into the static mroute table for the source range specified by the ***<source>*** and ***<mask>*** qualifiers. Sources that match the specified range will RPF to either the IP address specified by ***<rpf-address>*** or a local interface on the router specified by the ***<interface>*** value. When an ***<rpf-address>*** is specified, a recursive lookup is done from the unicast routing table on this address to find the directly connected neighbor router.

The administrative distance of an mroute may be specified by the use of the optional ***<distance>*** value. (If this value is not specified, the distance of the mroute defaults to zero.) If the static mroute has the same distance as another RPF source, the static mroute will take precedence. There are only two exceptions to this rule: directly connected routes and the default unicast route.

In addition to the normal ***<source>*** and ***<mask>*** matching qualifiers, other matching criteria may be specified to further tune the matching of source addresses. For example, if the ***<protocol><as-number>*** value is specified, the mroute applies to only those sources that have routes that have been learned by the specified routing process. If the **route-map** ***<map>*** clause is specified, further classification can be accomplished by using **match** clauses in the specified route map ***<map>***.

Static Mroute Example

The order that static mroutes are configured is important. The router searches the static mroute table in the order that they were configured. If a matching entry is found, the search terminates and the information in the matching static mroute is used. (Remember that the distance of this matching static mroute is compared to the distance of any other matching routes found in the other sources of RPF information. The static mroute is used if its distance is equal to or less than the distance of the other routes.) The example in Figure 16-3 demonstrates the use of static mroutes as well as their order-specific nature.

Figure 16-3   *Static Mroute Example*

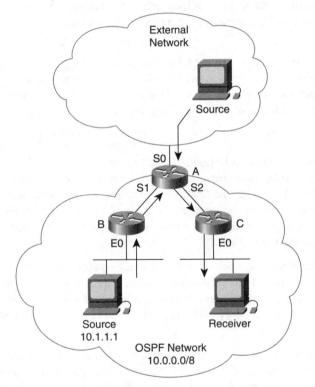

In this example, Router A is a border router that connects a PIM multicast network using Open Shortest Path First (OSPF) Protocol as the unicast routing protocol to an external network via a serial interface. The goal here is to use static mroutes to get Router A to RPF to **Serial0** for all multicast traffic from sources in the external network. At the same time, Router A should correctly RPF for sources inside the OSPF network. Consider the following possible static mroute configuration:

```
ip mroute 0.0.0.0 0.0.0.0 Serial0
ip mroute 10.0.0.0 255.0.0.0 ospf 1 Null0 255
```

In this configuration, the first mroute is a default route, which matches on any source. This mroute returns an RPF interface of **Serial0** and an administrative distance of zero. The second mroute matches on sources in the 10.0.0.0/8 network that have been learned via OSPF in the internal network. This mroute returns an RPF interface of **Null0** and an administrative distance of 255. Consider what happens when this configuration is used.

When Router A receives multicast traffic from a source in the external network, a search of the static mroute table matches on the first entry (the default mroute) and the search terminates. Because the distance of this mroute is zero, it is preferred over all other sources of RPF information and is used for the RPF calculation. The result is that Router A can RPF correctly to interface **Serial0** for all multicast traffic arriving from sources in the external network. However, when Router A receives multicast traffic from a source inside the OSPF network, a search of the static mroute table again matches on the first entry and terminates. Unfortunately, this behavior causes Router A to RPF to interface **Serial0,** which, in turn, results in RPF failures for all multicast traffic originated by sources inside the OSPF network. Obviously, this does not meet our needs.

Now, consider what happens when the static mroute entries are reordered as shown in the following configuration:

```
ip mroute 10.0.0.0 255.0.0.0 ospf 1 Null0 255
ip mroute 0.0.0.0 0.0.0.0 Serial0
```

Now, the first mroute is the one that matches sources in the 10.0.0.0/8 network that have been learned via OSPF in the internal network. The default route is now the second entry in the static mroute table. Consider what happens when this new configuration is used.

When Router A receives multicast traffic from a source in the external network, a search of the static mroute table does not match on the first entry but matches on the second entry. Again, the distance of the second mroute is zero and is therefore preferred over all other sources of RPF information. Router A will therefore RPF correctly to interface **Serial0** for multicast traffic arriving from the external network. This time, when multicast traffic is received from the source inside the OSPF network, a search of the static mroute table matches on the first entry and the search terminates. (The search matches on the first entry because the source address is in the 10.0.0.0/8 network and there is a route for this network that was learned by OSPF.) The information in this first mroute indicates an RPF interface of **Null0** and an administrative distance of 255. However, the RPF calculation doesn't stop here. Because the normal administrative distance of the 10.0.0.0/8 route in the OSPF route table is 90, it is preferred over the static mroute. Therefore, the matching static mroute is not used to calculate the RPF interface. Instead, the information in the OSPF route table is used to calculate the RPF interface, which causes Router A to RPF to **Serial1** for traffic from source 10.1.1.1. This situation causes Router A to RPF as desired for both external and internal multicast sources.

The currently defined static mroutes in a Cisco router may be displayed by the use of the **show ip mroute static** IOS command. Example 16-13 depicts the output of this command, assuming that the static mroutes presented in the previous configuration have been defined.

Example 16-13   *Sample* **show ip mroute static** *Output*

```
Router-A# show ip mroute static
Mroute: 10.0.0.0/8, interface: Null0
  Protocol: ospf 1, distance: 255, route-map: none
Mroute: 0.0.0.0/0, interface: Serial0
  Protocol: none, distance: 0, route-map: none
```

Traffic Engineering with DVMRP Routes

DVMRP routes may be exchanged between Cisco routers and used as the source of RPF data. Chapter 13 points out that the default administrative distance of DVMRP routes is zero. This distance generally makes them preferred over unicast routes, although it is possible to modify the distance of DVMRP routes by using other IOS configuration commands.

If it becomes desirable to use DVMRP routes between Cisco routers for multicast traffic engineering purposes, the fact that an inherent unicast route to DVMRP route redistribution of connected routes is on by default becomes important. In addition, if DVMRP routes are used for multicast traffic engineering, this default redistribution of connected routes is generally extended to all routes in the unicast routing table. This situation can introduce redistribution problems similar to those encountered when unicast route redistribution is in use. Therefore, care must be taken that this redistribution doesn't introduce route loops or other instabilities to the multicast routing process.

Figure 16-4 shows what can happen if this redistribution is not considered. Here are two routers with parallel links between them.

Figure 16-4   *Unicast-DVMRP Route Redistribution Problem*

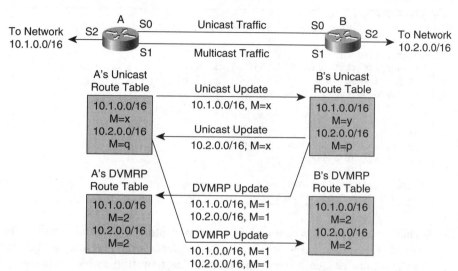

One is to be used for multicast traffic and the other for unicast traffic. The detailed configuration that a network engineer might initially try to use for these two routers is shown in Example 16-14 and Example 16-15.

Example 16-14   *Initial Router A Configuration*

```
interface Serial0
 ip address 10.1.255.1 255.255.255.252

interface Serial1
 ip address 10.1.255.5 255.255.255.252
 ip pim sparse-dense
 ip dvmrp unicast-routing
 ip dvmrp metric 1


interface Serial2
 ip address 10.1.1.1 255.255.255.252
 ip pim sparse-dense

eigrp 1 network 10.0.0.0
 passive-interface serial1
```

Example 16-15 *Initial Router B Configuration*

```
interface Serial0
 ip address 10.1.255.2 255.255.255.252

interface Serial1
 ip address 10.1.255.6 255.255.255.252
 ip pim sparse-dense
 ip dvmrp unicast-routing
 ip dvmrp metric 1

interface Serial2
 ip address 10.2.1.1 255.255.255.252
 ip pim sparse-dense

eigrp 1 network 10.0.0.0
 passive-interface serial1
```

Serial0 on each router is configured for unicast routing only so that it will be used for forward-only unicast traffic between the two routers. **Serial1** is configured on both routers as a PIM multicast interface with **ip dvmrp unicast-routing** enabled so that only multicast traffic will flow over the link. In addition, the network engineer has added the **ip dvmrp metric 1** command on **Serial1** so that all the unicast routes are advertised between the two routers. Unfortunately, this command introduces a problem that can be seen in Figure 16-4. Notice that as a result of the unicast to DVMRP redistribution in Router B, a DVMRP route to network 10.1.0.0/16 is advertised to Router A. This step results in an entry in Router A's DVMRP route table for network 10.1.0.0/16. Because the default distance of DVMRP routes is zero, Router A will prefer this route over the unicast route table entry, which causes Router A to incorrectly RPF to **Serial1** for all 10.1.0.0 traffic, instead of to **Serial2** as it should.

To advertise the correct DVMRP routing information, the router configurations should be modified to be more specific about which routes to advertise by the use of access-lists as shown in Examples 16-16 and 16-17.

Example 16-16 *Modified Router A Configuration*

```
interface Serial0
 ip address 10.1.255.1 255.255.255.252

interface Serial1
 ip address 10.1.255.5 255.255.255.252
 ip pim sparse-dense
 ip dvmrp unicast-routing
 ip dvmrp metric 1 10

interface Serial2
 ip address 10.1.1.1 255.255.255.252
 ip pim sparse-dense

access-list 10 permit 10.1.0.0 0.0.255.255
access-list 10 deny all

eigrp 1 network 10.0.0.0
 passive-interface serial1
```

Example 16-17 *Modified Router B Configuration*

```
interface Serial0
 ip address 10.1.255.2 255.255.255.252

interface Serial1
 ip address 10.1.255.6 255.255.255.252
 ip pim sparse-dense
 ip dvmrp unicast-routing
 ip dvmrp metric 1 10

interface Serial2
 ip address 10.2.1.1 255.255.255.252
 ip pim sparse-dense

access-list 10 permit 10.2.0.0 0.0.255.255
access-list 10 deny all

eigrp 1 network 10.0.0.0
 passive-interface serial1
```

This example of the unicast to DVMRP redistribution problem is highly simplified. Real-world networks tend to be more complex and require careful attention to detail to ensure that this sort thing doesn't happen. For example, consider the more complex scenario that occurs if **Serial2** on both Routers A and B had a unicast route to networks 10.1.0.0/16 and 10.2.0.0/16.

Traffic Engineering Example

I have frequently encountered customers who are using IP multicast to distribute important data that needs a high degree of reliable delivery. Although some application layer techniques provide forms of reliable multicast, most of these techniques rely on some form of retransmission. However, some applications just cannot wait for the loss to be detected and the retransmission requested and received. In these cases, I've seen customers use what I loosely call *physical multicast diversity* to deliver redundant multicast streams.

NOTE   Contrary to what you might think, physical multicast diversity is not a lecture topic at a company political-correctness meeting. I actually borrowed the concept from the radio communications industry where two (or more) redundant radio signals are transmitted from one site to the next. The two transmitted radio signals are sent from two antennas that are a short distance apart (in radio wavelength terms). The benefit of this system is that when radio wave fading occurs, both transmission paths are rarely affected at the same time. The result is that the receiving station is able to receive the information via one signal or the other because a fade on both signals at the same time is unlikely to occur.

Figure 16-5 shows physical multicast diversity being used to send redundant multicast traffic from two central sources via different physical paths through the network.

Figure 16-5   *Example of Physical Multicast Diversity*

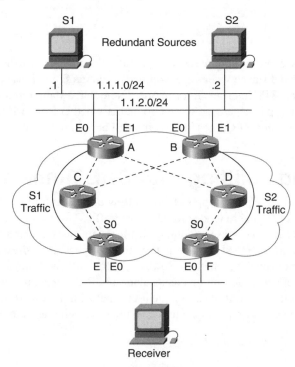

Both of these flows are arriving at the receiving node simultaneously, and the application level program simply discards packets from one of the duplicate flows. However, if a failure in the network results in the loss of one flow, the redundant flow is unlikely to be affected (if the network is designed well).

By using multicast traffic engineering, it is possible to achieve two physically diverse paths. The most obvious way might be to carefully craft the unicast route metrics so that the best route to source S1 is always path E-C-A and the best route to source S2 is always path F-D-B. This arrangement will result in (S1, G) Joins being always sent through Router C while (S2, G) Joins are always sent via Router D, thereby creating physically diverse paths.

Another way to build physically diverse paths would be to define the following static mroutes in routers E and F, as shown in Examples 16-18 and 16-19.

Example 16-18   *Configuration in Router E*

```
ip mroute 1.1.1.1 255.255.255.255 serial0
ip mroute 1.1.2.2 255.255.255.255 ethernet0
```

Example 16-19 *Configuration in Router F*

```
ip mroute 1.1.2.2 255.255.255.255 serial0
ip mroute 1.1.1.1 255.255.255.255 ethernet0
```

Because static mroutes are preferred over all other sources of RPF data (unless default administrative distance values are modified), Routers E and F use this information to calculate their RPF interface information. (Note that a static mroute was entered for each source. This step is necessary so that no matter whether Router E or Router F is the Designated Router (DR), the (S, G) Joins will be sent in the correct direction.)

Multicast Load Splitting with GRE Tunnels

Although it is possible to support load splitting of unicast traffic over equal-cost links, it is generally not possible to load split multicast traffic. This limitation occurs because even if multiple, equal-cost routes to a source exist in the unicast table, multicast can have only one incoming interface. (PIM uses the path with the highest IP address as the tiebreaker when presented with equal-cost paths.) However, with a little additional creative configuration and the use of a generic routing encapsulation (GRE) tunnel, it is possible to perform load splitting of multicast traffic across equal-cost paths. In Figure 16-6, for example, two routers connected with parallel equal-cost links are being used to carry unicast traffic.

Figure 16-6 *Pseudo Load Splitting over a Tunnel*

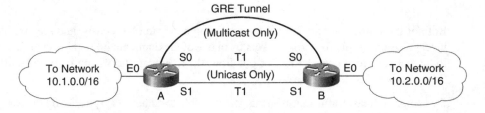

In addition, in Figure 16-6 a GRE tunnel is configured between these two routers to carry only multicast traffic. Using this configuration, multicast packets will be encapsulated in a GRE header and unicast across the T1 links between the two routers. Because the multicast packets are now being unicast via the tunnel mechanism, they can take advantage of the unicast load splitting over the two T1 links.

Configuring Multicast Load Splitting

Examples 16-20 and 16-21 show a configuration that accomplishes multicast load splitting.

Example 16-20 *Configuration in Router A for Multicast Load Splitting*

```
interface Tunnel0
 ip unnumbered Ethernet0
 ip pim sparse-dense
 tunnel source 10.1.1.1
 tunnel destination 100.1.5.3

interface Ethernet0
 ip address 10.1.1.1 255.255.255.0
 ip pim sparse-dense

interface Serial0
 ip address 10.1.255.1 255.255.255.252

interface Serial1
 ip address 10.1.255.5 255.255.255.252

ip mroute 10.2.0.0 0.0.255.255 Tunnel0

eigrp 1 network 10.0.0.0
 passive-interface Tunnel0
```

Example 16-21 *Configuration in Router B for Multicast Load Splitting*

```
interface Tunnel0
 ip unnumbered Ethernet0
 ip pim sparse-dense
 tunnel source 10.2.1.1
 tunnel destination 10.1.1.1

interface Ethernet0
 ip address 10.2.1.1 255.255.255.0
 ip pim sparse-dense

interface Serial0
 ip address 10.1.255.2 255.255.255.252

interface Serial1
 ip address 10.1.255.6 255.255.255.252

ip mroute 10.1.0.0 0.0.255.255 Tunnel0

eigrp 1 network 10.0.0.0
 passive-interface Tunnel0
```

Because multicast traffic is sent over the tunnel and unicast traffic via the two parallel serial links, the multicast topology is now incongruent with the unicast topology. Extra steps are now required to get Routers A and B to RPF correctly over the tunnel. In this particular example, static mroutes have been configured to force Routers A and B to RPF correctly via the tunnel for networks 10.2.0.0/16 and 10.1.0.0/16, respectively. (Notice also that care has been taken to ensure that the unicast routing protocols do not try to use the tunnel for unicast routing by the use of the **passive-interface** command.)

The approach to forcing multicast traffic to RPF correctly via the tunnel shown in this example is appropriate because networks 10.1.0.0/16 and 10.2.0.0/16 are both stub networks interconnected via Routers A and B. However, some other method for forcing multicast traffic to RPF correctly may be necessary for a different topology. One approach would be to run a different unicast routing protocol over the tunnel than is used for the rest of the network.

Process Versus Fast Switching

The same basic algorithms for the load splitting of unicast traffic apply to multicast load splitting using a tunnel. If fast switching is enabled on the tunnel (the default), load splitting over the equal-cost links will be done on a flow basis. The reason is that the fast-switching cache for multicast is made up of special Media Access Control (MAC) header fields in each outgoing interface entry of each entry of the mroute table.

The output shown in Example 16-22 of a **show ip mcache** command executed on Router A illustrates how the multicast fast-switching cache is organized.

Example 16-22 *Sample **show ip mcache** Output*

```
RouterA# show ip mcache
IP Multicast Fast-Switching Cache
(10.1.1.6/32, 224.1.1.1), Ethernet0, Last used: 00:00:00  Tunnel0
        MAC Header: 0F000800 (Serial1)
(10.1.1.6/32, 224.1.1.2), Ethernet0, Last used: 00:00:00  Tunnel0
        MAC Header: 0F000800 (Serial1)
(10.1.1.5/32, 224.1.1.3), Ethernet0, Last used: 00:00:00  Tunnel0
        MAC Header: 0F000800 (Serial0)
(10.1.1.5/32, 224.1.1.4), Ethernet0, Last used: 00:00:00  Tunnel0
        MAC Header: 0F000800 (Serial0)
```

Notice that the multicast fast-switching cache contains four (S, G) entries, each with an incoming interface of **Ethernet0**. As the output in Example 16-22 shows, each (S, G) flow has a separate MAC header and is associated with only one of the T1 links. This pattern clearly indicates that load splitting is being done on a flow basis.

NOTE	To be precisely correct, load splitting of multicast traffic over a tunnel is performed on an mroute table entry (that is, distribution tree) basis. However, because multicast traffic is normally forwarded using (S, G) entries by default, it is generally correct to say that the traffic is load split on a flow basis. However, if the forwarding uses (*, G) entries (as would be the case when an SPT-Threshold of infinity is used), then this statement is no longer correct. In this case, load splitting occurs on a shared tree basis, and all traffic of a particular shared tree flows over one of the serial links.

If process switching is in use on the tunnel, individual multicast packets are simply transmitted over the equal-cost links in a round-robin fashion. In this case, the multicast fast-switching cache entries are never populated, and new MAC header and physical interface information is computed every time a multicast packet is forwarded. Although this approach guarantees the most balanced usage of the physical interfaces that make up the tunnel, it comes at a much higher router CPU load. Therefore, just as in unicast process switching, multicast process switching should be used only on tunnels composed of links at T1 speeds and lower.

Broadcast-Multicast Traffic Conversion

Suppose that a network engineer wants to take advantage of a multicast-capable network but finds that the source, the receiver(s), or both do not support IP multicast. This situation often occurs in financial networks when a host has been IP broadcasting stock market data feeds to nodes on the local wire. As the network grows, the demand for this information usually begins to extend beyond the local wire out to hosts in other parts of the network. Frequently, the broadcast hosts do not support IP multicast, and network engineers resort to using UDP flooding techniques across the entire IP network. This approach usually meets with limited success, at least initially. However, UDP flooding is difficult to maintain, particularly as the network grows in size and complexity and typically quickly becomes an administrative nightmare. What is needed is a way to get this data to flow across a growing, IP multicast-capable network until the source and all receivers can be upgraded to new technology that supports native multicast.

Beginning with Cisco IOS release 11.1, it became possible to have the Cisco routers convert local wire IP broadcast traffic to multicast traffic at one end and reconvert that traffic to local wire IP broadcast at the other end.

The **ip multicast helper-map** command has the following two forms:

```
[no] ip multicast helper-map { broadcast | <broadcast-address> }
                             <group-address> <extended-acl> [ttl <ttl>]

[no] ip multicast helper-map  <group-address> <broadcast-address>
                             <extended-acl>
```

The first form of the command converts the destination address of any IP broadcast packets received on the interface that matches the specified ***<extended-acl>*** to the multicast group address specified by the ***<group-address>*** value. After the destination address conversion has been done, the packet appears to the Cisco router's multicast forwarding code as if it had actually been multicast by the source to ***<group-address>***. As a result, the packet is forwarded in the normal fashion and can take advantage of multicast fast switching.

It is important to note that the broadcast to multicast translation does not normally modify the TTL of the packet. However, if the optional **ttl *<ttl>*** clause is specified, the TTL value of the received broadcast packet is rewritten with the specified ***<ttl>*** value. This *ttl-remapping* feature can be very useful because it is not always possible to configure the broadcasting host to use a specific TTL value for IP broadcasts. For example, if the broadcast host is using a TTL value of 255, then the router will forward the translated broadcast packets as a multicast packet with a TTL of 254. (Remember that a router normally decrements the TTL value of all incoming packets before forwarding them.) If the network engineer is planning to use any TTL-Thresholds in the network, a TTL value of 255 may be too large and may allow these translated packets to leak out of the intended TTL-Threshold boundaries.

The second form of the command performs the inverse operation. That is, when the interface receives an IP multicast packet for the multicast group specified by the ***<group-address>*** value that also matches the ***<extended-acl>***, the destination address of the packet is converted to the IP broadcast address specified in the ***<broadcast-address>*** value. As long as this IP broadcast address is for a subnet directly attached to the router, the packet will be output to its associated interface.

NOTE   The preceding two commands translate incoming multicast or broadcast traffic. A common mistake is to configure the **ip multicast helper-map** command on an outgoing interface where non-multicast-capable receivers reside, which does not accomplish the desired goal.

Figure 16-7 shows broadcast-to-multicast conversion in action, using multicast helper maps. In the example, a non-multicast-capable host (at the top of the figure) is sending broadcast traffic with a destination UDP port number of 2000 to all hosts on the local network (10.1.1.0/24) via IP broadcasts. At the bottom of the figure is a non-multicast-capable host that wants to receive the traffic. By using the Cisco **ip multicast helper-map** interface configuration command at the points shown in the figure, local wire broadcasts received by Router A can be translated into IP multicast traffic, transmitted over the multicast-capable network, and converted back to local wire broadcasts by Router B.

Figure 16-7 *Broadcast-to-Multicast Conversion*

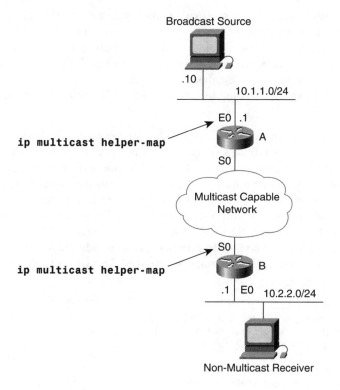

The details of the router configurations used in Figure 16-7 are given in Example 16-23 and Example 16-24.

Example 16-23 *Router A Configuration*

```
Interface Ethernet0
 ip address 10.1.1.10 255.255.255.0
 ip directed-broadcasts
 ip multicast helper-map broadcast 224.1.1.1 100 ttl 15

access-list 100 permit any any udp 2000
access-list 100 deny any any udp

ip forward-protocol udp 2000
```

In this configuration, the **ip multicast helper-map** command and its associated access-list instructs the router to translate any broadcast packets arriving on **Ethernet0** with a UDP destination port of 2000 to a multicast packet with a destination group address of 224.1.1.1. Notice also that the **ttl** clause was specified so that the TTL value of these received broadcast packets will be remapped to a value of 15. This step prevents the translated broadcast packets from being transmitted with a TTL value that is too large for this network.

In addition to the **ip multicast helper-map** command, the **ip directed-broadcasts** command was added to the **Ethernet0**. This command is necessary to enable the router to process the incoming broadcast packets on **Ethernet0**. If this command were not added, the router would simply ignore all incoming broadcast packets on this interface and they would not get translated to multicast. Even with this command added, the router will process only those broadcast packets with certain standard UDP port numbers (TFTP, BOOTP, DNS, NetBIOS Name Server, NetBIOS Datagram Server, and TACACS) by default. Therefore, it is also necessary to add the **ip forward-protocol udp 2000** command to instruct the router to also process the incoming broadcast packets with a UDP destination port of 2000.

Example 16-24 *Router B Configuration*

```
Interface Serial0
 ip address 172.16.255.2 255.255.255.252
 ip multicast helper-map 224.1.1.1 10.2.2.255 100
 ip igmp join-group 224.1.1.1

interface Ethernet0
 ip address 10.2.2.1 255.255.255.0
 ip directed-broadcast

access-list 100 permit any any udp 2000
access-list 100 deny any any udp

ip forward-protocol udp 2000
```

In the above configuration, interface **Serial0** on Router B has also been configured with an **ip multicast helper-map** command. This command and its associated access-list instructs the router to translate any incoming multicast packets with a destination group address of 224.1.1.1 and a UDP destination port of 2000 to a local wire broadcast to the 10.2.2.0/24 network. (10.2.2.255 is the broadcast address for the subnet configured on **Ethernet0**.) Again, it is necessary to also add the **ip directed-broadcast** interface command to **Ethernet0** and to add the **ip forward-protocol udp 2000** global command so that the router will properly forward the directed broadcast packets (that were translated from multicast packets) to **Ethernet0**.

In addition to these commands, the **ip igmp join-group** command was configured on **Serial0**. This command is necessary to get the router to join multicast group 224.1.1.1 so it can receive this multicast traffic. (This command was automatically added by IOS to the configuration of **Serial0** when the **ip multicast helper-map** command was entered.)

NOTE   The configurations shown in Example 16-23 and Example 16-24 assumed that both the sending host and all the receivers were not multicast capable. However, if the receiving hosts are multicast capable, then the configuration shown for Router B is not necessary. Likewise, if the sending host is multicast capable, the configuration shown for Router A is not necessary.

Summary

This chapter has examined several advanced, although reasonably common, multicast traffic engineering concepts and techniques. The first of these, bandwidth control, is a frequently used advanced technique, particularly as the volume of multicast traffic continues to increase. Traffic engineering of multicast traffic paths is also a commonly encountered requirement in multicast network design. Traffic engineering techniques can be used to increase the reliability of multicast traffic delivery and avoid congestion in the network. Finally, the use of tunneling and broadcast-to-multicast conversion features round out a short but important set of advanced multicast tools that should be in every multicast network engineer's toolkit.

CHAPTER 17

Inter-Domain Multicast Routing

Up to this point in the book, primarily all the discussion of IP multicast routing has been focused on intra-domain routing. Some may argue that Chapter 13, "Connecting to DVMRP Networks," offered some limited possibilities for inter-domain multicast routing and that the use of Distance Vector Multicast Routing Protocol (DVMRP) in the MBone constitutes a workable inter-domain multicast routing solution. However, the fact is that much work remains before truly scalable, inter-domain multicast routing is fully deployed throughout the Internet.

This chapter takes a brief look at some of the work on inter-domain multicast routing protocols that promises to extend IP multicast to the entire Internet. A brief description of two new protocols that provide improved inter-domain multicast routing is presented. These two protocols are

- Multiprotocol BGP (a.k.a. Multicast BGP) (MBGP)
- Multicast Source Discovery Protocol (MSDP)

Both protocols are taking off in popularity with many Internet service providers (ISPs) that are currently using MBGP and MSDP to provide reasonably scalable inter-domain multicast routing solutions, while the Internet Engineering Task Force (IETF) is working on protocols that will permit multicast to scale to even greater numbers. These future protocols currently in design by working groups of the IETF are

- Border Gateway Multicast Protocol (BGMP)
- Multicast Address Set-Claim (MASC)

Keep in mind that complete coverage of the topic of inter-domain multicast routing in general and the preceding protocols in particular is way beyond the scope of this book and is planned for another Cisco Press release.

Issues in Inter-Domain Multicast Routing

When the topic of extending inter-domain multicast beyond the outdated DVMRP-based MBone was first discussed by several ISPs, it was generally agreed that some sort of sparse mode protocol was necessary. (Clearly, the flood-and-prune behavior of dense mode protocols is unacceptable for use as an inter-domain multicast solution.)

In the summer of 1997, development engineers from Cisco Systems met with network engineers from all the major ISPs to discuss the topic of extending native IP multicast to the entire Internet. At that time, the IETF was just beginning to work on some new protocols (described briefly in the section titled "Future Protocols") that promised to provide solutions to the complex issues of inter-domain multicast routing. However, initial indications were that these protocols would be nontrivial to implement and would not be available and stable for quite some time. Therefore, the goal of this discussion was to see whether any alternatives could be found to deploy native IP multicast in the Internet in the immediate future.

Early in these discussions, it became clear that the consensus was that PIM sparse mode (PIM-SM) was the preferred multicast protocol for use inside the ISP's networks. This choice, however, introduced some problems because it is very problematical to interconnect multiple sparse mode domains.

NOTE	Although the current PIMv2 specification defines the function of PIM Multicast Border Routers (PMBR) and the concepts of (*, *, RP) multicast routing table entries, these techniques have some potential deficiencies. In the case where a PIM-SM domain serves as a transit network between two other PIM-SM clouds, these techniques cause the network to degenerate to dense-mode-like operation. Therefore, the Cisco Systems current implementation of PIM-SM does not support these concepts. Additionally, the major ISPs do not seem to be interested in pursuing this approach to inter-domain multicast routing for this reason.

In general, the problem revolves around the fact that in PIM-SM, receivers and senders learn of each other through a single rendezvous point (RP). Furthermore, if each ISP network is to remain autonomous and not be dependent on its competition, it must maintain its own RP for all groups. This requirement clearly rules out the idea of using a single RP for a group across the entire Internet. On the other hand, by using independent RPs in each ISP domain, learning of senders and receivers in other domains becomes a problem.

During these meetings, other issues regarding inter-domain multicast in the Internet were discussed. In the end, the ISPs listed the following major requirements that must be met before they could consider deployment of native multicast in the Internet to be feasible:

- An Explicit Join protocol inside the domain for efficiency
- Use of an existing (unicast) operations model for multicast peering
- Not dependent on competitor's RPs
- Flexibility regarding RP placement

The first item was, in general, already met by normal PIM-SM operation. However, at that time, the last three items required the development of two new solutions: MBGP and MSDP. Both of these are introduced briefly in the next two sections.

Multiprotocol BGP

One of the key concerns of the ISPs was to minimize the learning curve for dealing with the additional operational burden of multicast peering. In addition, they wanted to have the same set of highly flexible peering controls for multicast routing that they have in their current Border Gateway Protocol (BGP) based unicast routing environment. The solution to this was simple: Use the recently defined extensions to BGP (defined in RFC 2283, Multiprotocol Extensions to BGP-4) to carry multicast routing information that can be used for Reverse Path Forwarding (RPF) calculations between autonomous systems.

New Multiprotocol BGP Attributes

The basic idea behind MBGP (when used in multicast circles, the *M* of MBGP is understood to mean *multicast* and not *multiprotocol*) is the definition of two new multiprotocol BGP attributes: MP_REACH_NLRI and MP_UNREACH_NLRI. These attributes would then be used to exchange reachability information for different address families and would be carried inside BGP update messages. Inside of these two new BGP attributes are the *Address Family Identifier* (AFI) and *Subsequent Address Family Identifier* (Sub-AFI) fields that are used to identify the protocol for which the reachability information is applicable.

In the case of IPv4, the AFI value is 1, and the Sub-AFI values used are shown in Table 17-1. From this information, one can see how these new multiprotocol BGP attributes can be used to have BGP carry both unicast routing and multicast RPF information in the same updates. In addition, it is now possible to configure BGP to advertise different paths for unicast and multicast traffic flow between to autonomous systems. This feature is important if an ISP wants to build incongruent multicast and unicast networks.

Table 17-1   *IPv4 (AFI=1) Sub-Address Family Identifiers*

Sub-AFI = 1	Network layer routing information (NLRI) is used for unicast routing.
Sub-AFI = 2	NLRI is used for multicast RPF calculation.
Sub-AFI = 3	NLRI is used for both unicast routing and multicast RPF calculation.

NOTE   The prefixes passed in the attributes shown in Table 17-1 contain unicast prefixes, not
multicast group addresses and are used for multicast RPF calculations. A common
misconception is that MBGP is a replacement for PIM. MBGP does not perform any form
of multicast distribution tree building. It simply permits multicast RPF information to be
carried inside the new multiprotocol attributes.

Cisco's MBGP Implementation

Cisco's implementation of MBGP uses the same basic BGP configuration command set
with which the ISP's operations staff is already familiar. One of the key additions to the
BGP command syntax is the **nlri** clause, which can be added to the usual BGP **neighbor**
<foo> **remote-as** command.

This addition results in the following new BGP neighbor configuration command format:

```
[no] neighbor <address> remote-as <asn> [nlri unicast multicast]
```

This command configures a BGP peer and associates the autonomous system number
specified by the **remote-as** *<asn>* clause. If the **multicast** keyword is supplied in the
optional **nlri** clause, multicast NLRI is sent to the neighbor. On the other hand, if the
unicast keyword is supplied, unicast NLRI is sent to the neighbor. If both keywords are
supplied, the neighbor is sent both unicast and multicast NLRI. If the **nlri** clause is omitted,
only unicast NLRI is sent.

Multicast NLRI is sent in the new MP_REACH_NLRI and MP_UNREACH_NLRI
attributes, whereas unicast NLRI is sent using conventional BGP encoding to maintain
compatibility with existing BGP neighbors. This newer version of Cisco BGP negotiates
NLRI in the Capabilities option of the Open message to make sure that its neighbor can
handle these new attributes. Therefore, both sides of a BGP connection must be configured
to have at least one NLRI in common or the Transmission Control Protocol (TCP)
connection will not be established. If, for example, one side is configured for unicast only
and the other for multicast only, the connection will not come up and error messages will
be displayed on the Cisco router console port.

In addition to the modification to the BGP neighbor command syntax to support MBGP,
several other new commands were added to provide additional tuning and route
redistribution control to MBGP. For example, Cisco also added configuration commands to
allow the ISPs to redistribute existing DVMRP routing information into the new MBGP
domains. This step was necessary to provide the ISPs with a smooth transition strategy from
any existing DVMRP infrastructures that they might have had.

Again, a complete tutorial on MBGP or the associated new configuration commands
implemented in recent versions of Cisco Internetwork Operating System (IOS) is beyond
the scope of this book. (For up-to-date information on Cisco's MBGP implementation and
command set, refer to the following Web site: ftp://ftp-eng.cisco.com/ipmulticast.html.)

MBGP Example

Figure 17-1 shows an example of incongruent unicast/multicast traffic flow between two autonomous systems. In this example, Router B has been configured to advertise both unicast and multicast information to its neighbor MBGP router, Router A. Notice that the BGP update sent to Router A contains an old-style unicast NLRI attribute, advertising that network 192.192.25.0/24 is reachable via a next hop of 192.168.100.2. This information tells Router A that it must send any unicast traffic for this network via the top link in the figure.

Figure 17-1   *Incongruent Unicast/Multicast MBGP*

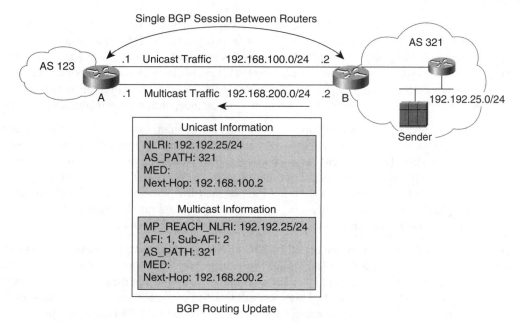

In addition, the BGP Update message contains a new style MP_REACH_NLRI attribute with an AFI/Sub-AFI that indicates this information is to be used for multicast RPF calculations for multicast sources in the 192.192.25.0/24 network. Specifically, the next-hop information in this attribute indicates that Router A should RPF to 192.168.200.2 for sources in the 192.192.25.0/24 network. If PIM-SM is being used between these two networks, Router A sends (S, G) Joins for sources in this network via the bottom link shown in the figure, which causes multicast traffic to flow via this link.

Multicast Source Discovery Protocol

At this point, the combination of PIM-SM and MBGP has enabled us to meet the first two ISP requirements for deploying native multicast in the Internet. The last two requirements—allowing independent RPs with flexible placement—required some rather creative thinking before a solution was found. Before launching into the details of this solution (which, if you haven't guessed by now, is MSDP), it would be beneficial to take a look at some history behind the birth of this solution.

A Little History

Once the decision to use PIM-SM and MBGP had been made, several ideas on how to solve the problem of interconnecting the shared trees of multiple PIM-SM networks were explored. These included such ideas as using some form of dynamic DNS to keep track of Group-to-RP mapping across the Internet. This particular idea was abandoned since it required a multicast group to be mapped to a single RP somewhere in the network. This failed to meet the ISP's third requirement (that is, independence from competitor's RPs).

Eventually, a temporary solution that met this requirement was found by having all ISP's place their network's RP on a PIM-DM network at a single Multicast Internet Exchange (MIX) point. This PIM-DM network was assigned its own unique autonomous system domain (10888) for the specific purpose of multicast peering. Each ISP would then externally MBGP peer with the other ISPs on the PIM-DM network, and multicast traffic would flow between the ISPs using dense mode flood-and-prune methods. This approach worked during the initial test phase but had several obvious drawbacks.

The first drawback was that not all ISPs that wished to participate had a presence at this IX, and, therefore, the AS 10888 PIM-DM network was extended to multiple IXs across the United States. This allowed other ISPs to participate by placing their network's RP on this extended PIM-DM network. This approach was fine as a temporary solution but was not desirable in the long run because the growing size of the PIM-DM cloud meant that multicast traffic was being transmitted across the United States using inefficient flood-and-prune techniques. In addition to these drawbacks, this method forced the ISPs to always place their RPs on the PIM-DM, AS 10888 domain, which was contrary to their last requirement (that is, must have flexibility regarding RP placement).

Even if the ISPs had agreed to forego this requirement, they still faced the problem of how to connect their customers' multicast networks to the PIM-SM network. Obviously, some other solution was needed to meet these requirements and tie together all these shared trees.

Finally, one of the ISPs proposed a totally different approach. Instead of trying to use the shared trees to tie together the PIM-SM networks, why not tie them together with source trees? If the RPs in each domain could somehow learn which sources were active in the other PIM-SM domains, the RPs could send Joins across the domains to join the (S, G) source tree when there were active receivers in their domain for group G. Furthermore, after last-hop routers receive traffic from these external sources down the shared tree, they too can join the source tree. This elegantly simple idea resulted in the development of MSDP.

MSDP Concepts

The key behind MSDP is that an RP in a PIM-SM domain knows about all active sources in its domain. If this first RP is peered with a second RP in another domain using MSDP, the first RP can send MSDP *Source Active* (SA) messages to the second.

Figure 17-2 shows several PIM-SM domains, each with their own independent RP that is MSDP peered to other RPs in other domains. To see how MSDP works, assume that a receiver in Domain E has joined multicast group 224.2.2.2, as shown in the upper right of Figure 17-2.

Figure 17-2 *MSDP Example—Step 1*

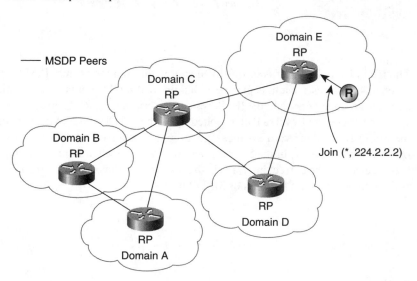

At this point, assume that a multicast source begins sending to this multicast group in Domain A, as shown in Figure 17-3.

Figure 17-3 *MSDP Example—Step 2*

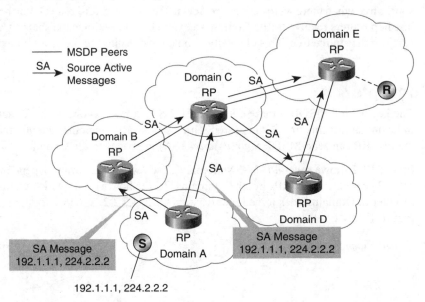

The RP in Domain A learns of this local source through the normal PIM Register mechanism and, as a result, begins periodically sending SA messages containing the source address, group address, and the IP address of the originating RP address to its MSDP peers. These messages are Reverse Path Flooded by all the MSDP nodes in the network away from the originating RP to avoid SA message looping. (Reverse Path Flooding uses the originators RP address in the SA message to determine whether an incoming SA message was received on the correct interface in the direction of the originator. If so, the SA message is flooded downstream to all other MSDP peers.)

When the SA messages reaches the RP for Domain E, the RP checks its mroute table and finds that it has active receivers for multicast group 224.1.1.1. This information causes the RP to send an (S, G) Join toward source 192.1.1.1, as shown in Figure 17-4.

Figure 17-4   *MSDP Example—Step 3*

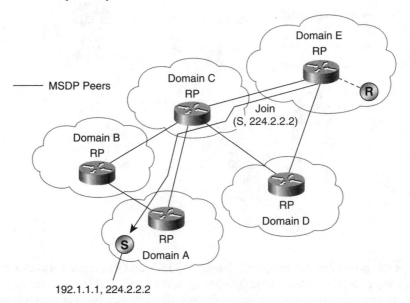

After this (S, G) Join reaches the first-hop router for the source in Domain A, a branch of the (S, G) source tree has been built from the source to the Domain E's RP, as shown in Figure 17-5. Multicast traffic can now flow from the source across the source tree to the RP and then down the shared tree in Domain E to the receiver.

Figure 17-5 *MSDP Example—Step 4*

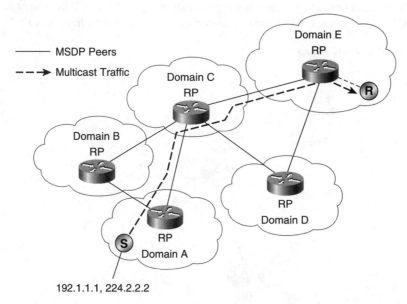

As this book went to press, MSDP usage by ISPs and enterprise network engineers was growing rapidly. Although MSDP does solve the initial problem of tying together PIM-SM domains, some critics question how far MSDP can scale. This concern is based on the fact that all active sources in the Internet result in SA messages being sent to identify them. Although this concern is valid, it should be pointed out that the IETF is still working on MSDP, and it will therefore most likely continue to evolve just as other protocols have to meet the increasing demands of the Internet. It is hoped that as MSDP evolves it will continue to improve in scalability for some time (or at least until the IETF develops the next protocol that accomplishes the same tasks in some other way).

Future Protocols

Although the combination of PIM-SM, MSDP, and MBGP is allowing many ISPs to deploy native inter-domain multicast service in their networks, the IETF is still defining other inter-domain multicast protocols. The hope is for these new protocols to permit multicast in the Internet to scale even further.

Although several multicast-related protocols are under design in the IETF, two key protocols deserve particular attention because they will have the biggest potential impact on IP multicast. These two protocols are

- Border Gateway Multicast Protocol (BGMP)
- Multicast Address Set-Claim (MASC)

The first protocol will provide a new inter-domain multicast routing protocol, and the second provides a method of dynamic multicast address allocation across the Internet. Both of these protocols are described in more detail in the following sections.

Border Gateway Multicast Protocol

BGMP is currently the IETF's proposed inter-domain multicast routing protocol for the future. The basic idea is that for any multicast group that is active in the Internet, there would be a single bidirectional shared tree that spans all domains that contain senders or receivers of this group. One of these domains (in this case, a domain is generally synonymous with an autonomous system) would be designated the root domain and would function as the root of the bidirectional shared tree. All other domains would send Joins and Prunes toward this root domain in the same fashion as routers do in a PIM-SM network. The key difference is that because the resulting shared tree is bidirectional, traffic can flow both up and down the tree.

Given that for any group only a single domain can function as the root of the shared tree in BGMP, it becomes important to have some sort of mechanism to determine which domain is to be root. The premise of BGMP is that there is (or will be by the time BGMP is implemented) some other mechanism in place that performs this function so that Joins can be forwarded through the Internet toward the root domain. The current IETF plans are to use a hierarchical multicast address allocation method that permits domains to request blocks of multicast addresses. The primary protocol currently slated by the IETF to accomplish this task is the MASC protocol and is briefly discussed in a following section. Therefore, the root domain for any multicast group would be the domain that was currently assigned that particular multicast address range.

Figure 17-6 shows a BGMP shared tree of domains in action. In this example, Domain B has allocated a multicast group range that includes address 224.2.2.2 and is, therefore, designated as the root domain for this group. In addition, Domains E, F, and G each have receivers that have just joined the multicast group. This process results in the Border Routers for those domains sending BGMP Joins toward the root domain as shown.

Figure 17-6   *BGMP Root Domain*

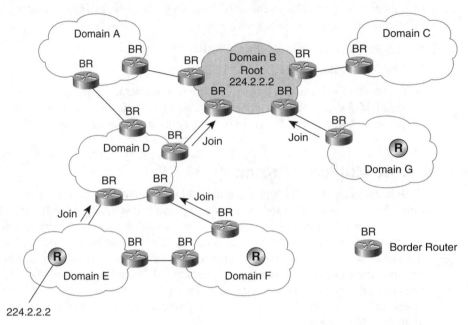

Figure 17-7 shows the shared tree of domains that result from the BGMP Joins that were sent in Figure 17-6.

Figure 17-7 also shows that a multicast source for this group has now gone active in Domain D and is transmitting traffic to the group. The intra-domain multicast routing protocol running inside of Domain D routes this traffic internally (indicated by the dashed arrows) to those BGMP Border Routers that are on the shared tree of domains. These Border Routers in turn forward the traffic up and down the bidirectional shared tree to the other domains (as shown by the solid arrows). When the traffic arrives at the Border Routers in Domains E, F, and G, the intra-domain multicast routing protocol running in those domains once again forwards this traffic internally (dashed arrows) to the receivers.

Figure 17-7 *BGMP Shared Tree of Domains*

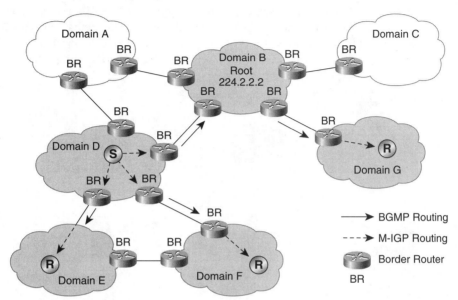

Multicast Address Set-Claim

Multicast address allocation has for some time been an area needing improved tools and techniques. The use of SDR (described in Chapter 4, "Multimedia Multicast Applications") for multicast allocation worked fine for the initial days of the Mbone. However, SDR's lack of scalability and its insuitability to non-multimedia applications has left the Internet in want of a better scheme for some time.

Presently, the IETF is hard at work on several protocols that will provide dynamic multicast allocation services both in the global Internet and inside enterprise intranets. Heading up this list of new protocols is MASC, which is a protocol that uses a hierarchical address allocation method.

Figure 17-8 briefly shows how MASC will work. At some key location(s) in the Internet (possibly at certain Internet Exchange points), a top-level MASC server will reside. This root MASC server will be responsible for the allocation of the global multicast address range into smaller contiguous blocks of addresses to the next lower level of MASC servers. Currently, it is envisioned that this first level of MASC servers would primarily consist of first-tier ISPs.

Figure 17-8 *MASC Hierarchy*

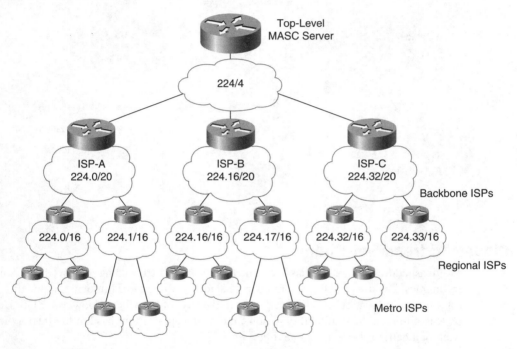

Each MASC server in the first-tier ISPs would send a *Set-Claim* message containing a requested range of multicast addresses to the root MASC server. If this range is available, the root MASC server would acknowledge the Set-Claim message and mark the range as allocated in its database. If, for some reason, some portion of the range has already been successfully claimed by another MASC server, the root server will propose an alternative range of available addresses to the requester. This back and forth negotiation would continue until the requester had successfully claimed an acceptable range of addresses (or finally gave up).

Once a MASC server has claimed a range of addresses, it can then make use of these addresses in its internal network as well as allocate smaller contiguous blocks of addresses to lower-tier MASC servers as shown in Figure 17-8. (The actual protocol that an end station will use inside of a domain to request a multicast address from a MASC server or one of its agents will be the Multicast Address Dynamic Client Allocation Protocol, or MADCAP. This protocol is also being defined by one of the working groups of the IETF.)

Because a successful MASC Set-Claim on a range of addresses is typically valid only for some finite period of time, a MASC server must periodically renew its claim. If the parent MASC server is experiencing address exhaustion, it may reduce the size of a lower-tier server's range in an attempt to free up some address space. Alternatively, a MASC server that is beginning to experience address exhaustion can also issue additional Set-Claims to its parent in an attempt to allocate more space.

It should be obvious that MASC is a very nontrivial protocol that must be carefully designed to avoid causing massive fragmentation of the limited resources of multicast addresses. If serious fragmentation does occur, one of the most incredibly complex, distributed, *garbage collection* problems that the computer industry has ever seen is bound to result. For this reason alone, the design of MASC is moving at a very cautious pace.

Summary

Inter-domain IP multicast is an area that is still in the early stages of development. Solutions to the problem of interconnecting several sparse mode domains such as MSDP and MBGP have only recently been developed enough for ISPs to begin converting their old DVMRP-based networks to more scalable PIM-SM networks. These ISPs are taking the first few steps toward truly enabling native IP multicast in the Internet. As the current protocols used for inter-domain IP multicast mature and/or new ones are introduced, the migration to a fully IP multicast–enabled Internet will be complete. At that time, a new age of Internet communication will have truly begun and exciting new IP multicast applications will become available to all Internet users.

PART VI

Appendix

PIM Packet Formats

This appendix contains the formats of all PIMv2 protocol messages and was largely taken directly from the current RFCs that define PIM-SM and PIM-DM. It is presented here primarily as a reference to the reader and is shown in the same textual formatting style that appears in the Requests for Comments (RFCs).

PIMv2 Packet Headers

All PIMv2 control messages have a protocol number of 103, which has been assigned by the Internet Assigned Numbers Authority (IANA). In addition, PIM messages are either unicast (for example, Registers and Register-Stop) or multicast hop by hop to All-PIM-Routers group 224.0.0.13 (for example, Join/Prune, Asserts). The format of all PIMv2 packet headers follows.

```
 0                   1                   2                   3
 0 1 2 3 4 5 6 7 8 9 0 1 2 3 4 5 6 7 8 9 0 1 2 3 4 5 6 7 8 9 0 1
+-+-+-+-+-+-+-+-+-+-+-+-+-+-+-+-+-+-+-+-+-+-+-+-+-+-+-+-+-+-+-+-+
|PIM Ver| Type | Reserved     |            Checksum            |
+-+-+-+-+-+-+-+-+-+-+-+-+-+-+-+-+-+-+-+-+-+-+-+-+-+-+-+-+-+-+-+-+

    PIM Ver
          PIM Version number is 2.

    Type  Types for specific PIM messages.  PIM Types are:

        0 = Hello
        1 = Register
        2 = Register-Stop
        3 = Join/Prune
        4 = Bootstrap
        5 = Assert
        6 = Graft (used in PIM-DM only)
        7 = Graft-Ack (used in PIM-DM only)
        8 = Candidate-RP-Advertisement

    Reserved
            set to zero. Ignored upon receipt.

    Checksum
          The checksum is the 16-bit one's complement of the one's
          complement sum of the entire PIM message, (excluding the
          data portion in the Register message).  For computing the
          checksum, the checksum field is zeroed.
```

Address Encoding

All unicast addresses, source addresses, and multicast group addresses are encoded in PIMv2 packets in separate formats. These formats are described in the following sections.

Unicast Address Encoding

Unicast addresses are encoded in the following format:

```
 0                   1                   2                   3
 0 1 2 3 4 5 6 7 8 9 0 1 2 3 4 5 6 7 8 9 0 1 2 3 4 5 6 7 8 9 0 1
+-+-+-+-+-+-+-+-+-+-+-+-+-+-+-+-+-+-+-+-+-+-+-+-+-+-+-+-+-+-+-+-+
| Addr Family  | Encoding Type |        Unicast Address         |
+-+-+-+-+-+-+-+-+-+-+-+-+-+-+-+-+-+-+-+-+-+-+-+-+-+-+-+-+-+-+-+-+
```

Addr Family
> The address family of the `Unicast Address' field of
> this address.

> Here is the address family numbers assigned by IANA:

```
Number    Description
--------  ----------------------------------------------------------
   0      Reserved
   1      IP (IP version 4)
   2      IP6 (IP version 6)
   3      NSAP
   4      HDLC (8-bit multidrop)
   5      BBN 1822
   6      802 (includes all 802 media plus Ethernet "canonical format")
   7      E.163
   8      E.164 (SMDS, Frame Relay, ATM)
   9      F.69 (Telex)
  10      X.121 (X.25, Frame Relay)
  11      IPX
  12      Appletalk
  13      Decnet IV
  14      Banyan Vines
  15      E.164 with NSAP format subaddress
```

Encoding Type
> The type of encoding used within a specific Address
> Family. The value `0' is reserved for this field,
> and represents the native encoding of the Address
> Family.

Unicast Address
> The unicast address as represented by the given
> Address Family and Encoding Type.

Group Address Encoding

Multicast group addresses are encoded in the following format:

```
 0                   1                   2                   3
 0 1 2 3 4 5 6 7 8 9 0 1 2 3 4 5 6 7 8 9 0 1 2 3 4 5 6 7 8 9 0 1
+-+-+-+-+-+-+-+-+-+-+-+-+-+-+-+-+-+-+-+-+-+-+-+-+-+-+-+-+-+-+-+-+
¦ Addr Family  ¦ Encoding Type ¦   Reserved   ¦  Mask Len       ¦
+-+-+-+-+-+-+-+-+-+-+-+-+-+-+-+-+-+-+-+-+-+-+-+-+-+-+-+-+-+-+-+-+
¦                   Group multicast Address                     ¦
+-+-+-+-+-+-+-+-+-+-+-+-+-+-+-+-+-+-+-+-+-+-+-+-+-+-+-+-+-+-+-+-+
```

    Addr Family
         described above.

    Encoding Type
         described above.

    Reserved
         Transmitted as zero. Ignored upon receipt.

    Mask Len
         The Mask length is 8 bits. The value is the number of
         contiguous bits left justified used as a mask which
         describes the address. It is less than or equal to the
         address length in bits for the given Address Family
         and Encoding Type. If the message is sent for a single
         group then the Mask length must equal the address
         length in bits for the given Address Family and
         Encoding Type. (e.g. 32 for IPv4 native encoding and
         128 for IPv6 native encoding).

    Group multicast Address
         contains the group address.

Source Address Encoding

Source addresses are encoded in the following format:

```
 0                   1                   2                   3
 0 1 2 3 4 5 6 7 8 9 0 1 2 3 4 5 6 7 8 9 0 1 2 3 4 5 6 7 8 9 0 1
+-+-+-+-+-+-+-+-+-+-+-+-+-+-+-+-+-+-+-+-+-+-+-+-+-+-+-+-+-+-+-+-+
¦ Addr Family  ¦ Encoding Type ¦ Rsrvd  ¦S¦W¦R¦  Mask Len       ¦
+-+-+-+-+-+-+-+-+-+-+-+-+-+-+-+-+-+-+-+-+-+-+-+-+-+-+-+-+-+-+-+-+
¦                       Source Address                          ¦
+-+-+-+-+-+-+-+-+-+-+-+-+-+-+-+-+-+-+-+-+-+-+-+-+-+-+-+-+-+-+-+-+
```

    Addr Family
         described above.

    Encoding Type
         described above.

    Reserved
         Transmitted as zero, ignored on receipt.

    S,W,R See Section 4.5 for details.

Mask Length
     Mask length is 8 bits. The value is the number of
     contiguous bits left justified used as a mask which
     describes the address. The mask length must be less
     than or equal to the address length in bits for the
     given Address Family and Encoding Type. If the message
     is sent for a single group then the Mask length must
     equal the address length in bits for the given Address
     Family and Encoding Type. In version 2 of PIM, it is
     strongly recommended that this field be set to 32 for
     IPv4 native encoding.

Source Address
     The source address.

Hello Message

PIM Hello messages are sent periodically by routers on all interfaces.

```
 0                   1                   2                   3
 0 1 2 3 4 5 6 7 8 9 0 1 2 3 4 5 6 7 8 9 0 1 2 3 4 5 6 7 8 9 0 1
+-+-+-+-+-+-+-+-+-+-+-+-+-+-+-+-+-+-+-+-+-+-+-+-+-+-+-+-+-+-+-+-+
|PIM Ver| Type | Reserved    |             Checksum            |
+-+-+-+-+-+-+-+-+-+-+-+-+-+-+-+-+-+-+-+-+-+-+-+-+-+-+-+-+-+-+-+-+
|          OptionType        |           OptionLength          |
+-+-+-+-+-+-+-+-+-+-+-+-+-+-+-+-+-+-+-+-+-+-+-+-+-+-+-+-+-+-+-+-+
|                         OptionValue                          |
+-+-+-+-+-+-+-+-+-+-+-+-+-+-+-+-+-+-+-+-+-+-+-+-+-+-+-+-+-+-+-+++
|                                                              |
|                              .                               |
|                              .                               |
|                              .                               |
+-+-+-+-+-+-+-+-+-+-+-+-+-+-+-+-+-+-+-+-+-+-+-+-+-+-+-+-+-+-+-+-+
|          OptionType        |           OptionLength          |
+-+-+-+-+-+-+-+-+-+-+-+-+-+-+-+-+-+-+-+-+-+-+-+-+-+-+-+-+-+-+-+-+
|                         OptionValue                          |
+-+-+-+-+-+-+-+-+-+-+-+-+-+-+-+-+-+-+-+-+-+-+-+-+-+-+-+-+-+-+-+++
```

PIM Version, Type, Reserved, Checksum
     Described above.

OptionType
     The type of the option given in the following OptionValue
     field.

OptionLength
     The length of the OptionValue field in bytes.

OptionValue
     A variable length field, carrying the value of the option.

The Option fields may contain the following values:

*   OptionType = 1; OptionLength = 2; OptionValue = Holdtime;
     where Holdtime is the amount of time a receiver must keep the
     neighbor reachable, in seconds. If the Holdtime is set to
     `0xffff', the receiver of this message never times out the
     neighbor. This may be used with ISDN lines, to avoid keeping
     the link up with periodic Hello messages. Furthermore, if the
     Holdtime is set to `0', the information is timed out
     immediately.

* OptionType 2 to 16: reserved

* The rest of the OptionTypes are defined in another
  document.

In general, options may be ignored, but a router must not ignore the **Holdtime OptionType**.

Register Message

A Register message is sent by the Designated Router (DR) to the rendezvous point (RP) when a multicast packet needs to be transmitted on the RP Tree. The source address is set to the address of the DR; the destination address is set to the RP's address.

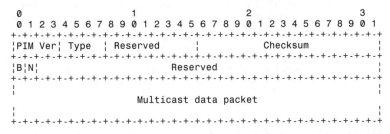

```
 0                   1                   2                   3
 0 1 2 3 4 5 6 7 8 9 0 1 2 3 4 5 6 7 8 9 0 1 2 3 4 5 6 7 8 9 0 1
+-+-+-+-+-+-+-+-+-+-+-+-+-+-+-+-+-+-+-+-+-+-+-+-+-+-+-+-+-+-+-+-+
|PIM Ver| Type | Reserved      |            Checksum            |
+-+-+-+-+-+-+-+-+-+-+-+-+-+-+-+-+-+-+-+-+-+-+-+-+-+-+-+-+-+-+-+-+
|B|N|                        Reserved                           |
+-+-+-+-+-+-+-+-+-+-+-+-+-+-+-+-+-+-+-+-+-+-+-+-+-+-+-+-+-+-+-+-+
|                                                               |
                        Multicast data packet
|                                                               |
+-+-+-+-+-+-+-+-+-+-+-+-+-+-+-+-+-+-+-+-+-+-+-+-+-+-+-+-+-+-+-+-+
```

PIM Version, Type, Reserved, Checksum
    Described above. Note that the checksum for Registers
    is done only on the PIM header, excluding the data packet
    portion.

B   The Border bit. If the router is a DR for a source that it
     is directly connected to, it sets the B bit to 0. If the
     router is a PMBR for a source in a directly connected
     cloud, it sets the B bit to 1.

N   The Null-Register bit. Set to 1 by a DR that is probing
     the RP before expiring its local Register-Suppression
     timer. Set to 0 otherwise.

Multicast data packet
    The original packet sent by the source.

For (S,G) null Registers, the Multicast data packet portion
contains only a dummy header with S as the source address, G as
the destination address, and a data length of zero.

Register-Stop Message

A Register-Stop message is unicast from the RP to the sender of the Register message. Source address is the address to which the Register was addressed. Destination address is the source address of the Register message.

```
0                   1                   2                   3
0 1 2 3 4 5 6 7 8 9 0 1 2 3 4 5 6 7 8 9 0 1 2 3 4 5 6 7 8 9 0 1
+-+-+-+-+-+-+-+-+-+-+-+-+-+-+-+-+-+-+-+-+-+-+-+-+-+-+-+-+-+-+-+-+
|PIM Ver| Type  | Reserved      |            Checksum           |
+-+-+-+-+-+-+-+-+-+-+-+-+-+-+-+-+-+-+-+-+-+-+-+-+-+-+-+-+-+-+-+-+
|                    Encoded-Group Address                      |
+-+-+-+-+-+-+-+-+-+-+-+-+-+-+-+-+-+-+-+-+-+-+-+-+-+-+-+-+-+-+-+-+
|                Encoded-Unicast-Source Address                 |
+-+-+-+-+-+-+-+-+-+-+-+-+-+-+-+-+-+-+-+-+-+-+-+-+-+-+-+-+-+-+-+-+
```

PIM Version, Type, Reserved, Checksum
   Described above.

Encoded-Group Address
   Format described above. Note that for Register-Stops the
   Mask Len field contains full address length * 8 (e.g. 32
   for IPv4 native encoding), if the message is sent for a
   single group.

Encoded-Unicast-Source Address
   host address of source from multicast data packet in
   register. The format for this address is given in the
   Encoded-Unicast-Address in 4.1. A special wild card value
   (0's), can be used to indicate any source.

Join/Prune Message

A Join/Prune message is sent by routers toward upstream sources and RPs. Joins are sent to build shared trees (RP trees) or source trees (SPTs). Prunes are sent to prune SPTs when members leave groups, as well as sources that do not use the shared tree.

```
0                   1                   2                   3
0 1 2 3 4 5 6 7 8 9 0 1 2 3 4 5 6 7 8 9 0 1 2 3 4 5 6 7 8 9 0 1
+-+-+-+-+-+-+-+-+-+-+-+-+-+-+-+-+-+-+-+-+-+-+-+-+-+-+-+-+-+-+-+-+
|PIM Ver| Type  | Reserved      |            Checksum           |
+-+-+-+-+-+-+-+-+-+-+-+-+-+-+-+-+-+-+-+-+-+-+-+-+-+-+-+-+-+-+-+-+
|            Encoded-Unicast-Upstream Neighbor Address          |
+-+-+-+-+-+-+-+-+-+-+-+-+-+-+-+-+-+-+-+-+-+-+-+-+-+-+-+-+-+-+-+-+
|  Reserved     |  Num groups   |           Holdtime           |
+-+-+-+-+-+-+-+-+-+-+-+-+-+-+-+-+-+-+-+-+-+-+-+-+-+-+-+-+-+-+-+-+
|                Encoded-Multicast Group Address-1              |
+-+-+-+-+-+-+-+-+-+-+-+-+-+-+-+-+-+-+-+-+-+-+-+-+-+-+-+-+-+-+-+-+
|  Number of Joined  Sources    |   Number of Pruned Sources   |
+-+-+-+-+-+-+-+-+-+-+-+-+-+-+-+-+-+-+-+-+-+-+-+-+-+-+-+-+-+-+-+-+
|                Encoded-Joined Source Address-1                |
+-+-+-+-+-+-+-+-+-+-+-+-+-+-+-+-+-+-+-+-+-+-+-+-+-+-+-+-+-+-+-+-+
|                             .                                 |
|                             .                                 |
+-+-+-+-+-+-+-+-+-+-+-+-+-+-+-+-+-+-+-+-+-+-+-+-+-+-+-+-+-+-+-+-+
|                Encoded-Joined Source Address-n                |
+-+-+-+-+-+-+-+-+-+-+-+-+-+-+-+-+-+-+-+-+-+-+-+-+-+-+-+-+-+-+-+-+
|                Encoded-Pruned Source Address-1                |
+-+-+-+-+-+-+-+-+-+-+-+-+-+-+-+-+-+-+-+-+-+-+-+-+-+-+-+-+-+-+-+-+
|                             .                                 |
|                             .                                 |
+-+-+-+-+-+-+-+-+-+-+-+-+-+-+-+-+-+-+-+-+-+-+-+-+-+-+-+-+-+-+-+-+
|                Encoded-Pruned Source Address-n                |
```

```
+-+-+-+-+-+-+-+-+-+-+-+-+-+-+-+-+-+-+-+-+-+-+-+-+-+-+-+-+-+-+-+-+
|                              .                                |
|                              .                                |
|                              .                                |
+-+-+-+-+-+-+-+-+-+-+-+-+-+-+-+-+-+-+-+-+-+-+-+-+-+-+-+-+-+-+-+-+
|              Encoded-Multicast Group Address-n                |
+-+-+-+-+-+-+-+-+-+-+-+-+-+-+-+-+-+-+-+-+-+-+-+-+-+-+-+-+-+-+-+-+
|  Number of Joined  Sources   |   Number of Pruned Sources    |
+-+-+-+-+-+-+-+-+-+-+-+-+-+-+-+-+-+-+-+-+-+-+-+-+-+-+-+-+-+-+-+-+
|                Encoded-Joined Source Address-1                |
+-+-+-+-+-+-+-+-+-+-+-+-+-+-+-+-+-+-+-+-+-+-+-+-+-+-+-+-+-+-+-+-+
|                              .                                |
|                              .                                |
|                              .                                |
+-+-+-+-+-+-+-+-+-+-+-+-+-+-+-+-+-+-+-+-+-+-+-+-+-+-+-+-+-+-+-+-+
|                Encoded-Joined Source Address-n                |
+-+-+-+-+-+-+-+-+-+-+-+-+-+-+-+-+-+-+-+-+-+-+-+-+-+-+-+-+-+-+-+-+
|                Encoded-Pruned Source Address-1                |
+-+-+-+-+-+-+-+-+-+-+-+-+-+-+-+-+-+-+-+-+-+-+-+-+-+-+-+-+-+-+-+-+
|                              .                                |
|                              .                                |
|                              .                                |
+-+-+-+-+-+-+-+-+-+-+-+-+-+-+-+-+-+-+-+-+-+-+-+-+-+-+-+-+-+-+-+-+
|                Encoded-Pruned Source Address-n                |
+-+-+-+-+-+-+-+-+-+-+-+-+-+-+-+-+-+-+-+-+-+-+-+-+-+-+-+-+-+-+-+-+
```

PIM Version, Type, Reserved, Checksum
     Described above.

Encoded-Unicast Upstream Neighbor Address
     The address of the RPF or upstream neighbor. The format
     for this address is given in the Encoded-Unicast-Address in
     4.1. .IP "Reserved"
     Transmitted as zero, ignored on receipt.

Holdtime
     The amount of time a receiver must keep the Join/Prune
     state alive, in seconds. If the Holdtime is set to
     `0xffff', the receiver of this message never times out the
     oif. This may be used with ISDN lines, to avoid keeping the
     link up with periodical Join/Prune messages. Furthermore,
     if the Holdtime is set to `0', the information is timed out
     immediately.

Number of Groups
     The number of multicast group sets contained in the
     message.

Encoded-Multicast group address
     For format description see Section
     4.1. A wild card group in the (*,*,RP) join is represented
     by a 224.0.0.0 in the group address field and `4' in the
     mask length field. A (*,*,RP) join also has the WC-bit and
     the RPT-bit set.

Number of Joined Sources
     Number of join source addresses listed for a given group.

Join Source Address-1 .. n
     This list contains the sources that the sending router
     will forward multicast datagrams for if received on the
     interface this message is sent on.

     See format section 4.1. The fields explanation for the
     Encoded-Source-Address format follows:

Reserved
     Described above.

S   The Sparse bit is a 1 bit value, set to 1 for PIM-SM.
      It is used for PIM v.1 compatibility.

W   The WC bit is a 1 bit value. If 1, the join or prune
      applies to the (*,G) or (*,*,RP) entry. If 0, the join
      or prune applies to the (S,G) entry where S is Source
      Address. Joins and prunes sent towards the RP must
      have this bit set.

R   The RPT-bit is a 1 bit value. If 1, the information
      about (S,G) is sent towards the RP. If 0, the
      information must be sent toward S, where S is the
      Source Address.

Mask Length, Source Address
     Described above.

Represented in the form of
< WC-bit >< RPT-bit ><Mask length >< Source address>:

A source address could be a host IPv4 native encoding
address :

 < 0 >< 0 >< 32 >< 192.1.1.17 >

A source address could be the RP's IP address :

 < 1 >< 1 >< 32 >< 131.108.13.111 >

A source address could be a subnet address to prune from
the RP-tree :

 < 0 >< 1 >< 28 >< 192.1.1.16 >

A source address could be a general aggregate :

 < 0 >< 0 >< 16 >< 192.1.0.0 >

Number of Pruned Sources
     Number of prune source addresses listed for a group.

Prune Source Address-1 .. n
     This list contains the sources that the sending router
     does not want to forward multicast datagrams for when
     received on the interface this message is sent on. If the
     Join/Prune message boundary exceeds the maximum packet
     size, then the join and prune lists for the same group must
     be included in the same packet.

Bootstrap Message

Bootstrap messages are multicast to All-PIM-Routers group, out all interfaces having PIM neighbors (excluding the one over which the message was received). Bootstrap messages are sent with a Time To Live (TTL) value of 1. Bootstrap messages originate at the bootstrap router (BSR) and are forwarded by intermediate routers.

Bootstrap messages are divided up into semantic fragments if the original message exceeds the maximum packet-size boundaries.

The semantics of a single fragment follows:

```
 0                   1                   2                   3
 0 1 2 3 4 5 6 7 8 9 0 1 2 3 4 5 6 7 8 9 0 1 2 3 4 5 6 7 8 9 0 1
+-+-+-+-+-+-+-+-+-+-+-+-+-+-+-+-+-+-+-+-+-+-+-+-+-+-+-+-+-+-+-+-+
|PIM Ver| Type | Reserved      |            Checksum           |
+-+-+-+-+-+-+-+-+-+-+-+-+-+-+-+-+-+-+-+-+-+-+-+-+-+-+-+-+-+-+-+-+
|            Fragment Tag       | Hash Mask len | BSR-priority  |
+-+-+-+-+-+-+-+-+-+-+-+-+-+-+-+-+-+-+-+-+-+-+-+-+-+-+-+-+-+-+-+-+
|                  Encoded-Unicast-BSR-Address                  |
+-+-+-+-+-+-+-+-+-+-+-+-+-+-+-+-+-+-+-+-+-+-+-+-+-+-+-+-+-+-+-+-+
|                   Encoded-Group Address-1                     |
+-+-+-+-+-+-+-+-+-+-+-+-+-+-+-+-+-+-+-+-+-+-+-+-+-+-+-+-+-+-+-+-+
| RP-Count-1    | Frag RP-Cnt-1 |            Reserved           |
+-+-+-+-+-+-+-+-+-+-+-+-+-+-+-+-+-+-+-+-+-+-+-+-+-+-+-+-+-+-+-+-+
|                  Encoded-Unicast-RP-Address-1                 |
+-+-+-+-+-+-+-+-+-+-+-+-+-+-+-+-+-+-+-+-+-+-+-+-+-+-+-+-+-+-+-+-+
|        RP1-Holdtime          | RP1-Priority |    Reserved    |
+-+-+-+-+-+-+-+-+-+-+-+-+-+-+-+-+-+-+-+-+-+-+-+-+-+-+-+-+-+-+-+-+
|                  Encoded-Unicast-RP-Address-2                 |
+-+-+-+-+-+-+-+-+-+-+-+-+-+-+-+-+-+-+-+-+-+-+-+-+-+-+-+-+-+-+-+-+
|        RP2-Holdtime          | RP2-Priority |    Reserved    |
+-+-+-+-+-+-+-+-+-+-+-+-+-+-+-+-+-+-+-+-+-+-+-+-+-+-+-+-+-+-+-+-+
|                              .                                |
|                              .                                |
+-+-+-+-+-+-+-+-+-+-+-+-+-+-+-+-+-+-+-+-+-+-+-+-+-+-+-+-+-+-+-+-+
|                  Encoded-Unicast-RP-Address-m                 |
+-+-+-+-+-+-+-+-+-+-+-+-+-+-+-+-+-+-+-+-+-+-+-+-+-+-+-+-+-+-+-+-+
|        RPm-Holdtime          | RPm-Priority |    Reserved    |
+-+-+-+-+-+-+-+-+-+-+-+-+-+-+-+-+-+-+-+-+-+-+-+-+-+-+-+-+-+-+-+-+
|                   Encoded-Group Address-2                     |
+-+-+-+-+-+-+-+-+-+-+-+-+-+-+-+-+-+-+-+-+-+-+-+-+-+-+-+-+-+-+-+-+
|                              .                                |
|                              .                                |
+-+-+-+-+-+-+-+-+-+-+-+-+-+-+-+-+-+-+-+-+-+-+-+-+-+-+-+-+-+-+-+-+
|                   Encoded-Group Address-n                     |
+-+-+-+-+-+-+-+-+-+-+-+-+-+-+-+-+-+-+-+-+-+-+-+-+-+-+-+-+-+-+-+-+
| RP-Count-n    | Frag RP-Cnt-n |            Reserved           |
+-+-+-+-+-+-+-+-+-+-+-+-+-+-+-+-+-+-+-+-+-+-+-+-+-+-+-+-+-+-+-+-+
|                  Encoded-Unicast-RP-Address-1                 |
+-+-+-+-+-+-+-+-+-+-+-+-+-+-+-+-+-+-+-+-+-+-+-+-+-+-+-+-+-+-+-+-+
|        RP1-Holdtime          | RP1-Priority |    Reserved    |
+-+-+-+-+-+-+-+-+-+-+-+-+-+-+-+-+-+-+-+-+-+-+-+-+-+-+-+-+-+-+-+-+
|                  Encoded-Unicast-RP-Address-2                 |
+-+-+-+-+-+-+-+-+-+-+-+-+-+-+-+-+-+-+-+-+-+-+-+-+-+-+-+-+-+-+-+-+
|        RP2-Holdtime          | RP2-Priority |    Reserved    |
+-+-+-+-+-+-+-+-+-+-+-+-+-+-+-+-+-+-+-+-+-+-+-+-+-+-+-+-+-+-+-+-+
|                              .                                |
|                              .                                |
+-+-+-+-+-+-+-+-+-+-+-+-+-+-+-+-+-+-+-+-+-+-+-+-+-+-+-+-+-+-+-+-+
|                  Encoded-Unicast-RP-Address-m                 |
+-+-+-+-+-+-+-+-+-+-+-+-+-+-+-+-+-+-+-+-+-+-+-+-+-+-+-+-+-+-+-+-+
|        RPm-Holdtime          | RPm-Priority |    Reserved    |
+-+-+-+-+-+-+-+-+-+-+-+-+-+-+-+-+-+-+-+-+-+-+-+-+-+-+-+-+-+-+-+-+
```

PIM Version, Type, Reserved, Checksum
    Described above.

Fragment Tag
    A randomly generated number, acts to distinguish the
    fragments belonging to different Bootstrap messages;
    fragments belonging to same Bootstrap message carry the
    same `Fragment Tag'.

Hash Mask len
    The length (in bits) of the mask to use in the hash
    function. For IPv4 we recommend a value of 30. For IPv6 we
    recommend a value of 126.

BSR-priority
    Contains the BSR priority value of the included BSR. This
    field is considered as a high order byte when comparing BSR
    addresses.

Encoded-Unicast-BSR-Address
    The address of the bootstrap router for the domain. The
    format for this address is given in the Encoded-Unicast-
    Address in 4.1. .IP "Encoded-Group Address-1..n"
    The group prefix (address and mask) with which the
    Candidate RPs are associated. Format previously described.

RP-Count-1..n
    The number of Candidate RP addresses included in the whole
    Bootstrap message for the corresponding group prefix. A
    router does not replace its old RP-Set for a given group
    prefix until/unless it receives `RP-Count' addresses for
    that prefix; the addresses could be carried over several
    fragments. If only part of the RP-Set for a given group
    prefix was received, the router discards it, without
    updating that specific group prefix's RP-Set.

Frag RP-Cnt-1..m
    The number of Candidate RP addresses included in this
    fragment of the Bootstrap message, for the corresponding
    group prefix. The `Frag RP-Cnt' field facilitates parsing
    of the RP-Set for a given group prefix, when carried over
    more than one fragment.

Encoded-Unicast-RP-address-1..m
    The address of the Candidate RPs, for the corresponding
    group prefix. The format for this address is given in the
    Encoded-Unicast-Address in 4.1. .IP "RP1..m-Holdtime"
    The Holdtime for the corresponding RP. This field is
    copied from the `Holdtime' field of the associated RP
    stored at the BSR.

RP1..m-Priority
    The `Priority' of the corresponding RP and Encoded-Group
    Address. This field is copied from the `Priority' field
    stored at the BSR when receiving a Candidate-RP-
    Advertisement. The highest priority is `0' (i.e. the lower
    the value of the `Priority' field, the higher). Note that
    the priority is per RP per Encoded-Group Address.

Assert Message

The Assert message is sent when a multicast data packet is received on an outgoing interface corresponding to the (S,G) or (*,G) associated with the source. This message is used in both dense mode and sparse mode PIM:

```
0                   1                   2                   3
0 1 2 3 4 5 6 7 8 9 0 1 2 3 4 5 6 7 8 9 0 1 2 3 4 5 6 7 8 9 0 1
+-+-+-+-+-+-+-+-+-+-+-+-+-+-+-+-+-+-+-+-+-+-+-+-+-+-+-+-+-+-+-+-+
|PIM Ver| Type  | Reserved      |             Checksum          |
+-+-+-+,+-+-+-+-+-+-+-+-+-+-+-+-+-+-+-+-+-+-+-+-+-+-+-+-+-+-+-+-+
|                      Encoded-Group Address                    |
+-+-+-+-+-+-+-+-+-+-+-+-+-+-+-+-+-+-+-+-+-+-+-+-+-+-+-+-+-+-+-+-+
|                  Encoded-Unicast-Source Address               |
+-+-+-+-+-+-+-+-+-+-+-+-+-+-+-+-+-+-+-+-+-+-+-+-+-+-+-+-+-+-+-+-+
|R|                      Metric Preference                      |
+-+-+-+-+-+-+-+-+-+-+-+-+-+-+-+-+-+-+-+-+-+-+-+-+-+-+-+-+-+-+-+-+
|                            Metric                             |
+-+-+-+-+-+-+-+-+-+-+-+-+-+-+-+-+-+-+-+-+-+-+-+-+-+-+-+-+-+-+-+-+
```

```
PIM Version, Type, Reserved, Checksum
     Described above.

Encoded-Group Address
     The group address to which the data packet was addressed,
     and which triggered the Assert.  Format previously
     described.

Encoded-Unicast-Source Address
     Source address from multicast datagram that triggered the
     Assert packet to be sent. The format for this address is
     given in the Encoded-Unicast-Address in 4.1. .IP "R"
     RPT-bit is a 1 bit value. If the multicast datagram that
     triggered the Assert packet is routed down the RP tree,
     then the RPT-bit is 1; if the multicast datagram is routed
     down the SPT, it is 0.

Metric Preference
     Preference value assigned to the unicast routing protocol
     that provided the route to Host address.

Metric The unicast routing table metric. The metric is in units
     applicable to the unicast routing protocol used.
```

Graft Message (Dense Mode Only)

Graft messages are sent by a downstream router to a neighboring upstream router to reinstate a previously pruned branch of a SPT. (This is done for dense mode groups only.) The format is the same as a Join/Prune message except that the value in the Type field is 6.

Graft-Ack Message (Dense Mode Only)

Graft-Ack messages are sent in response to a received Graft message. The Graft-Ack is sent only if the interface in which the Graft was received is not the incoming interface for the respective (S,G). (This procedure is done for dense mode groups only.) The format is the same as a Join/Prune message except that the value of the message Type field is 7.

Candidate-RP-Advertisement

Candidate-RP-Advertisements are periodically unicast from the candidate-RPs to the BSR.

```
 0                   1                   2                   3
 0 1 2 3 4 5 6 7 8 9 0 1 2 3 4 5 6 7 8 9 0 1 2 3 4 5 6 7 8 9 0 1
+-+-+-+-+-+-+-+-+-+-+-+-+-+-+-+-+-+-+-+-+-+-+-+-+-+-+-+-+-+-+-+-+
¦PIM Ver¦ Type  ¦ Reserved      ¦          Checksum             ¦
+-+-+-+-+-+-+-+-+-+-+-+-+-+-+-+-+-+-+-+-+-+-+-+-+-+-+-+-+-+-+-+-+
¦ Prefix-Cnt    ¦  Priority     ¦          Holdtime             ¦
+-+-+-+-+-+-+-+-+-+-+-+-+-+-+-+-+-+-+-+-+-+-+-+-+-+-+-+-+-+-+-+-+
¦                 Encoded-Unicast-RP-Address                    ¦
+-+-+-+-+-+-+-+-+-+-+-+-+-+-+-+-+-+-+-+-+-+-+-+-+-+-+-+-+-+-+-+-+
¦                 Encoded-Group Address-1                       ¦
+-+-+-+-+-+-+-+-+-+-+-+-+-+-+-+-+-+-+-+-+-+-+-+-+-+-+-+-+-+-+-+-+
¦                          .                                    ¦
¦                          .                                    ¦
¦                          .                                    ¦
+-+-+-+-+-+-+-+-+-+-+-+-+-+-+-+-+-+-+-+-+-+-+-+-+-+-+-+-+-+-+-+-+
¦                 Encoded-Group Address-n                       ¦
+-+-+-+-+-+-+-+-+-+-+-+-+-+-+-+-+-+-+-+-+-+-+-+-+-+-+-+-+-+-+-+-+
```

```
    PIM Version, Type, Reserved, Checksum
         Described above.

    Prefix-Cnt
         The number of encoded group addresses included in the
         message; indicating the group prefixes for which the C-RP
         is advertising. A Prefix-Cnt of `0' implies a prefix of
         224.0.0.0 with mask length of 4; i.e. all multicast groups.
         If the C-RP is not configured with Group-prefix
         information, the C-RP puts a default value of `0' in this
         field.

    Priority
         The `Priority' of the included RP, for the corresponding
         Encoded-Group Address (if any). highest priority is `0'
         (i.e. the lower the value of the `Priority' field, the
         higher the priority). This field is stored at the BSR upon
         receipt along with the RP address and corresponding
         Encoded-Group Address.

    Holdtime
         The amount of time the advertisement is valid. This field
         allows advertisements to be aged out.

    Encoded-Unicast-RP-Address
         The address of the interface to advertise as a Candidate
         RP.  The format for this address is given in the Encoded-
         Unicast-Address in 4.1. .IP "Encoded-Group Address-1..n"
         The group prefixes for which the C-RP is advertising.
         Format previously described.
```

Differences Between PIMv1 and PIMv2 Packets

PIMv1 packets contain the same functional information (albeit with some minor formatting variations) that is carried inside their PIMv2 packet equivalents. One key exception is that PIMv1 packets are transmitted using Internet Group Membership Protocol (IGMP) headers, whereas PIMv2 packets use their own assigned protocol (103). In addition, the address encoding method used in PIMv1 is much simpler than the method used in PIMv2, which was extended to permit the use of other protocol address families. Finally, some PIMv1 messages were made obsolete when PIMv2 was introduced. All these differences are discussed briefly in the following sections.

PIMv1 Headers

All PIMv1 messages (as well as DVMRP and Mtrace messages) ride inside IGMP headers. PIMv1 messages are identified by a special PIM Type code (0x14) in the Type field of the IGMP message. Therefore, all PIMv1 headers have the following format:

```
 0                   1                   2                   3
 0 1 2 3 4 5 6 7 8 9 0 1 2 3 4 5 6 7 8 9 0 1 2 3 4 5 6 7 8 9 0 1
+-+-+-+-+-+-+-+-+-+-+-+-+-+-+-+-+-+-+-+-+-+-+-+-+-+-+-+-+-+-+-+-+
|     Type      |     Code      |           Checksum            |
+-+-+-+-+-+-+-+-+-+-+-+-+-+-+-+-+-+-+-+-+-+-+-+-+-+-+-+-+-+-+-+-+
|PIM Ver|                    Reserved                           |
+-+-+-+-+-+-+-+-+-+-+-+-+-+-+-+-+-+-+-+-+-+-+-+-+-+-+-+-+-+-+-+-+
```

Type   There are eight types of IGMP messages currently in use:

        0x11 = IGMP Membership Query
        0x12 = IGMPv1 Membership Report
        0x13 = DVMRP Message
        0x14 = PIMv1 Message
        0x16 = IGMPv2 Membership Report
        0x17 = IGMPv2 Leave Group
        0x1E = Mtrace Response
        0x1F = Mtrace Request

Code   Codes for specific PIM message types:

        0 = Query (basically equivalent to PIMv2 Hello)
        1 = Register
        2 = Register-Stop
        3 = Join/Prune
        4 = RP-Reachability (Not used in PIMv2)
        5 = Assert
        6 = Graft (used in PIM-DM only)
        7 = Graft-Ack (used in PIM-DM only)

Checksum
        The checksum is the 16-bit one's complement of the one's
        complement sum of the entire IGMP message. For computing the
        checksum, the checksum field is zeroed.

PIM Ver
        PIM Version number is 1.

Reserved
        set to zero. Ignored upon receipt.

PIMv1 Address Encoding

In general, addresses are not encoded in PIMv1 messages. Instead, the 32-bit IP address (group, unicast, or source address) is simply used in the message. The exception to this convention is in PIMv1 Join/Prune messages, where source addresses are encoded in the following manner:

```
 0                   1                   2                   3
 0 1 2 3 4 5 6 7 8 9 0 1 2 3 4 5 6 7 8 9 0 1 2 3 4 5 6 7 8 9 0 1
+-+-+-+-+-+-+-+-+-+-+-+-+-+-+-+-+-+-+-+-+-+-+-+-+-+-+-+-+-+-+-+-+
¦  Reserved    ¦S¦W¦R¦ Mask Len    ¦    Source Address ...      ¦
+-+-+-+-+-+-+-+-+-+-+-+-+-+-+-+-+-+-+-+-+-+-+-+-+-+-+-+-+-+-+-+-+
¦ ... Source Address            ¦
+-+-+-+-+-+-+-+-+-+-+-+-+-+-+-+-+
```

S   The Sparse bit is a 1 bit value, set to 1 for PIM-SM.
        It is used for PIM v.1 compatibility.

W   The WC bit is a 1 bit value. If 1, the join or prune
        applies to the (*,G) entry. If 0, the join or prune
        applies to the (S,G) entry where S is Source Address.
        Joins and prunes sent towards the RP must have this bit set.

R   The RPT-bit is a 1 bit value. If 1, the information
        about (S,G) is sent towards the RP. If 0, the
        information must be sent toward S, where S is the
        Source Address.

Mask Len
        The Mask length is 6 bits. The value is the number of
        contiguous bits left justified used as a mask which
        describes the address. It must be less than or equal to the
        address length in bits.

Source Address
        This address is either an RP address (WC bit = 1) or a source
        Address (WC bit = 0). When it is a source address, it is
        coupled with the group address to make (S,G).

PIMv1 Messages Not Used in PIMv2

In PIMv1, the RP sends RP-Reachability messages down the shared tree to notify all routers that it is still active and reachable. The original idea was to have a timer that would expire if these messages were not received periodically. Then, a router would send a Join message toward a backup RP. Unfortunately, this PIMv1 RP switchover mechanism had problems and never worked properly. Therefore, RP-Reachability messages were dropped from the PIMv2 protocol and are used only in PIMv1.

INDEX

Symbols

(*, G) entries
>show ip mroute command 251–252
>state rule 243–244

(S, G) entries
>show ip mroute command 253–254
>state rule 244

A

ABRs (area border routers) 201
acceptance filtering, DVMRP Route Reports 379
Accept-Any state, PIMv2 BSR message flooding 335
accepting DVMRP neighbors 366–367
Accept-Preferred state, PIMv2 BSR message flooding 335
accept-rp command 346
access lists, configuring candidate RPs 318
accumulation, prune delay (PIM-DM) 140
ACLs (access control lists). See rate limiting
Adaptive Pulse Code Modulation (ADPCM) 80
adding
>neighbors to outgoing interface lists 234–237
>port numbers to CAM table entries 413
address encoding, PIMv1 540
Address Family Identifier (AFI) 511
addresses
>administratively scoped 29
>Class D, assigning 26
>Ethernet, mapping 30–32
>IP
>>IP-to-ATM 469–470
>>LIS 446
>>multicast group addresses 6
>>OUIs 31
>MAC
>>mapping 31–34
>>mapping to Ethernet addresses 30–32
>>mapping to FDDI addresses 32
>>mapping to Token Ring addresses 32–33
>>multicast, leasing 26
>>reserved multicast 28–29
>>scoped zones, BSR 489
>>Token Ring, functional 33

adjacencies
>DVMRP 107–108
>PIM
>>displaying 131–132
>>establishing 130
>>expiration time 130
adjusting bandwidth consumption (VIC) 100
administrative distance
>DVMRP routes 379
>static mroutes 491
administratively scoped boundaries 45–46
administratively scoped multicast addresses 29
administrative-scoped announcements, SAP 83
ADPCM (Adaptive Differential Pulse Code Modulation) 80
advertised routes, over MBone 21
advertisements
>Candidate-RP-Advertisements 538
>connected unicast routes 369–370
>DVMRP
>>controlling 372–375
>>metrics 111
>>Poison Reverse 112–114
>LSAs, MOSPF 196–197
AFI (Address Family Identifier) 511
aggregate rate limiting 477–478
Ahem packets 15
algorithms, load splitting 502–503
allocating
>administratively scoped addresses 29
>dynamic IP addresses 26–27
>multicast addresses 26, 521–523
>reserved multicast addresses 28–29
announcements, SAP 82–83
>caching 88
>viewing 87–88
applications
>audio conferencing, RTP 80–81
>IP address allocation 27
>launching via SDR 89
>MBone freeware 86–87
>>SDR 87–90
>>VAT 91–93
>>VIC 94–98
>>Whiteboard 100
>multicast address assignment 28–29

D

J

M

N

O

P

T

W

X

Z

CCIE Professional Development

Cisco LAN Switching

Kennedy Clark, CCIE; Kevin Hamilton, CCIE

1-57870-094-9 • AVAILABLE NOW

This volume provides an in-depth analysis of Cisco LAN switching technologies, architectures, and deployments, including unique coverage of Catalyst network design essentials. Network designs and configuration examples are incorporated throughout to demonstrate the principles and enable easy translation of the material into practice in production networks.

Advanced IP Network Design

Alvaro Retana, CCIE; Don Slice, CCIE; and Russ White, CCIE

1-57870-097-3 • AVAILABLE NOW

Network engineers and managers can use these case studies, which highlight various network design goals, to explore issues including protocol choice, network stability, and growth. This book also includes theoretical discussion on advanced design topics.

Large-Scale IP Network Solutions

Khalid Raza, CCIE; and Mark Turner

1-57870-084-1 • AVAILABLE NOW

Network engineers can find solutions as their IP networks grow in size and complexity. Examine all the major IP protocols in-depth and learn about scalability, migration planning, network management, and security for large-scale networks.

Routing TCP/IP, Volume I

Jeff Doyle, CCIE

1-57870-041-8 • AVAILABLE NOW

This book takes the reader from a basic understanding of routers and routing protocols through a detailed examination of each of the IP interior routing protocols. Learn techniques for designing networks that maximize the efficiency of the protocol being used. Exercises and review questions provide core study for the CCIE Routing and Switching exam.

Cisco Press   **www.ciscopress.com**

Cisco Press Solutions

Enhanced IP Services for Cisco Networks
Donald C. Lee, CCIE

1-57870-106-6 • AVAILABLE NOW

This is a guide to improving your network's capabilities by understanding the new enabling and advanced Cisco IOS services that build more scalable, intelligent, and secure networks. Learn the technical details necessary to deploy Quality of Service, VPN technologies, IPsec, the IOS firewall and IOS Intrusion Detection. These services will allow you to extend the network to new frontiers securely, protect your network from attacks, and increase the sophistication of network services.

Developing IP Multicast Networks, Volume I
Beau Williamson, CCIE

1-57870-077-9 • AVAILABLE NOW

This book provides a solid foundation of IP multicast concepts and explains how to design and deploy the networks that will support appplications such as audio and video conferencing, distance-learning, and data replication. Includes an in-depth discussion of the PIM protocol used in Cisco routers and detailed coverage of the rules that control the creation and maintenance of Cisco mroute state entries.

Designing Network Security
Merike Kaeo

1-57870-043-4 • AVAILABLE NOW

Designing Network Security is a practical guide designed to help you understand the fundamentals of securing your corporate infrastructure. This book takes a comprehensive look at underlying security technologies, the process of creating a security policy, and the practical requirements necessary to implement a corporate security policy.

Cisco Press

www.ciscopress.com

Cisco Press Solutions

EIGRP Network Design Solutions
Ivan Pepelnjak, CCIE
1-57870-165-1 • AVAILABLE NOW

EIGRP Network Design Solutions uses case studies and real-world configuration examples to help you gain an in-depth understanding of the issues involved in designing, deploying, and managing EIGRP-based networks. This book details proper designs that can be used to build large and scalable EIGRP-based networks and documents possible ways each EIGRP feature can be used in network design, implmentation, troubleshooting, and monitoring.

Top-Down Network Design
Priscilla Oppenheimer
1-57870-069-8 • AVAILABLE NOW

Building reliable, secure, and manageable networks is every network professional's goal. This practical guide teaches you a systematic method for network design that can be applied to campus LANs, remote-access networks, WAN links, and large-scale internetworks. Learn how to analyze business and technical requirements, examine traffic flow and Quality of Service requirements, and select protocols and technologies based on performance goals.

Cisco IOS Releases: The Complete Reference
Mack M. Coulibaly
1-57870-179-1 • AVAILABLE NOW

Cisco IOS Releases: The Complete Reference is the first comprehensive guide to the more than three dozen types of Cisco IOS releases being used today on enterprise and service provider networks. It details the release process and its numbering and naming conventions, as well as when, where, and how to use the various releases. A complete map of Cisco IOS software releases and their relationships to one another, in addition to insights into decoding information contained within the software, make this book an indispensable resource for any network professional.

Cisco Press   **www.ciscopress.com**

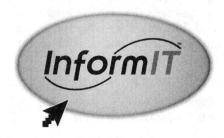